Lecture Notes in Computer Science 16333

Founding Editors

Gerhard Goos
Juris Hartmanis

Editorial Board Members

Elisa Bertino, *Purdue University, West Lafayette, IN, USA*
Wen Gao, *Peking University, Beijing, China*
Bernhard Steffen, *TU Dortmund University, Dortmund, Germany*
Moti Yung, *Columbia University, New York, NY, USA*

The series Lecture Notes in Computer Science (LNCS), including its subseries Lecture Notes in Artificial Intelligence (LNAI) and Lecture Notes in Bioinformatics (LNBI), has established itself as a medium for the publication of new developments in computer science and information technology research, teaching, and education.

LNCS enjoys close cooperation with the computer science R & D community, the series counts many renowned academics among its volume editors and paper authors, and collaborates with prestigious societies. Its mission is to serve this international community by providing an invaluable service, mainly focused on the publication of conference and workshop proceedings and postproceedings. LNCS commenced publication in 1973.

Hirohiko Mori · Yumi Asahi ·
Dylan D. Schmorrow · Cali M. Fidopiastis
Editors

HCI International 2025 – Late Breaking Papers

27th International Conference on
Human-Computer Interaction, HCII 2025
Gothenburg, Sweden, June 22–27, 2025
Proceedings, Part III

 Springer

Editors
Hirohiko Mori
Tokyo City University
Tokyo, Japan

Dylan D. Schmorrow
Soar Technology, Inc.
Orlando, FL, USA

Yumi Asahi
Tokyo University of Science
Tokyo, Japan

Cali M. Fidopiastis
Katmai Government Services
Orlando, FL, USA

ISSN 0302-9743   ISSN 1611-3349 (electronic)
Lecture Notes in Computer Science
ISBN 978-3-032-12659-7   ISBN 978-3-032-12660-3 (eBook)
https://doi.org/10.1007/978-3-032-12660-3

This Springer imprint is published by the registered company Springer Nature Switzerland AG
The registered company address is: Gewerbestrasse 11, 6330 Cham, Switzerland

If disposing of this product, please recycle the paper.

Foreword

The HCI International (HCII) conference was founded in 1984 by Gavriel Salvendy (Purdue University, USA, Tsinghua University, P.R. China, and University of Central Florida, USA) and the first event of the series, "1st USA-Japan Conference on Human-Computer Interaction", was held in Honolulu, Hawaii, USA, on 18–20 August. Since then, HCI International has been held jointly with several Thematic Areas and Affiliated Conferences, with each one under the auspices of a distinguished international Program Board and under one management and one registration. Twenty-seven HCI International Conferences have been organized so far (every two years until 2013, and annually thereafter).

Last year, we celebrated 40 years since the establishment of the HCII conference, which has been a hub for presenting groundbreaking research and novel ideas and collaboration for people from all over the world. Over the years, this conference has served as a platform for scholars, researchers, industry experts, and students to exchange ideas, connect, and address challenges in the ever-evolving HCI field. The conference has evolved itself, adapting to new technologies and emerging trends, while staying committed to its core mission of advancing knowledge and driving change.

The 27th International Conference on Human-Computer Interaction, HCI International 2025 (HCII 2025), was held as an 'on-site' conference at the Gothia Towers Hotel and Swedish Exhibition & Congress Centre, in Gothenburg, Sweden, on June 22–27, 2025, with the additional option for 'on-line' participation. It incorporated the 21 thematic areas and affiliated conferences listed below.

A total of 7972 individuals from academia, research institutes, industry, and government agencies from 92 countries submitted contributions. 1430 papers and 355 posters (as short research papers) were included in the volumes of the proceedings published just before the start of the conference. Additionally, 439 papers and 104 posters were included in the volumes of the proceedings published after the conference, as "Late Breaking Work". The contributions thoroughly cover the entire field of human-computer interaction, highlight the evolving role of computers in diverse contexts, and demonstrate how HCI research is shaping and improving user experiences across a wide range of domains, influencing technological progress and its effective integration into various sectors. The volumes constituting the full set of the HCII 2025 conference proceedings are listed on the following pages.

I would like to thank the Program Board Chairs and the members of the Program Boards of all thematic areas and affiliated conferences for their contribution towards the high scientific quality and overall success of the HCI International 2025 conference. Their manifold support including paper reviews (via a single-blind review process, with a minimum of two reviews per submission), session organization, and their willingness to act as goodwill ambassadors for the conference is most highly appreciated.

This conference would not have been possible without the continuous and unwavering support and advice of Gavriel Salvendy, founder, General Chair Emeritus, and Scientific Advisor. For his outstanding efforts, I would like to express my sincere appreciation to Abbas Moallem, Communications Chair and Editor of HCI International News.

September 2025   Constantine Stephanidis

HCI International 2025 Thematic Areas and Affiliated Conferences

- HCI: Human-Computer Interaction Thematic Area
- HIMI: Human Interface and the Management of Information Thematic Area
- EPCE: 22nd International Conference on Engineering Psychology and Cognitive Ergonomics
- AC: 19th International Conference on Augmented Cognition
- UAHCI: 19th International Conference on Universal Access in Human-Computer Interaction
- CCD: 17th International Conference on Cross-Cultural Design
- SCSM: 17th International Conference on Social Computing and Social Media
- VAMR: 17th International Conference on Virtual, Augmented and Mixed Reality
- DHM: 16th International Conference on Digital Human Modeling & Applications in Health, Safety, Ergonomics & Risk Management
- DUXU: 14th International Conference on Design, User Experience and Usability
- C&C: 13th International Conference on Culture and Computing
- DAPI: 13th International Conference on Distributed, Ambient and Pervasive Interactions
- HCIBGO: 12th International Conference on HCI in Business, Government and Organizations
- LCT: 12th International Conference on Learning and Collaboration Technologies
- ITAP: 11th International Conference on Human Aspects of IT for the Aged Population
- AIS: 7th International Conference on Adaptive Instructional Systems
- HCI-CPT: 7th International Conference on HCI for Cybersecurity, Privacy and Trust
- HCI-Games: 7th International Conference on HCI in Games
- MobiTAS: 7th International Conference on HCI in Mobility, Transport and Automotive Systems
- AI-HCI: 6th International Conference on Artificial Intelligence in HCI
- MOBILE: 6th International Conference on Human-Centered Design, Operation and Evaluation of Mobile Communications

Conference Proceedings – Full List of Volumes

1. LNCS 15766, Human-Computer Interaction — Part I, edited by Masaaki Kurosu and Ayako Hashizume
2. LNCS 15767, Human-Computer Interaction — Part II, edited by Masaaki Kurosu and Ayako Hashizume
3. LNCS 15768, Human-Computer Interaction — Part III, edited by Masaaki Kurosu and Ayako Hashizume
4. LNCS 15769, Human-Computer Interaction — Part IV, edited by Masaaki Kurosu and Ayako Hashizume
5. LNCS 15770, Human-Computer Interaction — Part V, edited by Masaaki Kurosu and Ayako Hashizume
6. LNCS 15771, Human-Computer Interaction — Part VI, edited by Masaaki Kurosu and Ayako Hashizume
7. LNCS 15772, Human-Computer Interaction — Part VII, edited by Masaaki Kurosu and Ayako Hashizume
8. LNCS 15773, Human Interface and the Management of Information: Part I, edited by Hirohiko Mori and Yumi Asahi
9. LNCS 15774, Human Interface and the Management of Information: Part II, edited by Hirohiko Mori and Yumi Asahi
10. LNCS 15773, Human Interface and the Management of Information: Part III, edited by Hirohiko Mori and Yumi Asahi
11. LNAI 15776, Engineering Psychology and Cognitive Ergonomics: Part I, edited by Don Harris and Wen-Chin Li
12. LNAI 15777, Engineering Psychology and Cognitive Ergonomics: Part II, edited by Don Harris and Wen-Chin Li
13. LNAI 15778, Augmented Cognition, Part I, edited by Dylan D. Schmorrow and Cali M. Fidopiastis
14. LNAI 15779, Augmented Cognition, Part II, edited by Dylan D. Schmorrow and Cali M. Fidopiastis
15. LNCS 15780, Universal Access in Human-Computer Interaction: Part I, edited by Margherita Antona and Constantine Stephanidis
16. LNCS 15781, Universal Access in Human-Computer Interaction: Part II, edited by Margherita Antona and Constantine Stephanidis
17. LNCS 15782, Cross-Cultural Design: Part I, edited by Pei-Luen Patrick Rau
18. LNCS 15783, Cross-Cultural Design: Part II, edited by Pei-Luen Patrick Rau
19. LNCS 15784, Cross-Cultural Design: Part III, edited by Pei-Luen Patrick Rau
20. LNCS 15785, Cross-Cultural Design: Part IV, edited by Pei-Luen Patrick Rau
21. LNCS 15786, Social Computing and Social Media: Part I, edited by Adela Coman and Simona Vasilache

https://2025.hci.international/proceedings

27th International Conference on Human-Computer Interaction (HCII 2025)

The full list with the Program Board Chairs and the members of the Program Boards of all thematic areas and affiliated conferences of HCII 2025 is available online at:

http://www.hci.international/board-members-2025.php

HCI International 2026 Conference

The 28th International Conference on Human-Computer Interaction, HCI International 2026, will be held jointly with the affiliated conferences at the Montréal Convention Centre (Palais des congrès de Montréal), in Montreal, Canada, 26–31 July 2026. It will cover a broad spectrum of themes related to Human-Computer Interaction, including theoretical issues, methods, tools, processes, and case studies in HCI design, as well as novel interaction techniques, interfaces, and applications. The proceedings will be published by Springer (part of Springer Nature) in a multi-volume set. More information will become available on the conference website: https://2026.hci.international/.

General Chair
Constantine Stephanidis
University of Crete and ICS-FORTH
Heraklion, Crete, Greece
Email: general_chair@2026.hci.international

https://2026.hci.international/

Contents

Human Factors in Intelligent and Autonomous Systems

Computational Methods for Human Behavior Analysis

Human Experience in Virtual Environments

Impact of a VR Environment on Divergent Thinking During Walking Meetings

Eisuke Aoki[1], Keita Nishida[2], and Takehiko Yamaguchi[2(✉)]

[1] School of Engineering and Management, Suwa University of Science Graduate, Chino City Toyohira 5000-1, Japan
gh24501@ed.sus.ac.jp
[2] Suwa University of Science, Chino City Toyohira 5000-1, Japan
t121109@ed.sus.ac.jp, tk-ymgch@rs.sus.ac.jp

Abstract. Type 2 diabetes is a chronic disease characterized by high blood glucose levels mainly owing to lifestyle habits such as overeating and a lack of exercise. One approach for preventing and treating type 2 diabetes is through exercise; however, patients often face challenges in finding time to sufficiently exercise. Thus, options where patients can exercise while working are currently being investigated. Active workstations, where a patient can work at a desk while performing aerobic exercises, have been considered. However, previous studies have shown that users have difficulty in balancing physical activity and work. Therefore, a more viable option may be walking meetings, where participants hold discussions while walking, because precision manipulation is not required and the physical activity does not interfere with cognitive loads. Furthermore, walking meetings may encourage divergent thinking, thus improving productivity and creativity. However, walking meetings are limited by distance- and weather-related restrictions as well as difficulties in note-taking. To address these issues, this study investigated the effectiveness of walking meetings occurring in a virtual reality (VR) environment using a 360° treadmill. Experiments were conducted to investigate the differences between walking and the associated divergent thinking when participants walked in real space and in a VR environment. The results reveal remarkable differences in walking but not in divergent thinking.

Keywords: Diabetes · Walking meeting · 360° treadmills · Exercise therapy · Virtual Reality

1 Introduction

Diabetes mellitus is a chronic disease characterized by high blood sugar levels owing to a lack of insulin action. In particular, type 2 diabetes, or insulin-independent diabetes, is caused by a combination of genetic factors and lifestyle habits such as overeating and a lack of exercise. In Japan, approximately one in six adults or 18.7 million people are suspected of having type 2 diabetes [1]. Exercise therapy uses exercises to treat or prevent disorders and diseases and is effective at combating type 2 diabetes. In general, moderate-intensity and full-body aerobic exercises for at least three times a week, a duration of

H. Mori et al. (Eds.): HCII 2025, LNCS 16333, pp. 3–18, 2026.
https://doi.org/10.1007/978-3-032-12660-3_1

at least 20 min each session, and a total duration of at least 150 min each week are recommended for preventing or treating type 2 diabetes [2]. However, approximately half of the patients with type 2 diabetes could not find enough time to engage in exercise therapy owing to their work–life balance [3].

An active workstation is a desk environment that can help users improve their posture and activate muscles while working. It has been termed as a possible solution for helping patients with diabetes exercise sufficiently. However, Podrekar et al. [4] found that using an active workstation can remarkably reduce typing speed and increase typing errors. Cho et al. [5] found that active workstations do not decrease performance at low workloads but decrease performance at high workloads. Thus, active workstations make it difficult to balance physical activity and work performance. Walking meetings are a type of meetings in which participants hold discussions while walking rather than sitting. Such meetings have been gaining attention as a way to address sedentary lifestyles and increase physical activity. Oppezzo and Schwartz [6] found that walking promotes divergent thinking, which is necessary for creativity and productivity, more than sitting. However, walking meetings require large spaces, especially when many people are involved, and are difficult to hold in office environments such as meeting rooms and corridors. Holding walking meetings outdoors is a potential solution. However, external factors such as weather and noise can affect the comfort of participants.

Virtual reality (VR) is a technology that attempt to mimic real-world experiences in terms of three major elements: three-dimensional spatiality, real-time interactivity, and self-projection [7]. Combining VR with a 360° treadmill can allow unlimited walking by the user even when the real-world space is small. The Research Question of this study was to investigate the differences between walking meetings held in real space and VR space using a 360° treadmill, especially in terms of gait and divergent thinking. The purpose of this study is to evaluate the feasibility of VR as a walking meeting environment that resolves the tradeoff between exercise and work performance and that can be conducted anytime and anywhere.

2   Methods

Figure 1 shows the developed system, including a 360° treadmill, head-mounted display (HMD), heart rate sensor, and motion sensor. The HMD (Meta Quest 2, Meta) was used to provide the virtual environment. The heart rate sensor (Magene) was used to measure the heart rate of the user. The 360° treadmill (KATWALK C2 +, KATVR) was used to allow the user to walk in any direction. Motion sensors (VIVE Trackers Ultimate, HTC) were used to track foot and waist movements. Fig. 2, 3, 4,und 5 demonstrate the above devices.

A total of ten healthy male participants (mean age = 21.9 years) took part in the study. Of these, six had previous experience with virtual reality (VR), whereas the remaining four did not. [Information on 10 participants]

An experiment was conducted to investigate the differences in walking in the real world (RL condition) and in VR space (VR condition). To unify the visual input across conditions, participants wore the HMD in both conditions and continuously walked along a 7 m × 2.5 m course displayed by the HMD. In the VR condition, the movements

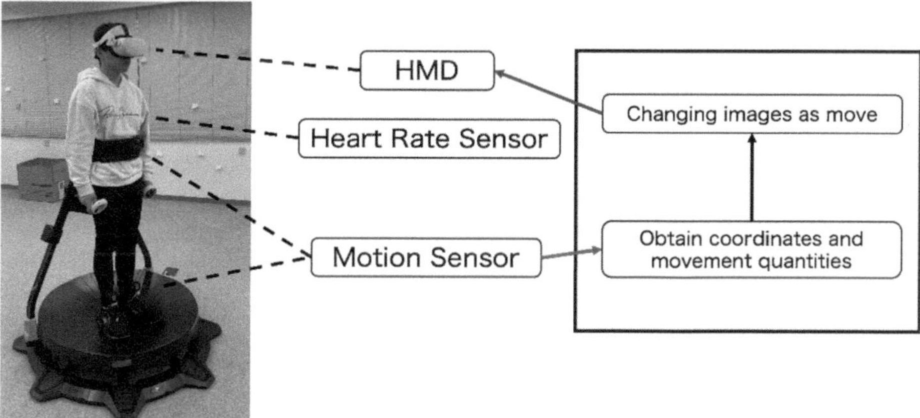

Fig. 1. Framework of the developed system.

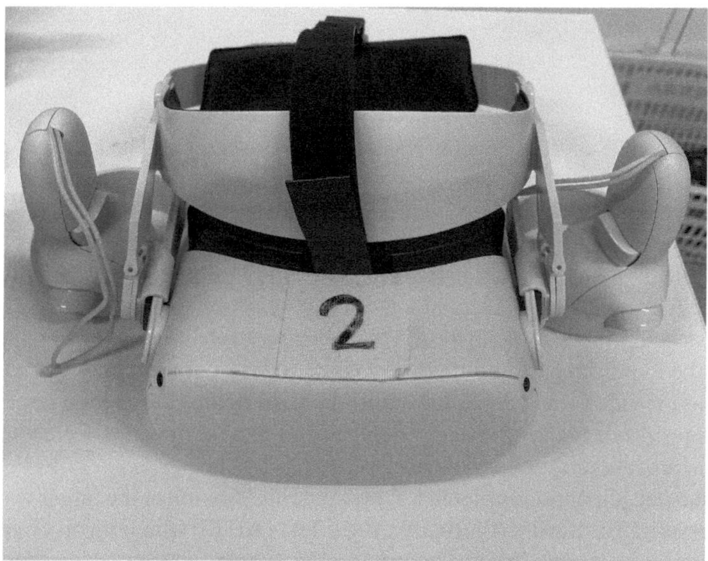

Fig. 2. Meta Quest 2 (Meta).

of the participants were synchronized with those of a virtual avatar as they walked on the treadmill. In the RL condition, the participants walked along the same course in a physical space. Figure 6 and 7 show the course in the VR and physical spaces, respectively.

The experiment was conducted in a room set at 19 °C. Participants who entered the room were instructed to attach the heart rate sensor to their heart, and their resting heart rate was measured for 5 min. The participants were then fitted with motion trackers. Based on the resting heart rate, the target heart rate for moderate intensity was calculated by employing the Karvonen method. Each participant first performed one of the

Fig. 3. Heart rate sensor (Magene).

two conditions (VR or RL), which was randomly assigned. The other condition was conducted on a separate day, with an interval of at least two days between the sessions to avoid carryover effects. During each session, participants were instructed to walk one lap under the assigned condition. While walking, the experimenter verbally monitored their heart rate and gave simple instructions to either maintain or increase their walking speed. Specifically, if the participant's heart rate was below the target level, the experimenter instructed them to walk faster. If their heart rate was close to or had reached the target, the experimenter told them to maintain their current pace. The experimenter continued to provide these verbal cues until the participant reached the target heart rate. Once the appropriate walking speed was identified, the participants were allowed to rest until their heart rate returned to its baseline.

Then, the participants completed a 5-min practice session at the target walking speed while performing Guilford's Alternative Uses Test (AUT), which involves generating as many unusual uses as possible for common objects (e.g., a brick, newspaper, or paperclip). AUT is widely used as a measure of divergent thinking, which is a key component of creativity. Following the work of Fukada et al. [8], the present experiment used four items for AUT: a plastic sheet, chopsticks, a plastic bottle, and a jump rope. During this session, auditory cues were used to help participants internalize the appropriate walking speed. Following the practice session, participants rated their fatigue on the Borg Rating of Perceived Exertion (RPE) scale [8]. The main experiment comprised two 5-min walking sessions during which participants performed AUT under either the RL or VR condition. After each 5-min session, the participants again reported their subjective fatigue on the Borg RPE scale. At the end of the experiment, they completed the questionnaire provided in Table 1 to assess their divergent thinking and the simulator sickness questionnaire (SSQ) developed by Kennedy et al. [9] to evaluate any symptoms

Fig. 4. KATWALKC2 + (KATVR).

of video sickness or physical discomfort. Responses were collected using a five-point Likert scale (1: Not at all; 5: Very much).

The AUT results were evaluated based on the total number of ideas (responses), number of nonredundant ideas (fluency), and number of different categories of nonredundant ideas (flexibility). The three authors independently evaluated the responses for fluency and flexibility, after which they discussed their evaluations and reached a consensus on the final scores.

Table 1. Questionnaire on divergent thinking.

Q1	Felt that the avatar's walking speed in VR was too slow
Q2	Felt more fatigued than usual walking
Q3	Felt that many ideas came to mind in a short time
Q4	Felt that new ideas kept coming
Q5	Felt able to quickly come up with multiple solutions or ideas
Q6	Felt able to think from a different perspective than usual

(continued)

Table 1. (continued)

Q7	Felt able to smoothly shift ideas when stuck
Q8	Felt able to flexibly try multiple approaches to solve the problem
Q9	Felt that the ideas were original
Q10	Felt able to generate new ideas different from others
Q11	Felt ideas were unconventional and reflected originality
Q12	Felt confident in tackling creative tasks
Q13	Felt ideas could be valuable
Q14	Felt capable of coming up with new solutions to any problem
Q15	Felt so focused on generating ideas that I lost track of time
Q16	Felt deeply engaged in creative thinking
Q17	Felt deeply immersed in thinking with little awareness of anything else

3   Results and Discussion

3.1   Walking Performance

All data were analyzed using the open-source statistical software JASP. A two-way analysis of variance (ANOVA) was conducted using the condition (RL vs. VR) and phase (first session vs. second session) as within-subject factors. The results for the mean heart rate are presented in Table 2 and Fig. 8. The mean heart rate was remarkably higher in the VR condition than in the RL condition, which indicated that it involved a higher level of physical exertion under the current experimental settings.

Table 2. ANOVA results for the mean heart rate.

Case	F	p	ω^2
Condition	14.478	0.005	0.432
Phase	14.263	0.005	0.295

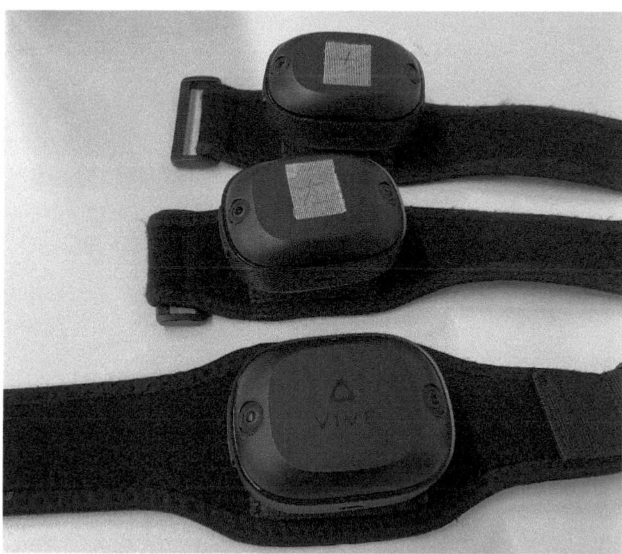

Fig. 5. VIVE Ultimate tracker (HTC).

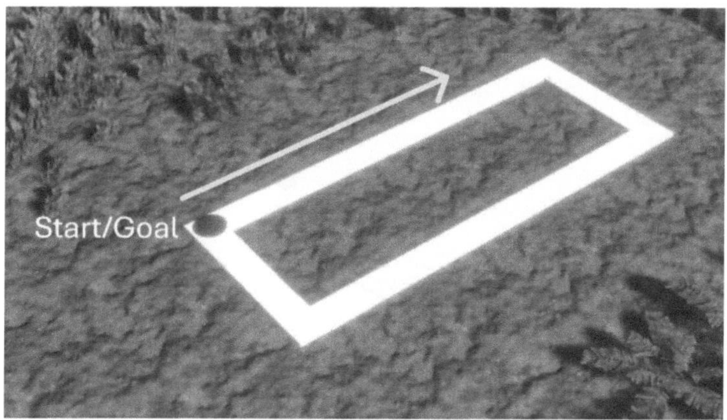

Fig. 6. Course in VR space.

Fig. 7. Course in physical space.

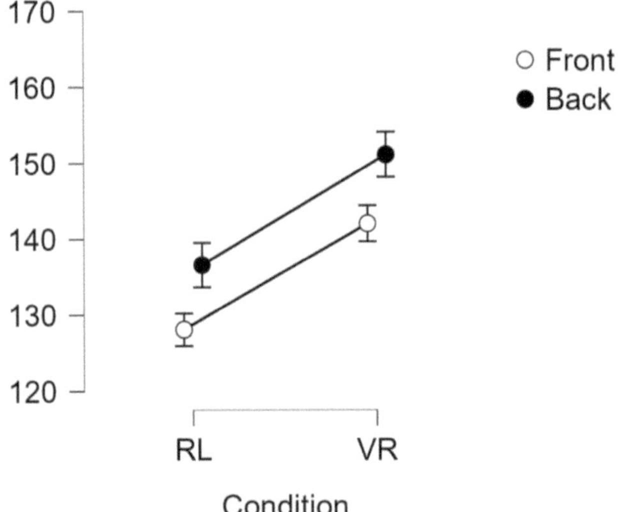

Fig. 8. Mean and standard error of the heart rate.

Table 3 and Fig. 9 present the results for the mean walking speed. The walking speed was remarkably slower under the VR condition than in the RL condition.

Table 3. ANOVA results for the mean walking speed.

Case	F	p	ω^2
Condition	210.476	< .001	0.846
Phase	0.223	0.164	0.006

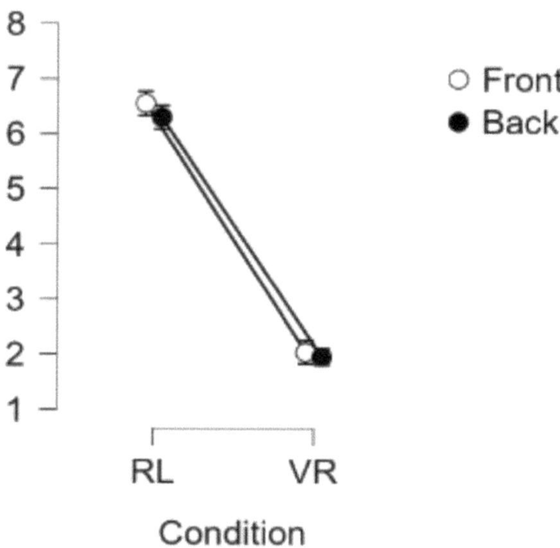

Fig. 9. Mean and standard error of the walking speed.

Table 4 and Fig. 10 present the results for the mean stride length. The stride length was considerably shorter under the VR condition than in the RL condition.

Table 4. ANOVA results for the mean stride length

Case	F	p	ω^2
Condition	249.032	< .001	0.940
Phase	0.836	0.396	0.000

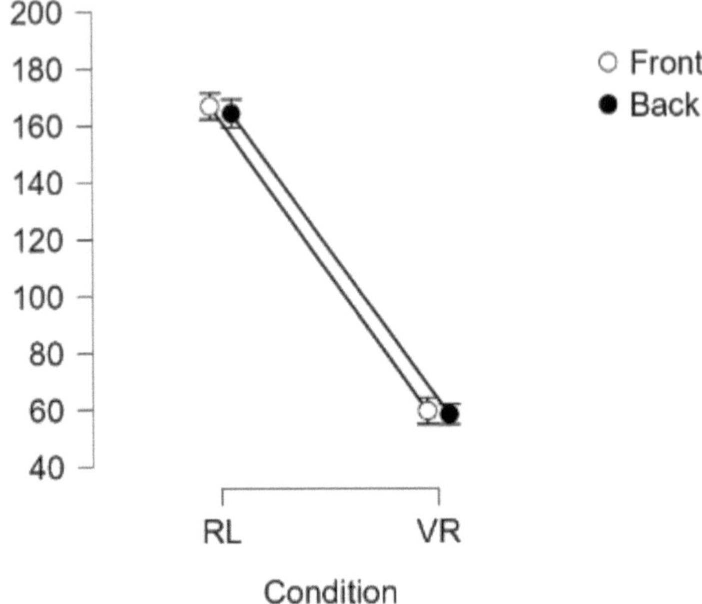

Fig. 10. Mean and standard deviation of the stride length.

Table 5 and Fig. 11 present the results for the mean foot clearance. No remarkable differences were observed between the conditions.

Table 5. ANOVA results for the mean foot clearance.

Case	F	p	ω^2
Condition	1.090	0.337	0.007
Phase	2.524	0.163	0.090

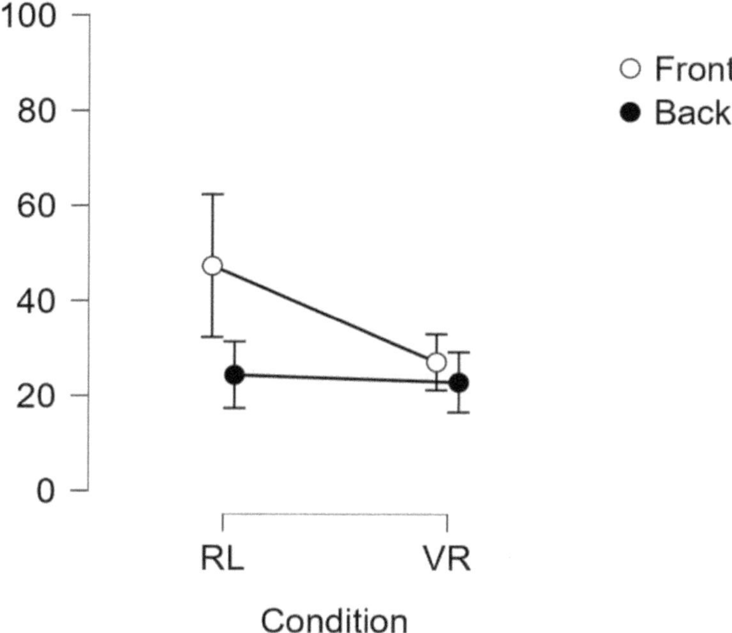

Fig. 11. Mean and standard deviation of the foot clearance.

Figure 12 shows the walking trajectories under the RL and VR conditions. To evaluate the straightness, the walking trajectories were only evaluated along the x-axis, which represented the longest straight section of the course. The mean y-coordinate for each participant during this segment was defined as the ideal walking line, and the standard deviation of the y-coordinate was used as an evaluation index. Table 6 and Fig. 13 present the results of a paired t-test on the standard deviation of the walking trajectories. The standard deviation of the walking trajectory was considerably greater under the VR condition than in the RL condition. This indicates that the participants had more difficulty walking in a straight line under the VR condition.

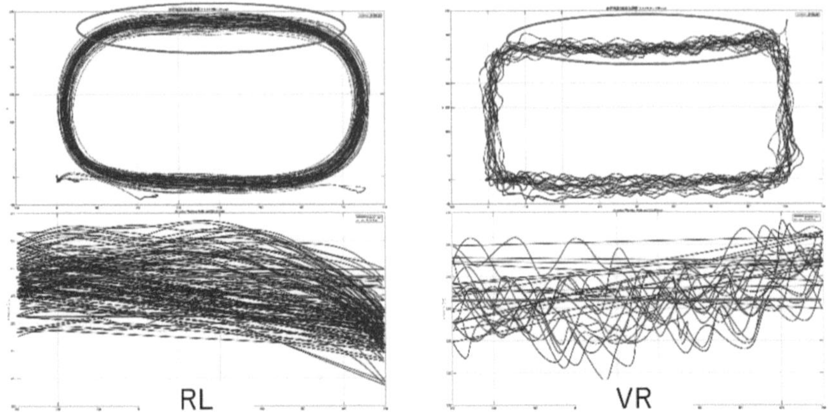

Fig. 12. Walking trajectories and the ideal line under RL and VR conditions.

Table 6. Results of a paired t-test on the standard deviation of the walking trajectories under the RL and VR conditions.

Case	*t*	*df*	*p*
Condition	-2.897	9	0.018

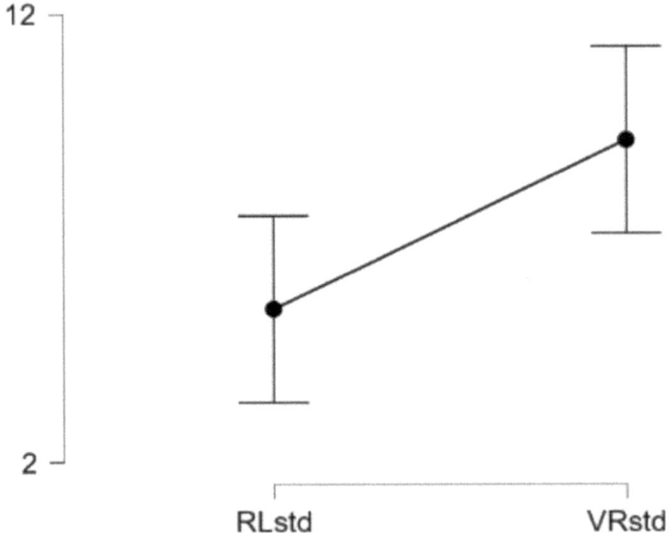

Fig. 13. Mean and standard deviation of the walking trajectories.

3.2   Subjective Evaluation of Divergent Thinking

Tables 7 and 8 include the results of the questionnaire on divergent thinking under each condition. Because of missing data from two participants, eight data points were collected. The mean scores of responses to specific question groups were used as the indicators of various dimensions: (Q2–Q4) fluency, (Q5–Q7) flexibility, (Q8–Q10) originality, (Q11–Q13) self-efficacy, and (Q14–Q16) immersion.

Table 7.   Results of the questionnaire on divergent thinking under the RL condition.

Subject No.	Fluency	Flexibility	Originality	Self-Efficacy	Immersion
1	2.67	4.00	1.25	3.00	4.67
2	1.33	1.00	1.50	1.00	2.00
3	1.33	2.00	3.25	1.67	3.33
4	2.00	2.00	0.75	2.33	4.33
5	2.00	2.00	1.50	1.67	3.67
6	3.00	2.67	0.75	1.00	2.00
7	2.00	2.00	1.50	2.00	2.00
8	2.00	2.33	1.25	2.00	5.00

Table 8.   Results of the questionnaire on divergent thinking under the VR condition.

Subject No.	Fluency	Flexibility	Originality	Self-Efficacy	Immersion
1	2.67	4.00	1.67	3.00	4.67
2	3.33	2.67	2.00	3.33	3.00
3	1.00	1.67	3.00	1.33	1.33
4	3.33	2.67	2.00	3.33	5.00
5	1.00	1.33	2.00	1.00	3.00
6	2.00	1.33	2.00	1.33	4.00
7	1.00	1.00	1.00	1.00	3.67
8	2.00	2.00	2.00	2.00	4.33

According to these results, the Wilcoxon signed-rank test was used to compare the VR and RL conditions for each measure. The results are presented in Table 9. No remarkable differences were found in any of the selected dimensions of divergent creativity.

Table 9. Results of the Wilcoxon signed-rank test on divergent creativity

Case	W	p
Fluency	11.000	1.000
Flexibility	10.000	0.554
Originality	31.000	0.078
SelfEfficacy	11.500	0.916
Immersion	18.000	0.553

3.3 Evaluation of Divergent Thinking

Tables 10–12 present the evaluation of the ANOVA results for the number of responses, fluency, and flexibility. No remarkable differences were observed for any item.

Table 10. ANOVA results for the number of responses

Case	F	p	ω^2
Condition	0.372	0.774	0.000

Table 11. ANOVA results for fluency

Case	F	p	ω^2
Condition	0.458	0.714	0.000

Table 12. ANOVA results for flexibility

Case	F	p	ω^2
Condition	0.519	0.673	0.000

3.4 Discussion

The experimental results indicated that the exercise intensity was higher under the VR condition. However, variables typically associated with an increased physical load such as the walking speed, stride length, and cadence were actually greater under the RL condition. This suggests that the higher exercise intensity under the VR condition may be attributed to other factors. One possible factor is the lateral balance. Under the VR condition, the participants were able to walk less in a straight line. This was likely because of the walking mechanism of the treadmill, which requires the user to move one foot forward while simultaneously sliding the other foot backward. The friction generated during the backward movement may disrupt the lateral balance and make it difficult to maintain a straight walking trajectory. As a result, participants may have exerted additional effort to compensate for the imbalance, which increased the intensity of the exercise. This effect may be mitigated with greater familiarity and practice.

The results on divergent creativity revealed that no remarkable differences were observed between the experimental conditions. However, the subjective evaluations generally had low scores suggesting that the RL and VR conditions did not sufficiently enhance divergent creativity. One possible reason may be the discomfort associated with VR use, which may have interfered with divergent thinking. However, the lack of difference between the RL and VR conditions implies that conducting walking meetings in a VR environment is a potentially viable option for improving divergent thinking if the conditions are modified or optimized.

4 Conclusion and Outlook

This study investigated the differences between walking in physical and VR spaces on exercise intensity and divergent thinking. The VR condition resulted in a higher exercise intensity, which may be owing to reduced lateral balance caused by the friction generated by the walking mechanism of the treadmill. No remarkable differences were observed for the divergent creativity in either the subjective ratings or the response-based measures. However, the difference in walking experience may influence divergent thinking. To determine whether a VR environment can match or exceed the effects of real-world walking on divergent creativity, further empirical studies are necessary. Future research is required to address the issues identified in this study, such as the increased exercise intensity and reduced balance during walking in the VR environment.

References

1. Ministry of Health, Labour and Welfare. https://www.e-healthnet.mhlw.go.jp/information/dictionary/metabolic/ym-048.html
2. Ministry of Health, Labour and Welfare. https://www.e-healthnet.mhlw.go.jp/information/exercise/s-05-005.html
3. Arakawa, S., et al.: Current status of diet and exercise therapy in diabetes care: Results of a nationwide survey of diabetic patients. Diabetes **58**(4), 265–278 (2015)
4. Podrekar, N., Kozinc, Ž, Šarabon, N.: The effects of cycle and treadmill desks on work performance and cognitive function in sedentary workers: A review and meta-analysis. Work **65**(3), 537–545 (2020)
5. Cho, J., Freivalds, A., Rovniak, L., Sung, K., Hatzell, J.: Using a desk-compatible recumbent bike in an office workstation. Proceedings of the Human Factors and Ergonomics Society Annual Meeting **58**(1), 1662–1666 (2014)
6. Oppezzo, M., Schwartz, D.L.: Give your ideas some legs: The positive effect of walking on creative thinking. J. Exp. Psychol. Learn. Mem. Cogn. **40**(4), 1142–1152 (2014)
7. Tachi, A.: Virtual reality and transversal core science and technology. Measurement and Control **42**(3), 196 (2003)

8. Borg, G.: Borg's perceived exertion and painscale. Champaign IL: Human Kinetics (1998)
9. Kennedy, R.S., Lane, N.E., Berbaum, K.S., Lilienthal, M.G.: Simulator sickness questionnaire: An enhanced method for quantifying simulator sickness. Int. J. Aviat. Psychol. **3**(3), 203–220 (1993)
10. Ariga, A., Lleras, A.: Brief and rare mental "breaks" keep you focused: Deactivation and reactivation of task goals preempt vigilance decrements. Cognition **118**(3), 439–443 (2011)

Enhancing Navigation in Virtual Reality with Naturally Recallable Wall Decorations

Misuzu Hasegawa[1], Mana Nakai[1] (ID), Shinji Miyake[1] (ID), and Daiji Kobayashi[2(✉)] (ID)

[1] Graduate School of Chitose Institute of Science and Technology, Hokkaido, Japan
[2] Chitose Institute of Science and Technology, Hokkaido, Japan
{m2240360,d-kobaya}@photon.chitose.ac.jp

Abstract. As public and commercial facilities grow in scale and complexity, wayfinding within such environments has become an increasingly challenging task. Conventional aids, such as floor guides, are often insufficient because their fixed locations and limited accessibility, particularly for foreign visitors navigating multilingual signage. This study investigates the potential of wall decorations as continuous, language-independent visual cues to support pedestrian navigation. In the first phase, ten participants evaluated the memorability of eight types of three-dimensional wall decorations in a virtual environment. Decorations featuring identifiable motifs were determined to be more naturally recallable. In the second phase, 18 participants performed wayfinding tasks in virtual mazes simulating a three-story hotel, with the conditions varying according to the presence and type of wall decorations. The results indicated significantly shorter return journey times in environments with naturally recallable decorations ($p < .001$), suggesting enhanced spatial memory. Participants under these conditions relied less on alternative cues, such as room numbers or route features. Qualitative feedback emphasized the importance of decoration distinctiveness and density. These findings suggest that strategically designed wall decorations can serve as effective navigational aids, enhancing route memory and supporting intuitive movement in complex architectural spaces.

Keywords: Virtual Reality · Navigation · Biomorphic Design · Wall Decoration

1 Introduction

1.1 Expansion of Commercial Facilities

Recently, commercial facilities have continuously expanded, with numerous stations and shopping malls undergoing extension or renovation into large-scale complexes. In general, as commercial facilities grow, their structures become increasingly complex. However, navigating large facilities with intricate layouts can be challenging, which makes it difficult to locate destinations.

In numerous cases, floor guides are installed to assist the visitors. Although these guides facilitate the easy identification of the current location and intended destination of an individual, their installation locations are limited. Moreover, as facilities become

H. Mori et al. (Eds.): HCII 2025, LNCS 16333, pp. 19–30, 2026.
https://doi.org/10.1007/978-3-032-12660-3_2

larger and more complex, floor guides evolve accordingly, incorporating multilingual information owing to the increasing number of foreign tourists. Consequently, the volume of information has increased, presenting both convenience and challenges.

These factors further hinder the discovery of destinations and memorization of routes. Therefore, to prevent visitors from getting lost in facilities with intricate layouts, devising methods that encourage spatial awareness and help individuals retain their sense of direction and location is essential.

Regarding the relationship between navigation and memory, a study demonstrated that the memory of landmarks is superior to that of streets (Tom et al., 2004) [1]. Furthermore, Credé et al. (2019) revealed that local landmarks, such as storefronts along streets, cause less navigation-related stress than global landmarks, such as distant towers [2].

Based on these findings, this study proposes a method for incorporating easily memorable decorations throughout walls to provide continuous visual cues. Because this approach does not rely on the language of the user, it can effectively accommodate multilingual tourists.

1.2 Biomorphic Design

Biomorphic design plays an important role as a wall element that directs attention toward space as a landmark. Biomorphic design is a type of biophilia that reflects the innate biological connections between humans and nature. People find the sounds of campfires and ocean waves appealing, and nature walks provide restorative and soothing effects. Biomorphic design embodies this connection through curvilinear and fluid forms inspired by natural elements, such as living organisms and water. Developed from research demonstrating that shifting focal points can reduce stress and enhance concentration, the purpose of biomorphic design is to create visually pleasant environments that foster a sense of connection to nature, improve cognitive abilities, and aid in stress reduction. Two primary approaches to implementing biomorphic design exist: incorporating decorative elements within a larger design, or integrating them into structural or functional aspects. Architects known for employing biomorphic design include Antoni Gaudí, who designed Casa Milà and the Sagrada Familia [3], as well as Toyo Ito [4]. Figures 1 and 2 illustrate examples of their architectural works.

Fig. 1. Antoni Gaudí's Casa Milà.

Regarding biomorphic design and spatial memory, Mirkia et al. (2022) reported that in static images of spaces incorporating biomorphic design, participants who exhibited

Fig. 2. Toyo Ito's National Taichung Theater.

higher visual attention to biomorphic elements tended to achieve higher spatial memory scores [5]. Furthermore, Nakai (2025) determined that in a virtual environment, integrating biomorphic design helped individuals who were prone to losing better recall of previously traveled routes [6].

However, both studies utilized static images or simple pathways as the experimental environments, and the characteristics of wall decorations specifically aimed at enhancing memory and their effects on navigation have not been thoroughly examined.

1.3 Purpose of this Study

Therefore, this study aims to investigate the features of wall decorations that are more memorable to pedestrians and to identify spatial elements that contribute to more efficient pedestrian navigation. This study was reviewed and approved by the Research Ethics Committee of the Chitose Institute of Science and Technology (Approval No. 2023-6).

2 Investigation of Recallable Wall Decoration Features

2.1 Methods

We assessed the ease with which eight decoration samples could be recalled using a paired comparison method to examine the characteristics of recallable decorations. The paired comparison method is an evaluation technique that quantifies the relative strength of sensations or preferences by systematically comparing pairs of samples. Specifically, this approach involves assessing two samples at multiple stages without considering the order of presentation, thereby ensuring that all possible pairs are evaluated.

We developed decoration samples based on biomorphic design principles to enhance spatial recognition within virtual environments by seamlessly integrating design elements into space. The decoration samples created for this study are shown in Fig. 3. During the design process, specific motifs were selected (1: Flower, 2: Sun, 3: Leaf, 4: Wind, 5: Snow, 6: Honeycomb, 7: Water, 8: Flame), and Blender 3.5 was utilized for their creation.

Participants. Ten healthy students, aged 21–27 years (*mean* = 22.5, *SD* = 1.8), participated in this study. Prior to the experiment, all participants received a comprehensive explanation of the study procedures and provided informed consent.

Experimental Environment. Decoration samples were presented in a virtual environment developed using Unity (2021.3.28f1) and displayed on a VIVE Pro Eye of head-mounted display (HMD). The virtual space used in the experiment is depicted in Figs. 4

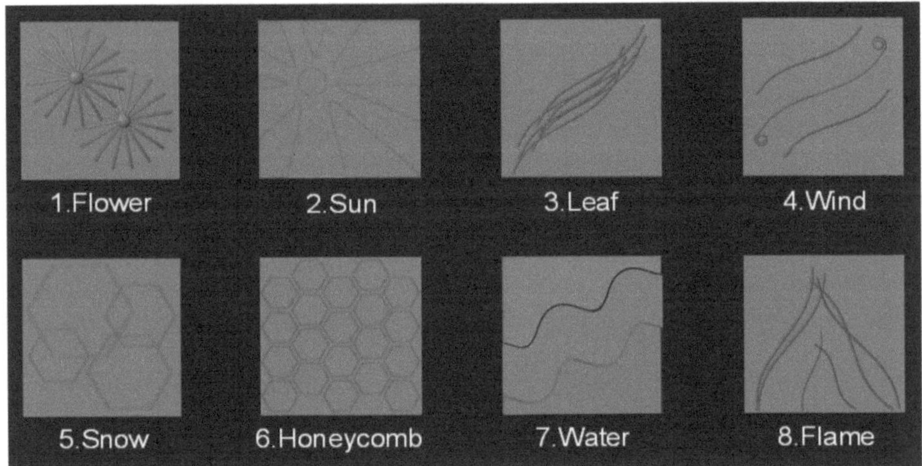

Fig. 3. Motifs established with reference to biomorphic design and the eight types of decoration samples created.

and 5, and the HMD is shown in Fig. 6. Participants evaluated the recallability of the two decoration samples using a 7-point scale ranging from -3 to + 3, as summarized in Table 1. Given that eight types of decoration samples were present; 28 evaluations were performed. The presentation sequence was randomized for each participant to mitigate order effects.

The evaluations were selected using the HMD controller, and the responses were recorded in an Excel file. Upon completion of the evaluations, the participants were asked to complete a questionnaire.

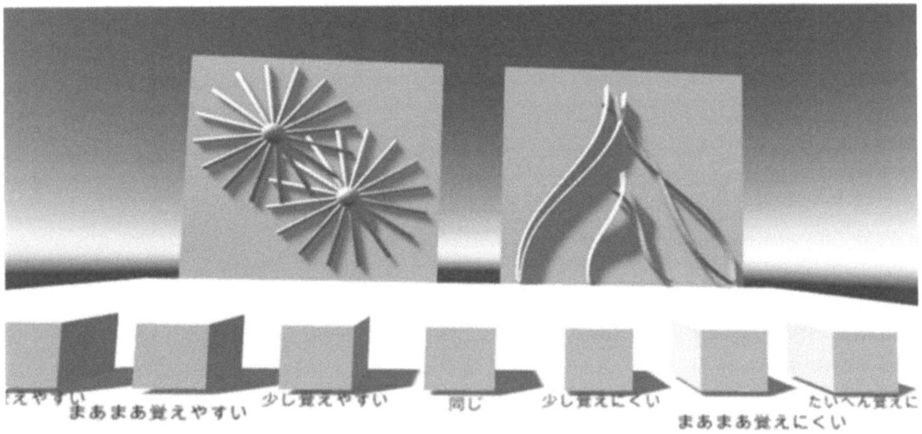

Fig. 4. Virtual space used in the experiment.

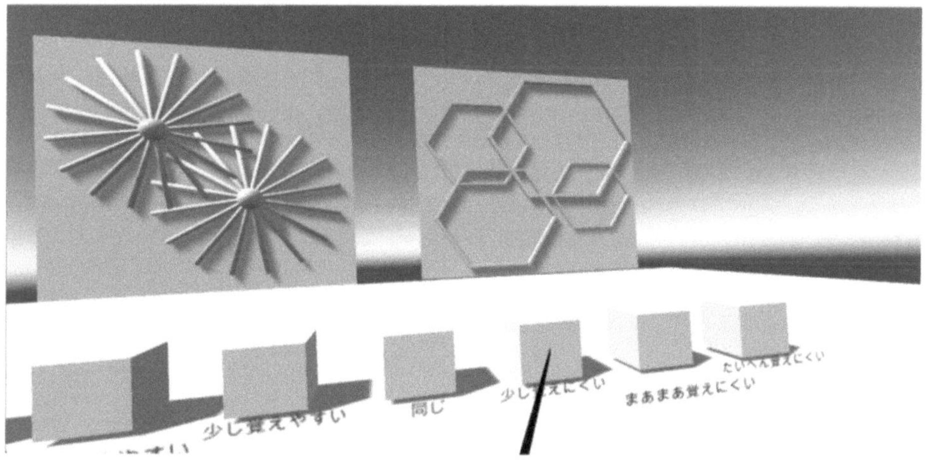

Fig. 5. Scene of participants selecting evaluations using a VR controller.

Fig. 6. HMD used in the experiment.

Table 1. Seven-point evaluation criteria presented to participants.

Score	Description
+ 3	The decoration on the left is significantly more recallable than that on the right.
+ 2	The decoration on the left is considerably more recallable than that on the right.
+ 1	The decoration on the left is slightly more recallable than that on the right.
± 0	The decoration on the left is equally recallable as that on the right.
-1	The decoration on the left is slightly less recallable than that on the right.
-2	The decoration on the left is considerably less recallable than that on the right.
-3	The decoration on the left is significantly less recallable than that on the right.

2.2   Results and Discussion

Using the paired comparison ratings ranging from -3 to + 3, the average preference score (α) was calculated, as shown in Fig. 7. A higher average preference score indicates that the participants rated the decoration sample as more recallable. The decoration sample rated as the most recallable was Sample 1 (Motif: Flower, $\alpha = 0.9$), whereas the least recallable sample was Sample 3 (Motif: Leaf, $\alpha = -1.1875$). However, no significant differences were observed between Samples 1 and 3.

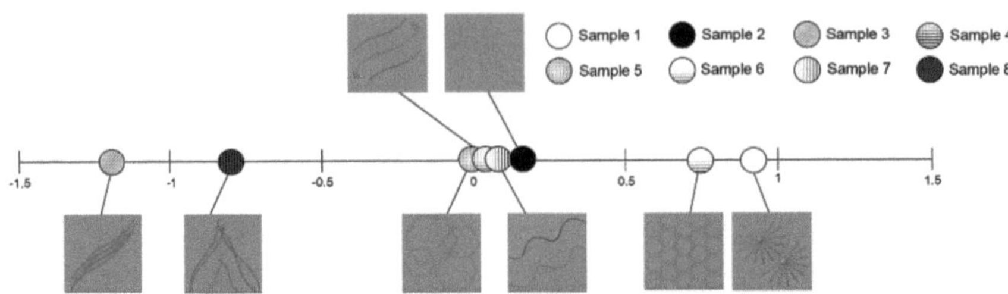

Fig. 7.   Average preference score calculated from the evaluation points.

Regarding the criteria for a "recallable" decoration sample, eight out of ten participants cited size and clarity as key factors. Additionally, six out of ten participants stated that motifs that were easily recognizable and could be intuitively named contributed to recallability.

An analysis of the decoration samples that participants named revealed that for the most recallable samples, seven out of ten participants referred to Sample 1 as "Sun" or "One Sun," whereas Sample 2 was labeled as "Sun" or "Two Suns." Furthermore, seven out of ten participants identified Sample 6 as "Honeycomb" or "Hexagonal Structure."

In contrast, although six out of ten participants labeled Decoration Sample 8 as "Flame," its average preference score was relatively low. Participant feedback on Sample 8 included comments such as "I only realized it was a flame midway through" and "After recognizing it as a flame, my perception shifted from recalling it as a difficult-to-recall decoration to an easier-to-recall one." These observations suggest that the difficulty in recognizing the motif contributed to the lower recallability rating.

The average preference scores derived from the paired comparison evaluation, along with participant feedback, indicated that decorations with a large and distinct appearance, as well as easily identifiable and nameable motifs, tended to be more recallable.

Based on the findings of this study, the three decoration samples with high average preference scores (Samples 1, 2, and 6) were classified as "recallable decorations," whereas the three samples with low average preference scores (Samples 3, 5, and 8) were categorized as "less recallable decorations."

3   Verifications of Recallable Wall Decorations

3.1   Methods

Participants. A total of eighteen healthy students, aged 21–27 years (*mean* = 22.5, *SD* = 1.2), participated in this study. Prior to the experiment, all participants received a comprehensive explanation of the study procedures and provided informed consent.

Experimental Environment. The participants performed navigation tasks in a maze in decorated and undecorated virtual environments. The maze was designed to resemble a three-story hotel and created using Unity (2021.3.28f1).

The experiment involved the following three tasks: Task 1 featured walls with recallable decorations; Task 2 featured walls with less recallable decorations; and Task 3 featured undecorated walls. The virtual environment was constructed using Unity 2021.3.28f1 (Unity Technologies), whereas the decorations were designed using Blender 4.1 (Blender Foundation) and placed on the maze walls. The structures of Tasks 1–3 are illustrated in Figs. 8, 9, and 10. In the figure for Task 1, the orange line represents Sample 1, green line represents Sample 2, and blue line represents Sample 6. Similarly, in the figure for Task 2, the orange line represents Sample 3, green line represents Sample 5, and blue line represents Sample 8. Based on the results of Experiment 1, which suggested that large and distinct decorations enhance recallability, decoration samples were placed to fill the entire vertical span of the maze walls. The state of the maze during the experiment is shown in Fig. 11.

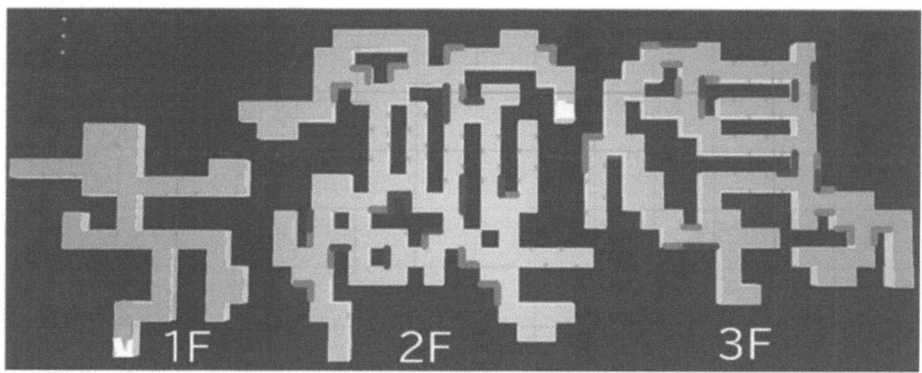

Fig. 8. Structure of the maze used in Task 1.

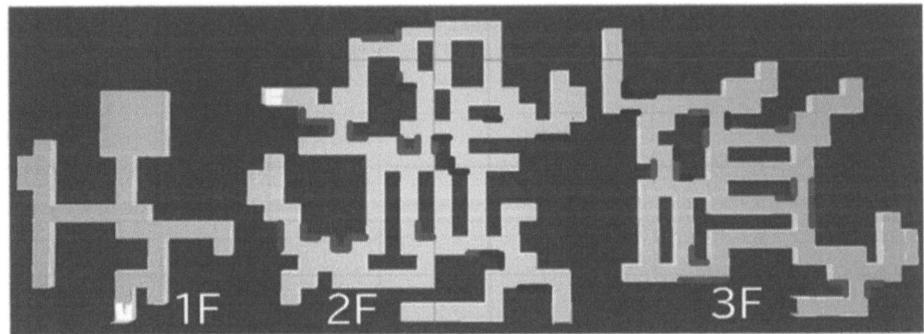

Fig. 9. Structure of the maze used in Task 2.

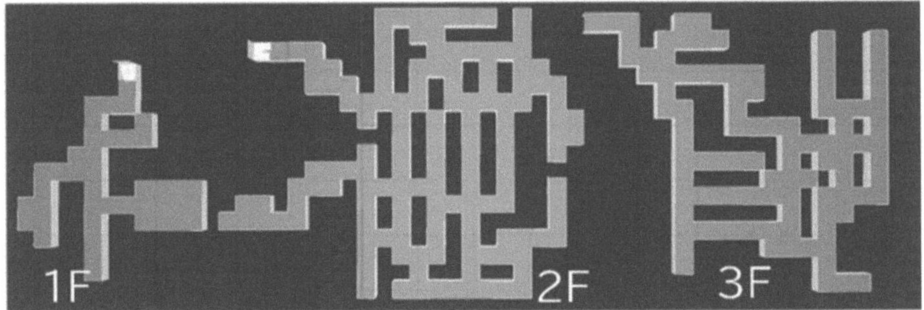

Fig. 10. Structure of the maze used in Task 3.

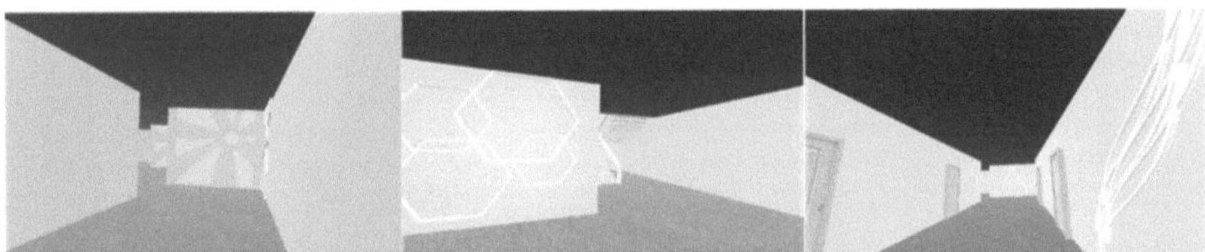

Fig. 11. Interior of the virtual space used in the experiment.

During the outbound task, participants explored the environment while navigating from the starting point on the first floor to a designated goal door on the third floor. In the return task, participants retraced their route based on prior experience and selected what they perceived as the shortest path back to the starting point. The outbound and return tasks for Task 1 are referred to as Task 1–1 and Task 1–2, respectively. Each participant was assigned a randomized task execution sequence to control order effects.

Throughout the experiment, the completion times for both the outbound and return tasks were recorded, followed by a post-task questionnaire survey. Additionally, gaze coordinates were tracked using the VIVE Pro Eye of HMD, with data output to a CSV file at intervals of 0.01 s for precise recording.

3.2 Results and Discussion

Completion Time. Before analyzing the completion time, the experimenter navigated each maze environment using the shortest possible route and recorded the time required to travel from the starting point to the goal. This process was repeated five times for each environment, and the average time was established as the baseline time for each environment. The baseline time was subtracted from each participant's recorded completion time to obtain pure completion time. In this study, the completion time obtained through this process was referred to as the standard completion time.

A statistical test was performed to compare the standard completion times of the outbound and return tasks in each environment. Significant differences were observed between Task 1–1 and Task 1–2, as well as between Task 2–1 and Task 2–2 ($p < .001$). Additionally, a significant difference was observed between Task 3–1 and Task 3–2 ($p < .05$). The standard completion times for the return tasks in different environments are shown in Fig. 12.

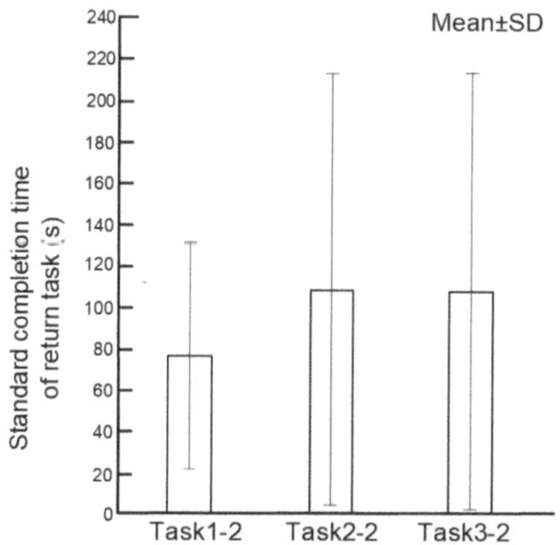

Fig. 12. Standard completion time and standard deviation for the return task ($n = 18$).

Analysis of standard deviations revealed that Task 1 exhibited a lower variance than Tasks 2 and 3, indicating that individual differences in completion time were more pronounced in the return tasks for Tasks 2 and 3 than for Task 1. This suggests that participants' completion times were more consistent in the return task for Task 1, whereas greater individual variation was observed in Tasks 2 and 3.

Gaze Duration. For Task 1, the participants were categorized into three groups based on their standard completion times. Those who completed the return task faster than the standard completion time minus one standard deviation (Participants B and I) were assigned to Group 1, whereas those who completed the task slower than the standard completion time plus one standard deviation (Participants C, N, and G) were assigned to Group 3. Participants who did not fall into either category were classified into Group 2. This classification allowed for the analysis of gaze duration spent on decorations across the three groups. CSV files containing recorded coordinates and timestamps were converted into Excel format to extract gaze data, and Visual Basic was used to filter out cells corresponding to the decoration areas. From this, the gaze duration was calculated, and the average gaze duration for each group was determined. The results indicated that the average gaze duration was 31.7 s for Group 1, 36.0 s for Group 2, and 34.7 s for Group 3.

Participants in Group 1 reported selectively remembering decorations that were critical for navigation, stating: "I only remembered the decorations around the staircase" and "I memorized the shape of distinctive corridors along with the decorations." Their ability to filter relevant decorations appeared to support efficient navigation during the return task. Group 2 participants largely exhibited similar recall patterns to Group 1, but Participants K and J noted: "I noticed the decorations but did not actively try to remember them during the outbound task" and "I navigated by following the right-side wall during the outbound task, which helped me retain a sense of spatial orientation." This suggests that some participants executed the task without relying on the decorations as navigational cues. Therefore, Group 2 was further refined by excluding Participants K and J, forming Group 2–2, which had an average gaze duration of 38.7 s.

The analysis of Group 3 revealed differences in individual gaze behaviors. Participant C exhibited a shorter gaze compared with Participants G and N. Regarding task difficulty, Participant G stated that the return task was "not easy," and Participant N indicated that it was "rather difficult." In contrast, Participant C reported that the task was "somewhat easy" and commented, "I relied on decorations for navigation and felt confident in the return task but still made an error in route selection." This highlights the differences in the perceived difficulty among the participants. Therefore, after excluding Participant C from Group 3, the remaining two participants were classified as Group 3–2. The average gaze duration for this group was determined to be 42.8 s.

Based on these results, the gaze durations of the participants are summarized in Fig. 13. Evidently, several participants selectively focused on wall decorations by categorizing participants into three groups based on Task 1–2 completion times and analyzing their gaze duration and feedback, integrating them with other spatial cues to aid in navigation during the return task. In addition, participants who spent more time gazing at decorations tended to have shorter completion times in the return task. Conversely, some participants with extremely short completion times completed the task without relying on decorations, rather relying on their intrinsic directional sense. In contrast, some participants with significantly longer completion times appeared confident in their memory, yet they did not actively focus on decorations, leading to navigation errors during the return task.

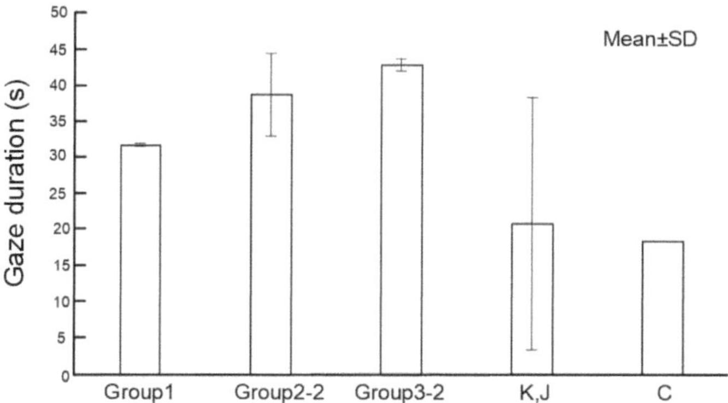

Fig. 13. Average gaze duration and standard deviation for each group classified based on the standard completion time of the return task ($n = 18$).

4 Conclusion

These findings suggest that several participants utilized wall decorations as navigational cues, with recallable wall decorations particularly enhancing their ability to memorize complex pathways. In addition, a selective gaze at decorations and their integration with other spatial cues contributed to efficient navigation during the return task.

However, further investigation is required to enhance the effectiveness of wall decorations in navigation for a broader range of participants, particularly focusing on the gaze duration patterns of Group 3. Specifically, optimizing decoration design, color schemes, and presentation methods to ensure that visual elements can be passively remembered and recalled when needed, even without conscious effort, is crucial.

As this experiment was conducted in a virtual reality (VR) environment, future research should focus on validating these findings in real-world settings or replicating them in virtual spaces that closely resemble real environments. This approach can enhance wayfinding strategies in commercial facilities, potentially reducing instances of disorientation and navigation errors.

In summary, this study indicates the potential role of recallable decorations in supporting navigation and spatial memory. Future research should refine decoration design strategies and optimize presentation methods to facilitate seamless navigation experiences in both virtual and real-world environments.

Acknowledgments. We would like to thank Editage (www.editage.jp) for English language editing.

Disclosure of Interests..   The authors have no competing interests to declare that are relevant to the content of this article.

References

1. Tom, A., Denis, M.: Language and spatial cognition: Comparing the roles of landmarks and street names in route instructions. Appl. Cogn. Psychol. **18**(9), 1213–1230 (2004). https://doi.org/10.1002/acp.1045

2. Credé, S., Thrash, T., et al.: The acquisition of survey knowledge for local and global landmark configurations under time pressure. Spat. Cogn. Comput. **19**(3), 190–219 (2019). https://doi.org/10.1080/13875868.2019.1569016
3. Casa Milà, La Pedrera. https://www.lapedrera.com/en, Accessed 2025/5/29
4. Ito T et al. Architects. http://www.toyo-ito.co.jp/WWW/index/index_en.html, Accessed 2025/5/29
5. Mirkia, H., Nelson, M.S.C., et al.: Recognition memory for interior spaces with biomorphic or non-biomorphic interior architectural elements. J Interior Des **47**(3), 47–66 (2022). https://doi.org/10.1111/joid.12224
6. Mana, N., Misuzu, H., Daiji, K.: Late breaking papers the effect of visual design using biomorphic designs on walking behavior in virtual world. HCI International **2024**, 182–192 (2025)

The Avatar as an Extension of the Self: How Personal Avatar Embodiment Influences Self-Perception

Chisato Kasahara and Mamiko Sakata[(✉)]

Graduate School of Culture and Information Science, Doshisha University,
Kyotanabe, Kyoto 610-0394, Japan
`msakata@mail.doshisha.ac.jp`

Abstract. The phenomenon whereby users' cognition and behavior are altered through avatar embodiment—commonly referred to as the Proteus effect [1]—has been extensively studied. However, prior research has predominantly focused on the effects of ready-made avatars experimenters have designed. In contrast, this study explores the psychological effects of personal avatars—those that users customize for the purpose of interacting with others. Specifically, we examine how different forms of self-projection onto personal avatars (i.e., projection of the real self vs. the ideal self) influence changes in users' self-perception during avatar embodiment. Our findings indicate that using personal avatars can induce shifts in self-perception. Moreover, the type of self projected onto the avatar significantly modulates the direction and magnitude of these changes. Finally, the results suggest that the timing of avatar use (i.e., whether users view their real selves before or after avatar embodiment) also plays a critical role in shaping self-perceptual outcomes.

Keywords: Personal Avatar · Self-Perception · Avatar embodiment · Self-Projection Strategy

1   Introduction

In recent years, user-customized avatars have become increasingly prevalent as tools for communication in digital spaces. In this study, we define a personal avatar as an one that users design to serve as their alter ego, specifically for interactions with others. We examine how the embodiment of a personal avatar influences users' self-perception.

Embodiment is interpreted differently across academic disciplines [2]. In avatar research, embodiment typically refers to the sense of embodiment (SoE)—the subjective experience of feeling as if one is inside, owning and controlling an avatar. It is often defined as, "the ensemble of sensations that arise in conjunction with being inside, having, and controlling a body," or as, "the sense that emerges when avatar's properties are processed as if they were the properties of one's own biological body" [3]. In this study, we refer to the use of an avatar synchronized with the user's movements as "embodiment."

H. Mori et al. (Eds.): HCII 2025, LNCS 16333, pp. 31–42, 2026.
https://doi.org/10.1007/978-3-032-12660-3_3

2 Related Work

The Proteus effect refers to the phenomenon in which users' cognition and behavior change because of embodying an avatar [1]. A substantial body of research has demonstrated this effect. For example, embodying an Einstein avatar has been shown to improve performance on the Tower of London Task (TOL) [4], embodying a casually dressed Black avatar with an Afro hairstyle increases arm swing during drumming compared to embodying a formally dressed White avatar [5], and using a dragon avatar can reduce fear of heights [6]. Most of these studies have focused on the effects of *ready-made avatars*—those the experimenter designed and provided. However, no mention has been made of the fundamental role of avatars as an alter ego of oneself.

Recent studies have begun to investigate how using an avatar as one's alter ego influences behavior. For example, Koulouris et al. (2020) demonstrated that avatars resembling one's appearance led to better performance compared to idealized avatars [7]. Similarly, avatars that match the user's gender and ethnicity tend to enhance the sense of embodiment, that is, the feeling that the avatar's body is one's own [8]. In this way, by focusing on the aspect of avatars as one's alter ego, avatar embodiment and its impact on users has been explored. However, these studies focus on the effects of embodying avatars that were created based on pre-instructed conditions or avatars the experimenter prepared to reflect the users' characteristics. Nevertheless, the effects of embodying self-created avatars remain underexplored.

As mentioned earlier, studies have shown that embodied avatars can influence users' cognition and behavior (the Proteus effect). As discussed above, the Proteus effect demonstrates that avatar embodiment can alter cognition and behavior. However, the examination of the impact of avatar use on the self has mostly focused on the effects of using "ready-made avatars" the experimenter prepared. However, given that an avatar's body can be freely customized and used as a representation of the self [9], it is essential to explore what users seek in their alter ego. We refer to such self-designed avatars as personal avatars. In our prior research, we examined how users project aspects of their real and ideal selves onto these avatars [10]. This suggests that avatars may contribute as a mirror reflecting their self. We found that personal avatars may reflect not only latent desires and aspirations such as, "what they want to become," but also perceived shortcomings and feelings of inferiority related to their "real self".

3 Research Objectives

Previous research on the impact of avatars—particularly within the framework of the traditional Proteus effect—has largely focused on how avatar embodiment influences cognitive processing and behavioral outcomes, typically using ready-made avatars. However, we argue that changes in self-perception may occur prior to these cognitive and behavioral shifts. Despite this possibility, the effect of avatar embodiment on self-perception remains underexplored.

In this study, we aim to investigate how embodying a personal avatar—one the user creates and customizes—affects self-perception. Specifically, we examine whether the degree and type of self-projection (e.g., projection of the real self vs. the ideal self) onto the avatar modulates these effects.

4   Method

We conducted an experiment in which participants created personal avatars, followed by an interview-based embodiment session using the avatars they had designed.

4.1   Personal Avatar Creation

Fifty-two university and graduate students participated (19 male, 33 females; $M =$ 19.04 years, $SD = 1.19$). Participants were recruited on the condition that they had no prior experience using avatars in metaverse spaces designed for communication, such as virtual reality (VR) social networking services. For avatar creation, we used the 3D character design tool "VRoid Studio,"[1] that Pixiv Inc. Developed. This software offers an intuitive interface that supports extensive customization of facial features, hairstyles, body shapes, clothing, and accessories. Prior to the experiment, participants were asked to complete the Self-Presentation Motivation Scale [11] to assess their self-perception by indicating the extent to which each item applied to themselves. After completing the questionnaire, we introduced the basic features of VRoid Studio, including how to modify the avatar's face, hair, body, clothing, and accessories (see Fig. 1).

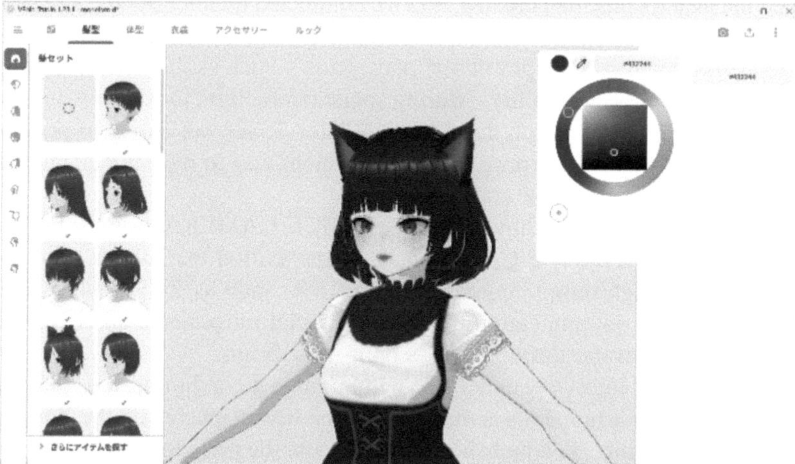

Fig. 1. Avatar customization interface. Participants created personal avatars using VRoid Studio, which allows customization of face, hairstyle, body, clothing, and accessories.

After explaining how to operate the tool, we provided the following instruction: "Imagine communicating online with someone who has no knowledge of your real appearance and never will. Create the avatar you would use in that situation." Participants had 30 min to create their avatars (see Fig. 2). After the avatar creation, we asked participants to respond to the Self-Projection Strategy Scale [10], which measures how participants projected their self onto the avatar.

---

[1] https://vroid.com/studio (accessed 03–01-2025).

Fig. 2. Examples of avatars participants created

4.2   Personal Avatar Creation Experiment

We invited the same 52 participants to participate in an additional session, in which they embodied the avatars they had created, and we conducted an interview. Each participant assumed the role of an interviewer in an online interview scenario. We adopted this setting to assess potential changes in self-perception—such as those related to physical appearance, personality, and ability—during social interaction. In addition, by assigning participants the task of taking on the role of an interviewer, we aimed to prevent them from realizing that the true purpose of the experiment was to measure changes in self-perception resulting from avatar embodiment.

To enable real-time embodiment, we used NICE CAMERA,[2] developed by Kids Plates Inc., in this study. NICE CAMERA is an application that allows users to easily operate avatars through remote communication tools such as Zoom and Teams. This tool enables natural communication by allowing facial movements and expressions to be reflected onto the avatar through a PC's built-in webcam.

We conducted the interview under two within-subject conditions: the "real-self condition," in which the participant's actual appearance was displayed on the Zoom screen, and the "avatar condition," in which the personal avatar the participant previously created was displayed. Participants who underwent the interview in the order of the avatar condition followed by the real-self condition were assigned to the "avatar-first embodiment group," and those who underwent the interview in the order of the real-self condition followed by the avatar condition were assigned to the "avatar-second embodiment group." We randomly assigned participants to these between-subject conditions.

The experimenter guided participants to a PC and explained the experiment, which involved conducting an online interview in the role of an interviewer. Participants were instructed to take on the role of an interviewer by reading aloud the interview script and asking questions. The experimenter gave interview responses from a separate room,

---

[2] https://nicecamera.kidsplates.jp/ (accessed 2025–03-01).

using the Zoom chat function and based on a pre-prepared script (Fig. 3). In this experiment, each participant took part in two interview sessions. Therefore, the replies to the interviewer's questions were the same for all participants. In addition, care was taken to ensure that the replies in the first and second interview sessions did not overlap.

Using the chat function eliminated as much as possible the influence that responses containing nonverbal elements—such as voice and facial expressions—might have on the interview conducted by the participant acting as the interviewer. Participants were then instructed: "While looking at the screen, please act as the interviewer to make it easier for the respondent to answer." At the end of each interview session, we reassessed self-perception using the same Self-Presentation Motivation Scale administered prior to the experiment. Finally, we conducted a debriefing session and concluded the experiment.

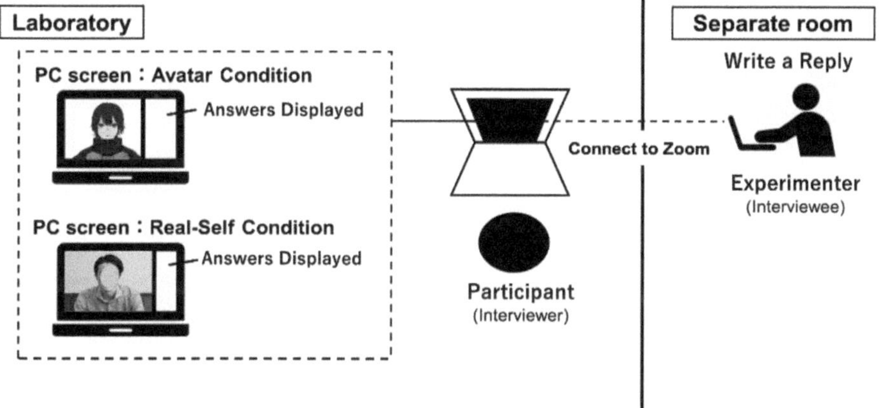

Fig. 3. Experimental environment. The participant conducted interviews from a laboratory PC under avatar and real-self conditions. The experimenter (interviewee) responded remotely via Zoom using the chat function.

5 Results

5.1 Patterns of the Self-Projection Strategy

To examine how participants projected their sense of self onto the avatars they created, we used an exploratory factor analysis on the raw scores of the nine items from the Self-Projection Strategy Scale. We used the maximum likelihood method with Promax rotation. One item, "The avatar is cohesive as a whole," was excluded due to a factor loading below 0.40. After reanalysis, two factors emerged, explaining 52.50% of the cumulative variance (Table 1). As a result, two factors were extracted, and the cumulative contribution rate was 52.50%. We labeled the first factor the Reality Projection Factor because it included items such as, "The avatar reflects my real self" and "The avatar is not far from how I usually am." We labeled the second factor the Ideal Projection Factor because it contained items such as, "The avatar embodies my ideal self" and "The avatar is designed to be likable to others."

The raw scores of the items comprising each factor were summed and then divided by the number of items to calculate the factor scores. These scores were used as self-presentation strategy scores in the subsequent analyses.

Table 1. Factor loadings in items of the Self-Projection Strategy Scale.

Items of the self-projection strategy scale		The Reality	The Ideal
The avatar is not far from how I usually am.		0.95	0.03
The avatar reflects my real self.		0.87	0.00
The avatar features a look only possible in virtual space.		-0.72	0.30
The avatar conveys my individuality.		0.46	0.20
The avatar is designed to be likable to others.		0.00	0.79
The avatar reflects my feelings at the time.		0.16	0.70
The avatar is dressed in fashionable clothing.		-0.08	0.47
The avatar embodies my ideal self.		-0.31	0.46
Inter-factor correlation	The Reality	1.00	
	The Ideal	-0.10	1.00

5.2 The Impact of Embodiment of Personal Avatars on Self-Perception

We conducted a factor analysis on the 11 items of the Self-Presentation Motivation Scale to assess self-perception. The analysis used the maximum likelihood method with Promax rotation. As a result, four factors were extracted, with a cumulative contribution rate of 60.40%. Based on [12], the first factor was labeled "Competence," the second "Physical Attractiveness" the third "Ethicality," and the fourth "Approachability" (Table 2). Based on the factor structure obtained through factor analysis, factor scores were calculated separately for the real self and the avatar. For each, the raw scores of the items comprising each factor were summed and then divided by the number of items.

This study examines whether differences in the type of self-projected onto a personal avatar led to changes in self-perception following avatar embodiment. To examine the effects of personal avatar embodiment, difference scores were calculated by subtracting the pre-experiment self-perception scores from the self-perception scores. A positive difference score reflects an increase in self-perception following avatar embodiment.

Because the timing of personal avatar embodiment differed between the avatar-second embodiment group and the avatar-first embodiment group, correlation coefficients were calculated separately for each group (Table 3). The analysis used the difference between post-embodiment self-perception scores and pre-experiment scores, along with the self-projection strategy scores obtained from the factor analysis. In addition, Figs. 4, 5, and 6 present scatter plots for the variable pairs that showed statistically significant correlations at the 5% level.

As Table 3 shows, in the avatar-second embodiment group, moderate correlations were observed between the reality projection scores and the factors of physical attractiveness and approachability. This suggests that in the avatar-second embodiment group, participants who evaluated their created personal avatar as a "projection of their real self" tended to show increases in physical attractiveness and approachability scores after avatar embodiment, compared to their scores before the experiment.

Table 2. Factor loadings of the Self-Presentation Motivation Scale.

The Self-Presentation Motivation Scale	Competence	Physical Attractiveness	Ethicality	Approachability
I am a capable person.	1.01	0.07	-0.17	-0.04
I am someone who can do things reasonably well.	0.70	-0.12	0.05	0.09
I am an intelligent person.	0.55	0.16	0.09	0.02
I am a person with strong beliefs.	0.50	-0.04	-0.01	-0.02
I am a handsome person.	-0.03	1.02	-0.09	-0.07
I am an attractive person.	0.01	0.76	0.03	0.03
I am a moral person.	-0.02	-0.06	0.76	-0.07
I am an ethical person.	0.00	0.03	0.87	-0.13
I am an approachable person.	0.03	-0.12	-0.18	0.71
I am a likable person.	-0.02	0.21	-0.01	0.79
I am a socially desirable person.	0.03	-0.01	0.38	0.43

Inter-factor correlation		Competence	Physical Attractiveness	Ethicality	Approachability
	Competence	1.00			
	Physical Attractiveness	0.43	1.00		
	Ethicality	0.31	0.16	1.00	
	Approachability	0.65	0.35	0.31	1.00

Table 3. Correlation between the self-projected onto personal avatars and changes in perseption scores.

Self-Presentation Motivation Factors	Experimental Conditions	The Reality	The Ideal
Physical Attractiveness	Avatar-First	0.03	0.28
Physical Attractiveness	Avatar-Second	0.49*	0.07
Ethicality	Avatar-First	0.27	0.07
Ethicality	Avatar-Second	0.22	0.33
Competence	Avatar-First	-0.21	0.01
Competence	Avatar-Second	0.17	-0.02
Approachability	Avatar-First	-0.20	-0.07
Approachability	Avatar-Second	0.41*	0.49*

p < .05*

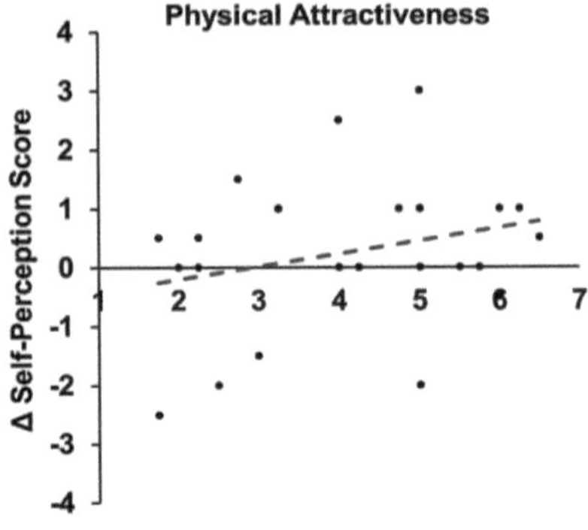

Fig.4. Physical Attractiveness × Reality Projection Factor

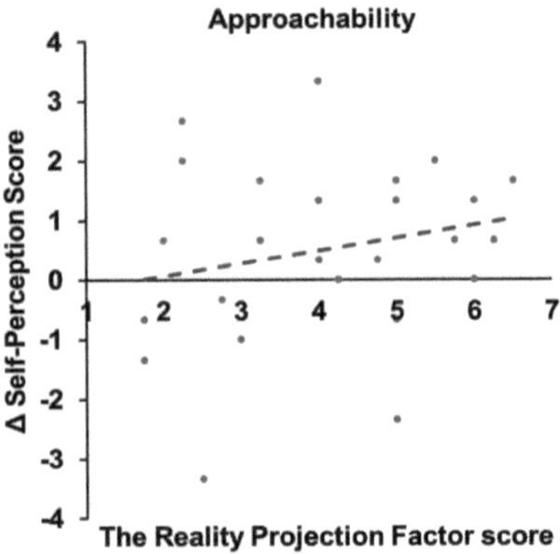

Fig.5. Approachability × Reality Projection Factor.

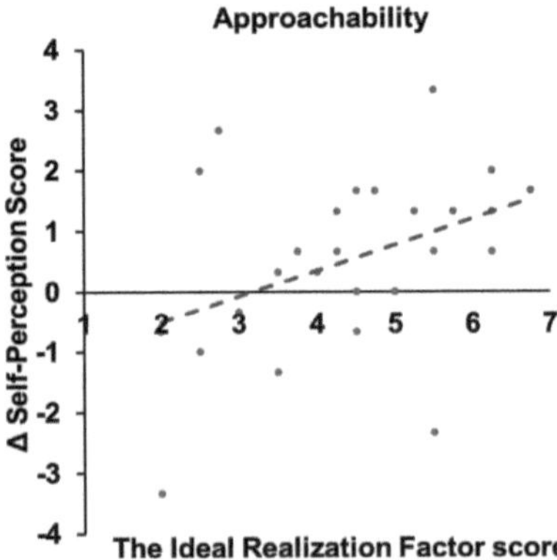

Fig.6. Approachability × Ideal Realization Factor.

Figure 4, 5 and 6. Scatter plots showing the relationship between projection factor scores and changes in self-perception (post–pre avatar embodiment).

5.3 The Potential for Self-Expansion Through Personal Avatars

We examined whether using a self-created personal avatar altered users' self-perception by comparing self-perception scores measured before the experiment with those obtained after the avatar embodiment task. As a result, we found that in the avatar-second embodiment group—where participants viewed their real appearance before embodying their avatar—those who evaluated their created avatar as a projection of their real self-exhibited increases in self-perception scores for physical attractiveness and approachability after avatar embodiment, compared to their pre-experiment baseline scores. This suggests that participants who perceived their avatar as a projection of their real self were more likely to experience enhanced self-perception in terms of physical attractiveness and approachability after using the avatar. We also found that, within the avatar-second embodiment group, participants who evaluated their self-created avatar as a projection of their ideal self-showed larger increases in their approachability scores following avatar embodiment compared to their baseline scores.

These results suggest that participants who perceived their avatar as an embodiment of their ideal self-experienced a greater increase in approachability after using the avatar. This finding indicates that the way in which the self is projected onto a personal avatar—whether as a reflection of the real or ideal self—differentially influences changes in self-perception following avatar embodiment.

Furthermore, we found that the relationship between avatar evaluation and changes in self-perception was present only in the avatar-second embodiment group—where participants saw their real appearance before embodying the avatar. In contrast, no such relationship was observed in the avatar-first embodiment group, where participants embodied their avatar before seeing their real appearance. These results suggest that, in the avatar-second embodiment group, viewing one's real appearance before embodying the avatar may influence the outcome. People are known to evaluate themselves more positively than is objectively warranted—a phenomenon Taylor (1988) termed the "positive illusion" [13]. In other words, even when there is a discrepancy between one's actual appearance and self-perception, individuals can maintain a positively biased self-evaluation by holding a "positive illusion" [14]. Based on this perspective, seeing oneself through a camera may have unexpectedly confronted individuals with the gap between their actual appearance and their prior self-perception, making them realize that their previous self-image was in part a positive illusion. Therefore, our findings suggest that embodying an avatar after seeing one's actual appearance may help positively restore self-perception that has temporarily declined.

Self-evaluations fluctuate not only because of long-term developmental processes but also in response to short-term experiences such as success or failure [15]. As self-perception is not fixed, our findings suggest that using personal avatars can lead to shifts in self-perception, potentially enhancing users' self-evaluation.

5.4 Self-Expansion as the Proteus Effect

Many studies on the Proteus effect have focused on behavioral-level transformations of the self. For example, Banakou et al. (2018) demonstrated that embodying an Einstein avatar improved performance on the Tower of London task (a measure of executive function) [4], while Kilteni et al. (2013) found that users embodied in an Afro-haired Black avatar wearing casual clothing showed larger arm swings while drumming compared to when embodying a formally dressed White avatar [5]. While numerous studies have demonstrated that avatars' stereotypical traits can influence users' cognition and behavior, the underlying mechanisms driving the Proteus effect remain a topic of ongoing debate. Despite various theoretical discussions, there is still no consensus on how this phenomenon emerges [16]. While prior studies on the Proteus effect have primarily focused on behavioral outputs—such as task performance or action changes before and after avatar use—our study demonstrates that avatar embodiment can lead to a transformation in self-perception. This finding suggests that changes in self-perception may play a key role in the underlying mechanisms of the Proteus effect. We believe this perspective offers valuable theoretical insight and broadens our understanding of how avatar use shapes the self.

Most prior studies investigating the Proteus effect have conducted experiments using head-mounted displays (HMDs). The average effect size observed across these studies remains small to moderate, with a mean correlation of $r = 0.24$ [16]. In contrast, our study did not use HMDs; instead, we synchronized participants' movements with their avatars displayed on a standard PC screen. Despite this non-immersive setup and the short avatar use duration, most of the observed changes in self-perception demonstrated medium effect sizes. Immersion in avatars is known to depend on the perspective used for display—first-person perspectives generally evoke greater embodiment than third-person ones do [17]. In addition, HMDs tend to induce stronger feelings of presence and immersion compared to 2D displays [18]. Considering these findings, our results demonstrate that even when avatars are presented on a standard monitor, their use can still lead to meaningful changes in self-perception. This suggests that self-transformation through avatar embodiment does not necessarily require immersive hardware such as HMDs.

6 Conclusion

In this study, we examined how the way users project themselves onto their self-created personal avatars, whether as a reflection of their real self or as a realization of their ideal self, influences changes in self-perception following avatar embodiment. Our experiment—where participants created and used their own personal avatars—demonstrated that embodying a personal avatar can lead to changes in self-perception. Furthermore, our findings suggest that differences in how individuals project the self onto their personal avatars—as well as the timing of avatar use—may differentially influence changes in self-perception. These findings suggest that embodying a personal avatar may help elevate self-evaluations that have temporarily declined for various reasons, thus implying that intentionally modulating self-perception through avatar use could have a positive impact in contexts requiring self-presentation, such as job interviews or public presentations. From this perspective, the social significance of our study is considerable.

This study has several limitations. The avatar creation tool used in the experiment defaults to highly attractive, anime-style appearances. As a result, it is possible that the tool's stylistic constraints influenced participants' responses. Additionally, the embodiment task involved only the avatar's upper body. Further studies are needed to determine whether similar effects on self-perception would be observed when using full-body avatars.

Acknowledgments. This work was supported by JST SPRING, Grant Number JPMJSP2129.

References

1. Yee, N., Bailenson, J.: The Proteus effect: The effect of transformed self-representation on behavior. Hum. Commun. Res. **33**(3), 271–290 (2007)
2. Kiverstein, J.: The meaning of embodiment. Top. Cogn. Sci. **4**(4), 740–758 (2012)
3. Kilteni, K., Groten, R., Slater, M.: The sense of embodiment in virtual reality. Presence: Teleoperators and Virtual Environments, **21**(4), 373–387 (2012)
4. Banakou, D., Kishore, S., Slater, M.: Virtually being Einstein results in an improvement in cognitive task performance and a decrease in age bias. Front. Psychol. **9**, 368309 (2018)
5. Kilteni, K., Bergstrom, I., Slater, M.: Drumming in immersive virtual reality: The body shapes the way we play. IEEE Trans. Visual Comput. Graphics **19**(4), 597–605 (2013)
6. Oyanagi, A., Narumi, T. Lugrin, J., Ando, H., Ohmura R.: Reducing the fear of height by inducing the Proteus effect of a dragon avatar. Transactions of the Virtual Reality Society of Japan, **25**(1), 2–11 (2020) (in Japanese)
7. Koulouris, J., Jeffery, Z., Best, J., O'neill, E., Lutteroth, C.: Me vs. Super (wo) man: Effects of Customization and Identification in a VR Exergame. In Proceedings of the 2020 CHI conference on human factors in computing systems, 1–17. (2020)
8. Do, T.D., Protko, C.I., McMahan, R.P.: Stepping into the right shoes: The effects of user-matched avatar ethnicity and gender on sense of embodiment in virtual reality. IEEE transactions on visualization and computer graphics. (2024)
9. Nowak, K.L., Fox, J.: Avatars and computer-mediated communication: A review of the definitions, uses, and effects of digital representations. Review of Communication Research **6**, 30–53 (2018)
10. Kasahara, C., Sakata, M.: Basic research on strategies for creating self-avatars as a means of self-presentation. J. Hum. Interface Soc. **26**(4), 399–410 (2024). (in Japanese)
11. Leary, M.R., Nezlek, J.B., Downs, D., Radford-Davenport, J., Martin, J., McMullen, A.: Self-presentation in everyday interactions: Effects of target familiarity and gender composition. J. Pers. Soc. Psychol. **67**(4), 664–673 (1994)
12. Taniguchi, J., Daibo, I.: Examination of self-presentation motives in close relationships with opposite-sex partners. The Japanese Journal of Experimental Social Psychology, **45**(1), 13–24. (2005) (in Japanese)
13. Taylor, S.E., Brown, J.D.: Illusion and well-being: A social psychological perspective on mental health. Psychol. Bull. **103**(2), 193–210 (1988)
14. Saito, I., Ogino, N., Kojima, M.: An empirical study on positive self-evaluation and negative self-presentation. Bull. Fac. Psychol. Rissho Univ. **4**, 27–46 (2006). (in Japanese)
15. Heatherton, T.F., Polivy, J.: Development and validation of a scale for measuring state self-esteem. J. Pers. Soc. Psychol. **60**(6), 895 (1991)

16. Martin Coesel, A., Biancardi, B., Buisine, S.: A theoretical review of the Proteus effect: Understanding the underlying processes. Front. Psychol. **15**, 1379599 (2024)
17. Lenggenhager, B., Tadi, T., Metzinger, T., Blanke, O.: Video ergo sum: Manipulating bodily self-consciousness. Science **317**(5841), 1096–1099 (2007)
18. Hepperle, D., Purps, C.F., Deuchler, J., Wölfel, M.: Aspects of visual avatar appearance: Self-representation, display type, and uncanny valley. Vis. Comput. **38**(4), 1227–1244 (2022)

Influence of Other's Spatial Behavior on Whole-Body Movement - Re-thinking Personal Space from Precise Motion Analysis

Yosuke Kinoe[✉], Hana Matsuo, and Asuka Takahashi

Hosei University, 2-17-1, Chiyoda City, Tokyo 102-8160, Japan
kinoe@hosei.ac.jp

Abstract. The present paper described an experimental study on the effect of other's approach on whole-body movements of approached person. Participants' 3D movements while other person approached and crossed beyond participants' personal space boundaries were analyzed. To quantify difference among probability distributions of movements, we proposed a combined method of precise motion analysis and KL divergence. As a result, the study had an initial threefold outcome.

First, this study demonstrated the possibility of capturing the influence of others' spatial behavior on individual from the perspective of physical movement. Second, the results suggested even in the area *outside* their interpersonal space boundary, other's approach influenced a person's movements. Third, the study suggested our combined method of precise motion analysis based on human-musculoskeletal model and KL divergence was an effective tool for detecting the difference of probability distribution of movements.

Keywords: Personal space · Motion analysis · Kullback–Leibler divergence

1 Introduction

Personal space is a dynamic spatial component of interpersonal relations in a relatively closer domain [3, 10]. It can be defined as "an area individuals actively maintain around themselves into which others cannot intrude without arousing some sort of discomfort" [5, 11].

1.1 Spatial Interaction Between Self and Other Person

Interpersonal distance, or spatial relationship between self and other is one of the most fundamental elements of social behavior of human being as well as social animals. People automatically and reliably attempt to regulate the distance maintained between themselves and others and reinstate a safety and appropriate interpersonal distance during social interaction in relation to their social situations [1, 4, 6].

Previous studies demonstrated that the others' intrusion into one's preferred interpersonal distance (PID) elicits negative emotional reactions in individuals which could

H. Mori et al. (Eds.): HCII 2025, LNCS 16333, pp. 43–55, 2026.
https://doi.org/10.1007/978-3-032-12660-3_4

be recorded as an explicit behavior such as an unpleasant facial expression and a withdrawal tendency [11]. However, few studies so far were concerned with an entire process of approaching and crossing their interpersonal space boundary, from the viewpoints of a combined aspect of physical, physiological, and psychological response (e.g. [2, 7]).

The present paper describes an experimental study on visible and *invisible* physical movements during other's approach reaching and crossing one's interpersonal space boundary.

1.2 Research Questions

The following research questions were established in this study.

1. Does a person make any physical movement during the process of other's approaching, according to the change of spatial relation between a person and other? Especially, does that movement differ from that during quiet-standing alone? (RQ1)
2. Even before a person begins to subjectively feel strange about their spatial relation with other person, does any characteristic movement occur? (RQ2)

1.3 Our Approach

The following were difficulties we had for tackling the research issues.

1. First of all, it is unclear whether a change in spatial relation with other person affect their physical movements.
2. Even if an influence appears in their physical movement, it was hard to identify it. It was assumed to contain almost invisible and quick or extremely subtle, slow phenomena. It may involve unconscious process.
3. It's unknown when, where and how the phenomenon will occur.

Figure 1 shows the overall scheme of our approach. In order to overcome those difficulties for investigating an effect on micro body movements, we adopted a new approach by combining (1) precise motion analysis using MoCap based on human musculoskeletal model, and (2) statistical technique using Kullback-Leibler divergence [9] based on probability distributions from precise motion analysis.

Precise Motion Analysis using MoCap based on Human Musculoskeletal Model. To capture quick and micro 3D movements, participants' whole-body movements were captured from eight different directions using Qualisys Tracking Manager (QTM) software with synchronized high-speed cameras (300 Hz). We defined a marker set that consisted of eighty-six musculoskeletal landmarks, which included back/fore-head, CV7, TV10, R/L acromions, R/L hip, R/L knees lateral and medial and tips of R/L feet, etc. Standard deviation of motion tracking error in the calibration is less than 1 mm in the average. Approximately 4.6 million of data points of the 3D movements is obtained from 60s of each trial of iterations.

Precise motion analysis can be performed according to the predefined analysis viewpoints on huge 3D motion data based on human musculoskeletal model, by using Visual3D software. Analysis viewpoints include bodily-orientation, joint-angle displacement as well as translation of segments and the center of gravity (CoG).

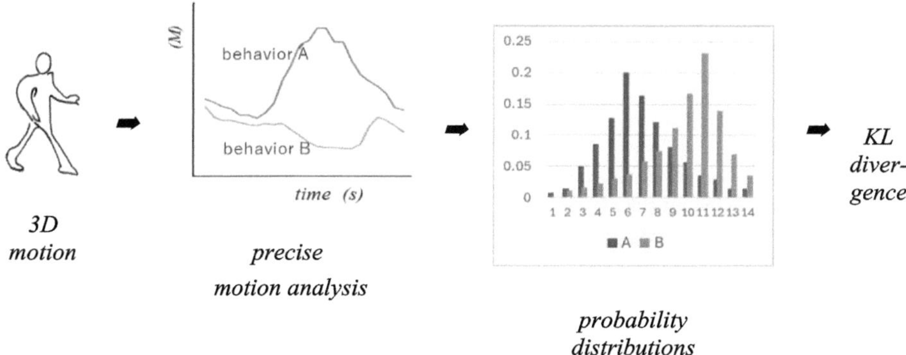

Fig. 1. Our approach combining (1) precise motion analysis using MoCap and (2) Kullback-Leibler divergence based on probability distributions from motion analysis.

Kullback–Leibler divergence. Kullback-Leibler divergence is a standard measurement that is used to quantify a difference between two probability distribution in the information theory [9]. When two probability distribution P and Q are given, KL divergence is used to measure how distribution P deviates from distribution Q. While KL divergence is a type of statistical distance, it is not actually a metric.

Kullback-Leibler (KL) divergence, denoted $D_{KL}(P\|Q)$, for discrete distributions $P(x)$ and $Q(x)$ defined on the same sample space is defined as

$$D_{KL}(P\|Q) = \sum_{x \in X} P(x) \log\left(\frac{P(x)}{Q(x)}\right). \tag{1}$$

2   Experiment

The present paper concentrated to this study purpose described above, a part of our whole experimental study.

2.1   Method

The experimental conditions are shown in Table 1. There were two conditions in the present study. In the AP_7 conditions, other person (an assistant experimenter) stands quietly apart from 7 M in the same room for a while (approx. One minute). Then, an assistant experimenter constantly approaches a participant slowly (prox. a step per second) from the front direction, but in the moment unknown to a participant In QS_A condition, a participant stands *alone* quietly for one minute. Each participant and an assistant experimenter were not an acquaintance.

Participants. Thirteen healthy university students participated. All participants provided informed consent prior to their inclusion in the study. The participants were recruited individually and were informed that the study dealt with spatial preferences. In this paper, five participants (A1-A5; age range: 18–22) were analyzed.

Table 1. Experimental conditions.

condition	task and situation (participant)	task (by other person)
AP_7	A participant and an unknown person stand apart at 7M. Other person approaches slowly from front, but in the moment unknown to a participant.	To stand apart for a while and then approach a participant.
QS_A	A participant stands *alone* quietly for one min.	N/A. No other person in the room.

Procedure. The experimental condition and its order were unknown to the participant. Each participant was asked to stand quietly on a floor in an upright position, with her/his arms relaxed on either side of body, and the eyes opened. The assistant experimenter randomly executed different conditions (Table 1) in a random order. In a single session, each participant performed five to ten trials for each condition. Each participant gave their informed consent before participation. The data collection was performed during daytime between December 2021 and December 2022, in Tokyo.

Measurements.

Motion data. 3D full-body motions of all the participants were tracked with eighty-six markers predefined for human full body, by using Qualisys track manager (QTM) with synchronized high-speed cameras (300 Hz). Standard deviation of motion tracking error in the calibration was 0.69 mm in the average. Approximately 5.2 millions of data points of the 3D movements were obtained from each trial of iterations.

Spatial Orientation and Direction. In coordinate system of laboratory, the forward direction along the sagittal plane of a participant is the positive of Y axis, and their right side is the positive direction of X axis. For example, in AP_7 condition, a participant and an assistant experimenter initially stand approximately at (0, 0, 0) and (0, 7000, 0) in mm respectively and then an assistant experimenter approaches in Y(-) direction.

Video recording and time stamp. Each participant's movement was recorded with time-stamp at a one-300th seconds accuracy.

Preferred interpersonal distance. Preferred interpersonal distance (PID) was measured by employing the stop-distance method [5] in a separated session of data collection after the MoCap session. Their preferred interpersonal distance was determined by the average of three trials of the measurements.

An assistant experimenter constantly approached the participant slowly from 7 M. The participant was asked to verbalize "stop" when they began feeling something strange or restless about a distance with other person, and then an assistant experimenter stopped walking. According to the surface model [6], the distance between their tips of toes of a participant and an assistant experimenter was measured.

3   Analysis

3.1   Analysis 1: Precise Motion Analysis

A set of whole-body motion data was collected from thirteen participants, in five to ten iterations of three experimental conditions, with eighty-three markers attached on landmarks of a participant's body. In this paper, a part of dataset, that is, motion data from five participants were analyzed. Butterworth low-pass filter (cut-off 40Hz) was utilized for data pre-processing.

Analysis Viewpoints. We defined 129 viewpoints of whole-body 3D movements. Biomechanical analysis based on human musculoskeletal model was conducted by using the combination of Qualisys Tracking Manager (QTM) and Visual3D according to the analysis viewpoints. In this study, the analysis viewpoints including joint angle displacements, translational movement of segments and CoG (center-of-gravity) were established for analyzing 3D micro movements of the whole human body.

Comparison of Trajectories of Different Conditions. Figure 2-a illustrates overlapped trajectories of model-based CoG (center of gravity) of five trials under the condition of QS_A (quiet-standing alone) of participant A1. Figure 2-b overlapped furthermore trajectories of five trials under the conditions of AP_7 (approach by other person from 7M) of participant A1. The vertical line at fame 6900 in Fig. 2-b indicates the time corresponding to preferred interpersonal distance (PID) of participant A1.

The overall trend of five trajectories of CoG under the AP_7 condition differed from those under the QS_A condition. The movements of five trajectories of AP_7 recognizably changed, at least after the time of participant A1's preferred interpersonal distance (PID). On the other hand, in QS_A, slow movements were continuously observed, but fast and noticeable movements were not.

Comparison of Specific Joint-angle Displacement. Figure 3 illustrates overlapped trajectories of five trials each under the conditions of QS_A and AP_7 of a specific joint-angle displacement y (+abduction/ adduction) of Right Shoulder of participant A1.

The overall trend of five trajectories under the AP_7 condition differed from those under the QS_A condition, at Right Shoulder joint angle y (abduction/adduction). The results suggested the effect of social spatial relation between self and other person possibly be identified from the viewpoint of body movements.

The results of analysis 1 indicated that the time of PID roughly corresponded to the start time of visible movement. The movements of participant A1 under the AP_7 condition began noticeably changing at the time preferred interpersonal distance (PID) or thereafter.

At Right Shoulder joint angle y, although quick movements of participant A1 were not but slow ones were recognized in the QS_A condition. Kinoe et, al (2020) suggested the approached person made a characteristic movement before the time of PID [8]. However, it was difficult to simply compare the movements bents between the AP_7 condition especially before the time of PID and the QS_A condition according to the results of the Analysis 1 alone based on precise motion analysis.

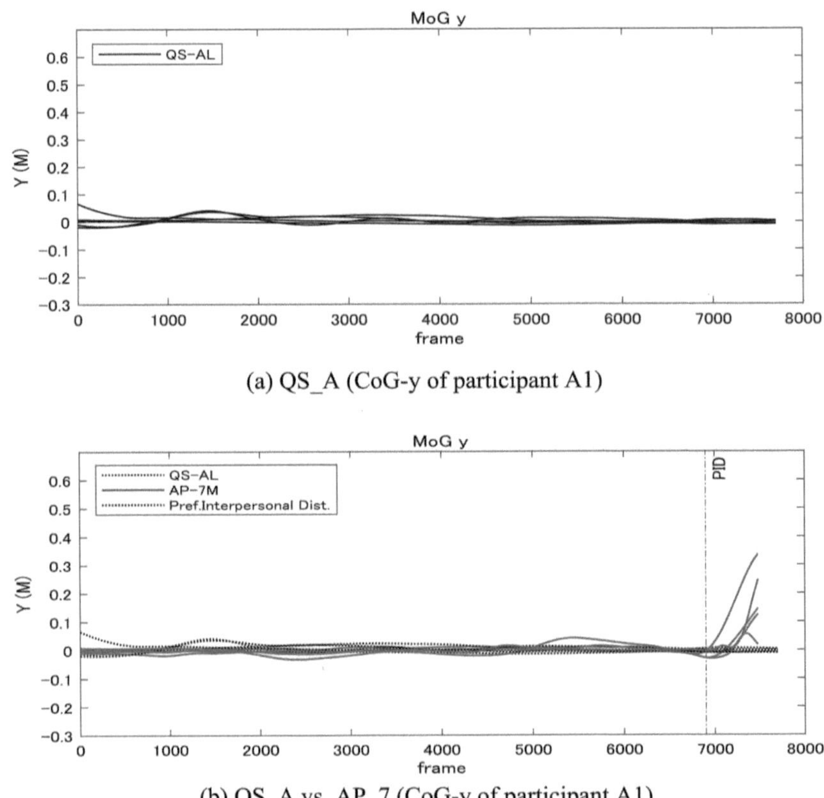

(a) QS_A (CoG-y of participant A1)

(b) QS_A vs. AP_7 (CoG-y of participant A1)

Fig. 2. Trajectories of five trials each of (a) QS_A, and (b) QS_A & AP_7, of participant A1's CoG-y (+: forward). The vertical line at frame 6900 in (b) indicates the time corresponding to participant A1's preferred interpersonal distance.

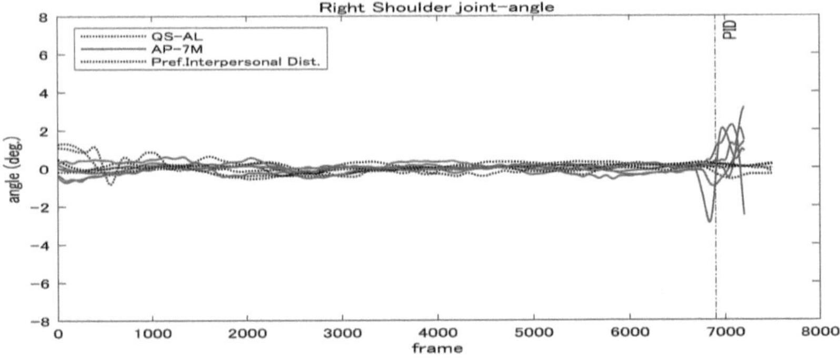

Fig. 3. Overlapped trajectories of five trials each of the QS_A and the AP_7 conditions, at Right Shoulder joint-angle y (+abduction/-adduction) of participant A1. The vertical line at frame 6900 indicates the time corresponding to participant A1's preferred interpersonal distance.

3.2 Analysis 2: Investigating Effect of Other's Approach using KL Divergence

We investigated an effect of dynamic spatial relation with other person by applying statistical analysis based on Kullback-Leibler divergence. KL divergence is a standard measurement that is used to quantify a difference between two probability distribution. The captured body movement data can be considered as a kind of discrete-time stochastic process, as well as time-series data.

An Example: Comparison of Movements using KL Divergence. When two probability distribution P and Q are given, KL divergence is used to measure how distribution P deviates from distribution Q.

For example, movement at Right Shoulder joint-angle y (abduction/adduction) was considered. The analysis process consisted of three steps.

1. Let P and Q be the probability distributions of the movements of a particular trial under a particular condition, respectively.
2. Histograms of P and Q were created based on corresponding motion data derived from precise motion analysis in the Analysis 1 (*eg.* Figure 4-a). The histograms were normalized by probability.
3. Based on probability distributions of P and Q, KL divergence ($D_{KL}(P\|Q)$) was calculated using formula 1 defined in previous chapter.

Figure 4 shows overlapped histograms obtained from movement at Right Shoulder joint-angle y of participant A1; which were based on movements of trials #1 and #2 of the same condition QS_A (Fig. 4-a), and based on different trials of different conditions QS_A trial #1 and AP_7 trial #2 (Fig. 4-b).

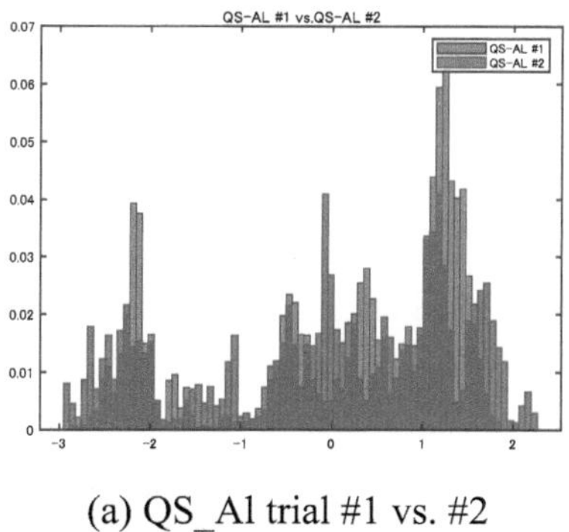

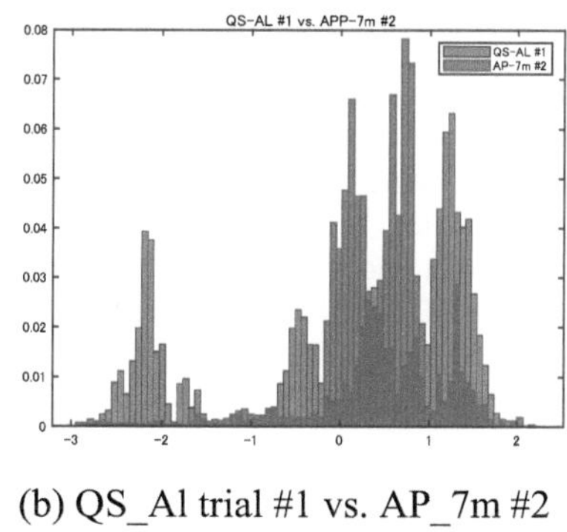

(a) QS_Al trial #1 vs. #2   (b) QS_Al trial #1 vs. AP_7m #2

Fig. 4. Histogram of Right Shoulder joint-angle y (abduction/adduction) of participant A1: (a) trial #1 vs. #2 of QS_A, (b) trial #1 of QS A vs. trial #2 of AP_7.

According to formula 1, KL divergence was calculated. KL divergence for (a) was 0.950, and 2.447 for (b). In this example, KL divergence for a combination of heterogeneous conditions QS_A vs. AP_7 was higher than that of a combination within the same condition QS_A.

Comparison based on KL Divergence. We conducted statistical comparison based on KL divergence. The analysis coverage had been expanded to 129 items of movements, five trials of iteration, five participants.

In this section, comparisons between KL divergence for pairs of the same QS_A condition and those for a pair of different conditions QS_A - AP_7 were investigated. An example of the results were shown in Fig. 5.

Figure 5 consisted of five charts (a)-(e), which compared the values of KL divergence for the probability distributions of the movements of Right Shoulder joint-angle y (abduction/adduction) from participant A1. In Fig. 5-a to 5-e, let P be the probability distributions of the movements of trial #1 to #5 under QS_A condition respectively. Each figure is divided into five bars in left and five bars in right. In left five bars, let Q be the probability distributions of the movements of trial #1 to #5 under QS_A condition respectively[1]. In right five bars, let Q be the probability distributions of the movements of trial #1 to #5 under AP_7 condition respectively. KL divergence were calculated for probability distributions P and Q. For instance, five bars in right side of Fig. 5-a represent KL divergence for a combination of P (i.e. QS_A trial #1) and Q (i.e. AP_7 trial #1 to #5).

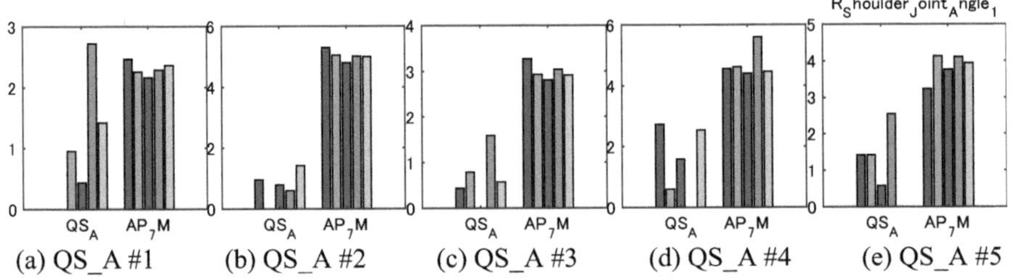

Fig. 5. Five charts (a)-(e) compare KL divergence from R Shoulder joint-angle y (abduction/adduction) of participant A1. In (a)-(e), P be the probability distributions from trial #1 to #5 of QS_A condition respectively. Each chart involves five bars in left and five bars in right. In left five bars, let Q be the probability distributions from trial #1 to #5 of QS_A condition respectively. In right ones, let Q be the probability distributions from trial #1 to #5 of AP_7 condition respectively. That is, left five bars show KL divergence for a pair of the same QS_A condition and right ones show that for a pair of QS_A vs. AP_7 conditions.

KL divergence is a measurement that quantifies a difference between two probability distribution P and Q. In Fig. 5-a to 5-e, either five bars of right side were higher than any five bars of left side except for a pair of QS_A #1 and #4 (see Fig. 5-a).

Furthermore, by employing the same analysis procedure, we also conducted comparisons based on KL divergence as for other participants. The results from participant A5 were shown in Fig. 6.

Similarly, Fig. 6 consisted of five charts (a)-(e), which compare the values of KL divergence for the probability distributions of the movements of Left Wrist joint-angle

---

[1] Please note that KLD divergence is zero for the same probability distributions such as trial #1 and trial #1 of QS_A.

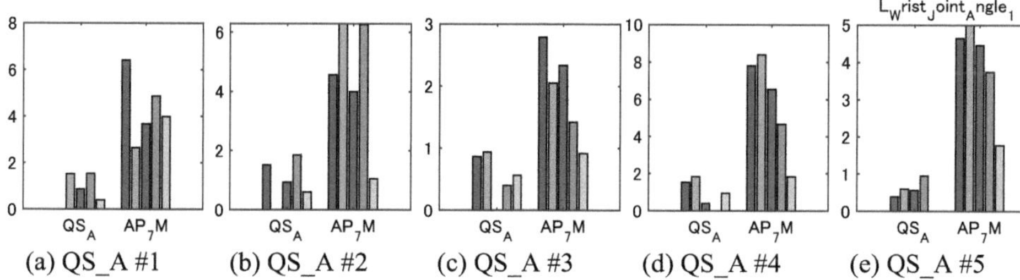

(a) QS_A #1   (b) QS_A #2   (c) QS_A #3   (d) QS_A #4   (e) QS_A #5

Fig. 6. Five charts (a)-(e) compare KL divergence from Left Wrist joint-angle y (abduction) of participant A5. In (a)-(e), let P be the probability distributions from trial #1 to #5 of QS_A condition respectively. Each chart involves five bars in left and five bars in right. In left five bars, let Q be the probability distributions from trial #1 to #5 of QS_A condition respectively. In right ones, let Q be the probability distributions from trial #1 to #5 of AP_7 condition respectively. That is, left five bars show KL divergence for a pair of the same QS_A condition and right ones show that for a pair of QS_A vs. AP_7 conditions.

y from participant A5. The composition of five bar-graphs in left and right side were the same in Fig. 5 and 6.

In Fig. 6-a to 6-e, either five bars of right side were higher than any five bars of left side except for a pair of QS_A #2 and AP_7 #5 (see Fig. 6-b).

Similar results were obtained also from other participants A2, A3 and A4. However in either case, a few exceptions related to high and low values were observed. There were individual differences in the body-parts where this phenomenon was observed.

3.3 Analysis 3: Effect of Changing Spatial Relation with Other (Pre-PID)

The process of other's approaching was divided at the timing of reaching the participant's preferred interpersonal distance (PID) into two periods, *pre-PID* and *post-PID* (Fig. 7). Authors [8] had shed light on characteristic phenomena especially during the *pre-PID* period, prior to reaching their preferred interpersonal distance.

The period of *pre-PID* is an interesting duration like an inertial period. In *pre-PID* period, objectively spatial relation between a participant and other person dynamically changed. However, a participant subjectively didn't yet begin feeling strange or discomfort with the distance to other until reaching their personal space boundary.

On the other hand, as explained in earlier section, it was difficult to directly compare 3D movements visually using a time-series graph for the purpose of examining the effect of other's approaching especially during *pre*-PID period (see Fig. 2).

To directly compare the movements between QS_A and AP_7 (*pre-PID*), we adopted our analysis method based on KL divergence.

Comparison based on KL Divergence: QS_=A vs. AP_=7 (pre-PID). We conducted statistical comparison based on KL divergence. Comparisons between KL divergence for pairs of the same QS_A condition and for those of different conditions QS_A - AP_7 (*pre-PID*). Figure 8 shows an example of the result.

The composition of Fig. 8 was the same as Fig. 6. Figure 8-A and 8-B consisted five charts (a)-(e) that involved five bars each on the left and the right side individually. In

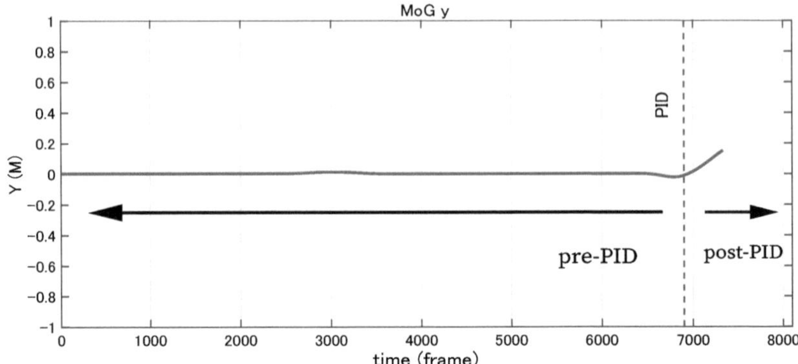

Fig. 7. The periods of pre-PID and post-PID are shown in a trajectory of participant A1's CoG-y (+: forward) in AP_7 condition. The vertical line at frame 6900 indicates the time corresponding to participant A1's preferred interpersonal distance (PID).

Fig. 8-A, the charts were created based on KL divergence for the probability distributions of the movements of A1's Right Elbow joint angle x (flexion/extension). The charts of Fig. 8-B was created based on KL divergence for A3's Left Wrist joint-angle y (abduction/).

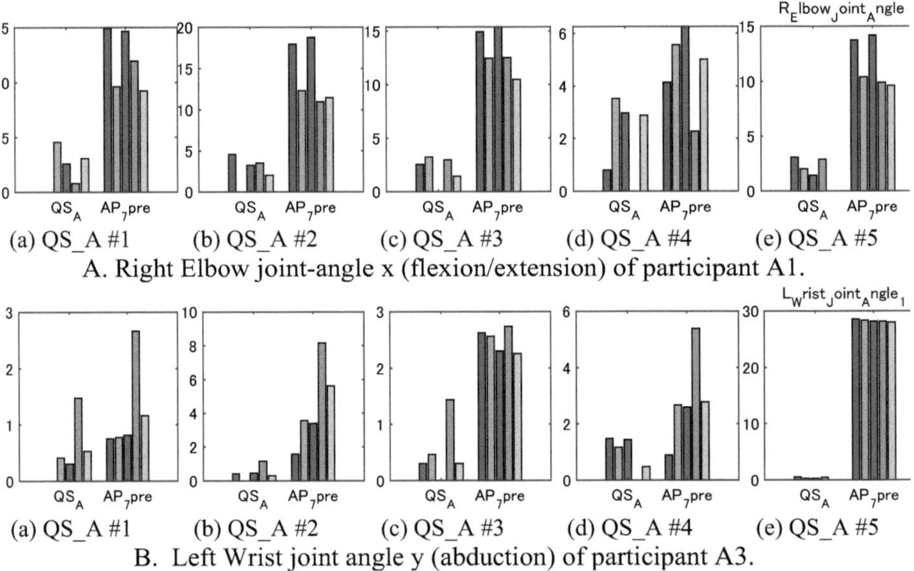

A. Right Elbow joint-angle x (flexion/extension) of participant A1.

B. Left Wrist joint angle y (abduction) of participant A3.

Fig. 8. Comparisons between KL divergence for pairs of the same QS_A condition and those for pairs of different conditions QS_A vs. AP_7 (*pre-PID*). The five bars on the left side of each graph are KL divergence calculated from the combination of QS_A conditions, and the five bars on the right side are KL divergence calculated from the combination of QS_A and AP_7 (*pre-PID*). Figure 8-A shows the result of Right Elbow joint-angle x (flexion/extension) of participant A1. Figure 8-B shows the result of Left Wrist joint-angle y (abduction) of participant A3.

In Fig. 8-A (a) to (e), the five bars on the right side were higher than either on the left side except for KL divergence from AP_8 #4 in Fig. 8-A (d). Similarly, in Fig. 8-B (a) to (e), the five bars on the right side were higher than either on the left side except for KL divergence from QS_A #4 in Fig. 8-B (a) and KL divergence from AP_7 #1 in Fig. 8-B (d).

Furthermore, similar results were obtained from other participants, A2 and A4. However, a few exceptions in either case, but more than those in Fig. 6 were observed.

Comparison between QS$_=$A vs. AP$_=$7 (pre-PID) using Improved Method.

Improvement of Analysis Accuracy. The purpose of the study was to compare movements between different conditions. Naturally, there was some variability between trials in iteration. One-by-one comparison of movement in trials was beyond current research issue. To improve analysis accuracy, we combined the five trials of movement data from the same condition. The data of five trials were normalized based on the average of its middle portion that excluded its 4s initial and 4s final portions and then concatenated. Succeeding analyses employed KL divergence based on probability distribution from the combined data.

Analyses based on KL divergence using the combined data of five trials each of QS_A and AP_7 were conducted. The analysis was expanded to 129 items of analysis viewpoints. A part of the results from the participants A1 to A5 were shown in Fig. 9.

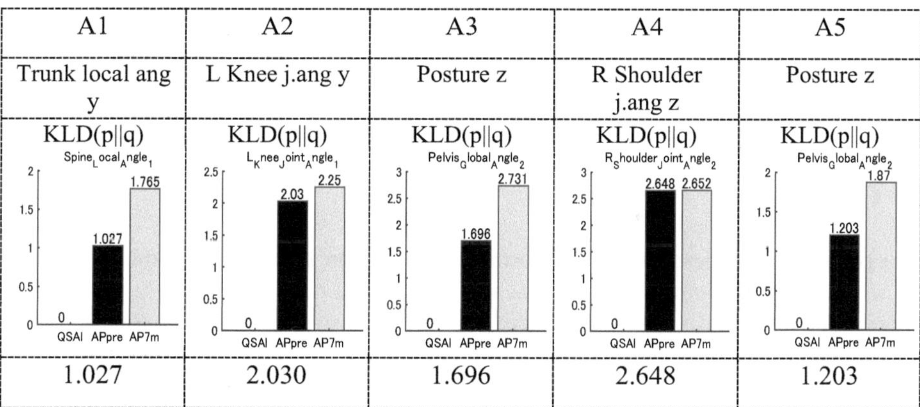

A1	A2	A3	A4	A5
Trunk local ang y	L Knee j.ang y	Posture z	R Shoulder j.ang z	Posture z
1.027	2.030	1.696	2.648	1.203

Fig. 9. Comparison based on KL divergence using the combined data of five trials. Left bar: among QS_A condition. Middle bar: between QS_A vs. AP_7 (*pre-PID*). Right bar: QS_A vs. AP_7 (whole) for reference. KL divergence for QS_A vs. QS_A is zero.

In this example, in either participant, KL divergence for a pair of QS_A and AP_7 (*pre-PID*) indicated meaningful values greater than zero. For example, KL divergence were 1.027 from A1's Trunk local angle y (bend), 2.030 from A2's Left Knee joint-angle y (abduction), 1.696 from A3's Posture z (rotation), 2.648 from A4's Right Shoulder joint-angle z (ext. Rotation), and 1.203 from A5's Posture z (rotation) respectively. However, they were lower than KL divergence for AP_7 (whole) condition. The results revealed that the probability distribution of AP_7 (*pre-PID*) differed from that of QS_A.

4   Discussion

Figure 10 illustrates a heatmap of a matrix of KL divergence (combined data of five trials) from A1's Left Wrist joint angle y (abduction) for a combination of QS_A, AP_7 (pre-PID), and AP_7 condition. In this study, a set of heatmaps was created for 129 body-parts. This chart was helpful for roughly exploring body-part candidates that generated a significant movement which differed from quiet-standing.

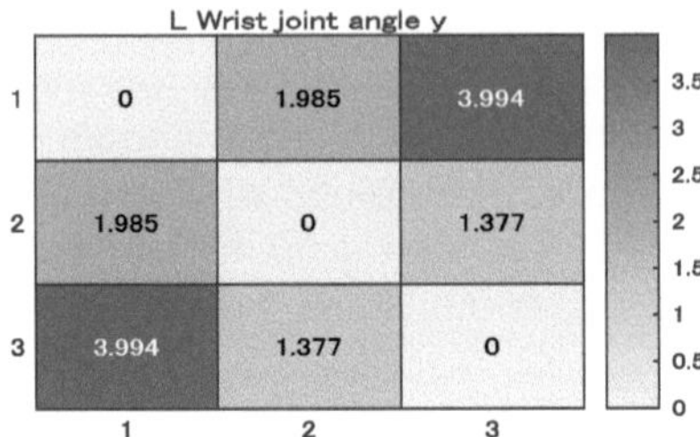

Fig. 10. Heatmap of a matrix of KL divergence using the combined data of five trials from Left Wrist joint angle y (abduction) of participant A1. (1) QS_A, (2) AP_7 (*pre-PID*), and (3) AP_7. KLD divergence for the same probability distribution such as AP_7 vs. AP_7 is zero.

Based on the results of this study, our method of analyzing physical movements using KL divergence was an effective tool for the analysts to take a bird's-eye view of whole-body movements and narrowing down specific body-part candidates needed to be analyzed in depth and detail.

5   Conclusion

The present paper described an experimental study on the effect of other's approach on whole-body movements of approached person. 3D movements while other person approached and crossed beyond participants' personal space boundaries were analyzed. To quantify difference among movements, we applied a method that combined precise motion analysis and KL divergence. As a result, the study had a threefold outcome.

First, this study demonstrated the possibility of capturing the influence of others' spatial behavior on individual from the perspective of physical movement.

Second, the results suggested even in the area *outside* their interpersonal space boundary (i.e. *pre*-PID), other's approach influenced a person's movements.

Third, the study suggested our combined method of precise motion analysis and KL divergence was an effective tool for detecting the difference of probability distribution of movements.

By expanding the coverage of participants and experimental conditions, the validation of those initial results is underway.

Acknowledgments. Acknowledgments. We thank all the study participants. We appreciate devoted support from Konatsu, Yu, Maino, Aro, Marina, and our lab members 2021- 2022. We thank Toshiyuki, who encouraged improving our early analysis framework.

Disclosure of Interests..   The authors have no competing interests to declare that are relevant to the content of this paper.

References

1. Candini, M., Giuberti, V., Santelli, E., di Pellegrino, G., Frassinetti, F.: When social and action spaces diverge: A study in children with typical development and autism. Autism **23**(7), 1687–1698 (2019). https://doi.org/10.1177/1362361318822504
2. Candini, M., Battaglia, S., Benassi, M., et al.: The physiological correlates of interpersonal space. Sci. Rep. **11,** 2611 (2021). https://doi.org/10.1038/s41598-021-82223-2
3. Gifford, R.: Environmental psychology: principles and practice. Optimal Books (2014)
4. Hall, E. T.: The hidden dimension. Doubleday (1966)
5. Hayduk, L.A.: Personal space: where we now stand. Psychol. Bull. **94**(2), 293–335 (1983)
6. Kinoe, Y., Mizuno, N.: Situational Transformation of Personal Space. In: Yamamoto, S. (eds) Human Interface and the Management of Information. Lecture Notes in Computer Science, vol 9173, pp.15–24. Springer, Cham (2015). https://doi.org/10.1007/978-3-319-20618-9_2
7. Kinoe, Y., Tatsuka, S.: Effect on postural sway of the invasion to preferable interpersonal distance. In: Yamamoto, S. (ed.) Human Interface and the Management of Information. LNCS, vol. 10273, pp. 539–553. Springer, Cham (2017). https://doi.org/10.1007/978-3-319-58521-5_42
8. Kinoe, Y., Akimori, Y.: Appeal of Inconspicuous Body Movements during Spatial Invasion: Frequency Analysis of Movements. In: Yamamoto, S., Mori, H. (eds.) Human Interface and the Management of Information. Interacting with Information. LNCS, vol. 12185, pp. 175–193. Springer, Cham (2020). https://doi.org/10.1007/978-3-030-50017-7_12
9. Kullback S., Leibler R.A.: On information and sufficiency. Annals of Mathematical Statistics, **22**(1), 79–86 (1951)
10. Sommer, R.: Personal space in a digital age. In: Bechtel, R.B., Churchman, A. (eds.) Handbook of environmental psychology, pp. 385–504. Wiley, NY (2002)
11. Sommer, R.: Personal space: The behavioral basis of design, Updated edition. Bosko Books, Bristol (2008)

Assessing Differences Between Perception and Impression Evaluations in Immersive Virtual Environments

Eriko Kitamoto[1]([⊠]) [iD] and Satoshi Yamada[2] [iD]

[1] Department of Information Media, Faculty of Information Technology, Kanagawa Institute of Technology, 1030 Shimogino,Kanagawa Ken, Atsugi Shi 243-0292, Japan
e_kitamoto@ic.kanagawa-it.ac.jp
[2] Department of Architecture and Urban Design, College of Science and Engineering, Ritsumeikan University, 1-1-1 Nojihigashi, Kusatsu Shi, Shiga 525-8577, Japan
sy@fc.ritsumei.ac.jp

Abstract. Head-mounted displays (HMDs) are used to create immersive virtual reality experiences. However, the methods for generating HMD environments and delivering stimuli can lead to discrepancies between the real world and HMD environments. This study assesses the impressions of "sufficient openness of space" and "presence of visual objects" across three settings: real spaces, spaces created with display panels (DP spaces), and immersive HMD spaces. Subsequently, we evaluated the mean values and standard deviations for these impressions. We analyzed and verified the differences and similarities among real, DP, and HMD spaces using correlation coefficients and confidence intervals. The results indicate that the HMD space resembled the real space more closely than the DP space regarding sufficient openness. However, even within the same virtual spatial configuration, the similarity between perception of distance and impression of space did not always align. In conclusion, although there are differences depending on the question items, the HMD space could potentially provide an experience similar to that of real space.

Keywords: Immersive virtual environment · Impression evaluation · Distance perception

1 Introduction

Cross-reality or extended reality (XR) technologies, including virtual reality (VR), augmented reality, mixed reality, and simulated reality, are rapidly evolving owing to advancements in next-generation communication technologies (e.g., the Internet of Things, 5G, and 6G), as well as their improved affordability and user-friendliness. XR superimposes real and virtual elements using smartphone displays and head-mounted displays (HMDs), which offer diverse immersive experiences. For example, XR is utilized in fields such as remote medical treatment [1], VR-based practical classes [2], virtual shopping [3], and sports simulations [4]. Furthermore, VR spaces are used in designing and studying product prototypes [5], urban spaces [6], digital twins, metaverses, and innumerable other applications.

H. Mori et al. (Eds.): HCII 2025, LNCS 16333, pp. 56–73, 2026.
https://doi.org/10.1007/978-3-032-12660-3_5

VR spaces make particularly valuable contributions to architectural design [7], often being used to simulate natural environments and behaviors for structural analysis, construction, and maintenance management. In the planning stage, clients and designers often use VR to study spatial components, such as the size and brightness of spaces, material textures, furniture arrangement, and occupant traffic flow. Creating a full-scale mockup is time-consuming, costly, and limits the design scope. Additionally, scale models do not offer interior views of spaces. Presentations typically use three-dimensional (3D) models and still or moving images, with viewpoints predetermined by the creator; which may restrict the client's understanding of the space regarding the creator's perspective. In contrast, VR users can explore such spaces from many vantage points, thereby resolving the aforementioned limitations and providing the immersive experience of being physically present [8].

Since VR's advent in 2016, HMDs have frequently been used to deliver immersive VR experiences. These devices expand the visualization and presentation opportunities even for users who lack any prior exposure to HMDs, such as those examining interior designs or participating in urban development workshops. However, the methods for creating VR spaces and delivering stimuli can cause discrepancies between real and HMD environments, leading to a diminished sense of immersion, discomfort during movement, and reluctance to use an HMD to engage in VR spatial experiences [9]. Consistency of perception may be lost, and the results observed in an HMD environment may differ from their appearance in real space [10].

This study investigated whether immersive VR spaces can provide perceptions and impressions similar to those experienced in real spaces created with flat displays (DP spaces), which is a commonly used spatial design method. Mabuchi et al. [11] verified spatial perception accuracy by varying the object distances and viewing angles in immersive VR. Furthermore, by measuring skin activity, Kobayashi et al. [12] explored the relationship between the mental burdens of crossers emerging from the blind spots at intersections and corners in an HMD space. Finally, Ishida et al. [13] studied the home design process using immersive VR, and Nishida et al. [14] evaluated impressions by projecting full-sky images of various U-shaped spaces onto an HMD screen.

However, these studies did not compare the perception of distance and spatial impressions between real and experience spaces (such as flat displays). Although many studies have examined the comfort [15] offered by HMDs and the positioning [16] of objects, few have focused on spatial perception and impression. The similarity of displays and HMDs to real spaces was verified by the author's previous studies on immersive VR spaces.

In one of these studies [17–19], the superiority of a display installed on the left-hand side of the participant was analyzed by verifying the distance perception and psychological evaluation of the personal space. However, the study was limited to a single direction; hence, it could not induce the "looking around the space" behavior that is characteristic of HMDs. Therefore, we examined the perception and impression of spatial components when participants felt their personal space being enclosed by objects placed in front of them and on both sides (left and right), compelling them to look around the space.

Previous research showed that HMDs were superior to flat displays regarding distance perception, as the former perceived distances to be shorter. However, this superiority was not evident in a single direction, and the impression of space was not evaluated. This study created and evaluated a space based not on viewing it from a particular direction but rather on the characteristics of the HMD, which allows the user to move their head and "search the peripheral space." We also examined the relationship between perceived distance and spatial impression and discussed whether the immersive VR environment provides a better perception and impression of spatial components than existing methods with respect to similarity and consistency with the real space.

2   Methods

The relevant target space, components, and question items were established to conduct the "impression evaluation" of three different posting methods. Hereafter, the three different posting methods are denoted as "Real space," "DP space," and "HMD space." In addition, the results were analyzed and discussed for similarity and consistency.

This study received ethical approval from Ritsumeikan University Ethics Review Committee for Research Involving Human Subjects (approval number: Kinugasa-Human-2022–76). Informed consent was voluntarily obtained from participants after they received oral explanations on the 12 items (such as the significance, purpose, and methods of the study, as well as data handling methods) stipulated by their respective institutions.

2.1   Spatial Organization of the Experiment

The experimental space was a laboratory designed to emulate environments such as a café or study room, where various tasks (meetings and conversations) were undertaken around a desk at which participants worked. A table (0.7 m long, 0.7 m wide, and 0.7 m high) and a chair (0.45 m long, 0.50 m wide, and 0.45 m high) were centrally placed in the room. Three seats, for individuals not involved in the participant's work, were positioned in front and to the left and right of the participant. Additionally, partitions (0.9 m × 0.9 m) were placed directly in front and to the left and right of the participant, creating a line connecting the participant at the center with the surrounding seats.

Whenever the partitions were repositioned, the participants were asked to provide their "impressions of the space." We selected a space with minimal detail, i.e., without tiling, shelves, lighting fixtures, and furniture (e.g., desks and chairs) to examine the impression of space based on the dimensions of the partitioned space (see Fig. 1). Measurements and positions were acquired to create 3D models of both the DP and HMD spaces; owing to a lack of detailed drawings, the models were required to mimic the Real space.

A university conference room (7.9 m long, 17.66 m wide, and 2.61 m high) served as the Real space. People sat in front and to the left and right of the participant with partitions equidistantly placed from the latter, who remained at the center (see Figs. 2 and 3). The participants were not informed about the actual dimensions or distances of the space. During the experiment, the partitions were randomly placed at four different distances (0.8 m, 1.4 m, 2.1 m, and 2.6 m).

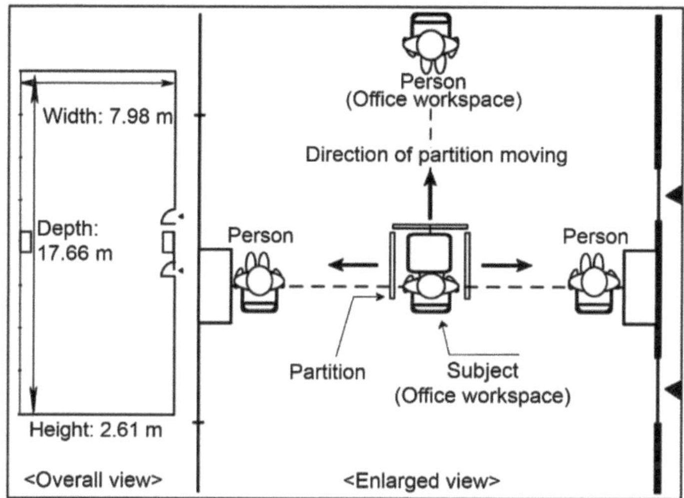

Fig. 1. Plan of the space used for the experiment.

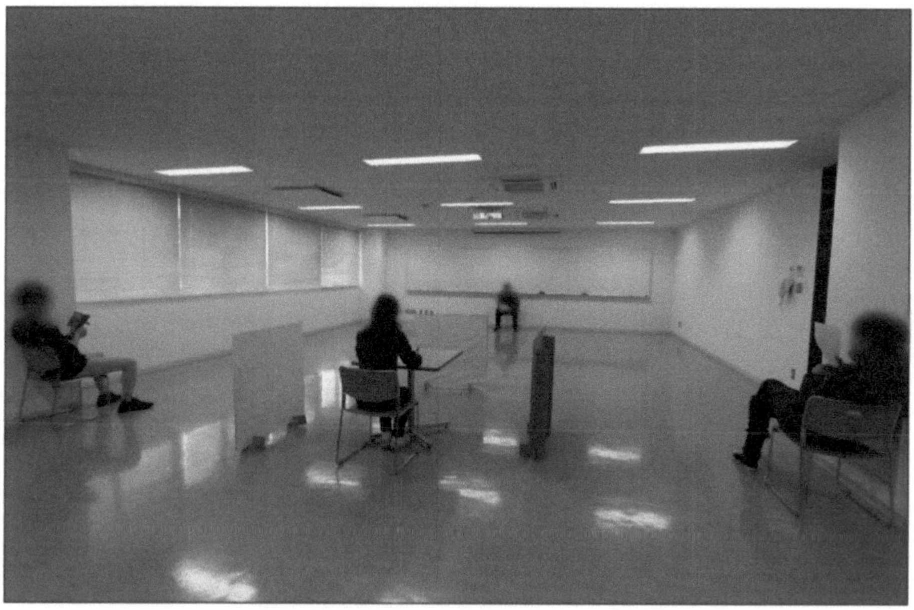

Fig. 2. Experimental scene of the Real space.

2.2 Contents of the Impression Survey

Two questions were posed regarding the participant's impression of the personal space when sitting in the center of the room (see Appendix 1). Details of the experimental space are provided in Sect. 2.3. The participants in this study included 59 undergraduate and graduate architecture students (40 men and 19 women) aged between 18 and 23 years. These students mainly attended classes on the fundamentals of architectural planning, design, structure, and production. This study did not focus on differences in responses based on gender or the participants' architectural proficiency or knowledge. In addition, the HMD used in the experiment had a narrow gap between the face and lens, thus because it butted against any eyewear individuals who typically wore glasses were excluded from the experiment.

The first survey item was "Openness and oppressiveness." We assessed whether the participant considered their personal space oppressive or open (hereafter, referred to as openness) on a five-point scale (1: oppressive–5: open) for each partition position.

The second survey item was "Human presence." We evaluated the impression of "presence" or "absence" (hereafter, referred to as presence) of people outside the personal space of the participant on a five-point scale (1: presence–5: absence) for each partition position.

Further details concerning the questionnaire and participant responses are discussed in Sect. 2.4.

2.3 Creation of the Experience Space

Three types of spaces were created for the experiment: Real, DP, and HMD spaces. The DP and HMD spaces were designed to replicate the dimensions, texture, and brightness of the Real space. The specifications of the personal computer used for space creation were as follows: Intel Core i7–6700 central processing unit, NVIDIA GeForce GTX 980 graphics card (GM204 core, 28 nm process, 2048 CUDA cores, core clock 1126–1216 MHz, 4096 MB memory, memory clock 7010 MHz), HDMI video output, USB 3.0, and 16 GB system memory.

As detailed in Sect. 2.1, the Real space was established without additional spatial components to avoid distractions and allow focus solely on the participant, chair, desk, partitions, real humans (as external workers), and other elements outside the primary space (Fig. 2).

The DP space was a 3D model created using Autodesk 3ds Max 2019, which was imported into Unreal Engine and displayed on a DP (EIZO, 27 inches, 2560 × 1440 resolution) using real-time rendering. The dimensions of the furniture and size of the rooms were the same as those in the Real space. While real people were placed as additional workers in the Real space, a motionless, expressionless, white-colored 3D model was placed in the DP space. The camera in the DP space was set to a viewing angle of 110° based on preliminary experiments and the study by Mabuchi et al. [11]. The camera height was adjusted vertically to match the sitting height of the participant. A desk and chair of the same height as those in the Real space were positioned in front of the display, which was placed 60 cm from the participant's face. The participant used the keyboard arrow keys (←, ↑, ↓, and →) instead of head movements to look around in the DP space (see Fig. 3).

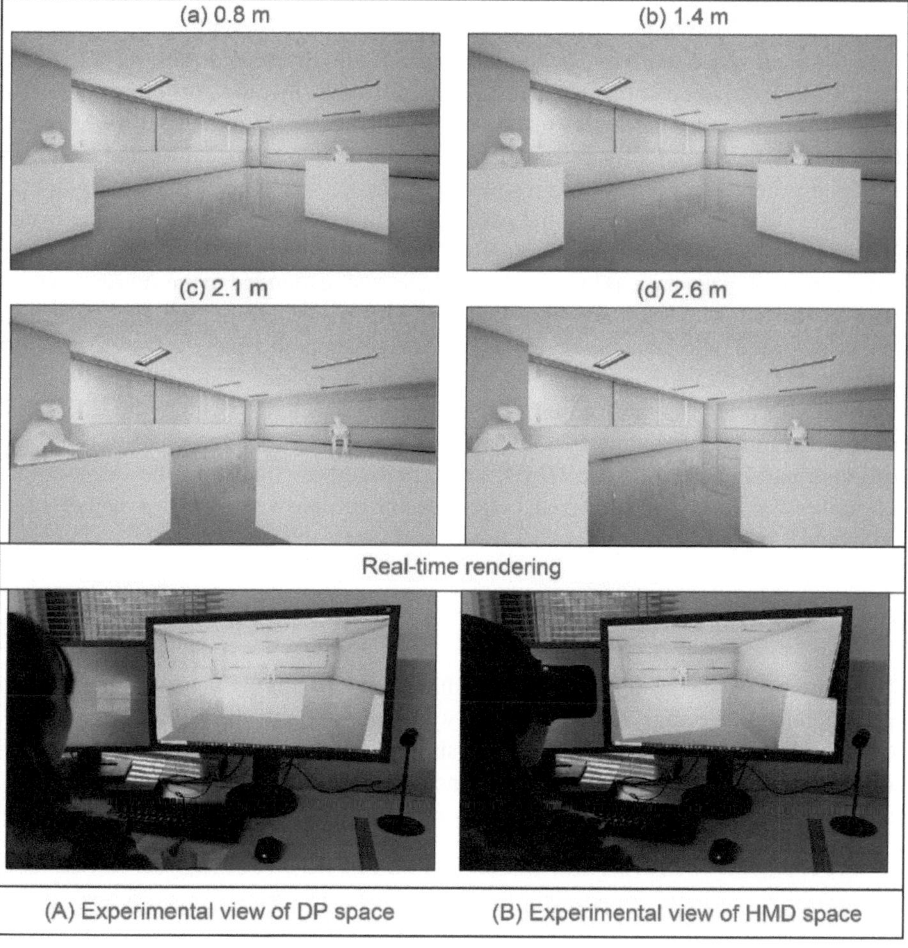

Fig. 3. The experimental scene and real-time rendering in the flat display (DP) and head-mounted display (HMD) spaces.

The images, displayed on an HMD (Oculus Rift: 2160 × 1200 pixels total resolution, 1080 × 1200 pixels per eye, 90 Hz refresh rate, outside-in tracking sensor), were created with 3ds Max and Unreal Engine 4 and used in the HMD space. The dimensions of the furniture and the sizes of the rooms were the same as those in the Real space. While real people were placed as external workers in the Real space, as in the DP space, a similarly motionless white 3D model was placed in the HMD space. Participants sat at a desk and chair set to the same height as in the Real space. The viewpoint in the HMD space was vertically adjusted to match the participant's seated height (see Fig. 3).

2.4 Procedures

The participants underwent a question-and-answer procedure regarding each experience space. Before the experiments began, it was explained that the experiment would be set in a freely navigable space resembling a café. The participants were instructed to explore the space in front and to their left and right visually before responding to questions.

In the Real space experiment, the participants initially seated themselves facing a desk. Subsequently, partitions were installed; following this, the participants observed the space and answered the survey questions given in Sect. 2.2 for each partition position. The partitions were randomly placed at distances of 0.8 m, 1.4 m, 2.1 m, and 2.6 m. The participants directly recorded their responses on the answer sheet using a ballpoint pen.

For the DP space experiment, the participants first positioned themselves in front of the display and adjusted their viewpoints. Subsequently, using the keyboard arrow keys, they explored the DP space akin to the Real space, and responded to the survey questions posed in Sect. 2.2 for each partition location. Using a ballpoint pen, the participants directly recorded their answers on the answer sheet where the questions were provided.

In the HMD space experiment, the participants were seated and fitted with HMDs with their viewpoints suitably adjusted. They were instructed to explore the HMD space and respond to the survey questions (outlined in Sect. 2.2) for each partition position. While the participant wore the HMD, the experimenter conducted the question-and-answer session orally and entered responses on the answer sheet on behalf of the participant.

3 Results and Discussion

This section presents an overview of the three types of spaces based on the response values obtained. We analyzed the similarity of impression of the DP and HMD spaces to the Real space using correlation analysis and used confidence intervals to clarify their relationships. The perception of distance and impression of space are discussed in Sect. 4.

3.1 Openness of Space

The respondents were asked to rate their response to the question of openness or oppressiveness using a five-point scale, where the "sense of pressure" was rated with 1 point and the "sense of openness" was rated with 5 points. Figure 4 summarizes the response values across distances of 0.8 m, 1.4 m, 2.1 m, and 2.6 m. Further, in Fig. 5, "DP-R" represents the response value in the DP space minus the response value in the Real space, whereas "HMD-R" represents the response value in the HMD space minus that in the Real space. The results of the descriptive statistics are presented in Table 1.

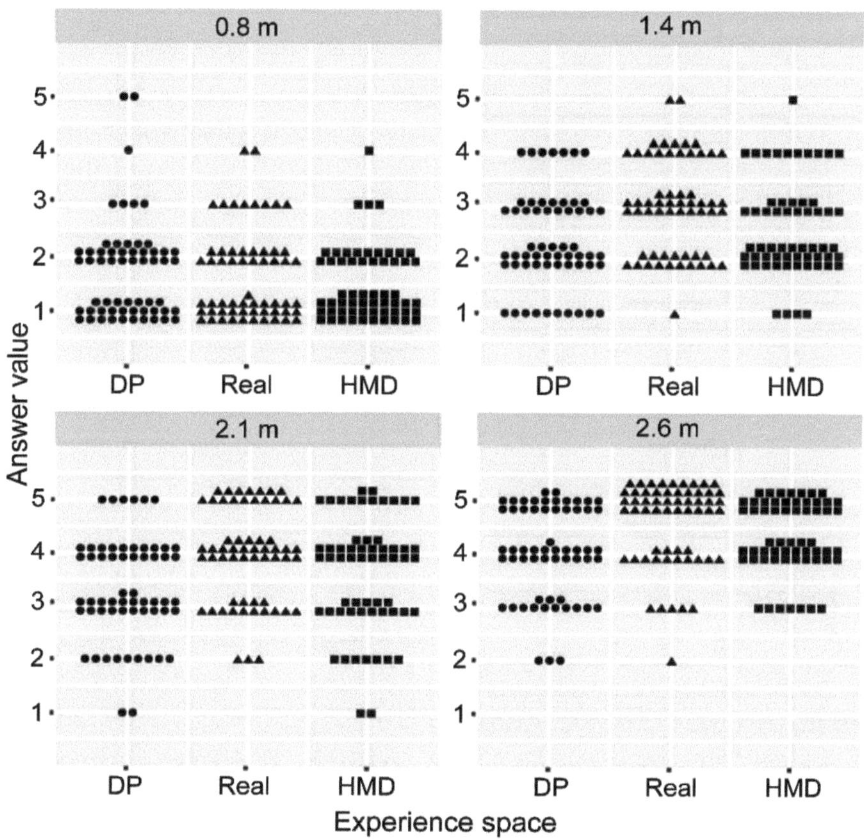

Fig. 4. Answer values according to the distance and sense of openness (openness of space).

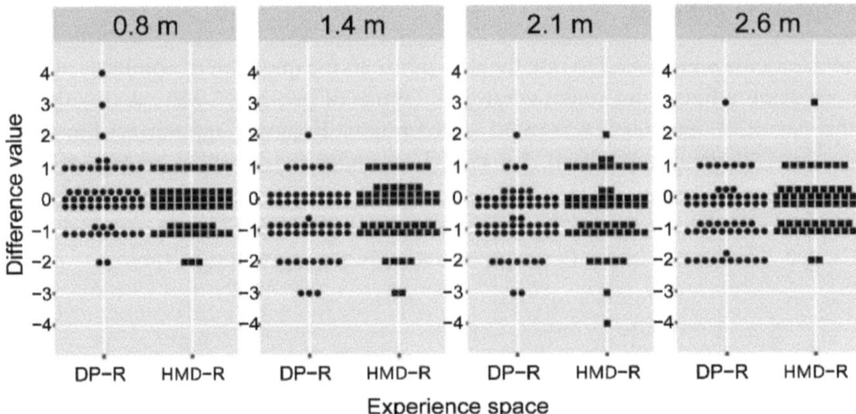

Fig. 5. Differences in answer values from the Real space (openness of space) (DP-R: The response value in the DP space minus the response value in the Real space, HMD-R: The response value in the HMD space minus that in the Real space).

Table 1. Average/standard deviation (openness of space).

	Distance level	0.8 m	1.4 m	2.1 m	2.6 m
Real	ave.	1.678	3.000	3.949	4.542
	SD	0.832	0.864	0.852	0.721
DP	ave.	1.746	2.356	3.322	4.051
	SD	0.913	0.898	0.964	0.891
HMD	ave.	1.475	2.576	3.610	4.339
	SD	0.673	0.906	1.042	0.679
DP-R	ave.	0.068	-0.644	-0.627	-0.492
	SD	1.023	1.054	0.937	1.031
HMD-R	ave.	-0.203	-0.424	-0.339	-0.203
	SD	0.776	0.924	1.099	0.839

ave.: average; SD: standard deviation; DP: flat display; HMD: head-mounted display; DR-R: the response value in the DP space minus the response value in the Real space; HMD-R: the response value in the HMD space minus that in the Real space.

Figure 6 shows the trends of the average Real, DP, and HMD values in Table 1. Except for the case of partitions at 0.8 m, Real exhibited the largest value. In addition, the difference between the DP and Real spaces and between the HMD and Real spaces (Table 1) was negative, except for 0.8 m for DP-R. Furthermore, a comparison of the absolute values of DP-R and HMD-R revealed that HMD-R was always smaller than DP-R, except at 0.8 m.

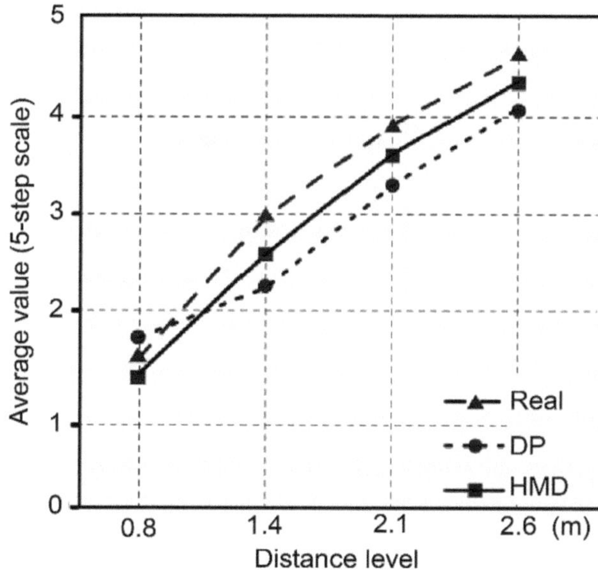

Fig. 6. Average response values (openness of space). The participants in this study included 59 undergraduate and graduate architecture students (40 men and 19 women) aged between 18 and 23 years.

Subsequently, the correlation coefficients (Pearson's product rate correlation coefficient) and 95% confidence intervals were analyzed to determine the relationship between the DP and HMD spaces and the Real space. The correlation coefficients (Pearson's product factor correlation coefficient) and confidence intervals are shown in Fig. 7. Regarding whether the threshold crossed zero and whether the null hypothesis of the lack of correlation could be rejected, "DP and Real" crossed zero at 2.6 m and was near zero at 0.8 m and 1.4 m. This suggests that the DP space may not exhibit notable similarity to the Real space. Regarding the correlation coefficient values, "HMD and Real" showed a moderate correlation at 0.8 m and 1.4 m, indicating that the HMD space may be similar to the Real space. Furthermore, a comparison of the correlation coefficients between DP and Real and between HMD and Real reveals that HMD and Real yielded higher values, except at 2.1 m.

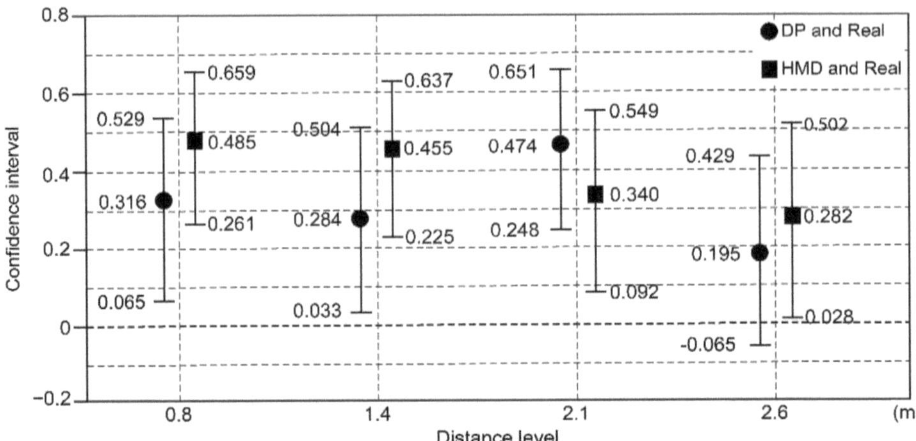

Fig. 7. Pearson's product rate correlation coefficient and 95% confidence intervals (openness of space). The horizontal axis is the distance level, and the vertical axis is the confidence interval. The error bars extend up and down from each marker and represent the width of the confidence interval for each data point.

The descriptive statistics indicate that the users' impression was slightly more prominent in the HMD space than the Real space regarding the impression of openness. Additionally, the HMD space tended to be more similar to the DP space in providing a comparable impression to the Real space. Based on the correlation coefficients and confidence intervals, it can be inferred that the HMD space exhibited a stronger correlation with the Real space than the DP space and overall possessed greater similarity to the Real space.

3.2 Human Presence

The respondents were tasked with rating the question of sensing or not sensing the presence of a human on a five-point scale, with the response "feel a presence" rated with 1 point and "do not feel a presence" rated with 5 points. Figure 8 shows the response values for the four distance levels (0.8 m, 1.4 m, 2.1 m, and 2.6 m). Figure 9 is similar to Fig. 5, where DP-R corresponds to the response value in the DP space minus that in the Real space, and HMD-R corresponds to the response value in the HMD space minus that in the Real space. The results of the descriptive statistics are listed in Table 2.

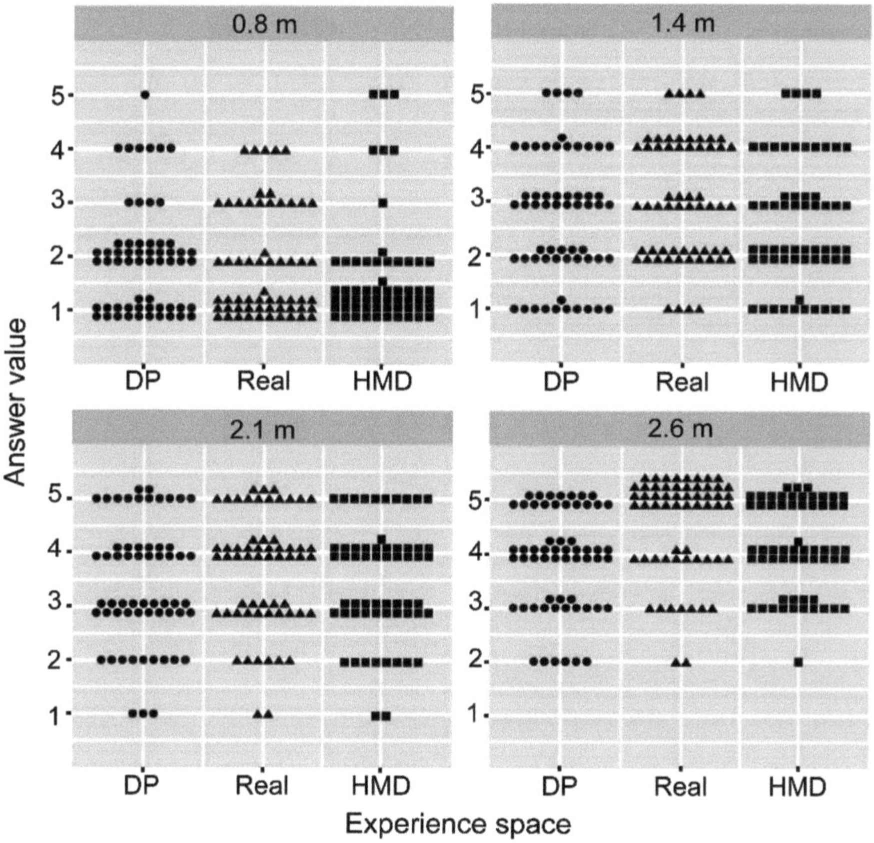

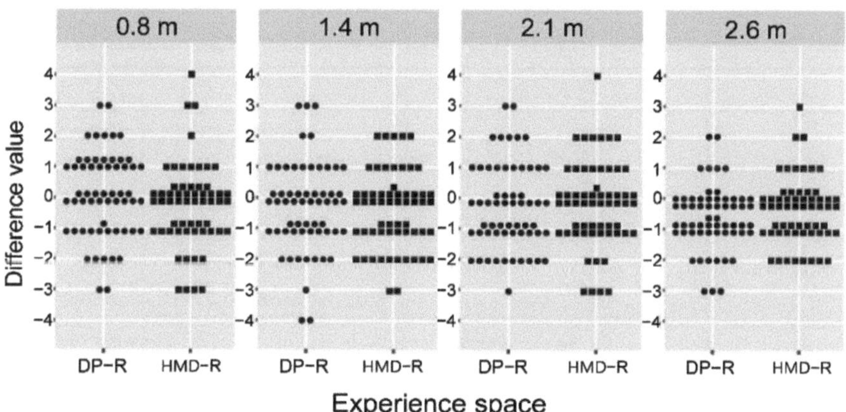

Fig. 8. Answer values according to the distance and experience space (human presence).

Fig. 9. Differences in answer values from the Real space (human presence).

Table 2. Average/standard deviation (human presence).

	Distance level	0.8 m	1.4 m	2.1 m	2.6 m
Real	ave.	1.847	2.983	3.661	4.458
	SD	1.022	1.081	1.035	0.830
DP	ave.	1.949	2.695	3.424	3.864
	SD	0.999	1.168	1.123	0.947
HMD	ave.	1.576	2.593	3.492	4.119
	SD	1.092	1.166	1.031	0.825
DP-R	ave.	0.102	-0.288	-0.237	-0.593
	SD	1.324	1.450	1.370	1.043
HMD-R	ave.	-0.271	-0.390	-0.169	-0.339
	SD	1.351	1.235	1.367	1.051

Figure 10 shows the trends of the average values for Real, DP, and HMD listed in Table 2. Except for the case of partitions at 0.8 m, Real yielded the largest value for the response "openness of space." In addition, the difference between the DP and Real spaces and that between the HMD and Real spaces (Table 2) yielded negative values, except for 0.8 m for DP-R. Furthermore, a comparison of the absolute values of DP-R and HMD-R revealed that HMD-R was larger at 0.8 m and 1.4 m but smaller at 2.1 m and 2.6 m.

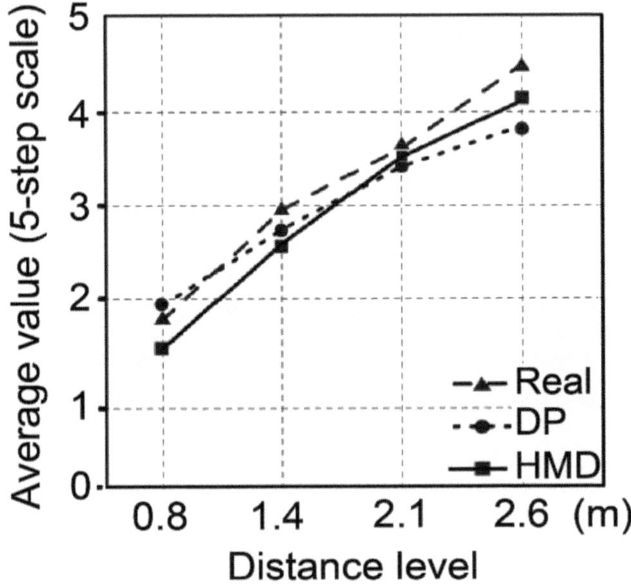

Fig. 10. Average response answer values (human presence).

Subsequently, Pearson's product-moment correlation coefficients and their 95% confidence intervals were analyzed to assess the relationship between the DP and HMD spaces compared with the Real space. The coefficients and confidence intervals are depicted in Fig. 11. Concerning the null hypothesis being rejected for lack of correlation (crossing the threshold of zero), all correlations crossed zero, except for HMD and Real at 1.4 m and DP and Real at 2.6 m. An examination of the correlation coefficient values for HMD and Real at 1.4 m and DP and Real at 2.6 m showed moderate correlations. However, at most distances, the DP and HMD spaces did not exhibit significant similarity to the Real space. A comparison of the correlation coefficients between DP and Real and between HMD and Real revealed that HMD-R was higher at 0.8 m and 1.4 m but lower at 2.1 m and 2.6 m.

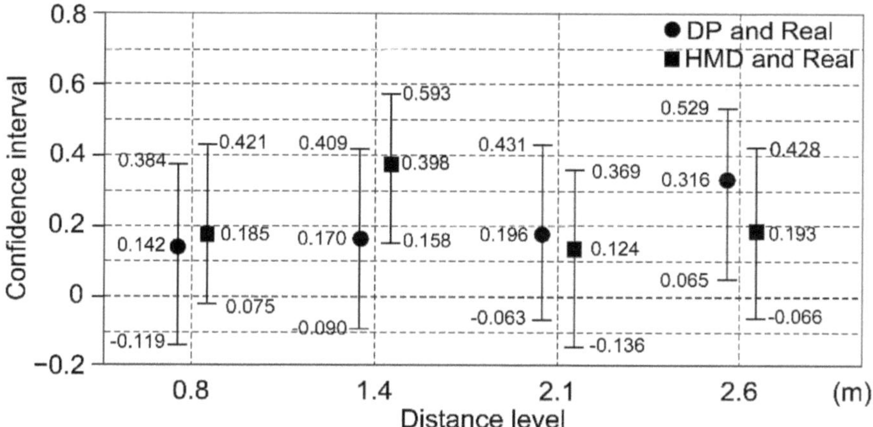

Fig. 11. Pearson's product rate correlation coefficient and 95% confidence intervals (human presence).

The descriptive statistics indicate that users were slightly more aware of humans being present in the HMD space than in the Real space regarding their impressions of presence. However, concerning a similar impression being provided in the Real space, when considering the correlation coefficients and confidence intervals, the HMD space showed a correlation with the Real space at a specific distance (1.4 m). Overall, the HMD space exhibited a lower similarity to the Real space than the DP space.

3.3 Discussion Summary

The similarities between the impressions of spaces and the Real space were statistically verified by comparing three posting modalities; significant differences are discussed in Sect. 3. First, we calculated and reviewed the mean and standard deviation of the response values on a five-point scale for the three types of experience spaces. Second, we calculated the differences between the Real and DP spaces and between the Real and HMD spaces to verify their differences from the Real space. However, for presence, they may have incorrectly evaluated the visibility of people outside the partition [20].

4 Conclusions

This study analyzed and discussed the impressions of space across three experimental conditions using partitions placed in the front, left, and right directions. Our findings are summarized as follows:

The difference in the impression of spatial openness across varying distances was examined based on the mean differences between DP-R and HMD-R (the difference of mean differences). The trend in mean values indicated that the HMD space felt more oppressive than the Real space, even at equivalent distances. The correlation coefficient and confidence interval analyses suggested that the HMD space exhibited greater similarity to the Real space regarding the impression of openness than to the DP space.

Similarly, the difference in the impression of the presence of observed objects across varying distances was verified using the mean difference between DP-R and HMD-R. The findings revealed that the HMD space felt more present than the Real space, even at comparable distances. However, an analysis of the correlation coefficients and confidence intervals indicated that the HMD space may not be more similar to the Real space than the DP space concerning the impression of presence.

These results align with the findings of previous studies [17–19]. However, a discrepancy was observed between the results of the perception of distance [21] and impression of space. Accordingly, the mean values for the perception of distance and impression of space were plotted on the horizontal axis (see Fig. 12) to examine the differences between the perception of distance and the impressions of openness and presence.

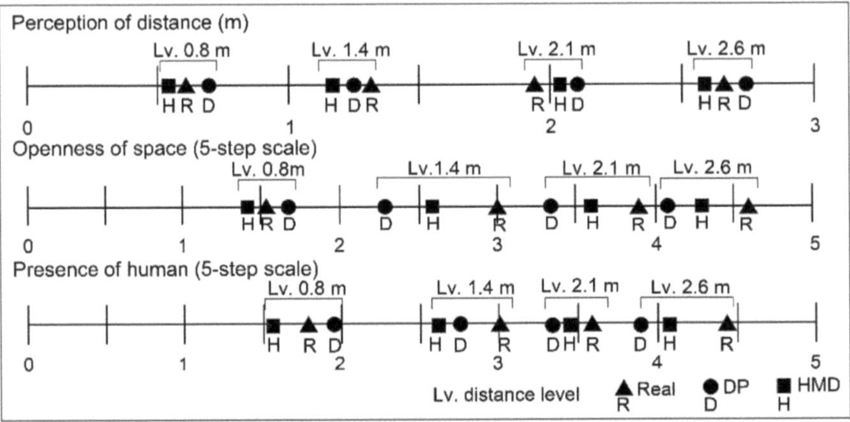

Fig. 12. Results for different settings. The average of the responses for each space for the perception of distance and the impression of space (openness and presence) were plotted on the horizontal axis.

Both the perception of distance and the impressions of openness and presence consistently showed lower values in the HMD space compared to the Real space [22]. However, the magnitude of the difference varied depending on the position of the partition. In particular, for impression evaluations, the difference from the Real space increased as the installation distance became larger, and participants tended to feel more pressure and more presence in the HMD space. Additionally, for distance perception, there were cases in which distances in the HMD space were perceived as longer than those in the Real space, depending on the position of the partition.

These results suggest that factors such as the immersive characteristics of HMDs—including head movements to look around, stereoscopic rendering, and exploratory behavior—as well as participants' psychological sense of distance, may contribute to these differences.

This study's findings highlight the utility of HMDs for investigating visual perception and impression in immersive environments. As technological advancements continue to narrow the gap between real and virtual spaces, future research should explore not only qualitative evaluation methods but also the impact of spatial scale, including applications in natural and urban environments. Additional aspects such as safety and comfort also warrant further investigation. The fundamental data and insights provided by this study will support the ongoing development and diffusion of VR technology, especially for innovative approaches in architecture and spatial design. To address current limitations, future work should validate these findings with a broader range of participants and spatial settings.

In summary, this study directly compared and assessed the differences between the perception of distance and impressions (openness and presence) in immersive virtual environments. While distance perception was relatively similar across all conditions, impressions in the HMD space were distinct from those in the real space, especially depending on the position of the partition. These findings highlight that perception and impression do not always align in immersive environments, underscoring the importance of treating these aspects as independent yet complementary. This provides valuable insights for advancing the evaluation and design of VR spaces.

Acknowledgments. Acknowledgments. This research was supported by JSPS KAKENHI [grant number 22K18145, research category: Grant-in-Aid for Early-Career Scientists]. In addition, we express our deepest gratitude to all the participants, assistants, and teachers involved in this study. Further, we thank Editage (www.editage.com) for the English language editing.

Author Contributions.. Conceptualization, E.K., and S.Y.; methodology, E.K., and S.Y.; software, E.K.; validation, E.K.; formal analysis, E.K., and S.Y.; investigation, E.K.; resources, E.K., and S.Y.; data curation, E.K.; writing—original draft preparation, E.K.; writing—review and editing, E.K., and S.Y.; visualization, E.K.; supervision, E.K., and S.Y.; project administration, E.K.; funding acquisition, E.K. All authors have read and agreed to the published version of the manuscript.

Disclosure of Interests.. The authors have no competing interests to declare that are relevant to the content of this article.

Appendix 1

The following points should be considered when you experience the space and answer the questionnaire.

1) Do not move; remain seated in the chair; and make as few big movements as possible.

2) When you experience any space, first look around the space while being seated.
3) Do not use other components as cues.

I set the partitions four times. Please evaluate the following questions on a scale of 1 to 5 each time setting a partition.

i)Do you feel a sense of oppressiveness or a sense of open in your personal space?
ii)Do you feel the presence of human or not outside the partitions?

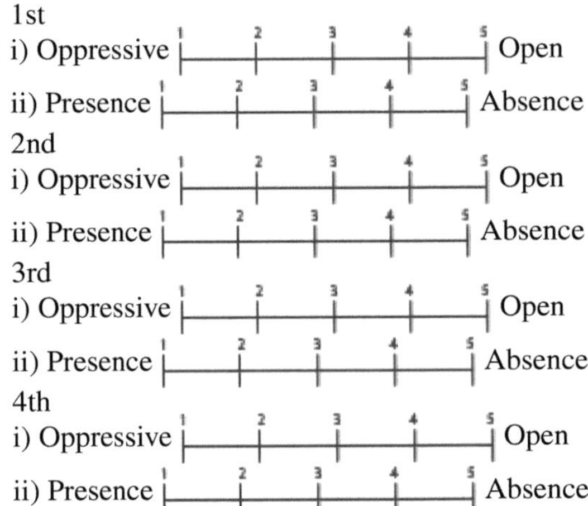

Note that the four distances (0.8 m, 1.4 m, 2.1 m, and 2.6 m) are posted at random.

References

1. Salmimaa, M., et al.: Live delivery of neurosurgical operating theater experience in virtual reality. J. Soc. Inf. Disp. **26**, 98–104 (2018). https://doi.org/10.1002/jsid.636
2. Zhang, Z., Li, Y., Guo, J., Weng, D., Liu, Y., Wang, Y.: Vision-tangible interactive display method for mixed and virtual reality: towards the human-centered editable reality. J. Soc. Inf. Disp. **27**, 72–84 (2018). https://doi.org/10.1002/jsid.747
3. Pizzi, G., Scarpi, D., Pichierri, M., Vannucci, V.: Virtual reality, real reactions?: comparing consumers' perceptions and shopping orientation across physical and virtual-reality retail stores. Comput. Hum. Behav. **96**, 1–12 (2019). https://doi.org/10.1016/j.chb.2019.02.008
4. Cheng, L.Y., Lin, C.J.: The effects of depth perception viewing on hand–eye coordination in virtual reality environments. J. Soc. Inf. Disp. **29**, 801–817 (2018). https://doi.org/10.1002/jsid.1068
5. Maria-Jesus, A., Margarita, V., Vicente, B.: Perceiving design features in new interaction environments: Comparing rendered images, 360° rotation, AR, immersive and non-immersive VR, and real product interaction. Appl. Sci. **14**, 4470 (2024). https://doi.org/10.3390/app14114470
6. Tianning, Y., et al.: Research on range of appropriate spatial scale of underground commercial street based on psychological perception evaluation. Appl. Sci. **14**, 5435 (2024). https://doi.org/10.3390/app14135435
7. Shinomiya, S., Sakatani, S., Tanaka, Y., Chiba, M.: A process of dialogue with situation in VR as a design space. J. Archit. **86**, 1409–1419 (2021). https://doi.org/10.3130/aija.86.1409
8. Kusumoto, M., Kubota, Y.: The projection of astronomical simulation to improve the azimuth recognition. Jpn. Soc. Sci. Educ. **35**, 452–453 (2011) (in Japanese). https://doi.org/10.14935/jssep.35.0_452

9. Kuliga, S.F., Thrash, T., Dalton, R.C., Hölscher, C.: Virtual reality an empirical research tool—exploring user experience in a real building and a corresponding virtual model. Comput. Environ. Urban Syst. **54**, 363–375 (2015). https://doi.org/10.1016/j.compenvurbsys.2015.09.006

10. Pizzolante, M., Bartolotta, S., Sarcinella, E.D., Chirico, A., Gaggioli, A.: Virtual vs. real: exploring perceptual, cognitive and affective dimensions in design product experiences. BMC Psychol. **12**, 10 (2024). https://doi.org/10.1186/s40359-023-01497-5

11. Mabuchi, D., Yoshioka, Y., Fujii, K., Enta, A., Sano, T.: Verification of the influence factors concerning the accuracy of distance perception in immersive virtual environment. AIJ J. Technol. Des. **23**, 223–228 (2017) (in Japanese). https://doi.org/10.3130/aijt.23.223

12. Kobayashi, W., Mabuchi, D., Yoshioka, Y.: Corner shapes for decreasing psychological stress by pedestrian approaching from blind spot of intersection. AIJ J. Technol. Des. **25**, 845–850 (2019) (in Japanese). https://doi.org/10.3130/aijt.25.845

13. Ishida, K., Sakatani, S., Tanaka, Y., Chiba, M.: Influence of experience of space using VR on design process: A study on VR as a dialogical tool supporting the creative process in architectural design Part 1. J. Archit. Plan. (Trans. AIJ). **84**, 1579–1587 (2019) (in Japanese). https://doi.org/10.3130/aija.84.1579

14. Nishida, T., Ito, T., Yamamoto, Y., Han, Y.: Effects of side length in U shape partition on perceived shapes and visual impressions. J. Archit. Plan (Trans. AIJ). **85**, 2517–2527 (2020) (in Japanese). https://doi.org/10.3130/aija.85.2517

15. Chiuhsiang, J., Cheng, L.Y., Wang, M.C.: Performance of estimating depth in projection based stereoscopic virtual display. J. Soc. Inf. Display. J. SID. **23**, 76–83 (2015). https://doi.org/10.1002/jsid.309

16. Ping, J., Weng, D., Liu, Y., Wang, Y.: Depth perception in shuffleboard: depth cues effect on depth perception in virtual and augmented reality system. J. Soc. Inf. Disp. **28**, 164–176 (2020). https://doi.org/10.1002/jsid.840

17. Kitamoto, E., Yamada, S., Oikawa, K.: Study on space perception on using HMD-providing enclosed feel on the subject experiment; In: Proceedings of the 39 Symposium on Computer Technology of Information, Systems and Applications, Tokyo, Japan, 9 December 2016, pp. 169–172. Architectural Institute of Japan, Tokyo, Japan (2016) (in Japanese)

18. Kitamoto, E., Yamada, S., Oikawa, K.: Study on space perception on using HMD-providing enclosed feel on the subject experiment. Architectural Institute of Japan; Instruction for Summaries of Technical Papers of Annual Meeting *Inf. Syst. Technol.* 17–18 (2017) (in Japanese)

19. Yamada, S., Kitamoto, E., Jincho, N., Oikawa, K.: A study on spatial perception in immersive virtual space-perception and psychological evaluation of distance with consideration of personal space. AIJ J. Technol. Des. **24**, 1303–1307 (2018) (in Japanese). https://doi.org/10.3130/aijt.24.1303

20. Blais, C., Jack, R.E., Scheepers, C., Fiset, D., Caldara, R.: Culture shapes how we look at faces. PLoS ONE **3**, e3022 (2008). https://doi.org/10.1371/journal.pone.0003022

21. Kitamoto, E., Yamada, S., Jincho, N.: A study on spatial perception in immersive virtual space: -Perception and psychological evaluation of distance about enclosed feeling for personal space. AIJ J. Technol. Des. **27**, 1104–1109 (2021) (in Japanese). https://doi.org/10.3130/aijt.27.1104

22. Itaguchi, Y.: Size perception bias and reach-to-grasp kinematics: an exploratory study on the virtual hand with a consumer immersive virtual-reality device. Front. Virtual Real. **2**, 712378 (2021). https://doi.org/10.3389/frvir.2021.712378

Effects of Virtual Experiences on Enhancing Social Acceptance of Autonomous Buses

Daiji Kobayashi[1]([✉]) [iD], Shuto Uji-ie[1], and Takehiko Yamaguchi[2]

[1] Chitose Institute of Science and Technology, Bibi 758-65,, Chitose, Hokkaido, Japan
d-kobaya@photon.chitose.ac.jp
[2] Suwa University of Science, Toyohira, Chino, Japan

Abstract. In response to challenges such as driver shortages and the need for improved accessibility, many developed countries, including European Union nations and Japan, are implementing pilot programs for autonomous bus systems. These initiatives aim to enhance public transportation, particularly for aging populations. In Japan, municipalities are conducting trials to verify the safety and reliability of these systems within existing transportation networks. However, public skepticism remains a challenge owing to limited understanding and safety concerns. To improve public acceptance, municipalities have introduced various outreach efforts, including the distribution of informational guidebooks, use of social media and public relations materials, and organization of trial ride events. Research has shown that direct experience with autonomous buses increases familiarity and acceptance, especially when users perceive the systems as safe and useful. Building on these insights, a study developed virtual reality content that simulates a ride on an autonomous bus. The simulation was created using 360-degree video and presented via a head-mounted display. This simulation allowed users to experience boarding, riding, and exiting a bus. The video included explanatory text and was filmed from a third-person perspective to reduce motion sickness. The study assessed changes in perception among 21 participants using a questionnaire based on the Unified Theory of Acceptance and Use of Technology. Results showed increased trust and perceived safety, with many participants expressing confidence in the reliability and convenience of autonomous buses. Views on privacy and fares varied.

Keywords: Autonomous Bus System · Social Implementation · Social Acceptability · Virtual Experience

1 Introduction

Pilot programs for the implementation of autonomous bus systems are currently being introduced in many developed countries, including those within the European Union. These initiatives are designed to address critical challenges, such as driver shortages, which are increasingly exacerbated by aging populations. Simultaneously, these initiatives aim to enhance public transportation infrastructure to better serve elderly residents and improve overall accessibility. For example, Wicki et al. (2018) conducted a study

H. Mori et al. (Eds.): HCII 2025, LNCS 16333, pp. 74–86, 2026.
https://doi.org/10.1007/978-3-032-12660-3_6

on public opinion regarding autonomous driving, focusing specifically on a pilot test of an automated bus service in Neuhausen am Rheinfall, Switzerland. The study identified several key issues that must be addressed, including data privacy, safety in complex traffic environments, and the effectiveness of public communication [1].

In Japan, various municipalities are actively working to integrate autonomous buses into their public transportation networks. These efforts primarily concentrate on validating and optimizing the reliability and safety of autonomous bus systems to ensure their smooth integration into existing infrastructure. In Chitose, Hokkaido, trials were scheduled to begin in 2024, with the objectives of improving the performance of autonomous buses under severe winter conditions, particularly on icy roads, and refining the artificial intelligence systems that control them. Despite continuous technological advancements, achieving widespread social acceptability remains a significant challenge.

The municipality of Chitose City, which is seeking to implement autonomous bus systems, faces several obstacles. Some residents have limited awareness of the functionality and benefits of these systems, express concerns about safety, and demonstrate reluctance to use them. In response, local authorities have introduced a range of measures to enhance public understanding, including the distribution of user guidebooks, dissemination of information through social media platforms and public relations publications, and organization of trial events and community forums. Collectively, these initiatives aim to improve public perception and establish the conditions necessary for the social acceptability of autonomous bus systems.

Research on the social acceptance of autonomous bus systems includes a study by Camps-Aragó et al. (2022) that examined public perception in two scenarios: commuting to a hospital and commuting to a workplace in Brussels, Belgium [2]. The findings suggest that experiencing a ride on an autonomous bus increases familiarity with the technology and enhances individuals' willingness to adopt autonomous buses. Furthermore, individuals who perceive autonomous buses as safe and useful are more likely to express a willingness to use them. These results indicate that effectively communicating the safety and utility of autonomous bus systems can contribute to greater social acceptance. European studies have primarily examined user experience following the implementation of autonomous bus systems, and the concept of social acceptability refers to the extent to which society is willing to accept such technologies prior to their full deployment. Therefore, in the case of Chitose City, focusing on social acceptability, which is shaped by the expectations and perceptions of potential future users, is essential.

Additional insights were provided by Nastjuk et al. (2020), who identified key factors that influence social acceptability [3]. Uhde et al. (2021) proposed an approach based on social practice theory to better understand and design for social acceptability [4]. According to this theory, human behavior results from the interaction of meanings, competences, and material conditions. Public relations efforts and community forums that provide information regarding the safety and efficiency of autonomous bus systems can help shape the public understanding of this new technology. Trial events can also enhance users' competence in interacting with autonomous buses and thereby reduce the likelihood of usage errors or incidents. Furthermore, the safety and reliability of the systems themselves must continue to be improved. Human behavior is also influenced by implicit social norms and assumptions, which are often referred to as doxa. In this context, Hosotsubo et al. (2020) examined public attitudes toward science and technology, comparing responses from Japan and the European Union [5]. The study found that Japanese respondents were generally more positive about artificial intelligence than were their European counterparts, although they did not view artificial intelligence and robotics as unequivocally beneficial or in need of strict regulation. The findings also suggest that higher levels of awareness and an understanding of the benefits and safety of these technologies contribute to increased social acceptance, thus highlighting the importance of cultural perceptions in shaping public attitudes.

Jammes et al. (2024) explored social acceptability in the context of service experiences and developed a model to assess the social acceptability of technological innovations and the behavioral responses they elicit, including acceptance, rejection, and indifference [6]. Their model was based on two key dimensions: perceived social desirability and perceived accessibility. Perceived social desirability refers to the subjective evaluation of a the moral, social, and political benefit of a service, relative to its costs. Perceived accessibility encompasses cognitive, financial, service-related, and physical accessibility. This model suggested that the perceived benefits and accessibility of a technology, when weighed against its societal costs, are critical factors in ensuring its sustainable adoption.

The existing literature suggests that providing individuals with an opportunity to experience autonomous bus systems, accompanied by appropriate instruction, can significantly enhance social acceptability. However, offering such experiences to all residents is not a practical solution. Therefore, this study aims to simulate the experience of riding an autonomous bus via virtual reality technology. This approach allows residents to engage with the technology without temporal or logistical constraints and examines the impact of this virtual experience on the social acceptance of autonomous buses in Chitose City.

2 Methods

In this study, we conducted investigations in two steps. The first step involved designing a prototype of the virtual experience content to allow users to experience riding on an autonomous bus via a head-mounted display (HMD) and evaluating its effectiveness in influencing their acceptance of autonomous buses before and after the virtual experience. The second step focused on refining the prototype design based on the results and evaluating its effectiveness in shaping the acceptance of autonomous buses among residents who may use them in the near future. Furthermore, in this step, we investigated the factors influencing the acceptability of autonomous bus services.

2.1 Creating Virtual Experience Contents

In Chitose City, autonomous buses were not yet available prior to the proof-of-concept experiment. Therefore, to provide a guided experience of riding an autonomous bus, we created virtual experience content using a 360-degree video presented to participants. The video was recorded inside an autonomous bus during a proof-of-concept experiment conducted in Tokoname City, Aichi Prefecture. The autonomous bus used in the experiment in Tokoname was the same type as that planned for the experiment in Chitose City. This bus had a capacity of 24 passengers and operated at level-two autonomy, meaning that a driver controlled the bus on demand. The virtual content consisted of three scenes: boarding, riding, and getting off the bus, each of which was presented from a first-person perspective. Additionally, a narration by an official from the Chitose City Office was included to provide an overview of autonomous buses and explain how drivers support autonomous operations during proof-of-concept experiments. The total duration of the virtual content was 4 min and 17 s. The recording was made using a Ricoh 360-degree camera, THETA SC2, and edited using CyberLink's PowerDirector. The virtual content was presented using two types of head-mounted displays (HMDs): Meta's Quest 2, which featured an 1832×1920-pixel display, and the Quest Pro, which featured an 1800×1920-pixel display. Participants were randomly assigned to one of the two HMDs and experienced the virtual ride using the assigned device. By rotating their heads, participants were able to view a 360-degree visual field, allowing for an immersive and interactive experience (Fig. 1).

Fig. 1. A scene in the virtual content depicts the autonomous bus being operated by a partially autonomous system, with the human driver keeping their hands off the steering wheel while monitoring the performance of the vehicle.

2.2 Evaluation of the Content's Effectiveness

The effectiveness of autonomous bus acceptance through the virtual ride experience was evaluated by 38 participants (mean age $= 48 \pm 3.3$ years). Participants who expressed interest in this survey during a public festival event in Chitose City voluntarily took part in this study and were provided instructions for the evaluation following their experience with the virtual content. Informed consent was obtained from all participants in advance. Given these circumstances, a concise questionnaire containing a minimal number of items was developed to investigate changes regarding the acceptability of autonomous buses while minimizing participant burden. The effectiveness of the content was then evaluated based on the questionnaire results.

To develop the questionnaire items, prior research was consulted, including a systematic literature review by Pigeon et al. [7] as well as theoretical frameworks such as the Technology Acceptance Model (TAM) [8] and Unified Theory of Acceptance and Use of Technology (UTAUT) [9]. The literature review identified 70 distinct factors that influenced the acceptability and acceptance of non-rail autonomous public transport vehicles. These factors were categorized into individual-related (micro-level) and system-related (meso-level) domains. The individual-related factors included age, gender, possession of a driver's license, frequency of bus use, and prior experience with autonomous buses. Accordingly, questionnaire items addressing these variables were incorporated into the participant face sheet. Furthermore, system-related factors included in the main section were selected based on their relevance to key dimensions associated with user acceptance, including trust, safety, perceived usefulness, ease of use, and usability. In addition, intention to use was included as a behavioral indicator to reflect the level of user acceptance, which is consistent with its role in TAM and UTAUT. These dimensions are known to be influenced by experiences such as virtual autonomous bus rides, which may result in changes in user acceptability over time. The 10 main questionnaire items are presented in Table 1.

Table 1. Questionnaire items included in the main section.

No	Questionnaire Items
1	I feel I can use it with peace of mind
2	I trust autonomous driving technology
3	I believe it will be beneficial to everyone
4	It allows for efficient transportation
5	I find it is easy to use
6	It takes a lot of time to understand how to use it
7	I would recommend it to my family and friends
8	I would try it if my family or friends used it
9	I would like to use it if it were introduced in Chitose City
10	I would prefer to use it over my private car

Participants were asked whether their responses to each questionnaire item had changed positively or negatively as a result of the virtual riding experience. Subsequently, their subjective feedback was collected to explore ways to enhance the effectiveness of the virtual content.

2.3 Enhancing Virtual Content to Investigate the Acceptability of Autonomous Bus Services

To prepare for a future investigation involving residents living along the autonomous bus route, the virtual autonomous bus riding content was revised based on subjective feedback collected during earlier trials. The specific feedback that informed these improvements, along with the design of the updated content, is described in a later section.

Furthermore, the three scenes included in the revised content were created using video footage recorded during the experiment conducted in Chitose City. The equipment used for recording and editing as well as the HMDs for presenting were the same as those employed in the previous version of the content.

2.4 Investigation into the Acceptability of Autonomous Bus Services from a Service-Oriented Perspective

For residents who are likely to utilize autonomous bus systems, considering not only their acceptance of the underlying technology but also their recognition of the broader values offered by services as a form of public transportation is essential, particularly in the context of implementation within Chitose City. To explore this perspective, a service-oriented investigation was conducted using a questionnaire developed to assess the acceptability of autonomous bus services among 21 residents living near the bus routes identified for potential deployment. The participants consisted of 11 males and 10 females with a mean age of 63 years ($SD = 3.1$), all of whom regularly attended events at the local community center and voluntarily took part in this survey. Accordingly, the investigation was conducted at the community center prior to a regularly scheduled event, and informed consent was obtained from all participants before the study began.

The questionnaire consisted of a face sheet and main section. The face sheet had been used in a previous study; however, additional items related to future autonomous bus use were added. These items included questions on the frequency of private car use, main purpose of local bus use, current employment status, means of transportation to the workplace, and anticipated future modes of transportation. The main section was designed based on service-related factors and incorporated items examining trust, safety, usability, privacy, and perceptions of safety as a traffic participant. Wicki et al. (2018) reported that a significant proportion of respondents opposed the transfer of autonomous vehicle data to government entities, as observed in the initial survey of the pilot experiment that involved an autonomous bus service [1]. The autonomous bus contained multiple cameras that monitor both internal and external environments, which may raise privacy concerns among users.

Regarding service-related factors that influence acceptability or acceptance, Mouratidis et al. (2021) noted that attitudes toward the use of autonomous buses vary depending on their operating frequency [10]. In addition, Piao et al. (2016) examined public attitudes toward the introduction of automated vehicles, particularly automated buses, in urban environments. They concluded that the most attractive benefit was the potential for lower fares resulting from the elimination of driver-related costs [11]. Based on these previous studies, the main items considered in this research are presented in Table 2.

In this study, participants experienced a simulated enhanced virtual autonomous bus ride that was followed by the administration of a questionnaire. As a significant proportion of the participants were older adults, the questionnaire was conducted orally. Their verbal responses were carefully transcribed by the researchers to ensure both accuracy and respect for the participants' input. Responses were recorded using a five-point Likert scale, consisting of the options *Strongly Agree, Agree, Neutral, Disagree,* and *Strongly Disagree,* with the exceptions of Questions 7 and 8, which used a different response format. Furthermore, the researchers sought to obtain explanatory comments or reasons for each response. As a result, the survey process required approximately 15 min per participant.

Table 2. Main items for addressing the acceptability of autonomous bus services.

No	Questionnaire Items
1	As a passenger, do you feel that autonomous buses are safe?
2	How much do you trust autonomous buses as a passenger?
3	As a passenger, do you feel that autonomous bus services are usable?
4	As a passenger, do you feel that autonomous buses ensure privacy?
5	As a road user, do you think that autonomous buses are safe?
6	If autonomous buses operated more frequently than they do now, would you be more likely to use them?
7	What is the maximum fare you would be willing to pay to use an autonomous bus operating on the same route as the current local bus?
8	Would you be willing to use autonomous buses if they replaced the existing local bus service?

3 Results and Discussion

3.1 Participant Responses to the Virtual Autonomous Bus Ride Experience

Seventy percent of the 38 participants who experienced the developed virtual content prototype have a driver's license, including the young participants. Seven participants reported using local buses at least once a week, and three participants had prior experience participating in a pilot test of an autonomous bus in another city, although the type of autonomous bus was different. The participants' responses to the questionnaire items presented in Table 1 are summarized in Table 3.

As shown in Table 3, participant responses to most questionnaire items indicated a positive change, with the exception of Questions 6 and 10. However, more than half of the participants reported no changes in their responses to Questions 1 and 2. In particular, Question 1 used the Japanese term anshin, which encompasses multiple dimensions, including trust, safety, and well-being, although it is often translated as "peace of mind." This concept reflects a culturally specific sense of emotional and social security. Although Question 2 was designed to investigate trust in autonomous technology, it is reasonable that the results of Questions 1 and 2 are similar. To address this issue, the Japanese term for trust was used instead of anshin in the corresponding questionnaire item for the subsequent survey.

Question 6 was designed to investigate the usability of autonomous bus riding, specifically the procedures of boarding, riding, and getting off the bus. For this question, eight participants were estimated to have had difficulty understanding the procedure through the virtual content. Therefore, it is reasonable that three participants preferred using their private cars over autonomous buses.

Table 3. Participant responses to the virtual autonomous bus experience ($n = 38$).

No	Questionnaire Items	Negative Change	No Change	Positive Change
1	I feel I can use it with peace of mind	0	20	18
2	I trust autonomous driving technology	0	20	18
3	I believe it will be beneficial to everyone	0	6	32
4	It allows for efficient transportation	0	11	27
5	I find it is easy to use	0	17	21
6	It takes a lot of time to understand how to use it	8	22	8
7	I would recommend it to my family and friends	0	21	17
8	I would try it if my family or friends used it	0	14	24
9	I would like to use it if it were introduced in Chitose City	0	13	25
10	I would prefer to use it over my private car	3	28	7

Furthermore, after experiencing the virtual content, participants expressed various concerns and thoughts regarding autonomous buses. Some mentioned safety-related worries, such as, "I became scared after seeing news about an autonomous bus catching fire," and "I would use it if its safety is guaranteed." Others envisioned using autonomous buses in the future, providing comments such as, "I might use an autonomous bus when I get older and can no longer drive." Additionally, some participants raised questions such as, "How would an autonomous bus operate if there is a road under construction?".

Consequently, participants' responses to the virtual experience were mostly positive; however, their responses regarding the comprehensibility of the autonomous bus service were questionable. Therefore, the virtual content should be improved based on participants' perspectives. Such improvements are described in the next section.

3.2   Enhancing Virtual Content Based on Participants' Perspectives

As described in the previous section, the virtual content was enhanced based on participants' subjective opinions. In this section, we explain the participants' opinions regarding their experience with the virtual content and how these opinions informed the improvements made to address the identified issues.

In the virtual content, participants reported that they were more likely to feel motion sickness during the boarding and alighting scenes. In this regard, the original virtual content consisted of three scenes from a passenger's point of view. However, participants experienced these scenes while standing still, and it is considered that the perceptual gap between stimuli from different sensory modalities led to perceptual conflict and fatigue. To address this issue, these scenes were replaced with a third-person view. Furthermore, some participants pointed out that the duration of the experience was too long. Therefore, the content was successfully shortened by 32 s.

As indicated by the results of the preceding questionnaire survey, improving the comprehensibility of the presented content was necessary. The original material included a narration by an official from the Chitose City Office, who provided an overview of autonomous bus systems and described the roles of drivers in supporting autonomous operations. Nevertheless, within the virtual content, it was challenging for viewers to determine whether the bus was being operated by an onboard human operator or by autonomous systems. This ambiguity is particularly relevant in the context of level-two autonomy, which requires human intervention when necessary.

Clayton et al. (2024) demonstrated that the inclusion of an indicator panel displaying whether the bus was in autonomous mode or under human control contributed to increased user trust [12]. In response to this finding, the virtual scenes were modified to include explicit textual captions, such as "Autonomous Mode" and "Human Control Mode," to enhance the clarity of the operational status for viewers.

The questionnaire survey also revealed that participants experienced usability issues related to autonomous bus riding, particularly difficulties in understanding the procedures for boarding, riding, and alighting. To address this concern, a scene depicting a passenger pressing the stop button inside the bus as it approached the designated stop was recorded and incorporated into the original footage. Additionally, the narration was enhanced to clarify the procedure. This scene is shown in Fig. 2.

Fig. 2. A scene from the enhanced virtual content, showing the caption "Autonomous Mode" in Japanese and a passenger pressing the stop button, which is visually emphasized by enclosing it in a circle.

3.3   Residents' Perspectives on the Acceptability of Autonomous Bus Services

Each participant held a valid driver's license; however, two had voluntarily returned theirs. Eighteen participants reported driving their cars twice a week, and 13 indicated that they expect to continue driving 10 years from now. Thus, most participants used their personal vehicles instead of the public bus service, with the exception of one resident who uses the bus for commuting. Additionally, six participants had experienced autonomous bus riding near their residential area in Chitose City.

3.4   Results of the Questionnaire Survey (Questions 1–5).

The numbers of responses to Questions 1 through 5 are shown in Table 4. Regarding safety, trust, usability, and privacy from the perspectives of the passengers, the numbers of responses indicating "Agree" or "Strongly Agree" exceeded those for other response options. In contrast, responses to the question regarding safety from the perspectives of road users were more varied.

Table 4. Numbers of responses to the questionnaire on the acceptability of autonomous bus services (Questions 1–5, $n = 21$).

No	Questionnaire Items	Strongly Disagree	Disagree	Neutral	Agree	Strongly Agree
1	As a passenger, do you feel that autonomous buses are safe?	0	1	4	12	4
2	How much do you trust autonomous buses as a passenger?	0	1	6	12	2
3	As a passenger, do you feel that autonomous bus services are usable?	0	1	5	13	2
4	As a passenger, do you feel that autonomous buses ensure privacy?	1	0	7	9	4
5	As a road user, do you think that autonomous buses are safe?	1	7	1	6	6

In response to Question 1, participants who experienced autonomous bus riding in virtual reality for the first time commented that they understood that the bus could stop properly at traffic signals and that they felt safe owing to the presence of a driver in the virtual scene. Conversely, some participants voiced concerns, including doubts about whether the bus would remain safe in the event of a malfunction and the view that all technologies inevitably involve some level of risk.

With respect to safety and privacy, a participant expressed concern regarding the possibility of human error or malicious use involving the autonomous driving program and its configuration. Additionally, another participant noted that the presence of an in-vehicle camera could help prevent crime, and therefore, having such cameras installed would be desirable. One participant also remarked that, in today's world, if we worry too much about privacy, then nothing can be accomplished.

In contrast, regarding Question 6, many participants expressed concerns about safety from the perspectives of other traffic users, such as pedestrians, car drivers, and cyclists. For example, some participants stated: "If an autonomous bus were operating near me, I would worry about whether it might make a dangerous move toward me," "I wonder whether the autonomous bus can accurately and precisely recognize the surrounding traffic environment," "I'm concerned about whether there are any blind spots in the bus's sensors," "If an elderly person is slowly crossing the road, I would trust a bus with a human driver more," and "I'm worried about what would happen in the event of a malfunction."

In this regard, our developed virtual content we developed did not provide information regarding safety from perspective of road users. As a result, participants experienced the virtual ride as passengers but later reflected on safety from the viewpoints of other traffic users. The participants deduced that the autonomous bus might not be entirely safe for road users.

Although these results suggest that the virtual content positively influenced social acceptability, it is necessary for future autonomous bus users to experience interactions with autonomous buses not only as passengers but also as road users to better understand and trust the safety of autonomous bus services from the perspectives of traffic users.

3.5   Responses to the Acceptability of Autonomous Bus Services (Questions 6–8).

This section presents participants' responses to Questions 6 through 8, which examined the perceived social acceptability of autonomous bus services. Specifically, Question 6 focused on assessing the extent to which participants desire or expect frequent bus operations. According to the responses, all participants expressed a willingness to use autonomous bus services, provided that the service frequency exceeds those of conventional public bus systems. For example, one participant stated, "I will use the autonomous bus service after I voluntarily return my driver's license," and another noted, "I will use the service instead of using my car if the autonomous bus frequency is between ten and fifteen minutes." According to De Vos et al. (2020), when public transportation services meet users' desired frequency, service satisfaction increases and the willingness to use the service is enhanced [13]. Therefore, to enhance the acceptance of autonomous bus services in Chitose City, providing more frequent autonomous bus operations than are provided by the existing public bus service, which operates at a frequency of fewer than one bus per hour, is necessary.

Regarding the acceptable fare for autonomous bus services, responses to Question 7 varied. Nevertheless, participants generally perceived bus fares as more economical, compared with taxi fares. Although the current bus fare was considered somewhat expensive, many participants expressed a willingness to use autonomous bus services if the fare remained at the same level.

In contrast, Question 8 asked whether participants would accept autonomous bus services as a replacement for the current public bus system. In this regard, participants who currently drive a car noted, "Given the current shortage of bus drivers, I would have no choice but to use it," and "I would use it if the fare is cheaper than a taxi."

4 Conclusion

This study suggests that the virtual riding experience of autonomous buses generally has a positive impact on social acceptability. Although it is often said that seeing is believing, the findings indicate that the exclusion of certain information or a lack of clarity in the provided content may raise concerns regarding trust, safety, usability, and privacy.

Through the questionnaire survey on autonomous bus services, numerous important opinions and needs were gathered from individuals who may be directly affected by the services. Although governments do not serve as technology providers, those leading pilot programs are actively involved in the deployment and management of autonomous bus systems. Therefore, to implement new technologies, such as autonomous bus systems, with higher social acceptability in today's transportation society, governments have a responsibility to provide clear and accessible information to stakeholders. In this context, simulated experiences using virtual technology can play key roles in enhancing stakeholder engagement.

Acknowledgments. This study was supported by JSPS KAKENHI (grant number: JP24K15031). We would like to thank Editage (www.editage.jp) for English language editing.

Disclosure of Interests.   The authors have no competing interests to declare that are relevant to the content of this article.

References

1. Wicki, M., Bernauer, T.: Public opinion on Route 12: Interim report on the first survey on the pilot experiment of an automated bus service in Neuhausen am Rheinfall. ISTP Paper Series, vol. 3, ETH Zurich (2018). https://doi.org/10.3929/ethz-b-000282577
2. Camps-Aragó, P., Temmerman, L., Vanobberghen, W., Delaere, S.: Encouraging the sustainable adoption of autonomous vehicles for public transport in Belgium: Citizen acceptance, business models, and policy aspects. Sustainability **14**(2), 921 (2022). https://doi.org/10.3390/su14020921
3. Nastjuk, I., Herrenkind, B., Marrone, M., Brendel, A.B., Kolbe, L.M.: Autonomous vehicles and sustainable mobility: The role of positive anticipated emotions and regulatory focus in intentions to adopt AVs. Technol. Forecast. Soc. Change **155**, 119942 (2020). https://doi.org/10.1016/j.techfore.2020.119942
4. Uhde, A., Hassenzahl, M.: Towards a better understanding of social acceptability. In: CHI Conference on Human Factors in Computing Systems Extended Abstracts (CHI EA '21), ACM, New York (2021). https://doi.org/10.1145/3411763.3451649

5. Hosotsubo, M., Tsunoda, H., Kano, K., Okamura, A., Hoshino, T.: Public attitudes to science and technology: Social acceptance of new technologies. NISTEP Research Material, No. 296, National Institute of Science and Technology Policy, Japan (2020). https://doi.org/10.15108/rm296

6. Jammes, J., N'Goala, G., Folcher, P.: Conceptualizing social acceptability of technological innovation in frontline service experiences: A qualitative study. In: 18th Int. Res. Conf. in Service Management, La Londe-les-Maures, France (2024). https://hal.science/hal-04643340v1

7. Pigeon, C., Alauzet, A., Paire-Ficout, L.: Factors of acceptability, acceptance and usage for non-rail autonomous public transport vehicles: A systematic literature review. Transp. Res. Part F: Traffic Psychol. Behav. **81**, 251–270 (2021). https://doi.org/10.1016/j.trf.2021.06.008

8. Vervier, L., Glawe, F., Brauner, P., Ziefle, M.: Beyond agreements: A semantic differential for technology acceptance measurement. In: Kurosu, M., Hashizume, A. (eds.) Human-Computer Interaction. HCII 2025, LNCS, vol. 15771, pp. 126–143. Springer, Cham (2025). https://doi.org/10.1007/978-3-031-93965-5_9

9. Venkatesh, V., Morris, M.G., Davis, G.B., Davis, F.D.: User acceptance of information technology: Toward a unified view. MIS Q. **27**(3), 425–478 (2003). https://doi.org/10.2307/30036540

10. Mouratidis, K., Cobeña Serrano, V.: Autonomous buses: Intentions to use, passenger experiences, and suggestions for improvement. Transp. Res. Part F: Traffic Psychol. Behav. **76**, 321–335 (2021). https://doi.org/10.1016/j.trf.2020.12.007

11. Piao, J., McDonald, M., Hounsell, N., Graindorge, M., Graindorge, T., Malhene, N.: Public views towards implementation of automated vehicles in urban areas. Transp. Res. Procedia **14**, 2168–2177 (2016). https://doi.org/10.1016/j.trpro.2016.05.232

12. Clayton, W., Adeel, M., Flower, J., Clark, B., Parkhurst, G., Parkin, J.: Passenger experiences of an autonomous bus service: The MultiCAV project. In: Universities' Transport Study Group Conference 2024, University of the West of England, Bristol (2024). https://uwe-repository.worktribe.com/OutputFile/13391952

13. De Vos, J., Waygood, E.O.D., Letarte, L.: Modeling the desire for using public transport. Travel Behav. Soc. **19**, 90–98 (2020)

Effects of Virtual Environment Presentation on Sweating Function During Exercise in a Hot Environment

Kentaro Kotani[✉] [ID], Tatsuyuki Aso, Satoshi Suzuki, and Takafumi Asao

Kansai University, Suita, Osaka 564-8680, Japan
kotani@kansai-u.ac.jp

Abstract. This study was conducted based on the idea that presenting virtual environmental images via HMD during exercise in a hot environment may cause the brain to misunderstand the effects of such images on thermoregulation and that the misunderstanding may be used to reduce the risk of heat stroke. If this is clarified, presenting a virtual hot and cold environment as a visual stimulus by HMD during exercise in a hot environment may somehow affect the human sweating function. Finding new ways to cope with heat stroke and other diseases involving thermoregulation may be possible. Thus, we created environmental images that give several different impressions to people during exercise, played them on an HMD to create an irregular situation, and measured the body's reaction to the images. As a general trend, the results for the desert video exceeded those for the snowstorm video during the exercise. Also, the results showed significant differences from 70 to 90, 120, and 240 to 260 s ($p < 0.05$). The results showed significant differences between the two environments ($p < 0.05$), and no significant differences were observed in the amount of perspiration between the two environments. However, it is possible that the deep temperature at which sweating begins differs depending on the brightness of light entering the visual system and that circadian rhythms may be related, indicating the need for further detailed investigation.

Keywords: Virtual environment · Sweating function · Exercise

1 Introduction

The widespread use of VR-based information presentation technology has made it easy to experience visual environments that could not have occurred during human evolution. If the human thermoregulatory system is sensitive to visual stimuli with no thermal energy, the current artificial environment may interfere with maintaining homeostasis, such as thermoregulation. Many people suffer from heat stroke yearly due to exercising in hot environments. As global warming continues, the risk of such cases occurring in the future is potentially increased.

We hypothesized that the risk of heat stroke could be reduced by using the effects of VR on the body's thermoregulation, which causes the brain to mislead the virtual environment during exercise in a hot environment.

H. Mori et al. (Eds.): HCII 2025, LNCS 16333, pp. 87–96, 2026.
https://doi.org/10.1007/978-3-032-12660-3_7

In the previous study, the experiment was conducted by projecting images on a display 1.9 m in front of the participant's eyes. Hot, Control, and Cold conditions were used for the video images. The temperature was measured in a room at 28 °C for 20 min and then lowered to 16 °C for 80 min to measure rectal and skin temperatures. The results showed that skin and rectal temperatures were significantly higher and lower in the Hot condition than in the Control condition. That homeostasis of body temperature regulation was disrupted in the previous study. These results suggest that thermoregulation is sensitive to visual stimuli in addition to the actual temperature of the environment to which it is exposed. It may consequently affect the effectors of thermoregulation.

However, in previous studies, only skin and deep temperatures were measured to see the thermoregulation function. In other words, we have not been able to confirm what effects are produced on the amount of sweating when stimuli without thermal energy are given in a high-temperature environment. Therefore, the objective of this study was to investigate the effects of visual stimuli without thermal energy on sweating during exercise in a high-temperature environment.

2   Model of Visual Input and Autonomic Thermoregulatory Mechanisms

Based on previous studies [1], we constructed a prediction model based on how thermoregulation is involved in this study. For thermoregulation to function, thermoregulation begins with the stimulation of thermoreceptors by external and internal temperatures. This environmental background is physical information and thermal energy transfer activates thermoregulation and maintains human homeostasis. In this study, however, we focused on visual information as a factor related to thermoregulation. Visual information is information about light in the surrounding environment obtained through photoreceptors in the retina, enabling humans to recognize objects' color and shape. However, visual information itself does not have any thermal energy. Despite this, it has been suggested that visual information may influence thermoregulation [2]. Figure 1 shows the predictive diagram of this point based on previous studies.

In a previous study [1], body temperature changes differed between hot and cold environments. This study suggested that thermoregulation has a pathway that allows a particular input to visual information, which is projected to the preoptic area and influences the effector. Figure 2 shows the relationship between vision and the preoptic area. The figure shows the pathway of visual information transmission, in which visual information obtained from the retina of the eye is sent to the visual cortex of the brain via the lateral pallidum of the thalamus. Visual information is transmitted from the lateral pallidum to the primary visual cortex, secondary visual cortex, and higher visual cortex. The higher-order visual cortex provides feedback of hot and cold information, which is transmitted to the hypothalamus via the lateral pallidum of the thalamus.

Although it is unclear to what extent semantic information is processed in this pathway, it is possible that visual stimuli without thermal energy, which are provided by HMDs and monitors as input devices, induce impressions of heat and cold, which in turn affect thermoregulation.

Therefore, the purpose of this experiment is to examine the risk of heat stroke, obtain knowledge for countermeasures against the risk, and create a usable system. We will investigate whether viewing hot images changes the function of body temperature regulation and consequently affects the amount of sweating and whether it is related to the risk of heat stroke.

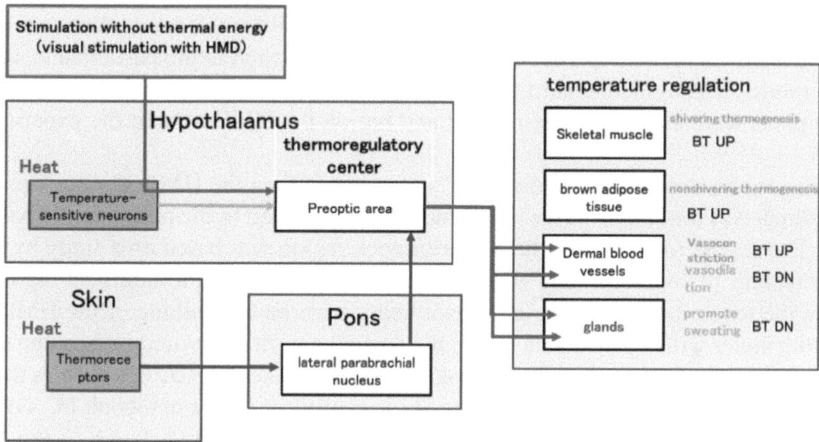

Fig. 1. Model for visual presentation of temperature and cooling information and change in body temperature.

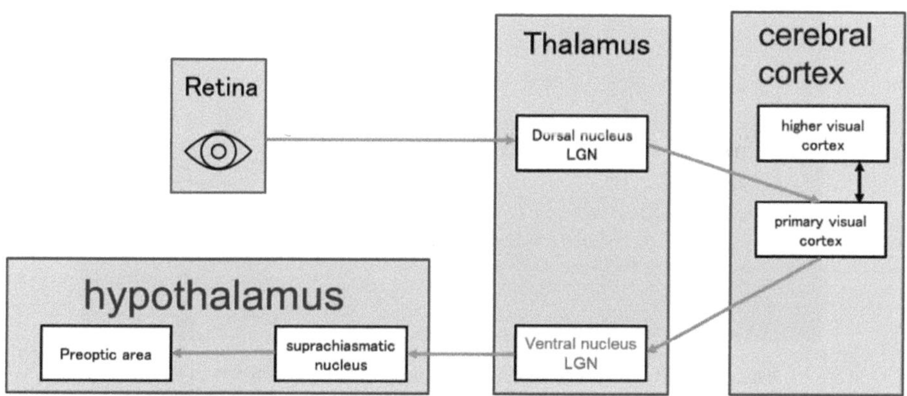

Fig. 2. Relationship between vision and the prefrontal cortex for visual input.

3 Methods

3.1 Participants

The participants in this experiment were 20 male undergraduate and graduate students with an average age of 20.9 years. Participants gave their written consent after receiving an explanation of the purpose and significance of the experiment.

3.2 Apparatus

The participants' skin and deep body temperatures and perspiration rates were measured. A Core-temp CM-210 was used to measure body temperature. The HMD (Meta Quest 2) was used to provide visual information to the participants. An air conditioner controlled the room temperature. SKW-1000 (Skinos) was used to measure the amount of perspiration.

The experimental room consisted of two rooms. Room 1 was mainly used as a waiting area where the experimental apparatus was attached to the participants, and the temperature measurement condition stabilized. After the temperature data stabilized, the participants were asked to enter room 2 and put on the HMD to start the experimental task.

Images of a desert and a snowstorm were projected on the HMD screen. The probe part, which was the sensor of the sweat meter, was attached to the participant's posterior neck. The reason for selecting the posterior neck region was based on a study by Smith and Havenith [3], which found that the back neck region was a relatively high sweat area in the whole body without the sensor being covered by clothing or the HMD. The sweating meter with a probe attached to the posterior neck was wired to the central unit, and the unit was connected to a notebook PC wirelessly so that settings such as the start of measurement could be made from the Skinos software on the notebook PC side. The visual information given by the HMD used in this experiment is shown in Fig. 3 and overall configuration of the apparatus is illustrated in Fig. 4.

Fig. 3. Cold (snowstorm) and heat (desert) images shown in HMD.

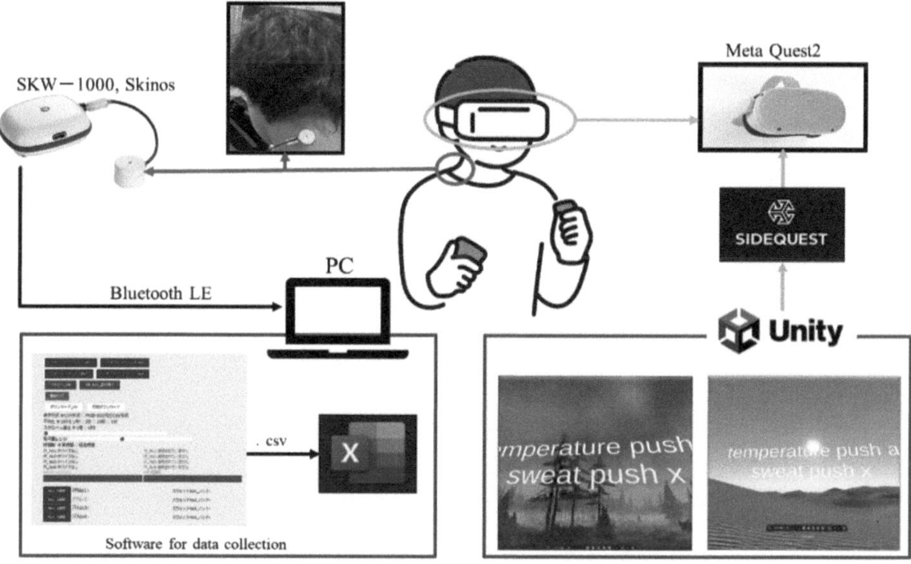

Fig. 4. Overall configuration of the apparatus.

3.3 Procedure

At the beginning of the experiment, the participants first performed a 5-min warm-up exercise in Room 2. The exercise consisted of ascending one step every three seconds while holding a handrail and descending from the right foot to the left foot with both feet. The warm-up was performed beforehand, taking into account studies that have shown an influence on post-exercise sweating thresholds [4].

The participants were then asked to take a 10-min break while the experiment was explained in Room 1. After the explanation, the participants were fitted with an HMD on their heads and a sweat sensor attached to their posterior neck. After the HMD was attached, the participants performed an elevation exercise for 10 min while wearing the HMD in Room 2. To maintain the pace once every five seconds, the HMD emitted a sound to alert the participant of the timing, and the participant performed the ascending and descending exercise when the sound was confirmed. Figure 5 shows the participants as they ascend and descend the stairs.

The experimenter constantly monitored the participants next to them to avoid the possibility of them stepping off the elevator. After the end of the exercise, the participants took a 10-min break in Room 2 and then performed the same 10-min ascending and descending exercise in Room 1 while wearing the HMD, but with a different thermal image. A flowchart showing the sequence of these steps is shown in Fig. 6, and the time chart of the experiment is shown in Fig. 7.

Fig. 5. Participant performing exercise with platform in the experiment.

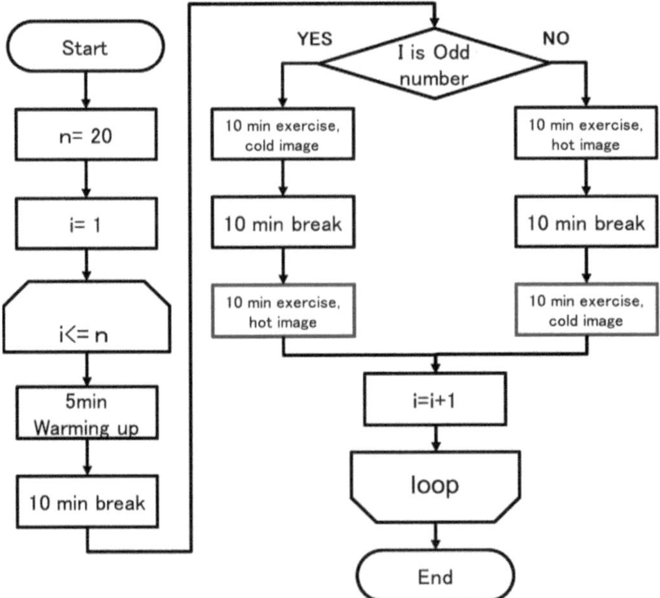

Fig. 6. Flow of the experiment.

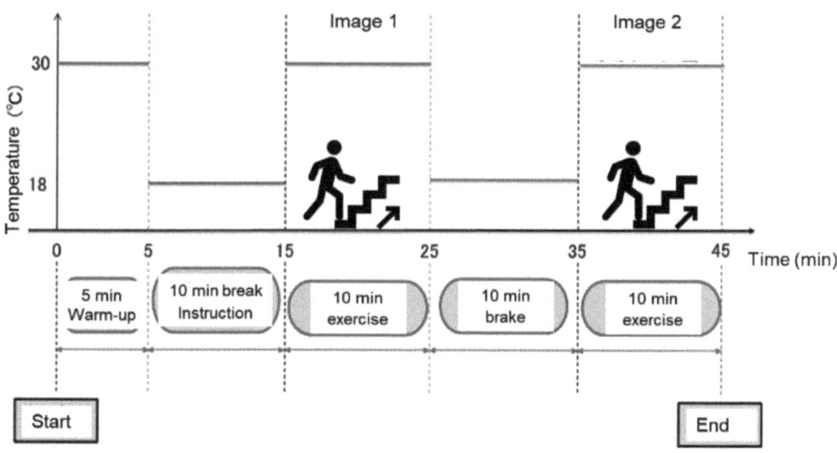

Fig. 7. Time chart of the experiment.

3.4 Data Analysis

A within-participants design was used for both the thermal images. The order of the images was counterbalanced to remove noise caused by the order of the images. Perspiration and skin temperature were measured, but the perspiration data were reported in this study. A t-test was conducted, at each 1-min interval, between the desert and snowstorm images to confirm the change in perspiration caused by the desert and snowstorm images.

4 Results

Figure 8 shows the results of the experiment. This figure illustrates the averages of the hot and cold images for all participants at all times. The overall trend of the graph was that the results for the desert image were higher than those for the snowstorm image at all time intervals. Statistical test results showed significant differences from 70 to 90, 120, and 240 to 260 s ($p < 0.05$). No significant differences were observed between the two environments regarding the amount of perspiration.

Figure 9 shows an example of a participant who experienced a peak during the experiment. This peak may have been caused by stress-induced psychogenic sweating [5], although the source of the stress could not be clarified, such as whether it was due to the wearing of the HMD or a change in environment.

The amygdala is deeply involved in stress-induced psychogenic sweating. The amygdala is a region that performs emotional processing when stressed by sensory organs, and it plays a role in the fight-or-flight response to some fearful stimulus [6]. In addition, there are high-load and low-load pathways in the brain that lead to the amygdala after being stressed [7]. The difference between these two pathways is that they take time but process information with high precision, causing a precise fear response. In contrast, they are instantaneous, causing an instinctive and immediate fear response.

Stress factors in this experiment may include exercise and the tightness of the continuous wearing of HMD. However, since the amygdala receives input from all sensory organs, it is difficult to identify the cause of stress.

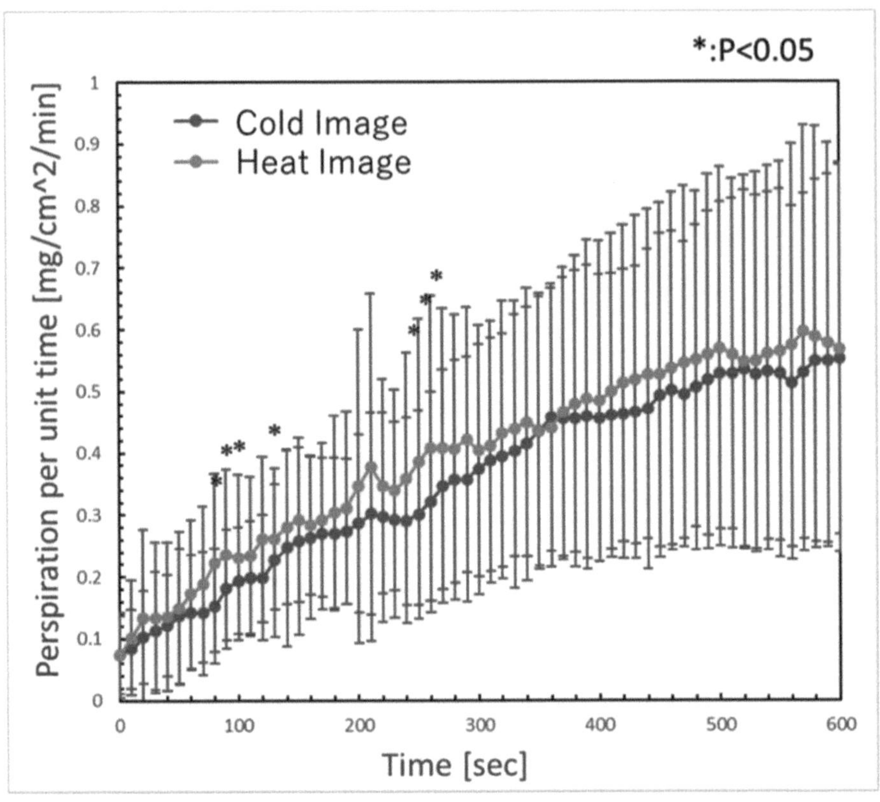

Fig. 8. Differences in perspiration rates by two image conditions.

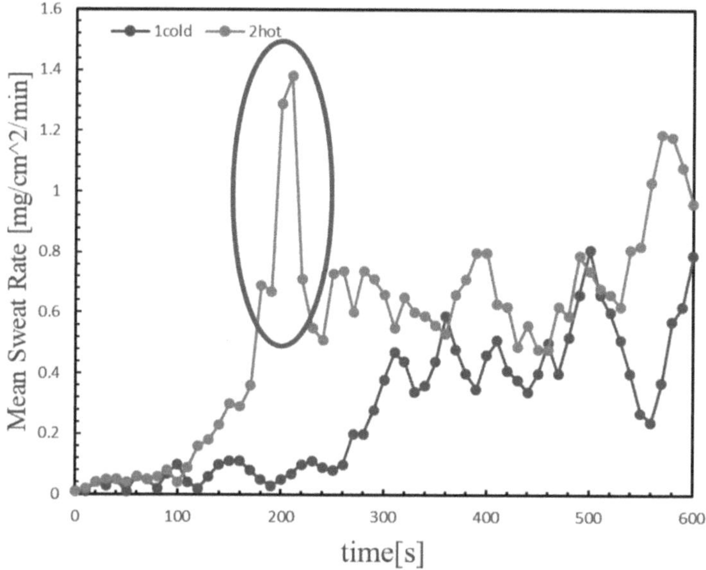

Fig. 9. Change in perspiration per unit time for a participant.

5   Discussion

The presentation of the heat image by the HMD may affect sweating during exercise in a hot environment. In particular, a significant difference appeared before the 300-s point, suggesting that the onset of sweating was accelerated and heat acclimatization was promoted. Conversely, however, the cold environment may lead to a decrease in sweating, which may increase the risk of heat stroke in this context.

The current data was obtained with 20 participants, yet the number of participants needs further increase. In addition, it has been suggested that the brightness of light entering the visual system affects the deep temperature at which sweating begins [8], and the possibility that circadian rhythms are related should also be considered [9]. In addition, there is literature showing that the amount of perspiration varies with the season [10], and the influence of this on the amount of perspiration has not been ruled out.

Although there are still many points to be considered, the results suggested that exercise while viewing a heat environment with an HMD can be used as a countermeasure against heat stroke to promote heat acclimatization. On the other hand, exercise while viewing a cold environment with an HMD increases the risk of heat stroke, and exercise should be avoided under such conditions.

6   Conclusion

The purpose of this study was to investigate the effects of heat stroke on the risk of heat stroke and to obtain knowledge on the construction of a system that can be used as a countermeasure and vice versa. As shown in the previous section, many points remain to be considered. However, the results obtained at this point suggest that the presentation of heat images as visual stimuli may promote heat acclimatization and accelerate the onset time of sweating. This may reduce the risk of heat stroke.

By utilizing this experiment, it is possible that some effects can be obtained simply by playing a heat image on a monitor during exercise in an inorganic space indoors, such as a gym or rehabilitation facility. In addition, using HMDs in rehabilitation, which have been the focus of attention in recent years, may also be effective by incorporating heat-related images into the background. Thus, this research has many possible applications in various systems, and if we can reduce the risk of heat stroke, we can contribute to the adaptation to global warming.

Acknowledgement. This study was partially supported by Research Group on Biological Response and Sensory Models of Human-Environmental Systems, Organization for Research and Development of Innovative Science and Technology, Kansai University and JSPS Kakenhi (Grant number 24K15031).

References

1. Nakamura, K.: Central circuitries for body temperature regulation and fever. American journal of Physiology. Regul. Integr. Comp. Physiol. **301**(5), 1207–1228 (2011)
2. Takakura, J.: Influence of images evoking hot and cold environments on human thermoregulation, Ph.D. Dissertation (2021)
3. Smith, C.J., Havenith, G.: Body mapping of sweating patterns in male athletes in mild exercise-induced hyperthermia. Eur. J. Appl. Physiol. **111**(7), 1391–1404 (2011)
4. Glen, P. K., Julien, P., Journey, W. S., Ronald, J. S., Francis, D. R.: Effect of exercise intensity on the postexercise sweating threshold. J. Appl. Physiol. **95**(6), 2355–2360 (2003)
5. Mori, K., Sakaguchi, M., Yokochi, H., Nakashima, K., Ohashi, T.: A new sweating ratemeter utilizing with a hygrometer and its thermal characteristics, Proceeding of Japanese Society of ME and BE, 302 (1989)
6. Lee, G., Bechara, A., Adolphs, R., Arena, J., Meado, K., Loring, D., Smith, J.: Clinical and physiological effects of stereotaxic bilateral amygdalotomy for intractable. Aggression. J. Neuropsychiatry Clin. Neurosci. **10**(4), 413–420 (1998)
7. Carr, J. A.: I'll take the low road: the evolutionary underpinnings of visually triggered fear, Frontiers in Neuroscience, 9, 414(2015)
8. Kakitsuba, N.: The Effect of Season and Light Intensity on the Core Interthreshold Zone. J. Physiol. Anthropol. **30**(4), 161–167 (2011)
9. Stephenson, L.A., Wenger, C.B., O'Donovan, B.H., Nadel, E.R.: Circadian rhythm in sweating and cutaneous blood flow. Am. J. Physiol. **246**(3), 321–324 (1984)
10. Okamura, K., Nakamura, Y.: Seasonal changes in perspiration response based on the same thermal environment experiment. Proceedings of the Kinki Branch of the Society of Air-Conditioning and Sanitary Engineers of Japan, 107–110 (1998)

Effects of Sensory Intake Tasks on Flow State and Cardiac Responses in Virtual Reality Environment

Hiroyuki Kuraoka[1]([🖂]) [ID], Ibuki Yoshida[2], and Daiji Kobayashi[1] [ID]

[1] Chitose Institute of Science and Technology, Hokkaido, Japan
h-kuraok@photon.chitose.ac.jp
[2] Graduate of Chitose Institute of Science and Technology, Hokkaido, Japan

Abstract. This study explored the flow experience and physiological responses during a mirror-tracing task performed in both real-world (REAL) and virtual reality (VR) environments. Seventeen healthy participants completed the task under two feedback conditions—a self-paced tracing condition (NORMAL) and a self-competitive condition (GHOST)— where participants attempted to trace faster than their own prior trajectory. Both conditions were carried out in REAL and VR environments that replicated an identical workspace. Each session included a 5-min resting phase followed by two 5-min task trials. Subjective measures (flow experience, mental workload, and simulator sickness) and physiological responses (heart rate [HR] and heart rate variability [HRV]) were collected and compared across conditions. The results indicated that, regardless of the environment, the GHOST condition significantly enhanced perceived feedback and task accomplishment scores on the Flow State Scale. Mental workload was lower in GHOST, whereas temporal demand and frustration scores were notably higher, particularly under the VR condition. Simulator sickness scores indicated a mild increase in oculomotor symptoms during VR use; however, no severe discomfort was reported. HR did not show significant differences between conditions; however, HRV indices showed notable changes. Specifically, low-frequency (LF) power and the LF/HF ratio decreased substantially during task performance in both environments, indicating parasympathetic dominance typically associated with sustained attention. In the VR condition, a transient reduction in LF/HF during the first task block may reflect initial sensory adaptation to the immersive environment. These findings suggest that while self-competitive feedback can facilitate components of the flow state, immersive VR environments introduce sensory and cognitive demands that may disrupt the sustained flow. Additionally, HRV indices such as LF and LF/HF emerged as sensitive indices of attentional engagement. Although HR was less responsive to task variations, it demonstrated temporal stability and may serve as a complementary indicator for real-time monitoring in VR-supported task environments.

Keywords: Flow State · Virtual Reality · Sensory Intake · Heart rate

H. Mori et al. (Eds.): HCII 2025, LNCS 16333, pp. 97–107, 2026.
https://doi.org/10.1007/978-3-032-12660-3_8

1 Introduction

The advancements in virtual reality (VR) technology have expanded its applications beyond education and entertainment to include business domains such as office work and meetings. VR is particularly recognized for its ability to enhance user concentration and comprehension through high levels of immersion and presence. For instance, immersive VR conferencing systems have been shown to improve social presence among participants, resulting in more speaking opportunities and enhanced collaborative behaviors [1, 2]. Additionally, VR-based training has proven effective in improving the acquisition of complex task skills and emergency response performance [3]. However, despite these advantages, VR environments are still associated with several negative effects. One notable issue is simulator sickness, which occurs when there exists a mismatch between visual and vestibular systems, causing symptoms such as nausea, dizziness, and visual fatigue [4]. Furthermore, immersive VR environments may increase visual and cognitive load, which can elevate psychological stress [5, 6]. For instance, in learning environments that employ 360° VR content, changes in heart rate variability (HRV) have been shown to negatively affect learners' concentration and performance [7]. Additionally, fatigue and psychological discomfort after VR use are often linked to inconsistencies between the sense of presence and perceived reality [8].

Despite the physiological and psychological concerns associated with VR, it has gained significant attention as a medium that facilitates positive mental states, such as "flow." Flow, as proposed by Csikszentmihalyi [9, 10], describes an optimal experiential state in which individuals are completely immersed in an activity, losing awareness of time and self. This state is associated not only with improved learning and creativity but also with job satisfaction and increased productivity [9, 10]. The immersive and interactive nature of VR enables users to disconnect from their physical surroundings and focus intensely on tasks, creating ideal conditions for flow. For instance, research has shown that in VR gaming, the balance between task difficulty and a player's skill level significantly influences the intensity of flow experiences [11]. Additionally, Faiola et al. [12] demonstrated that self-regulated behavior and visual feedback in VR environments promote flow, highlighting the significance of interface design and usability.

Traditionally, flow has been assessed using self-report questionnaires such as the Flow State Scale [13]. However, these methods are subjective and retrospective, making it challenging to capture real-time dynamics. As a result, research has increasingly focused on the use of physiological indicators—such as heart rate (HR), HRV, and respiration rate—for objective flow assessment. For instance, Tian et al. [14] demonstrated in a PC-based experimental setting that HR may be useful for detecting pre-flow states, suggesting a potential link between flow and sympathetic nervous system activity. Other studies have identified an inverted U-shaped relationship between flow experience and HRV components (LF and HF) during Stroop task performance [15]. Another study showed that HRV, approximated by the standard deviation of HR, tends to be lower during flow states compared to boredom or frustration [16]. Although these findings highlight a growing interest in the psychophysiology of flow, no consistent trends have yet emerged.

According to the "sensory intake/sensory rejection" model proposed by Lacey and Lacey [17], different patterns of cardiovascular response emerge depending on the direction and type of attentional engagement. Specifically, tasks that require sustained selective attention to external stimuli—categorized as sensory intake—are associated with a pattern 2 response characterized by decreased HR and increased blood pressure [18]. In most existing flow studies, pattern 1 responses involving increases in HR HR have been more commonly reported [14, 15]. However, it appears that different types of tasks may elicit distinct autonomic patterns, highlighting the need for context-sensitive physiological assessment of flow. In our previous research, we explored the relationship between flow and autonomic nervous activity using the mirror drawing task, a representative sensory intake task. We observed pattern 2 responses, including reductions in both HR and pulse amplitude, under conditions associated with high flow states, suggesting that these responses could serve as effective indicators of flow [19]. Nonetheless, these studies were conducted exclusively in real-world (non-VR) environments. Little is known about how VR-specific factors—such as increased cognitive load from immersion or physiological symptoms like simulator sickness—affect flow-related autonomic responses. Understanding how VR environments influence both flow experience and autonomic nervous system activity, particularly in sensory intake tasks, is a crucial step toward practical applications of VR.

Given this background, this study aims to clarify the physiological characteristics of flow in VR environments by simultaneously measuring subjective flow experience and cardiac indicators (HR and HRV) during the mirror drawing task, a typical sensory intake task. The findings are expected to contribute to the development of real-time flow monitoring using wearable devices, inform optimal intervention design in VR-based work support and educational applications, and offer insights into performance enhancement and mental health promotion in modern work environments.

2   Method

2.1 Participants

Seventeen healthy male participants (mean age: 22.7 ± 1.2 years) participated in the study. This study was reviewed and approved by the Research Ethics Committee of Chitose Institute of Science and Technology (Reception No. 2024-8), and informed consent was obtained from all the participants.

2.2 Procedure

Before the experimental trials, participants engaged in a mirror-drawing task (ZTRACE) for approximately 15 min. Each trial began with the attachment of electrodes and sensors, after which participants remained seated at rest in the experimental space for 10 min. This was followed by a 5-min resting phase (REST), after which they performed a 5-min self-paced drawing task (first trial), followed by a second 5-min drawing trial. In the second trial, the trajectory from the first task was displayed on the screen at task onset, and participants were instructed to trace the path "as quickly as possible compared to the previous trial."

The first and second drawing conditions were labeled as the NORMAL and GHOST conditions, respectively. One REST–NORMAL–GHOST sequence constituted a single set. The entire procedure was conducted twice under two environmental conditions (Fig. 1): in the REAL condition, participants worked within a partitioned physical space, while in the VR condition, participants performed the same task in a virtual space designed to replicate the REAL condition. The order of environmental conditions was counterbalanced across participants. Subjective fatigue was assessed after each rest and task phase. Following the final task in each condition, participants completed flow and mental workload evaluations. Additionally, in the VR condition, assessments of VR-induced motion sickness were conducted after both rest and task phases.

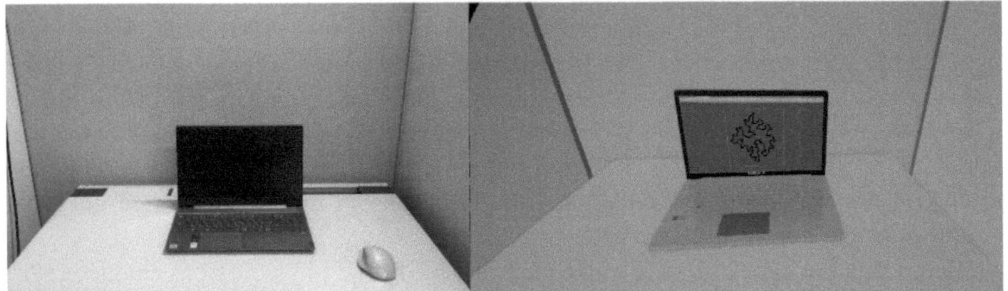

Fig. 1. Experimental condition (Left: REAL condition; Right: VR condition)

The mirror-drawing task required participants to trace a visually complex and angular path (Fig. 2) displayed on a computer screen using a mouse with reversed control axes (X and Y axes swapped). Both drawing trials used the same path, and participants were instructed to continue tracing laps until the 5-min time period had elapsed, even after completing a full circuit.

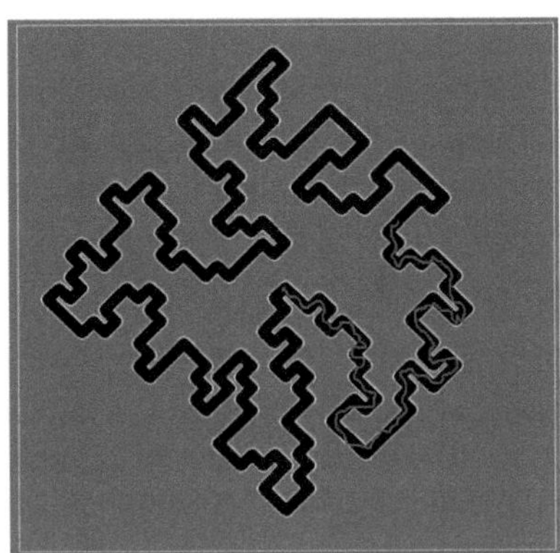

Fig. 2. Screenshot of ZTRACE.

2.3 Subjective Assessments

Flow experience was evaluated using the Flow State Scale (FSS) [13], which consists of 12 items rated on a 7-point Likert scale. Scores were calculated for four subdimensions: "Goals," "Time Perception," "Challenge," and "Feedback."

Subjective mental workload (MWL) scores were obtained using the National Aeronautics and Space Administration Task Load Index (NASA-TLX) [20]. This index includes six subscales: mental demand (MD), physical demand (PD), temporal demand (TD), own performance (OP), effort (EF), and frustration (FR). The weighted mean (Adaptive Weighted Workload: AWWL) of these six subscales was calculated. It is a weighted average score of the six subscales calculated using the weighting coefficients defined by the rank order of the raw scores without the paired comparisons [21].

To assess virtual reality sickness, the Japanese version of the Simulator Sickness Questionnaire (SSQ) was employed [22]. Participants responded to the questionnaire using a 4-point rating scale. Scores were calculated by applying the scoring criteria by Kennedy et al. [23], including sub-items such as Oculomotor (O), Disorientation (D), and Nausea (N), with a total score representing the overall tendency.

2.4 Physiological Assessments

An electrocardiogram (ECG) was continuously recorded throughout the experiment. ECG parameters, including RR intervals and heart rate, were obtained from the waveform acquired through CM5 leads placed on the chest. For heart rate variability analysis, power spectral analysis using autoregressive modeling was performed to extract the power spectrum in the low-frequency components (LF: 0.05–0.15 Hz) and high-frequency components (HF: 0.15–0.40 Hz). Subsequently, the LF/HF ratio was calculated.

2.5 Statistical Analysis

FSS and NASA-TLX scores were analyzed using two-way repeated measures analyses of variance, considering task condition (NORMAL[N], GHOST[G]) and environment (REAL, VR). When a significant main effect or interaction was detected, Bonferroni-adjusted pairwise comparisons were conducted. SSQ scores were evaluated using one-way repeated measures ANOVAs across three phases: REST[R], NORMAL[N], and GHOST[G]. Greenhouse–Geisser corrections were applied where appropriate, and Bonferroni correction was used for post hoc pairwise comparisons. SFF scores were subjected to two-way repeated measures ANOVA with block (3 levels) and environment (2 levels) as within-subject factors. Bonferroni-corrected comparisons were performed in the presence of significant effects. If a significant interaction was observed, additional one-way repeated measures ANOVAs were performed across all eight blocks (3 blocks × 2 environments + repetition), followed by Bonferroni-adjusted comparisons.

Physiological indices were standardized within each participant across six blocks (R, N, G × two environments), and analyzed using two-way repeated measures ANOVA with block and environment as factors. Bonferroni correction was applied to all post hoc tests following significant main effects or interactions. The significance level was set at $p < .05$.

3   Results

3.1   Subjective Scores

FSS scores. The FSS scores are exhibited in Fig. 3. Under the REAL environment con-dition, the FEEDBACK score was significantly higher in the GHOST (G) condition compared to the NORMAL (N) condition ($p < .05$). No significant differences were observed between task conditions (N vs. G) or between environmental conditions (REAL vs. VR) for the other subscales.

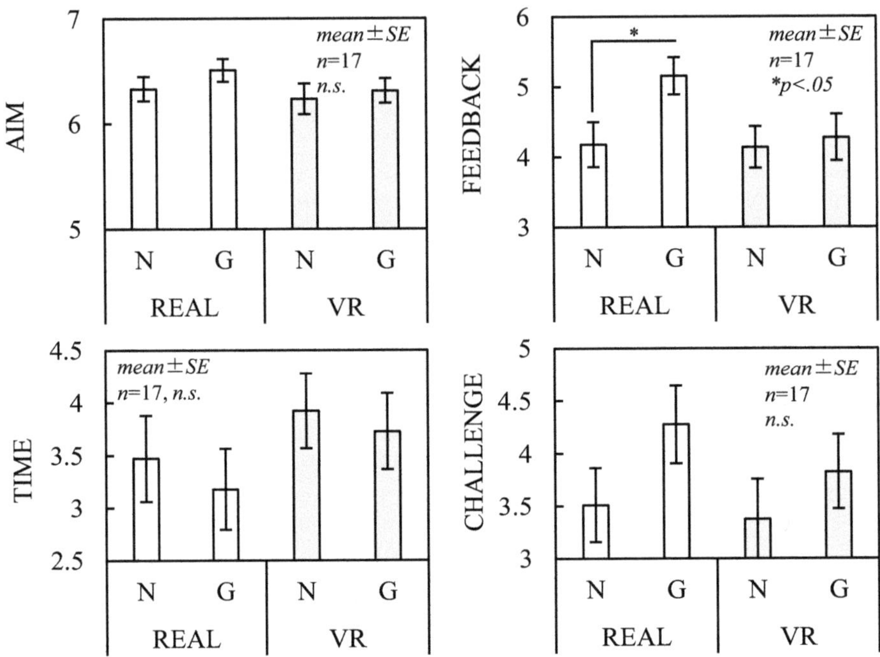

Fig. 3. FSS scores.

NASA-TLX scores. Figure 4 depicts the subscales and the overall workload score (AWWL) for which significant differences were found. Comparing task conditions, TD score was significantly higher in the G condition than in the N condition under the REAL environment ($p < .05$). For Own Performance (OP), scores were significantly lower in the G condition than in the N condition under both environments (REAL: $p < .01$; VR: $p < .01$). A similar pattern was observed in AWWL, with significantly lower scores in the G condition compared to the N condition in both environments (REAL: $p < .01$; VR: $p < .01$). When comparing environment conditions, OP and Frustration (FR) scores were significantly higher in the VR environment than in the REAL environment during the G condition (OP: $p < .01$; FR: $p < .01$).

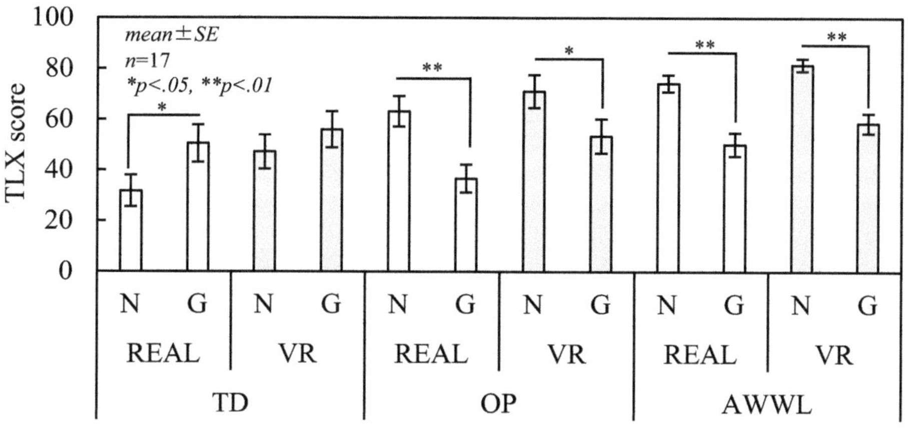

Fig. 4. NASA-TLX Scores.

SSQ scores. SSQ results for subscales and Overall score with significant differences are illustrated Fig. 5. Oculomotor score was significantly higher in the G condition than in the REST (R) condition ($p < .05$)

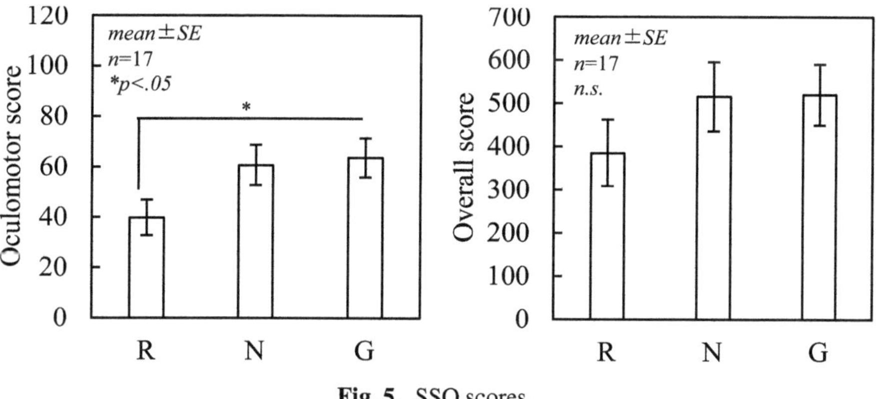

Fig. 5. SSQ scores.

3.2 Physiological Indices

Figures 6, 7 and 8 depict the results for HR and HRV indices. Letters in the figures indicate statistically homogeneous subgroups identified by Bonferroni-adjusted comparisons. No significant main effects or interactions were observed for HR across blocks or environment conditions. Conversely, significant main effects of block were observed for the LF and LF/HF components of HRV ($p < .01$), while no significant interactions were detected. LF were significantly lower in the two task blocks than during in REST under both environments ($p < .01$). No significant main effects or interactions were observed for the HF. LF/HF under the VR environment was significantly lower in TASK1 (N) compared to REST ($p < .05$) (Fig. 9).

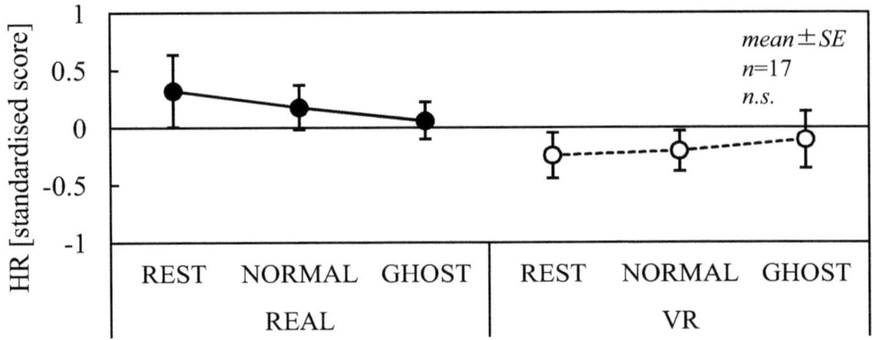

Fig. 6. Changes in HR.

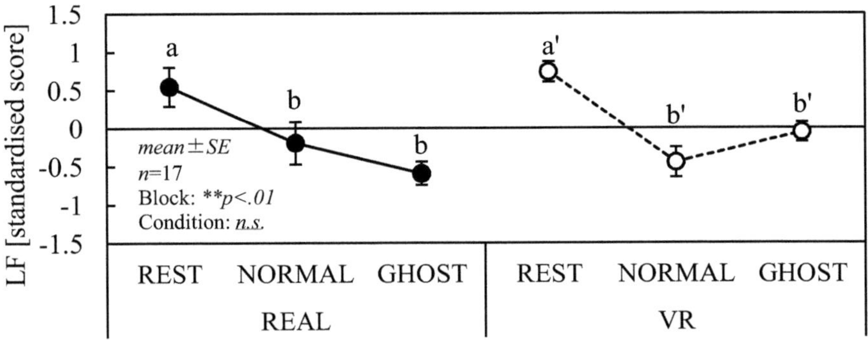

Fig. 7. Changes in LF of HRV indices.

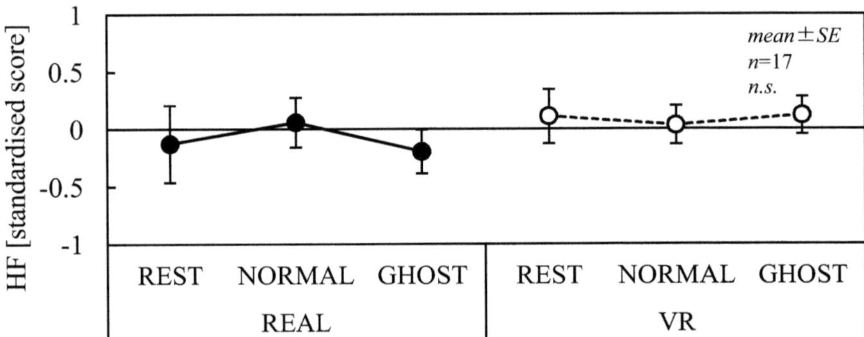

Fig. 8. Changes in HF of HRV indices.

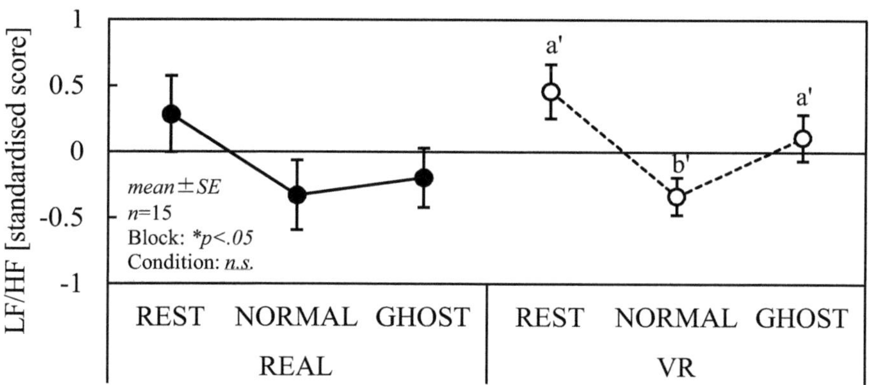

Fig. 9. Changes in LF/HF of HRV indices.

4   Discussions

This study aimed to clarify how immersive VR environments influence flow states and autonomic nervous activity during a sensory intake task. The findings revealed consistent changes across both subjective measures and physiological indices depending on task and environmental conditions.

Subjective evaluations indicated that under the GHOST (G) condition, participants experienced enhanced feedback clarity and a heightened sense of task accomplishment (OP), accompanied by a reduction in average cognitive workload (AWWL), suggesting facilitation of flow states. However, the G condition also led to increased temporal demand (TD), and the VR environment was associated with elevated frustration (FR) levels. These findings imply that while enhanced feedback and perceived task efficacy contributed to elements of the flow experience, temporal constraints and interaction-specific demands within the VR environment may have introduced cognitive or sensory stressors that partially disrupted flow experience. The coexistence of facilitative and inhibitive factors in subjective evaluations aligns with the observed increase in oculo-motor strain in the SSQ, particularly under the G condition. Even in the absence of pronounced cybersickness, the sensory load specific to VR environments can augment concentration demands, potentially impacting user comfort and engagement [24].

These subjective patterns were largely consistent with autonomic responses. While HR remained stable across conditions, HRV indices (LF and LF/HF) significantly decreased during task execution in both NORMAL and GHOST conditions. This decrease indicates parasympathetic dominance typically associated with focused attention and low arousal. This pattern aligns with the Pattern 2 response observed in sustained perceptual intake tasks [17]. Although, HR did not show sensitivity to task or environmental condition, its temporal stability across blocks suggests that it may function as a reliable index of general task engagement or attentional state. Prior studies have reported that modest reductions in HR can occur just before deep engagement or flow onset, particularly in low-arousal but cognitively demanding contexts [14]. When combined with HRV-based measures, HR may provide complementary information regarding the onset and maintenance of attentional states in real time. Its relative robustness and ease of interpretation also make it a practical candidate for use in adaptive VR systems. Furthermore, the observed changes in HRV indices, particularly LF and LF/HF ratios, highlight their utility as physiological indices for assessing flow states in VR contexts. These metrics can inform real-time monitoring and adaptive interventions in human-computer interaction applications, facilitating personalized adjustments to task difficulty and interface design to optimize user experience and performance.

5 Conclusion

This study examined how immersive VR environments influence flow states and autonomic activity during a sensory intake task. Trajectory-based feedback in the GHOST condition enhanced perceived task accomplishment and feedback clarity, and was accompanied by reduced cognitive workload and decreased LF and LF/HF in HRV, suggesting parasympathetic activation. However, increased temporal demand, frustration, and oculomotor strain in VR indicated that sensory and interaction demands may partially disrupt sustained flow. While HR did not vary by condition, its temporal stability suggests utility in monitoring engagement.

These findings demonstrate that immersive VR can support elements of flow in attention-demanding tasks. However, maintaining flow requires balancing feedback design with interaction comfort. HRV indices—particularly LF and LF/HF—and HR may serve as effective physiological indices for real-time flow detection and adaptive VR interface design.

Acknowledgment. This study was supported by JSPS KAKENHI Grant Number JP24K17409.

References

1. Moore, S.M., Geuss, M.N.: Familiarity with teammate's attitudes improves team performance in virtual reality. PLoS ONE **15**(10), e0241011 (2020)
2. Macchi, G., De Pisapia, N.: Virtual reality, face-to-face, and 2D video conferencing differently impact fatigue, creativity, flow, and decision-making in workplace dynamics. Sci. Rep. **14**, 10260 (2024)
3. Lønne, T.F., Karlsen, H.R., Langvik, E., Saksvik-Lehouillier, I.: The effect of immersion on sense of presence and affect when experiencing an educational scenario in virtual reality: A randomized controlled study. Heliyon **9**(6), e17196 (2023)
4. Saredakis, D., Szpak, A., Birckhead, B., Keage, H.A.D., Rizzo, A., Loetscher, T.: Factors associated with virtual reality sickness in head-mounted displays: A systematic review and meta-analysis. Frontiers Human Neurosci. **14**, 96 (2020)
5. Juliano, J.M., Schweighofer, N., Liew, S.L.: Increased cognitive load in immersive virtual reality during visuomotor adaptation is associated with decreased long-term retention and context transfer. J. Neuroeng. Rehabil. **19**, 106 (2022)
6. Deblock-Bellamy, A., Lamontagne, A., McFadyen, B.J., Ouellet, M.C., Blanchette, A.K.: Virtual reality-based assessment of cognitive-locomotor interference in healthy young adults. J. Neuroeng. Rehabil. **18**(1), 53 (2021). https://doi.org/10.1186/s12984-021-00834-2
7. Hsin, L.J., Chao, Y.P., Chuang, H.H., et al.: Mild simulator sickness can alter heart rate variability, mental workload, and learning outcomes in a 360° virtual reality application for medical education: A post hoc analysis of a randomized controlled trial. Virtual Reality **27**, 3345–3361 (2023)

8. Jang, S., Vitale, J.M., Jyung, R.W., Black, J.B.: Direct manipulation is better than passive viewing for learning anatomy in a three-dimensional virtual reality environment. Comput. Educ. **106**, 150–165 (2017)

9. Csikszentmihalyi, M.: Beyond boredom and anxiety. Jossey-Bass Publishers, San Francisco, CA (1975)

10. Csikszentmihalyi, M.: Flow: The psychology of optimal experience. J. Leis. Res. **24**(1), 93–94 (1990)

11. Bian, Y., Yang, C., Gao, F., Li, H., Zhou, S., Meng, X.: A framework for physiological indicators of flow in VR games: Construction and preliminary evaluation. Pers. Ubiquit. Comput. **20**, 821–832 (2016)

12. Faiola, A., Newlon, C., Pfaff, M., Smyslova, O.: Correlating the effects of flow and telepresence in virtual worlds: Enhancing our understanding of user behavior in game-based learning. Comput. Hum. Behav. **29**(3), 1113–1121 (2013)

13. Jackson, S.A., Ford, S.K., Kimiecik, J.C., Marsh, H.W.: Psychological correlates of flow in sport. J. Sport Exerc. Psychol. **20**, 358–378 (1998)

14. Tian, Y., Bian, Y., Han, P., Wang, P., Gao, F., Chen, Y.: Physiological signal analysis for evaluating flow during playing of computer games of varying difficulty. Front. Psychol. **8**, 1–10 (2015)

15. Malinska, M., Zuzewicz, K., Bugajska, J., Grabowski, A.: Heart rate variability (HRV) during virtual reality immersion. Int. J. Occup. Saf. Ergon. **21**, 47–54 (2015)

16. Rácz, M., Becske, M., Magyaródi, T., Orosz, G.: Physiological assessment of the psychological flow state using wearable devices. Sci. Rep. **15**, 11839 (2025). https://doi.org/10.1038/s41598-025-95647-x

17. Lacey, J.I.: Psychophysiological approaches to the evaluation of psychotherapeutic process and outcome. In: Rubinstein, E.A., Parloff, M.B. (eds.) Research in Psychotherapy, pp. 160–208. American Psychological Association, Washington, DC (1959)

18. Kasprowicz, A.L., Manuak, S.B., Malkoff, S.B., Krantz, D.S.: Individual differences in behaviorally evoked cardiovascular response: Temporal stability and hemodynamic patterning. Psychophysiol. **27**(6), 605–619 (1990)

19. Kuraoka, H., Wada, C., Miyake, S.: Flow state induced by a sensory intake task and autonomic nervous system activities. J. Ergonomics Occup. Saf. Health **23**(1), 15–24 (2023). [in Japanese]

20. Hart, S.G., Staveland, L.E.: Development of NASA-TLX (Task Load Index): Results of empirical and theoretical research. In: Hancock, P.A., Meshkati, N. (eds.) Human Mental Workload, pp. 139–183. North-Holland, Amsterdam (1988)

21. Miyake, S., Kumashiro, M.: Subjective mental workload assessment technique: An introduction to NASA-TLX and SWAT and a proposal of simple scoring methods. Japan. J. Ergonomics **29**, 399–408 (1993)

22. Mishima, M., Ishida, T.: The subjective severity of simulator sickness induced by driving simulator and its correlation with the psychophysiological measurement results. Japan. J. Ergonomics **44**(5), 279–289 (2007)

23. Kennedy, R.S., Lane, N.E., Berbaum, K.S., Lilienthal, M.G.: Simulator sickness questionnaire: An enhanced method for quantifying simulator sickness. Int. J. Aviat. Psychol. **3**(3), 203–220 (1993)

24. Sevinc, V., Berkman, M.I.: Psychometric evaluation of Simulator Sickness Questionnaire and its variants as a measure of cybersickness in consumer virtual environments. Appl. Ergon. **82**, 102958 (2020). https://doi.org/10.1016/j.apergo.2019.102958

From Theory to Practice: Leveraging VR and CTF Competitions for Advanced Cybersecurity Education

Triin Muulmann[(✉)] [iD], Ricardo Gregorio Lugo [iD], and Rain Ottis [iD]

Tallinn University of Technology, Tallinn, Estonia
`triin.muulmann@taltech.ee`

Abstract. This study explores the integration of gamified approaches, such as Capture the Flag (CTF) exercises, within cybersecurity education to enhance engagement and skill development. Focusing on the use of virtual reality (VR), the research aims to examine its potential in improving student learning outcomes, fostering critical thinking, and simulating realistic cyber-attack and defense scenarios.

Drawing upon frameworks like the European Skills, Competences, Qualifications, and Occupations framework (ESCO) and the Digital Competence Framework for Citizens (DigComp), this study highlights their role in defining essential competencies in digital literacy and cybersecurity. ESCO is a multilingual classification system that connects the labor market with education by categorizing skills, competencies, qualifications, and occupations in Europe. DigComp, on the other hand, defines digital competence as the ability to confidently and critically use digital technologies for learning, work, and social participation. By aligning cybersecurity education with these frameworks, the study emphasizes the importance of immersive and interactive learning environments to develop relevant skills.

Using a systematic review methodology, articles were screened based on inclusion and exclusion criteria, resulting in a final selection of five relevant studies. These studies showcase the application of VR in cybersecurity education, ranging from virtual labs to augmented reality games, highlighting their impact on engagement and practical skill acquisition. The findings reveal that VR enhances situational awareness and provides a more engaging and realistic learning experience compared to traditional methods, despite challenges like high implementation costs and technical limitations.

This study underscores the evolving role of VR in cybersecurity education, demonstrating its capacity to address complex learning objectives and align with digital competence frameworks. Future research should further investigate the scalability and long-term effectiveness of VR-based approaches in fostering digital literacy and cybersecurity expertise. It details the key research questions guiding the study, the reasoning behind incorporating VR and CTF methodologies, and their relevance to cybersecurity competency frameworks like ESCO and DigComp. Additionally, it expands on the systematic review process, outlining the selection criteria, research methodology, and analytical framework used. The discussion of findings highlights the comparative advantages of VR-based cybersecurity training, its effectiveness in bridging skill gaps, and its potential to improve engagement and knowledge retention.

© The Author(s), under exclusive license to Springer Nature Switzerland AG 2026
H. Mori et al. (Eds.): HCII 2025, LNCS 16333, pp. 108–122, 2026.
https://doi.org/10.1007/978-3-032-12660-3_9

Keywords: Cybersecurity education · Virtual reality · Digital competence · Gamified learning · ESCO · DigComp

1 Introduction

1.1 Framework for Waterway Operational Technology (OT) and Information Technology (IT)

Water is a fundamental yet increasingly insufficient resource, with half of the global population experiencing significant water shortages at some point during the year. Additionally, one-quarter of the world's population faces extreme water stress, consuming more than 80% of their annual renewable freshwater resources [1]. Digitalization is increasing as industry strives for effectiveness and efficiency of water treatment and distribution systems, while improving efficiency and operational capabilities, also introduces new cybersecurity vulnerabilities. Water sector control systems, such as Supervisory Control and Data Acquisition (SCAD) play a critical role in overseeing and managing water distribution. Traditionally, these systems relied on isolation and restricted access for security. However, the integration of smart technologies and the Internet of Things (IoT) has created new vulnerabilities, exposing critical infrastructure to cyber-physical attacks [2].

The convergence of Operational Technology (OT) and Information Technology (IT) has expanded the attack surface of industrial control systems (ICS) and SCADA networks, making them increasingly susceptible to ransomware, cryptojacking, insider threats, and data breaches. The consequences of these cyber threats are severe, with potential risks including water contamination, operational disruptions, and financial losses [3]. Furthermore, insider threats remain a persistent challenge, as former employees can exploit privileged knowledge to manipulate systems. Weak cybersecurity measures, such as inadequate network segmentation, weak authentication mechanisms, and poor access controls, exacerbate these cyber threats [4].

The threat landscape of the water sector mirrors the challenges faced by other critical infrastructure domains, with cyber incidents ranging from denial-of-service (DoS) attacks and a system compromise by advanced persistent threats (APTs). Attackers can manipulate sensor data, disrupt remote control mechanisms, and inject malicious inputs, leading to degraded service quality and operational failures [5]. The reliance on real-time data transmission in SCADA systems heightens the risk of interception and unauthorized data modifications, further emphasizing the need for cyber resilience strategies [6].

To enhance cybersecurity resilience in water infrastructure, a multi-layered defense approach is required [4]. The integration of endpoint security, intrusion detection, and anomaly detection systems enhances the ability to identify and respond to cyber threats in real time. Moreover, fostering collaboration between IT and OT teams creates conditions for a coordinated response to security incidents, reducing operational disruptions [5].

Beyond technical defenses, governance frameworks such as the EU network and information systems (NIS2) Directive [7] play a pivotal role in shaping cybersecurity policies within the water sector. This directive mandates increased collaboration among IT, OT, and water management experts to secure infrastructure against cyberattacks while ensuring regulatory compliance and sustainability. As the governance landscape evolves, cybersecurity must be prioritized alongside environmental concerns, striking a balance between security, affordability, and long-term sustainability. [8] The integration of cybersecurity measures into governance models is essential for ensuring the continuous and safe operation of water systems in an era of increasing digitalization and cyber risk.

1.2 Cyber Security Competency Frameworks

1.2.1 ESCO

ESCO (European Skills, Competences, Qualifications, and Occupations framework), is a multilingual classification system designed to bridge the gap between the labor market and the education and training sectors in Europe [9]. Acting as a digital dictionary, ESCO identifies, describes, and categorizes professional occupations and their associated skills. It offers a systematic approach to illustrating the relationships between different professional roles and the knowledge required for each. The framework is publicly accessible through an ESCO online portal, enabling users to freely browse or download the datasets, which include detailed descriptions of occupations and related competences [9].

The ESCO system is structured into three main pillars: occupations, knowledge, skills and competences, and qualifications. These three interconnected pillars enable ESCO to maintain a consistent and transparent organizational structure. By providing an integrated terminology system, ESCO serves as a valuable resource for the European labor market, allowing users to search for specific occupations and view their detailed descriptions. Each occupation is broken down into essential and optional skills, competences, and knowledge areas, ensuring a comprehensive understanding of the requirements associated with various professional roles [9].

1.2.2 DigComp (Digital Competence Framework)

The DigComp (Digital Competence Framework for Citizens) provides a common understanding of digital competence [10]. It encompasses the "confident, critical, and responsible use of, and engagement with, digital technologies for learning, at work, and for participation in society." In other words, digital competence involves a combination of knowledge, skills, and attitudes [10].

DigComp identifies digital competence through a comprehensive lens, covering areas such as information and data literacy, communication and collaboration, digital content creation, safety, and problem-solving. These components outline the fundamental capabilities individuals need to navigate the digital age responsibly and effectively. Information literacy includes the ability to articulate information needs, retrieve digital content, and evaluate its reliability. Communication emphasizes the responsible use of digital tools for interaction, while content creation focuses on developing and integrating digital materials [10].

Safety, one of the critical areas of DigComp, involves protecting devices, data, and personal well-being in digital environments. This aspect includes the ability to safeguard against threats, protect personal information, and promote psychological and physical well-being while using technology. DigComp also highlights environmental awareness, encouraging the responsible and sustainable use of digital technologies [10].

1.2.3 DigComp and ESCO Analysis

ESCO and DigComp are intrinsically connected in their objectives, as ESCO integrates some of the skills outlined in DigComp into its classification system. This integration primarily focuses on IT-related fields, ensuring that professionals in these sectors are equipped with the necessary competences to thrive in a digitally driven environment. The relationship between these frameworks enhances the usability of both systems, particularly in areas such as ICT safety [11].

In the realm of ICT safety, ESCO and DigComp collectively address the need for robust digital security measures. ESCO emphasizes practical skills, such as using antivirus software, setting up firewalls, and implementing access controls. DigComp complements this by highlighting the broader implications of digital safety, including privacy protection, online well-being, and the responsible use of technology. Together, these frameworks provide a comprehensive foundation for understanding and addressing the challenges of modern digital environments [11].

The integration of ESCO and DigComp frameworks supports a more unified approach to skills development in Europe, fostering greater alignment between education and labor market demands. By combining the structured occupational classifications of ESCO with the detailed digital competence guidelines of DigComp, these frameworks enable individuals and organizations to navigate the evolving technological landscape with confidence and competence. Their continued evolution and integration will play a vital role in shaping the future of digital literacy and occupational expertise across Europe [11].

1.2.4 Cybersecurity Education and IT/OT Personnel

The growing integration of Operational Technology (OT) and Information Technology (IT) in critical infrastructure has introduced significant cybersecurity challenges, particularly in sectors such as energy grids, water treatment facilities, and industrial control systems (ICS). Traditionally, industrial networks operated in isolated environments; however, with the emergence of Industrial Internet of Things (IIoT) devices and cloud-based operations, these systems have become increasingly interconnected with corporate IT infrastructures. While this convergence enhances operational efficiency and cost savings, it also significantly expands the attack surface, making OT environments more vulnerable to ransomware, unauthorized access, and advanced persistent threats (APTs) [12]. The urgent need for skilled cybersecurity professionals to secure these systems has become a major concern, highlighting the importance of specialized education and workforce development. The 100 job postings in the critical infrastructure sector reveals that 95% of positions require relevant professional experience, while 82% demand a bachelor's degree in fields such as computer science or engineering [13].

Additionally, 64% of employers list cybersecurity certifications, including CISSP and GICSP, as key qualifications. Beyond technical expertise, employers seek candidates with strong communication skills to facilitate collaboration between technical and operational teams [13]. However, despite these demands, the lack of cybersecurity awareness and specialized training among operational personnel remains a critical issue. Many organizations still lack fundamental security measures, such as password policies, network segmentation, intrusion detection systems, and structured cybersecurity training. Even where security policies are in place, untrained employees remain the weakest link, increasing the risk of cyber incidents [12].

To address the workforce gap and enhance cybersecurity resilience in IT/OT environments, a multi-layered approach is essential. This involves integrating cybersecurity education into vocational and higher education programs, ensuring that graduates possess both technical expertise and regulatory knowledge. A comprehensive curriculum should cover OT frameworks, networking protocols, and industrial control security, aligning training with industry demands to produce a cybersecurity-literate workforce. Collaboration between educational institutions, policymakers, and industry leaders is necessary to develop targeted training programs that bridge the gap between theoretical knowledge and real-world cybersecurity challenges in critical infrastructure sectors [13].

The digital transformation of industrial environments requires cross-functional expertise to mitigate evolving cybersecurity risks. As IT and OT continue to merge, organizations must implement robust security strategies, including regulatory compliance, cross-functional collaboration, and advanced threat detection mechanisms. Without a skilled cybersecurity workforce, industries will remain vulnerable to the growing spectrum of cyber threats, underscoring the need for proactive education and workforce development as foundational pillars for securing Industry 4.0 [12].

1.3 Capture the Flag (CTF)

1.3.1 What is CTF?

CTFs are structured as gamified cybersecurity challenges, where individuals or teams attempt to solve security-related tasks to find or steal hidden "flags" and accumulate points. These competitions serve as an educational tool for training cybersecurity professionals and students in real-world attack and defense techniques [14].

The learning-through-practice approach is widely recognized as an effective pedagogical method, particularly in technical disciplines such as cybersecurity. Many cybersecurity courses incorporate structured, goal-oriented activities to enhance student engagement and skills development. Some educators further increase motivation and participation by integrating gamification elements, such as realistic, challenge-based scenarios in controlled environments. However, while these approaches have demonstrated effectiveness, they are not consistently implemented across cybersecurity education programs [15].

CTF competitions are one of the most effective gamified approaches as they provide an interactive learning environment where participants rely on their existing foundational cybersecurity knowledge and adapt it to solve unexpected and unconventional problems while engaging in problem-solving tasks. Studies show that CTFs are particularly effective in introducing cybersecurity concepts to high school and university students, increasing their interest and competence in the field [15]. The CTF format encourages students to adopt an attacker's mindset, an essential perspective for understanding cyber threats, vulnerabilities, and defense mechanisms [16].

Keeping students motivated in cybersecurity courses can be challenging due to the complex and demanding nature of the subject matter. A gamified teaching approach, developed over the past decade, integrates practical, engaging security exercises with a challenge-based format and a real-time scoring system is a common feature, it is not mandatory across all CTF formats and contexts. This competitive structure not only fosters engagement but also enhances students' ability to retain and apply cybersecurity knowledge effectively [17].

CTF competitions are widely used in cybersecurity education and training to enhance practical skills, problem-solving abilities, and teamwork. These competitions serve as hands-on learning environments where participants engage in security-related challenges designed to simulate real-world cyber threats. CTFs can be integrated into academic curricula, professional training programs, and cybersecurity exercises to provide interactive and engaging learning experiences [18].

CTF competitions generally fall into three primary categories: Jeopardy-style, Attack-Defense, and Mixed formats. Jeopardy-style CTFs consist of standalone challenges in areas such as web security, forensics, cryptography, and binary analysis. Participants solve progressively difficult tasks to earn points, with the highest-scoring team or individual winning the competition [19]. In contrast, Attack-Defense CTFs require teams to secure their own vulnerable network or host while simultaneously attempting to exploit opponents weaknesses [19]. These competitions can be either offensive or defensive, providing hands-on experience that differs from typical cybersecurity roles, where defense is the primary focus and offensive security is usually a separate specialization. The Mixed CTF format incorporates elements of both styles, alternating between challenge-based problem-solving and interactive wargames [20].

Although all CTF competitions are often categorized together, interactive CTFs best capture the real-time strategic elements of the format, requiring participants to actively apply cybersecurity skills in a dynamic environment. These competitions not only serve as training platforms for aspiring cybersecurity professionals but also contribute to the development of teamwork, critical thinking, and technical proficiency, essential for cybersecurity careers in both offensive and defensive roles [19].

1.3.2 How does CTF help in Teaching Cybersecurity?

The growing complexity of cyber threats demands innovative educational methods to prepare students for real-world security challenges. Traditional lecture-based cybersecurity education often fails to provide the hands-on experience necessary to develop technical skills. CTF competitions and other gamified approaches address this gap as they are effective tools forenhancing engagement, skill development, and real-world problem-solving abilities [21].

CTF competitions often simulate realistic cyberattack and defense scenarios, allowing students to apply theoretical knowledge in a controlled environment. These exercises expose participants to practical cybersecurity challenges, improving their technical expertise in penetration testing, cryptography, network security, and digital forensics. Students who engage in CTF activities report higher motivation, greater confidence, and an improved understanding of cyber threats and mitigation strategies. By bridging the gap between theory and practice, CTFs serve as is valuable component in preparing students for careers in cybersecurity [21].

To further expand accessibility and scalability in cybersecurity education, researchers have developed CTF-as-a-Service platforms [22]. These platforms allow educators and students to create and participate in CTF competitions with minimal technical overhead, enabling on-demand, hands-on cybersecurity training. By lowering entry barriers, CTF-as-a-Service facilitates broader participation and helps address the growing cybersecurity workforce shortage [22]. The CTF platforms enhances offensive and defensive security skills, critical thinking, and teamwork, mirroring real-world cyber incident response scenarios. However, challenges such as ensuring security within competition environments and keeping content updated with evolving cyber threats remain areas for further research and development [22].

A further key benefit of CTF competitions is their ability to generate learning analytics through digital datasets. The performance of participants can be tracked using technical metrics, such as time spent on tasks, frequency of correct and incorrect submissions, and command-line usage. These rich datasets enable organizers to assess learning effectiveness, provide targeted feedback, and improve future cybersecurity exercises [18].

Despite their effectiveness, CTFs present certain challenges. Many competitions focus primarily on technical skills, potentially overlooking cognitive and strategic aspects of cybersecurity training. Additionally, not all CTF challenges offer structured feedback mechanisms, making it difficult for participants to reflect on their learning progress [18].

Overall, CTF competitions and on-demand cybersecurity training platforms play a crucial role in modern cybersecurity education, offering engaging, skill-based learning experiences that align with industry needs. As cyber threats continue to evolve, incorporating gamified, challenge-based learning will be instrumental in equipping the next generation of cybersecurity professionals with the necessary skills and experience to protect digital infrastructure effectively.

1.3.3 Comparison of 2D, 3D, VR and CTF

Data visualization plays a critical role in transforming raw data into meaningful insights. Over time, advancements in technology have expanded the range of visualization techniques, with 2D, 3D, and Virtual Reality (VR) emerging as the most prominent methods. Each of these techniques offers unique benefits depending on the complexity of data and the user's needs. 2D visualizations, such as charts and heatmaps, provide clear and accessible representations suitable for general data analysis. 3D visualizations enhance depth and interactivity, making them ideal for spatially complex datasets in fields like engineering and scientific research. VR-based visualizations push boundaries by creating fully immersive environments where users can interact with data in a three-dimensional space, leading to greater engagement and comprehension [23].

Virtual reality (VR) technology creates a computer-generated, three-dimensional environment that users can interact with, typically through headsets like Oculus Rift or HTC Vive [28].

VR is gaining popularity for its valuable training applications, offering a multi-sensory and interactive experience that enhances visual learning [29].

The integration of VR and gamification in cybersecurity education has revolutionized learning by providing immersive, interactive experiences that traditional lectures and online courses often lack. VR-based simulations enable hands-on training in realistic cyber defense scenarios, improving decision-making and problem-solving skills. CTF competitions benefit significantly from VR-enhanced simulations, offering participants a more dynamic and engaging learning environment [24].

Remote and distance education also leverage VR technologies to enhance cybersecurity awareness programs. The ability to simulate complex cyber threats in a controlled yet realistic setting increases knowledge retention and situational awareness. VR-supported CTF competitions further improve hands-on experience in threat detection, incident response, and vulnerability assessment, ensuring students acquire practical cybersecurity skills [25]. Additionally, VR fosters collaboration and teamwork, both essential in real-world cybersecurity operations.

While the adoption of VR in cybersecurity education presents challenges such as high costs and technical limitations, its growing accessibility is expected to bridge the gap between theory and practice. As cybersecurity threats evolve, integrating VR-based learning environments into training programs will better prepare students and professionals to tackle emerging cyber risks. The combination of data visualization, immersive learning, and gamification not only enhances knowledge retention and engagement but also provides a more effective and interactive approach to cybersecurity education [26].

2 Methodology

Following the Preferred Reporting Items for Systematic Reviews and Meta-Analyses (PRISMA) guidelines [27], the first author (TM) conducted the literature search from 04 May 2024 to 04 July 2024 using Google Scholar. The databases searched included Tandfonline, IEEE, Elsevier, Springer, SAGE Publications, ACM, and ScienceDirect, ensuring a broad and credible academic scope.

The inclusion criteria for article selection were: 1) articles were published in English, 2) only articles published from 2014 to present were considered; 3) Considering the interdisciplinary research, full text available in Google Scholar (HTML, PDF, docx-format), 4) Peer-reviewed only and 5) relevance to cybersecurity education and VR-based learning.

Consequently, the exclusion criteria included: 1) articles not published in English, 2) Thesis, dissertations, consultancy papers, pre-prints, e-prints, e-books, books, research reports, manuals, guides, as the focus is on academic journal and conference articles as the authors are looking for scientifically validated technology, 3) non-peer reviewed academic literature including theses; and 4) articles that were published from 2014 is included and further back (> 13 years).

Considering the criteria, the author screened the titles and abstracts, which left the authors with three groups of articles: 1) the ones to include (those which meet all inclusion criteria); 2) the ones to exclude (those which do not meet at least one of the inclusion criteria) and 3) the ones that the authors were in doubt about.

This systematic review was guided by the following research questions:

1. How does VR enhance cybersecurity education compared to traditional learning methods?
2. What are the advantages and challenges of integrating VR into cybersecurity training?

3. How do gamified approaches like CTF exercises contribute to engagement and knowledge retention?

By structuring the review around these questions, the study establishes a clear connection between the research objectives and the findings. The selected studies showcase a diverse range of VR applications in cybersecurity education, from virtual labs to augmented reality games, illustrating their impact on engagement, situational awareness, and skill acquisition. The findings reveal that while VR significantly enhances learning experiences, challenges such as cost, scalability, and accessibility remain critical considerations for widespread adoption.

3   Results

3.1   Study Search Results

A total of 1,510 articles were initially identified through keyword searches related to "cybersecurity" OR "cyber security" AND "engineering" AND "education" OR "training" AND "evaluation" AND "feedback" AND "experiment" AND "quantitative" OR "qualitative" OR "correlation" AND "virtual reality" or "VR". After an initial screening of titles and abstracts, 260 articles remained for further review. Subsequent filtering based on inclusion criteria resulted in a final selection of five relevant studies that met the research requirements. Article results were collected in MS Excel and an initial total of N = 260 articles including duplications were collected. The flow diagram shows the process of article identification and selection for eligibility and inclusion into the scoping review (see Fig. 1).

After reviewing the articles, 5 papers were deemed relevant for the needs of this paper (see Table 1).

Table 1. Summary of the reviewed papers regarding virtual reality in cybersecurity education.

Reference	Domain	Use case	Goal	Population
Hassenfeldt, C, et al., (2020)	Digital Forensics education	Virtual and Physical lab	User study	57 participants
Mathis, F. et al., (2022)	Cybersecurity education	Lab-based	User study	18 participants
Korkiakoski, M. et al., (2023)	Cybersecurity education	Augmented reality game	User study	6 individuals
Chekhovskoy, Y. et al., (2022)	Cybersecurity training	VR testbed	Proof of concept	None
Munsinger, B. et al., (2023)	Cybersecurity training	VR based network monitoring tool	User study (experiment)	12 participants

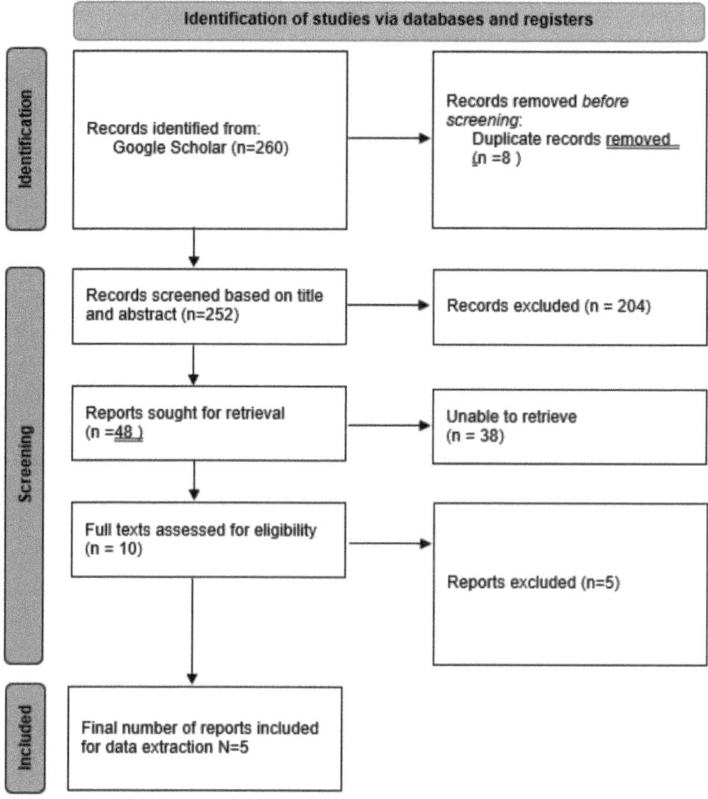

Fig. 1. PRISMA diagram– study screening and selection.

3.2 Study Summary

Hassenfeldt et al. (2020) conducted an experimental study with 57 participants to evaluate the learning efficacy of digital forensics concepts and the bagging & tagging of digital devices in an immersive virtual reality (VR) environment. The study employed a controlled experiment design, where participants were randomly assigned to either a VR-based training group or a traditional physical lab group. Both groups underwent the same lecture and hands-on lab exercise, with pre- and post-tests administered to assess learning outcomes. The study found no statistically significant differences in knowledge acquisition between the VR and physical lab groups. However, participants in the VR group completed the lab exercises faster, suggesting increased time efficiency. The average pre-test score was 7.26 (SD = 1.92), and the post-test average improved to 9.96 (SD = 1.79), demonstrating a statistically significant knowledge gain across both groups. Despite similar learning outcomes, the study highlights VR's potential for improving efficiency and engagement in digital forensics education [30].

Mathis et al. (2022) conducted an experimental study with 18 participants to explore the use of virtual reality (VR) in shoulder surfing research, specifically in authentication scenarios. The study investigated the effectiveness of immersive and non-immersive

VR observations compared to traditional 2D video-based methods in assessing participants' ability to shoulder surf ATM PIN entries, smartphone PIN authentication, and smartphone pattern authentication. They employed a within-subject experimental design where participants were exposed to all three observation conditions: 2D video observations (2DVO), 3D non-immersive observations (3DO), and immersive VR observations (VRO). Their findings indicated that participants' observation performance was highest in immersive VR (M = 93.14%, SD = 25.35%), followed by 2D video (M = 89.35%, SD = 30.92%) and non-immersive VR (M = 81.40%, SD = 39.01%). However, there was no significant difference between the immersive VR and 2D video conditions in terms of observation performance. Immersive VR resulted in a significantly higher sense of presence, spatial awareness, and involvement compared to both 2D video and non-immersive VR, suggesting its potential for more realistic shoulder surfing simulations [31].

Korkiakoski et al. (2023) conducted a pilot study with six participants to explore the potential of an augmented reality (AR) game, Hack the Room, in teaching cybersecurity concepts. The study aimed to assess whether AR-enhanced Capture the Flag (CTF) games could improve learning and increase cybersecurity situational awareness. They employed an experimental design, dividing participants into two groups: three cybersecurity experts and three novices. The experts were assessed on their situational awareness using the SART questionnaire, while the novices were evaluated on their learning outcomes and ability to recall cybersecurity commands used in the game. The results showed that experts reported high familiarity and information quantity in the game environment, while novices demonstrated knowledge retention, with two out of three correctly answering all cybersecurity-related questions [32].

Chekhovskoy et al. (2022) conducted an experimental study with 28 participants to evaluate the use of virtual reality (VR) technologies in training information security (IS) specialists. The study aimed to address the lack of effective educational tools for network attack simulations and cybersecurity training. They employed a comparative experimental design, dividing participants into two groups: one group used traditional lecture-based learning, while the other utilized a VR-based testbed developed using the Unity engine. Both groups received instruction on network attacks and defense mechanisms, followed by a knowledge assessment and feedback survey. The results showed that the VR-based group demonstrated a higher knowledge retention rate (89%) compared to the traditional learning group (71%). Additionally, participants reported greater engagement and interest in learning through VR. However, some technical limitations were identified, including minor issues with the accuracy of the virtual environment and the clarity of attack visualization [29].

Munsinger et al. (2023) conducted an experimental study with 12 participants to evaluate the impact of virtual reality (VR) on cyber situational awareness (SA) in Security Operations Centers (SOCs). The study explored whether VR-based network monitoring tools could improve SOC operator performance and reduce cognitive load compared to traditional tools. They employed a between-subjects experimental design, assigning participants to one of three conditions: VR headset only, traditional network monitoring tool (Wireshark) only, or a combination of both. Using the Situation Awareness Global Assessment Technique (SAGAT), they measured perception, comprehension, and projection abilities across different network attack scenarios. The results indicated that VR-only participants demonstrated higher perception performance (M = 2.25) compared to traditional tool users (M = 1.75). However, comprehension scores were similar between both groups (M = 2), and projection performance remained low across all conditions (VR: M = 1.25, traditional: M = 1.5). Participants also reported a lower cognitive load when using VR (M = 9.9) than Wireshark (M = 11.2), suggesting that VR may enhance ease of use [33].

3.3 Study Findings

Studies indicate that while VR simulations for tasks such as bagging and tagging do not show a significant difference in knowledge acquisition compared to traditional labs, they offer advantages in time efficiency and engagement [30]. Additionally, immersive VR provides a more realistic experience and improves observation performance compared to 2D video, reinforcing its effectiveness in cybersecurity training [31]. Studies also suggests that novices can quickly reach the skill level of experts during gameplay [32], highlighting VR's potential for accelerating learning. Given the growing need for advanced training methods in information security, VR technologies play a crucial role in studying network attacks [29] and enhancing cyber situational awareness, particularly for novice SOC operators [33].

4 Analysis of VR and AR Applications in Cybersecurity Education

The integration of VR and Augmented Reality (AR) in cybersecurity education has demonstrated significant potential in improving engagement, motivation, and learning efficiency. VR enhances situational awareness by providing realistic simulations that closely mimic real-world cybersecurity threats, making it an effective tool for both novice learners and experienced professionals. The use of AR-based CTF games has also been found to engage users effectively, offering an interactive approach to ethical hacking exercises.

Another notable advantage of VR and AR training is its efficiency in time management. Compared to traditional learning methods, VR-based exercises allow participants to complete tasks more quickly while maintaining high engagement levels. This time-saving aspect is especially valuable in practical cybersecurity training environments, as well as in OT and the water sector, where rapid decision-making is crucial for protecting critical infrastructure during cyber incidents.

While VR enhances realism in training scenarios, the extent to which this contributes to better learning outcomes remains an open question. In some cases, immersive VR environments provide a more lifelike experience, helping users better understand spatial and situational dynamics in cybersecurity threats. This is particularly beneficial for CTF style exercises, where participants must quickly analyze complex scenarios, navigate virtual infrastructures, and react to simulated cyber incidents in real time. The interactive and hands-on nature of VR enhances engagement, improves retention of security concepts, and allows for realistic adversarial simulations, making training more effective compared to traditional methods. Additionally, VR environments can simulate high-stakes, real-world cyberattacks in a controlled setting, fostering critical thinking and teamwork under pressure. However, certain studies found that realism improvements did not necessarily translate to better knowledge retention or performance compared to traditional methods. AR, on the other hand, has not significantly enhanced realism in cybersecurity training, likely due to its reliance on overlaying digital content onto real-world environments rather than creating fully immersive simulations.

Despite its advantages, VR-based cybersecurity training faces several challenges, including high hardware costs, technical complexity, and limited scalability. The initial setup and calibration required for VR systems can be a barrier, particularly for institutions or organizations with budget constraints. Motion sickness has been reported as a minor issue in immersive VR studies, though its impact on training effectiveness remains limited.

Scalability and accessibility present another challenge for widespread adoption. While VR offers potential for remote learning applications, hardware requirements and infrastructure limitations may restrict its reach. AR-based training appears to be more accessible due to its compatibility with mobile devices, making it a promising alternative for cybersecurity education in resource-constrained environments. This is particularly relevant for OT and the water sector, where cybersecurity training must be both cost-effective and easily deployable across geographically distributed sites. However, the long-term effectiveness of AR-based cybersecurity training compared to traditional CTF exercises still requires further investigation.

The effectiveness of VR and AR training in cybersecurity education remains a complex issue, particularly regarding knowledge retention. While some studies reported no significant improvement in retention compared to traditional methods, others found that VR participants demonstrated higher long-term memory retention rates. This discrepancy suggests that the benefits of VR and AR in cybersecurity education may depend on factors such as the complexity of the training environment, the specific skills being taught, and the experience level of the participants.

Further studies with larger samples could be beneficial in assessing if VR would be a suitable environment.

5 Conclusion

This study set out to explore the integration of VR and AR in cybersecurity education, particularly within CTF exercises and other hands-on training methods. The analysis of existing research demonstrates that VR and AR can significantly enhance engagement, motivation, and learning efficiency in cybersecurity education. This study highlights that immersive learning environments improve situational awareness, skill acquisition, and training effectiveness in complex cybersecurity scenarios.

Despite these promising findings, several challenges remain, including high hardware costs, technical complexity, and scalability issues, which may limit the widespread adoption of VR and AR-based training. Furthermore, the long-term effectiveness of AR-based cybersecurity training compared to traditional CTF exercises still requires further research. While some studies reported no significant improvement in knowledge retention compared to conventional methods, others found that VR participants demonstrated higher long-term memory retention rates. This discrepancy suggests that the effectiveness of immersive learning depends on multiple factors, such as the complexity of the training environment, the skills being taught, and the participants' prior experience.

Given these challenges, future research should prioritize optimizing VR and AR-based cybersecurity training by focusing on balancing engagement, realism, scalability, and learning outcomes. Additionally, more studies with larger sample sizes and comprehensive methodologies are needed to ensure that findings can be generalized and applied to broader cybersecurity education settings. Exploring AI-powered adaptive learning systems, scalable infrastructure, and advanced assessment methods can further contribute to the development of effective and accessible immersive learning environments.

Ultimately, while VR and AR technologies hold great promise for cybersecurity training, their full potential can only be realized through continued development, refinement, and integration into standardized educational frameworks.

Acknowledgments. This study was funded by Digital Europe Programme: Project ATHENA (grant number 101127970).

References

1. UNESCO World Water Assessment Programme: The United Nations World Water Development Report 2024: water for prosperity and peace. UNESDOC (2024)
2. Cardenas, A., Amin, S., Sastry, S.: Research Challenges for the Security of Control Systems. in 3rd USENIX Workshop on Hot Topics in Security, San Jose (2008)
3. Hassanzadeh, A., Rasekh, A., Galelli, S., Aghashahi, M., Taormina, R., Ostfeld, A., Banks, M.K.: A review of cybersecurity incidents in the water sector. J. Environ. Eng. (2020)
4. Paes, R., Mazur, D.C., Venne, B.K., Ostrzenski, J.: A guide to securing industrial control networks: Integrating IT and OT systems. IEEE Ind. Appl. Mag. **26**(2), 47–53 (2019)
5. Patriarca, R., Simone, F., Di Gravio, G.: Modelling cyber resilience in a water treatment and distribution system. Reliab. Eng. Syst. Saf. (2022)
6. Stouffer, K, Pease, M., Tang, C., Zimmerman, M., Pillitteri, V., Lightman, S., Hahn, A., Saravia, S., Sherule, A., Thompson, M.: Guide to Operational Technology (OT) Security. Computer security resource center (2023)
7. E. Commission, European Commission: https://eur-lex.europa.eu/eli/dir/2016/1148/oj/eng. Accessed 10 Febr 2025
8. Michalec, O., Milyaeva, S., & Rashid, A., Reconfiguring governance: How cyber security regulations are reconfiguring water governance., Regulation & Governance, pp. 1325–1342 (2022)
9. E. Commission, European Skills, Competences, Qualifications and Occupations (ESCO): European Commission. https://esco.ec.europa.eu/en. Accessed 03 Febr 2025
10. E. Commission, European Commission's Joint Research Centre: https://joint-research-cen tre.ec.europa.eu/digcomp/digcomp-framework_en. Accessed 14 June 2024
11. Muulmann, T.: D2.6 Raport on roles and competence needs. Manuscript submitted for Digital Europe Programme: Project ATHENA (2024)
12. Karampidis, K., Panagiotakis, S., Vasilakis, M., Markakis, E. K., Papadourakis, G., Industrial cybersecurity 4.0: Preparing the operational technicians for industry 4.0. In 2019 IEEE 24th international workshop on computer aided modeling and design of communication links and networks (CAMAD), pp. 1–6 (2019)
13. Ramazan, C.A., Coffy, P.M., Lemons, J.: Building the Operational Technology (OT) Cybersecurity Workforce: What are Employers Looking for? Journal of Cybersecurity Education Research and Practice (JCERP) (2024)
14. Caliskan, E., Topgul, M. O., Ottis, R.: Cyber security exercises: A comparison of participant evaluation metrics and scoring systems. In Strategic Cyber Defense, pp. 180–190 (2017)
15. Gonzalez, H., Llamas, R., Rivas, O. M.: Using a CTF Tournament for Reinforcing Learned Skills in Cybersecurity Course. Res. Comput. Sci. (2019)
16. Dabrowski, A., Kammerstetter, M., Thamm, E., Weippl, E., Kastner, W.: Leveraging competitive gamification for sustainable fun and profit in security education. In 2015 USENIX Summit on Gaming, Games, and Gamification in Security Education (2015)

17. Carlisle, M., Chiaramonte, M., Caswell, D.: Using {CTFs} for an Undergraduate Cyber Education. In 2015 USENIX Summit on Gaming, Games, and Gamification in Security Education (2015)
18. Maennel, K.: Learning analytics perspective: Evidencing learning from digital datasets in cybersecurity exercises. In 2020 IEEE European symposium on security and privacy workshops (EuroS&PW), pp. 27–36 (2020)
19. Vigna, G., Borgolte, K., Corbetta, J., Doupé, A., Fratantonio, Y., Invernizzi, L., ... Shoshitaishvili, Y.:Ten Years of {iCTF}: The Good, The Bad, and The Ugly. In 2014 USENIX Summit on Gaming, Games, and Gamification in Security Education (2014)
20. Time, C.: CTF Time. CTFtime. https://ctftime.org/ctfs. Accessed 1 Dec 2024
21. Leune, K., Petrilli Jr, S. J.: Using capture-the-flag to enhance the effectiveness of cybersecurity education. In: Proceedings of the 18th annual conference on information technology education, pp. 47–52 (2017)
22. Trickel, E., Disperati, F., Gustafson, E., Kalantari, F., Mabey, M., Tiwari, N., ... Vigna, G.: Shell we play a game? {CTF-as-a-service} for security education. In 2017 USENIX Workshop on Advances in Security Education (2017)
23. Pramod, D.: Gamification in cybersecurity education; a state of the art review and research agenda. J. Appl. Res. High. Educ. (2024)
24. Riva, G., Botella, C., Baños, R., Mantovani, F., García-Palacios, A., Quero, S., ... Gaggioli, A.: Presence-inducing media for mental health applications. Immersed in media: Telepresence theory, measurement & technology, pp. 283–332 (2015)
25. Chekhovskoy, Y., Plaksiy, K., Nikiforov, A., Miloslavskaya, N.: The Use of Virtual Reality Technologies in the Specialists' Training in the Field of Information Security. Procedia Comput. Sci. **213**, pp. 223–231 (2022)
26. Ahmed, A., Watterson, C., Alhashmi, S., Gaber, T.: How universities teach cybersecurity courses online: a systematic literature review. Frontiers Comput. Sci. **6** (2024)
27. Wagner, P., Alharthi, D.: Leveraging VR/AR/MR/XR Technologies to Improve Cybersecurity Education, Training, and Operations. J. Cybersecurity Educ. Res. Pract. (2024)
28. Oktavianto, R., Erik Sibarani, B.: Building Cyber-Savvy Generation: 15 Years of Research on Cybersecurity Education and Future Research Agendas. Build. Cyber-Savvy Gener. (2024)
29. Hutton, B., Salanti, G., Caldwell, D.M., Chaimani, A., Schmid, C.H., Cameron, C.: ... & Moher, D, The PRISMA extension statement for reporting of systematic reviews incorporating network meta-analyses of health care interventions: checklist and explanations. Ann. Intern. Med. **162**(11), 777–784 (2015)
30. Hassenfeldt, C., Jacques, J., Baggili, I.: Exploring the learning efficacy of digital forensics concepts and bagging & tagging of digital devices in immersive virtual reality. Forensic Sci. Int. Digit. Invest. **33** (2020)
31. Mathis, F., O'Hagan, J., Khamis, M., Vaniea, K.: Virtual reality observations: Using virtual reality to augment lab-based shoulder surfing research. In: 2022 IEEE Conference on Virtual Reality and 3D User Interfaces (VR), pp. 291–300 (2022)
32. Korkiakoski, M., Antila, A., Annamaa, J., Sheikhi, S., Alavesa, P., Kostakos, P.: Hack the Room: Exploring the potential of an augmented reality game for teaching cyber security. in in Proceedings of the Augmented Humans International Conference 2023 (2023)
33. Munsinger, B., Beebe, N., Richardson, T.: Virtual reality for improving cyber situational awareness in security operations centers. Comput. Secur. **132** (2023)
34. Vuorikari, R., Kluzer, S., Punie, Y.: The Digital Competence Framework for Citizens. 27 07 2024 (2024). https://joint-research-centre.ec.europa.eu/digcomp/digcomp-framework_en#definition-of-digital-competence

Three-Dimensional Spatial Instructional Design and Empirical Research from the Perspective of Embodied Cognition: A Case Study of the Course Transformation from 2D to 3D Forms

Li Ou-yang[1] , Yunyi Zhuang[1,1] , and Jie Ling[2(✉)]

[1] Guangzhou Academy of Fine Arts, Guangzhou, Guangdong, China
[2] Zhongkai University of Agriculture and Engineering, Guangzhou, Guangdong, China
47219382@qq.com

Abstract. In the teaching of three-dimensional space based on design in colleges and universities, it is the core task of teaching to improve students' understanding of the transformation from 2D to 3D morphology and their practical operation ability. Based on embodied cognition theory, this study focuses on the key content of two-dimensional to three-dimensional morphological transformation, and is committed to constructing an effective teaching design and teaching strategy system.

In this study, 33 first-year students majoring in art and design from Guangdong Comprehensive University were divided into experimental group and control group. The experimental group used teaching strategies based on embodied cognition, covering multiple aspects such as body perception, sensory experience, and situational simulation. Students experience first-hand the transformation of morphology from 2D to 3D through multi-sensory experiences such as body imitation of 2D graphics and 3D model shapes, with the help of VR technology, and participation in the "Space Sculpture Project" scenario simulation. The control group used traditional teaching methods.

In order to comprehensively evaluate the teaching effect, the study collected data from multiple dimensions through a combination of quantitative and qualitative methods. The quantitative analysis covers students' aptitude test scores and work evaluation scores; Qualitative analysis focuses on students' classroom performance and learning feedback. The results showed that the overall average score of the experimental group increased by 15.43% compared with that of the control group, the score of innovation of works increased by 20%, and the class participation reached 80%. These results show that the teaching strategy based on embodied cognitive design has achieved remarkable results, and the students' abilities in spatial perception, hands-on practice and innovative thinking have been significantly improved, and their works have outstanding performance in innovation, aesthetics and functionality, and their satisfaction with teaching methods is also higher.

H. Mori et al. (Eds.): HCII 2025, LNCS 16333, pp. 123–133, 2026.
https://doi.org/10.1007/978-3-032-12660-3_10

However, there are some limitations to this study. The small number of samples and narrow scope, the short experimental period, and the strong subjectivity in the data collection process affect the universality and accuracy of the research conclusions to a certain extent. Future studies may consider expanding the sample range, extending the experimental time, and further optimizing the research methodology. At the same time, the integration of embodied cognition and other educational theories should be explored in depth, and its application in different disciplines and courses should be expanded, so as to provide more powerful support for education and teaching reform.

Keywords: embodied cognition · three-dimensional spatial teaching · conversion from two-dimensional to three-dimensional forms · teaching design · teaching reflection

1 Introduction

Under the strategic goal guidance of "Modernization of Chinese Education 2035", the "Guidelines for Public Art Courses in Higher Education Institutions" (2022) clearly emphasizes the need for universities to strengthen three-dimensional thinking cultivation and the reform of practical teaching. The module of "Transformation from Two-Dimensional to Three-Dimensional Forms" in the design-related course "Three-Dimensional Space" has become the core teaching medium for implementing these policy requirements.

The current course presents three main contradictions: Firstly, 40% of first-year students majoring in Fine Arts and Design lack a foundational knowledge of three-dimensional coordinates, making it difficult for them to develop spatial cognition. Secondly, the course integrates knowledge from various disciplines, such as solid geometry, materials mechanics, and innovative design, which can lead to cognitive overload for students with weak foundational skills. Thirdly, the traditional 'demonstration - imitation' teaching model lacks physical engagement, resulting in a limited capacity for spatial processing and innovative thinking among students.

In international research, Porat & Ceobanu (2024) confirmed a strong correlation between the spatial abilities of architecture students and their academic performance through experiments [1]; Stefaniak (2020) [2], Moreira (2019)[3], and others have constructed frameworks for design thinking from the perspectives of systems theory and complexity. Domestically, scholars such as Jin Yaqing et al. (2025) [4] and Fan Yinliang (2024) [5] have respectively explored interdisciplinary theoretical integration and paths for curriculum reform. Although existing achievements are plentiful, there remains a lack of empirical support and systematic answers for the deep application of embodied cognition theory in three-dimensional spatial teaching.

2 Theoretical Basis and Strategy Construction

2.1 The Core Ideas of Embodied Cognition Theory

Body Centrality. Embodied cognition theory views the body as the foundation of cognition, emphasizing that cognition is formed through dynamic interactions between the body and the environment. For example, students transform a two-dimensional plane into a triangular prism through origami operations during three-dimensional spatial learning, or simulate the rotation of a cylinder with bodily movements; this bodily involvement can convert abstract spatial concepts into muscle memory.[6] Merleau-Ponty's theory of 'embodied subjectivity' indicates that spatial cognition originates from the interaction between the body and the world, providing theoretical support for the cultivation of spatial thinking in design education.

Situational Dependence. Cognitive processes rely on specific contexts, and the environment is an organic part of the cognitive system [7]. In teaching, virtual scenes are constructed using VR technology, combined with tactile materials, to enhance three-dimensional shape perception through multisensory collaboration. This design aligns with Lakoff's concept of 'embodied philosophy,' which posits that abstract concepts (such as 'spatial tension') originate from the interactive experiences between the body and the environment.

2.2 Multi-Theory Collaborative Framework

Constructivism. Constructivism provides a logical framework for knowledge construction in embodied cognitive instruction, advocating for real projects such as 'campus sculpture design' to enable students to combine bodily experiences (such as spatial scale perception) with theoretical knowledge in group collaborations, thereby forming a systemic understanding of the transformation from two dimensions to three dimensions. Vygotsky's theory of the 'Zone of Proximal Development' is reflected in teachers guiding students to overcome cognitive limitations through 'scaffolding' (such as step-by-step demonstrations).

Gestalt Psychology. Gestalt psychology emphasizes that "the whole is greater than the sum of its parts," guiding students to integrate elements such as points, lines, and planes into organic three-dimensional forms. For example, based on embodied perception experiences, students apply organizational principles to combine fragmented graphics into a cohesive sculpture, reflecting the theory of "aha learning," which emphasizes understanding spatial relationships through physical manipulation.

2.3 Teaching Strategy Construction Path

Physical Interactions. Construct a three-tier interaction of 'Body - Paper - Space': the basic layer establishes dimensional connections through origami to form triangular pyramids; the advanced layer understands dimensional transformation by simulating the trajectory of a cone with body movements and projecting drawings; the applied layer represents the projection surface with the body, providing an intuitive understanding of view transformation.

Multi-Sensory Engagement. Construct a "Virtual-Reality" dual-track perception system: The virtual layer disassembles models through VR and creates an immersive experience with sound effects; the reality layer perceives the limitations of shape through the tactile interaction with materials such as rice paper and metal mesh, achieving a synergy between visual and tactile sensations.

Scenario Simulation. Create design tasks that involve real constraints (such as "campus sculptures"). Students will measure the site, use cardboard modeling to verify structural stability, and utilize AI to simulate lighting effects to optimize the model, thereby forming a closed loop of "operation - verification - optimization" to enhance problem-solving skills.

3 Teaching Practice and Design Implementation

3.1 Fundamentals of Instructional Design

Course content. Based on embodied cognition theory, construct a progressive knowledge module system: Two-dimensional shape cognition: Establish intuitive understanding of planar forms through embodied operations; Three-dimensional transformation methods: Systematically explain basic techniques such as folding and cutting; Multi-sensory cognition construction: Enhance three-dimensional perception by combining VR technology with material touch; Contextual project practices: Utilize the 'Spatial Sculpture Project' as a medium to drive comprehensive application.

Learning Situation Analysis. Among first-year students majoring in fine arts and design, 40% lack a fundamental understanding of three-dimensional coordinates and therefore need to lower the cognitive threshold through bodily simulation (such as using body gestures to outline geometric shapes); the remaining students, although possessing knowledge in two dimensions, suffer from rigid patterns of innovative thinking and require stimulation through multi-sensory experiences and real projects to achieve breakthroughs.

3.2   Teaching Model

Somatic Perception. Operations such as 'forming a triangular pyramid with origami' (see Fig. 1) and 'mimicking the rotational trajectory of a cone with the body', a preliminary association between two-dimensional figures and three-dimensional space is established, transforming abstract spatial concepts into embodied experiences.

Sensory Experience. Construct a dual-path perception system of 'virtual-reality': on the virtual level, dynamically deconstruct models using VR technology, while on the reality level, achieve multi-sensory integration through touching diverse materials (such as rice paper and metal mesh), encompassing visual and tactile sensations (see Fig. 2).

Contextual Application. With the design of "Campus Cultural Square Sculpture" as the task carrier, the constraints of "3m × 2m × 1.5m size, 500-yuan budget, and embodying the concept of 'flow'" are set to promote students to transform theoretical knowledge into practical application ability (see Fig. 3).

Fig. 1. Body Perception Process.

Dynamic Interaction and Feedback Adjustment. Dynamic interaction: Conduct thematic discussions such as 'Transforming 2D Polyline into 3D Forms' through group collaboration, combining creative sharing to achieve knowledge co-construction; - Feedback adjustment: Based on student operational data (such as folding time, frequency of view errors), project evaluations (structural stability, creativity novelty), and questionnaire feedback, drive the iterative optimization of teaching strategies (see Figs. 4, 5, 6, 7, 8).

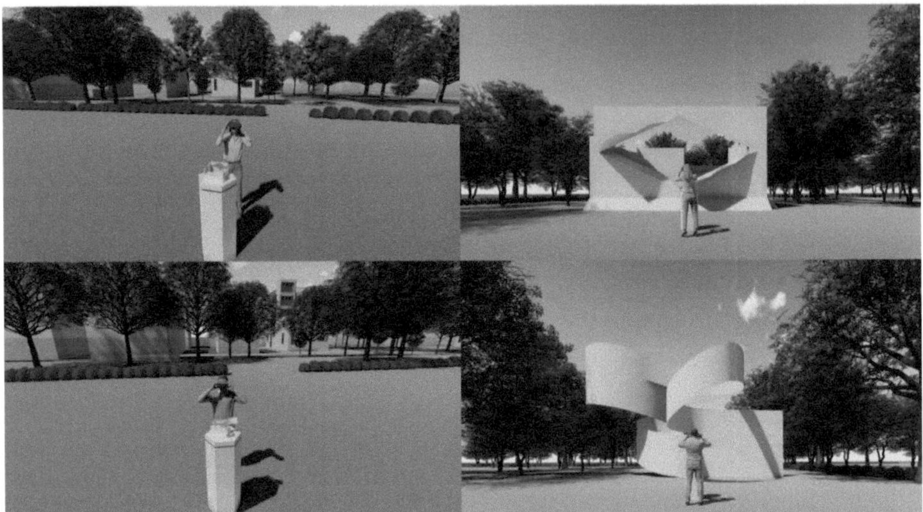

Fig. 2. Sensory Experience Phase.

Fig. 3. Contextual Application Segment.

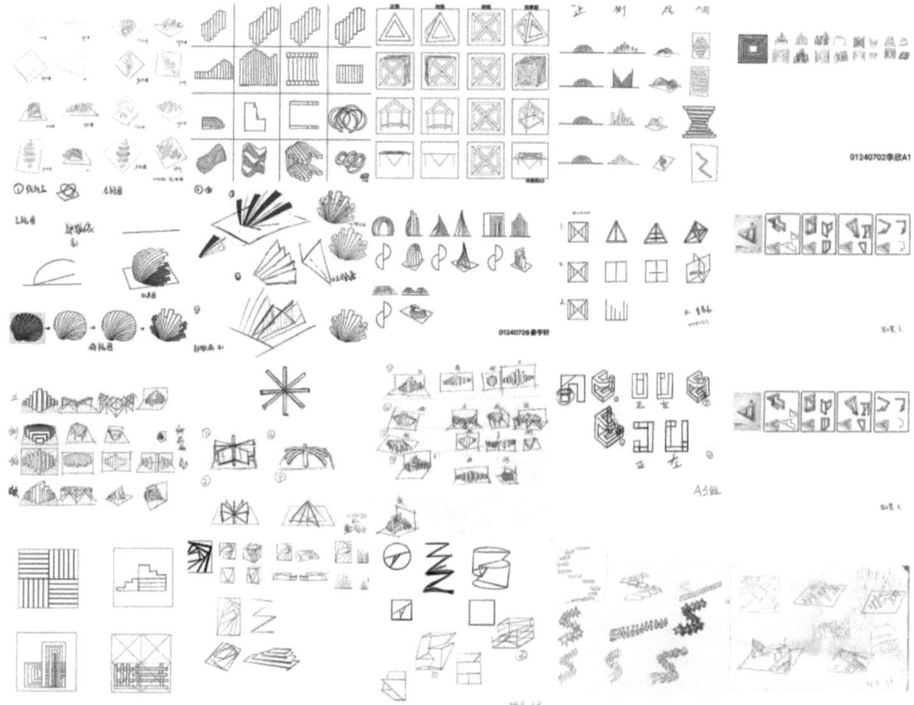

Fig. 4. Student Proposal Sketch.

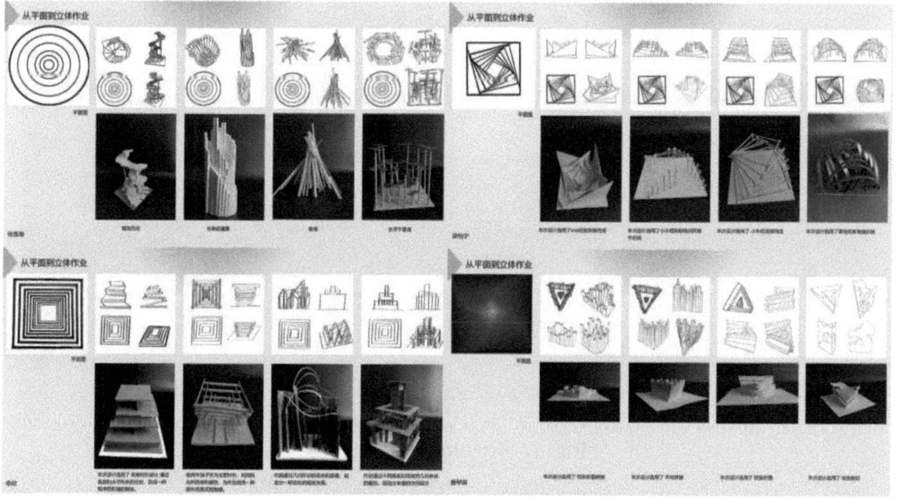

Fig. 5. Student Plan1.

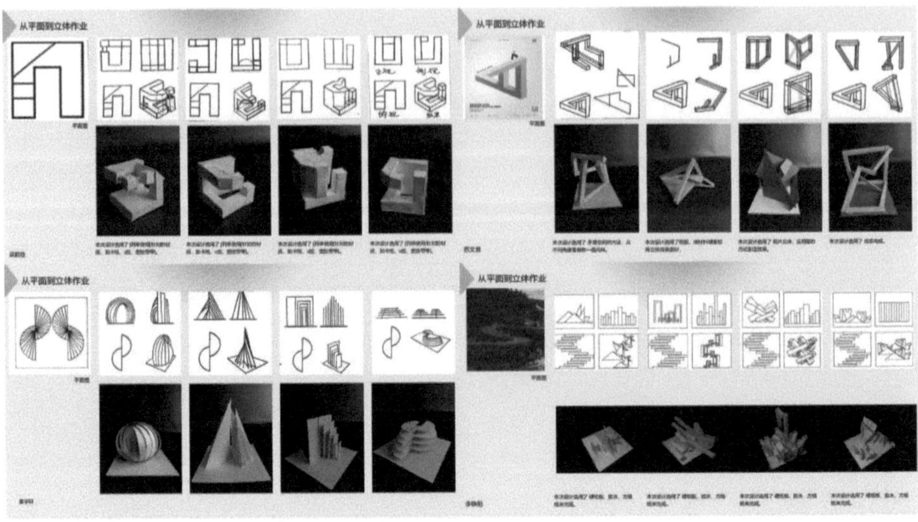

Fig. 6. Student Plan2.

Fig. 7. Simulation Diagram1.

Fig. 8. Simulation Diagram2.

4   Empirical Research and Result Validation

4.1   Research Design

Sample. This study selected 33 first-year students majoring in Fine Arts and Design from a comprehensive university in Guangdong as the research subjects. This group is at the initial stage of their professional studies, with similar knowledge foundations and yet to establish fixed learning patterns, which makes them highly adaptable to teaching methods. The students were randomly divided into an experimental group (16 individuals) and a control group (17 individuals) to compare the effectiveness of embodied cognitive teaching strategies versus traditional teaching models.

Tool. The research employs various tools to evaluate teaching effectiveness: measuring students' spatial rotation cognitive abilities regarding three-dimensional shapes through a psychological rotation task scale; examining students' orientation judgment and structural organization skills in three-dimensional space using a spatial positioning ability scale; and simultaneously utilizing VR equipment to create virtual space scenarios to assist students in immersive exploration and perception of three-dimensional shapes.

4.2   Key Research Findings

Experimental data indicate that embodied cognitive teaching strategies significantly enhance students' three-dimensional spatial cognition abilities: the overall scores of the experimental group increased from 9.91 before the intervention to 13.27, reflecting an improvement of 33.91%, while the control group's scores rose from 10.55 to 12.50, with an improvement of 18.48%. The enhancement in the experimental group is significantly superior to that of the control group. In the spatial visualization tests, the effect size for both groups was d = 0.917, which, based on effect size assessment criteria, indicates a medium to large difference between the two groups in this dimension, further validating the effectiveness of embodied cognitive teaching strategies.

4.3 Recommendations for Teaching Improvement

Expand the Sample to Cover Different Disciplines. The expanded research sample only selected 33 first-year students majoring in Fine Arts and Design from a comprehensive university in Guangdong. The sample size is relatively small, and the specific major may affect the generalizability of the research results. Future studies could broaden the sample scope to include students from different regions and various majors, in order to explore the application effects of embodied cognition theory in teaching more comprehensively.

Integrating AI Technology to Optimize Scenario Simulation. Despite the positive effects of embodied cognition theory in education, there remains room for further optimization. In terms of teaching content, AI technology can be integrated to enhance the richness of situational simulation cases, introducing more projects related to real-life situations and career development, enabling students to better apply their learned knowledge to future work. Additionally, leveraging AI technology to develop more interactive and engaging educational software can provide students with a more enriched learning experience.

5 Conclusions and Prospects

5.1 Research Conclusions

This study confirms that embodied cognition teaching strategies are highly effective in the instruction of 'Transformation from Two-Dimensional to Three-Dimensional Forms'. Experimental data indicates that the experimental group experienced an improvement of 33.91% in their scores, significantly higher than that of the control group. Moreover, students' abilities in spatial perception, hands-on practice, and innovative thinking have been effectively enhanced. The research has established a five-phase teaching model comprising 'Body Perception - Sensory Experience - Situational Application - Dynamic Interaction - Feedback Adjustment'. Through the organic integration of embodied operations and multidimensional perception, this model systematically promotes students' cognitive transformation from two-dimensional to three-dimensional thinking, providing a replicable practical paradigm for teaching three-dimensional spatial design in design-related disciplines.

5.2 Insufficiencies and Future Directions

The study has limitations such as a small sample size, short experimental duration, and high requirements for teaching resources. Future research can be deepened in three aspects: first, expanding the sample to include students from different regions, majors, and grades to enhance the generalizability of the conclusions; second, conducting long-term follow-up studies to assess the lasting impact of the strategies; and third, expanding interdisciplinary applications to explore the applicability of this theory in fields such as architectural design and engineering drawing, providing broader theoretical and practical support for educational reform.

Acknowledgments. We gratefully acknowledge the financial support from the following programs: Provincial-Level Top-Tier Offline Course (KA24YY044, 6040324137), 2024 Guang-dong Provincial Graduate Education Innovation Plan (2024SFKC_054), Guangzhou Academy of Fine Arts Graduate Demonstration Course Program, New Agricultural Science Teaching Re-search and Reform Practice Project at Zhongkai University of Agriculture and Engineering (PX-44231059), and Design Fundamentals Virtual Teaching and Research Office (ZG2023011).

Disclosure of Interests.. The authors have no competing interests to declare that are relevant to the content of this article.

References

1. Porat, R., Ceobanu, C.: The Role of Spatial Ability in Academic Success: The Impact of the Integrated Hybrid Training Program in Architecture and Engineering Higher Education. Educ. Sci. **14**(11), 1237 (2024)
2. Stefaniak, J.: The utility of design thinking to promote systemic instructional design practices in the workplace. TechTrends **64**(2), 202–210 (2020)
3. Moreira, M.: Making Design Education (Even More) Complex: Exploring complexity for an amplified mindset of design. Int. J. Art Des. Educ. **38**(4), 769–784 (2019)
4. Jin, Y., Lin, S., Zou, Z., et al.: On the Effective Integration of Visual Communication and Architectural Design. Earthq. Resistant Eng. Retrofitting **47**(01), 185 (2025)
5. Fan, Y.: Spatial and Plastic Thinking Construction: A Preliminary Exploration of Teaching Reform in Cross-Professional Design Foundation Courses. ZHUANGSHI (Art & Design) **05**, 119–123 (2024)
6. Shi, W., Ye, H.: Embodied Cognition: A Buddhist Perspective. Psychol. Explor. **30**(05), 15–19 (2010)
7. Ye, H.: The dilemma of mind-body dualism and the rise of embodied cognition research. Psychol. Sci. **34**(04), 999–1005 (2011)

The Use of Virtual Agents in Cybersecurity Education and Training - a Systematic Literature Review

Vanessa Roberts[(✉)] [iD] and Ricardo Gregorio Lugo [iD]

Tallinn University of Technology, Tallinn, Estonia
`vanessa.roberts@taltech.ee`

Abstract. Virtual agents (VA) are transforming the field of education and learning. Cybersecurity is a domain with an acknowledged skill gap as there is an urgent need to build competencies. Traditional learning approaches for obtaining cybersecurity skills are struggling to scale due to the shortage of trained personnel and the increasing number of cyber threats. Virtual agents can assist with the development of competencies as they can support decision-making and automation of processes related to cybersecurity. An obstacle in reaching this goal is the lack of a foundational understanding as to what kind of virtual agents exist for assisting cybersecurity skills learning, how they are implemented and what are the effects of the virtual agent. The aim of this study is to provide a foundational understanding of virtual agents for obtaining cybersecurity skills and knowledge to researchers and practitioners that would advance the field. To achieve this, a systematic literature review was conducted focusing on conference and journal publications within cybersecurity education. The PRISMA protocol was used to evaluate systematic literature reviews. The review findings reveal that there is a gap concerning empirical studies as a means to evaluate the impact of virtual agents for obtaining cybersecurity skills.

Keywords: virtual agents · systematic review · cybersecurity education and training

1 Introduction

Learning and educational technology are transforming to incorporate cutting edge technology, such as virtual (VR) and augmented reality (AR) and artificial intelligence (AI). Virtual Agents (VA) integrate these technologies, providing a digital character that can simulate aspects of human learning in an interactive environment. Cybersecurity is an area where there is a fundamental need to explore innovative educational technology to enhance skills and situational awareness. 2024 has seen exponential growth in cyberattacks, fuelled by increased geopolitical tensions and proliferation of cybercrime. These attacks have predominantly targeted critical infrastructure sectors, such as transport, finance and public administration (ENISA, 2024). The primary threats faced by these

H. Mori et al. (Eds.): HCII 2025, LNCS 16333, pp. 134–146, 2026.
https://doi.org/10.1007/978-3-032-12660-3_11

organisations are attacks which exploit weaknesses in the human aspects of the organisation. These include social engineering attacks which aim to manipulate users to download or interact with malicious system properties which would enable an attacker to access the victim's network and deliver malware, ransomware (remove or restrict access to systems) or steal data. A workforce which is situationally aware and skilled to detect and respond to cyber threats is essential. In this work, we are motivated to investigate VAs and their utility to cybersecurity.

To achieve this, we conduct a systematic literature review that investigates the types of VAs used and how they are utilised or can be utilised for cybersecurity situational awareness and skills development.

2 Background

2.1 Defining Virtual Agents

This paper will use the term Virtual Agents, (VAs) also referred in the literature as *pedagogical agents (PA), conversational agents (CA), embodied conversational agents (ECAs),* or *avatar-based agents (ABA)*—which are computer-generated characters designed to simulate aspects of human interaction in digital learning or communication environments (Martha & Santoso, 2019; Schroeder et al., 2015a; Bente et al., 2023). The term virtual agents will also encompass *virtual assistants and digital assistants* as noted in the literature where terms have been used interchangeably. These agents may appear as 2D or 3D characters and may often include verbal (spoken or written) and non-verbal (facial expressions, gestures, body language) cues to enhance their social presence and effectiveness. *Pedagogical agents* are typically goal-oriented and serve instructional roles such as mentors, facilitators, or motivators, and supporting learners by providing guidance, feedback, and encouragement (Martha & Santoso, 2019; Schroeder et al., 2015a). *Embodied conversational agents* differ by characterising human-like traits and are programmed to engage users in dialogue, using human-like speech and gestures, to convey emotion and intent (Schroeder et al., 2015a). Bente et al. (2023) defines that agents function within *avatar-mediated environments,* where their social cue intensity—such as facial responsiveness or gestural richness—can significantly influence user perceptions of trust, credibility, and realism. Together, these definitions underscore that virtual agents are not just functional tools, but socially and emotionally interactive entities designed to enhance learning, engagement, and user experience. Schroeder et al. (2015b) and Bente et al. (2023) provide support for Martha & Santoso (2019), particularly in relation to the use of pedagogical agents and social cues in digital environments.

Schroeder et al. (2015b) explored the impacts of different types of pedagogical agents on learning outcomes and found that agent realism and embodiment can positively influence user engagement and perceived learning, especially when agents convey social cues that simulate human interaction showing how there is a need for more naturalistic, socially engaging interactions in cybersecurity training tools. Similarly, Bente et al. (2023) investigated the role of social cue intensity in avatar-mediated communication and found that stronger social cues enhanced trust, credibility, and social presence. These results show that interventions must feel personal and trustworthy to be effective, particularly in countering social engineering (Martha & Santoso, 2019). These results also show the importance of designing interventions that leverage socially rich, human-like agents to enhance user engagement and behavioural change—highlighting the role of affective and social design elements in training efficacy.

Cognitive Aspects of Virtual Agents. A growing body of research highlights the potential of virtual agents to enhance learning outcomes and engagement across diverse educational contexts (Jondahl & Mørch, 2002). Social cues and emotional expressiveness can influence learners' affective responses and engagement, leading to improved learning outcomes. Petersen et al. (2021) tested the use of virtual museum guides in VR and found that agents with high behavioural realism significantly improved conceptual learning (Cohen's $d = 0.7$), although they could negatively impact factual retention suggesting that PAs may be particularly suited to abstract, concept-driven instruction rather than detail-heavy factual recall. Jondahl and Mørch (2002) tested PAs in collaborative settings using the Wizard-of-Oz method and showed that PAs acting as collaboration agents improved group awareness and task division, but did also find unanticipated social effects, such as exclusion of group members. Petersen et al. (2021) and Schroeder and Gotch (2015) further demonstrated that perceived realism, especially through embodied cues, such as gestures and facial expressions, significantly contributes to social presence and learning engagement. Together, these studies converge on the idea that the effectiveness of VAs depends heavily on the match between their design features and instructional goals. While Martha and Santoso (2019) emphasize generalizable design principles across media, more recent empirical work in immersive environments (e.g., Petersen et al., 2021) reveals nuanced trade-offs that need to be considered when deploying VAs in VR or cybersecurity training settings.

In a recent randomised control experiment (Nguyen-Thinh & Wartschinski's, 2018), 74 participants were divided between a group using the dialogue-based agent LIZA and a control group using a non-interactive online course. Across the seven reasoning tasks, learners who interacted with LIZA consistently outperformed the control group. For example, in tasks like regression to the mean, LIZA users improved their scores by 43% on average, compared to just 13% in the control group—a difference that translates to roughly three to four more students out of ten answering correctly after training. In tasks like covariation detection and the Wason Selection Task, interacting with LIZA led to gains of 17% compared to minimal or even negative change in the control group. While some effects were small (Cohen's $d = .14-.21$) such as for the Gambler's Fallacy and Sunk Cost Fallacy, this still amounted to nearly twice the gain seen in the passive learning condition (control). These results indicate that even brief interactions with a conversational agent can lead to meaningful improvements in reasoning performance across a range of cognitive tasks. But there are many limitations to this study. Besides using a small, non-representative sample, the study used a single-item test measures per task, which reduces its reliability.

Additionally, there was no follow-up to assess if there was long-term retention. Looking further into the application of virtual agents and how they enhance competency development, there are studies that have investigated virtual agents supporting digital literacy (Sriwisathiyakun & Dhamanitayakul, 2022), on communication through language (Istrate, 2019), on collaboration (David et al., 2022), on problem solving (Winkler et al., 2021).

2.2 Cybersecurity

Cybersecurity is a predominant area where VAs can be used to enhance situational awareness and develop skills.

Growing Threat Environments. Cyber-attacks to critical infrastructure are growing in prevalence. A recent report of the cyber threat landscape in the EU by ENISA revealed the most prevalent cyber threats as ransomware, malware, social engineering and information manipulation (ENISA, 2024).

In the example of drinking water supply and distribution, which is a highly critical sector and part of critical infrastructure, ENISA´ incident reporting tool (CIRAS, 2023) shows 47% of 141 reported incidents from 2020-2024 are from malicious actions. The categorisation attributing to technical causes of the incident under the ENISA incident reporting mechanism is difficult to attribute due to sensitive nature of cyber breaches, however, ransomware, malware and phishing are clearly attack types which dominate. Social engineering techniques, such as phishing, are used by attackers to exploit vulnerabilities of the human aspects to deliver ransomware and malware. ENISA identifies that the assets impacted by these malicious actions are mostly OT (31%) and critical supporting IT infrastructure related (CIRAS, 2023). These assets control the water supply and distribution operations and are therefore highly critical for the sector. The ENISA incident report highlights how vulnerabilities of the human aspects can be exploited by a cyber-attack causing cascading affects into the technical systems. Under reporting needs to be considered as the actual number of incidents may be higher.

Lack of Trained Personnel. Considering the growing threat environment, globally, there is a concern as to a lack of cybersecurity skills in critical infrastructure areas, especially to confront sector specific issues, such as ageing infrastructure and a lack of situational awareness to cyber threats emanating from digitised networks.

Periodic security awareness and tailored trainings is recommended (ENISA, 2024) for different departments within the company considering the most recent trends and evolving threats being critical for the personnel to possess the knowledge and skills to perform their tasks in a way that cybersecurity is kept in mind. In other words, as the attacks are reoccurring, but also evolving in ways that it keeping getting harder to detect them, in there is a need to teach in a way that supports knowledge retention also months after the training.

In addition, considering the advancements related to Industry 4.0, more emphasis is recommended to be put on introducing cyber-culture and cyber-hygiene to OT personnel while the IT personnel would require more on safety-culture and safety-hygiene (ENISA, 2019).

There is a need for collective efforts from a range of stakeholders to enable further continuous education and training to the employees and management to enhance resilience towards cyber-attacks.

2.3 Research Gaps and Defining Questions for Current Study

Currently, there is the lack of a foundational understanding as to what kind of virtual agents exist for assisting cybersecurity skills learning, how they are implemented and what are the effects of the virtual agent.

The aim of this study is to provide a foundational understanding of VAs for obtaining cybersecurity skills and knowledge to researchers and practitioners that would advance the field. This systematic literature focuses on the effects of virtual agent in cybersecurity education. The reporting of this systematic review was guided by the standards of the Preferred Reporting Items for Systematic Review and Meta-Analysis (PRISMA) Statement (Moher et al., 2009).

There are virtual agents that will act as teachers by instructing, but the focus of this paper are virtual agents that help users learn through interaction.

The focus is on 3 Research Questions (RQ):

RQ1: What type of Virtual Agents are in use?

RQ2: How are Virtual Agents implemented for cybersecurity education?

RQ3: What is the effect of the Virtual Agent compared to the traditional way of obtaining cybersecurity education?

3   Method

The systematic review was carried out according to the PRISMA guidelines (Moher et al., 2009). We reviewed original research articles with experimental research design that was human-centered and used VAs for obtaining cybersecurity skills.

3.1   Review Procedure

The review procedure was conducted as follows. First, identify original research from journals and conferences on the topic of humans interacting with virtual agents. Second, adjust the query with experts. Third, categorize the publications according to type, area of research, type of virtual agents, research design and results. Fourth, summarise selected articles. Finally, synthesis and discussion on findings following thoughts on future research.

3.2   Literature Collection Methodology

For the retrieval of the different papers, inclusion and exclusion criteria were defined to analyze the papers relevant to the needs of this article (Table 1).

Databases, ACM Digital Library (ACM), Database IEEE Xplore (IEEE), Springer Publishing Platform (Springer), Taylor & Francis Online (T & F) are used as a source to conduct research as the articles there are mostly peer-reviewed on information technology and social sciences. The last search was done on April 1st, 2025.

The following query was used:

("virtual assistant" OR "digital assistant" OR "intelligent agent" OR "dialogue agent" OR "conversational agent" OR "pedagogical agent") AND (education OR training OR learning) AND (cybersecurity OR "cyber security") AND experiment

The following Table 2 displays the consolidated results of the query search.

Considering the inclusion and exclusion criteria, the selection process took place by two authors. The article authors worked independently to decide based on the abstract what kind of a study it was. Then the authors also worked together on decisions based

Table 1. Inclusion and exclusion criteria

Number	Inclusion criteria	Exclusion criteria
1	Articles in all languages	
2	Articles published 2014-2024	
3	Peer-reviewed journal articles and conference proceedings	Thesis/dissertations, reports etc.
4	Experimental research design	
5	Articles that focused on experimentation with humans and virtual agents in cybersecurity training and education	

Table 2. Consolidated results of the query search

Number	Database	Publications
1	ACM	27
2	IEEE	42
3	Springer	327
4	T & F	21

on the abstract (and if needed, the full paper) understanding the design of the study and if it was included or not in this review.

Abstracts which left three possible considerations:

- The ones to include (those which meet all inclusion criteria).
- The ones to exclude (those which meet at least one of the inclusion criteria) and
- the ones that the authors were in doubt about, confirmation from the other author was asked.

To reduce the bias in doing a systematic literature review, after the initial screening, the authors worked together to identify possible relevant articles by screening again the selected titles and full articles. Further, the authors consulted independent experts from the institution's library and information management department to ensure the quality of the literature search process.

3.3 Descriptive Information

Methods of collecting secondary data from publications were used from journals and conference papers. Area of the paper was mapped, also which VA technology was used in the study, what type of research design the paper had and what were the effects. Figure 1 displays the flow of the literature review process from identification to the final list of included papers. Due to the low number of articles, after inclusion and exclusion criteria were applied, all articles were screened manually based on abstracts, so there was no removing of duplicates.

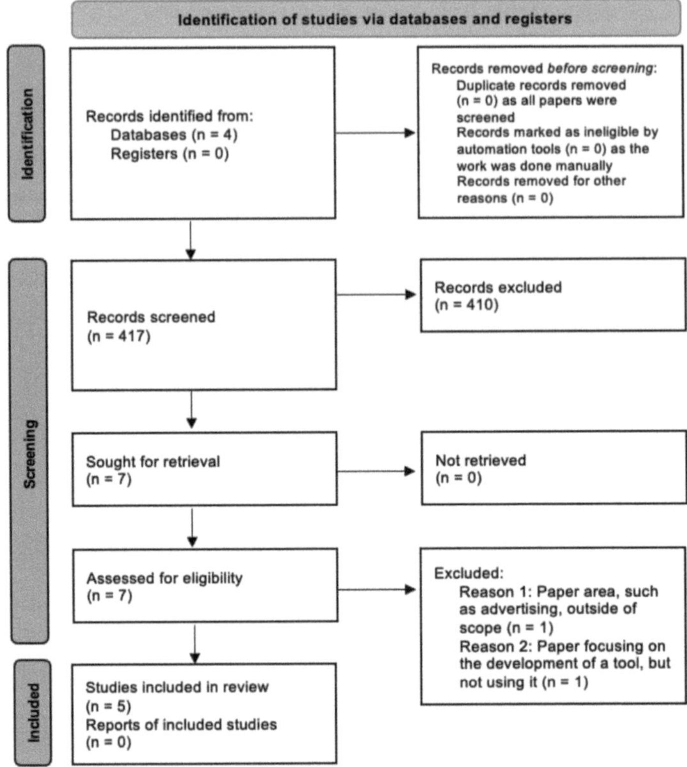

Fig. 1. Flow diagram, PRISMA diagram

Due to the low number of articles, all articles were screened manually based on abstracts, so there was no removing of duplicates.

4   Analysis of Results of the Literature Review

The literature exhibited a diverse range of VA technologies and utilized both qualitative and quantitative methods for assessing their use. The following Table 3 displays the studies analysed in our literature review.

Quantitative Results. One quantitative study—Sriwisathiyakun & Dhamanitayakul (2022) was included in the synthesis. Table following 4 presents the design, effect sizes, and approximate conversions to Cohen's d for each quantitative study included in the review. The study explored the use of immersive or intelligent digital tools that were designed for content delivery, foster deeper cognitive and emotional engagement with learning or persuasive content, and to support learning-related outcomes (Table 4).

Table 3. Study type with details.

Author (Year)	Study Type	Technology Tested	Participants (*n*)
Adinolf et al. (2020)	Qualitative	Digital agent in VR centred around cybersecurity training	24
Dickelman & Greenberg (2024)	Qualitative/Narrative Review	AI integration across early to adult learning	Not applicable
Şimşek (2025)	Qualitative	General AI tools in education	6
Sriwisathiyakun & Dhamanitayakul (2022)	Quantitative	A chatbot as a type of an intelligent conversational agent in education	422
Zhong et al. (2024)	Qualitative	AI-assisted learning tools (e.g., ChatGPT)	20

Table 4. The design, effect sizes with details

Study	Design	Effect Size(s)	p-value (s)	Cohen's *d*
Sriwisathiyakun & Dhamanitayakul (2022)	Expert review	Not given	Not reported	Not reported

Sriwisathiyakun & Dhamanitayakul (2022) conducted a research and development design to create and evaluate an intelligent chatbot—*"Senior See Net"*—aimed at enhancing digital literacy among older adults in Thailand. A total of 422 senior citizens participated in the initial needs assessment, which identified widespread smartphone and platform use but only moderate levels of digital literacy. Based on these findings, the chatbot was designed using the Software Development Life Cycle (SDLC) model and implemented via Google Dialogflow within the LINE messaging app. The content focused on five core digital literacy domains: Access, Analyze, Evaluate, Participate, and Act. It included interactive features, multimedia lessons, and tools for validating fake news, scheduling, and safety. Rather than testing learning outcomes with inferential statistics, the study relied on expert evaluations to assess the tool's quality and relevance. Experts rated the chatbot's media quality, accessibility, and functionality very highly, with average ratings exceeding 4.5 on a 5-point scale.

Quantitative Studies – Methological Aspects. The quantitative study findings warrant cautious interpretation due to methodological limitations and the risk of overestimating effects in single-study contexts.

Sriwisathiyakun & Dhamanitayakul (2022) developed and implemented a chatbot intervention for older adults but did not report any inferential statistical testing. While expert review was used to assess media quality, accessibility, and content relevance, the study lacked empirical outcome data, such as pre/post measures or user-level digital literacy improvements. As a result, conclusions about the effectiveness of the intervention remain speculative.

While the study offers promising insights into the potential of AI-based tools, their methodological designs—particularly the absence of control conditions, longitudinal data, and robust outcome measures—limit the generalizability and evidential strength of the findings. These limitations underscore the need for more rigorously controlled evaluations in future research.

Qualitative Results. The following Table 5 summarizes key qualitative themes and their interpretations from the included qualitative and mixed-methods studies.

Table 5. Table captions should be placed above the tables.

Study	Themes	Meaning/Interpretation
Adinolf et al. (2020)	Relational connection, agent-human interaction, engagement	Use of digital agents fosters trust and deeper engagement through simulated social presence and personalized interaction.
Dickelman & Greenberg (2024)	AI in lifelong learning, media literacy, early childhood integration	Early integration of AI shapes cognitive development. Advocated cross-disciplinary AI literacy and ethical alignment across educational stages.
Şimşek (2025)	Pre-service teacher attitudes, ethical awareness, AI perception	Explored qualitative insights on ethical concerns and conceptual understanding of AI among teacher trainees.
Zhong et al. (2024)	AI utility, ethical ambiguity, workload implications	Teachers found AI useful but raised concerns about ethical implications and increased responsibilities. Reflected duality of opportunity and anxiety.

Qualitative Studies. For continuity in interaction, the value of social presence and emotional responsiveness, and a strong preference for agent behaviours that mirrored supportive, conversational human dialogue. These design-oriented insights on how relational dynamics within virtual agents could foster trust and deeper learning engagement in immersive contexts.

Şimşek (2025) conducted a qualitative case study designed to explore how pre-service teachers conceptualize artificial intelligence in educational settings. The study involved six participants from a teacher education program, and data were gathered through a multi-phase process combining interviews with visual elicitation techniques. The research was structured to not only capture participants' knowledge and perceptions of AI, but also to probe their emotional and ethical associations with the concept. The main data collection strategy was the use of domain prompts, a reflective exercise in which participants were asked to define what "AI in education" meant to them using keywords or short phrases. These responses were then transformed into individual word clouds, visually representing the most salient concepts each participant associated with AI. This visual artifact served as both data and stimulus: following the word cloud creation, participants took part in semi-structured interviews where they elaborated on the meanings behind their chosen terms and discussed how they envisioned AI influencing teaching and learning and three primary domains were identified: conceptual understanding, emotional tone, and perceived professional impact. For conceptual understanding, participants described AI as a tool that could support personalization, automate feedback, and potentially serve as an assistive tutor. However, most acknowledged an uncertain understanding of how these technologies functioned. The emotional tone domain identified ambivalence with terms like "future," "unknown," "help," "threat," and "replacement" were commonly featured in the word clouds, reflecting a dual sentiment of intrigue and caution. Lastly, in terms of professional impact, participants expressed concerns about teacher autonomy, ethical use of data, and the preparedness of future educators to integrate such technologies meaningfully.

Zhong et al. (2024) conducted a qualitative interview study with 20 primary and secondary school teachers to examine their perspectives on AI-assisted learning tools. The study was structured around in-depth, open-ended interviews that allowed participants to elaborate on their experiences with and expectations of AI in educational contexts. The findings were synthesized into several key themes: (1) AI was frequently regarded as a useful tool for personalized instruction and workload reduction, (2) ethical ambiguity emerged as a prominent concern, especially around student data privacy and decision-making transparency, and (3) teachers expressed ambivalence about the extent to which AI should replace or augment human interaction in the classroom. Zhong's study painted a nuanced picture of educators navigating the tension between technological promise and pedagogical responsibility.

Dickelman and Greenberg (2024) contributed a narrative review that examined the developmental implications of introducing AI in early learning environments. Drawing on a wide range of sources—including expert interviews, policy analyses, and empirical literature—the authors explored how exposure to AI technologies from an early age might influence cognitive development, media literacy, and learning trajectories extending into higher education and the workplace. The article was structured around a central inquiry: how can early experiences with AI be aligned with performance-centred and ethical learning goals across the lifespan? The review emphasized the importance of human-centred AI design that integrates insights from neuroscience, cognitive psychology, and pedagogy. One notable contribution was the framing of AI tools as part of a broader media ecology, where their role is not only technological but also has social and developmental implications.

The qualitative studies included in this review—Adinolf et al. (2020), Şimşek (2025), and Zhong et al. (2024)—demonstrated adherence to established qualitative research principles, which enhances the credibility and trustworthiness of their findings. All three studies clearly articulated their research aims and justified the use of qualitative designs to explore subjective experiences and perceptions related to AI and virtual agents. Data collection methods—ranging from participatory workshops to semi-structured interviews and domain-prompt activities—were well-suited to the exploratory nature of their inquiries. For example, Adinolf et al. (2020) incorporated iterative, co-creative workshops that allowed participants to engage meaningfully with the design and evaluation of a virtual agent, while Şimşek (2025) triangulated interview data with participant-generated word clouds, offering a multimodal lens on conceptual and emotional responses to AI. Zhong et al. (2024) employed in-depth interviews with a selected sample of educators, allowing for saturation of themes related to ethical ambiguity and pedagogical responsibility. Although the narrative review by Dickelman and Greenberg (2024) did not include original empirical data, it demonstrated theoretical triangulation by synthesizing insights across disciplines and data sources, contributing to the conceptual depth of the review.

5 Discussion

Our systematic literature review on virtual agents in cybersecurity education and training, from which out of 417 records from 4 databases, 5 papers are analysed in detail in this work, showed that there is a gap concerning empirical studies as a means to evaluate the impact of virtual agents for obtaining cybersecurity skills. This contrasts with the rise of using new technologies that educational technology is aiming to incorporate, such as AI, VR and AR.

Based on the analysed academic articles, this study is able to partially answer the research questions. Only 1 qualitative study presented the virtual agent in the area of cybersecurity education. The study conducted by Adinolf et al. (2020) finds that the use of a digital (pedagogical) agent as a learning companion in the context of cybersecurity training may lead to better interactions and outcomes. The study also highlights that the partner agent does not need to be in human form, but can be a anthropomorphic robot or an animal. Due to the nature of the study, assessing the effect of virtual agents in the field defined in this study was not possible.

To address the limitations of this study, the number of studies analysed, the sample in studies and method should be addressed. The number of suitable studies and the sample sizes in studies are very small, so no generalisations can be made. While experimental design is considered appropriate for research that aims to understand the effect of the tool, not reported effect sizes make it impossible to generalize the study results. Also, the most recent articles from 2025 have not been included but could be a consideration for the future when conducting an updated systematic literature review. Finally, this article does include a Risk of Bias (RoB) process that aims to consider the risk of bias in the findings but is an opportunity for the authors when writing a journal article.

While we believe these limitations have not impacted the primary outcome of the study, for future work, it is important to consider experimental design for conducting studies to measure the effect of the virtual agents.

5.1 Future research direction

First and foremost, there exists a sparsity of research which use both qualitative and quantitative research methods (especially experimental design) to evaluate VAs.

In addition, there is potential of integrating of VAs into workforce skills frameworks. As the (European Cybersecurity Skills Framework (ECSF) (2025)) and The Digital Competence Framework for Citizens (DigComp) (2025)) address different aspects of digital skills, they have the potential to give valuable input on aspects where virtual agents can help. Moreover, for future research, skills-up platforms can employ virtual agents guiding the users in their skill development.

Finally, there is a lack of sector specific skills development. However, with the help of virtual agents supporting training related to a specific sector and the necessary skills, this would enable to enhance skills to protect the sector more effectively.

6 Conclusion

The study showed that there is a gap when it comes to empirical studies as a way of evaluating the impact of virtual agents for obtaining cybersecurity skills.

Firstly, this is an opportunity for researchers interested in understanding the effects of virtual agents, to invite them to conduct research on this. We recommend future studies to consider experimental design to be able to measure the effect of the virtual agents.

Secondly, if ENISA or any other company were to adopt VAs (including assistants) for cybersecurity education and training, then the VAs need to be rigorously tested and evaluated before implementing.

Acknowledgments. This study is conducted as part of the ATHENA project (DEP: Project 101127970). In addition, it was supported by the EU Horizon 2020 project MariCybERA (agreement No. 952360).

Disclosure of Interests.. The authors have no competing interests to declare that are relevant to the content of this article.

References

Adinolf, S., Wyeth, P., Brown, R., Simpson, L.: Near and Dear: Designing Relatable VR Agents for Training Games. In: Australasian Computer-Human Interaction Conference, pp. 413–425. ACM (2020). https://doi.org/10.1145/3441000.3441007

Bente, G., Schmälzle, R., Jahn, N.T., Schaaf, A.: Measuring the effects of co-location on emotion perception in shared virtual environments: An ecological perspective. Front. Virtual Reality **4**, 13 (2023). https://doi.org/10.3389/frvir.2023.1032510

David, B., Chalon, R., Zhang, X.: Virtual assistants (chatbots) as help to teachers in collaborative learning environment. In: International Conference on Interactive Collaborative Learning (pp. 135–146). Cham: Springer International Publishing (2022)

DigiComp Framework | European Commission. https://joint-research-centre.ec.europa.eu/pro jects-and-activities/education-and-training/digital-transformation-education/digital-compet ence-framework-citizens-digcomp/digcomp-framework_en. Accessed 25 May 2025

Dickelman, G., Greenberg.: AI in Early Learning and How it Affects Higher Education and Workplace Learning (2024). 10.1007/978-3-031-72430-5_12

European Cybersecurity Skills Framework (ECSF) - User Manual | ENISA. https://www.enisa.europa.eu/topics/skills-and-competences/skills-development/european-cybersecurity-skills-framework-ecsf. Accessed 25 May 2025

Industry 4.0 - Cybersecurity Challenges and Recommendations | ENISA (2019). https://www.enisa.europa.eu/publications/industry-4-0-cybersecurity-challenges-and-recommendations. Accessed 25 May 2025

ENISA Threat Landscape 2024 | ENISA (2024). https://www.enisa.europa.eu/publications/enisa-threat-landscape-2024. Accessed 25 May 2025

Incident reporting CIRAS | ENISA (2023). https://ciras.enisa.europa.eu. Accessed 25 May 2025

Istrate, A.M.: The impact of the virtual assistant (VA) on language classes. In: Conference Proceedings of eLearning and Software for Education, Vol. 15, No. 01, pp. 296–301. Carol I National Defence University Publishing House, Romania (2019). https://doi.org/10.12753/2066-026X-19-040

Jondahl, S., Mørch, A.I.: Simulating pedagogical agents in a virtual learning environment. In: Proceedings of the Conference on Computer Support for Collaborative Learning: Foundations for a CSCL Community (CSCL '02). International Society of the Learning Sciences, 531–532 (2002)

Le, N.-T., Wartschinski, L.: A Cognitive Assistant for improving human reasoning skills. Int. J Hum Comput Stud. / Int. J. Man Mach. Stud. **117**, 45–54 (2018). https://doi.org/10.1016/J.IJHCS.2018.02.005

Martha, A.S.D., Santoso, H.B.: The design and impact of the pedagogical agent: A systematic literature review. J. Educ. Online **16**, 15 (2019). https://doi.org/10.9743/JEO.2019.16.1.8

Moher, D., et al.: Preferred Reporting Items for Systematic Reviews and Meta-Analysis. PRISMA Statement. PLOS Med. **6**, e1000097 (2009). https://doi.org/10.1371/journal.pmed.1000097

Petersen, G.B., Mottelson, A., Makransky, G.: Pedagogical Agents in Educational VR: An in the Wild Study (2021). https://doi.org/10.1145/3411764.3445760

Schroeder, N.L., Adesope, O.O.: Impacts of pedagogical agent gestures on social presence, cognitive load, and learning outcomes. Comput. Educ. **91**, 56–72 (2015). https://doi.org/10.1016/j.compedu.2015.08.004

Schroeder, N.L., Gotch, C.M.: Emotional design in multimedia learning: Effects of shape and color on affect and learning. Learn. Instr. **44**, 74–84 (2015). https://doi.org/10.1016/j.learninstruc.2016.03.005

Sriwisathiyakun, K., Dhamanitayakul, C.: Enhancing digital literacy with an intelligent conversational agent for senior citizens in Thailand. Educ. Inform. Technol. **27**, 6251–6271 (2022). https://doi.org/10.1007/s10639-021-10862-z

Şimşek, N.: Integration of ChatGPT in mathematical story-focused 5E lesson planning: Teachers and pre-service teachers' interactions with ChatGPT. Educ. Inf. Technol. (2025). https://doi.org/10.1007/s10639-024-13258-x

Winkler, R., Söllner, M., Leimeister, J.M.: Enhancing Problem-Solving Skills with Smart Personal Assistant Technology. Comput. Educ. **165**, 104148 (2021). https://doi.org/10.1016/J.COMPEDU.2021.104148

Zhong, T., Zhu, G., Hou, C., Wang, Y., Fan, X.: The influences of ChatGPT on undergraduate students' demonstrated and perceived interdisciplinary learning. Educ. Inform. Technol. (2024). https://doi.org/10.1007/s10639-024-12787-9

Impact of Virtual Natural Environments on Workers' Creativity and Workload

Ibuki Yoshida[1], Hiroyuki Kuraoka[2] (iD), Jun Ito[2], Shinji Miyake[1] (iD), and Daiji Kobayashi[2(✉)] (iD)

[1] Graduate of Chitose Institute of Science and Technology, Hokkaido, Japan
[2] Chitose Institute of Science and Technology, Hokkaido, Japan
{d-kobaya,m2240500}@photon.chitose.ac.jp

Abstract. Recently, virtual reality (VR) technology has evolved beyond mere visual experience to become a tool that influences creativity and cognitive ability. Its immersive nature is increasingly utilized and studied in fields such as education, healthcare, and office work. Recent studies suggest that VR environments can enhance creativity, particularly when simulating natural settings. Ichimura (2023) found that VR platforms with natural landscapes, such as beaches, boost divergent thinking. Similarly, Nanjappan et al. (2023) and Li et al. (2022) demonstrated that nature-inspired VR environments enhance creativity more effectively than urban VR settings. However, the cognitive workload for creative tasks in VR has not been fully explored. This study investigated the effects of natural VR environments on creativity and workload using divergent thinking tasks and subjective evaluations. A total of 36 male university students experienced three conditions: a real office (CTRL), virtual office (VR), and virtual natural landscape (VR-N). They performed two tasks: the alternative uses task (AUT) and the creative uses task (CUT). The results demonstrated that CTRL conditions led to higher elaboration scores in the AUT, whereas the VR conditions enhanced flexibility and fluency in the CUT. Subjective assessments indicated higher eyestrain and mental workload under the VR conditions but reduced discomfort under the VR-N conditions. Future studies should explore different work environments and tasks to further understand the impact of VR on creativity and workload.

Keywords: Creativity · Virtual Reality · Immersive Nature · Office Work

1 Introduction

Recently, urbanization and advancements in digital technology have led to a decline in opportunities for human interaction with nature. Simultaneously, numerous studies have demonstrated the beneficial effects of natural environments on human health and cognitive function [1–4]. One theory that explains restorative effects in natural environments, as demonstrated in these studies, is the attention restoration theory (ART) by Kaplan (1995) [5]. The ART suggests that attention should be classified into two categories. The first involves involuntary attention. This type does not require effort to focus on interesting or important stimuli. The second type of attention is directed. This type requires

H. Mori et al. (Eds.): HCII 2025, LNCS 16333, pp. 147–159, 2026.
https://doi.org/10.1007/978-3-032-12660-3_12

focusing on things that are not particularly interesting. Furthermore, in ART, four elements are considered important for promoting recovery from fatigue caused by directed attention: being away, extent, fascination, and compatibility. Previous studies indicate that natural environments have restorative effects, which can be explained by the fact that they are rich in these elements. Additionally, several studies have shown that natural environments not only enhance cognitive function but also human performance, such as creativity. Konishi (2023) examined the effects of natural and office environments on participants' creativity and psychological states under real conditions and found that creativity scores were higher in natural environments than in office environments [6].

Recently, the utilization of virtual reality (VR) has progressed in various fields such as healthcare and education. Studies on creativity have reported the effects of simulated natural environments on the creative thinking of the participants. Ichimura (2023) demonstrated that highly immersive VR platforms, such as head-mounted displays (HMDs), in conjunction with open and natural environments such as beaches, can effectively enhance divergent thinking [7]. Similarly, Nanjappan et al. (2023) highlighted the potential of nature-inspired and familiar environments for enhancing individual creativity [8]. Furthermore, Li et al. (2022) demonstrated that restorative virtual environments featuring natural elements, such as forests, elicit greater improvements in creativity than virtual environments replicating urban settings [9]. These studies have revealed that virtual environments that simulate natural scenery enhance the creativity of workers. However, it has been highlighted that daily and long-term use of a VR device can cause symptoms such as increased fatigue and VR sickness and reduce productivity [10]. This study aimed to investigate the effects of natural environments in virtual spaces on creativity and workload in creative tasks.

2   Method

2.1   Participants

A total of 36 healthy male students with a mean age of 21.1 ± 0.2 years participated in the study. This study was reviewed and approved by the Research Ethics Committee of the Chitose Institute of Science and Technology (Approval No. 2024-4), and informed consent was obtained from all participants.

2.2   Experimental Conditions

The experiment was conducted under three conditions sequentially: a real desk in an office environment (CTRL), a virtual environment simulating a CTRL setting (VR), and a virtual environment simulating a natural landscape (VR-N). These scenes are illustrated in Fig. 1.

Fig. 1. CTRL condition (left panel), VR condition (center panel), and VR-N condition (right panel).

2.3 Procedure

The experiment was conducted with one participant at a time. The experimental procedure is illustrated in Fig. 2. After explaining the experiment, participants were instructed to perform the experimental tasks. They then completed the subjective feeling of fatigue (SFF) test and performed experimental task 1 for 9 min. Next, the participants responded to the SFF, flow short scale (FSS), and NASA Task Load Index (NASA-TLX); performed experimental task 2 at 9 min; and completed the SFF, FSS, and NASA-TLX once again. Finally, interviews were conducted. Additionally, when using the VR device (VR, VR-N), the participants responded to the simulator of sickness questionnaire (SSQ) before and after each task.

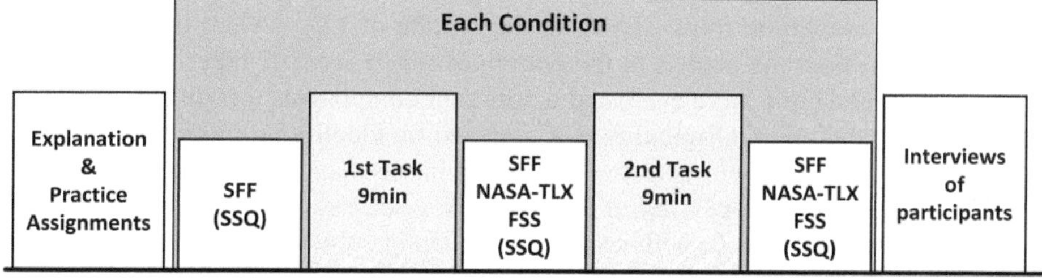

Fig. 2. Experimental procedure. SSQ was administered exclusively under conditions utilizing virtual environments.

2.4 Divergent Thinking Task

In this study, we employed two types of divergent thinking tasks to evaluate creativity: divergent and convergent. As Guilford argued, divergent thinking is essential for creative cognition, and tasks designed to elicit divergent thinking, where individuals generate logically possible and diverse ideas as they can from given information, are considered suitable for measuring creativity [11]. Tasks assessing divergent thinking are widely used, including the alternative uses task (AUT) and Torrance Tests of Creative Thinking (TTCT). In the experiment, the AUT was selected as one of the tasks. This decision was made because the TTCT includes both figural and verbal tasks, which may require a significant amount of time to complete. Given that this study involved three experimental conditions, it was determined that the TTCT would impose a substantial burden on participants. Several previous studies on creativity have used the AUT. Therefore, the AUT was adopted in this study to facilitate comparisons with previous research and to support the theoretical discussions.

The AUT is a divergent thinking task proposed by Guilford [12]. This is a method of evaluating divergent creative thinking, wherein participants are requested to propose as many alternative uses for a single object. In this study, the participants were presented with three objects under each experimental condition, with a time limit of 3 min allocated for each object. Under the CTRL condition, cardboard, swim ring, and slippers were presented; under the VR condition, iron, water bottle, and scourer were presented; and under the VR-N condition, a flying pan, hanger, and boot were presented. The difficulty of the objects was adjusted to be equivalent across conditions through preliminary experiments. The participants recorded their responses to the tasks on paper.

In addition, the creative uses task (CUT) was selected for the second task. This newly developed task was designed specifically for the present study. Previous research suggests that extensive prior knowledge can impede creativity. Consequently, the AUT, which prompts participants to generate ideas related to familiar everyday objects, may introduce cognitive biases. The CUT was developed and implemented to mitigate this effect. While its fundamental procedure aligns with that of the AUT, the CUT differs in the type of objects presented. Instead of familiar items, it utilizes novel 3D objects created in Blender, featuring unfamiliar and abstract forms. To facilitate recognition of their shapes, these objects are presented in videos alternating between rotation and still frames.

Under the CTRL condition, the objects depicted at the top of Fig. 3 were presented; under the VR condition, those shown in the middle of Fig. 3 were used; and under the VR-N condition, the objects at the bottom of Fig. 3 were displayed. Responses to both the AUT and CUT were evaluated across four components: originality, flexibility, fluency, and elaboration. Originality was assessed by identifying infrequent responses relative to the entire dataset. Responses occurring in less than 5% of cases were assigned 1 point, whereas those appearing in less than 1% of cases received 2 points; all other responses were scored as 0, with scores subsequently summed. Flexibility was determined based on the number of distinct response categories, excluding overlapping classifications. Fluency reflected the total number of responses, including those excluded owing to excessive abstraction, infeasibility, or ambiguity. Elaboration was quantified by calculating the number of words per response.

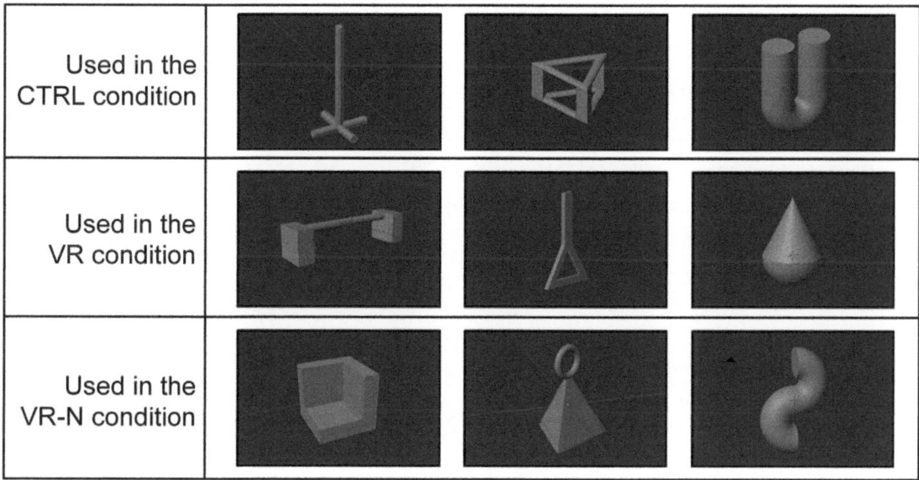

Fig. 3. Objects of CUT.

2.5 Subjective Assessments

The SFF evaluates changes in fatigue associated with a task over time. The participants responded to 25 questions on a 5-point scale. The 25 questions were grouped into five categories: drowsiness, instability, uneasiness, local pain or dullness, and eyestrain. The participants were asked to answer the same set of questions before and after the task to capture temporal changes.

The FSS investigated the flow experience of the work. The experiment used a short-scale checklist comprising ten questions. The checklist comprised three factors: ability (confidence in ability), immersion (conscious experience through positive emotions and immersion), and challenge (challenging goals). The average score for each indicator and the overall average were calculated. Moreover, this checklist does not have a reference point for whether a flow state has occurred; a score of four or more was considered as a flow state because it references several prior studies [6, 13].NASA-TLX subjectively evaluates mental workload according to six scales: mental demand (MD), physical demand (PD), temporal demand (TD), own performance (OP), effort (EF), and frustration level (FR). They were evaluated on a visual analog scale of 0–100 points. The values of "low-high" and "bad-good" were presented as polar extremes, and the average scores for each indicator were calculated. Additionally, weights ranging from 6 to 1 were assigned to the six scales to calculate the adaptive weighted workload (AWWL).

The SSQ is used to assess the discomfort and motion sickness caused by the use of VR devices. Participants responded to 16 questions on a 4 point scale. Questions were categorized into three groups: nausea, oculomotor symptoms, and disorientation. The mean score for each assessment and the overall average were calculated.

3 Results

3.1 Creativity Performance

Finding on AUT Score. The AUT scores are shown in Fig. 4; the elaboration score was significantly higher under the CTRL condition than under the VR and VR-N conditions ($p < .01$, $p < .05$). Furthermore, other scores were not significant.

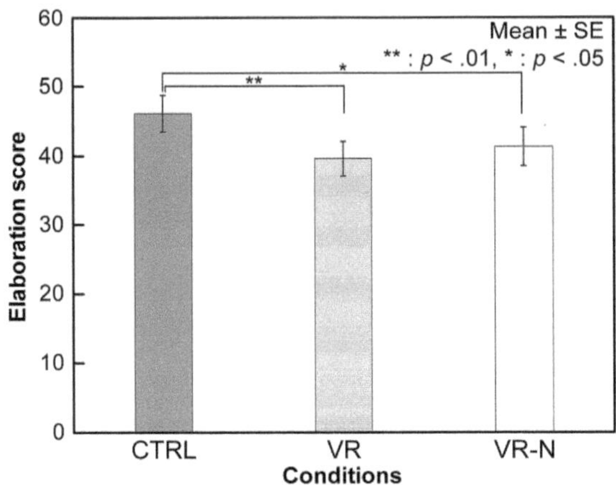

Fig. 4. Creativity performances during the AUT ($n = 36$).

Finding on CUT Score. The CUT scores are shown in Fig. 5; the flexibility score was significantly higher under the VR condition than under the VR-N and CTRL conditions ($p < .01, p < .01$). Additionally, the fluency score was significantly higher under the VR condition than under the VR-N and CTRL conditions ($p < .01, p < .001$).

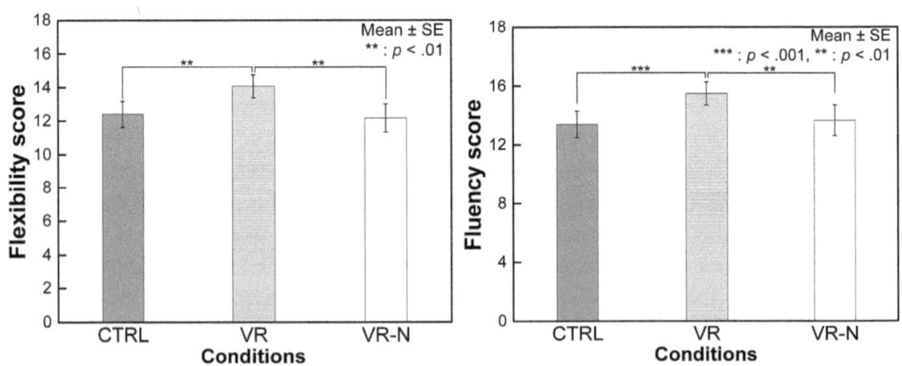

Fig. 5. Creativity performances during the CUT ($n = 36$)

3.2 Subjective Feeling of Fatigue

During the AUT. The SFF scores are shown in Fig. 6. Focusing on the transitions before and after the task, drowsiness and instability were significantly elevated under the VR-N condition ($p < .05$). Furthermore, the results of the comparison under each condition revealed that pre-task drowsiness was significantly higher under the VR-N condition than under the CTRL condition ($p < .01$). Pre-task uneasiness was significantly higher under the VR condition than under the CTRL condition ($p < .05$). Additionally, pre- and post-task eyestrain was higher under the VR condition than under the CTRL condition ($p < .05, p < .05$).

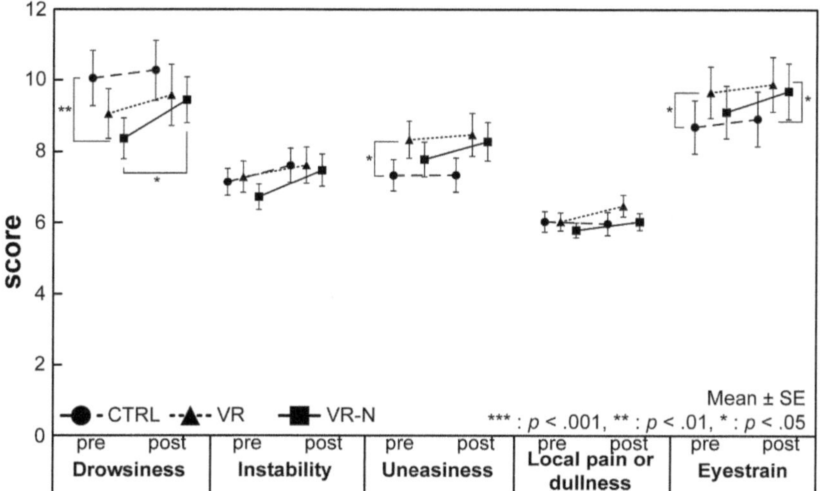

Fig. 6. Results of SFF during the AUT ($n = 36$).

During the CUT. The SFF scores are shown in Fig. 7. Focusing on the transition before and after the task, drowsiness and eyestrain were significantly elevated under the VR condition ($p < .05, p < .01$). Additionally, drowsiness and instability were significantly elevated under the VR-N condition ($p < .05, p < .05$). Furthermore, the results of the comparison under each condition, pre- and post-task drowsiness, were significantly lower under the VR-N condition than under the CTRL condition ($p < .001, p < .05$). Pre- and post-task uneasiness were significantly lower under the CTRL condition than under the VR condition ($p < .05$).

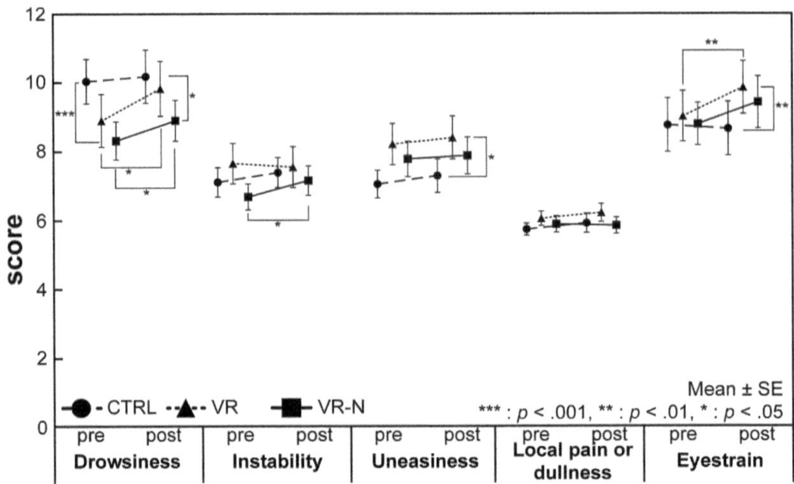

Fig. 7. Results of SFF during the CUT ($n = 36$)

3.3 NASA Task Load Index

During the AUT. The NASA-TLX scores are shown in Fig. 8. MD was significantly higher under the VR condition than under the CTRL and VR-N conditions ($p < .01$, $p < .01$). Furthermore, PD was significantly higher under the VR-N and VR-N conditions than under the CTRL condition ($p < .001$, $p < .001$). Additionally, FR and AWWL were significantly higher under the VR condition than under the CTRL condition ($p < .01$, $p < .01$).

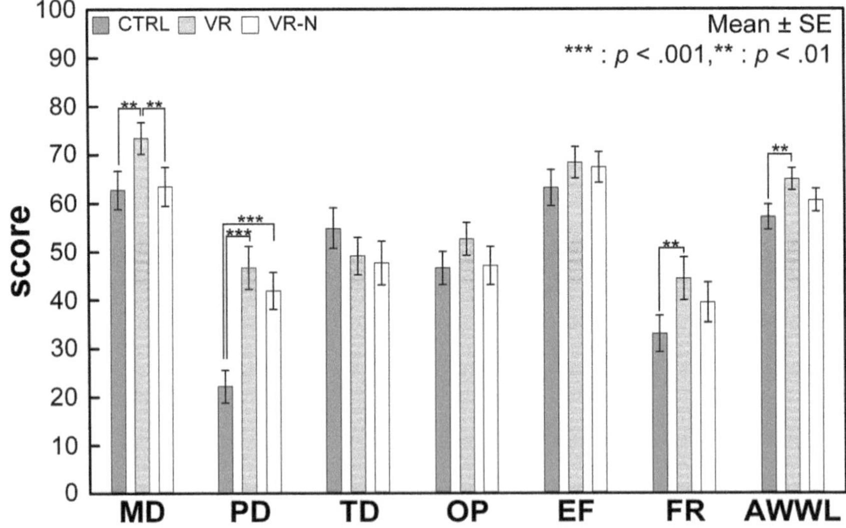

Fig. 8. Results of NASA-TLX during the AUT ($n = 36$).

During the CUT. The NASA-TLX scores are shown in Fig. 9. PD was significantly higher under the VR-N and VR-N conditions than under the CTRL condition ($p < .001$, $p < .001$).

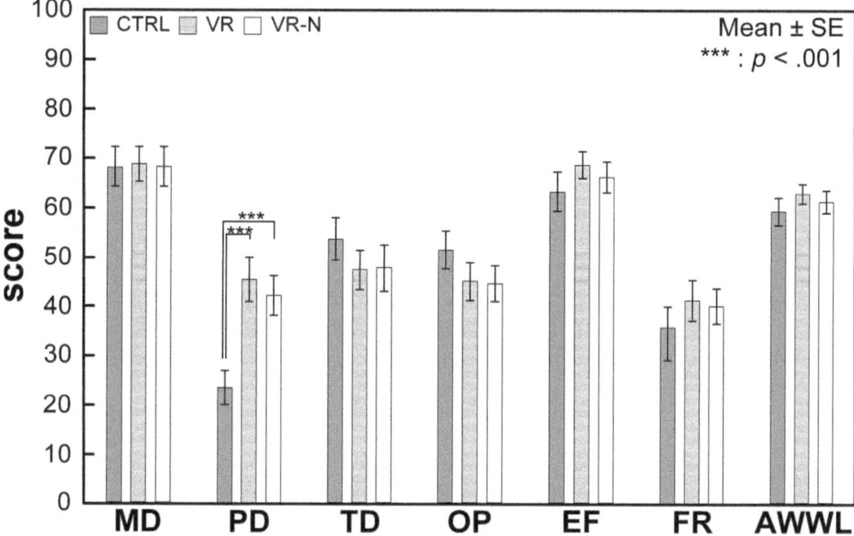

Fig. 9. Results of NASA-TLX during the CUT ($n = 36$)

3.4 Flow Short Scale

During the AUT. The FSS scores were not significantly different under the conditions across the four assessments. Therefore, all scores exceeded the four-point flow state criterion.

During the CUT. The FSS scores were not significantly different under the conditions across the four assessments. Therefore, all scores exceeded the four-point flow state criterion.

3.5 Simulator of Sickness Questionnaire

During the AUT. The SSQ scores are shown in Fig. 10. Transition before and after the task, oculomotor function was significantly elevated under the VR condition ($p < .05$). Focusing on the comparison of the two conditions; post-task total severity was significantly lower under the VR-N condition than under the VR condition ($p < .05$).

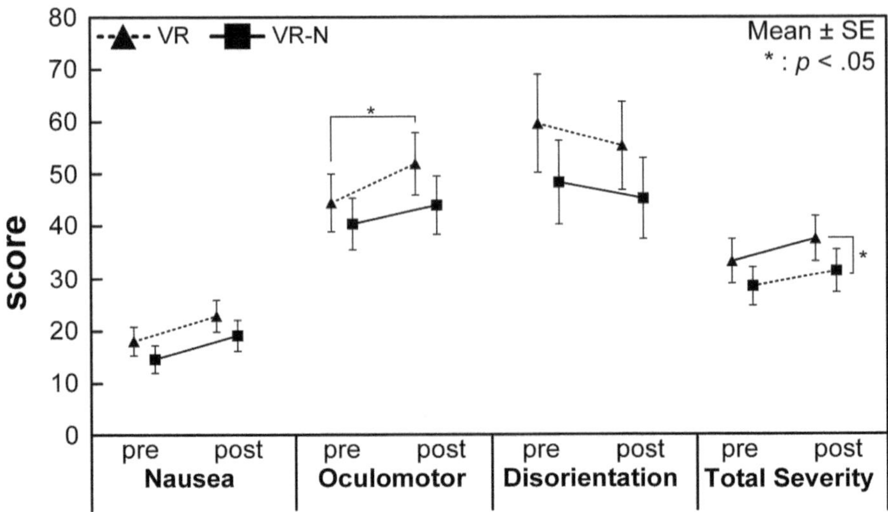

Fig. 10. Results of SSQ during the AUT ($n = 36$).

During the CUT. The SSQ scores are shown in Fig. 11. Transition before and after the task; total severity was significantly elevated under the VR and VR-N conditions ($p < .01$, $p < .05$). Additionally, pre-task disorientation, total severity, post-task disorientation, and total severity were significantly lower under the VR-N condition than under the VR condition ($p < .05, p < .05, p < .05, p < .05$).

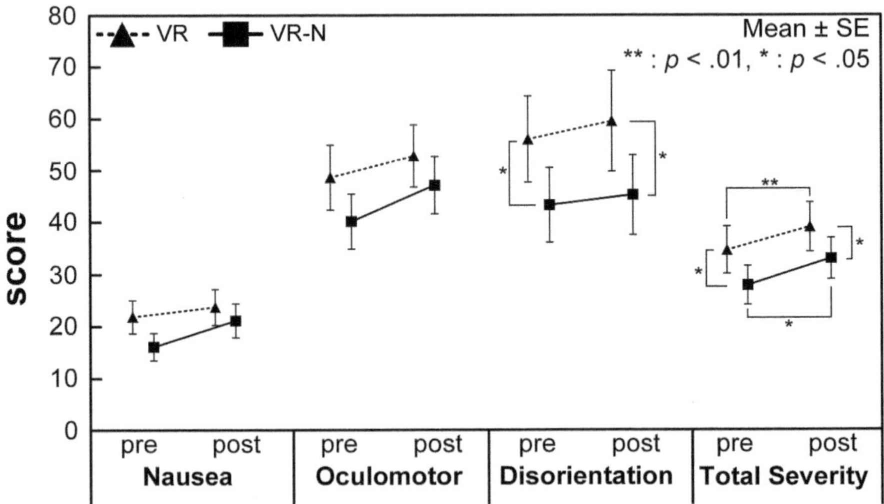

Fig. 11. Results of SSQ during the CUT ($n = 36$).

4 Discussion

The results indicate that creativity scores differ depending on the task performed, even within the same work environment. Specifically, in the AUT, a significant difference was observed in the elaboration scores among the environments, with the CTRL condition yielding higher results than the other two. An examination of the SFF scores revealed that pre-task drowsiness was higher under the CTRL condition than under the VR-N condition, whereas uneasiness was lower under the CTRL condition than under the VR condition. This suggests that the CTRL condition, which did not involve wearing an HMD, was perceived as more natural and closer to everyday experience. However, this result also indicates that the presentation of a natural environment was unable to mitigate the discomfort and cognitive load associated with HMD and VR use, leaving a challenge in improving task performance within VR. Furthermore, the NASA-TLX scores were significantly lower under the CTRL condition than under the VR or VR-N conditions, implying that the CTRL environment imposed the lowest perceived workload, and thus did not impede performance. The AUT involves considering well-known, everyday objects. A participant's comment that "the ability to see my own hands in the CTRL condition made it easier to imagine manipulating everyday objects" suggests that the nature of the task—proposing novel uses for familiar items—may have influenced the level of elaboration achieved across the different environments.

In contrast, for the CUT, significant differences emerged in flexibility and fluency, with the VR condition scoring higher than the other two conditions for both metrics. Focusing on the NASA-TLX items revealed significant differences during the AUT, and it was evident that the scores under the VR condition did not change substantially during the CUT. However, the scores under the CTRL and VR-N conditions increased, eliminating the previously observed significant differences. Therefore, it can be inferred that performance under the VR condition was maintained at a consistent level across both the AUT and CUT. The CUT requires participants to devise uses for an unfamiliar object, necessitating deep observation and an understanding of the object itself. The simple VR condition, which was free of extraneous information, could possibly be the most conducive to the performance of this focused task. This inference is supported by participant feedback, such as, "In the VR-N environment, I was distracted by the surrounding objects," and "I felt I could concentrate on the task in the VR environment because it contained only the bare essentials."

Furthermore, this study demonstrated that the inclusion of natural elements in a virtual space can suppress the workload and fatigue associated with task execution. The results from the SSQ demonstrated that, for all items, the scores under the VR-N condition were lower than those under the VR condition, following both the AUT and CUT. Moreover, regarding the total severity scores for both the AUT and CUT, the post-task score was significantly lower for VR-N than for VR. This indicates that the fatigue resulting from wearing the HMD and experiencing the VR space was lower under the VR-N condition. In addition, several participants commented that "the presence of green scenery like grass and trees in the VR-N environment allowed me to feel refreshed while performing the task," suggesting a high likelihood that exposure to nature, even in a virtual context, can help maintain concentration and performance. Additionally, compared with the VR condition, fewer participants under the VR-N condition reported eye strain or a sense of pressure associated with VR use after the task. This indicates that visual exposure to nature has the potential to alleviate discomfort associated with using VR.

5   Conclusion

This study investigated the impact of virtual environments on creative performance. The results generally indicate that performing creative tasks in VR can decrease creativity scores while increasing perceived workload and discomfort compared with a real-world setting. However, a key nuance emerged: for tasks that are inherently three-dimensional or require engagement with unfamiliar concepts, VR has the potential to enhance creative processes. Interestingly, in contrast to previous research, the introduction of a natural environment into the virtual space did not directly increase creativity scores; in some instances, performance was significantly lower than under the control condition. Despite this, the virtual natural environment yielded a clear and vital benefit: it effectively mitigated user fatigue, workload, and symptoms of VR sickness associated with task performance.

Therefore, we conclude that while current VR setups present challenges to creative work, the integration of natural elements is crucial for user well-being. By reducing the inherent strain of VR, these environments can foster sustained concentration, which may in turn support overall performance over longer periods. Future research should focus on redesigning virtual spaces and experimental conditions to build upon these fatigue-reducing benefits, aiming to create an environment where creativity can flourish without being compromised by the discomfort of the medium.

Acknowledgments. We would like to thank Editage (www.editage.jp) for English language editing.

Disclosure of Interests..   The authors have no competing interests to declare that are relevant to the content of this article.

References

1. Berman, M.G., Jonides, J., Kaplan, S.: The cognitive benefits of interacting with nature. Psychol. Sci. **19**(12), 1207–1212 (2008)
2. Berto, R., Baroni, M.R., Zainaghi, A., Bettella, S.: An exploratory study of the effect of high and low fascination environments on attentional fatigue. J. Environ. Psychol. **30**(4), 494–500 (2010)
3. Ulrich, R.S.: Effects of gardens on health outcomes: theory and research. In: Marcus, C.C., Barnes, M. (eds.) Healing Gardens: Therapeutic Benefits and Design Recommendations, pp. 27–86. Wiley, New York (1999)
4. Frances, E.K.: Coping with poverty: Impacts of Environment and Attention in the Inner City. Environ. Behav. **33**(1), 5–34 (2001)
5. Kaplan, S.: The restorative benefits of nature: toward an integrative framework. J. Environ. Psychol. **15**(3), 169–182 (1995)

6. Konishi, R., Miyake, S., Kobayashi, D.: Comparison of nature and office environments on creativity - A field study -. In: Stephanidis, C., et al. (eds.) HCI International 2023 – Late Breaking Papers. LNCS, vol. 14058, pp. 499–508. Springer, Cham (2023)
7. Ichimura, K.: Effects of virtual reality's viewing medium and the environment's spatial openness on divergent thinking. PLoS ONE **18**(3), e0283632 (2023). https://doi.org/10.1371/journal.pone.0283632
8. Nanjappan, V., Uunila, A., Vaulanen, J., Välimaa, J., Georgiev, G.V.: Effects of immersive virtual reality in enhancing creativity. Proc. Des. Soc. **3**, 1585–1594 (2023)
9. Li, H., Du, X., Ma, H., Wang, Z., Li, Y., Wu, J.: The effect of virtual-reality-based restorative environments on creativity. Int. J. Environ. Res. Public Health **19**(19), 12083 (2022). https://doi.org/10.3390/ijerph191912083
10. Biener, V., et al.: Quantifying the effects of working in VR for one week. IEEE Trans. Vis. Comput. Graph. **28**, 3810–3820 (2022)
11. Sisk, D.A.: J.P. Guilford: A Pioneer of Modern Creativity Research. In: Reisman, F. (ed.) Celebrating Giants and Trailblazers: A-Z of Who's Who in Creativity Research and Related Fields, pp. 171–185. KIE Publications, London (2021)
12. Guilford, J.P.: Creativity: Yesterday, today and tomorrow. J. Creative Behav. **1**(1), 3–14 (1967)
13. Kurosaka, C., Kuraoka, H., Maruyama, T.: Mental workload task modeled on office work: Focusing on the flow state for well-being. PLoS ONE **18**(9), e0290100 (2023). https://doi.org/10.1371/journal.pone.0290100

Human Factors in Intelligent and Autonomous Systems

Q+blind: A Game Adaptation for the Blind

Anabela Gomes[1,2(✉)], Rodrigo Nogueira[1], and Álvaro Santos[1]

[1] Polytechnic University of Coimbra,
Rua da Misericórdia, Lagar Dos Cortiços, S. Martinho Do Bispo, 3045-093 Coimbra, Portugal
anabela@isec.pt
[2] Center for Informatics and Systems of the University of Coimbra, Coimbra, Portugal

Abstract. In this work, we present an adaptation of the well-known game *Q*bert* for blind players. This game is a classic arcade game that has become a staple of puzzle games of the time. The gameplay is simple yet challenging, and the game combines action and strategy elements in a colorful and unique aesthetic. Adapting *Q*bert* for blind people is a creative challenge that requires significant changes in design and gameplay, focusing on sensory accessibility. Therefore, this paper aims to illustrate a set of suggestions and respective implementations to make the game more inclusive, especially for blind people. The enhancements leverage sensor technology to improve accessibility, provide intuitive controls, and create a multi-sensory gaming experience for blind players. The adaptations would allow the game to maintain its essence while offering an accessible, immersive and fair experience for blind players. Although a true evaluation of the new version of the game is planned to be done, including participants with and without visual problems, we have been conducting informal discussions and tests with players to try to include the best game options.

Keywords: Accessible games · Blind players · Game adaptation · Inclusive games · Sensory accessibility

1 Introduction

Nowadays, games play an important role in our society and have gained ground in recent years in all age groups. However, they do not promote equal opportunities for people with disabilities, and more than 2.2 billion people worldwide are blind or visually impaired [1]. Nevertheless, the games industry and researchers have taken these concerns into consideration and are increasing the development of accessible games and experiences. Sightlence [2], Papa Sangre [3] and Blind Legend [4] are examples of non-visual-first approaches. There are also examples of traditional game adaptations such as Tic-Tac-Toe [5], AuditoryPong [6], Blind Hero [7], Pinball [8] or BlindBattle [9]. The adapted versions use strategies such as binaural technology to provide players with localized auditory signals, touch controls, basic vocal instructions, sonification strategies, or tactile feedback, ensuring a clear and concise gaming experience for visually impaired players.

   This paper addresses this gap by proposing an adaptation of the classic arcade game *Q*bert*, released in 1982, for blind players. *Q*bert* is known for its challenging gameplay

H. Mori et al. (Eds.): HCII 2025, LNCS 16333, pp. 163–173, 2026.
https://doi.org/10.1007/978-3-032-12660-3_13

and unique aesthetics, where the player controls an orange character that jumps on a pyramid of isometric blocks, changing their colors to create specific patterns. The adaptation for blind players, called *Q+blind*, maintains the essence of the original game while introducing significant innovations to make it accessible and engaging for people with visual impairments. The current proposed game includes auditory feedback, haptic feedback, dynamic narration and sensor integration. The goal is to create an inclusive and immersive gaming experience, contributing to the advancement of accessibility in digital games.

Some works include general techniques for designing more accessible games [10–15], proposing modifications to the original games, however, the proposed work, *Q+blind*, advances the state of the art in several aspects:

- Innovative adaptation: Transforms a classic game into an accessible experience for blind players, while maintaining the essence of the original game;
- Multisensory approach: Implements directional auditory feedback, haptic feedback, and dynamic narration to replace visual elements;
- Customization: Provides adjustable difficulty modes to suit the needs of both beginners and advanced players;
- Technological integration: Uses motion and proximity sensors to improve the gaming experience and make it more intuitive;
- Inclusive design: Considers aspects such as speed of sound/speech, voice options, and the distinction between essential and optional sounds.

By addressing these aspects, *Q+blind* not only adapts an existing game but also introduces a set of new ideas to encourage more accessible game development, helping to foster greater inclusion in the field of digital games.

2   Original Game *Q*bert*

Q*bert is a classic arcade game released in 1982 by Gottlieb [16], which quickly became a landmark among platform and puzzle games of the time. Combining elements of action, strategy and skill, the game is known for its challenging gameplay and unique aesthetics.

The game takes place in a pyramid of 28 isometric blocks (see Fig. 1), with the main objective being to change the colors of the blocks by jumping on them. The player must create a specific pattern of colors to advance to the next level.

The player controls *Q*bert*, the main character, an orange character with an elongated nose. He is friendly but vulnerable, relying solely on his movement ability to avoid enemies and complete objectives.

The game features a variety of enemies that hinder progression: *Coily* – A snake chasing Q*bert through the pyramid; *Ugg and Wrong-Way* – Creatures that move along the sides of the pyramid; *Slick and Sam* – Characters that undo color changes on blocks, creating additional challenges. Additionally, mistimed jumps can cause Q*bert to fall off the pyramid, leading to the loss of a life, and when no lives remain, a game over. Occasionally, colored balls will appear and bounce down. Red balls cost one life on contact, while green ones temporarily freeze enemies. Floating disks on the sides of the pyramid allow Q*bert to escape, especially from Coily. Jumping on a disk transports him

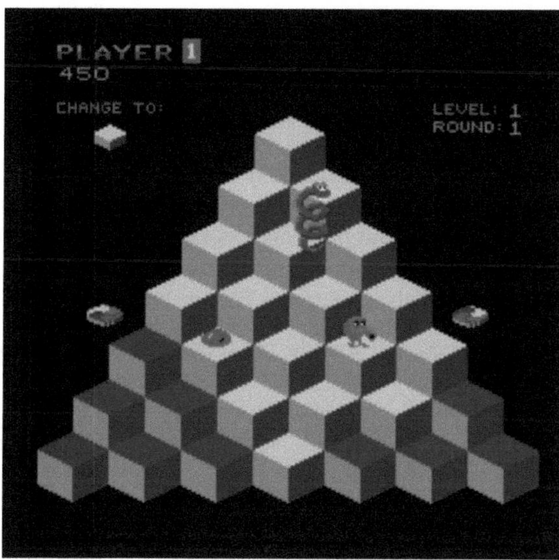

Fig. 1. Q*Bert screenshot [4].

to the top, and if Coily follows, he falls, earning bonus points and clearing all enemies and balls for a few seconds.

The game has multiple stages with increasing difficulty. Each level adds more enemies, more complex color patterns, and increased gameplay speed. The player moves Q*bert in diagonals (upper left, upper right, lower left, and lower right). This control scheme requires precision and coordination, especially at advanced levels. The pyramid of blocks creates an illusion of three-dimensional depth, innovative for the time. Iconic sound effects such as Q*bert's jump sound and enemy noises enhance the gameplay experience.

The game has a set of Challenges, which are the Movement Scheme, Enemy Management and Obstacles; Color Patterns and Reversals; Increasing Difficulty and Dependent Visual Feedback. The diagonal movement scheme, unusual for the time, is intuitive but can be difficult to master, especially in pressure situations with multiple enemies. Enemy and Obstacle Management, in which the player must deal with several enemies that present different behaviors, makes it necessary to plan movements to avoid being cornered or hit, requiring a careful strategy. Color Patterns and Reversals, implying changing blocks to the correct pattern requires focus and memory, and characters like *Slick and Sam* add complexity by reversing the changes made. Difficulty increases as you progress through the stages, and the speed and number of enemies increase significantly, putting the player's reflexes and planning skills to the test. Dependent Visual Feedback, in which all gameplay is based on visual information such as Q*bert's location, enemy positions, and block color status, makes the game inaccessible to visually impaired players.

*Q*bert* is an iconic example of a simple yet deeply challenging design, where the reliance on quick reflexes, strategic planning, and precision movement keeps the player engaged. However, its limited accessibility, especially for people with visual impairments, presents an opportunity for innovative adaptations, such as the *Q+blind* proposal.

3 *Q*bert* Adaptation

To adapt the *Q*bert* game for blind players, it is essential to implement modifications that replace visual elements with auditory and tactile stimuli, in addition to adjusting the gameplay to meet the needs of these players. The proposed changes include:

- Auditory Feedback: Directional sounds, pitch changes, and enemy detection;
- Haptic Feedback: Vibrations for alerts and enemy interactions;
- Dynamic Narration: Real-time updates on progress, events, and goals;
- Custom Difficulty Modes: Adjustable settings for both beginners and advanced players;

In Auditory Feedback, aspects such as Directional Sounds, Pitch Changes and Enemy Detection were considered. Regarding Directional Sounds, aspects such as player movement and enemy location were taken into consideration. Regarding Movement: Each of *Q*bert*'s jumps is accompanied by a sound that indicates the direction of movement jointly with an audio description helping the player understand the current position in the pyramid. When moving upward, the sounds follow an ascending musical scale, while descending movement produces a descending scale. The sounds change in pitch depending on *Q*bert*'s position on the pyramid. Higher blocks produce higher-pitched sounds, while lower blocks generate deeper tones. Left and right movements are represented using stereo sound, with the tones shifting from left to right or right to left, depending on the direction of movement. Regarding Enemy Location: Enemies emit specific sounds that vary in volume as they move closer or further away from *Q*bert*, allowing the player to perceive the proximity and direction of threats. A clear, directional sound for each jump, indicating the direction (upper left, upper right, etc.). For example, the first change is a short, sharp sound; the second change is a longer sound or a rising tone. Regarding Tone Changes, the Color Change of the Blocks was taken into consideration, so each changed block produced a specific tone. Besides the colour description, a specific sound is associated with each colour change, indicating to the player that the action was successful. Different tones represent different states of the blocks.

In Haptic Feedback, vibrations were considered for alerts and interactions with enemies. Regarding Vibrations for Alerts, situations of Immediate Danger were taken into consideration, in which the controller can vibrate with variable intensity to warn of the proximity of enemies or risks of falling. On the easiest levels, if the player attempts a move that would cause Qbert to fall off the pyramid, haptic feedback is triggered, and the move is blocked. Only if the player insists and repeats the action will Qbert actually fall. In Enemy Interactions, special attention has been paid to contact situations, where different vibration patterns can indicate possible collisions with specific enemies, helping the player identify the type of threat faced. For example, Jump Feedback: Short vibrations when jumping on safe blocks; Danger alerts: Pulsating or continuous vibration when an enemy is close.

In Dynamic narration, aspects such as Progress, events, and objectives in real-time were considered. Regarding Progress, Real-Time updates were considered, in which the user can choose a synthesized voice (among those existing) to inform the player about the current progress, such as the number of blocks remaining to complete the level. Regarding Events, particular emphasis was placed on Important Occurrences using narration to announce significant events, such as the entry of a new enemy into the scene or the activation of a power-up. One aspect considered crucial was the clear indication of the objectives in real-time, through Clear Instructions such as Guidelines on the objectives of each level and strategic tips provided to help understand the gameplay. A radar feature was also introduced. The player can pause the game and activate the radar in a specific direction to have a narration of what lies ahead, including the colors of the blocks, the number of blocks to the edge of the pyramid, and the distance (in blocks) to the enemy.

Custom Difficulty Modes have been adjusted for beginners and advanced players. For Beginner players, we have opted for Reduced Speed considerations: Slowing down the game to allow new players to familiarize themselves with the controls and auditory/haptic feedback and providing Frequent Guidance, providing more frequent and detailed tips through narration to assist in learning. For Advanced Players, we opted for Increased Challenge, introducing additional enemies and more unpredictable behaviors to increase complexity, and Reduced Feedback, decreasing the amount of auditory/tactile guidance to challenge the player's memory and skills. For example, adjusting the pace of the game so that blind players have more time to process auditory and tactile information, or introducing modes with more serious or less complex enemies, especially for beginners. At the easiest levels, enemies only move to another block when *Q*bert* makes a move.

Also, some considerations that resulted from the investigation of auditory information were followed in the implementation [17–19]. Considerations such as the speed at which sound/speech is played and the choice between a male or female voice were considered. Also contemplated was the possibility of switching off/on different sounds, especially if the sounds are not essential for advancing the game. Sound can motivate, but may also be very distracting, so a distinction was made between essential and optional sounds. In text-existing situations, it may be an advantage to use synthetic speech and text-to-speech. Also, in this specific game, it was considered that the textual description of the symbols used could be simpler than their association with specific sounds.

The issue of feedback was also an important aspect to reflect. Thus, not only should the messages be audible, but also it should be possible to repeat speech messages, either automatically when there is no response from the player after some time or at the user's request. Also, the possibility to start/stop/pause the reproduction of a message and the existence of other elements like rewards and associated auditory feedback were foreseen.

The game will always use the same sounds to signal errors, to symbolize counters and others. Much like the Windows operating system, it always uses the same sound when the user makes a mistake. When the user advances in level, the sound will always be the same. The study of what kind of sounds would work better to help users recall the last sequence planned was also a considered aspect.

These adaptations aim to provide an inclusive and engaging gaming experience for blind players, while maintaining the challenging and fun essence of the original *Q*bert*.

4   Implementation

In developing the project *Q+blind* (see Fig. 2),), the following tools were used: *Lucidchart* (lucid.app) [20], *Unity Engine* [21], *Colorblind Effect* [22] and *Arduino IDE* [23].

Lucidchart is a visual collaboration platform that lets to create diagrams, flowcharts, and wireframes. In the context of this project, Lucidchart was instrumental in: Planning and Design (Helped with the creation of game flow diagrams, level mapping, and user interface structuring, ensuring a clear and organized vision of the project before implementation) and Team Collaboration (it facilitated communication between team members, allowing simultaneous editing and sharing of ideas in real-time, which is essential to maintain cohesion and efficiency in development).

Unity Engine is a robust platform for 2D and 3D game development. Its use in the project provided Multiplatform Development (It enabled the creation of a game compatible with several platforms, expanding the reach and accessibility for different audiences) and Resource Integration (It facilitated the incorporation of several assets and plugins, such as visual effects and control systems, essential for adapting the game to the needs of blind players).

Colorblind Effect is a plugin available on the Unity Asset Store; it simulates the three most common types of colour blindness. Its application in the project was important for future colorblind testing, including Accessibility Testing (it allowed the development team to view the game from the perspective of people with different color vision deficiencies, ensuring that design choices were inclusive and accessible) and Visual Enhancement (helped identify game elements that needed adjustments to improve color distinction, contributing to a more inclusive experience).

The integration of these tools was crucial to the success of the project, enabling an efficient, collaborative workflow focused on accessibility and user experience.

Fig. 2. Q+blind screenshot.

Additionally, to provide haptic feedback through vibration, a belt with eight evenly spaced vibrating motors was designed to signal approaching danger from different directions (see Fig. 3). If a threat (e.g.: an enemy) comes from an angle, the vibration intensity is distributed accordingly, with a stronger effect on one motor and, eventually, weaker vibrations on its adjacent motors. The motors are controlled using an ESP32-S [24], enabling multiple communication methods with the computer running the game.

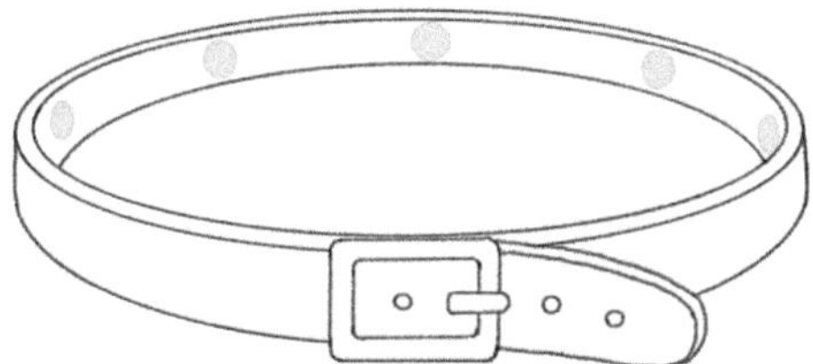

Fig. 3. Belt with vibrating motors.

The Arduino IDE (Integrated Development Environment) was used to develop the control system for the vibration motors using an ESP32-S. This IDE is an easy-to-use platform for programming and uploading code to Arduino boards. It supports multiple programming languages, primarily C and C++, and provides a simple interface with essential tools for writing, compiling, and debugging code. The IDE includes a built-in serial monitor for real-time communication with connected boards, making it useful for debugging and monitoring sensor data. It also includes a library manager that allows users to easily integrate additional functionality. The Arduino IDE is compatible with Windows, macOS, and Linux, and is widely used for prototyping and developing embedded systems.

5   Assessment

To ensure that a game adapted for blind players offers an inclusive and satisfying experience, it is essential to conduct a series of comprehensive tests. The following are the recommended approaches:

Although informal tests have already been carried out, formal tests are planned. These tests will include Structured Game Sessions with blind participants, following predefined scripts to evaluate specific aspects of gameplay and accessibility. Standardized questionnaires will be used to measure user satisfaction, ease of use and effectiveness of implemented adaptations. Various performance analyses will also be carried out, monitoring metrics such as time to complete levels, number of errors made or frequency of requests for help. In addition to the structured sessions, we also intend to carry out Informal Tests to collect Spontaneous Feedback, allowing players to experience the game freely and provide opinions and suggestions without the rigidity of a formal protocol. Participatory Observation will be another of the techniques that we intend to use. Thus, the aim is to observe players while using the game in natural environments, noting behaviors and difficulties encountered and other types of reactions.

Evaluation criteria relating to accessibility, gameplay and user experience will be used. In terms of accessibility, the aim is to assess Perceptibility, Operability and Comprehensibility. In terms of Perceptibility, assessing whether auditory and tactile feedback is clear and easily distinguishable; in terms of Operability, checking whether the controls are intuitive and adapted to the needs of blind players; in terms of Understandability, checking whether the information and instructions provided are easily understood by players.

With regard to Gameplay, the aim is to assess the suitability of the game by checking whether the game offers an appropriate level of challenge, without being frustrating or excessively easy; engagement, checking whether the player feels motivated to continue playing and Replayability, checking whether there is an incentive for the player to return to the game after the first experience.

Regarding Player Experience, it is important to check: Overall Satisfaction, whether the player is satisfied with the experience provided by the game; Ease of Learning, whether the player can learn the game mechanics quickly; as well as Immediate Feedback aspects, checking whether the game provides immediate responses to the player's actions, confirming their interactions.

6 Results

In informal discussions with blindfolded, non-vision-impaired players, the following comments were obtained. Regarding Auditory Feedback, directional sounds were found to be useful for navigation, although some players suggested the need for greater distinction between certain sound effects. Regarding Haptic Feedback, vibrations for alerts were well received, but there were suggestions to diversify the vibration patterns, better differentiating the types of alerts. Regarding Dynamic Narration, this was seen as a positive point, providing context and guidance, although some players suggested options to customize the frequency and detail of narrated information. Regarding Difficulty Modes, beginner players appreciated the existence of an easier mode, while experienced players requested additional challenges in the advanced levels.

It was mentioned that the game's difficulty may not be the most suitable for a first game using the developed platform. It may be more appropriate to choose a game with simpler characteristics, possibly just a 2D side-scrolling game.

Thus, these insights are valuable in guiding adjustments and improvements to the game, ensuring that it meets the expectations and needs of the blind gaming community.

7 Conclusion and Future Work

The adaptation of Q*bert for blind players, resulting in Q+blind, demonstrates the potential to make classic games accessible to a wider audience. Implemented modifications such as directional auditory feedback, haptic feedback through vibrations, dynamic narration and sensor integration offer a rich and immersive gaming experience for visually impaired players.

Using tools like *Lucidchart, Unity Engine,* and the *Colorblind Effect plugin* was critical to the development and testing of the game, ensuring a collaborative and accessibility-focused approach.

These adaptations not only maintain the challenging essence of the original *Q*bert* but also open up new possibilities for creating inclusive games. While a formal evaluation with both blind and sighted participants is still planned, informal discussions with players have been valuable in refining the game options.

This project represents an important step towards more accessible and inclusive gaming, demonstrating that it is possible to adapt classic games to meet the needs of players of different abilities, without compromising the quality of the gaming experience.

The development of this game led to the creation of a platform that could be adapted for other games. More importantly, its evolution could include implementation on mobile devices, leveraging the capabilities of modern smartphones and tablets to enhance accessibility and engagement. This adaptation could integrate various sensor technologies to provide an immersive and intuitive gaming experience. With motion sensors for motion controls using accelerometers and gyroscopes, players could control Q*bert's movement by tilting or shaking the device, offering a gesture-based and tactile experience rather than relying on traditional touch-based inputs. With proximity sensors for gesture detection the player could use hand movements near the screen to activate specific commands and make specific actions, such as pausing the game or activating power-ups, reducing the need for on-screen controls. Proximity Sensors could also be used to detect approaching edges or enemies and trigger tactile or auditory warnings. With touch sensors with multi-touch gestures for gameplay interactions and navigating menus, players could interact with the game using swipes, taps, and pinches, with haptic and auditory feedback ensuring accurate control and confirmation of actions. With environmental sensors (Light and Noise Adaptation), players could dynamically adjust game difficulty or sound intensity based on ambient conditions, making the game more accessible in different environments and ambient conditions. With pressure sensors, to allow nuanced control, the game could interpret variations in touch pressure to adjust movement speed or trigger specific interactions, allowing for a more refined and adaptive control scheme. Wearable sensors integration for haptic feedback is also an idea being studied to support haptic gloves or suits that could provide spatial feedback, enhancing immersion by indicating enemy proximity or changes in game state like proximity to pyramid edges through vibrations.

References

1. World Health Organization: World Report on Vision. https://www.who.int/publications-det ail/world-report-on-vision. Accessed: 04 Nov 2024
2. Nordvall, M. 2013. The Sightlence game: Designing a haptic computer gameinterface. In: DiGRA'13, Proceedings of the 2013 DiGRA International Conference: DeFragging Game Studies. http://www.digra.org/digital-library/publications/the-sightlence-game-designing-a-haptic-computer-game-interface/
3. Hugill, A.: Towards an analysis of Papa Sangre, an audio-only game for the iPhone/iPad. The Online Repository for Electroacoustic Music Analysis. (2012)

4. Spöhrer, M.: Binaural gaming arrangements: Techno-sensory configurations of playing the audio game A Blind Legend. Techniques of Hearing, Routledge, 114–124 (2022)

5. Chundru, S.D.V., Chintapalli, M.R.: BlindBattle: Tactile Game For Blind. 2024 IEEE International Conference on Communication, Computing and Signal Processing (IICCCS), ASANSOL, India, pp. 1–6, (2024) https://doi.org/10.1109/IICCCS61609.2024.10763650

6. Heuten, W., Henze, N., Boll, S. and Klante, P.: AuditoryPong–playing pong in the dark. In: Proceedings of audio mostly 2007: the 2nd conference on interaction with sound, pp. 134–147. (2007)

7. Yuan, B., Folmer, E.: Blind Hero: enabling Guitar Hero for the visually impaired. In: Proceedings of assets '08: The 10th international ACM SIGACCESS conference on computers and accessibility, pp. 169–176. (2008)

8. Berge, D., Bettencourt, D., Lageweg, S., Overman, W., Zaidi, A. and Bidarra, R.: Pinball for the visually impaired—an audio spatialization and sonification mobile game. In: Proceedings of CHI PLAY '20: the annual symposium on computer-human interaction in play, pp. 43–46. (2020)

9. Chundru, S.D.V., Chintapalli, M.R.: BlindBattle: Tactile Game For Blind. In: Proceedings of 2024 IEEE International Conference on Communication, Computing and Signal Processing (IICCCS), ASANSOL, India, pp. 1–6. (2024) https://doi.org/10.1109/IICCCS61609.2024.10763650

10. Agrimi, E., Battaglini, C., Bottari, D., et al.: Game accessibility for visually impaired people: a review. Soft. Comput. **28**, 10475–10489 (2024). https://doi.org/10.1007/s00500-024-098 27-4

11. Aguado-Delgado, J., Gutiérrez-Martínez, J.M., Hilera, J.R., et al.: Accessibility in video games: a systematic review. Univ. Access Inf. Soc. **19**, 169–193 (2020). https://doi.org/10. 1007/s10209-018-0628-2

12. da Rocha, T., Filho, F., Mirza-Babaei, P., Kapralos, B., Moreira, M., Junior, G.: Let's play together: adaptation guidelines of board games for players with visual impairment. In: Proceedings of CHI'19: CHI conference on human factors in computing systems, article no. 631, pp. 1–14. (2019)

13. Gao, Z., Wang, H., Feng, G., Lv, H.: Exploring sonification mapping strategies for spatial auditory guidance in immersive virtual environments. ACM Trans. Appl. Percept. **19**(3), 9 (2022)

14. Grabski, A., Toni, T., Zigrand, T., Weller, R. and Zachmann, G.: Kinaptic—techniques and insights for creating competitive accessible 3D games for sighted and visually impaired users. In: Proceedings of haptics symposium '16: the 2016 IEEE haptics symposium, pp 325–331. (2016)

15. Brown, M., Anderson, S.L.: Designing for Disability: Evaluating the State of Accessibility Design in Video Games. Games and Culture **16**(6), 702–718 (2021). https://doi.org/10.1177/ 1555412020971500

16. Hodges, J.A.: How do I hold this thing? Controlling reconstructed Q* berts. New Media Soc. **19**(10), 1581–1598 (2017)

17. Sekhavat, Y.A., Azadehfar, M.R., Zarei, H., Roohi, S.: Sonification and interaction design in computer games for visually impaired individuals. Multimedia Tools Appl **81**, 7847–7871 (2022)

18. Torres, M.J.R., Barwaldt, R., Pinho, P.C.R., de Topin, L.O.H., Otero, T.: An auditory interface to workspace awareness elements accessible for the blind in diagrams' collaborative modeling. In: Proceedings of the 2020 IEEE Frontiers in Education Conference (FIE'2020), pp. 1–7. (2020)

19. Battal, C., Rezk, M., Mattioni, S., Vadlamudi, J. and Collignon, O.: Representation of auditory motion directions and sound source locations in the human planum temporale. J Neurosci 39(12), 2208–2220. Beeston J, Power C, Cairns P, Barlet M (2018) Characteristics and motivations of players with disabilities in digital games. arXiv: 1805.11352 (2019)

20. Sonchack, J., Loehr, D., Rexford, J., Walker, D.: Lucid: a language for control in the data plane. In: Proceedings of the 2021 ACM SIGCOMM 2021 Conference (SIGCOMM '21). Association for Computing Machinery, New York, NY, USA, pp. 731–747. (2021). https://doi.org/10.1145/3452296.3472903

21. Singh, S., Kaur, A.: Game development using unity game engine. In: Proceedings of the 2022 3rd International Conference on Computing, Analytics and Networks (ICAN), pp. 1–6. (2022)

22. Gulti Co. 2017. Color Blindness Simulator for Unity. https://assetstore.unity.com/packages/vfx/shaders/fullscreen-camera-effects/color-blindness-simulator-for-unity-1903 Last accessed on July 1, 2024

23. Ismailov, A. S., & Jo'Rayev, Z. B. (2022). Study of arduino microcontroller board. Science and Education, 3(3), 172–179

24. Bahtiti, A.: Redeveloping a mixing system in a biomedical device to improve system control and increase its intelligence and effectiveness: redeveloping a mixing mechanism using ESP32, TMC5130, Bluetooth and CAN-bus. (2023)

Effect of eHMI on Driver Situation Awareness in Autonomous-Bus Environment

Yuga Kato[1], Naomi Kuwata[1], Yu Ichihashi[1], Kai Kitayama[2], Takehiko Yamaguchi[3], Shinji Miyake[1] (iD), and Daiji Kobayashi[2(✉)] (iD)

[1] Graduate School of Chitose Institute of Science and Technology, Hokkaido, Japan
[2] Chitose Institute of Science and Technology, Hokkaido, Japan
`{m2240180,d-kobaya}@photon.chitose.ac.jp`
[3] Suwa University of Science, Nagano, Japan

Abstract. Owing to the increasing prevalence of autonomous vehicles in mixed-traffic environments, developing effective approaches for them to interact with road users is essential. One widely investigated method is external human-machine interfaces (eHMIs), which help communicate a vehicle's intentions. However, most previous studies have focused on interactions with pedestrians. This study investigates the effect of eHMI messages on the situation awareness of drivers following autonomous buses. Using a virtual-reality driving simulator, we recreated realistic traffic scenarios to examine this interaction. The findings indicate that eHMI messages can improve the awareness of the following drivers. Additionally, we observed that the timing of these messages involves balancing between helping drivers decide more rapidly and avoiding potential safety risks. Although this study was conducted in a simulated environment, the results provide useful insights into the future implementation of autonomous buses in real-world traffic systems.

Keywords: Situation Awareness · Autonomous Vehicle · External Human-Machine Interface · Virtual Simulation

1 Introduction

Autonomous buses are increasingly being perceived as a solution to the shortage of bus drivers in Japan and are expected to be key in supporting public transportation. Hence, several local governments, such as Sakai Town in Ibaraki Prefecture and Chitose City in Hokkaido, are conducting pilot programs to establish continuous autonomous-bus operations. These buses must operate in conventional traffic environments, interact with various road users, and form a mixed-traffic system [1–4].

Previous studies on human-autonomous vehicle interaction demonstrated that external human-machine interfaces (eHMIs) can effectively communicate vehicle intentions to road users, including pedestrians, drivers, and cyclists. For example, De (2019) demonstrated that eHMIs conveyed an autonomous vehicle's intention to yield to pedestrians [5]. Similarly, Rettenmaier (2020) found that eHMI displays on autonomous vehicles

H. Mori et al. (Eds.): HCII 2025, LNCS 16333, pp. 174–187, 2026.
https://doi.org/10.1007/978-3-032-12660-3_14

reduced passing times and led to fewer collisions involving drivers of conventional vehicles [6]. These findings emphasize the importance of designing eHMIs that facilitate intuitive decision-making in environments where autonomous and conventional vehicles coexist.

The design and evaluation of eHMIs should consider the cognitive processes that influence effective decision-making and the behavior of road users [7]. According to the international standard ISO 9241 810:2020, situational awareness refers to the ability of human operators, including drivers, supervisors, and other stakeholders, to perceive, comprehend, and respond to critical information related to autonomous systems and their operational context [8]. In contrast, Endsley (1988) presents a distinct conceptual framework for situation awareness (SA), which involves perceiving environmental elements, understanding their significance, and anticipating their future states [9]. This model has been widely adopted in human factors research and continues to serve as a foundational reference. Enhancing SA is essential for ensuring safe and efficient interactions, as it directly influences human decision-making and behavior. However, systematic evaluations of the impact of eHMIs on the SA of road users remain limited. Moreover, most existing studies on eHMIs have focused on pedestrian interactions [10], whereas the effect of eHMIs on surrounding drivers is rarely examined, thus resulting in a significant gap in the current body of knowledge [11]. Therefore, the present study investigates the effect of eHMIs on the SA of surrounding drivers using a driving simulator. Furthermore, a separate experiment is conducted to devise strategies for enhancing SA in similar driving contexts.

2 Methods

In this study, we conducted an experiment to investigate the effect of information presented by an autonomous bus's eHMI on the SA of surrounding drivers. Furthermore, we examined the effect of different timings for presenting eHMI information on the SA of surrounding drivers.

2.1 Experiment: Effect of eHMI on Following-Driver SA

Participants. The participants were 20 healthy males and 4 female student volunteers aged 20 to 23 years (mean = 20.7 ± 0.9 years), all with a valid driver's license, adequate visual acuity for driving, and high driving frequency. This study was approved by the Research Ethics Committee of the Chitose Institute of Science and Technology (Approval No. 2024–5), and informed consent was obtained from all participants.

Experimental Environment and Apparatus. Virtual reality (VR) was employed in a driving simulator to increase experimental immersion and enable the observation of driving behaviors that are comparable to those exhibited in real-world scenarios [12]. The autonomous bus, private passenger vehicle, and roads used in the driving simulator were created using Blender, which is a three-dimensional computer graphics software package. The size of the autonomous bus was modeled after the Isuzu Erga, i.e., measuring 11.13 m (length) × 2.485 m (wide) × 3.1 m (high). The road was designed as a straight, two-lane road in each direction, with intersections placed at 450 m intervals.

The autonomous bus was driven at 40 km/h in a VR environment developed using the Unity game engine, as shown in Fig. 1.

Fig. 1. Virtual reality environment.

The driving simulator was equipped with a head-mounted display (HMD) (HTC Vive Pro Eye) connected to a PC (Lenovo Legion T5), along with a steering wheel, an accelerator, and a brake pedal (Hori Co.). This setup provided the participants with realistic driving experience in a virtual traffic environment.

Scenario Design. The participants were instructed to maintain a speed of 50 km/h and change lanes as necessary until the scenario concluded. They were tasked with driving in three scenarios: (1) the bus approaching and stopping at a bus stop before an intersection, (2) the bus changing to the right lane to avoid a parked vehicle and then turning right at an intersection, and (3) the bus turning left at an intersection. Each scenario commenced when the participants passed through one intersection and concluded upon passing through the subsequent intersection. Scenarios 1 and 3 were included as common occurrences [13]. Conversely, Scenario 2, in which the bus executes a right turn at an intersection and changes lanes to avoid a parked vehicle, was selected due to its relative infrequency and complexity.

Schieben et al. (2018) argued the necessity of presenting information regarding autonomous-vehicle maneuvers to support traffic participants in anticipating the vehicle's current and future behaviors [1]. Therefore, based on this design consideration, we selected the next maneuver of a vehicle as the key information for communication to enhance the SA of surrounding drivers.

We installed an eHMI measuring 2.65 m (wide) × 1.49 m (high) at the rear of an autonomous bus. Text messages pertaining to the autonomous bus's maneuvers, which were displayed in a highly visible white-on-black format, were shown from initiation to the conclusion of each of the following scenario: "Bus stop ahead" in Scenario 1, "Turning right at the next traffic light" in Scenario 2, and "Turning left at the next traffic light" in Scenario 3, as shown a Fig. 2.

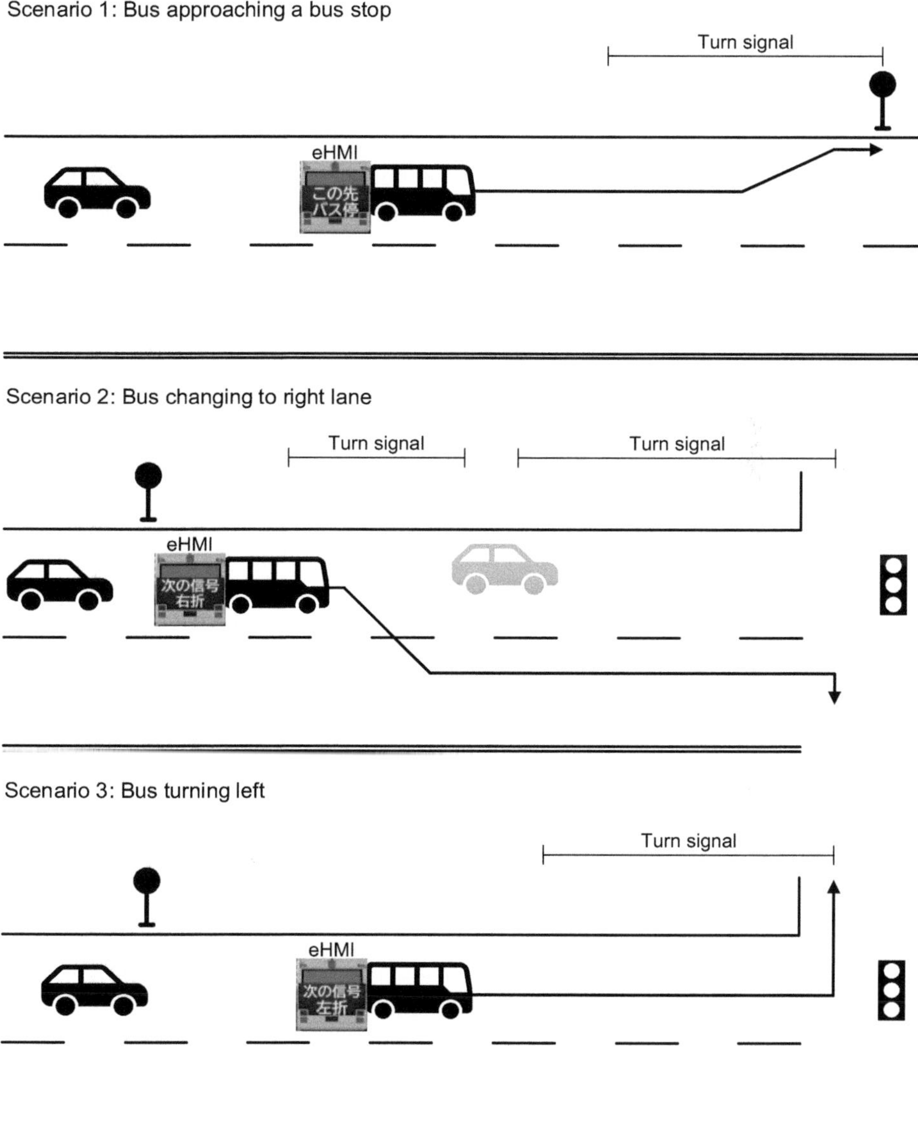

Fig. 2. Experimental scenarios and associated eHMI.

Procedure and Metrics. This study employed a within-subjects experimental design. The participants first completed the driving task without an eHMI. After an interval of more than two weeks, they recompleted the task with an eHMI to minimize learning effects. In both conditions, the participants were instructed to drive primarily in the left lane at a constant speed of 50 km/h. If smooth driving was impossible, they were permitted to change lanes to overtake the autonomous bus.

Prior to the main trials, the participants were briefed regarding the experimental procedure and practiced driving using an HMD and a driving simulator to become familiar with the task. Once they demonstrated sufficient proficiency, they were randomly assigned to one of three driving scenarios. At the end of each scenario, the participants were instructed to stop driving and complete a questionnaire to assess their SA. After completing the questionnaire, the participants resumed driving and proceeded to the next scenario. Upon completion of all scenarios, the HMD was removed and the participants were instructed to provide feedback on both the experiment and eHMI system.

Driving behavior data, including steering, acceleration, and braking inputs, were recorded at a sampling rate of 90 Hz. Eye-tracking data were obtained at 30 Hz, and gaze points were categorized into three areas: bus, driver's vehicle mirrors, and other elements. Gaze durations were calculated for instances where the gaze remained fixed for 300 ms or longer. Participants with more than 25% missing-gaze data were excluded from the analysis. SA during driving was assessed using the reworked version of the situational awareness rating technique (SART) developed by Taylor (2011) [14]. This instrument evaluates three dimensions: Demands on Attentional Resources (Instability, Complexity, Variability) (D), Supply of Attentional Resources (Arousal, Concentration, Division of Attention, Spare Capacity) (S), and Understanding of the Situation (Information Quantity, Information Quality, Familiarity) (U). The individual factor scores and overall SA scores were calculated using Eq. (1): The reworked SART was translated into Japanese and supplemented with five additional items based on the SA model (see Table 1).

$$\text{Overall score} = U - (D - S) \tag{1}$$

Table 1. Five additional questionnaire items in reworked SART.

Category	Question Items
Perception	Was the information necessary for smooth driving easily obtainable?
Comprehension	Was the information required for smooth driving easily understood?
Projection	Was the next event easily predictable?
Decision	Were the decisions necessary for smooth driving easy to make?
Action	Were the actions necessary for smooth driving easy to perform?

Following each scenario, questionnaire items were displayed within the VR environment, and the participants provided their responses by verbally stating their rating for each item on a 7-point scale, based on the instruction that a rating of "4" should correspond to their normal driving behavior.

2.2 Experiment on the Effect of Timing in Information Presentation to Following Drivers

Participants. The participants were 18 healthy male and 2 female student volunteers aged 20 to 24 years (mean = 22.4 ± 1.2 years), all with a valid driver's license, adequate visual acuity for driving, and a driving frequency of at least once per week. This study was approved by the Research Ethics Committee of the Chitose Institute of Science and Technology (Approval No. 2024–5), and informed consent was obtained from all participants.

Scenario Design. The participants were instructed to maintain a speed of 50 km/h and change lanes as necessary until the scenario concluded. They were tasked with driving in two scenarios. In Scenario 4, the bus changed lanes to the right after being overtaken by another vehicle in the right lane, in order to execute a right turn at the intersection. In Scenario 5, the bus drove in the right lane to overtake a stopped vehicle in the left lane, returned to the left lane after overtaking, and stopped at a bus stop located in the left lane, as shown in Fig. 3. The eHMI was installed as described in Sect. 2.1.

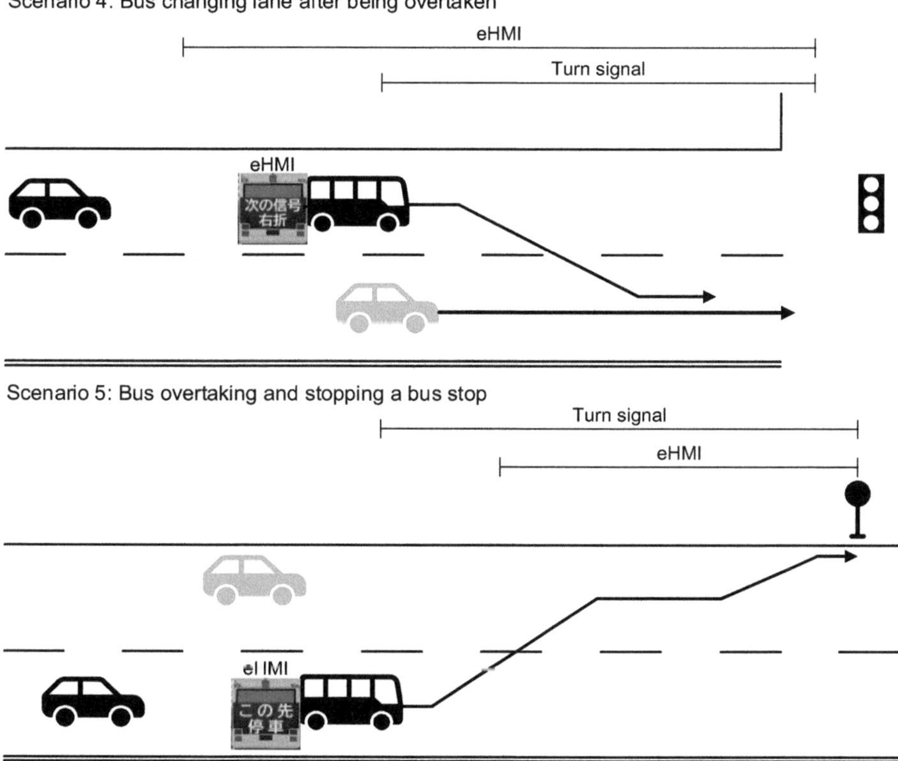

Fig. 3. Experimental scenarios and associated eHMI for difference in timing of information presentation.

In Scenario 4, the message "Turning right at the next traffic light" was displayed to participants driving behind the bus approximately 6.8 s before the turn signal was activated. This interaction was designed with the expectation that, even if participants initially considered changing lanes to overtake the bus, the displayed message would encourage them to refrain from unnecessary overtaking maneuvers, thereby enabling smoother driving.

In Scenario 5, the message "Stopping ahead" was displayed approximately 3.3 s after the turn signal was activated, i.e., during the bus's lane-change maneuver. This interaction was intended to help participants understand the bus's intention early via the eHMI, prompting them to remain in the right lane instead of instinctively following the bus back into the left lane. This allowed them to pass the stopped bus smoothly from the right side, avoiding unnecessary lane changes. To ensure that participants observed these movements, they were instructed to turn left at the subsequent intersection.

Procedure and Metrics. The experimental environment and apparatus for the second experiment were identical to those described in Sect. 2.1. The experiment was conducted under two scenarios: Scenario 4 and 5. In one scenario, the experiment was conducted without an eHMI, followed by the second with an eHMI. To ensure that the participants could not predict the behavior of the bus under the condition with the eHMI, an additional scenario with different bus behaviors was prepared and presented either before or after without eHMI condition. Under each condition, the participants were instructed to drive primarily in the left lane at a speed of 50 km/h. When smooth driving was not feasible, the drivers changed lanes to overtake the bus. Additionally, the participants were directed to proceed straight at the intersection in Scenario 4 and turn left at the intersection in Scenario 5.

After an explanation regarding the experiment was provided, participants wearing the HMD were instructed to practice driving on a driving simulator to familiarize themselves with the driving task. Once the participants achieved proficiency, the first scenario was presented, which included conditions without the eHMI, with different bus behavior, and with the eHMI. The participants completed the reworked SART after driving in each condition. Upon the completion of all conditions, the HMD was removed, and the participants were instructed to provide feedback regarding the experiment and eHMI. Subsequently, the second scenario was conducted using the same procedure, and feedback regarding the overall experiment was obtained upon the scenario completion.

Inputs from the steering wheel, accelerator, and brake pedal were measured and recorded at 90 Hz during driving, whereas gaze points were measured and recorded at 90 Hz. The gaze points were categorized into bus, driver's vehicle mirrors, and others. The gaze duration for each category was calculated using data in which the gaze remained for 300 ms or longer. Participants with more than 25% missing-gaze data were excluded from the analysis.

3 Results

3.1 Effect of eHMI on Following-Driver SA

Driving Performance. In Scenario 2, the duration from the onset of the scenario to the initiation of the turn signal for the right lane change was significantly longer under the "with eHMI" condition ($p < .01$). By contrast, no significant differences were observed in the other scenarios for the same duration.

Gaze Behavior. For the gaze-behavior analysis, 12 participants were excluded because their datasets contained more than 25% missing data. Table 2 shows that the gaze duration directed at the bus under the "with eHMI" condition was significantly longer than that under the "without eHMI" condition in Scenario 1 ($p < .01$). Additionally, the gaze duration at the others under the "with eHMI" condition was significantly shorter under the "without eHMI" condition in Scenario 2 ($p < .05$).

Table 2. Gaze duration for three Scenarios ($n = 12$).

Scenario	Category	Without eHMI (s)		With eHMI (s)		p-value
		Mean	SD	Mean	SD	
1	Bus	5.641	3.330	8.700	1.975	0.007
	Mirror	1.150	0.837	0.728	0.669	0.138
	Others	3.236	2.694	1.889	1.375	0.080
2	Bus	10.608	5.595	12.803	2.203	0.228
	Mirror	1.228	0.706	0.964	0.686	0.381
	Others	6.325	4.293	3.947	2.679	0.010
3	Bus	7.950	3.872	9.631	3.133	0.113
	Mirror	0.919	0.640	0.600	0.631	0.086
	Others	3.320	2.989	4.058	2.709	0.466

Reworked SART. In Scenario 1, the S score for the "with eHMI" condition was lower, whereas the projection score was higher than that for the "without eHMI" condition ($p < .001, p < .05$). In Scenario 2, both the U and projection scores for with the "with eHMI" condition were higher than those for the "without eHMI" condition ($p < .01, p < .01$). In Scenario 3, the U and projection scores for the "with eHMI" condition were higher, whereas the S score was lower than that for the "without eHMI" condition ($p < .05, p < .001, p < .01$).

3.2 Effect of Timing in Information Presentation to Following Drivers

Driving Performance. In Scenario 4, the McNemar's test revealed a significant reduction in the number of participants who engaged in unnecessary lane changes in the "with eHMI" condition, i.e., decreasing from eleven to two (χ^2 (1) $= 5.818, p < .05$). Under the same condition for Scenario 5, the number of participants who engaged in unnecessary lane changes decreased from eighteen to seven (χ^2 (1) $= 9.091, p < .01$).

Gaze Behavior. One participant was excluded from the gaze-behavior data analysis, specifically for Scenario 4, owing to missing data exceeding 25%. Table 3 shows that the gaze duration directed at the driver's vehicle mirrors under the "with eHMI" condition was significantly shorter than that under the "without eHMI" condition in Scenario 4 ($p < .05$). By contrast, no significant differences in gaze duration were observed in Scenario 5.

Table 3. Gaze duration in two scenarios (Scenario 4, $n = 19$; Scenario 5, $n = 20$).

Scenario	Category	Without eHMI (s)		With eHMI (s)		p-value
		Mean	*SD*	Mean	*SD*	
4	Bus	7.671	6.543	9.555	7.542	0.082
	Mirror	2.538	1.389	1.725	1.491	0.036
	Others	26.502	11.925	28.820	14.459	0.362
5	Bus	7.479	4.760	6.364	5.242	0.155
	Mirror	3.708	1.835	3.119	1.831	0.080
	Others	39.396	6.894	37.893	8.248	0.247

Reworked SART. In Scenario 4, the U score and the five additional question scores under the "with eHMI" condition were higher while S score was lower compared with those under the "without eHMI" condition ($p < .01, p < .001, p < .001, p < .001, p < .001, p < .001, p < .01$), as shown in Fig. 4. In Scenario 5, U score, overall score, and the five additional question scores under the "with eHMI" condition were higher, while D score was lower, compared with those under the "without eHMI" condition ($p < .001, p < .001, p < .001, p < .001, p < .001, p < .001, p < .01, p < .05$), as shown in Fig. 5.

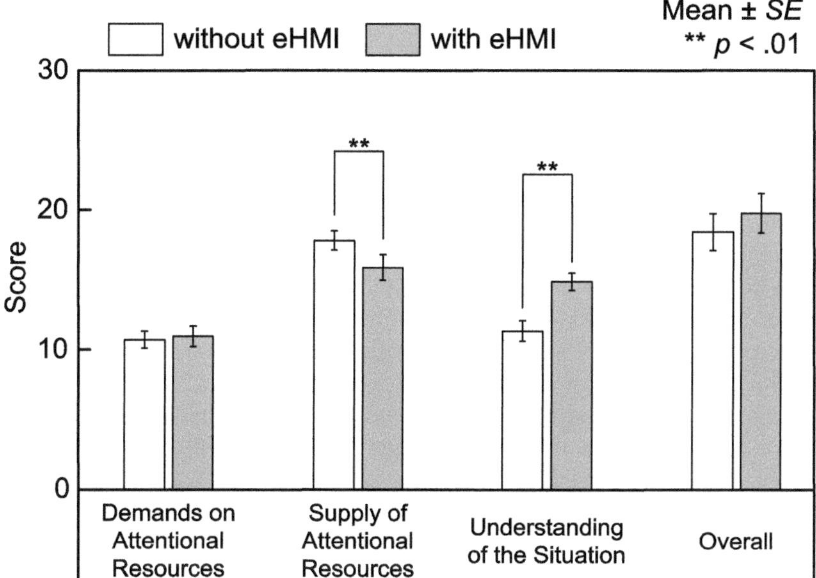

Fig. 4. Result of SART scores for Scenario 4.

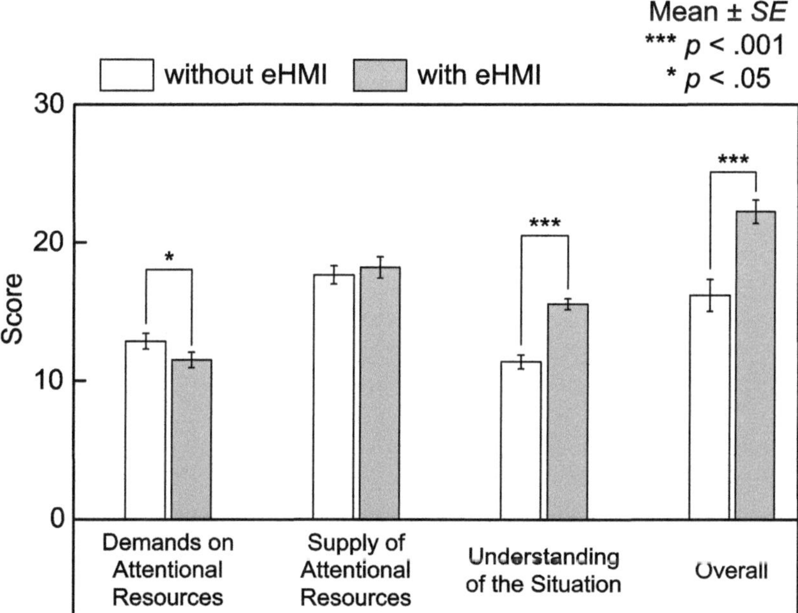

Fig. 5. Result of SART scores for Scenario 5.

4 Discussion

4.1 Effect of eHMI on Following-Driver SA

Scenario 1. No statistically significant difference was observed in the duration of turn-signal activation for right-lane changes between the conditions with and without the eHMI. However, the twenty-one participants whose supply of attentional resource scores did not improve required a significantly longer time to activate their turn signals to avoid the bus from preparing to stop ($p < .05$). Because the activation of turn signals is regarded as a stage in the driver's behavioral decision-making process, the delays in this process are attributable to the message presented by the eHMI, which interferes with the even distribution of attentional resources. In this regard, the participants reported, "Although the eHMI indicated a bus stop ahead, it was unclear if or when the bus would stop or pass through." Therefore, eHMI messages with low predictability concerning specific bus actions appeared to have induced an attentional bias toward the bus and delays in the decision-making process.

Furthermore, when information is displayed concurrently with the initiation of a scenario, predicting the subsequent action location based on the timing of the display is not feasible. Therefore, the differential effects of display timing must be examined and the optimal timing required for more effective information presentation must be determined.

Scenario 2. Owing to the longer time required for turn-signal activation, the participants reported, "The eHMI display appeared blurred when the distance to the bus was relatively large" and "The message content only became clearly visible after participants had changed lanes and reduced the distance to the bus." Therefore, attempting to read the less-visible eHMI had likely interfered with the participant's ability to observe the activation of the bus's turn signal, thus causing a delayed lane change compared with the condition without the eHMI.

The increase in both the U and projection scores is attributable to the participants' feedback, thus indicating that after the bus had completed lane change, proceeding by changing to the left lane was recognized as the appropriate course of action. Additionally, no significant attentional bias was observed in this scenario. This is attributable to the presence of a parked vehicle in the same lane, which required the participants to focus on the bus and other relevant elements in the driving environment. Therefore, in situations where the drivers are required to allocate attention to both the bus and other traffic elements, the eHMI may support a more efficient driving behavior without disproportionately focusing on the bus.

Scenario 3. This Scenario is distinct from the others in that the traffic conditions are relatively simple and the location where the bus is expected to initiate its next maneuver is clearly discernible. Among the 24 participants, eleven identified Scenario 3 as the easiest to drive. Therefore, in a relatively simple Scenario, the implementation of the eHMI did not result in measurable changes in driving performance. Nevertheless, the message conveyed by the eHMI enhanced the driver's SA and fostered a greater sense of ease during driving.

4.2 Effect of Timing in Information Presentation to Following Drivers

Scenario 4. The number of participants who performed unnecessary lane changes decreased from eleven to two when the eHMI message was presented. Additionally, the scores for the additional questions improved under the "with eHMI" condition. In this regard, participants reported that "Receiving the message in advance provided greater flexibility in decision-making and facilitated smooth driving." Therefore, conveying the bus's intended next action through the eHMI before the activation of the turn signal is considered effective in enhancing the drivers' SA and promoting more efficient driving behavior. However, two participants who performed unnecessary lane changes despite the presence of the eHMI reported that they understood the bus was about to turn right based on the eHMI; nonetheless, they attempted to overtake the bus before it began to change lane. This observation highlights that whereas the eHMI can support decision-making, individual strategies may result in divergent behavioral outcomes. Furthermore, the presence of the eHMI is associated with a reduction in gaze duration directed at the mirror of the vehicle, accompanied by a decrease in the S score. In this regard, the participants reported that reading the eHMI message from a distance was challenging, which unintentionally piqued their attention. Therefore, conveying the bus's intended next action through the eHMI before the activation of the turn signal appeared to have biased attentional resources toward the bus from an earlier stage. This shift in attention had likely contributed to the reduction in time allocated to mirror observation.

Scenario 5. In this scenario, although the number of participants who performed unnecessary lane changes decreased because of the eHMI message, seven individuals exhibited such behavior, which exceeded the number observed in Scenario 4. Among them, six participants activated their turn signals during the interval between signal onset and eHMI message display. Upon noticing the eHMI message, they aborted their intention to change lanes. These observations suggest that the message was presented after the decision-making process had already been completed, which was likely triggered by the initial turn-signal activation.

Moreover, unlike the case in Scenario 4, the D score decreased in the presence of the eHMI. Based on the participants' reports, decisions made in Scenario 4 were primarily based on the eHMI message. By contrast, in Scenario 5, the bus's movement was first interpreted through the turn signal, with the eHMI serving as supplementary information to support that interpretation. Hence, in Scenario 5, delaying the timing of the eHMI message allowed information to be presented while the drivers were already attending to the lane-changing bus. Consequently, the supplementary message was conveyed without requiring additional allocation of attentional resources to the bus. Therefore, Scenario 4 successfully promoted efficient decision-making, although an attentional bias was induced. Conversely, Scenario 5 avoided this bias and reduced attentional demand; however, it failed to foster efficient decision-making for seven participants. These findings suggest that presenting eHMI information—either before or after a conventional communication method such as a turn signal—involves a trade-off between decision-making efficiency and potential safety implications, as reflected by shifts in driver attention.

5 Conclusion

We examined the effect of an eHMI on the SA of following drivers on an autonomous bus using a driving simulator, with emphasis on the effects of different presentation timings. The results revealed that the predictability of information affected attentional resource bias and delayed the decision-making of the following drivers. Additionally, the difference in timing involved a trade-off between decision-making efficiency and potential safety implications. In future studies, we shall leverage these insights to investigate eHMI information requirements that can promote efficient decision-making without sacrificing safety. However, because this study was conducted using a VR simulator, further investigation is required to determine whether similar effects are observed by implementing autonomous buses in real-world environments. Furthermore, more diverse scenarios shall be considered in future studies to obtain more generalizable findings.

Acknowledgments. This study was supported by JSPS KAKENHI (grant number: JP24K15031). We would like to thank Editage (www.editage.jp) for English language editing.

Disclosure of Interests.. The authors have no competing interests to declare that are relevant to the content of this article.

References

1. Schieben, A., Wilbrink, M., Kettwich, C., et al.: Designing the interaction of automated vehicles with other traffic participants: design considerations based on human needs and expectations. Cogn. Technol. Work **21**, 69–85 (2019)
2. Dinneweth, J., Boubezoul, A., Mandiau, R., et al.: Multi-agent reinforcement learning for autonomous vehicles: a survey. Autonomous Intell. Syst. **2**(27) (2022)
3. Zhang, J., Shu, Y., Yu, H.: Human-machine interaction for autonomous vehicles: a review. In: Meiselwitz, G. (eds.) Social Computing and Social Media: Experience Design and Social Network Analysis. HCII 2021. Lecture Notes in Computer Science, vol. 12774, pp. 1–13. Springer, Cham (2019). https://doi.org/10.1007/978-3-030-77626-8_13
4. Carmona, J., Guindel, C., Garcia, F., et al.: EHMI: review and guidelines for deployment on autonomous vehicles. Sensors **21**(9), 2912 (2021)
5. De Clercq, K., Dietrich, A., Núñez Velasco, J.P., et al.: External human-machine interface on automated vehicles: effects on pedestrian crossing decisions. Hum. Factors **61**(8), 1353–1370 (2019)
6. Rettenmaier, M., Albers, D., Bengler, K.: After you?! – Use of external human-machine interfaces in road bottleneck Scenarios. Transport. Res. F: Traffic Psychol. Behav. **70**, 175–190 (2020)
7. Zheng, Y., Wu, K., Shi, R., Zhu, X., Zhang, J.: A literature review of current practices to evaluate the usability of external human machine interface. In: Harris, D., Li, W. C. (eds.) Engineering Psychology and Cognitive Ergonomics. HCII 2023. Lecture Notes in Computer Science, vol. 14018, pp. 1–13. Springer, Cham (2023). https://doi.org/10.1007/978-3-031-35389-5_40
8. ISO/TR 9241-810: Ergonomics of human-system interaction—Part 810: Robotic, intelligent and autonomous systems (2020)

9. Endsley, M.R.: Design and evaluation for situation awareness enhancement. Proceedings of the Human Factors and Ergonomics Society Annual Meeting **32**(2), 97–101 (1988)

10. Avsar, H., Utesch, F., Wilbrink, M., et al.: Efficient communication of automated vehicles and manually driven vehicles through an external human-machine interface (eHMI): evaluation at T-junctions. In: Stephanidis, C., Antona, M., Ntoa, S. (eds.) HCI International 2021 - Posters. HCII 2021. Communications in Computer and Information Science, vol. 1421, pp. 1–13. Springer, Cham (2021). https://doi.org/10.1007/978-3-030-78645-8_28

11. Dey, D., Habibovic, A., Löcken, A., et al.: Taming the eHMI jungle: a classification taxonomy to guide, compare, and assess the design principles of automated vehicles' external human-machine interfaces. Transp. Res. Interdisc. Perspect. **7**, 100174 (2020)

12. Walch, M., Frommel, J., Rogers, K., et al.: Evaluating VR driving simulation from a player experience perspective. Proceedings of the 2017 CHI Conference on Human Factors in Computing Systems 2982–2989 (2017)

13. Chen, Y., Guo, Y., Gu, X., et al.: Investigating the effect of school bus stopping process on driver behavior of surrounding vehicles based on a driving simulator experiment. Int. J. Environ. Res. Public Health **18**(23), 12538 (2021)

14. Taylor, R. M.: Situational awareness rating technique (SART): The development of a tool for aircrew systems design. In: Situational Awareness, pp. 111–128 (2011)

Enhancing Situational Awareness in Autonomous Vehicle Environments with External Human–Machine Interfaces from Drivers' Perspective

Naomi Kuwata[1], Yuga Kato[1], Yu Ichihashi[1], Kai Kitayama[2], Kentaro Kotani[3], Shinji Miyake[1] , and Daiji Kobayashi[2(✉)]

[1] Graduate School of Chitose Institute of Science and Technology, Hokkaido, Japan
[2] Chitose Institute of Science and Technology, Hokkaido, Japan
{m2240200,d-kobaya}@photon.chitose.ac.jp
[3] Kansai University, Osaka, Japan

Abstract. As autonomous vehicles (AVs) become more prevalent, the absence of traditional driver-to-human communication (e.g., gestures and eye contact) may hinder the ability of other road users to infer vehicle intentions, potentially disrupting traffic flow. Consequently, external human–machine interfaces (eHMI) have been proposed for conveying AV intentions. Although previous studies have focused on pedestrian interactions, few have examined the impact of eHMI on the surrounding drivers. This study investigated the effects of eHMI content on driver behavior and situation awareness (SA) in a virtual environment simulating urban traffic using autonomous buses. A total of 20 licensed drivers participated in driving tasks under two scenarios: a pedestrian crossing in front of a stopped bus, and a bus waiting to turn right while another vehicle proceeded straight. The participants experienced both eHMI-present and eHMI-absent conditions. Results demonstrated that eHMI significantly improved SA and gaze behavior, particularly when displaying context-specific messages (e.g., 'Pedestrian Crossing' and 'Oncoming Vehicle'). However, generic messages (e.g., 'Pay Attention to Traffic') did not enhance SA and were often disregarded. Although the informative eHMI improved awareness, it also focused on the bus, potentially reducing attention to other elements. These findings highlight the importance of designing informative and contextually relevant eHMI content.

Keywords: eHMI · Autonomous Bus · Situation Awareness

1 Introduction

Traditionally, communication between vehicles and pedestrians has been performed through driver gestures and eye contact. However, in the case of autonomous vehicles (AVs) without a driver, pedestrians experience difficulty predicting the movements of the AVs, which may impact traffic. The interactions between autonomous systems, including autonomous buses and humans, were evaluated using situation awareness (SA), a model defined by Endsley [1]. This interaction influences human decision-making and behavior [2]. Guerty (1997) highlighted that a decline in driver SA could be a contributing factor to traffic accidents [3]. Therefore, the research and development of external human–machine interfaces (eHMI) as a means of communication with AVs is being advanced. Messages from AVs can be effectively communicated to other traffic participants by conveying the movements and intentions of AVs to surrounding drivers through eHMI, thereby influencing their decision-making and behavior. Designing an eHMI to relay information regarding the presence of pedestrians and obstacles ahead, obtained through sensor and network technologies, can enhance the SA of the surrounding drivers. This approach has the potential to improve the overall safety of traffic systems significantly. Eisma et al. (2020) demonstrated that displaying 'Driving' and 'Waiting' on eHMI displays provides pedestrians with cues to make crossing decisions [4]. Furthermore, Alhawit et al. (2024) demonstrated that eHMI displays installed on autonomous buses significantly enhance pedestrians' willingness to cross, reduce their crossing response times, and deepen their understanding of AVs [5].

Simulations using virtual environments are effectively utilized to prevent traffic accidents and address the new challenges associated with the introduction of autonomous driving technologies. According to John et al. (2023), in the field of traffic research, virtual reality technology has been widely applied for data collection, and analyses of driving patterns and behavioral characteristics using driving simulators have advanced [6].

Although studies on messages from AVs to pedestrians are underway, few studies have evaluated eHMI from the perspective of the surrounding drivers. Therefore, this study aimed to clarify the impact of bus eHMI on drivers through experiments in a virtual environment in which autonomous buses operate.

2 Method

In this study, experiments were conducted on buses equipped with an eHMI and those without to investigate the SA of drivers influenced by the eHMI installed on the buses. Additionally, experiments were conducted in settings where electric scooters were in operation to elucidate the impact of eHMI in complex environments. This study was approved and reviewed by the Research Ethics Committee of the Chitose Institute of Science and Technology (Reception No. 2024–5).

2.1 Investigate SA of Drivers with and without eHMI.

Experimental Virtual Environment. We first created a simplified driving simulation in a virtual environment to conduct the experiment. The experimental setup was constructed using Unity to simulate an urban area in which autonomous buses and passenger cars operate. The vehicles used in the experiment, including the autonomous bus and urban areas, were created using the Blender software. The autonomous bus conceptualized for the experiment was a large bus, whereas the car driven by the participants was a passenger car. The constructed virtual environment was presented through a head-mounted display

(HMD) (HTC VIVE Pro Eye) connected to a personal computer (Lenovo Legion T5). In the experiment, participants drove the vehicle using a steering controller and foot pedals (HORI SPF-004). The maximum speed of the car driven by participants was set at 50 km/h.

The driving tasks were performed in two scenarios. Scenario A included a situation in which an autonomous bus stopped at a bus stop, and a pedestrian crossed in front of it. Scenario B included a situation in which the autonomous bus waited to make a right turn at an intersection while another vehicle proceeded straight. In Scenario A, the participants were instructed to proceed straight through the traffic signal, whereas in Scenario B, they were instructed to make a right turn at the signal. The participants were instructed to drive safely in these scenarios. Additionally, the driving tasks were performed under two conditions: with and without the eHMI on the autonomous bus. First, experiments were conducted without the eHMI, followed by a period of more than one week before conducting the experiments with the eHMI. The eHMI displayed the message 'Pedestrian Ahead of Bus' when a pedestrian was walking in front of the bus, and 'Oncoming Vehicle Approaching' when a vehicle was approaching the intersection where the bus was waiting to make a right turn. The experimental setup is shown in Figs. 1 and 2.

Fig. 1. Scenario A experimental setup. The eHMI displayed 'Pedestrian in Front of Bus'.

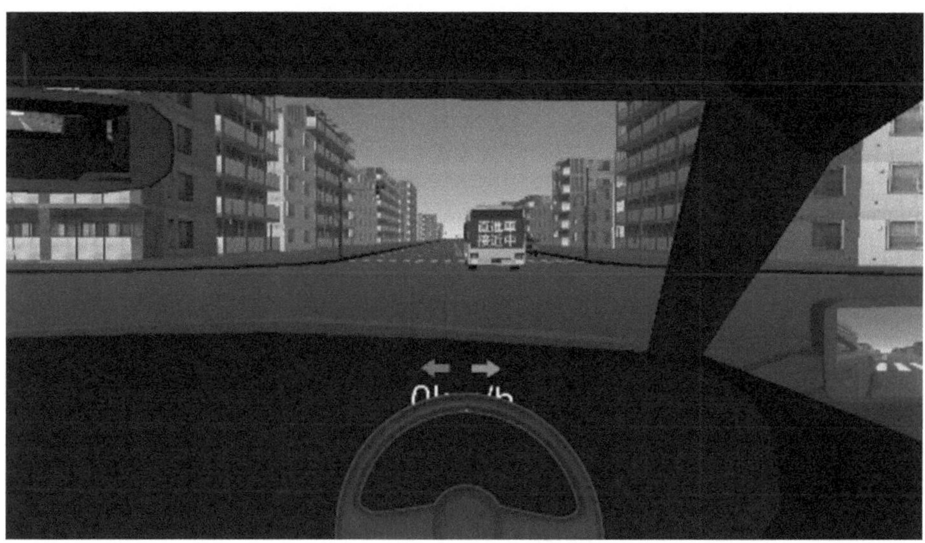

Fig. 2. Scenario B experimental setup. The eHMI displayed 'Oncoming Vehicle Approaching'.

Participants' SA was assessed using the situation awareness rating technique (SART), a subjective evaluation method defined by Taylor (2011) [7], to evaluate their understanding of the surrounding traffic conditions for safe driving. After completing each scenario, the participants were asked to respond to a questionnaire projected within the virtual environment. In addition, the gaze points of the drivers during the driving tasks were measured.

Participants. The participants were 20 students (mean age $= 21.5$, SD $= 1.3$), who held a standard driver's license and had driven a car within the past year. Informed consent was obtained from all participants prior to the experiment.

Procedure and Metrics. As a preliminary practice for driving tasks, participants underwent driving training in a virtual environment. The training was continued until the participants felt proficient in driving within the virtual environment. After completing the training, the participants were asked to remove the HMD, and the SA questionnaire to be answered during the task was explained to them. The participants read the SA questionnaire before the driving tasks to ensure that they understood its content before proceeding with the tasks. The participants were asked to put on the HMD again, and after running the calibration to measure the gaze points, the driving tasks began. After each scenario, the participants completed the SA questionnaire. After completing all the scenarios, the participants removed the HMD and provided feedback on the experiment.

The SART measured SA through 10 questions comprising 'Demand on Attentional Resources,' 'Supply of Attentional Resources,' and 'Understanding of the Situation.' Participants responded using a 7-point Likert scale ranging from 'low' to 'high.' In its reworked form, the SART was translated from English to Japanese and further augmented with five supplementary questions pertaining to the SA model (as summarized in Table 1).

Table 1. Five additional questions in the reworked SART.

Category	Question
Perception	Was the information necessary for smooth driving easy to obtain?
Comprehension	Was the information required for smooth driving easy to understand?
Projection	Was the next event easily predictable?
Decision	Were the decisions necessary for smooth driving easy to make?
Action	Were the actions necessary for smooth driving easy to perform?

For the SART, a composite score was calculated for each participant using Eq. (1), and the sum of the evaluation points for each factor and the composite scores were compared between scenarios at a 5% significance level. In Eq. (1), D represents 'demand on attentional resources,' S represents 'Supply of attentional resources,' and U represents 'understanding of the situation.'

$$SART = U - (D - S)$$

(1)

Additionally, to measure SA, a questionnaire comprising five items was created: 'perception', 'comprehension', 'projection', 'decision making,' and 'action' during driving. Participants responded using a 7-point Likert scale ranging from 'low' to 'high,' similar to the SART. Gaze points were measured using VIVE Pro Eye and SRanipal Runtime (version 1.3.2.0). The coordinates of the gaze points and objects being gazed at were sampled at 90 Hz using a C# script and recorded in a CSV file. The gaze points data for the mirrors of the autonomous bus and participant-driven passenger car, pedestrians, and oncoming vehicles were extracted. Following Card's (1981) model [8], data with a fixation duration of less than 300 ms were excluded. The total fixation time for each gaze target (hereinafter referred to as total fixation time) was calculated.

2.2 Impact of Ehmi in Complex Environments

Experimental Virtual Environment. The experimental setup is the same as that described in Sect. 2.1. The driving tasks were performed in two scenarios. In Scenario C, the autonomous bus in the oncoming lane stops at a bus stop, and a pedestrian crosses behind the bus. In Scenario D, the autonomous bus waits to turn right at an intersection while other vehicles proceed straight. In addition to these two scenarios, dummy scenarios were introduced to account for variations, such as the absence of crossing pedestrians or oncoming vehicles, as well as instances where the bus suddenly stops. The six scenarios were grouped into a single set, and each set was repeated four times during the experiment. The order of the scenarios within each set was randomized to mitigate order effects. In this experiment, the participants were instructed to make a right turn at an intersection with specific buildings. In this experiment, the participants were divided into two groups based on the type of eHMI message presented. Group A was shown a general cautionary message, 'Pay Attention to Surroundings,' whereas Group B received scenario-specific messages tailored to the context: 'Pedestrian Behind Bus' for Scenario C and 'Oncoming Vehicle Approaching' for Scenario D. The experimental setup is shown in Fig. 3.

Fig. 3. Illustration of Scenario C, with the eHMI displaying the cautionary message 'Pay Attention to Surroundings'.

Participants. The participants were 16 students (mean age $= 22.5$, SD $= 1.1$), who held a standard driver's license and had driven a car within the past year. Informed consent was obtained from all participants prior to the experiment.

Procedure and Metrics. First, the driving tasks were explained, followed by an explanation of the SA questionnaire that the participants were required to answer during the driving tasks. Next, the participants were equipped with HMD and underwent driving training in a virtual environment as preliminary practice for the driving tasks. The training continued until the participants felt proficient in driving within the virtual environment. After running the calibration to measure the gaze points, the driving tasks commenced. The participants completed the SA questionnaire after completing each scenario. Upon completing all scenarios, the participants' HMD were removed, and their feedback on the experiment was collected.

2.3   Investigation of Attentional Bias in Complex Scenarios

Experimental Virtual Environment and Participants. An auxiliary experiment was conducted under conditions consistent with those described in Sect. 2.2 to explore the effects of the additional variables, including the experimental environment and participant demographics. In this experiment, Scenarios C and D were modified to include a person riding an electric scooter. The eHMI messages remained the same as those used in Sect. 2.2, and the same participant groups were retained. Group A was presented with the message 'Pay Attention to Surroundings,' whereas Group B received scenario-specific messages: 'Pedestrian Behind Bus' in Scenario C and 'Oncoming Vehicle Approaching' in Scenario D. A practice scenario was provided before the main trials and the experiment was conducted using a set of four scenarios. The presence of a scooter is shown in Fig. 4.

Fig. 4. Scenario C: Scooter Present.

Procedure and Metrics. The experiment began with an explanation of the driving task, followed by an overview of the SA questionnaire that participants were required to complete during the task. The participants were thereafter equipped with HMD and underwent a driving training session in a virtual environment as a pre-task practice. This training was continued until the participants reported feeling sufficiently familiar with the virtual driving environment. The main driving task commenced after the eye-tracking calibration procedure was completed. Participants completed the SA questionnaire after each scenario set. Scenarios C and D were fixed as the fourth scenario in each set, and the participants were instructed to respond to the SA questionnaire based on the final scenario. Given the relatively short duration of the driving task, no breaks were scheduled during the experiment.

3   Results

3.1   Investigation of Driver SA with and without eHMI

In the environment where the bus was not equipped with an eHMI, 6 out of 20 participants collided with a pedestrian who suddenly appeared in front of the bus in Scenario A. The results of the SART questionnaire are described as follows: In Scenario A, scores for supply, understanding, and overall SART were significantly higher when messages were present on the eHMI ($p < .01$, $p < .001$, and $p < .001$, respectively). Furthermore, scores related to perception, comprehension, projection, decision-making, and action were significantly higher in the presence of eHMI messages ($p < .001$, $p < .001$, $p < .001$, $p < .01$, and $p < .01$, respectively). No significant differences were observed in the other scores. In Scenario B, the scores for understanding and SART were significantly higher ($p < .001$ and $p < .01$, respectively). Furthermore, for perception, comprehension, projection, decision-making, and action, scores were significantly higher when messages were present on the eHMI ($p < .001, p < .01, p < .01, p < .05$, and $p < .001$, respectively). No significant differences were observed in the other scores.

The gaze duration results demonstrated that, in Scenario B, the gaze duration on the bus displaying the eHMI was significantly longer than that on the bus not displaying the eHMI.

3.2 Investigation of Attentional Bias Based on eHMI Display Content

In the first set (Set 1) of Scenario C, no participants in Group A collided with the pedestrian. In contrast, in Group B, five of eight participants collided with the pedestrian. In the fourth set (Set 4), no participants in either group collided with the pedestrian.

The SART results are described as follows: First, regarding Scenario C, a comparison between Sets 1 and 4 for Group A indicated that scores for 'action' were significantly higher in Set 4 ($p < .05$). No significant differences were observed in other SART-related measures in this group. Furthermore, for Group B, comparing Sets 1 and 4 revealed that the scores for understanding and overall SART were significantly higher in Set 4($p < .01$ and $p < .05$, respectively). Next, for Scenario D, a comparison between Sets 1 and 4 for Group A revealed that the scores for understanding were significantly higher in Set 4 ($p < .05$). For Group B, a similar comparison indicated that the scores for demand, supply, understanding, and overall SART were significantly higher in Set 4 ($p < .05, p < .05, p < .01$, and $p < .001$, respectively). No other significant differences were observed for Group B in this comparison.

Regarding gaze duration, no significant differences were observed in either Scenarios C or D.

3.3 Investigation of Attentional Bias in Complex Scenarios

The SART and gaze point data were compared with the data from Set 4 in Sect. 2.2. First, the SART results are described. In Scenario C, for Group A, scores for 'action' were significantly lower when an electric scooter was present ($p < .05$). For Group B, in the presence of an electric scooter, scores for demand were significantly higher ($p < .05$), whereas those for understanding and overall SART were significantly lower ($p < .05$ and $p < .05$, respectively). Next, in Scenario D, when an electric scooter was present: for Group A, scores for understanding, overall SART, and 'perception' were significantly lower ($p < .01, p < .001$, and $p < .05$, respectively). For Group B, scores for understanding and overall SART were also significantly lower ($p < .01$ and $p < .05$, respectively).

Regarding eye-tracking metrics: in Scenario C, when an electric scooter was present, both the total gaze duration and number of fixations on the bus and the eHMI were significantly lower ($p < .05$). Additionally, under this condition, the number of fixations on the crossing pedestrian was significantly lower ($p < .05$). For Scenario D, the presence of an electric scooter was also associated with a significantly lower total gaze duration and number of fixations on the bus and the eHMI ($p < .05$).

4   Discussion

4.1   Investigation of Driver SA with and without eHMI

Results concerning the presence or absence of eHMI suggest that providing drivers with information about the blind spots of a bus can lead to improved situational understanding and serve as a basis for making safer driving decisions. Furthermore, it is believed that the presence of context-adaptive eHMI messages not only enhances participants' awareness of the surrounding environment but also improves their ability to understand, predict, and respond to traffic conditions.

However, the finding that gaze duration was longer on buses displaying the eHMI suggests that the participants' attention might have been captured by the eHMI, potentially at the expense of attending to other critical visual cues. Moreover, feedback from some participants raised concerns that, with increased familiarity or prolonged exposure to an eHMI-equipped environment, they might develop an over-reliance on eHMI. This could lead to a reduced tendency to verify information personally, and such over-reliance could potentially increase the risk of accidents.

4.2   Investigation of Attentional Bias Based on eHMI Display Content

Experiments were conducted by dividing participants into two groups based on the eHMI display content: one group received displays prompting general caution, whereas the other received displays with specific informational content. Feedback from the participants offered several insights. A general sentiment expressed by some was, 'The display does not provide a complete understanding of the surroundings, so I verify the situation with my own eyes.' Participants from the group that received only caution-prompting messages commented, 'If the display only shows cautionary information, I would eventually stop looking at it.' In contrast, several from the group that received specific information stated, 'It was helpful because it provided information about blind spots that I wouldn't have known otherwise.'

Therefore, it was concluded that displaying specific, attention-relevant content on an eHMI enhances SA. However, this could also lead to a focused concentration of attention on the bus, potentially resulting in the neglect of other surrounding areas. Furthermore, it was suggested that, if the content is not perceived as sufficiently beneficial, drivers may ultimately stop focusing on the eHMI display.

4.3   Investigation of Attentional Bias in Complex Scenarios

The findings from experiments involving the operation of an electric scooter indicate that when an attention-demanding entity, such as an electric scooter requires focused vigilance, attention may be diverted from the eHMI itself. This was further supported by feedback from the participant interviews, where some participants reported not recalling whether the eHMI display was active or admitted to not looking at the eHMI at all in the presence of an electric scooter. These observations strongly suggest that the effectiveness of eHMI depends on the complexity of the traffic environment.

5 Conclusion

In this study, experiments were conducted in a virtual driving environment, simulating a traffic environment with operating autonomous buses, to investigate the impact of the eHMI of the bus on other drivers. This study demonstrated that displaying specific messages on the eHMI is effective when critical objects requiring attention are present. Furthermore, it was revealed that, in complex scenarios, drivers may not notice the eHMI, potentially undermining its role in hazard anticipation.

Future research will explore eHMI display strategies that remain effective even in complex environments, such as when unexpected obstacles appear or when attentional demands are high because of vulnerable road users, such as cyclists or scooter riders on the roadside. Additionally, considering the concerns expressed by participants regarding potential over-reliance on eHMI displays, issues of trust in and reliance on the eHMI will also be investigated.

Acknowledgments. This study was supported by JSPS KAKENHI (grant number: JP24K15031). We would like to thank Editage (www.editage.jp) for English language editing.

Disclosure of Interests.. The authors have no competing interests to declare that are relevant to the content of this article.

References

1. Endsley, M.R.: Design and evaluation for situation awareness enhancement. Proceedings of the Human Factors Society 32nd Annual Meeting **32**(2), 97–101 (1988)
2. Endsley, M.R.: Toward a theory of situation awareness in dynamic systems. Hum. Factors J. **37**(2), 32–64 (1988)
3. Guerty, L.: Situation awareness during driving: Explicit and implicit knowledge in dynamic spatial memory. J. Exp. Psychol. Appl. **3**(1), 42–66 (1996)
4. Eisma, Y.B., van Bergen, S., ter Brake, S.M., Hensen, M.T.T., Tempelaar, W.J., de Winter, J.C.F.: External Human–Machine Interfaces: The Effect of Display Location on Crossing Intentions and Eye Movements. Information **11**(1), 13 (2020). https://www.mdpi.com/2078-2489/11/1/13
5. Alhawiti, A., et al.: The Effectiveness of eHMI Displays on Pedestrian-Autonomous Vehicle Interaction in Mixed-Traffic Environments. Sensors **24**(15), 5018 (2024). https://doi.org/10.3390/s24155018
6. John, A.P., Sadu, J., Dong, J., Li, Y., Chen, S., Labi, S.: Using virtual reality techniques to investigate interactions between fully autonomous vehicles and vulnerable road users. In: Transportation Research Board Annual Meeting 2024, 1–10. TRB, Washington, D.C. (2024)
7. Taylor, R.M.: Situational awareness rating technique (SART): The development of a tool for aircrew systems design. In: Banbury, S., Tremblay, S. (eds.) A Cognitive Approach to Situation Awareness: Theory and Application, pp. 111–128. Ashgate, Aldershot (2011)
8. Card, S.K.: The model human processor: A model for making engineering calculations of human performance. In: Proc. of the Human Factors and Ergonomics Society Annual Meeting **25**(1), 1–5 (1981)

A Revised Method of AI Quality-In-Use Evaluation and Its Application to AI-Enhanced Drone

Ryuichi Ogawa[1]([✉]), Yoichi Sagawa[1], Shigeyoshi Shima[1,2], Toshihiko Takemura[1,3], and Shin-ichi Fukuzumi[4]

[1] Information-Technology Promotion Agency, Japan, Tokyo 113-6591, Japan
r-ogawa@ipa.go.jp
[2] University of Nagasaki, Nagasaki 851-2195, Japan
[3] Josai University, Saitama 350-0295, Japan
[4] Riken AIP, Tokyo 103-0027, Japan

Abstract. Building trustworthiness in AI has become a critical task of AI governance to secure trustworthiness of AI systems/services. Since the trustworthiness concept is highly broad, its evaluation and implementation are tough tasks both for AI system/service providers and users. The authors previously developed a process to evaluate AI systems' triste worthiness in terms of quality-in-use components. Using the systems' functional requirements, but the mapping design was complicated and application specific. In this paper we propose an improved method to evaluate the quality-in-use components, utilizing quality components and these measurement indices based on ISO/IEC software quality standards. The method provides a unified, cross-application process by mapping vendor-implemented product/service quality components to quality-in-use components to derive quantitative evaluation results. We apply this method to an autonomous drone case study and analyze its effectiveness.

Keywords: AI System · Non-functional requirements · Quality in Use · Software quality evaluation

1 Introduction

Maintaining trustworthiness has become critical for AI governance to provide safe, secure, and beneficial AI systems/services. AI governance has been discussed in terms of ethics and trust, and the term trustworthiness has been used to describe items that embody ethical and trust values such as fairness, accountability, sustainability, safety, and transparency. Since such trustworthiness concept is highly broad, its evaluation and implementation are tough tasks for AI system/service providers.

In order to ease implementation/evaluation load, AI system management standards such as ISO/IEC 42001:2023 [1] have included these items. Also system software quality standard model ISO/IEC 25010:2023 [2], SQuaRE, has been extended for AI as ISO/IEC 25059:2023 [3]. However, these standards are described in general terms and their relationship is not clear, so it is still difficult to practically implement and evaluate trustworthiness items such as safety, security, privacy, sustainability.

To cope with this problem, the authors proposed a comprehensive process to evaluate AI trustworthiness items using revised quality-in-use standard model, ISO/IEC 25017:2023 [4]. The process provides a method to map AI system/service requirements to quality-in-use components, usability, safety, and social acceptance, so that the evaluation can be quantitatively specified without user-testing [5].

We applied this model to evaluate quality-in-use components of AI-enhanced drone, which autonomously flies and respond emergency risks. We derived quantitative evaluation figure of quality-in-use component by summing up levels of requirement implementation that were mapped to the component. The mapping method proved to be effective to evaluate quality-in-use from product/service implementation data. It also proved to be effective to see how non-functional requirements such as level of learning, safety, and security contributed to quality-in-use.

However, the process includes development of a complex mapping model whose functional requirements are application dependent. It requires expert knowledge both on application area and requirement specification. Otherwise the model easily become inconsistent in granularity and complexity.

Another problem is that the model lacks the concept of clarifying product requirement and service requirement. The mixture of the two requirement types can again easily cause confusion and misunderstanding. We need a better mapping method whose process is simple, applicable to different applications with unified granularity, and yet structured so that product/service requirements are clarified.

Considering these, we propose a revised process model to employ a new mapping method consisting of trustworthiness-related requirements (reliability, safety, security, resilience, etc.). Reasons we focus on these requirements are: 1) they are common across various AI application area, 2) they are not too fine-grained and the mapping method can stay manageable, 3) we can take advantages of SQuaRE based quality components and their measurement indices, and 4) evaluation of implementation level of trustworthiness, both in terms of AI system product and its service requirement in a unified manner is meaningful for users. It helps their evaluating how trustworthy the corresponding AI system/service is in actual use.

Based on these ideas we re-design our previous process model. Quality requirements in the mapping method are reorganized with SQuaRE based quality components, and requirement structure in the mapping becomes two-steps, product quality part and corresponding service quality part. We apply this method to the autonomous drone case in [3] to derive quantitative evaluation of quality in use. Then we analyze the effectiveness of the method and remaining issues.

2 Problem Definition

2.1 Previous Work

We have attempted to develop a process of AI system/service evaluation in terms of quality-in-use perspective [5, 6, 7, 8 and 9]. Quality in use is important for AI systems/services since their quality is heavily environment dependent and they can change in actual use if they are capable of continuity learning.

Our method provides a quantitative evaluation process for AI users to see quality-in-use value, including trustworthiness, of AI system/service to help them judging if they accept the service or not. Figure 1 shows the overall process model. It comprises three parts: service quality requirement (left), quality-in-use components (center), and service value perceived by its user (right).

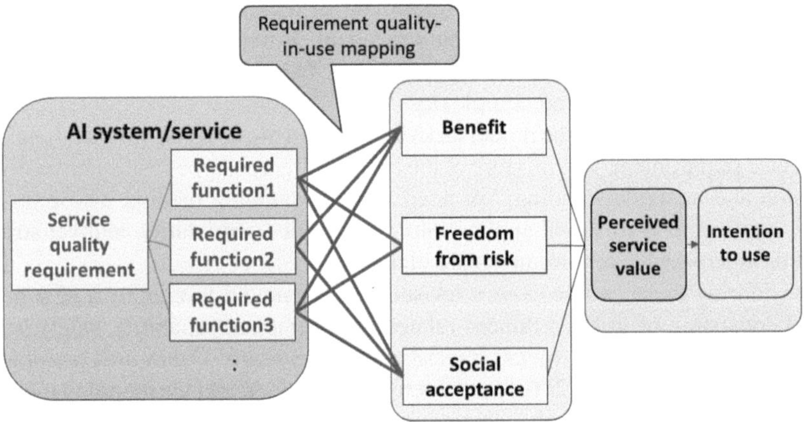

Fig. 1. AI system/service evaluation process model.

Here we assume that service requirement critically affects quality-in-use, and the quality-in-use critically affects service value perception. Mapping diagrams between required functions and quality-in-use components are important since they can visualize each function's impact to the components in quantitative form. The evaluation process is summarized as follows:

1. Develop AI system/service required function structure (usually tree based)
2. Map the requirement subcomponents in the structure to quality-in-use components/subcomponents
3. Determine quantitative level of implementation fulfilment of each required function subcomponent. Quantification must be common and simple such as three levels.
4. Sum up levels of subcomponents connected to each quality-in-use subcomponent. Summed-up figures indicate magnitude of the requirement fulfilment.

Here we are assuming that system/service requirement critically affects quality-in-use, and the quality-in-use critically affects service value perception to determine if users accept the service. Mapping diagrams between required functions and quality-in-use components are important since they can visualize each function's impact to the components in quantitative form.

2.2 Application to Autonomous Drone Case

We applied this method to a case of fictional autonomous drone which flies without a human operator. Also with the AI help, the drone reacts to emergency risks such as some malfunction, collision, severe weather. Figure 2 shows an example map of autonomous drone functional requirements and quality-in-use components. Required function structure is green colored. It includes machine learning requirements such as flight rules, geographical knowledge for routing and safety risk mitigation measures. Each subcomponent has an implementation requirement fulfilment level figure, ranging from 1 to 3, where level 2 indicates 'average quality.' Quality-in-use components/subcomponents are light yellow colored and red figure in each subcomponent shows summed-up levels. The figures show that the current requirement implementation impacts 'acceptability' most.

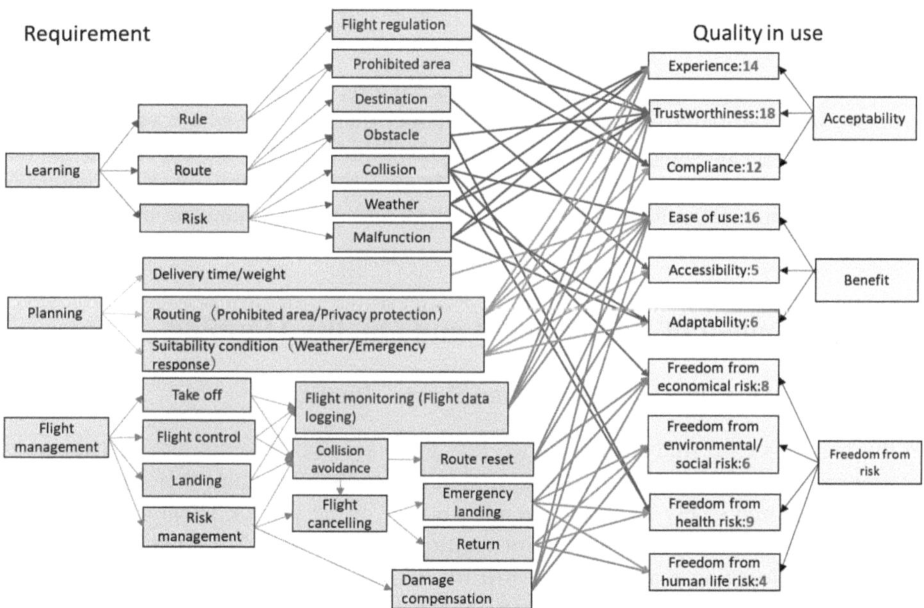

Fig. 2. AI drone functional requirements and their impact to quality-in-use components.

This method enables quantitative evaluation of quality in use without user testing. Also relative relationship of summed-up figures shows overall quality characteristics and provides meaningful feedback for system/service vendors regarding to see which requirement implementation should be more enhanced.

2.3 Problems of Requirement Mapping

The drone case study showed that quantitative quality-in-use evaluation can be possible by mapping the requirement implementation levels, but it also revealed the method's drawbacks. We summarize them as follows:

1. Method of developing requirement structure (green colored part of Fig. 2) is complicated and application dependent. Although expertise of application domain and product/service quality evaluation is needed, there is no guideline or support tools for that.
2. Role of stakeholders are not well specified. As for the drone case, operability of drone itself and drone control system is important for drone service vendor, but the operability is not priority issue for user who use the drone delivery service. Requirements and responsibilities of drone vendor and service vendor should be clarified in the mapping method.
3. Requirements for product quality and service quality are not specified. Regarding the above issue (2), service user often judge reliability by service quality issues such as delivery service continuity, compensation for accidents, etc. On the other hand, product reliability of drone is critical for service vendor, who is regarded as a 'user' of the drone. For precise evaluation mapping should be designed not to mix the two qualify types.

In the following we tackle these problems. We first divide the function requirement structure into two parts. The first step is 'product quality part' where product vendor is responsible for product requirement implementation, and the second step is 'service quality part' where service vendor is responsible for service requirement implementation. We then introduce SQuaRE based quality components and their measurement indices in each part of the requirement structure.

3 Improvement of Requirement and Quality Mapping

3.1 Separation of Product Quality and Service Quality

In the previous case study, we assumed that there are two stakeholders, drone service vendor and drone service user. This is reasonable in the viewpoint that service quality should be assured solely by service vendor, not by drone vendor. However, drone vendor should be indirectly responsible for requirements asking technological background and machine learning readiness to fulfill trustworthiness such as safety, security, and reliability. Here we assume the requirement mapping has two steps:

1. Product quality part

This part defines requirements for quality of product functions and product vendor is responsible for fulfilling the requirements. The quality components are critical for service vendor, from which the requirements come. Some of them such as safety and security can directly affect service user satisfaction.

2. Service quality part

This part defines quality requirements of service. Service vendor is responsible for fulfilling the requirements and secure product quality needed for it.

Note that product vendor and service vendor can be in one organization. But this separation is more precise expression of mapping of requirements and its fulfilment levels. Also this separation contributes who is responsible to maintain service quality. Figure 3 shows the two step mapping image. In the figure leftmost block (AI system function) is application dependent, but other requirement blocks need to be application independent. Bold arrows indicate that product quality can be directly a part of service quality and affect quality in use.

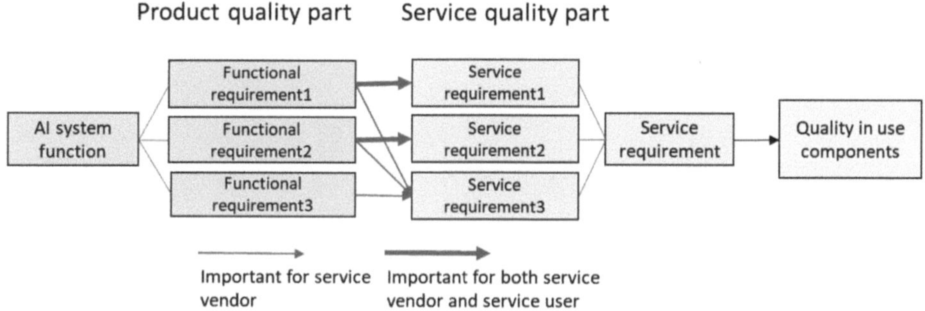

Fig. 3. Two step requirement mapping.

3.2 SQuaRE Based New Product Quality Model

For securing application independence in the mapping, we introduce SQuaRE based quality components and their evaluation measures. The newest version of SQuaRE standard, ISO/IEC 25010:2023 [2], is extended to include safety component. Also SQuaRE is extended for AI system as ISO/IEC 25059:2023 [3]. It includes AI specific quality subcomponents such as functional adaptability, user controllability, transparency, robustness and intervenability. However AI extended ISO/IEC 25059:2023 is based on the previous SQuaRE model, ISO/IEC 25010:20010, so safety extension is not included. As for software quality measurement, we refer to ISO/IEC 25023:2016 [10] for product quality evaluation and ISO/IEC 25011:2017 [11] for service quality, but they are also based on ISO/IEC 25010:2010 and need updating.

As shown above, the standards are not consistent and complete adoption of current versions are not desirable. In this paper we employ our own software quality models and measurement indices by adding necessary extension/subtraction to the standards. Accordingly we add evaluation items/measurement indices for updated models to the current components. Figure 4 shows parts of newly developed software quality components and subcomponents, including safety and AI extension. In the figure we have excluded compatibility and portability which have been regarded not significant for the drone case study.

Also we have excluded quality-in-use components, which are included in SQuaRE model, in our model. Reasons are: 1) quality-in-use components relates to both product and service quality and its clear separation is difficult, 2) standards say that measuring quality-in-use should be by user feedback. Such user evaluation process is inherently included in our quality-in-use evaluation process model shown in Fig. 1.

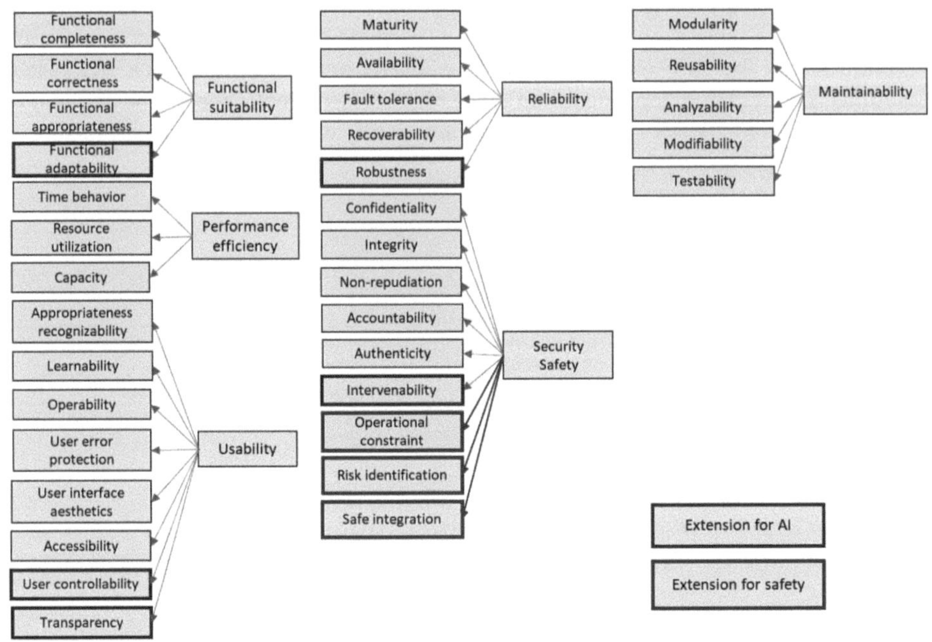

Fig. 4. Product quality model with safety and AI extension.

3.3   SQuaRE Based Service Quality Model

As for service quality, we first adopt ISO/IEC 25011:2017 components. We temporally add security components with the same subcomponents in the product quality model. We do not add AI extension, since we think that AI quality is clearly separable in product layer, but the quality separation become difficult in service layer. In the service layer, trustworthiness related components are already included and we must examine what new AI related categories are necessary. Currently we see the issue as a future work. Figure 5 shows the current version of service quality model.

The main task of the revised mapping method is to connect subcomponents of Figs. 4 and 5 and assign fulfilment level figures to the connections. Figure 6 shows a schematic relationship between product quality subcomponents and service quality subcomponents. Bold arrows show that quality of a product quality connected by the arrow significantly affects corresponding service quality. Keeping this relationship in mind, service vendor is required to implement service quality.

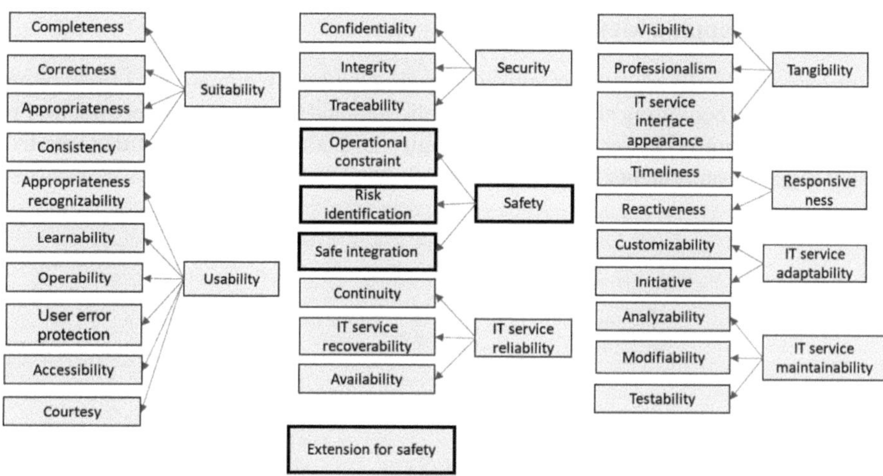

Fig. 5. Service quality model with safety extension.

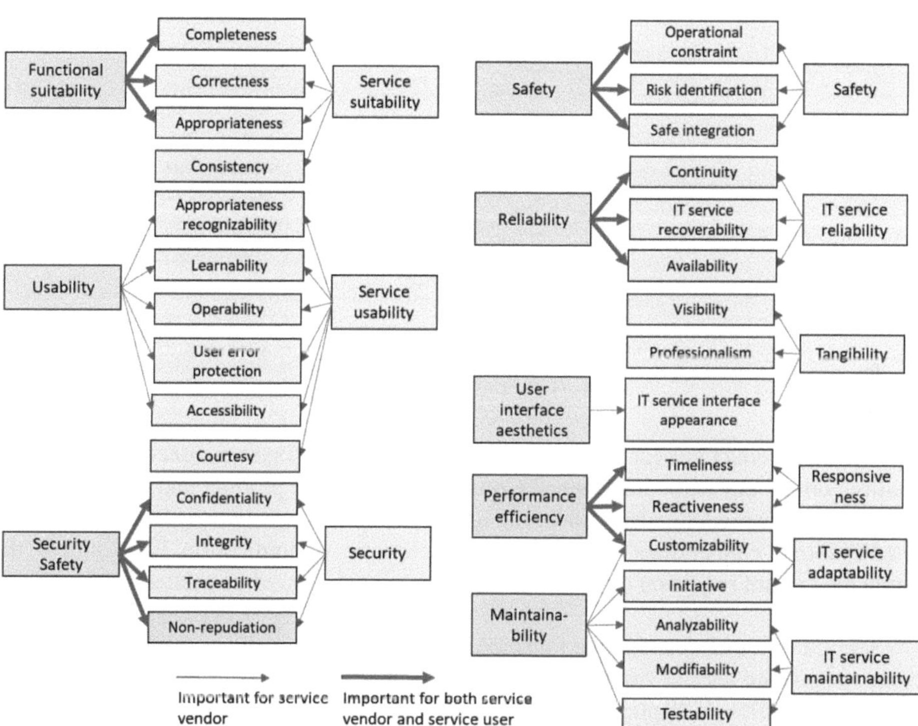

Fig. 6. Relationship of product quality and service quality.

3.4　Revised Mapping Method

Figure 7 schematically shows our revised mapping method. Compared to Fig. 2, requirement structure is becoming simple, less complicated and application independent. Product vendor is required to secure product quality and connect required functions to the product quality components.

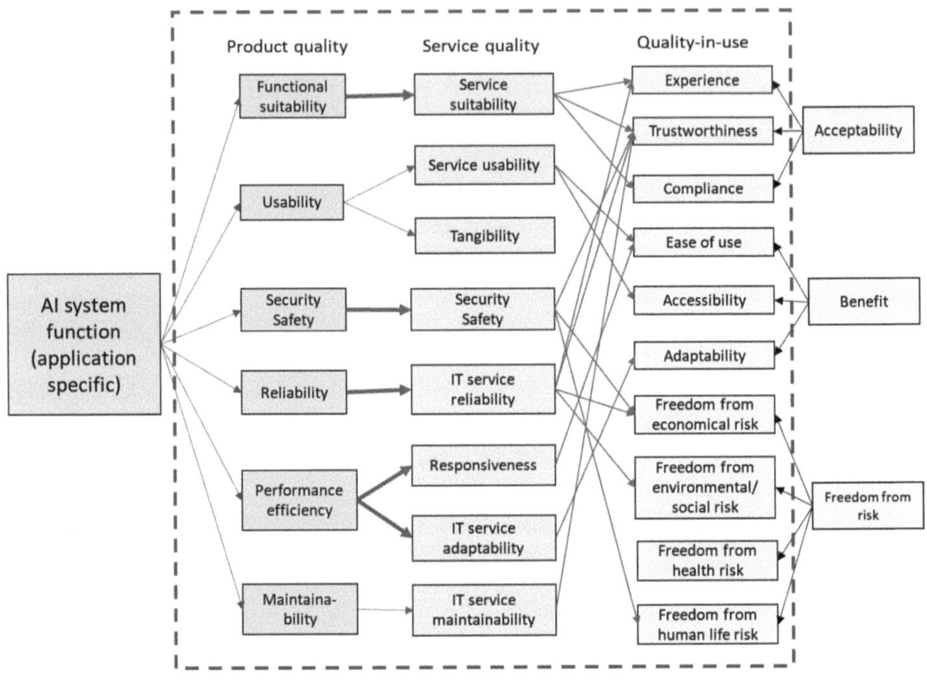

Fig. 7. Revised mapping model

Also the product vendor is responsible for connecting AI system functions to product quality components/subcomponents. Connections between product and service quality components are predefined as shown in Fig. 6, but product and service vendors can agree to add/subtract connections according to characteristics of application. For example, the drone case is not requiring evaluation of system portability, so its related connection is not defined.

Service vendor is responsible for implementing service quality and connecting components between service quality and quality-in-use. The connections heavily relies on the characteristics of application, so that this method assigns its role to service vendor. The vendor is required to define connections, determine fulfilment level of their implementation and sum up them to derive quantitative evaluation of the quality-in-use components.

In actual use of the application, the quality-in-use evaluation should be updated by user feedback. With the feedback product vendor and service vendor need to implement necessary enhancements and refine connections..

3.5 Quality Measurement

In the mapping process vendors make connections between product quality and service quality having the same component/subcomponent names such as 'usability,' 'operability,' and 'testability.' But their evaluation target and measurement are different between product and service. For example, operability of AI drone product should be measured by the operational functions of drone, but operability of AI drone service need to be evaluated by the whole operability including Web interface for users. To clarify the difference of product and service measurement, we adopt abovementioned ISO/IEC 25023:2016 and ISO/IEC 25011:2017. Since they are not updated to the newest SQuaRE, we do not mandate full compliance.

Both standards provide application-independent measurement indices (such as number of measures taken, ratio of measure implemented), but in this paper we employ 'interpretation' approach. That is, we interpret application-independent indices into drone specific terms. As for newly emerging quality indices (such as 'risk identification of risks' in 'safety') we introduce new drone-specific indices (such as 'AI identifiable risks: malfunction, obstacle, collision, bad weather'). Table 1 shows examples of interpreted product/service measurement indices.

Table 1. Examples of quality measurement indices.

Quality component	Subcomponent	Interpreted measurement indices
Product Functional suitability Performance efficiency Usability Reliability	Correctness Resource utilization Transparency Robustness	Precision of auto re-routing, landing Precision of risk condition detection Power consumption during one flight Number of explainable AI decisions Number of risk avoidance measures
Service Suitability Security IT service reliability IT service reliability Responsiveness	Appropriateness Traceability Recoverability Availability Reactiveness	Ratio of successful services without delay Frequency of delivery trace reporting Number of successful retry delivery Serviceable time, area, weather, frequency Time lag of responding emergency request

4 Analysis

4.1 Effectiveness of the Mapping Method

1. Derivation of quality-in-use evaluation measurements

SQuaRE standards request product vendors to implement quality in use. But it could be a tough task for the vendor since relationship of quality components with product/service quality is not clearly defined in the standards. Also quality-in-use evaluation is thought to be highly environment dependent and it is hard to assume a 'most common user environment' at initial stages of development. This issue becomes more intense for

AI systems with 'continuity learning' capability. Such AI system continues to learn user environments, so that its quality also continues to change along with learning.

The mapping method provides quantitative measurements of quality-in-use components, based on the fulfilment level of product and service quality implementation. This is a simple and straightforward approach to derive quality-in-use by implemented product/service quality, reducing vendors' load such as function tuning for individual user environments. The measurements derived by the method can be a 'first approximation' or a start point of quality-in-use evaluation and should be refined by reflecting user feedback later. The mapping can be a useful tool for reflecting user requests to product/service quality improvement.

2. Advantages of SQuaRE based mapping

Adding to the clarification of quality category relationship, assuring universality is another motivation to integrate SQuaRE based product/service components in the mapping method. The mapping provides a unified view of quality implementation across application areas, avoiding inconsistency of model granularity and semantic difference. Also the view shows clear separation of product and service quality. Without SQuaRE models' assistance, the separation/integration of the two quality types would be hard for vendors (service vendor in particular).

4.2 Issues of the Mapping Method

1. Quality measurement

The mapping method provides examples of quality fulfilment measurement indices. A problem here is that the indices are required to be quantitative and specific, so that many of them tend to be application dependent (see Table 1). Such application specific indices might be easy to measure but might not be appropriate for expressing required quality. There could be as many application-specific indices as the number of use cases, so that measuring all of them become expensive and hard to manage. Simple and abstract index (such as number of errors) could be better for the measurement. Deriving suitable indices would need time for trial and error. Guideline for measurement index selection for important use cases would be required.

2. Level assignment

Assigning fulfilment levels to quality-in-use connections needs deliberate preparation. There is no common rules/guidelines to determine to what extent product/service quality should be for a service except for regulations (such as safety and security), so the whole implementation is up to service vendors' design. The vendor should clearly define the requirements and assign fulfilment levels. Also this would require a level-assigning process guideline.

3. AI extension toward trustworthiness

In recent years providing 'trustworthy AI' has become a critical issue and AI governance policies/guidelines are based on the concept (such as [12]). The trustworthiness concept is partially incorporated into newest SQuaRE model [3], but more work might be needed to align the concept to trustworthiness-related components already in SQuaRE (safety, security, reliability etc.). Also emerging AI quality issues such as 'fairness' or 'biased judgement' might require more extension. Regarding AI quality, our mapping method is based on the current SQuaRE scheme of integration. Along with the progress of SQuaRE model and trustworthiness concept implementation, the mapping method should be reviewed for improvement.

5 Conclusion

We have proposed a revised request-quality mapping method for AI system evaluation process. The method separates product quality model and service quality model to derive evaluation measurements for quality in use of AI system provides in unified manner. The method is based on the current SQuaRE models and their measurement indices, with its own extension. Autonomous drone case study showed that the method is effective for 1) clarifying and reducing the load of vendors quality evaluation tasks and 2) providing process of continuous quality evaluation and improvement. Also reducing measurement cost, requirement-fulfilment-level assignment support and AI extension have been identified as remaining issues. We will attempt to apply the method for more detailed use case to tackle these issues.

References

1. ISO/IEC 42001:2023 Information technology -Artificial intelligence - Management system. https://www.iso.org/standard/81230.html
2. ISO/IEC 25010:2023 Systems and software engineering - Systems and software Quality Requirements and Evaluation (SQuaRE) - Product quality model
3. https://www.iso.org/standard/78176.html
4. ISO/IEC 25059:2023 Software engineering - Systems and software Quality Requirements and Evaluation (SQuaRE) - Quality model for AI systems
5. https://www.iso.org/standard/80655.html
6. SO/IEC 25019:2023 Systems and software engineering - Systems and software Quality Requirements and Evaluation (SQuaRE) - Quality-in-use model
7. https://www.iso.org/standard/78177.html
8. Ogawa, R., Sagawa, Y., Shima, S., Takemura, T., Fukuzumi, S.: A Case Study on AI System Evaluation from Users' Viewpoints. Human Interface and the Management of Information (HCII2024), Springer, pp. 238–248, (2024)
9. Ogawa, R., Shima, S., Takemura, T., Fukuzumi, S.: A Study on Trust Building in AI Systems Through User Commitment. Human-Computer Interaction Design and User Experience (HCII2023), Springer, pp.557–567 (2023)
10. Shima, S., Ogawa, R., Sagawa, Y., Takemura, T.: Quantitative measurement of the decline in quality in use due to AI misjudgment (in Japanese). Proceedings of Computer Security Symposium 2022, pp.759–766 (2022)
11. Shima, S., Ogawa, R., Sagawa, Y., Takemura, T.: Impact analysis of the influence of AI misjudgment risk on intention to use AI systems (in Japanese). Proceedings of 2023 Symposium on Cryptography and Security (SCIS2023), 4E-2 (2023)
12. Fukuzumi, S., Hirasawa, N., Wada, N., Komiyama, T., Azuma, M.: Proposal of quality in use in software quality. Human-Computer Interaction Design and User Experience (HCII2020), Springer, pp.431–438 (2020)

13. ISO/IEC 25023:2016 Systems and software engineering - Systems and software Quality Requirements and Evaluation (SQuaRE) - Measurement of system and software product quality
14. https://www.iso.org/standard/35747.html
15. ISO/IEC TS 25011:2017 Information technology - Systems and software Quality Requirements and Evaluation (SQuaRE) - Service quality models
16. https://www.iso.org/standard/35735.html
17. NIST Trustworthy and Responsible AI NIST AI 600-1 Artificial Intelligence Risk Management Framework: Generative Artificial Intelligence Profile

Tracking Expressions and Emotions: The Experience of Virtual Youtubers in Building Their Avatars

Marcos Silbermann[(✉)] [iD] and Hanah Correa [iD]

SIDIA, Manaus, Brazil
`Marcos.silbermann@sidia.com`

Abstract. Vtuber is the term used to define YouTubers and virtual influencers (Lee et al., 2022). This simplified definition relates the activity of digital content production to the use of 2d or 3d avatars modeled to respond to the physical and bodily reactions of these influencers. The content produced by Vtubers and the aesthetics of the avatars used visual and behavioral elements from Japanese Idol and Otaku culture (Regis et al, 2024; Azuma, 2009). The universe of Vtuber content creators and production agencies is intrinsically related to the technological development of sensors for tracking physical and body movements (Lehtovirta, 2023) in parallel with the improvement of 3D modeling software. Content producers and their followers relate the expressive potential of characters to the quality of tracking their visual reactions and the detailed modeling of the avatar. This has aroused the curiosity of vtubers in the development of 3D avatars and the acquisition of Head Mounted Devices to reproduce full body interactions and feel closer to their audience. The Vtuber market has expanded in recent years led by the emergence of agencies such as Vshojo, Hololive and Nijisanji (Regis et al, 2024) responsible for managing the careers of a growing number of this type of creators and structuring a content production model (Regis et al 2024). Together with the consolidation of agency vtubers, a growing number of autonomous Vtubers, called in this universe as Independent Vtubers (Lehtovirta, 2023), who produce their own content and engage in the creation and modeling of their avatars. Independent vtubers present themselves as a consumer niche for modeling applications and mixed reality devices (XR).

The objective of this article is to present how Independent Vtubers develop and relate to their avatars, from the perspective of UX Design, the article discusses the values constructed by performers and the main difficulties encountered by users engaged in this new field of content production. In this way, the relationship between Vtuber, creator and user, with their avatar is understood as an object, which articulates the expressive capacity desired by users and the difficulties they encounter in modeling and performing with their avatars. This particularity places Vtubers' activity as a new form of content production that synthesizes work on digital platforms such as YouTube, new forms of artistic expression and technological development and innovation. This research was organized in two phases. Firstly, we entered social media groups and started monitoring the profiles of famous Vtubers and their communities on platforms such as X, Reddit and Youtube. In the second phase, we immersed ourselves in the experience of Independent Vtubers by conducting nine interviews with people who work as independent vtubers.

H. Mori et al. (Eds.): HCII 2025, LNCS 16333, pp. 211–226, 2026.
https://doi.org/10.1007/978-3-032-12660-3_17

These semi-structured interviews (Gil, 2021) allowed the collection of in-depth information about their daily lives and the challenges they faced, especially in their process of building and refining their avatars and their expectations related to reality technologies. Mixed.

The results found reveal how the avatar used by Vtuber is understood as a tool of personal expression, which allows the user to elaborate and express feelings and emotions that they are unable to express in their daily lives (Lee et al., 2022). It not only represents the image of the vtuber but circumscribes the construction of a new identity. Avatars are an ongoing project of vtubers this type of user is continually engaged in improving and refining their avatar's personality and 2D/3D model. In parallel, the research mapped opportunities for introducing emerging mixed reality technologies, identifying situations and usage scenarios in which these technologies can help these users' experiences. From the vtuber's point of view, there is always a level of improvements to be made, whether in the degree of complexity of body expressions, the type of avatar chosen, or the content formats generated. The vtubers interviewed revealed that they already intended to purchase XR devices or were studying the idea of editing their avatar into a 3D model to use immersive tools and applications. This is a desire fueled not only by large companies that already use studios equipped with sensors to promote live shows, but also by independent vtubers who use XR devices to interact closely with their audience through 3D virtual platforms. The article demonstrated the existence of a variety of opportunities for the development of digital products aimed at solving the daily problems of Independent Vtubers, with the intention of enhancing their experience by making it simpler and more expressive, by offering more customizable and easy-to-model forms. of your avatars.

Keywords: Vtuber · Content Production · Tracking

1 Introduction

This research was carried out during the exploratory phase of a project that aimed to understand the experience of using content producers with the support of 2D and 3D avatars. The article proposes a discussion about the strategies used by independent virtual youtubers (Regis et al 2024), to increase the 2D or 3D models used in the creation of content for social media in an anonymous way. Independent vtubers develop on the margins of the centralized market of agencies specialized in production and promotion of two-dimensional and three-dimensional avatars. More broadly, at this moment, we identify the emergence of new technological arrangements and forms of artistic and cultural expression among these producers of virtual content. The form of content production vtuber consolidates an innovative relationship between an arsenal of technologies for tracking body movements, two-dimensional and three-dimensional object modeling software and the performer's ability to express himself/herself and connect with his/her audience.

The article presents how the experience of vtuber content production has been structured, from the perspective of the non-agency vtubers, here called independent vtubers. The intention is to highlight the historical and cultural context of this emerging market and its relationship with concepts present in the idol and otaku universes through the look of independent performers in their mixed characteristic as consumers and producers of content in a market still in consolidation. This article presents how independent Vtubers find in the artistic and expressive potentials of easy tracking technologies and movement disseminated in recent smartphones and head mounted devices. At the same time, we draw attention to how this process is linked to the centralization carried out by agencies specialized in content Vtuber and their effort to establish the technological framework for content production of this market, besides indirectly defining parameters of style, quality and type of content produced.

In turn, the agencies that manage the career of vtubers have a socio-technical apparatus (Law, 2007) composed of designers and developers and motion capture studios necessary to build avatars, map the body of the performer, track their movements, and change your voice to perform livestreams and live concerts. For these vtubers the access to artists, animators, programmers and studios with cutting-edge technologies is part of the way content production. Unlike vtubers who start their activities independently without any kind of support, seeking on the internet and especially in social media communities the knowledge and support necessary to develop their avatars and finance the technical set-up for production.

Building 2D and 3D avatars can be a complicated task for those who have never had contact with modeling tools, as well as acquiring motion tracking equipment and devices that support the technologies necessary for vtuber activity, as microphone, webcam and desktop, can become a high financial investment. Faced with these obstacles the performer who wants to be a vtuber independently seeks affordable ways to overcome barriers, whether technological or financial limitations. Such as using smartphones with motion tracking technology to map the movements of the face allowing the realization of lives on platforms like Youtube and Twitch.

In this scenario, the agencies consolidate themselves in the vtuber market establishing the quality standard for the other members of this universe. The combination of different types of devices and technologies favors the development of this content creation sector where the performer uses an avatar whether it is bidimensional or three-dimensional as a tool for social and cultural expression without its identity being revealed, being thus an anonymous content creator under a totally different identity from his reality. In the vtuber market, the agencies determine the parameters of quality and professionalization of the vtuber activity as well as have the necessary technological apparatus for creating models and production of this type of content. As well as the technical configuration, the avatar itself is a property of the agency, which can replace your performer if necessary. Anonymity is mediated by the technological and social arrangements elaborated in the broader cultural context that reveals this market movements of this type of content, revealing new forms of interaction between technology and artistic expression.

Finally, the article highlights as a case of independent Vtubers has been presented as a specific use scenario for emerging technologies such as mixed reality devices (XR) (Hillmann, 2021) and helps to envision a future for using these technologies. Due to the presence of tracking tools with an accurate level integrated into the Head Mounted Devices and its potential for production of events and livestreams with the virtual presence of followers in immersive environments the mixed reality technologies arise as a possible advance to this emerging technology platform.

In its second session, the article presents how the unhired vtubers, named here, as independent vtubers seek to build their artistic and professional trajectories through community ties, which offer the social context for the formation of their performances, at the same time that it functions as a platform to overcome the social and technological barriers they encounter to become producers of this kind of specific content.

2 Methods and Materials

The research sought to explore the universe of virtual youtubers who act independently without association with specialized agencies. With the aim of developing an initial set of information and knowledge about this topic, focusing on performers and their behaviors, rituals and strategies used in the creation of content for social media. So that we could then understand aspects of the performer's relationship with technology and its practices of creating two-dimensional and three-dimensional models and use of body movement mapping devices. The study was structured in two stages using different methodological tools. We initially conducted an ethnographic process in the digital field (Hine, 2015) between May and June 2024, with the purpose of building a broad set of references and broadening our vision about the agents that compose this universe, such as fans, agencies, performers and artists. We monitor profiles of famous vtubers and the main communities on different social media such as X, Facebook and Reddit. This was a fundamental process to identify relationships and social dynamics established between the different actors of this universe, as well as for the identification of values and difficulties narrated in digital communities.

However, the collection of primary data and the monitoring of the interactions of vtubers and their followers through social media has limitations, mainly, regarding the identification of practices and routines of performers related to their daily content production. In this sense, the ethnography was complemented by semi-structured interviews (Gil, 2021) with independent vtubers. In the second phase of the research, we conducted semi-structured interviews with about 10 independent vtubers from countries such as Brazil, USA and Finland. What allowed us to deepen the understanding of the individual process that surrounds the transition of a fan who becomes performer as well as production practices in the use of motion tracking technologies and modeling tools.

3 The Origins of the Vtuber Universe: Between the Idol and Otaku Cultures

About two decades ago, the first virtual idol appeared in Japan. In Japanese culture idols are a consolidated element, they are models, singers, dancers and actors, who operate as symbols of youth and lifestyle. They are considered true lifestyle and behavior ideals for fans and receive, in return, the full manifestation of their support and affection (Galbraith und Karlin, 2012). In 2007, Hatsune Miku was launched into the market by a Japanese technology company to be the first virtual idol (Lee, 2023). To bring Hatsune to life, its creators used a voice synthesizer technology called Vocaloid, which consists of pre-recorded vocals from voice actors or singers (Le, 2014). Hatsune Miko's performances use holograms and led screens to reproduce animations without the presence of a human performer accompanied by facial and body tracking tools.

Later, in 2011, the youtuber Ami Yamato started his activities by making vlogs using an animated 3D avatar model, which represented her, while she kept anonymous, Ami is recognized as the first creator of content identified by Vtuber (Baitello et al., 2023; Gamesight, 2023). However, the term virtual youtuber would only be consolidated years later with the debut of Kizuna AI, a 2D youtuber sponsored by the company Active8 (Baitello et al., 2023). Starting her career in 2016 (Mamat, 2022), Kizuna AI has become a worldwide sensation, reaching more than 2 million subscribers on her channel in less than a year (Gamesight, 2023). Behind the 2D model of Kizuna AI there is an anonymous performer, who uses body tracking technologies to perform in concerts and live lives.

The concept of virtual youtubers, or vtubers, has been consolidated as an intercession of two niches of Japanese culture, the culture idol and the otaku culture. The idol sphere involves the performer character of vtuber where a real person assumes the role of a character to perform live performances and stands as a reference that depends on the approval and support of the public. The term Otaku was coined in the 70's (Regis et al, 2024) and comes from the Japanese meaning home, a word that referred to individuals who isolated themselves in their homes to consume Japanese multimedia content such as comics, series, actions figures (Azuma, 2009; Regis et al, 2024) (Fig. 1).

Fig. 1. The first virtual youtuber, Kizuna AI. Source: https://kizunaai.com/Imagem Kizuna.

These fields of Japanese culture have reached a wide contingent of people around the world and strongly influenced the formation of a vtuber content fan community, both in style, and in forms of production and interaction with the public. Vtubers create digital content with their 2d or 3D animated avatars for social media while maintaining their anonymous identities (Lee et al., 2022; Regis et al, 2024). The characteristics or personalities assumed by the Vtubers build a diversity of universes inhabited by these characters (Baitello et al., 2023) in frank dialogue with concepts, aspects and behaviors common to idol culture and Otaku, the vtubers merge the fictional with reality (Gailbraith, 2016).

Concepts like Moe and Kawaii are widely used by vtubers to build their personalities whether they reflect themselves or totally different from reality. The term Moe refers to the ability of a female personality to appear innocent and vulnerable, in an idealized way, to inspire feelings of affection and protection in its audience (Regis et al, 2024; Gailbraith und Karlin, 2016). In the same direction, the term kawaii means "cute" and refers to the cuteness of an object or person (Regis et al, 2024; Mamat et al., 2022).

In the case of vtubers the modeled characters have their stories composed by a diversity of narratives and references to pop culture as well as Otaku. As is the case of a Brazilian vtuber interviewed, who tells us how most independent vtubers develop a story for their characters and how these narrative aspects align the independent Vtuber with Asian cultural aspects, even she finds parallels with the culture of her home country, Brazil. This moment, according to her, is of anxiety about the construction of the character, since it defines his career as Vtuber:

"Most of the vtubers end up creating a background for the model. There are some people who really embody the character and end up acting. But I can't, so I'm myself. But I created a story for my character, she is an alien bunny that came from the moon. It is because of an Asian legend that comes from China and Japan. In Brazil people see Saint George on the moon, in Asia they see a rabbit. My character is a villain who came to dominate the Earth. I say that I and the Dark Lord, my mascot, will take over the world and start making Lives to raise subjects for our cause". (Interviewed 3, 2024) (Fig. 2).

Fig. 2. Independent vtuber interviewed. Source: Author's Compilation, 2024.

The vtubers stand out as a subfield of this larger universe that involves idols and members of the Otaku culture, taking advantage of these references to explore new narratives and modes of production. In this direction, the development of body mapping technologies over the years, together with new forms of content creation and expression of the Otaku culture, favored the emergence of the vtuber community.

Although the vtuber community has existed for almost a decade, it has achieved great relevance by crossing Japanese borders from the years of the covid-19 pandemic, between 2020 and 2022, (Regis et al, 2024; Rebuli et al., 2023; Byron, 2022), driven by the increase in internet consumption and Otaku content during the period of social isolation. The current, post-pandemic moment is of frank expansion of this universe. The consolidation of this market and the establishment of production modes and quality standards are largely determined by the centrality of agencies that recruit performers and manage all areas of their careers as vtubers (Regis et al, 2024).

The main economic activities related to the market of agencies and vtuber content are still strongly focused on the Asian public, however, there is an effort directed by the main agents of this market for a new portion of the globe, fans present in markets such as the US and Brazil. Currently in the market there are numerous vtubers agencies, the main companies, such as Hololive[1] and Nijisanji[2], are Japanese, which not only manage vtubers' careers, but provide advice for content creation, use of technology, modeling and tracking their avatars. These agencies were pioneers in the area and today set the quality parameters for format, content and style (Fig. 3).

Fig. 3. Hololive talents and Nijisanji talents. Source: Hololive[3] and Nijisanji[4] website.

As part of the vtuber community's overseas expansion plan, agencies have invested in groups of vtubers for specific audiences such as Indonesian and English speakers. Hololive, for example, founded the HoloMyth[5] group in 2020, which had five female figures speaking English. One of them vtuber Gawr Gura reached the milestone of 4 million subscribers on Youtube in 2025, being the vtuber with the highest number of subscribers in the world. The growth of the vtuber community around the world has been accompanied by the foundation of agencies in countries where this market is emerging as the Brazilian agency Neobaka[6] and the American agency Vshojo[7] (Fig. 4).

This is a strategy to connect with the public, agencies have sought to expand the market through the diversification of languages and types of content produced in the various existing platforms. In this way, both Vtubers managed and independents, have

---

[1] https://hololivepro.com/en/

[2] https://www.nijisanji.jp/en

[3] https://hololive.hololivepro.com/en/talents

[4] https://www.nijisanji.jp/en/talents

[5] https://hololive.hololivepro.com/en/talents?gp=myth

[6] https://www.youtube.com/neobaka

[7] https://www.vshojo.com/

Fig. 4. Vtuber Gawr Gura, part of the HoloMyth group. Source: Hololive website[8]

sought to test different audiences, as a strategy to reach a large number of viewers, who can become part of their community of fans.

4 Independent Vtuber: Between the Fan and the Content Creator

On the other hand, independent vtubers have a hybrid character formed between the idolatry and attention lived by the fan and concerns about monetization and improvement of performance of digital content producers. Acting in parallel to the development of agencies, they see them as references for content production, finding in the activity vtuber a way to express-creatively, while understanding it as a professional activity that can be performed from home and with sufficient earnings to maintain their livelihood.

These vtubers are at the margin of the process led by agencies and develop their own rituals and livelihoods. While the agent vtuber relies on the resources provided by its agency the independent vtuber builds its existence from scratch. From modeling their avatars to managing their careers. Generally, the independent vtuber starts his/hers activities even if it has not reached the quality standard observed in the agencies so that with its performance get the investment necessary to make improvements in your avatar and devices.

To start the performer needs to have a 2D or 3D model, so it is necessary to use modeling software such as Live2D Cubism to design and animate the avatar. The learning curve of this type of application is high and it is necessary to invest time to build a detailed model, with the amount of assets and layers required to achieve an acceptable quality

---

[8] https://hololive.hololivepro.com/en/talents/gawr-gura/

standard. In this universe the artistic, social and technological expression are at the same point. Through the interviews conducted with independent vtubers we identified the particularities of their creation processes in their initiation journey as virtual youtubers. Developing ways of appropriation of technology according to their reality and exploring the potential of the digital community independent vtubers walk on their own. In this initial trajectory, they develop particular processes in the modeling of their avatars, in the production of content and in the construction of their technical configurations, seeking to achieve the quality standards required in a market referenced by agencies.

The interviewed independent vtubers narrate common processes that occur during the initiation period of their activities. These processes are marked by rituals and terminology common to the idol culture and Otaku. In the context of the vtuber universe some boundaries are blurred, the boundary between the fan and the content producer are eclipsed, because the whole process involved to produce becomes collective (Jenkins, 2006).

The community has great influence on the performance of independent vtubers and companies. In such a way that the market sees the work of fans and artists as a crucial part of the success of their content creators. In this sense the fans, consumers of this niche, are important not only as a demonstration of relevance to the market, but also as drivers of the process (Jenkins, 2006). Fans not only consume the content provided by their idols, but absorb it, reformulate and share their own narratives across multiple platforms (Jenkins, 2006; Regis et al, 2024; Brandão, 2010). Participation in the vtuber community enables the different actors of this universe, artists, fans, animators and vtubers a channel for social, artistic and technological expression. Allowing the expression of feelings and the formation of bonds of belonging in digital communities. Practice that reinforces the concept of participatory culture proposed by Jenkins (2006), where the consumer is stimulated to be an active agent in the interaction, transformation and sharing of the knowledge produced.

5   The Beginning of Life of an Independent Vtuber

The independent vtubers interviewed were mostly young people who, at the time of the interview, were in training and looking for ways to work from home. Most of the interviewees came into contact with the vtuber culture during the period of the covid-19 pandemic, between 2020 and 2022. From this perspective, the gateway to vtuber content consumption was the universe involving idols and participants of the Otaku culture. Later, with the perceptions created during isolation, these young people began to see in the activity vtuber a monetary potential, which could play together with other activities.

This is the case of one of our interviewees who acts as an independent vtuber creating content for Youtube and Twitch, she says that her main source of income comes from artistic production of models and illustrations for vtubers. In this case she uses the production of content as vtuber to also promote her work as an artist, and thus receive commissions [9]:

---

[9] Commission is the term commonly used by artists to describe the act of commissioning an art or project.

"I am basically a digital illustrator; I work mainly in the area of vtubers. I do illustrations and in general my livestreams consist of these drawings because I use this as a form of marketing for my commissions (Orders of Modeled Avatars and other art assets received from other vtubers). I also end up doing Livestream games, chatting and react. Currently I'm living off the commissions focused on vtubers, which is my main base, but also survive from the money, which I earn from Youtube and Twitch." (Interviewed 2, 2024).

The interviewee's speech directly exposes how the Vtuber universe is based on the structure of a digital community, in which the fan and content creator roles are interspersed. Similarly, this type of activity is used as an indirect economic activity and the vtuber's own avatar, a kind of portfolio to capture customers for performance. This happens due to the indistinguishable character of the independent vtuber, who sees in his activity a professional life at the same time, in which it is part of a community of fans and consumers.

The initial period of the trajectory of independent vtubers as beginning content creators is an arduous time, which for the interviewees seems to involve making a large number of definitive choices of their careers and trajectories as virtual youtubers. It is a period in which the focus of vtubers is on an anxious work, in which they need to define the character's story, categories of content produced, build an avatar model and structure their strategies for reaching and connecting with the public (Fig. 5).

Fig. 5. Vtuber interviewed, her model is a moth girl. Source: Author's compilation, 2024.

In this phase of conceptualization, the independent vtubers build their characters based on the characteristics and concepts of the Japanese culture Otaku and idol to build their personality traits and aesthetics. Through what is consumed they build their own narratives in order to form a connection with their audience, which directly influences the way the avatar will be built.

The construction of an avatar is a central activity of the experience of the vtubers, it is at one time object of symbolic elaboration as well as work tool. In this circumstance it is necessary to idealize the identity of the character to which the performer will give life and define his personality, aesthetic references and physical attributes. There are two types of avatar models that performers use to act as vtubers, the most commonly used being the two-dimensional model (2D) and the second one the three-dimensional model (3D). The 2D model is an accessible format, because it is easier to make at the same time, which does not require a large processing capacity in the use of specific tools in the vtuber machine. The 3D model, has its performance and modes of interaction closer to the real, but its manufacture is complex and requires the use of software with high processing capacity, because each 3D model brings together numerous layers and assets to make every reaction as fluid as possible. This is also what the interview participant, a 26-year-old Brazilian vtuber who has been working as an independent professional for about five years: "When I started making the lives the 2D model was more popular. I believe it's easier and you have more creative freedom in 2D. I think you can convey what you want more accurately than in 3D." (Interviewee 3, 2024).

The construction of an avatar is a central activity of the experience of vtubers, it is the OS vtubers participants of the interview narrate the difficulties, that they find in the construction of their avatars given the complexity of the tools and the need for prior knowledge about illustration, modeling and rigging of 2D or 3D models. Any model involves many details and additional layers in its manufacture which may involve a high investment of labor and resources, because according to the interviewees modeling tools are expensive and require a long learning period. Just like ordering an avatar is a complex and expensive process that can take up to two months to complete, while the vtuber waits to receive his/her model. The work of artists and animators can go beyond four thousand reais (in brazilian currency, about 800 dollars) depending on the need of the vtuber and the amount of assets required.

In this sense the vtuber that is at this time can choose to hire artists and modelers, or independent studios that are specialized in creating avatars for vtubers. But if the investment is too expensive the vtuber can choose to make your avatar on their own which will require the acquisition of paid software and a period of learning complex practices. In this case they seek to acquire the knowledge and skills necessary to model their avatar through courses and tutorials available on the internet, tips from community participants and support from more experienced friends in the area.

Therefore, digital communities are of vital importance for the vtuber ecosystem. The incorporation of fans as content producers is one of the great strategies of the vtuber market. Even among the independent vtubers, with limited market share, active performance in multiplatform channels is a fundamental professionalization strategy to network, and especially to give and seek technical support among their peers. In these digital spaces there is a margin for creative production that generates even economic exchanges between fans-producers who act as artists and 3D modelers and independent vtubers. Due to the level of expertise and technical knowledge required to create and model 2D and 3D avatars, these independent professionals find an entry path to employment opportunities in this universe, supporting independent vtubers who are starting their activities.

Even after the end of modeling, the finished avatar becomes an open project for independent vtubers. The research participants showed a continuous interest in making improvements in their character by increasing rigging and acquiring new clothes, accessories or evolving the two-dimensional model to three-dimensional. Independent vtubers at the beginning of their career often face significant limitations, such as lack of financial resources, simple technical configuration and little familiarity with content creation and technological tools. Given this scenario, they develop strategies to gradually improve their equipment and virtual models to improve the quality of their productions and achieve more engagement with their audience.

For the young vtubers interviewed, being a vtuber is not only an opportunity for artistic and social expression (Baitello et al., 2023), but also an opportunity for financial gain without the need to leave home. Each vtuber has its own motivation, whether it is the need to work part-time on behalf of the faculty or the presence of a family member who needs special care at home. In conversation with a vtuber interviewed, she explained that she had chosen to work as vtuber as a result of specific personal issues. She lives with her boyfriend and younger brother who has special needs, so acting as a vtuber was the way she found to be able to work from home and take care of her brother. When she made her debut, the technical configuration she was using was poor and had the same computer support that she used in school. As a strategy to start its activities, it decided to perform lives and count on the donations, in money, of its audience to make improvements in its technical configuration, and thus continue producing content in social media.

Equipment such as microphone, computer with high processing capacity, and camera with motion capture are on the list of items required for the activity vtuber and that can also have high cost. That's why the independent vtubers we interviewed tell us to explore more accessible options, as in the case of our interviewee, who would like to acquire a webcam with motion capture but still could not buy-la, so he started his trajectory as a vtuber using the camera of his smartphone, which enabled motion capture, to perform in live broadcasts on her channel on Youtube:

"I currently use motion capture from my smartphone, it has facial motion capture. As the processing is carried out in the smartphone ends up being a little lighter for my computer to process. So we always have to try alternatives that consume less of the computer so that a little more for the streaming software and games."(Interviewee 6, 2024).

The vtubers interviewed reported that the search for low-cost alternatives, as reported by vtuber previously, is a recurring practice among vtuber content creators' beginners, that, in general, do not have an adequate technical configuration at the beginning of their trajectory. However, they also report that it is a risky practice, as the camera's motion tracking can fail at any time and reveal the vtuber's identity. In this context, acting as a vtuber becomes also a self-sustaining strategy, to the extent that these creators develop monetization methods on the platforms in which they produce content, to raise money and invest in the improvement of their avatars and equipment.

The production of content, besides being a form of social and artistic expression, acquires a new facet by being understood to obtain financial return. Among the interviewed vtubers, content creation is perceived as a professional activity, even when it does not constitute their main occupation. Still, there is a recurring effort to maximize the monetization capacity of your channels. For this, breeders develop specific strategies aimed at increasing the gains from their content production. Among these strategies, three main ways stand out: the direct monetization offered by the platforms when the channels reach a minimum number of views; the use of resources such as SuperChat (Google, 2025), which allows the public to send cash donations so that their messages are highlighted or fixed in the chat during live broadcasts; and finally, offering exclusive content and channels for subscribing members. These practices demonstrate not only the growing professionalization but also the dynamics of continuous strategy construction in the environment vtuber.

6   Mixed Reality is the Next Frontier to the Vtuber Universe

As stated in the introduction, we started this research on vtubers with a view to developing a platform for mixed reality, to explore the experience of virtual content production. During the interviews all independent vtubers reported knowing the Mixed Reality technologies available in the market and feed the interest to acquire and experiment with platforms focused on content production with their avatars for social media. In this scenario, the interviewees reported the growing interest in acquiring 3D avatars that can be used in virtual worlds of XR platforms, made possible by the use of body tracking technologies contained in Head Mounted Devices.

This desire stems from the curiosity generated by colleagues and other vtuber idols such as Vtuber Fillian[10], who uses a three-dimensional avatar, with the help of mixed reality devices, to perform lives in alternative worlds available in VR Chat[11]. We must note that these alternative worlds are customized by the own performer and greatly expands the scope of performance of the Vtubers and the possibilities of contact with fans.

In this field VR chat emerges as the main platform reference in the use of 3D avatars with opportunities for content creation and public approach vtuber. Users are looking for a way to approach their followers in VR chat more closely, due to the ability to perform events with public participation and explore new possibilities of interaction through simulated gestures by body tracking (VR Chat, 2024), like handshakes and hugs. The platform also allows users to model objects and entire worlds for use in the application and invite their friends or viewers to gather there (VR Chat, 2024). The possibility of customizing your objects and environments through modeling is a factor that positively contributes to the experience of the vtuber who wants to reproduce their narratives in their "ideal world" so as to involve their audience in their storytelling (Fig. 6).

The main motivation, which goes beyond references, for vtubers to keep an eye on the use of augmented reality technology involves improving the movement tracking of their avatars. The vtubers use 2D and 3D avatars that are animated by motion tracking, this means that a camera captures the expressions and movements of the person performer and "glue" directly in the avatar, imitating the person's movements. Most HMDs have hand tracking as standard technology, but there are other devices even more complete with adjacent sensors that can map the user's entire body. Reaching this level of tracking is the dream of most vtubers.

As a result of this movement, all the interviewees demonstrated to know the mixed reality devices, especially about the use scenarios related to vtuber activity. They describe their desire to acquire HMDs, especially the Meta Quest 2, because although it does

---

[10] https://www.youtube.com/watch?v=7lTzstzqmCo.

[11] https://hello.vrchat.com/

Fig. 6. Vtuber Fillian on Livestream. Source: https://www.youtube.com/watch?v=TOF_XPw T51c

not have full body tracking, according to them is the most affordable device available on the market and that corresponds to your tracking needs, of the upper body in the current scenario. They narrate that acquiring other options of HMD devices are out of the question because of the need to acquire complementary sensors for the experience which are equally expensive to obtain the desired full body tracking.

Our participants understand that these devices offer a new frontier of technical, artistic and social possibilities for the users of the Vtuber universe. In the technical aspect, XR devices have more powerful and integrated tracking features than the cameras of smartphones or webcams used by them for motion capture. Artistically, the improvement of body tracking makes more realistic and natural the expressions and movements projected in your characters facilitating the elaboration and use of 3D avatars. In the social sphere, experiences in immersive environments open up new forms of interaction between vtubers and followers, which go beyond the senses of 2D screens, commonly used on monitors and smartphones, and reach the real environment.

7   Conclusion

The universe Vtuber is in a moment of expansion and consolidation, therefore, there are concepts, rituals among other aspects of this universe that are still in the process of consolidation. Through the research process developed we were able to discuss certain aspects of the vtuber culture that mainly involve the understanding of the initial trajectory of the independent vtuber. This trajectory involves a wide set of decisions, concepts and tools that are used to create the content production experience of independent vtuber. The interviewees state that the production of content through an avatar connects the public with the image and narrative they developed, allowing them to live the reality they chose while protecting their real image from being exposed on the internet, ensuring your anonymity.

Therefore, the avatar is modeled by vtubers as a tool to help them overcome inhibitions and social barriers (Baitello et al., 2023). Through the avatars vtubers can express feeling and emotions that in everyday situations would feel inhibited by certain social constraints. The independent vtubers find in the use of the avatar an opportunity to express and exercise aspects of their lives, which they consider important, but which do not find space in their daily life.

The use of technology in the field of digital content production, especially through three-dimensional avatars driven by motion tracking systems, still presents a vast horizon of scenarios and opportunities to be explored. The creation of virtual content is a central element in the practice of VTubers, however, there is a shortage of consolidated platforms in the XR market for those who wish to develop content using avatars in mixed reality environments. In the context of Extended Reality, it is observed that most of the currently consolidated platforms have emerged in the scenario of digital games. Still, the challenge for companies and multidisciplinary teams to design experiences that incorporate interactions and everyday situations of users persists. In this sense, it becomes fundamental the continuous investigation of these use scenarios from the perspective of users, with the aim of understanding the opportunities that emerge from forms of interaction and technological appropriation. Such an approach is essential for the advancement of knowledge about modes of production and socio-technical practices associated with content creation through avatars in immersive virtual environments.

Acknowledgements. This paper was presented as part of the results of the project "SIDIA-M_VSTPLATFORM_AND_APPLICATIONS", carried out by the Institute of Science and technology – SIDIA, in partneship with Samsung Eletrônica da Amazônia LTDA, in accordance with the Information Technology Law n.8387/91 and article ate the.39 of Decree 10,521/2020.

References

Law, J.: Actor network theory and material semiotics. https://www.heterogeneities.net/publications/Law2007ANTandMaterialSemiotics.pdf. last accessed 2025/05/05 (2007)

Hine, C.: Ethnography for the Internet: Embedded, Embodied and Every Day, 1st edn. Bloomsbury Academic, London (2015)

Azuma, H.: Otaku: Japan's Database Animals. Univ. of Minnesota Press, 2009

Gamesight.: The Rise of Vtubers report (2023). Homepage: https://blog.gamesight.io/vtuber/. last accessed 2025/04/04

Lehtovirta, S.: Creating a Vtuber Avatar. Tampere University of Applied Sciences. (2023)

Galbraith, P., Karlin, J.: Media Convergence in Japan. 1st edn. Kinema Club. United states (2016)

Gailbraith, P., Karlin, J.: Idols and celebrith in Japanese media culture, 2012th edn. Palgrave Macmillan, London (2012)

Google Support. Homepage: https://support.google.com/youtube/answer/7288782?hl=pt-BR, last accessed 2025/05/04

VR Chat. https://docs.vrchat.com/docs/full-body-tracking, last accessed 2025/04/06

VR Chat. https://creators.vrchat.com/worlds/creating-your-first-world, last accessed 2025/04/08

Hillmann, C.: UX for XR. 1st end. Apress, Berkeley, CA (2021)

Baitello, N., Soares, G. Virtual Youtubers: Entre el cuerpo y la imagen. In: Mediaciones de la Comunicación, vol. 18, pp 145–170, Uruguay (2023)

Lee, S., Lee, J. My Idol My Streamer: A Case Study on Fandom Experience as Audiences and Creators of vtuber Concert. IEEE Acess, p. 1 (2023)

Gil, A. How to do qualitative research. 1st edn. Atlas. Brazil (2021)

Le. Linh.: Examining the rise of hatsune miku: the first international virtual idol. The UCI Undergraduate Research Journal, 13 (4), pp 268–285 (2014)

Regis, R., Diniz, G., Ferreira, J., & Gonçalves, P. (2022). Vtubers Concept Review the new frontier of virtual youtubers. SVR22: Proceedings of the 24th symposiun on virtual and augmented reality, 24, pp 83–96, Association for computing Machinery, United States (2024)

Brandao, D.: Participatory culture: Critical review of the work Convergence Culture, Where Old and New Media Collide by Henry Jenkins. Comunicação e Sociedade **18**, 245–255 (2010)

Regis, R., Diniz, G., Ferreira, J., & Gonçalves, P. Vtubers transmedia capacity: narrative and content production expansion based on the intersection with fan-culture by the hololive agency. Innovaciones en narrativa y Medios: Transmedia, Interacción y Cultura, vol. 25, (2024)

Mamat, R., Rashid, R.A., Paee, R., Ahmad, N.: VTubers and anime culture: A case study of Japanese learners in two public universities in Malaysia. Int. J. Health Sci. **6**(S2), 11958–11974 (2022)

Rebuli, L., Gonçalves, P., Regis, R., & Ferreira, J. Tecnologia, Trabalho e Relações Sociotécnicas: um estudo de caso das vtubers Kizuna AI e Kiryu Coco. VIII Encontro de Gestão de Pessoas e Relações de Trabalho (EnGPR 2023). São Paulo, Brazil (2023)

Byron, J. New collaboration in a virtual world: studying vtubers through identity, gender and fan engagement. Departament of media, communications, creative arts, languages and literature. Macquarie University. New South Wales, Australia. (2022)

Jenkins, H.: Convergence Culture: Where old and new media colide. New York University Press, New York (2006)

A Framework for Understanding and Modifying Cognitive Bias in Information Visualization

Xinyi Tang and Chengqi Xue[✉]

Southeast University, Nanjing 211189, China
`ipd_xcq@seu.edu.cn`

Abstract. With the increasing reliance on data-driven decision-making, information visualizations have become critical tools across various domains. However, cognitive biases frequently distort users' interpretation of visualized data, leading to suboptimal outcomes. While prior research has documented cognitive biases in specific visualization contexts, most studies remain at the behavioral level and lack a unified framework for systematic bias modification. This study proposes a novel framework for understanding and modifying cognitive biases in information visualizations using event-related potentials (ERP). The framework consists of four key stages: 1) identification of potential cognitive bias triggers, 2) neural and behavioral characterization of cognitive biases, 3) preliminary design plans for cognitive bias modification, and 4) design evaluation and design strategy optimization. A case study on automotive dashboard interfaces demonstrates the framework's effectiveness in addressing anchoring bias. Experimental results show that combined angular and textual encoding induces anchoring bias, as evidenced by specific ERP components (P2, P300, N400). Three design strategies were derived: context-appropriate textual warnings, vertical alignment of elements, and semantically consistent information positioning. This work bridges theoretical insights with practical applications, offering a structured and actionable guidance for creating bias-modified visualizations.

Keywords: Information Visualizations · Cognitive Bias · Anchoring Bia · Event-Related Potential (ERP) · Decision-Making

1 Introduction

In the era of big data, information visualizations have become indispensable tools for supporting critical decision-making across various domains including healthcare, finance, and public policy. However, the effectiveness of these visual tools is frequently compromised by cognitive biases—systematic patterns of deviation from rational judgment that distort users' interpretation of visualized data [1]. While the visualization community has made significant progress in improving the perceptual efficiency of data representations, the challenge of cognitive biases persists, often leading to suboptimal or even dangerous decisions in high-stakes environments.

Previous studies on cognitive biases in visualization have primarily examined the manifestation of various biases across different visualization types and decision-making

H. Mori et al. (Eds.): HCII 2025, LNCS 16333, pp. 227–241, 2026.
https://doi.org/10.1007/978-3-032-12660-3_18

tasks [2–5], building upon foundational work in cognitive psychology [1, 6, 7]. While this research has successfully demonstrated the existence of visualization-induced biases through behavioral measures such as accuracy rates and response times, the underlying neural mechanisms remain largely unexplored. Furthermore, current approaches typically focus on specific bias types or visualization contexts, rather than developing comprehensive solutions applicable across diverse scenarios. The present study addresses these limitations by proposing a unified neurocognitive framework that combines behavioral and neural measures to systematically identify, analyze, and modify cognitive biases in information visualizations.

This paper is innovative in the following aspects:

- Proposal of a novel framework for the structured identification, analysis, and modification of cognitive biases in information visualizations
- Integration of cognitive psychology principles with neuro-ergonomic approaches to investigate the emergence of biases from fundamental perceptual, attentional, and memory mechanisms, extending beyond conventional behavioral observations
- Demonstration of the framework's efficacy through rigorous case study implementation on automotive dashboard interfaces, with validation of anchoring bias identification and modification supported by converging behavioral and neurophysiological evidence

Our work bridges an important gap between theoretical understanding of cognitive biases and practical visualization design, offering concrete strategies to create more reliable information displays. The remainder of this paper is organized as follows: Sect. 2 reviews related work on cognitive biases in visualization and EEG-based evaluation methods. Section 3 details our proposed framework. Section 4 presents the automotive dashboard case study, and Sect. 5 discusses implications and future directions.

2   Related Work

This section provides an overview of the relevant theories and previous studies. Firstly, the related research combining information visualizations and cognitive biases are introduced. Secondly, the studies of EEG-based evaluation of information visualization are classified and summarized.

2.1   Cognitive Bias in Information Visualizations

Research at the intersection of cognitive psychology and information visualization has identified numerous biases that affect how users interpret visual data representations. Anchoring bias, where initial exposures to numbers or values disproportionately influence subsequent judgments [8], has been particularly well-documented in financial dashboards and forecasting displays. Primacy effect—the tendency to seek and overweight information that presents first in a visual sequence [9]—has been shown to distort analytical reasoning in intelligence analysis systems. Other prevalent biases include framing effects [10], where identical data presented differently leads to divergent interpretations, and priming bias [11], where visually prominent features receive disproportionate attention regardless of their actual importance.

While existing empirical studies have documented behavioral manifestations of cognitive biases, such as the disproportionate impact of presentation order and initial information on subsequent judgments in visual analytics [2, 4, 12], the quantitative assessment of these biases using physiological indicators remains largely unexplored. Current research lacks systematic approaches for measuring visualization-induced cognitive biases through physiological features, representing a critical gap in understanding the neural mechanisms underlying these phenomena.

2.2 EEG-Based Evaluation of Information Visualization

The application of neuroscientific methods, particularly electroencephalography (EEG), to visualization evaluation represents a promising but underdeveloped research direction. EEG's excellent temporal resolution makes it particularly suitable for studying the rapid cognitive processes involved in visual data interpretation [13, 14]. Several event-related potential (ERP) components have emerged as relevant neural markers for visualization cognition, including the P2 component that reflects early attentional selection [15–17], the P300 associated with context updating and working memory engagement [18–20], and the N400 that indexes semantic processing and expectation violations [21–23].

While these neural markers have begun to be applied in visualization evaluation studies, this approach has not yet been systematically employed to study cognitive biases in visualization contexts, representing a significant opportunity for advancing both theory and practice in the field.

3   The Proposed Framework

The proposed framework can be used to analyze potential cognitive bias triggers in information visualizations and provide a reliable analysis process and feasible design process for design improvement, as shown in Fig. 1. Four key stages can be classified as 1) identification of potential cognitive bias triggers, 2) neural and behavioral characterization of cognitive biases, 3) preliminary design plans for cognitive bias modification, and 4) design evaluation and design strategy optimization.

3.1   Stage 1: Identification of Potential Cognitive Bias Triggers

The initial stage focuses on systematically identifying potential sources of cognitive bias in existing or proposed visualization designs through a structured decomposition process. This involves analyzing the information architecture, coding methods, layout organization, and connectivity pathways of the visualization system to uncover potential bias triggers such as information ambiguity, information deficiency, and cross-channel semantic discrepancies (see Table 1). The output of this stage is a prioritized list of potential bias problems that require empirical validation in subsequent stages.

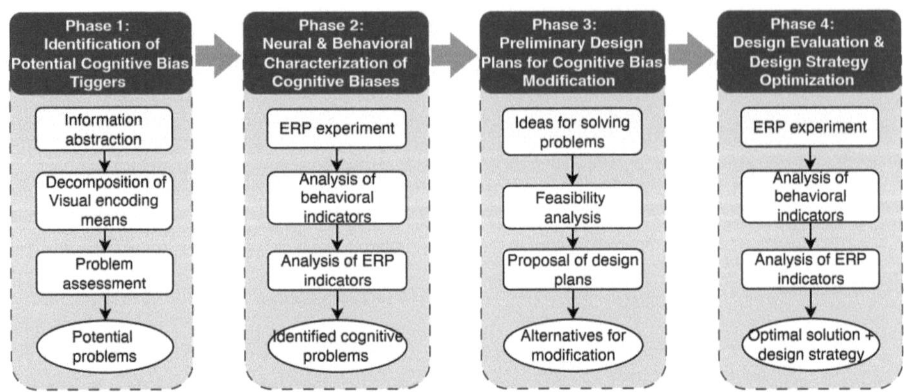

Fig. 1. The proposed framework for understanding and modifying cognitive bias in information visualizations.

Table 1. Potential cognitive bias triggers.

Source of the triggers	Potential triggers
Information	Information ambiguity (e.g., probabilistic data, value ranges)
Information architecture	Information deficiency/redundancy
Information coding	Cross-channel semantic discrepancies
Information layout	Spatiotemporal uncertainty of information display
Information connectivity path	Inconsistency with Operational Heuristics

3.2 Stage 2: Neural and Behavioral Characterization of Cognitive Biases

The second stage employs controlled ERP experiments to objectively characterize the cognitive biases identified in the first stage, using carefully designed visualization variants and ecologically valid decision tasks while recording both behavioral responses and EEG signals. The ERP experimental process of cognitive bias in information visualization is adopted for experimental research. The potential triggers identified in the first stage are imported into the experimental process, and the characterization of cognitive bias is carried out after variable setting, task arrangement and data collection, as shown in Fig. 2.

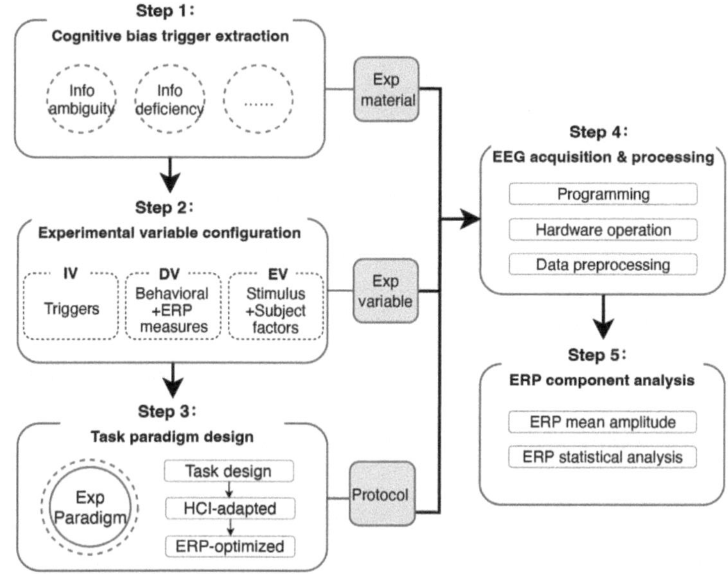

Fig. 2. The experimental process of cognitive bias in information visualization.

The characterization of cognitive bias is divided into two parts: behavioral analysis and ERP analysis. Behavioral analysis is used to determine whether a specific cognitive bias is induced and the uncertainty factors that play a role in inducing it; ERP analysis is used to obtain the ERP indicators that characterize the specified cognitive bias and to clarify the relevant cognitive processing processes, such as selective attention, perception, working memory and long-term memory.

This multimodal approach allows for comprehensive profiling of how, when, and why specific biases occur in the visualization context, with particular focus on key ERP components that serve as neural markers of bias manifestation. The combination of behavioral and neural measures provides a robust foundation for developing targeted interventions in the next stage.

3.3   Stage 3: Preliminary Design Plans for Cognitive Bias Modification

Building on the detailed bias characterization from the second stage, the third stage generates and evaluates potential design solutions through systematic exploration of the intervention space, considering data transformations, visual encoding adjustments, layout reorganizations, and interactive features. As illustrated in Fig. 3, common visualization design methods are employed to appropriately modify potential triggers of cognitive bias in visualization. The outcome of this stage is a set of prototype designs ready for empirical validation in the fourth stage, each accompanied by clear rationale linking the design choices to the identified bias mechanisms from the second stage.

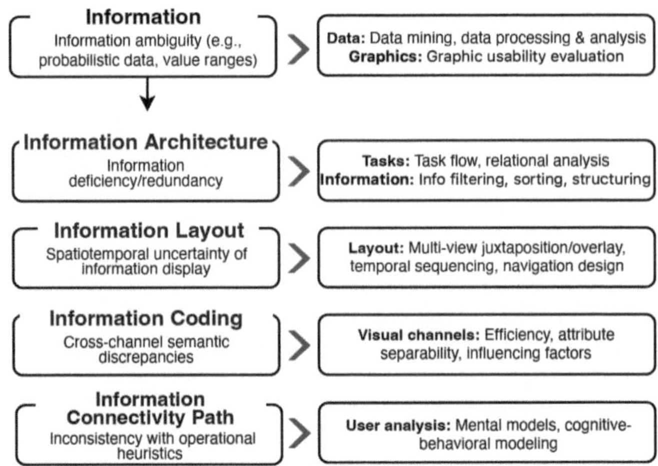

Fig. 3. Design methods for cognitive bias modification in information visualization.

3.4   Stage 4: Design Evaluation and Design Strategy Optimization

The most promising solutions then advance to the final stage for empirical validation using the same multimodal approach employed in the second stage to evaluate the efficacy of proposed design modifications while shifting focus from bias characterization to intervention validation. The modified design plans serve as experimental conditions against the original designs as controls, maintaining identical task protocols and counterbalanced presentation sequences to ensure direct comparability with the results from the second stage. Behavioral analysis now quantifies the reduction in bias magnitude rather than initial detection, while ERP analysis tracks the normalization of previously identified neural markers.

This stage systematically extends the methodology of the second stage by applying the same multimodal approach to evaluate interventions rather than characterize biases, creating a closed-loop framework where neural markers of bias manifestation become targets for measurable normalization. The continuum from detection (Stage 2) to modification (Stage 4) demonstrates how neurocognitive measures can guide and validate visualization design choices while maintaining experimental consistency across the research pipeline.

4   Case Study

To evaluate the feasibility of the proposed framework, this study selected automotive dashboard human-machine interfaces in driving scenarios as the research object, conducting comprehensive investigations into cognitive bias identification and modification. Five fully digital LCD dashboard interfaces were chosen as samples for analysis, with their design prototypes systematically categorized in Table 2.

Table 2. Summary of dashboard interfaces and prototype diagrams for each sample.

Vehicle Model	Dashboard Interface	Prototype Diagram
Infiniti-QX60		
Range-Rover-Autobiography		
Genesis- GV70		
Mitsubishi-Outlander		
Nissan Z		

4.1 Identification of Potential Cognitive Bias Triggers

In the first stage of the framework, a thorough analysis was conducted focusing on the original information, information architecture, visual encoding methods, and information connectivity pathways. This analysis led to the development of a potential cognitive bias trigger assessment for dashboard interface information displays, as presented in Table 3.

The evaluation revealed that cognitive biases primarily stemmed from variations in the effectiveness of different visual encoding channels. Specifically, angular encoding (e.g., pie-chart style indicators) demonstrated relatively poor effectiveness in conveying quantitative information, whereas textual encoding showed superior performance in ensuring accurate quantitative perception. Based on these findings, the combination of angular and textual encoding was identified as a primary source of information display uncertainty in automotive dashboard interfaces.

Table 3. Potential cognitive bias trigger assessment for dashboard interfaces.

	Case Analysis	Potential triggers	Yes/No	Note
Information	Speed, RPM, Fuel range, Coolant temp, Status, Trip info……	Information ambiguity (e.g., probabilistic data, value ranges)	No	
Information architecture	Primary: Driving-critical Secondary: Driving-related Tertiary: Non-driving	Information deficiency/redundancy	No	
Information coding	Angle, Text, Color (Hue, Brightness), Length, Area	Cross-channel semantic discrepancies	Yes	Angle Text
Information layout	Symmetry, Hierarchy	Spatiotemporal uncertainty of information display	No	
Information connectivity path	/	Inconsistency with Operational Heuristics	/	

4.2　Neural and Behavioral Characterization of Cognitive Biases

This study conducted an ERP experiment on cognitive biases in information display of dashboard interfaces, generating data for dual analysis through both behavioral metrics and ERP indicators. The experimental design incorporated the cognitive bias triggers identified in Sect. 4.1, utilizing angular encoding as the foundation for experimental materials while manipulating textual encoding as the independent variable.

Participants. We recruited 23 participants (12 males, 11 females), aged 19 to 28 (M = 23.52, SD = 2.14). Each of participants was voluntary and was provided the written informed consent approved by Ethics Committee of Southeast University affiliated ZhongDa Hospital.

Tasks. The task required participants to first observe an initial "anchor" pie chart (without reporting its value, but confirming their perception via mouse click) and then estimate the value of a second "target" pie chart on a 0–100 scale, with careful avoidance of bias-inducing terminology in the instructions. Each trial began with a 300ms fixation cross, followed by the anchor stimulus (until button-press response), a 200-400ms randomized blank interval, a 1500ms target presentation, and finally a response screen where participants entered their estimate before a 1000ms inter-trial interval.

All sessions were conducted in an EEG recording environment, allowing for simultaneous collection of behavioral responses (accuracy and reaction time) and EEG data during both the anchor processing and target estimation phases of each trial.

Behavioral and ERP analysis. Behavioral analysis served two primary objectives: establishing whether specific cognitive biases were successfully induced, and identifying the triggers contributing to such induction. As is shown in Fig. 4(A), the judgment deviation values demonstrated that combined angular and textual encoding stimuli reliably induced anchoring bias, whereas angular encoding alone failed to produce significant bias effects.

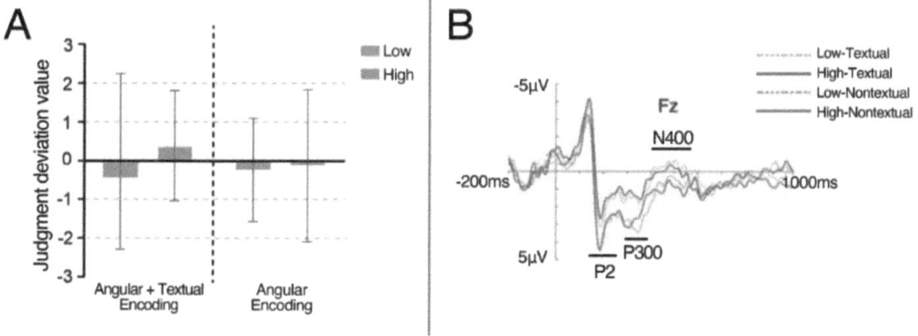

Fig. 4. Behavioral and neural characterization of cognitive biases.

The ERP analysis also pursued complementary goals: identifying specific ERP markers characteristic of the target cognitive bias, and clarifying associated cognitive processes including selective attention, perception, working memory, and long-term memory engagement. Figure 4(B) revealed three significant ERP components - P2 (170-250ms), P300 (300-375ms), and N400 (400-550ms) - that effectively characterized anchoring bias induced by visual information. The comprehensive behavioral and ERP findings are systematically summarized in Table 4.

Table 4. Comprehensive behavioral and ERP findings.

	Purpose	Conclusions
Behavioral Analysis	To determine whether specific cognitive biases are induced	Yes
	To identify triggers contributing to bias induction	Combination of angular and textual encoding
ERP Analysis	To obtain ERP markers characterizing targeted cognitive bias	1.P2 (170-250ms) 2.P300 (300-375ms) 3.N400 (400-550ms)
	To clarify related cognitive processes (selective attention, perception, working memory, long-term memory)	1. Attention resources: automatic vs. voluntary allocation 2. Working memory: task difficulty evaluation 3. Working memory: semantic processing of visual information

4.3   Preliminary Design Plans for Cognitive Bias Modification

Building upon the identified triggers from the second stage, this phase focused on extracting potential information display modification approaches in the automotive context, and developing preliminary design alternatives. Drawing from the cognitive bias modification framework established in Sect. 3.3, the study identified the current trigger as stemming from information encoding, specifically arising from salience disparities caused by varying effectiveness of visual channels.

Three potential modification approaches were evaluated: visual channel efficiency optimization, channel attribute separability enhancement, and visual perception factor adjustment. Feasibility analysis revealed that channel efficiency modification proved impractical due to drivers' established mental models. Furthermore, channel separability approaches were inapplicable to single-channel contexts. As a result, visual perception factors - particularly framing effects - offered promising intervention opportunities given the spatial constraints of automotive interfaces.

Guided by Weber's Law [24] of relative discrimination in human perception, the study developed three concrete modification alternatives: vertical alignment, clockwise orientation, and counterclockwise orientation. These solutions leveraged the well-established phenomenon that objects placed within shared frames and in aligned configurations yield more accurate perceptual judgments than randomly arranged elements, providing theoretically grounded approaches to bias modification.

4.4   Design Evaluation and Design Strategy Optimization

The final stage employed the same rigorous ERP experimental protocol used in the second stage to evaluate the proposed design modifications, integrating behavioral and neural indicators to derive comprehensive design strategies. The experimental design incorporated the modification alternatives from Sect. 4.3 as independent variables (vertical alignment, clockwise orientation, and counterclockwise orientation), maintaining the angular-textual encoding combination as the baseline while introducing control conditions for comparative analysis.

Participants. We recruited 23 participants (12 males, 11 females, mean age $= 23.65$, SD $= 2.80$). Each of participants was voluntary and was provided the written informed consent approved by Ethics Committee of Southeast University affiliated ZhongDa Hospital.

Tasks. The task design was consistent with the protocol detailed in Sect. 4.2.

Behavioral and ERP analysis. Behavioral analysis focused on two critical questions: determining whether the alternatives significantly differed from controls, and identifying the most effective modification approaches. As is shown in Fig. 5(A), absolute judgment deviation values demonstrated that vertical frame alignment produced the most substantial reduction in anchoring bias effects.

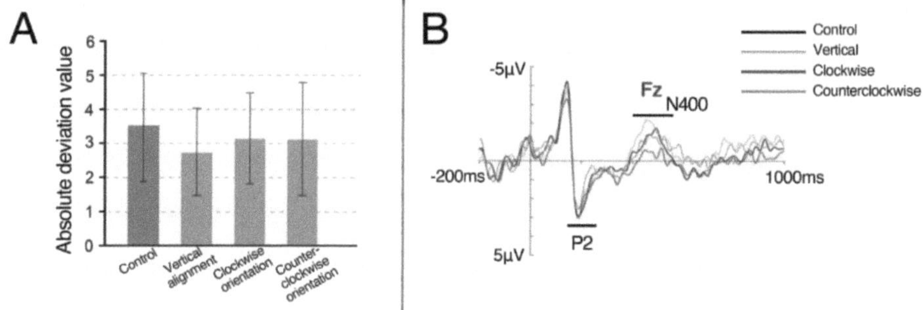

Fig. 5. Behavioral and ERP results for evaluation.

The ERP analysis examined whether the previously identified markers could characterize modification effects, and how different alternatives influenced cognitive processing. As is shown in Fig. 5(B), the results confirmed that P2 and N400 components effectively tracked bias modification, with clockwise orientation particularly enhancing semantic consistency between anchor and target stimuli. Notably, while different modifications showed comparable attention resource demands, textual elements maintained strong associations with attention allocation patterns. The comprehensive evaluation results are systematically presented in Table 5.

Table 5. Comprehensive evaluation results.

	Purpose	Conclusions
Behavioral Analysis	To determine whether alternative solutions vary from the control group significantly	Yes
	To identify which solution demonstrates modification effects	Vertical alignment
ERP Analysis	To analyze whether ERP indicators obtained in Step 2 can characterize modification effects	1.P2 (170-250ms) 2.N400 (400-550ms)
	To clarify impacts of different solutions on cognitive processing	1. Attention resources: correlated with presence of textual elements 2. 2. Working memory: semantic consistency in clockwise alignment

The integrated behavioral and ERP findings yielded three evidence-based interface design strategies: (1) context-appropriate textual warnings preceding critical decisions (Fig. 6), (2) relative discrimination through vertical framing (Fig. 7), and (3) semantic consistency via aligned information positioning (Fig. 8). These strategies collectively address the identified cognitive bias mechanisms while respecting the practical constraints of automotive interface design, offering actionable solutions grounded in both theoretical principles and empirical validation.

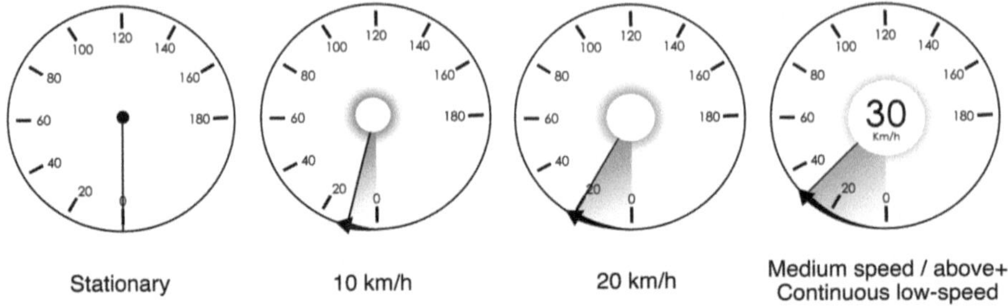

Fig. 6. Context-appropriate textual warnings preceding critical decisions.

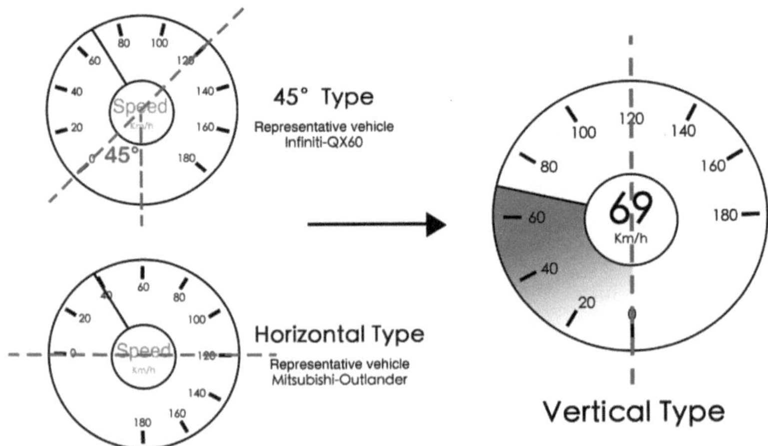

Fig. 7. Relative discrimination through vertical framing.

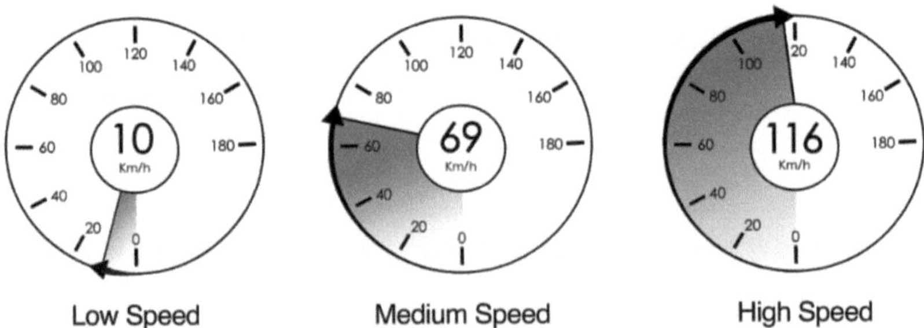

Fig. 8. Semantic consistency via aligned information positioning.

5 Discussion and Conclusion

This study presents a framework for understanding and modifying cognitive bias in visualization. The framework offers a novel, neuroscientific approach to addressing the challenge of cognitive biases in information visualization systems. By integrating rigorous behavioral measures with sensitive neural indicators of cognitive processing, we have advanced beyond design heuristics to develop interventions that target the fundamental mechanisms underlying bias effects. The automotive case study provides compelling evidence for the framework's practical value, demonstrating how anchoring bias can be modified through design strategies informed by neural evidence. The successful identification of specific ERP components as reliable neural markers of bias effects also establishes new possibilities for objective, theory-driven evaluation of visualization systems.

From a theoretical perspective, our work makes several important contributions to the field of information visualization. We have developed a unified model that explicitly links visualization design features to specific cognitive processing stages where biases emerge, providing a more nuanced understanding of how and why certain visual representations lead to systematic judgment errors. The empirical validation of ERP components as sensitive indicators of bias effects in complex visual decision tasks represents a significant methodological advance, offering researchers new tools for studying visualization cognition. Furthermore, our demonstration of how neuro-ergonomic principles can effectively inform visualization design establishes an important bridge between cognitive neuroscience and design practice that has been largely unexplored in previous work.

The practical implications of our findings are particularly relevant for designers creating interfaces for safety-critical applications such as automotive displays, medical diagnostics, and financial systems. The three evidence-based strategies developed through our case study provide concrete guidance for creating bias-resistant interfaces in these domains. These approaches are grounded in both theoretical understanding of cognitive processes and empirical validation through multimodal testing, offering a more reliable foundation for design decisions than conventional heuristic methods.

However, several limitations and future directions should be noted. Additional research is needed to validate the framework across a broader range of bias types and application domains, which would further establish its generalizability and refine its methodological approaches. The integration of complementary physiological measures such as eye-tracking and functional near-infrared spectroscopy (fNIRS) could provide additional insights by capturing different aspects of cognitive processing during visualization use. Furthermore, the development of automated tools for bias detection in visualization pipelines could help translate our research findings into practical applications for design practitioners.

In conclusion, this work establishes a new paradigm for understanding and mitigating cognitive biases in information visualization that effectively bridges the gap between cognitive neuroscience and design practice. By rooting visualization evaluation in the neural mechanisms of human cognition, we have developed an approach that not only advances theoretical understanding of visualization cognition but also provides practical tools for creating more effective designs. As data-driven decision-making continues to grow in importance across all sectors of society, such neuroscientific approaches to visualization design will become increasingly essential for supporting accurate, unbiased interpretation of complex information.

Acknowledgments. This work was supported by the National Natural Science Foundation of China (No. 72271053) and Postgraduate Research & Practice Innovation Program of Jiangsu Province (No. KYCX24_0375).

Disclosure of Interests.. The authors have no competing interests to declare that are relevant to the content of this article.

References

1. Tversky, A., Kahneman, D.: Judgment under Uncertainty: Heuristics and Biases. Science **185**(4157), 1124–1131 (1974)
2. Cho, I., R. Wesslen, A. Karduni, et al.: The anchoring effect in decision-making with visual analytics. In: 2017 IEEE Conference on Visual Analytics Science and Technology (VAST), pp. 116–126. IEEE (2017)
3. Valdez, A.C., Ziefle, M., Sedlmair, M.: Priming and Anchoring Effects in Visualization. IEEE Trans. Vis. Comput. Graph. **24**(1), 584–594 (2018)
4. Wesslen, R., Santhanam, S., Karduni, A., et al.: Anchored in a data storm: How anchoring bias can affect user strategy, confidence, and decisions in visual analytics. arXiv preprint arXiv: 1806.02720 (2018)
5. Wesslen, R., Santhanam, S., Karduni, A., et al.: Investigating Effects of Visual Anchors on Decision-Making about Misinformation. Computer Graphics Forum **38**(3), 161–171 (2019)
6. Wilson, T.D., Houston, C.E., Etling, K.M., et al.: A new look at anchoring effects: basic anchoring and its antecedents. J. Exp. Psychol. Gen. **125**(4), 387 (1996)
7. Furnham, A., Boo, H.C.: A literature review of the anchoring effect. J. Socio-Econ. **40**(1), 35–42 (2011)
8. Epley, N., Gilovich, T.: The anchoring-and-adjustment heuristic. Psychol. Sci. **17**(4), 311–318 (2006)
9. Mantonakis, A., Rodero, P., Lesschaeve, I., et al.: Order in Choice: Effects of Serial Position on Preferences. Psychol. Sci. **20**(11), 1309–1312 (2009)
10. Chong, D., Druckman, J.N.: Framing theory. Annu. Rev. Polit. Sci. **10**, 103–126 (2007)
11. Kuzyakov, Y., Friedel, J.K., Stahr, K.: Review of mechanisms and quantification of priming effects. Soil Biol. Biochem. **32**(11–12), 1485–1498 (2000)
12. Zhu, Z.M., Peng, N.Y., Niu, Y.F., et al.: The Influence of Commodity Presentation Mode on Online Shopping Decision Preference Induced by the Serial Position Effect. Applied Sciences-Basel **11**(20), 9671 (2021)
13. Sur, S., Sinha, V.K.: Event-related potential: An overview. Ind. Psychiatry J. **18**(1), 70 (2009)
14. Blackwood, D.H.R., Muir, W.J.: Cognitive Brain Potentials and their Application. Br. J. Psychiatry **157**(S9), 96–101 (2018)
15. Guo, F., Ding, Y., Wang, T., et al.: Applying event related potentials to evaluate user preferences toward smartphone form design. Int. J. Ind. Ergon. **54**, 57–64 (2016)
16. Cao, Y., Zhang, Y., Ding, Y., et al.: Is an anthropomorphic app icon more attractive? Evidence from neuroergonomomics. Applied Ergonomics, 97, 103545 (2021)
17. Guo, F., Li, M., Chen, J., et al.: Evaluating users' preference for the appearance of humanoid robots via event-related potentials and spectral perturbations. Behav. Inf. Technol. **41**(7), 1381–1397 (2022)

18. He, Y., Ao, H., Chen, Y., et al.: The Use of Smartphone Application Influence Human Visual Attention. Adv. Psychol. **7**, 518–530 (2017)
19. Li, F., Yi, C., Jiang, Y., et al.: Different contexts in the oddball paradigm induce distinct brain networks in generating the P300. Front. Hum. Neurosci. **12**, 520 (2019)
20. Zhang, Z., Xu, B., Zhang, T.: Aesthetic study of patterns based on event-related potential and eye-tracking: Taking the decorative patterns of the Tang dynasty as an example. J. Soc. Inform. Display **29**(2), 119–129 (2021)
21. Guo, F., Qu, Q.-X., Nagamachi, M., et al.: A proposal of the event-related potential method to effectively identify kansei words for assessing product design features in kansei engineering research. Int. J. Ind. Ergon. **76**, 102940 (2020)
22. Hou, G., Yang, J.: Measuring and examining traffic sign comprehension with event-related potentials. Cogn. Technol. Work **23**(3), 497–506 (2021)
23. Yang, J., Yang, Y., Xiu, L., et al.: Effect of emoji prime on the understanding of emotional words–evidence from ERPs. Behaviour & information technology **41**(6), 1313–1322 (2022)
24. Deco, G.: A neurophysiological model of decision-making and Weber's law. Eur. J. Neurosci. **24**, 901–916 (2006)

Artificial Intelligence and Machine Learning Aided Risk Assessment Methods and Event Management Scenario Simulations in Water Systems for Operators Training

Samuel Botts White[1,3]($\boxtimes$), Ilan Juran[1,3], and Marcello Serrao[2]

[1] New York University Tandon School of Engineering, Brooklyn, NY, USA
sbw323@nyu.edu
[2] Innovation & Technical Office, Engineering & Construction, SUEZ International, Paris, France
[3] Water Security Management Assessment Research and Technology (W-SMART), Paris, France

Abstract. In response to escalating climate-related challenges and evolving regulatory, operational, and environmental demands, metropolitan water and wastewater utilities are increasingly adopting advanced digital technologies. These include smart monitoring systems (e.g., SCADA, GIS, BIM), AI/ML-assisted process control, and twin modeling applications. This paper addresses the growing need for corporate-wide crisis management training for OT system managers and utility operators, spanning executive to technical levels. It presents a methodology for AI/ML-aided risk assessment and scenario-based simulations tailored to organizational structures, vulnerabilities, and operational conditions.

The proposed approach supports immersive tabletop training exercises that integrate AI/ML with real-time data and digital twin environments. These simulations enable early event detection, severity rating, and predictive impact assessment across interdependent systems such as hydraulic networks, energy supply, water quality, cybersecurity, and asset management. By leveraging high-frequency operational data, operators can build a dynamic, systemic situation picture to support preemptive decision-making during crises.

The methodology includes the use of SCADA-driven BIM platforms with potential GIS/VR integration for time-series visualization of anomalies and operational conditions. Applications are demonstrated for leak localization, bio-contamination detection in water distribution systems, and process control in wastewater treatment. Lessons learned from the design and implementation of these scenario exercises are discussed, offering guidance on integrating innovative AI/ML tools into utility crisis training programs.

Keywords: AI-driven models · Risk Assessment · Risk Prediction · Event Scenario Simulations · Water Utility Operations Training

H. Mori et al. (Eds.): HCII 2025, LNCS 16333, pp. 242–260, 2026.
https://doi.org/10.1007/978-3-032-12660-3_19

1   Introduction

Water and wastewater utilities face increasing complexity due to climate change, regulatory shifts, urbanization, and growing public expectations around water quality and resilience. To address these challenges, utilities are adopting digital transformation strategies incorporating SCADA, IIoT, GIS, and BIM; now increasingly enhanced by Artificial Intelligence (AI) and Machine Learning (ML) for predictive analytics, anomaly detection, and adaptive process control.

Beyond operational gains, AI/ML technologies offer new opportunities for training, especially in crisis preparedness. Traditional programs often fail to simulate the urgency and complexity of real emergencies. To bridge this gap, AI/ML-enabled Risk Assessment Methods (RAMs) and interactive scenario-based simulations are emerging as effective tools for operator training.

This paper presents a methodology for integrating AI/ML into risk assessment and crisis simulations, designed for in-house training through tabletop exercises. Leveraging real-time data, Digital Twins, and systemic vulnerability modeling, the approach enhances early event detection, impact forecasting, and cross-system awareness. Emphasizing human-computer interaction, the training framework supports accelerated learning and decision-making across operational, technical, and managerial roles; ultimately contributing to more resilient and intelligent water infrastructure.

2   State-Of-The-Art Review and Case Studies

Recent advances in AI and ML and simulation technologies are transforming risk assessment, event management, and operator training in water and wastewater utilities. This section reviews key developments and case studies that illustrate how AI/ML and Twin Modeling (TM) are being applied across five domains: risk and vulnerability assessment, asset management, water quality monitoring, process control, and crisis response.

AI/ML techniques have demonstrated strong capabilities in anomaly detection, event forecasting, and pattern recognition using real-time and historical data. In the context of crisis management, the following applications are highlighted:

- ML-based risk assessment for leak detection and geolocation in water distribution systems.
- AI-driven monitoring of water quality for early bio-contamination detection.
- AI/ML-supported control of wastewater treatment processes.

These case studies draw on a decade of applied research by PhD students at New York University and the University of Lille, within the EU-funded Smart Water for Europe (SW4EU) project, with the W-SMART as the SW4EU consortium partner, as well as doctoral work at the LEESU Laboratory (Université Paris-Est Créteil) in partnership with the SIAAP utility (Paris, France) through the MOCOPEE program. Key publications are referenced to provide further insight into emerging best practices.

2.1 Machine Learning Risk Assessment Methods for Leak Detection and Geolocation in Asset Management for Water Distribution Systems

Cantos et al. (2020) developed and validated a machine learning–based risk assessment method (ML-RAM) to enhance leak detection and geolocation in water distribution systems (WDS), addressing the limitations of current methods that rely on comparing distributed and consumed volumes at the district metering area (DMA) level.

Their approach integrated Support Vector Machines (SVM) and Artificial Neural Networks (ANN) as pattern recognition algorithms to classify flow and pressure patterns, distinguishing normal conditions from burst or leak events - with a GIS platform to analyze spatial and temporal flow data, allowing for early leak detection, severity estimation, and precise leak localization. The method was tested at a demonstration site at the University of Lille, France, campus using real-time flow data and historical consumption records. Serving 37,000 users and comprising 145 buildings and a 15-km WDS, the site was transformed into a smart city demonstration platform.

Fig. 1. Water system monitoring system at the University of Lille. (Cantos et al., 2020).

As shown in Fig. 1, the monitoring infrastructure includes 93 flow meters—13 at campus inlets and 80 automated meter readings (AMRs) at building connections—visualized in real time via a GIS platform. This network enabled the creation of a hydraulic database using AMR data and EPANET simulations to establish spatial-temporal flow patterns.

The methodology included four steps: (1) building the hydraulic and flow parameter database; (2) calculating LI distributions for training and validation; (3) applying SVM and ANN for spatial leak source identification; and (4) visualizing color-coded LI values on the GIS platform to support decision-making and filter false alarms.

The system architecture and Human-Machine Interface (HMI) employ SVM and ANN adapted and tested using MATLAB for an automated, expert-rule-based Risk Assessment Method (RAM). This method generates a spatial Leak Indicator (LI) time series across the WDS at both DMA and node/pipe levels. Integrated with a GIS platform, it enables early leak geolocation. The ML approach includes binary and multiclass SVM using Error-Correcting Output Codes (ECOC), and ANN for pattern recognition (see Fig. 2).

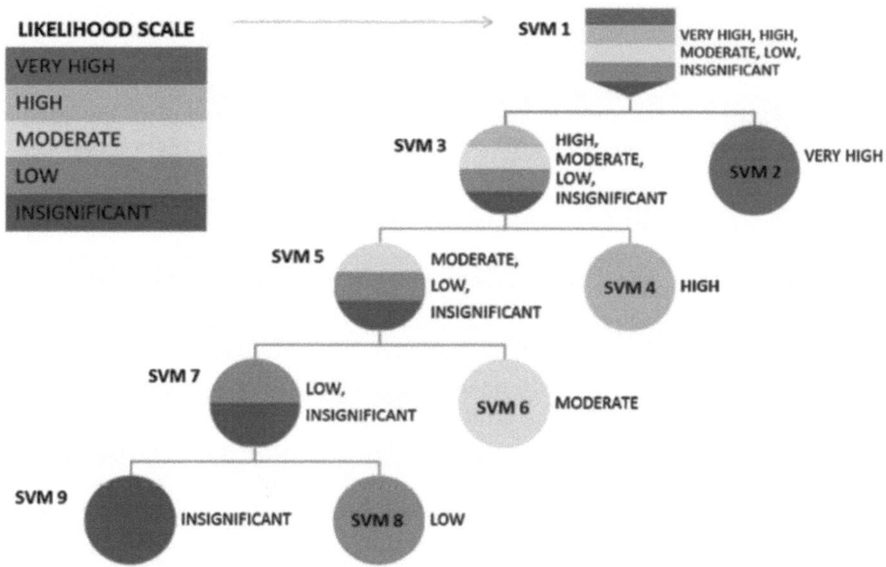

Fig. 2. SVM classification method. (Cantos et al., 2020).

The ML-RAM architecture (see Fig. 2) integrates SVM and ANN, trained using supervised learning. The system generates a Leak Indicator (LI), a time-series metric representing the likelihood of leak occurrence at both the DMA and node/pipe levels. The LI is based on anomaly frequency and severity, benchmarked against normal flow conditions using a 1-standard deviation risk matrix (Fig. 3).

The results of this study demonstrate that the ML-RAM significantly outperformed traditional leak detection approaches by enabling not only earlier detection but also accurate geolocation of potential leaks at the pipe and node level. Results showed high detection accuracy and low false alarm rates, supporting its potential for proactive maintenance and asset management.

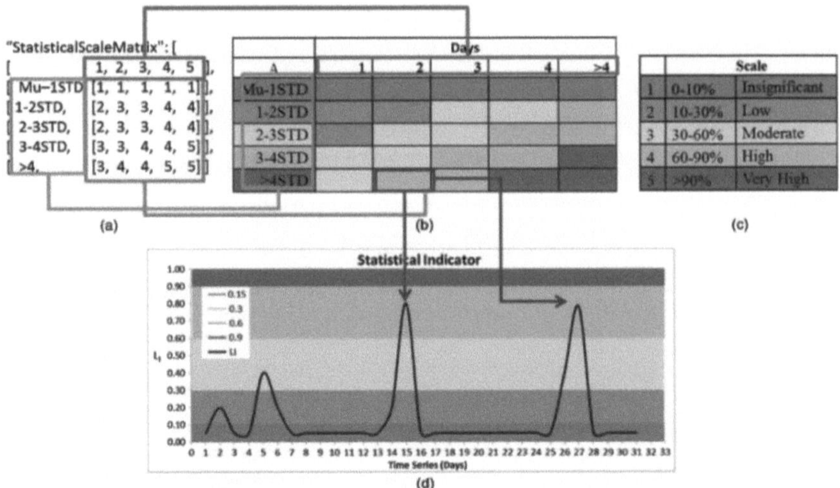

Fig. 3. Automated risk assessment method for establishing the time series of the leak likelihood indicator (LI): (a) configuration MATLAB; (b) matrix; (c) scale; and (d) indicator. (Cantos et al., 2020).

This work addresses a major challenge in managing aging water infrastructure, where traditional leak detection is reactive and imprecise. By leveraging machine learning and SCADA data, the method provides a scalable, cost-effective solution that can improve return on investment in system renewal and reduce non-revenue water losses. The case study underscores the role of AI in modernizing leak detection, supporting real-time decision-making, and strengthening utility resilience.

Integrated with GIS, the system enhances leak geolocation and, together with the HMI, improves operator awareness. This case demonstrates the operational benefits of combining machine learning, spatial analysis, and human-computer interaction for proactive leak management in aging infrastructure.

2.2 Artificial Intelligence-Based Monitoring System of Water Quality Parameters for Early Detection of Non-Specific Bio-Contamination in Water Distribution Systems

Tinelli and Juran (2019) proposed an AI-based approach for early detection of non-specific bio-contamination in water distribution systems, demonstrated on the Lille University campus in France. Their method addresses key limitations of traditional models by accounting for chemical decay and dynamic interactions among water quality parameters—such as free chlorine, pH, alkalinity, and TOC—thereby improving the accuracy of contamination detection and source identification. By integrating pattern recognition with adaptive thresholds, the system supports more realistic and responsive monitoring of contamination events.

The study combined ANNs and SVMs with dynamic thresholding to detect anomalies in water quality. Simulations of E. coli contamination were conducted using EPANET and EPANET-MSX to define normal baseline patterns and parameter thresholds. These simulations informed the training of AI algorithms, which were validated on the Lille campus network. The resulting models enabled non-specific anomaly detection and risk classification, with contaminated nodes visualized on a GIS interface according to severity levels, supporting spatial decision-making for timely intervention.

Baseline thresholds for each water quality parameter were first established through routine WDS monitoring. Deviations from these thresholds served as indicators of potential contamination. The primary objective of this case study was to demonstrate the feasibility of an AI-driven smart monitoring system that enables quasi-real-time detection of chemical and biological anomalies. Advanced pattern recognition techniques, specifically SVM and ANN, were employed to identify abnormal patterns and assess contamination severity. The system was able to classify these anomalies using a risk matrix and visualize them spatially across the network, facilitating targeted and timely interventions (Fig. 4).

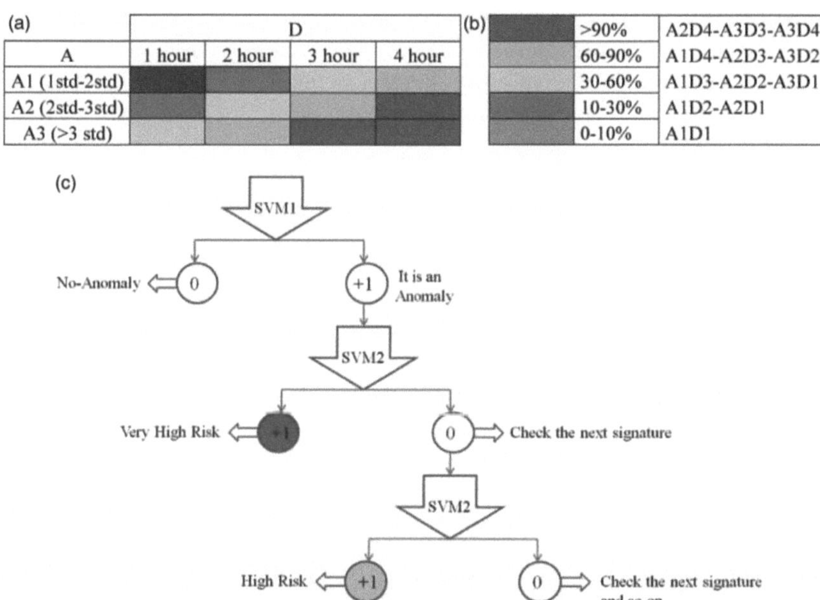

Fig. 4. Matrix used for the anomaly signature; (b) risk scale for the classification of the SVM out-put; (c) scheme of the multi-class anomaly detector (Tinelli & Juran, 2019).

This study introduced an innovative AI-based methodology for early detection of non-specific bio-contamination in water distribution systems, leveraging interrelated variations in key water quality parameters—such as chlorine, pH, alkalinity, and TOC—caused by the blending and diffusion of pollutants like E. coli. Once trained on baseline conditions, the algorithms accurately detected deviations and localized contamination events on a GIS interface using a color-coded risk severity scale. Among the supervised models tested, both SVMs and ANNs showed strong performance, with multi-class SVMs particularly effective in anomaly classification and decision support.

The approach minimizes false alarms and enhances operational efficiency by integrating real-time sensor data, pattern recognition, and spatial visualization. Applied on the Lille University campus network, the system successfully handled both single and multiple contamination scenarios. Its integration with platforms like Google Earth allows for intuitive geolocation and risk assessment, marking a significant step toward real-time decision support for utility managers. This methodology lays the groundwork for broader applications, including the detection of other contaminants such as pesticides and herbicides, advancing digital capabilities in water quality management.

2.3 AI/ML and Twin Modeling Application for Wastewater Treatment Process Control

Improving the performance of Wastewater Treatment Plants (WWTPs), now often referred to as Water Resource Recovery Facilities (WRRFs), requires optimizing complex, interdependent processes to meet goals such as energy efficiency, nutrient removal, reduced chemical use, and resource recovery. Traditional models like ASM1 and ASM2 have provided a strong foundation for process understanding but require extensive calibration, especially under atypical or biofiltration conditions. Recent advancements in Artificial Intelligence (AI), particularly machine learning (ML) and twin modeling (TM), are now being applied to enhance process control, fault detection, and influent/effluent prediction. These data-driven approaches offer greater adaptability to variable conditions and process nonlinearities, supporting more efficient, resilient, and sustainable operations across the wastewater sector (Serrao, 2024; Vanrolleghem et al., 2024).

Serrao et al. (2024) reviewed the evolution of mechanistic models for nitrogen removal in biofiltration systems over the past 25 years, noting their growing complexity in simulating interactions within biofilm, bulk liquid, and gas phases. Advancements include multi-layered biofilm structures (Bernier et al., 2014; Zhu, 2020), integration of nitrous oxide (N_2O) pathways (Fiat et al., 2019), and the inclusion of energy use and hydraulic behavior. While these models enhance accuracy, they require expert calibration, intensive data collection, and significant computing power—making them less practical for real-time applications. In contrast, data-driven models using AI/ML offer faster, more flexible alternatives well-suited for real-time control, although they require large datasets and frequent retraining due to process nonlinearity and time-dependence. The growing demand for improved effluent quality and environmental sustainability in the wastewater treatment sector has accelerated interest in digital innovations. As the volume of high-quality operational data increases, AI and ML are becoming increasingly central to wastewater management, mirroring their transformative impact across other industries.

The objective of the study by Serrao et al. (2024) was to improve the accuracy and operational applicability of nitrogen removal modelling in large-scale wastewater treatment plants (WWTPs) using submerged biofiltration. In response to growing demands for real-time decision-making and increased support of operators using digital transformation in water utilities, the researchers developed a parallel hybrid model designed to simulate nitrogen removal processes with high precision and computational efficiency. This hybrid approach aimed to support future integration into digital twin frameworks for advanced process control and monitoring.

To achieve this, the authors combined two modelling strategies: a mechanistic model based on a modified version of the Activated Sludge Model No. 1 (ASM1) and a data-driven model using an ANN. The mechanistic component captures the key biological, chemical, and physical processes in biofilm reactors and was carefully calibrated and validated using detailed operational data. This model, however, can exhibit residual errors due to real-world process variability and simplifications. To address this, a three-layer feedforward ANN—employing a rectified linear activation function—was trained on the model's residuals to improve its predictive accuracy. The resulting hybrid model shown in Fig. 5, effectively corrects and enhances the outputs of the mechanistic model.

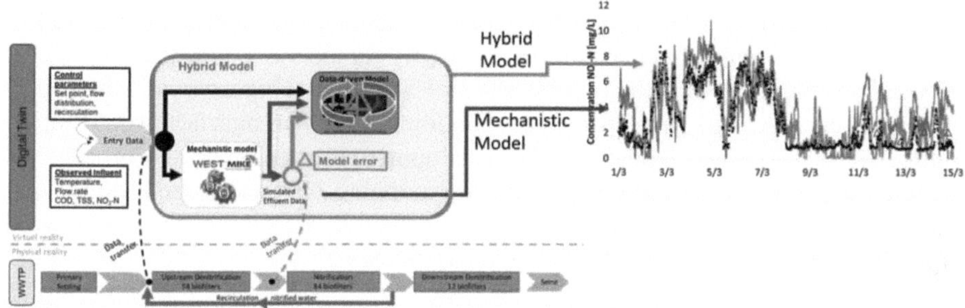

Fig. 5. Graphical abstract of the developed model (Serrao et al., 2024).

The study used high-frequency operational data collected from a large municipal WWTP over a 3.5-month period in 2020, combining online sensor data with daily laboratory analyses. This enabled both the mechanistic and ANN components to be calibrated and validated under real operational conditions. Among the tested machine learning approaches, feedforward neural networks delivered the best performance, reducing the validation error (at 15-min intervals) by a factor of three compared to the mechanistic model alone. The success of this approach marks a significant milestone—the first hybrid model applied to a full-scale biofilm system for nitrogen removal—and confirms its readiness for use in digital twin environments.

The study demonstrates that the hybrid modelling approach offers a significant improvement over the mechanistic model alone. During the training phase, the hybrid model reduced the relative mean error for effluent nitrate concentration from 12% (mechanistic-only) to just 2%. While this error increased to 8% during testing, it remained well below the standalone mechanistic model's error, confirming the added value of the machine learning component in operational scenarios.

The integration of a feed-forward neural network enabled the hybrid model to effectively correct the residual errors of the mechanistic simulation. By capturing complex or "hidden" dynamics not accounted for in the physical model, the data-driven module significantly enhanced predictive performance. The validation error at 15-min intervals was three times lower than that of the mechanistic model, and the model's robustness was further supported by strong Janus coefficients, indicating good generalization to unseen data.

However, the results also underline challenges that affect model accuracy, including high process variability, sensor noise, and data outliers. These factors suggest the need for more rigorous, possibly automated, data pre-processing and reconciliation workflows. Extending the duration of training and testing periods could further strengthen the model's generalizability.

Overall, the findings highlight that hybrid models can effectively bridge the gap between theoretical assumptions and real-world process variability. In particular, the machine learning component compensates for structural limitations in the mechanistic model—especially for complex systems like biofiltration—leading to more reliable predictions and greater confidence in their application for real-time decision support, including digital twin environments.

Looking ahead, a desktop or table-based version of the hybrid model could be integrated into Human-Machine Interfaces (HMI) for operator training and decision support. By simulating realistic process dynamics and allowing users to visualize system responses under different operational conditions, such an interface would serve as an effective learning and rehearsal tool. This approach aligns with the broader push for digital transformation in the water sector, equipping operators with intuitive, data-enriched platforms for understanding system behavior, managing uncertainties, and testing corrective actions in a safe, offline environment.

3 LSTM Application for WWTP Risk-Based Decision-Making in Energy-System Demand Response Participation

The use of energy in the water sector is significant. A study by EPRI in 2013 concluded that water and wastewater sectors use a combined 1.8% of the total energy use in the U.S., which accounts for 69.4 billion kWh per year. This estimation may be on the low end, as another report estimated that the water and wastewater sectors consumed between 2–4% of total energy used in the US per year (Liner and Stackin, 2013). This is a growth of 39% relative to the conclusion of a previous EPRI report completed in 1996. When only considering the growth in the electricity use in the wastewater sector, it is a 74% increase over the baseline established in 1996. Energy use in wastewater treatment is highest in the secondary treatment system, as the biological treatment system requires high amounts of energy to aerate the wastewater to facilitate the biological removal of N, C, and P. Aeration consistently accounts for more than 50% of electricity used by a treatment plant, and may be as high as 90%; the cost of consumed power for aeration may be between 15–49% of total costs with a plant (Drewnowski et al. 2019). The energy use for wastewater treatment will increase as standards for effluent discharge are made more stringent, and wastewater reuse becomes a critical drought protection plan in arid regions of the United States.

Given the importance of electricity energy for wastewater treatment, the demand for aeration energy is generally considered to be inelastic. Aeration interruption the effluent concentration of environmentally deleterious compounds such as total organic N and partially denitrified organic N (i.e. nitrite and nitrate). The criticality of electricity in wastewater treatment represents an opportunity for productive cooperation between energy and water systems.

An important way that water the water and energy sectors can cooperate in the present is for the water sector to begin to offer "grid services". These services are intended to maintain the reliability of the grid and are distinguished based on response speed, duration, and cycle time (Sparn and Hunsberger, 2015). Traditionally, these services have been provided by generation. This is done by centralized control centers sending out control signals to generating units that have the capability to rapidly adjust their energy dispatch. Technically, load can provide better reliability response than generation since full response is usually achieved immediately by tripping the load (Ela, et al. 2011). Electrical grids and the requirements for managing them are changing due to new energy and environmental goals for more renewable energy generation, policies to increase distributed generation of electricity, reduction of greenhouse gas emissions, and retirement of older power plants. These policies have brought on the new operating conditions for energy systems that require consumer control of electricity consumption:

- Short, steep ramps – ISO must bring on or shut down generation resources to meet increasing/decreasing electricity demand quickly over a short period of time;
- Oversupply risk – More electricity is supplied than is required;
- Decreased frequency response – Less resources are operating and available to automatically adjust electricity production to maintain grid reliability.

These three issues can be readily demonstrated in the projected net load curves produced by CAISO which is calculated by taking the forecasted load and subtracting the forecasted electricity production from variable generation resources of wind and solar (Fig. 6).

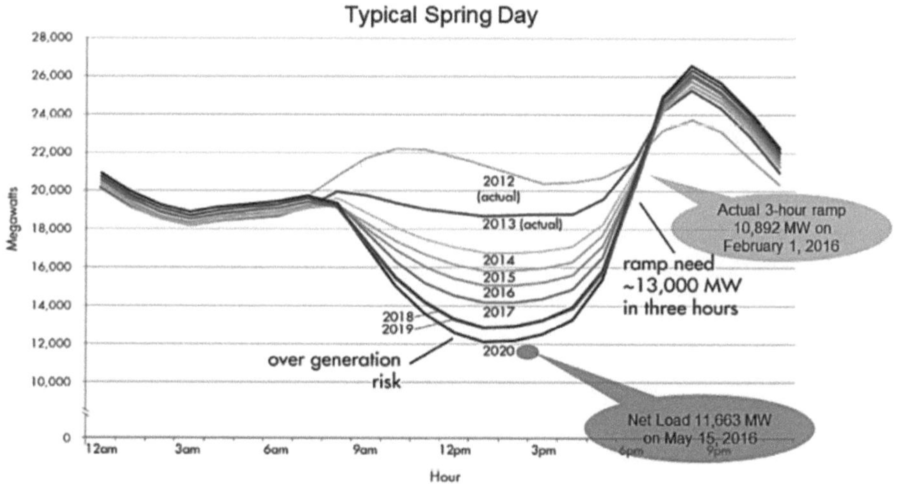

Fig. 6. CAISO Projected Net Load Curves, 2012 to 2020

The net load curve shows that as solar energy production increases in the morning hours, overgeneration from non-dispatchable energy resources attenuates; conversely, during sunset hours, demand loading increases, requiring large amounts of conventional energy generation to replace the missing solar energy. While replacement of missing renewable energy with conventional energy loads is one viable tactic to smoothing the net load curve, a more sustainable strategy is to incentivize customers to respond to requests from the ISO to bevel their flexible loads by shifting them to periods of low net load and curtailing them during periods of high net load. This is the essence of a demand response program.

Real-time WWTP demand response that involves the reduction of aeration is not currently considered a viable operational strategy for treatment operators. WWTPs are required to meet water quality standards for their treated effluent. Reduction in aeration energy necessarily results in a less efficient treatment process. While wastewater influent flow rates follow a predictable diurnal pattern, influent water quality parameters are random and do not follow any known distributions. Operators are therefore incentivized to not tailor their treatment strategies as the risk for violating effluent discharge standards increases as aeration rates are curtailed during potential demand response scenarios.

The nature of wastewater influent is chaotic and uncertain. There isn't a way to accurately predict the composition of loads that arrive at a treatment plant. For this reason, operators are necessarily risk averse in making treatment decisions, and this frequently results in treatment strategies that are energy inefficient. Advancements in sensors for monitoring Dissolved O_2 and Oxidation Reduction Potential (ORP) allow for feedback control loops to tailor aeration to maximize denitrification rates in the anoxic zone of biological reactors, known as Ammonia-Based Aeration Control (Rieger et al., 2014), however this comes with limitations. Lower aeration rates may adversely affect disinfection, induce sludge bulking, and cause foaming issues (ibid). While these challenges are not necessarily insurmountable to a skilled operator, aging treatment plants, lack of experience in fault isolation and resolution by operators, and the cost of additional infrastructure may make adaptive control methods unattractive to owners.

The Activated Sludge Model (ASM) in tandem with machine learning models are a viable combination of tools for assisting treatment plant operators in participating in demand response programs where aeration is curtailed without risking effluent discharge violations. The ASM can generate timeseries data of wastewater treatment parameters based on an experimental control strategy. An accompanying AI model can learn the aeration curtailment response pattern of water quality parameters leading to a given risk profile of the effluent using this data. By simulating an energy load reduction event in the aeration process in an ASM simulator, a learning algorithm can be trained to recognize the relationship between real-time treatment process parameters and the resultant effluent anomaly signatures due to aeration curtailment, allowing a forward look into the impact on aeration curtailment during energy system demand response events. Learning algorithms can thus perform risk-based extrapolation of future performance from real-time conditions based on this learned rule base. Put another way, the ASM generates a database of risk parameters in response to aeration curtailment, and the AI learning model acts as interface for the database through the training process by embedding the relationship between aeration settings, water quality parameters, and effluent risk.

The most suitable type of machine learning model are ones with a system architecture designed for sequence completion, such as recurrent neural networks (RNN). Applying an RNN system architecture known as a Long Short-Term Memory (LSTM) model will be explored.

3.1 Benchmark Simulation Model: Aeration Curtailment Database Generation.

Modelling wastewater treatment plants (WWTPs) is difficult as they are functionally nonlinear, and the influent characteristics are frequently subjected to random perturbations of volumetric flow rates and pollutant load concentrations. Another difficulty is that model inputs have non-stationary trends. This makes control strategy optimization a highly complex endeavor, historically managed through heuristics and experiential knowledge acquired by plant operators. In 1998, the IWAQ task force on control of activated sludge processes, proposed the concept of benchmarking WWTP control strategies through a standardized simulation protocol. This led to the development of an international research initiative that culminated in the Benchmark Simulation Model (BSM) series. This is a standardized simulation and evaluation procedures, including plant layout, simulation models and model parameters, and a detailed description of disturbances to be applied during testing and evaluation criteria for comparing the relative effectiveness of simulated strategies, grounded in fundamental transport and reaction principles.

The Benchmark Simulation Model (BSM) series, represents a standardized simulation protocol to enable unbiased, reproducible evaluation of WWTP operational strategies. The present study utilizes BSM2, which incorporates ASM1, an ODE-based representation of biological carbon and nitrogen removal dynamics. BSM2 includes a dynamic influent generator, capable of emulating the random nature of influent loads. BSM2's configuration consists of five biological reactors: two anoxic tanks followed by three aerobic reactors. The aeration profile of each aerobic chamber is defined via the KLa mass transfer coefficient, which defines the rate of transfer of O2 between its gas and liquid phases. The influent generator module parameterizes a complex mix of constituents—including soluble and particulate COD fractions, ammonium, nitrate, nitrite, and inert solids—based on empirical probability distributions to simulate day-to-day plant loading.

The combination of a standardized modelling protocol along with stochastic influent loads are key in developing a framework for creating robust databases of treatment system behavior under varying aeration loads required for simulating demand response in WWTPs. To generate training data for the LSTM architecture, an extended simulation is executed over a span of 609 operational days. This simulation period is partitioned into two distinct phases: an initial 245-day simulation period to establish a pseudo steady-state using dynamic influent and nominal aeration rates (Gernaey et al. 2014). After establishing the pseudo steady-state under dynamic influent is followed by a 365-day experimental phase involving recurring demand response (DR) events. Aeration is curtailed by reducing KLa to zero in all aerobic tanks for four hours during the first peak energy demand of the day (from 08:30AM to 12:30PM). The demand response scenarios are generated in 14-day batches, after which time-series data of water quality parameters under aeration curtailment in the biological treatment train is saved to a database. The model is re-initialized from the previous pseudo steady-state and run forward 14-days to prepare the next interval. In parallel, equivalent simulations under nominal aeration conditions are performed to serve as baseline reference datasets.

To mitigate adverse impacts on effluent quality during aeration curtailment, the internal recycle flow rate is dynamically increased to 1.5 times the standard value (from 20,648 m^3/day). This adjustment is intended to sustain microbial populations and nutrient removal kinetics within the biological train. Simulation results show elevated effluent concentrations of NH_3 and NH_{4+} during DR events, with these frequently exceeding BSM Total Nitrogen thresholds. In contrast, COD excursions remain comparatively moderate. These outcomes affirm that ammonium is the most sensitive and constraining variable in the context of energy-optimized WWTP operations.

Quantitative assessments of energy consumption indicate a daily savings of approximately 667 kilowatt-hours attributable to the curtailed aeration period. These reductions align with diurnal electricity pricing peaks, further enhancing the economic viability of the DR strategy. The energy burden associated with increased pumping for internal recycle is minor by comparison, representing approximately 15% of typical aeration energy consumption, and does not offset the net energy savings realized.

3.2   Data Preparation: Risk Scoring of Effluent Quality Time Series

Effective LSTM model training necessitates rigorous preprocessing of raw time series data. Given the objective of forecasting effluent risk levels under varying aeration conditions, simulated effluent time series are transformed into structured risk-annotated datasets. Central to this process is the computation of the Effluent Quality Index (EQI), formulated as a weighted aggregation of key regulatory constituents.

$$EQI = [B_{TSS}(t) + B_{COD}(t) + B_{BOD}(t) + B_{TKN}(t) + B_{NO}(t)]Q_e(t) \qquad (1)$$

Weight coefficients are extracted from existing literature and tailored to emphasize parameters disproportionately influenced by oxygen delivery reductions. The EQI time series is then discretized via a two-dimensional risk matrix incorporating both severity and frequency metrics (Table 1).

Table 1.   Effluent EQI Risk Matrix

		FREQUENCY				
		0	1	2	3	4
SEVERITY	4	2	3	3	4	4
	3	2	2	3	4	4
	2	1	1	2	3	4
	1	1	1	1	2	3
	0	0	0	1	1	2

Severity Score (based on deviation from nominal mean):

- $< 1\sigma$: 0
- $[1\sigma, 1.5\sigma)$: 1
- $[1.5\sigma, 2.0\sigma)$: 2
- $[2.0\sigma, 2.5\sigma)$: 3
- $\geq 2.5\sigma$: 4

Frequency Score (based on anomaly recurrence):

- > 3 contiguous anomalies (Severity $\geq$): 4
- Three contiguous anomalies: 3
- Two consecutive anomalies: 2
- Single anomaly followed by nominal: 1
- Isolated anomaly: 0

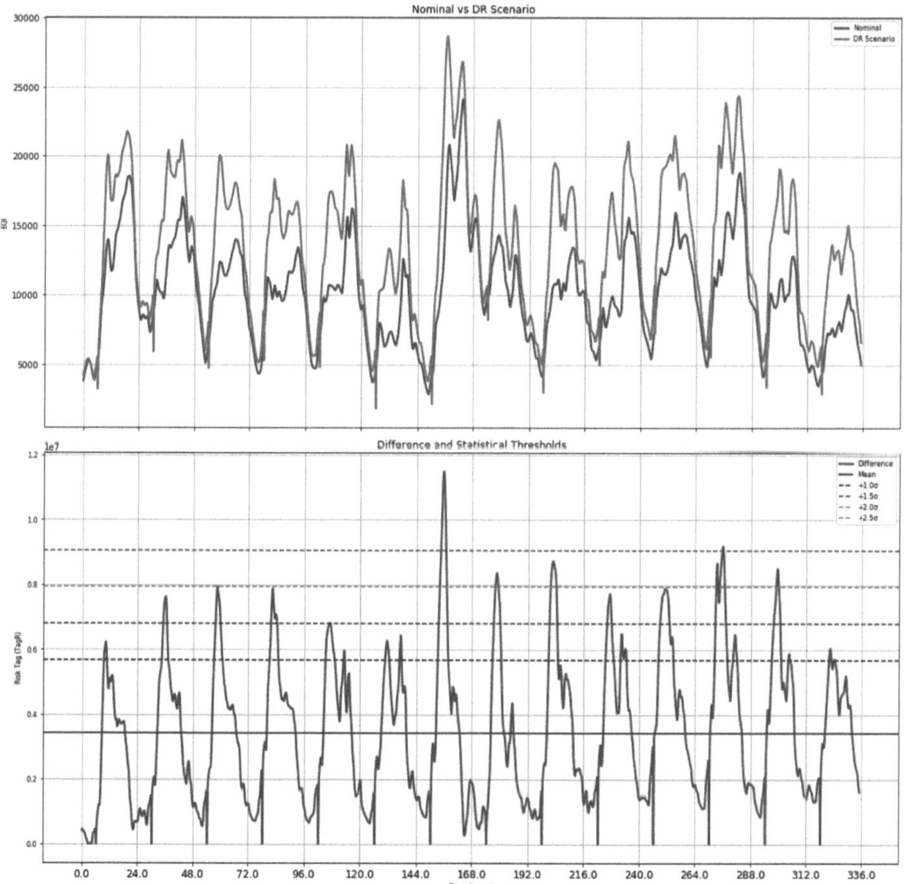

Fig. 7. EQI Timeseries and Raw Anomaly Signatures.

Each timestamped EQI value is assigned a composite risk score derived from this matrix. The resulting risk-labeled time series constitutes the supervised learning target for the LSTM model. Input features to the model include KLa values, diurnal temporal markers, and a suite of influent and in-process variables extracted from the underlying ASM1 framework (Fig. 7). Figures 8 and 9 show an example of the EQI anomaly signature before processing and the result of the risk timeseries processing.

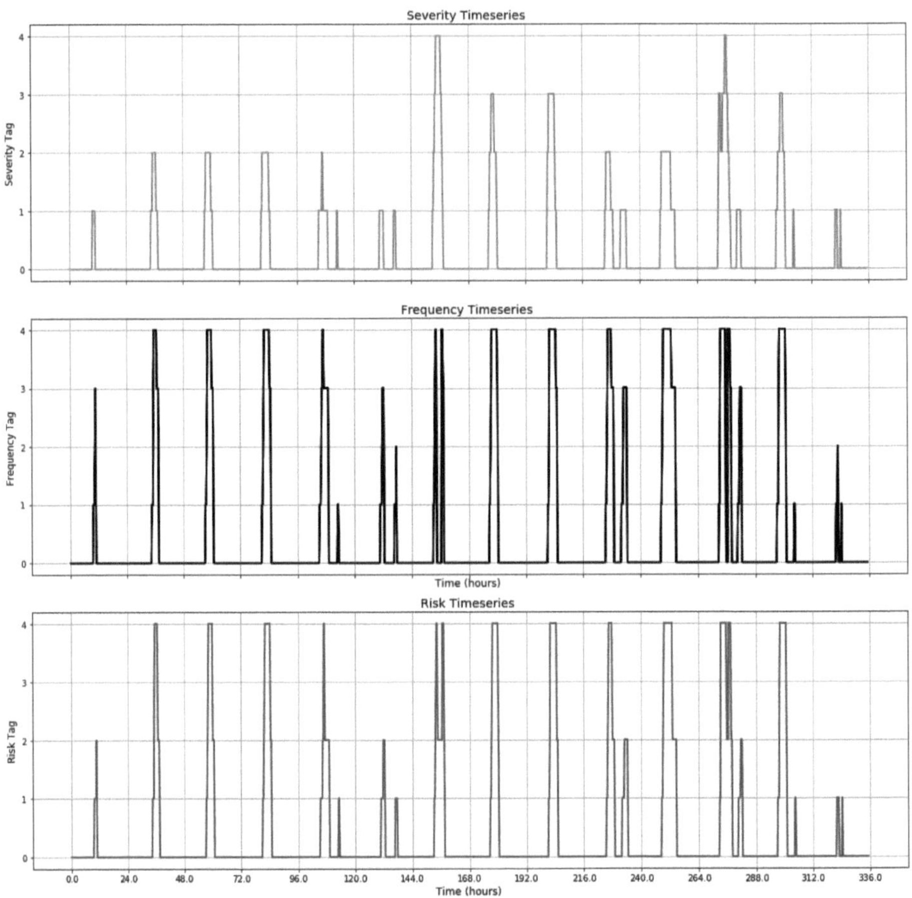

Fig. 8. Timeseries of Severity, Frequency, and Final Risk Scores of EQI Timeseries.

3.3 LSTM Architecture and Model Training Strategy

The LSTM architecture is uniquely suited for modeling multivariate, temporally dependent sequences such as those arising in wastewater treatment process modeling. In this context, temporal dependencies manifest in the lagged transformation of influent ammonia into downstream species such as nitrate and nitrite, contingent upon microbial activity and environmental conditions.

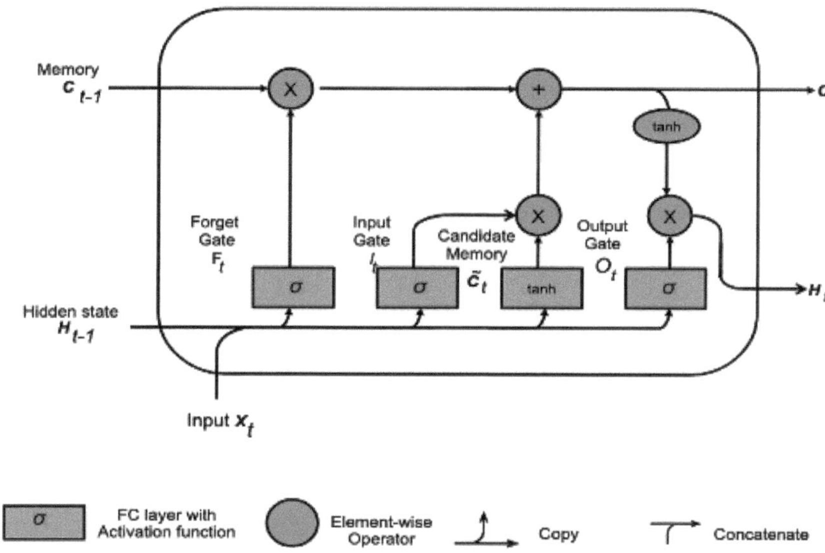

Fig. 9. LSTM System Architecture.

To inform LSTM sequence design, autocorrelation function (ACF) and partial autocorrelation function (PACF) analyses are conducted across effluent parameters. These diagnostics identify relevant time lags and inform sequence length hyperparameters. In variables exhibiting extended autocorrelation horizons, first-order differencing is applied to suppress temporal redundancy and compress sequence length (e.g., reducing lag from 11 h to approximately 2 h), thereby enhancing model generalization and computational efficiency (Fig. 10).

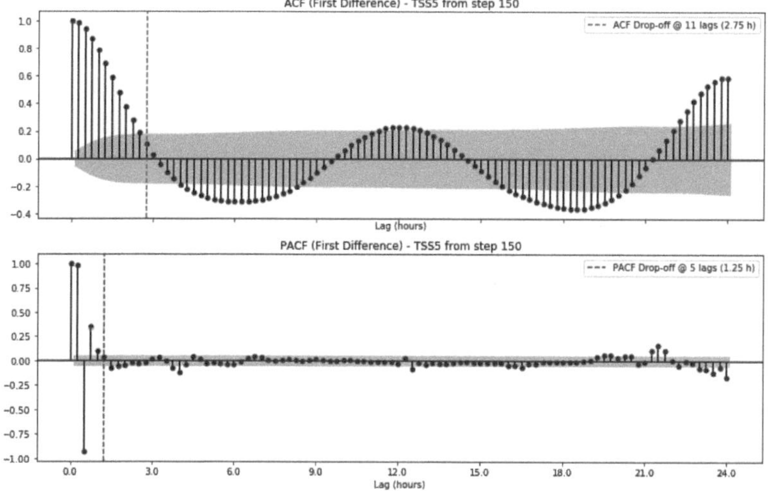

Fig. 10. ACF and PACF Plots of Bioreactor 1st Difference Timeseries Data.

Hyperparameter selection—including input window size, hidden layer dimensionality, dropout regularization, and learning rate—is iteratively tuned using validation loss minimization. The model is trained to minimize a categorical risk cross-entropy loss function, optimized via backpropagation through time using the Adam optimizer.

In conclusion, this methodology represents an integrated framework combining mechanistic process simulation with advanced machine learning techniques to forecast regulatory compliance risk under both planned and emergent energy demand scenarios. By leveraging BSM1 to generate large-scale, high-fidelity simulation data and systematically encoding effluent behavior into risk-labeled sequences, this study enables the development of LSTM models capable of providing operational foresight for WWTP operators. The resulting decision-support tool facilitates preemptive energy curtailment strategies that maintain compliance, minimize environmental impacts, and optimize operational costs under increasingly dynamic grid conditions.

4 Conclusion

This paper presented a methodology for AI/ML-aided risk assessment and interactive scenario simulation tailored for in-house corporate training in water and wastewater utilities. By integrating anomaly detection models, digital twin platforms, and immersive tabletop exercises, the proposed approach addresses the urgent need for enhanced crisis preparedness and accelerated learning in an increasingly complex and risk-prone operational environment. The proposed approach is applicable to both planned and unplanned events, including those triggered by cybersecurity incidents. A key challenge in crisis management for water systems lies in their nature as Systems of Systems (SoS), encompassing hydraulic, cyber, and energy domains. Based on the diversity of case studies reviewed, this approach demonstrates adaptability for SoS engineering and integrated risk analysis.

The role of AI and ML in water management is set to expand in the (near) future with increasing integration of real-time sensor data and advancements in deep learning that will further improve predictive accuracy and facilitate more autonomous operation and process control. This progress will contribute to more sustainable, cost-effective, and adaptive WWTP management systems. By leveraging AI and ML to optimize treatment processes, operators can make more informed decisions that lead to cost savings and greater sustainability, all while improving the quality of treated wastewater and supporting the development of smarter, resilient cities.

Given that cross-sector collaboration is required, it is essential to involve both technical OT and IT experts in training programs to provide a holistic understanding of the multi-system environment. In-house corporate training—both executive and technical levels—must expose personnel to the complexities of these interconnected systems. Using state-of-the-art technologies like virtual reality (VR) can offer immersive, hands-on training that simulates real-world crisis scenarios. This approach enables operators to practice handling multi-system crises, including cybersecurity threats, and equips them with a practical skillset, essential for effective decision-making and rapid response during emergencies.

The results demonstrate how artificial intelligence and human-computer interaction can be strategically combined to improve situational awareness, support early event detection, and foster adaptive decision-making across multiple operational domains. The tabletop simulations developed provide an effective and scalable training environment, enabling operators and managers to experience and respond to synthetic crisis scenarios in a controlled, role-specific, and system-aware setting.

From a human-computer interaction perspective, the use of intuitive interfaces, real-time data visualization, and adaptive feedback mechanisms plays a central role in supporting learning, trust in AI recommendations, and cross-functional communication. These elements are particularly critical when managing high-stakes operational events, where timely decisions and collaboration are essential.

Looking forward, the methodology can be extended along several dimensions:

- Integration of immersive technologies such as virtual reality (VR) and augmented reality (AR) to enhance realism and engagement in crisis scenario simulations.
- Validation through live exercises and multi-utility collaborations to evaluate performance under real-world constraints.
- Incorporation of behavioral models and user performance analytics to adapt training paths and measure individual learning outcomes over time.
- Expansion to other infrastructure sectors, enabling shared training across water, energy, and digital service domains through a unified systems-of-systems training framework.

Considering an accelerating technological and digital era and combined with societal and the effects of climate changes, building organizational resilience requires more than infrastructure investment—it demands new tools for learning, new models for decision-making, and new paradigms for human-computer collaboration. The work presented here contributes to this shift by combining AI/ML innovation with human-centered design for corporate training tools, enabling water utilities to better anticipate, manage, and learn from the complex risks they face.

Acknowledgments. The work by Samuel White at NYU Tandon was supported by experts at W-SMART. The work of Marcello Serrao on Hybrid Modelling of WWTP processes was performed at the Ecole de Ponts/LEESU in co-direction with model*EAU* at ULaval (Quebec, Canada) and was supported by W-SMART (Paris, France) and SIAAP (Paris, France) as part of the Mocopée research program. W-SMART cooperation is a part of the EU sponsored ATHENA project.

Disclosure of Interests. The authors have no competing interests to declare that are relevant to the content of this article.

References

Bernier, J., Rocher, V., Guerin, S., Lessard, P.: Modelling the nitrification in a full-scale tertiary biological aerated filter unit. Bioprocess Biosyst. Eng. **37**(2), 289–300 (2014)

Cantos, W.P., Juran, I., Tinelli, S.: Machine-learning–based risk assessment method for leak detection and geolocation in a water distribution system. J. Infrastruct. Syst. **26**(1), 04019039 (2020)

Drewnowski, J., Remiszewska-Skwarek, A., Duda, S., Łagód, G.: Aeration Process in Bioreactors as the Main Energy Consumer in a Wastewater Treatment Plant. Review of Solutions and Methods of Process Optimization. Processes **7**, 311 (2019)

Ela, E., Milligan, M., Kirby, B.: Operating reserves and variable generation. National Renewable Energy Lab. (NREL), Golden, CO (United States) (2011)

Fiat, J., et al.: Considering the plug-flow behavior of the gas phase in nitrifying BAF models significantly improves the prediction of N2O emissions. Water Res. **156**, 337–346 (2019)

Gernaey, K.V., Jeppsson, U., Vanrolleghem, P.A., Copp, J.B. (Eds.): Benchmarking of Control Strategies for Wastewater Treatment Plants. IWA Publishing (2014)

Liner, B., Stacklin, C.: Driving water and wastewater utilities to more sustainable energy management, in: ASME 2013 Power Conference. American Society of Mechanical Engineers Digital Collection (2013)

Rieger, L., Jones, R.M., Dold, P.L., Bott, C.B.: Ammonia-Based Feedforward and Feedback Aeration Control in Activated Sludge Processes. Water Environ. Res. **86**, 63–73 (2014). https://doi.org/10.2175/106143013X13596524516987

Sparn, B., Hunsberger, R.: Opportunities and challenges for water and wastewater industries to provide exchangeable services. National Renewable Energy Lab.(NREL), Golden, CO (United States) (2015)

Serrao, M., Jauzein, V., Juran, I., Tassin, B., Vanrolleghem, P.: Hybrid modelling of nitrogen removal by biofiltration using high-frequent operational data. Water Sci. Technol. **90**(5), 1416–1432 (2024)

Tinelli, S., Juran, I.: Artificial intelligence-based monitoring system of water quality parameters for early detection of non-specific bio-contamination in water distribution systems. Water Supply **19**(6), 1785–1792 (2019)

Tinelli, S., Juran, I., Cantos, W.P.: Development of risk assessment tools for early detection of bio-contamination in water distribution systems. Water Science and Technology: Water Supply **18**(6), 2151–2161 (2018)

Vanrolleghem P.A., Khalil M., Serrao M., Sparks J. & Therrien J-D.: Machine Learning in Wastewater: Opportunities and Challenges - "Not everything is a nail!". Current Opinion in Biotechnology (pending review) (2024)

Human-Centered Cognition Model for Human Digital Twins

Eloïse Zehnder[(✉)] and Yannick Naudet

Luxembourg Institute of Science and Technology, Esch-sur-Alzette, Luxembourg
`eloise.zehnder@list.lu`

Abstract. This paper presents an initial proposal for a human-centered cognition model intended to support the development and operation of Human Digital Twins (HDTs). Acknowledging the complexity and incomplete understanding of human cognition, this work adopts a systemic and interdisciplinary approach, integrating perspectives from cognitive sciences, social sciences, engineering, and cognitive informatics. The model aims to formalize the representation of human cognitive dimensions through a structured framework of domains, abilities, and processes, with particular attention to sensation, perception, memory, attention, motor skills, language, metacognition, and higher cognitive functions. Beyond offering a descriptive foundation, the model aspires to facilitate the integration of heterogeneous models and data sources into HDTs, thereby supporting more interpretable, adaptive, and context-aware digital representations of human behavior. While this work does not claim exhaustiveness, it seeks to contribute to ongoing efforts toward a more rigorous and interoperable conceptualization of human cognition within digital twin systems.

Keywords: Digital Twin · Cognitive Modeling · Explainable Artificial Intelligence · Interoperability

1 Introduction

A Human Digital Twin (HDT) is a digital replica of a human being, designed to simulate not only physical traits but also behavioral and cognitive dynamics, and their evolution. HDTs hold significant potential for applications in personalized healthcare, education, human–machine interaction, and adaptive systems. However, creating an effective and generalizable HDT requires more than real-time data streams and predictive algorithms. It requires a coherent, interpretable, and adaptable representation of the human being. Despite rapid progress in the field, most current HDT implementations remain narrow in scope. As noted recently *"Current HDT developments are highly specialized and typically seek to create models that focus on very few aspects of the individual and are restricted to specific contexts"* [41, p. 34]. These models are often built as proofs of concept, focusing on specific features such as movement, physiological data, or isolated behaviors. In addition, the dominant use of data-driven machine learning approaches,

H. Mori et al. (Eds.): HCII 2025, LNCS 16333, pp. 261–280, 2026.
https://doi.org/10.1007/978-3-032-12660-3_20

while effective at identifying patterns, often leads to black-box systems that lack explainability, semantic grounding, and transferability across contexts or individuals. To address these limitations, we introduce ontological models as a basis for knowledge representation and logical reasoning in HDTs. Ontologies enable a formal, machine-readable representation of expert knowledge, supporting reasoning, explainability, semantic integration, and hybrid architectures. Our approach does not oppose machine learning but rather complements it: ontological models can provide structure and interpretability to learned representations, helping to validate and contextualize predictions. The work presented here focuses on cognition modeling. In order to be as comprehensive as possible, it is grounded in an interdisciplinary perspective. We draw from cognitive sciences, social sciences, engineering, artificial intelligence, neuropsychology, education sciences, and cognitive informatics to build a descriptive model of human cognition. Finally, the central contribution of this paper is the definition of the cognitive sphere, a structured model of human cognition articulated through domains, abilities, and processes. The model aims to represent key cognitive functions such as sensation, perception, attention, memory, language, motor skills, metacognition, and higher cognitive functions.

2   Foundations of the Human Cognitive Model

Developing a comprehensive model of the human being constitutes a complex endeavor [1] constrained by the current limits of scientific knowledge, characterized by unresolved controversies and theoretical divergences. Several cognitive models and architectures have been proposed to represent aspects of human cognition [2], such as ACT-R [5], SOAR [6] (both being cognitive architectures), or neuroscience-inspired approaches [7], as well as models grounded in information processing theory [8]. While these frameworks provide valuable insights into specific mechanisms or domains of cognition, they often rely on domain-specific assumptions and diverge in terminology, scope, and underlying theoretical commitments.

Nevertheless, to build the digital twin of a human, the core part of a human model should be build on strong foundations and unambiguous concepts. In the literature on human cognition, terms like abilities, processes, or functions are often used interchangeably by different authors, depending on their specific fields. The first step in this work is to clarify and formalize these terms in order to create a clearer model of the human cognitive sphere. We draw upon the General System Theory (GST) [9], which provides a foundational framework. According to GST, the human can be seen as a system—a collection of interacting components working together as a whole to fulfill the system's objective, influenced by and influencing the environment.

A *human* is thus a *system* consisting of different subsystems (e.g., Cognitive, Physical, and Physiological systems), which can further be broken down into smaller subsystems. It has *properties* and *functions* that can be realized by any of its parts or by the whole. Thus, each subsystem performs specific functions that are the actions or processes that the subsystem is responsible for carrying out to maintain the overall functioning of the system. A *function* of a system refers to the specific tasks or actions that the system's components perform in order to achieve the system's overall goal or purpose. A *process* is the set of actions or steps that are carried out to perform a function. In other words, a function is what the system is meant to do, and a process is how it does it. The *ability* of a system is its capacity to carry out a function, meaning the system's potential to perform the required actions or tasks. Abilities are closely tied to the functions of the subsystems. For a system to have an ability, it must first possess the necessary functions. These functions may either originate from the system itself or be borrowed from other subsystems. For instance, a human's ability to walk relies on the functions of the motor subsystem (e.g., muscle movement, coordination).

Finally, we introduce the notion of *sphere*, which models a dimension of a system or a specific aspect according to which it can be considered, for whatever purpose. Any property, function, ability or (sub)system can be attached to a sphere or a sub-sphere, which we call a sphere *domain*. For example the cognitive sphere relates to all cognitive sub-systems with their functions. A different example is the psychological sphere, which relates to a set of properties attached to humans that are relevant for psychology (e.g. personality).

2.1   Establishing the Cognitive Model: Key Perspectives

Human digital twins refer to highly detailed and dynamic virtual models of a human beings that can mirror the physical, emotional, and cognitive states of the real human. In such models, the inclusion of cognition (the ability to think, reason, and understand) is critical for several reasons such as interactivity, personalization, predictive and adaptive capabilities, learning and adaptation or ethical and emotional considerations. In order to create a model of cognition which would be usable for both humans and machines, this work attempts to understand what defines and composes it.

Cognition has been studied across various fields like psychology, computer science, neurosciences or education, each using different terminologies, models and applications since the cognitive revolution in the 1950s and 1960s. This broad and diverse coverage raises the question of whether a single, unified model is achievable. Thus, our approach, although not exhaustive, combines insights from multiple models, focusing on traditional concepts like attention, memory, and perception, while incorporating relevant ideas that support the development of a comprehensive HDT.

The Social Sciences Perspective emphasizes the importance of understanding human behavior within biological, psychological, and social contexts. Neuropsychology explores how the physiological processes of the nervous system influence behavior and cognition, both in their normal and impaired states. In this field, Harvey [10] proposes a framework of cognitive domains (sensation and perception, motor skills and construction, attention and concentration, memory, executive functioning, processing speed and language skills). These domains can be assessed to detect cognitive impairments and provide a foundation for understanding human cognition.

In education sciences, cognitive processes are used to classify learning objectives, offering a deeper understanding of the cognitive demands placed on learners. Anderson and Krathwohl's taxonomy [11], classifies educational objectives along two dimensions: cognitive processes and knowledge. Our focus is on the cognitive process dimension, which includes stages such as Remembering (e.g., memorizing, listing), Understanding (e.g., interpreting, explaining), Applying (e.g., solving, demonstrating), Analyzing (e.g., comparing, critiquing), Evaluating (e.g., judging, defending), and Creating (e.g., designing, organizing). This perspective provides a focus on learning mechanisms and includes action verbs related to cognitive processes in humans. These verbs can be used to model the behaviors and interactions of Human Digital Twins.

The Cognitive Architecture Perspective focuses on understanding and replicating the structures and processes underlying human cognition. Cognitive architectures, rooted in cognitive science, provide computational models of the human mind to develop a unified theory of cognition. These architectures have evolved across various fields, including artificial intelligence, cognitive psychology, neuroscience, and robotics. Today, there are multiple designs and implementations [12,13]. The Common Model of Cognition (CMC), initially presented as a standard model of the mind [14] can be considered as a reference model for cognitive architectures. It offers a computational framework to build systems with human-like cognition, structured similarly to human thought processes. Recent experimental validations [15] show that the CMC's structure aligns with brain areas and their functions, supporting the model's accuracy.

The CMC structures cognition into five interacting functional components. The Perception component collects observations from the environment and sends them to the Working Memory, which acts as a buffer and communication hub for the other components. The Long-Term Declarative Memory stores feature-based information, while the Procedural Memory holds reactive rules, which are patterns that trigger specific actions based on situations. The Action (or Motor [14]) component acting in the environment. Overall, the CMC illustrates how perception, memory, and motor functions work together through working memory to facilitate the complete cognitive process. It provides a structured model of cognition, outlining how information flows from sensory input to action.

The Cognitive Informatics Perspective provides a framework for analyzing how cognitive processes can be represented and simulated in computational systems. Cognitive Informatics is an interdisciplinary field that combines cognitive science with computer science to understand and model cognition in both humans and machines [17]. A key framework within this perspective is the Layered Reference Model of the Brain (LRMB), proposed by Wang and collaborators [16]. This model offers a comprehensive structure for examining 37 human cognitive processes, dividing them into 6 layers: Sensation (e.g., vision, audition), Memory (e.g., short-term, long-term), Perception (e.g., self-consciousness, emotions, spatial awareness), Action (e.g., bodily and external actions), Metacognition (e.g., attention, abstraction, search), and Higher Cognitive Functions (e.g., recognition, learning, reasoning, decision-making). Given the model's broad scope, mapping the cognitive processes outlined in Anderson and Krathwohl's taxonomy to this framework, while linking them to neuropsychological findings, provides a richer understanding of human cognition. This approach lays a foundation for developing a more precise cognitive model. In the following subsection, we present our own model of the cognitive sphere, which integrates insights from the LRMB along with the perspectives discussed earlier.

3   The Cognitive Sphere

This section presents the key elements of cognition, or the cognitive sphere, that are essential for developing a Human Digital Twin. These elements are drawn from the various models and perspectives discussed earlier, as well as from common frameworks in psychology and cognitive science. Each element is described in a way that aims to provide a definition useful for both humans and digital twins. We also explore methods for assessing these cognitive elements, which helps understand how performance can vary among individuals and how it can be replicated in a digital twin. Additionally, we examine factors that could impair these cognitive functions.

3.1   Sensation

Sensation enables an organism to perceive and interact with its environment, playing a critical role in cognition. It is the ability to detect stimuli in one of the five sensory modalities: sight, sound, touch, taste, and smell [10]. From a cognitive informatics perspective, sensation is *"a subconscious layer of life functions of the brain for detecting and acquiring cognitive information from the external world via physical and/or chemical means"* (p. 125) [16]. Sensation also involves other modalities such as proprioception (the sense of position and movement of our body parts), vestibular sense (balance, contributing to our balance and spatial orientation), interoception (sensations inside the body), thermoception (perception of temperature externally and internally), nociception (perception of pain) or chronoception (perception of time). Measuring the ability for sensation in individuals can be done through methods like absolute and difference thresholds, which determine the minimum amount of stimulation needed for detection or the smallest detectable change in a stimulus [3]. Among individuals, sensation can be altered by a few factors such as neurological conditions (strokes, multiple sclerosis, brain injuries), psychiatric disorders (schizophrenia, anxiety), substance use, or developmental disorders (autism spectrum disorder). While sometimes interchanged in humans with perception, sensation allows to receive a sensory input which will then be processed by perception.

In the context of human digital twins which are virtual models replicating an individual's physical and cognitive characteristics, integrating sensation is required for accurately simulating human responses to stimuli. However, it is tightly coupled with perception and gathering data on human senses is not trivial. While sensors (sometimes wearable) such as cameras, microphones, or haptic devices can detect environmental or physical stimuli (light, sound waves, pressure, temperature,...) they emerge from a chain of processes characterizing sensation. Stimuli are transduced by specialized receptors into neural signals, which are then processed in primary sensory cortices to produce structured representations of the physical world. To replicate sensation in artificial systems, raw sensor data must undergo transduction, converting physical measurements into internal data structures suitable for downstream processing. Second, signal processing modules must extract low-level features in a manner analogous to early neural coding—such as spatiotemporal mapping in tactile sensing or edge detection in visual systems. Finally, dedicated computational layers must integrate these features into modality-specific representations, functionally equivalent to those generated by biological primary sensory cortices.

Finally, within this sensation domain and following the General Systems theory we draw from, we can assume that the stimulus detection function support the ability to sense environmental inputs, while the threshold detection function enable the distinction of minimal variations in stimulus intensity. Modality-specific functions support visual, auditory, tactile, gustatory, olfactory, chemo-, thermo-, photo- and nociceptive sensation. These sensory functions form the foundational input layer for perception and higher-level cognitive processing.

3.2   Perception

From a neuropsychological perspective, perception consists in the *"identification of previously experienced objects from sensory information"* (p. 228) [10]. Perception can be assessed in terms of ability to detect, discriminate identify objects, sounds, and also for the intactness of the perceptual fields. For cognitive informatics, perception belongs to the third layer of life functions and is part of the subconscious cognitive processes, along with memory and action. It is defined as *"a subconscious layer of life functions of the brain for maintaining conscious life functions and for browsing internal abstract memories in the cognitive models of the brain"* (p. 126) [16]. Perception is a fundamental aspect of cognition, serving as the process through which sensory information from the environment is gathered, processed, and interpreted by the brain. It involves both bottom-up processing, where sensory data is analyzed, and top-down processing, where prior knowledge, memories, and expectations shape how individuals interpret that data. While cognitive informatics described perception as subconscious [16] (as when an individual processing subliminal messages in advertisements), it can also be conscious, as when an individual may consciously recognize the scent of jasmine flowers. Perception in humans can be measured in very broad ways depending on the evaluated perception. It can consist for example in subjective reports (questionnaires, verbal descriptions) or behavioral tasks (with reaction time, categorization tasks, illusions to evaluate discrepancies between a sensory input and a perceived experience). Regardless of the sensory modality (visual, tactile, auditory,...), the domain of perception involves the capacity to recognize a meaningful stimulus. For instance, sensation may register nociceptive signals, but perception interprets them as pain, integrating contextual, emotional, and cognitive factors. In humans, perception can be altered by attention (priorization of certain stimulis), expectations or prior knowledge, emotions and mood, cognitive biases (confirmation bias for example), sensory adaptation (prolonged exposure to a stimuli), synesthesia, physiological factors (hearing impairments, color blindness, fatigue or sleep deprivation, substance use), health and neurological factors (chronic pain or neurological conditions like dementia or brain injuries).

In the context of human digital twins, replicating perception requires not only acquiring sensory data but also processing it through computational models that support interpretation and decision-making. Technologies such as computer vision, natural language processing, and pattern recognition contribute to this goal. For example, vision systems combine visual input from cameras with machine learning algorithms to identify objects, infer spatial relationships, or detect movement. Similarly, auditory perception can be approximated through speech recognition, sound localization, and affective audio analysis. These systems move beyond raw signal detection to emulate how humans derive meaning from their sensory environment.

Within the perception domain, the recognition function supports the ability to identify and interpret visual or auditory stimuli, while sensory integration enables the combination of information from multiple modalities. The spatial awareness function supports the ability to perceive position and orientation in space, and chronoception supports time perception. Proprioception and interoception functions allow the detection of body position and internal physiological states, respectively. These perceptual functions enable the interpretation and organization of sensory inputs.

3.3   Motor Skills and Sensorimotor Cognition

For Harvey [10], motor skills include manual dexterity and motor speed, but also reaction time and skills like balance which can be evaluated through finger tapping or grip strength tests (for example). He also mentions construction ability, which involves the ability to replicate or create a drawing and can be considered part of motor skills. In the work of Wang et al. [16], the cognitive process closest to motor skills is Action, defined as *"a set of subconscious Cognitive Processes of the brain at the subconscious cognitive function layers that executes both bodily (external) and mental (internal) actions via the motor systems of the body or the perceptional engine of the brain"* (p. 128). The awareness level involved in motor skills can vary. For example, some actions, like breathing, can be automatic, while others, like walking, are more voluntary. Other authors [18] describe motor skills broadly, stating that they range from basic, innate skills like walking and reaching, to learned skills like driving or touch-typing, and even elite-level skills like playing the violin. They define a motor skill as *"an acquired capability to successfully achieve a task goal"* with the key focus being movement [18]. Measuring motor skills in individuals can involve a broad range of tests, such as the Test of Motor Competence, which includes timed assessments of fine motor tasks, hand-eye coordination, and gross motor skills [4].

For accurate human digital twins, understanding the intricate link between motor skills and cognition is important. This requires considering not just specific motor components defined by Harvey [10] (dexterity, speed, reaction time, balance, construction ability), but also *Action* as a fundamental cognitive process encompassing both physical and mental activities [16]. These skills develop throughout the lifespan and involve purposeful, goal-oriented acquisition [18]. Encompassing the integration of sensory input with motor output (a core aspect of sensorimotor cognition) appears relevant for creating digital twins that can effectively mimic and predict human motor behavior. The brain areas involved in motor control, such as the motor cortex, cerebellum, and basal ganglia, work closely with cognitive regions, highlighting the deep intertwining of motor skills with cognitive processes. Integrating an individual's motor skills into a human digital twin serves the purpose of mimicking specific physical movements and interactions that individual. This allows for precise simulations of how the user would perform tasks, navigate environments, or respond to various physical challenges. Such integration is particularly valuable in fields like healthcare, where it can be used to tailor rehabilitation programs, in ergonomics for designing personalized workspaces, or in training environments to create realistic scenarios based on the individual's motor capabilities. By capturing and incorporating these motor skills, the digital twin could adapt a powerful tool for predicting and adapting physical interactions. Cognitive functions related to Motor/Action are subconscious cognitive processes according to [16].

Within the domain of motor skills, the motor planning function supports the ability to prepare and sequence movements; the motor execution function supports the ability to perform voluntary movements; the postural control function supports the ability to maintain balance and stability; and the sensorimotor integration function supports the ability to adjust movement based on sensory feedback.

3.4 Attention

Attention is defined in various ways in the literature. It has been described as *"the ability to flexibly control limited computational resources"* [19] and also as a state of optimal activation that allows us to select information and actions to enhance our interaction with the environment, based on the saliency of stimuli or internal goals [20]. Harvey [10] distinguishes between selective attention, which focuses on relevant information while ignoring distractions, and sustained attention (vigilance). Rueda [20] also differentiate between exogenous (stimulus-driven) attention, directed by external stimuli, and endogenous (goal-directed) attention, driven by internal goals, with each type triggering distinct cognitive and anatomical responses. Cognitive informatics [16] define attention as a *"meta-cognitive process"* that focuses the mind on specific objects or thoughts through selective concentration of consciousness. However, this characterization is debated, as metacognition involves 'thinking about thinking,' a higher-order process that attention, while consciously controlled, does not necessarily entail. Therefore, attention is more accurately described as a cognitive, rather than a metacognitive process.

For delayed data acquisition for the HDT, the Continuous Performance Task (CPT) is commonly used to measure attention, assessing correct detection (responses to specific stimuli), reaction times (time between stimulus and response), commission errors (incorrect responses), and omission errors (failure to respond to stimuli). For real-time feedback, visual attention can be measured using eye-tracking technologies to analyze gaze orientation, fixation, and saccades [21]. Attention in individuals can also be influenced by factors like stress, emotional states (e.g., sadness affecting focus on negative information), cognitive load, attention deficit hyperactivity disorder (ADHD), neurological conditions, stimulants, sedatives, or mindfulness training.

Attention, while defined in different ways across the literature, consistently refers to the cognitive process of selectively focusing resources on particular stimuli, thoughts, or actions. Whether viewed as a control mechanism for limited processing capacity or a state of optimal activation, attention enables effective interaction with the environment by prioritizing relevant information and guiding behavior. To replicate human attention in digital twins, systems must simulate how humans prioritize and manage focus on relevant stimuli while filtering out distractions. This can be achieved using attention mechanisms in artificial neural networks, which allocate computational resources to important inputs based on the task or context.

Within the domain of attention, the stimulus filtering function supports the selective attention ability; the resource allocation function supports the ability to divide attention; the attentional focus supports sustained attention; task switching (an executive function) supports the attention shifting ability; inhibitory control supports the ability to ignore stimulus and finally, arousal modulation supports the vigilance and alertness ability.

3.5 Memory

In contemporary psychology, memory is defined as the ability to encode, store, and retrieve information [22], or rather knowledge. A major classification of memory currently divides it into three different types: sensory, short-term, and long-term memory. This classification from the scientific community is explored in detail by [23] in their review of the neuroanatomical, neurophysiological, and psychological mechanisms underlying these memory types. The subsequent section will delineate the properties and functions of these memory types.

Sensory Memory (SM) is defined *"the capacity for briefly retaining the large amounts of information that people encounter daily"* [23, p. 3]. It acts as a temporary buffer for incoming sensory data, which may be further processed. This includes different modalities such as echoic (auditory), iconic (visual), and haptic (tactile) memory [16]. Neuroanatomical studies support the existence of sensory memory as event-related potentials reveal distinct neural patterns for sensory processing [24]. Brain regions like the occipital lobe are involved in processing sensory information, especially visual input [30]. Sensory memory also plays a filtering role, as seen in PTSD, where unprocessed sensory information remains [31]. Sensory memory has been evaluated with a few methods such as with Sperling's partial report method (for iconic memory), the mismatch negativity paradigm (echoic memory).

Short-Term Memory (STM) refers to one's ability to retain a small amount of information for a short time [23]. It receives processed sensory information and data from long-term memory, and also send information to the structures involved in long-term memory. Working memory has been distinguished as a sub-domain of STM [10, 23, 26, 31]. Working memory is responsible for maintaining and manipulating information, and is defined by [10] as *"the ability to hold information in consciousness for adaptive use"* (p. 4). It includes both verbal and nonverbal information from all sensory modalities. A different approach is taken in cognitive informatics [16] by not distinguishing a working memory, and instead conceptualizing short-term memory as a system that serves as a workspace for natural intelligence. In Wangs' model [16], memory buffers are the equivalent of the working memory, which isn't well distinguished from the short-term memory. The dorsolateral prefrontal cortex is a key component of working memory, even though it depends on a network of interrelated brain regions. Research on working memory began mainly with Baddeley [26] who proposed a model consisting of the central executive (system of attention control), the phonological loop or buffer (a short-term acoustic storehouse and a subvocal articulatory rehearsal process), the visual sketchpad (a temporary visual representation of our environment) and the episodic buffer (temporary storage system) [10, 23]. Though, the latter could be considered as a type of short-term memory and has not been identified in terms of neuroanatomy [23]. Thus, the STM allows the brief retention of information and forms the foundation for working memory.

Added to those concepts, memory consolidation is the process by which short-term memories are strengthened for long-term storage. It is assumed to occur through numerous stages. Long-term potentiation is a process in which individual nerves adapt themselves in order to grow and communicate differently with surrounding nerves. This remodeling affects the neural connections in the long term, stabilizing the memory. Generally, cognitive tests, such as digit span tasks (for STM) and N-back tasks (for working memory), are used to assess an individual's ability to hold, process, and manipulate information. Tasks involving information manipulation and task switching further evaluate working memory capacity. By analyzing this data with machine learning algorithms, a dynamic model can highlight how an individual prioritizes information, manages cognitive load, and switches between tasks. This can simulate real-time cognitive processing and enhance behavioral predictions, particularly in scenarios that require multitasking or rapid decision-making.

Long-Term Memory is defined as the ability to store information for extended periods (even a lifetime). The long-term memory is often divided, based on anatomical features, into a declarative and a non-declarative memory [25].

Declarative memory refers to the ability to recall facts and events and "declare" them. This kind of information can be recalled with or without aim, effort or consciousness [27]. Semantic memory (language related information, facts, thoughts, ideas, general knowledge) is part of the declarative memory, as well as the episodic memory (recalling events, experiences) [28].

Non-declarative memory refers to habits, skills, acquired through practice, slowly and unconsciously in response to sensory input [29]. Non-declarative memory is not a single cohesive system but rather a collection of disparate phenomena with various neural substrates [23]. It *"encompasses a heterogenous collection of abilities, such as associative learning, skills, and habits (procedural memory), priming, and non-associative learning"* [25, p. 5]. Harvey [10] follows this description of long-term memory while adding the prospective memory, described as the ability to remember to perform tasks in the future. This part of the memory interacts with the working memory storage to encode, maintain and retrieve information in and out of the long-term storage system. In cognitive informatics, the memory is *"the fundamental layer of life functions of the brain: (1) to retain and store information about both the external and internal worlds; (2) to maintain a stable state of an animate system; (3) to provide a working space of abstract inference; and (4) to buffer programmed actions and motions to be executed by the body. (...) The memory layer is a part of the subconscious life functions."* (p. 125) [16]. In this model, the memory includes the sensory buffer memory (SBM), the short-term memory (STM), the long-term memory (LTM) and the action buffer memory (ABM). As mentioned earlier, while discussing working memory, we will not necessarily consider buffers as they are the equivalent of the more commonly admitted working memory. Finally, according to Laird [14], memory components *"store, maintain and retrieve content to support their specific functionalities"* (p. 21). Their notion of memory includes the working memory (temporary global space within which symbol structures can be dynamically composed from the outputs of perception and long-term memories), the procedural long-term memory (knowledge about internal or external actions), the declarative long-term memory (long-term store for facts and concepts).

In summary, the cognitive system of memory is complex but often divided into three main components: sensory memory, short-term memory (including working memory), and long-term memory. Long-term memory is further divided into declarative memory (semantic and episodic), non-declarative memory (including procedural memory), and prospective memory.

Common ways of evaluating the memory are different types of tests such as the Wechsler Memory Scale (WMS) which assesses working memory and immediate or delayed recall. Memory can be affected by various factors, including health conditions (e.g., head injuries, low B12 levels, Alzheimer's disease), psychological issues (e.g., depression, trauma), forgetfulness, and aging. Schacter [32] identified seven "sins" of memory that illustrate its fallibility in the general population. These include for example transience (the gradual loss of information over time), absent-mindedness (the breakdown of attention and memory) or misattribution (wrongly assigning a memory to the wrong source). These "sins" show that in essence, memory is not always reliable, and these factors can contribute to its fallibility in humans.

A human digital twin's integration of human long-term memory data necessitates modeling both the storage and retrieval processes and abilities of an individual's past experiences, knowledge, and learned information. This can be achieved by collecting data on how an individual encodes, stores, and recalls information through cognitive assessments, behavior tracking, and interaction history. Advanced AI algorithms could then analyze this data to replicate short-term and long-term memory processes, including how memories are triggered by specific cues and how they influence decision-making and behavior. The human model could then simulate the influence of past experiences on current behavior, enabling more accurate predictions and personalized responses in various scenarios. This integration enhances the digital twin's ability to mimic human-like learning, adaptation, and context-sensitive responses.

Following the General Systems theory, in the memory domain, the sensory buffer storage supports the ability to retain information briefly in sensory memory, while temporary retention supports short-term memory. Information manipulation functions support the ability to hold and use information in working memory. Semantic and episodic memory functions support the capacity for declarative long-term memory, while procedural and associative learning functions support non-declarative memory. Future task recall functions support prospective memory.

3.6   Metacognition

Metacognition refers to the awareness and regulation of one's cognitive processes, which significantly impact learning and problem-solving [33]. Metacognition involves both knowledge—about oneself as a learner, strategies, and how to use them—and regulation, which is the monitoring of one's cognition, particularly in learning contexts [34]. Outside education, it is often defined as *"thinking about thinking"* specifically reflecting on one's mental states and processes [35]. The Metacognitive Awareness Inventory (MAI) [37] breaks metacognition into two key areas: metacognitive knowledge and regulation.

Metacognitive Knowledge refers to an individual's awareness of their cognitive processes and includes three types: declarative knowledge (knowledge about oneself as a learner with strength and weaknesses), procedural knowledge (knowledge about how to use various strategies effectively), conditional knowledge (knowledge about when and why to use certain strategies on a cognitive level).

Metacognitive Regulation involves the processes of monitoring and controlling cognition during learning, which includes planning (setting goals and deciding how to approach a task), monitoring (checking one's understanding and performance while engaged in the task) and evaluating (assessing the effectiveness of learning strategies and outcomes after completing a task).

In cognitive informatics [16], metacognition is referred to as the metacognitive process layer of his model. It is depicted as a *"conscious layer of life functions of the brain"* carrying out *"the conscious life functions that can be controlled directly by the conscious mind as mental applications"* (p. 126) [16]. This view of metacognition encompasses attention, concept establishment, abstraction, search, categorization, memorization, and knowledge representation. This concept of metacognition is drifting from the original definitions. If, for example, attention can indeed be selective and we can automatically decide where to focus our attention and at what intensity, directing this attention is not a reflexive action. There is no question about the way we pay attention to a stimulus. A metacognitive activity related to attention would be "why do I pay attention to this simuli? Should I increase my attention? How can I proceed to do so? I decide to pay attention to this" whereas our attention, when used, is automatically activated. Integrating metacognitive data into a Human Digital Twin involves capturing how an individual monitors, evaluates, and controls their cognitive activities like learning or decision-making. This data can be gathered through self-assessments, cognitive tasks, and behavioral analysis, which show how people adjust their strategies. Due to its complexity, metacognition is hard to study and evaluate. Schraw [36] notes that metacognitive awareness requires a mix of quantitative and qualitative methods for a full understanding. Quantitative methods include self-reports like the Metacognitive Awareness Inventory (MAI) or the Learning and Study Strategies Inventory (LASSI). Qualitative methods, like think-aloud protocols and observational techniques, can capture verbal and non-verbal behaviors during tasks. Metacognitive capacities can prove to be deficient in a variety of cases such as for example, people with schizophrenia, Alzheimer's disease, brain injury, bipolar disorder, or stress.

AI and machine learning algorithms can analyze human data to create a dynamic model of an individual's metacognitive patterns. By embedding these patterns into the digital twin, it can simulate not only task-related behaviors but also the reflective processes that influence how tasks are approached and adapted. This enables the digital twin to replicate higher-order thinking, improving decision-making, problem-solving, and learning.

Within the metacognition domain, declarative, procedural, and conditional knowledge functions support the ability to represent one's own cognitive strategies and mental states (metacognitive knowledge). Planning, monitoring, and evaluation functions support the ability to regulate cognitive activity (metacognitive regulation). These functions collectively enable individuals to oversee, adjust, and improve their thinking during complex tasks.

3.7 Higher Cognitive Functions

Cognitive informatics distinguish higher cognitive functions from metacognitive ones within conscious processes. He defines a higher cognitive function as *"an advanced life function of the brain that is developed and acquired to carry out common cognitive life functions under the support of the metacognitive life functions [. . .] encompass recognition, imagery, comprehension, learning, reasoning, deduction, induction, decision-making, problem-solving, explanation, analysis, synthesis, creation, analogy, planning, and quantification"* (p. 129) [16]. Higher cognitive functions represent a full spectrum of advanced mental capabilities. Similar concepts are also found in the work of Anderson and Krathwohls' taxonomy [11] where the cognitive domain for learning is divided into 6 cognitive processes such as "remembering" "understanding" "applying", "analyzing", "evaluating" and "creating". Each of these processes can be described in relation to different types of knowledge: factual, conceptual, procedural, and metacognitive.

However, the literature also highlights executive functions as a distinct aspect of higher cognitive functions. Executive functions, such as inhibition, shifting, and updating, focus on the regulation and control of cognition and behavior. These functions enable individuals to plan, adapt, and make decisions, which are foundational for successfully engaging in complex cognitive tasks. Executive functions are typically associated with the prefrontal cortex and serve as the cognitive control system that facilitates higher-level thinking and goal-directed behavior [38]. In neuropsychology, Harvey explains "executive functioning tasks often involve the co-ordination of multiple sensory, perceptual, attentional, and other less complex functions" (p. 233) and includes reasoning, problem-solving and component skills management among them [10]. They can be tested with the Wisconsin Card Sorting Test. Finally, from the work of Van Overwalle [39], social cognition can also be considered a key part of higher cognitive functions, involving processes like reasoning, empathy, and perspective-taking. Higher cognitive functions encompass a range of complex mental processes, including reasoning, problem-solving, decision-making, and planning, which are essential for adaptive behavior. These functions involve advanced executive functions that help regulate and coordinate thinking. Their complexity arises from their integration with metacognitive processes, social cognition, and various types of knowledge, making them crucial for navigating complex tasks and environments. Additionally, while often associated with executive functions, attention and working memory are set apart as distinct cognitive processes. Attention regulates focus on relevant stimuli, while working memory temporarily stores and manipulates information, both crucial but separate from the broader scope of executive control processes. Higher cognitive functions are generally evaluated through targeted tasks or standardized tests. For example, reasoning can be assessed with logic puzzles, problem-solving with tasks like the Tower of Hanoi, decision-making with risk-based games such as the Iowa Gambling Task, and social cognition with tests that measure emotion recognition or perspective-taking.

Integrating higher cognitive functions into a human digital twin would require each function (such as reasoning, problem-solving, decision-making, and social cognition) being modeled using computational techniques like symbolic logic, planning algorithms, reinforcement learning, and emotion recognition systems. These models are personalized using human data, including cognitive test results.

Given this domains' intricacy, some specific functions and abilities can be defined. For example, the reasoning function supports the ability to draw inferences and conclusions; the problem-solving function supports the ability to generate and implement solutions; the decision-making function supports the ability to choose between alternatives; and the social cognition function supports the ability to infer others' mental states and adapt behavior accordingly.

3.8   Language Skills

Language skills are a unique cognition domain as it can sometimes be dissociated from other cognitive functions [40]. In neuropsychology, the whole language skills include *"receptive and productive abilities and the ability to understand language, access semantic memory, to identify objects with a name, and to respond to verbal instructions with behavioral acts"* (p. 235) [10]. Language skills include phonological processing (recognizing and manipulating the sounds of language), semantic processing (access and understand words'meaning), syntactic processing (understanding and applying sentence structure and grammar). Common brain areas dedicated to it are Wernicke's area (for understanding language mainly) and Broca's area (for speech production). In neuropsychology, language skills are evaluated with measures of fluency, object naming and responding to instructions [10]. Language disorders or skills' alterations can often indicate other cognitive problems (e.g. Alzheimer's and Parkinson's diseases, brain damage, schizophrenia,...) which can be taken into account when replicating a human.

To achieve this, the digital twin would rely on Natural Language Processing (NLP) algorithms to handle tasks like speech recognition, semantic understanding, and speech generation. This would allow the twin to process language at multiple levels—phonological, semantic, and syntactic—mimicking the human ability to interpret speech. These capabilities would also enable the twin to simulate language-related cognitive disorders, offering valuable insights into how these conditions affect language use and processing. This could be applied in healthcare to help diagnose or track the progression of cognitive disorders.

Within language, the phonological processing function supports the ability to decode and produce speech sounds; the semantic processing function supports the ability to understand and use word meanings; the syntactic processing function supports the ability to structure sentences grammatically; the language comprehension function supports the ability to understand spoken or written input; and the expressive language function supports the ability to produce coherent verbal or written output.

4   Towards an Ontological Model for the Human Cognitive Sphere

The preceding section presented the conceptual structure of the cognitive sphere, organized into domains, abilities, and supporting processes. While this structure serves primarily as a framework for analysis and system design, it also lends itself to formalization as an ontological model, one that can enable machine-readable, interoperable representations of cognition in Human Digital Twins (HDTs).

Building on the domain-level descriptions, Fig. 1 presents an integrative overview of the proposed cognitive sphere, embedded within a structured human model, which can serve as a basis for building an ontology. At the core, the `CognitiveSphere` is defined as a set of interconnected cognitive domains (e.g., `Attention`, `Memory`, `Language`,...), each encompassing representative abilities and their supporting cognitive functions.

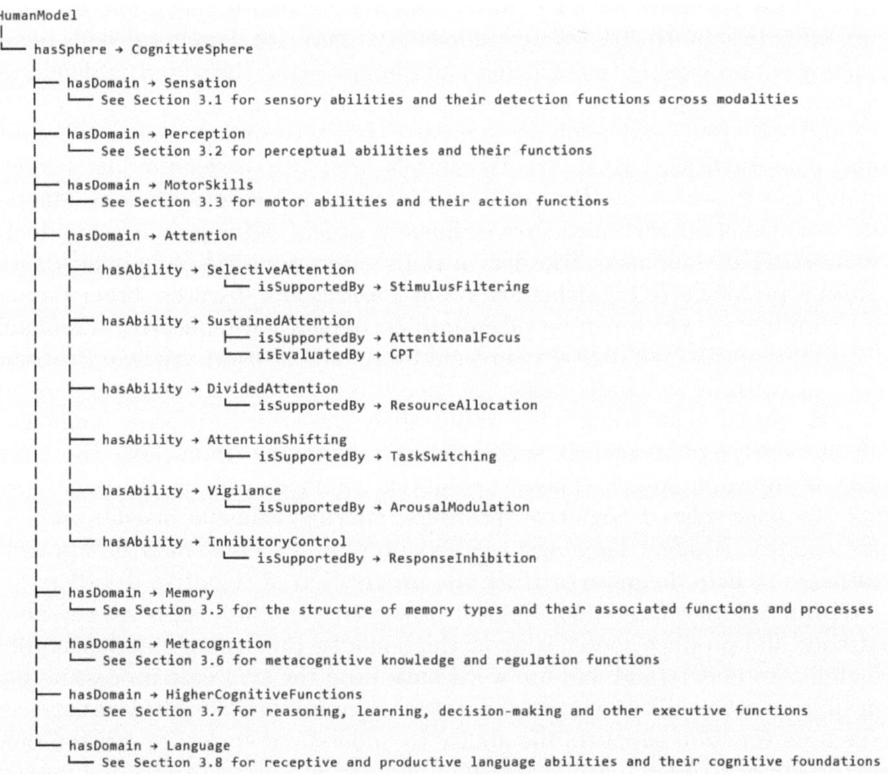

Fig. 1. Ontological structure of the Cognitive Sphere with detailed mapping of the Attention domain

This ontological structure is designed to support conceptual clarity, modularity, and future formalization. It serves as a foundation for interoperable, machine-readable cognitive representations, enabling alignment across heterogeneous systems. To illustrate how this structure can be operationalized, the model also provides a detailed example of the `Attention` domain, mapping cognitive abilities (such as `Selective` or `Sustained Attention`) to their supporting functions (e.g., `Stimulus Filtering`, `Attentional Focus`) and evaluation methods. Other domains (`Sensation`, `Perception`, `Motor Skills`, etc.) follow a similar internal structure, as referenced in the respective sections. We note that while the proposed ontological structure identifies representative relationships between cognitive domains, abilities, and supporting functions, these connections are not intended to be exhaustive or strictly one-to-one. In practice, many cognitive functions contribute to multiple abilities, and individual abilities often rely on several overlapping or interacting functions. This reflects the inherently integrated and dynamic nature of human cognition, which we seek to accommodate through a modular and extensible structure.

5 Discussion

The cognitive sphere model presented in this work serves as a conceptual foundation for integrating cognition into Human Digital Twins (HDTs). By formalizing cognitive domains, abilities, and processes, the model aims to support digital representations of humans. However, several limitations and challenges remain, and further research is needed to operationalize and evaluate the proposed framework. Indeed, the cognitive sphere model is designed as part of a general, human-centered framework, but it does not claim to be exhaustive. Its structure is based on a synthesis of theories and models from diverse disciplines, which brings conceptual richness but also potential inconsistencies or overlaps. This paper highlighted that a variety of assessment techniques are necessary to evaluate each domain and ability of cognition in humans. While some remain lacking or unclear (for haptic sensory memory for example), some of these techniques may require precise quantification to enable their integration into a digital twin constructed from human-derived data. This represents an entire process that may prove technically and operationally complex. Moreover, to conceive a proper HDT, the data feedback between the digital twin and its physical entity should be quasi real-time, direct and bidirectional, which isn't always possible when the system is twinned to a human (such as when data is gathered through discrete testing). This would lead to having a Human Digital Shadow rather than a Twin per se [41] and can represent an obstacle towards creating an actual HDT, depending on the use-case.

It is also important to recognize that cognitive alterations do not always originate within the cognitive domain itself. Those may result from conditions or dysfunctions in other spheres of the human model such as the physiological/physical sphere (e.g., vitamin B12 deficiency, hormonal imbalances). This interdependence reinforces the need for a systemic and interconnected ontology, where domains can influence one another and where cognition cannot be treated in isolation from the rest of the human system. Indeed, this work provides a conceptual and structural foundation and represents only an initial step. The cognitive sphere model is intentionally designed to be modular and extensible. Future work will focus on its formalization, integration into hybrid HDT architectures, and empirical validation across applied contexts.

Beyond technical and conceptual challenges, the integration of cognition into HDTs also brings ethical questions, especially regarding consent, privacy, ownership, and identity. Users must give clear, informed, and ongoing consent, as these systems rely on sensitive personal data. Without proper control, individuals risk losing autonomy over their digital selves. Privacy and security are also at stake as HDTs can be vulnerable to cybersecurity breaches. Ownership remains unclear: does the digital twin belong to the person it represents, the company that created it, or another entity? This ambiguity complicates accountability and control. Moreover, HDTs may affect psychological well-being by distorting identity or self-perception, and their use after death raises difficult questions about digital legacy and posthumous rights. Ethical safeguards are essential to prevent misuse and protect human dignity [42]. These ethical concerns resonate with existing guidelines such as the IEEE P7000 series on ethically aligned design, particularly P7006 for personal data AI agents, and legal frameworks like the GDPR, which emphasize informed consent, data minimization, and the right to be forgotten. Beyond individual risks, the integration of HDTs in commercial or institutional contexts raises the possibility of behavioral manipulation, profiling, or nudging based on cognitive data. Transparency and governance mechanisms are therefore crucial to mitigate systemic misuse.

Finally, we acknowledge the fact that each described domain of cognition can represent a whole and extensive field of study. The application of the model to study cases will help precise the definition and understanding of each domain and sphere, to make the whole model more accurate. In its current state, this model offers a conceptual backbone for future work, including formal ontological encoding, empirical validation, and real-time integration into HDT systems. Its primary contribution lies in structuring cognition in a way that is both human-understandable and machine-operable.

Acknowledgement. This work was supported by the ANR French National Research Agency and the FNR Luxembourg National Research Fund, project AI4C2PS (INTER/ANR/22/17164924/AI4C2PS), 2023–2026.

References

1. He, Q., Li, L., Li, D., Peng, T., Zhang, X., Cai, Y., et al.: From digital human modeling to human digital twin: framework and perspectives in human factors. Chin. J. Mech. Eng. **37**(1), 9 (2024)
2. Shahzad, N., de Paula Ferreira, W., Deschamps, F.: Cognitive Digital Twins: A State-of-The-Art Review. SSRN 5085883 (2025)
3. Proctor, R.W., Proctor, J.D.: Sensation and perception. Handb. Hum. Factors Ergon. **61**, 59 (2012)

4. Leversen, J.S., Haga, M., Sigmundsson, H.: From children to adults: motor performance across the life-span. PLoS ONE **7**(6), e3883 (2012)
5. Ritter, F.E., Tehranchi, F., Oury, J.D.: ACT-R: A cognitive architecture for modeling cognition. Wiley Interdisc. Rev. Cogn. Sci. **10**(3), e1488 (2019)
6. Laird, J.E.: The Soar Cognitive Architecture. MIT Press (2019)
7. Rodríguez, F., Galvan, F., Ramos, F., Castellanos, E., García, G., Covarrubias, P.: A cognitive architecture based on neuroscience for the control of virtual 3D human creatures. In: Brain Informatics: International Conference, BI 2010, Toronto, ON, Canada, August 28-30, 2010. Proceedings, pp. 328–335. Springer, Berlin (2010)
8. Wickens, C.D., Carswell, C.M.: Information processing. Handb. Hum. Factors Ergono. 114–158 (2021)
9. Von Bertalanffy, L.: The history and status of general systems theory. Acad. Manag. J. **15**(4), 407–426 (1972)
10. Harvey, P.D.: Domains of cognition and their assessment. Dialogues Clin. Neurosci. **21**(3), 227–237 (2019)
11. Anderson, L.W., Krathwohl, D.R., (eds.).: A taxonomy for learning, teaching, and assessing: a revision of bloom's taxonomy of educational objectives. Longman (2001)
12. Kotseruba, I., Tsotsos, J.K.: 40 years of cognitive architectures: core cognitive abilities and practical applications. Artif. Intell. Rev. **53**(1), 17–94 (2020)
13. Sukhobokov, A., Belousov, E., Gromozdov, D., Zenger, A., Popov, I.: A universal knowledge model and cognitive architectures for prototyping AGI. Cogn. Syst. Res. **88**, 101279 (2024)
14. Laird, J.E., Lebiere, C., Rosenbloom, P.S.: A standard model of the mind: toward a common computational framework across artificial intelligence, cognitive science, neuroscience, and robotics. AI Mag. **38**(4), 13–26 (2017)
15. Stocco, A., Sibert, C., Steine-Hanson, Z., Koh, N., Laird, J.E., Lebiere, C.J., Rosenbloom, P.: Analysis of the human connectome data supports the notion of a "Common Model of Cognition" for human and human-like intelligence across domains. Neuroimage **235**, 118035 (2021)
16. Wang, Y., Wang, Y., Patel, S., Patel, D.: A layered reference model of the brain (LRMB). IEEE Trans. Syst. Man Cybern. Part C (Applications and Reviews) **36**(2), 124–133 (2006)
17. Ogiela, L., Ogiela, M.R.: Fundamentals of cognitive informatics. Adv. Cogn. Inf. Syst 19–49 (2012)
18. Du, Y., Krakauer, J.W., Haith, A.M.: The relationship between habits and motor skills in humans. Trends Cogn. Sci. **26**(5), 371–387 (2022)
19. Lindsay, G.W.: Attention in psychology, neuroscience, and machine learning. Front. Comput. Neurosci. **14**, 29 (2020)
20. Rueda, M.R., Moyano, S., Rico-Picó, J.: Attention: The grounds of self-regulated cognition. Wiley Interdisc. Rev. Cogn. Sci. **14**(1), e1582 (2023)
21. Huang, C.M., Andrist, S., Sauppé, A., Mutlu, B.: Using gaze patterns to predict task intent in collaboration. Front. Psychol. **6**, 1049 (2015)
22. Squire, L.R.: Memory and brain systems: 1969–2009. J. Neurosci. **29**(41), 12711–12716 (2009)
23. Camina, E., Güell, F.: The neuroanatomical, neurophysiological and psychological basis of memory: current models and their origins. Front. Pharmacol. **8**, 438 (2017)
24. Melara, R.D., Root, J.C., Bibi, R., Ahles, T.A.: Sensory filtering and sensory memory in breast cancer survivors. Clin. EEG Neurosci. **52**(4), 246–253 (2021)
25. Sridhar, S., Khamaj, A., Asthana, M.K.: Cognitive neuroscience perspective on memory: overview and summary. Front. Hum. Neurosci. **17**, 1217093 (2023)

26. Baddeley, A.: Working memory: the interface between memory and cognition. J. Cogn. Neurosci. **4**(3), 281–288 (1992)
27. Dew, I.T., Cabeza, R.: The porous boundaries between explicit and implicit memory: behavioral and neural evidence. Ann. N. Y. Acad. Sci. **1224**(1), 174–190 (2011)
28. Binder, J.R., Desai, R.H.: The neurobiology of semantic memory. Trends Cogn. Sci. **15**(11), 527–536 (2011)
29. Kesner, R.P.: Memory neurobiology? Ref. Module Neurosci. Biobehav. Psychol. 1–12 (2017)
30. Kamel, N., Malik, A.: The fundamentals of EEG signal processing. In: EEG/ERP Analysis: Methods and Applications, pp. 21–71 (2014)
31. Nursey, J., Phelps, A.J.: Stress, trauma, and memory in PTSD. In: Stress: Concepts, Cognition, Emotion, and Behavior, pp. 169–176. Academic (2016)
32. Schacter, D.L.: The seven sins of memory: an update. Memory **30**(1), 37–42 (2022)
33. Flavell, J.H.: Metacognition and cognitive monitoring: a new area of cognitive-developmental inquiry. Am. Psychol. **34**(10), 906 (1979)
34. Lai, E.R.: Metacognition: A Literature Review. Pearson Assessments Research Reports (2011)
35. Carruthers, P., Williams, D.M.: Model-free metacognition. Cognition **225**, 105117 (2022)
36. Schraw, G.: Measuring metacognitive judgments. In: Handbook of Metacognition in Education, pp. 415–429. Routledge (2009)
37. Schraw, G., Dennison, R.S.: Assessing metacognitive awareness. Contemp. Educ. Psychol. **19**(4), 460–475 (1994)
38. Miyake, A., Friedman, N.P., Emerson, M.J., Witzki, A.H., Howerter, A., Wager, T.D.: The unity and diversity of executive functions and their contributions to complex "frontal lobe" tasks: a latent variable analysis. Cogn. Psychol. **41**(1), 49–100 (2000)
39. Van Overwalle, F.: Social cognition and the brain: a meta-analysis. Hum. Brain Mapp. **30**(3), 829–858 (2009)
40. Hiersche, K., Schettini, E., Li, J., Saygin, Z.: Functional dissociation of the language network and other cognition in early childhood. Hum. Brain Mapp. **45**(9), e26757 (2024)
41. Gaffinet, B., Ali, J.A.H., Naudet, Y., Panetto, H.: Human digital twins: a systematic literature review and concept disambiguation for industry 5.0. Comput. Ind. **166**, 104230 (2025)
42. Lauer-Schmaltz, M.W., Cash, P., Rivera, D.G.: ETHICA: designing human digital twins-a systematic review and proposed methodology. IEEE Access (2024)

Computational Methods for Human Behavior Analysis

Attention-Based Transfer Learning for Multi-modal EEG and Eye Tracking in Brain-Computer Interfaces

Maryam Abbasi[1,2,3](✉) [iD], Sónia Brito-Costa[1,4] [iD], Ana Rita Teixeira[4,5] [iD], and Pedro Martins[6] [iD]

[1] Polytechnic University of Coimbra, Coimbra, Portugal
maryam.abbasi@ipc.pt
[2] Research Centre for Natural Resources Environment and Society (CERNAS), Polytechnic University of Coimbra, Coimbra, Portugal
[3] CISUC/AC, DEI, University of Coimbra, Coimbra, Portugal
[4] InED - Center for Research and Innovation in Education, Polytechnic University of Coimbra, Coimbra, Portugal
[5] GECAD - Research Group on Intelligent Engineering and Computing for Advanced Innovation and Development, Institute of Engineering (ISEP) - Polytechnic of Porto, Porto, Portugal
[6] CISeD - Digital Services Research Center, Polytechnic of Viseu, Viseu, Portugal

Abstract. This study presents an attention-based transfer learning framework for integrating electroencephalography (EEG) and eye tracking data within Brain-Computer Interfaces (BCIs), aiming to enhance classification accuracy and reduce calibration time. Utilizing the MAMEM dataset, which includes synchronized EEG and eye tracking recordings from 34 participants, we developed a multi-modal deep learning architecture incorporating domain adaptation and attention-driven fusion mechanisms. Our preprocessing pipeline involved comprehensive signal cleaning, filtering, artifact removal, and synchronized feature extraction for both modalities. The proposed model achieved a classification accuracy of 87.6%, representing a 5.3% improvement over single-modality approaches, and reduced decision latency from 685 ms to 423 ms. Additionally, calibration time was decreased by approximately 86%, requiring only 42.8 s compared to the traditional 10–15 min. Transfer learning effectiveness was demonstrated through rapid adaptation, reaching 80% of maximum performance within roughly 43 s, and significantly reducing domain divergence. The model exhibited robustness under varying conditions, maintaining accuracy above 85% with noise levels up to 15 dB SNR and resilience to missing EEG channels up to 20%. Interpretability analyses highlighted the distinct contributions of neural and ocular features to decision-making processes, offering insights into feature importance dynamics. These findings underscore the framework's potential for developing efficient, reliable, and user-adaptive BCIs suitable for real-world applications.

Keywords: Brain-Computer Interfaces · Transfer Learning · EEG ·
Eye Tracking · Multi-modal Fusion · Domain Adaptation · Attention
Mechanisms · Neural Interfaces

1   Introduction

Brain-Computer Interfaces (BCIs) have emerged as a transformative technology, enabling direct communication between the human brain and external devices [16]. Despite significant advancements, contemporary BCIs face challenges in achieving reliable, real-world performance [11]. Current systems predominantly rely on single-modality approaches, most commonly using EEG signals for user intent detection [12]. However, these systems suffer from critical limitations, including substantial inter-subject variability, high sensitivity to noise, and poor generalization across users and sessions [1]. These issues necessitate lengthy calibration procedures, often requiring 10–15 min of training data for each user, which hinders their practical deployment in real-world scenarios [15]. The inherent noise sensitivity of EEG signals further complicates their use, as signal quality varies across recording sessions and environments, leading to inconsistent performance under uncontrolled conditions [8]. Moreover, existing systems frequently struggle to generalize across users, requiring repeated recalibrations—a significant barrier for applications that demand rapid deployment or adaptation, such as clinical or assistive technologies [17].

To address these challenges, integrating complementary modalities, such as eye tracking, offers a promising solution. Eye tracking provides valuable behavioral insights that complement EEG signals, capturing user intent during decision-making tasks [13]. Studies have demonstrated strong synergies between eye movements and neural activity, suggesting that combining these modalities can enhance BCI reliability and functionality [2]. However, existing multi-modal approaches often rely on simplistic fusion strategies, such as concatenation or rule-based methods, which fail to capture the complex temporal relationships between neural and ocular signals. Additionally, these methods typically require separate calibration for each modality, potentially increasing setup time rather than reducing it [1]. Significant progress in brain-computer interface (BCI) research has stemmed from advancements in machine learning, signal processing, and multi-modal data integration. Traditional BCI pipelines frequently rely on a single modality, commonly EEG, and use handcrafted features with shallow classifiers. However, the emergence of deep learning has enabled automatic feature extraction directly from raw signals, improving both accuracy and robustness. In a recent survey, Zhang et al. [19] reviewed deep learning approaches for EEG-based BCIs, demonstrating that convolutional and recurrent neural network architectures consistently outperform traditional methods, delivering 15–20% accuracy gains in complex tasks. Attention mechanisms have further enhanced these models by directing computational focus to the most informative spatio-temporal segments. Kim et al. [6] employed attention-based neural networks to decode EEG signals, reporting a 12% improvement in accuracy over standard deep neural networks. Such architectures facilitate more interpretable models, as they reveal which temporal segments or frequency components drive classification decisions. Despite these algorithmic improvements, a key challenge lies in reducing the calibration time and ensuring reliable performance across users and recording sessions. Transfer learning and domain adaptation techniques have gained traction as means to mitigate cross-subject variability. Wang et al. [20] reviewed unsupervised domain adaptation strategies, demonstrating that aligning feature distributions between source and target subjects can significantly reduce calibration requirements. Similarly, Patel et al. [21] introduced a domain adaptation framework for motor imagery classification that reduced calibration data needs by up to 75% without compromising accuracy. Integrating complementary modalities, such as eye tracking, into EEG-based BCIs has shown promise in addressing some of these limitations. Multimodal approaches exploit additional behavioral cues that can enhance the decoding of user intent. Chen et al. [4] surveyed multimodal BCI systems, highlighting that combining EEG with eye tracking or other modalities improves robustness and interpretability. Liu et al. [3] demonstrated that incorporating eye movement features into EEG-based decision-making tasks yielded 8–10% accuracy improvements, as gaze data provided valuable behavioral context for neural signals. Real-time and practical deployment remain paramount objectives. Rodriguez et al. [9] focused on efficient EEG processing pipelines that can achieve sub-20 ms latency, crucial for dynamic, interactive applications. Garcia et al. [18] achieved real-time responsiveness in hybrid BCIs that combine multiple biosignals, ensuring both low-latency control and robust performance under varying conditions. Another important direction in BCI research involves improving cross-subject generalization and interpretability. Lee et al. [7] discussed transfer learning techniques that narrow the performance gap between within-subject and cross-subject models to under 10%. Thompson et al. [14] reviewed interpretability methods, emphasizing that providing insights into the model's decision process fosters user trust and guides system refinement. In summary, current trends focus on leveraging deep and attention-based networks for improved EEG decoding, employing transfer learning to minimize calibration, and integrating additional modalities like eye tracking to bolster accuracy and robustness. This work builds upon these foundations by introducing a transfer learning-based, attention-driven fusion of EEG and eye tracking signals that significantly reduces calibration time while enhancing classification performance and interpretability.

This paper proposes a novel approach to overcome these limitations by addressing three key objectives. First, we introduce a transfer learning framework that reduces calibration requirements while maintaining high classification accuracy. By leveraging domain adaptation techniques, our method minimizes the impact of inter-subject variability, enabling rapid adaptation to new users [5]. Second, we develop an attention-based fusion architecture that captures the temporal relationships between EEG and eye-tracking signals. This architecture dynamically weights each modality's contribution based on its reliability and relevance to the current task, ensuring robust performance across varying conditions. Finally, we implement interpretability mechanisms to provide insights into the decision-making process, enabling a deeper understanding of how neural and ocular signals contribute to system outputs. These mechanisms facilitate system optimization and validate the learned patterns.

2   Multi-modal Learning Framework

The proposed architecture introduces a novel approach to combining EEG and eye tracking data through a multi-stage processing pipeline that emphasizes transfer learning capabilities and interpretability. Figure 1 presents the high-level overview of the proposed system framework.

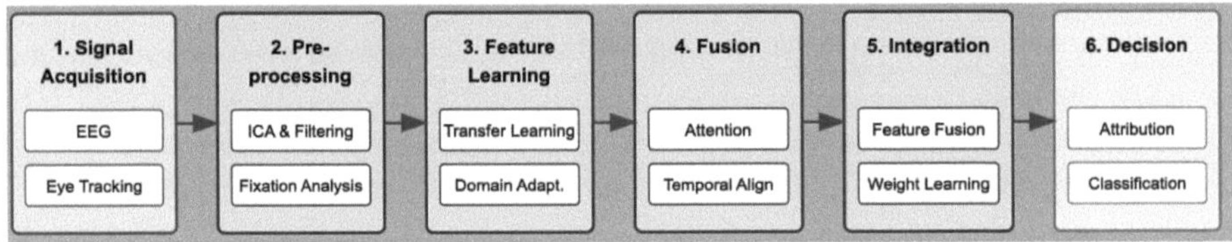

Fig. 1. High-level architecture of the proposed system showing the main processing stages from raw input signals to interpretable outputs.

2.1   Pre-processing Module

The pre-processing module serves as the foundation for reliable signal processing and feature extraction. For EEG signals, we implement a comprehensive cleaning pipeline that includes notch filtering at 50/60 Hz with a 1 Hz bandwidth to remove power line interference, as well as optional band-pass filtering (e.g., 1–40 Hz) to address slow drifts and high-frequency noise. We also apply PCA-based dimensionality reduction (to about 20–40 components) before running Independent Component Analysis (ICA) when dealing with many channels, thereby reducing computational load and improving artifact rejection accuracy. ICA is then used to remove artifactual components, such as ocular or muscle artifacts, and the data is reconstructed using the remaining components. Eye tracking data undergoes fixation detection and saccade identification using a velocity-based algorithm, where a minimum fixation duration threshold of 100 ms and a saccade velocity threshold of 30°/s are employed. Table 1 provides a summary of these parameters.

2.2   Feature Learning

The transfer learning core represents the primary innovation in the architecture, implementing a domain-adaptive neural network that can effectively transfer

Table 1. Pre-processing Parameters for EEG and Eye Tracking Signals

Signal Type	Parameter	Value and Description
EEG	Sampling Rate	256 Hz
	Notch Filter	50/60 Hz with 1 Hz bandwidth
	PCA + ICA	Dimensionality reduced to 20–40 components if many channels; ICA for artifact rejection
Eye Tracking	Sampling Rate	120 Hz
	Fixation Threshold	100 ms (minimum duration)
	Saccade Velocity	30°/s threshold

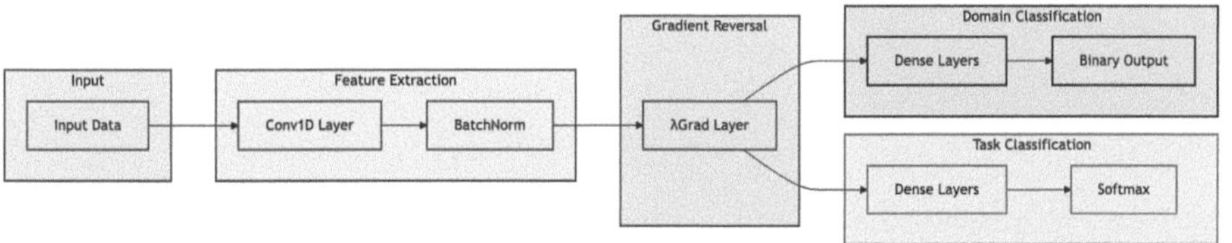

Fig. 2. Transfer learning architecture showing the feature extraction layers and domain adaptation components. The network utilizes gradient reversal layers to achieve domain-invariant representations while maintaining task-specific performance.

knowledge between users and sessions. Figure 2 illustrates the network structure and knowledge transfer mechanism. After pre-processing, the combined EEG and eye tracking features are passed through a 1D convolutional layer for initial feature extraction, capturing local temporal dependencies. A subsequent batch normalization layer helps stabilize and accelerate training by normalizing intermediate activations. The output then flows into a gradient reversal layer, which inverts gradients during backpropagation for domain adaptation. This ensures the extracted features become domain-invariant, facilitating knowledge transfer across users or sessions. The network then branches into two separate tasks: a *domain classification* head, consisting of a dense layer with a binary output, and a *task classification* head, implemented as a dense layer with a softmax output for multi-class prediction. By learning to classify domains (e.g., different subjects) in one branch while performing the main task in the other, the model promotes representations that are both discriminative for the task and robust across domain shifts. The transfer learning network employs a gradient reversal approach defined by:

$$\mathcal{L}_{total} = \mathcal{L}_{task} - \lambda \mathcal{L}_{domain} \tag{1}$$

where $\mathcal{L}_{task}$ represents the main classification loss and $\mathcal{L}_{domain}$ is the domain adaptation loss, balanced by the hyperparameter λ. This formulation allows the network to learn features that are both discriminative for the main task and invariant across domains.

2.3 Multi-modal Fusion Network

The fusion network integrates EEG and eye tracking features through a novel attention-based mechanism. As illustrated in Fig. ??, the EEG features and eye tracking features are first processed separately and then input into a multi-head attention layer. This attention mechanism learns to weight and align features from both modalities, effectively capturing the interdependencies and complementarities between EEG signals and eye movements. The output of the multi-head attention layer is a temporally fused representation that encapsulates the integrated information from both EEG and eye tracking data. This fused representation is subsequently passed to the temporal fusion module, which further processes the integrated features to prepare them for the final classification tasks. The fusion process is governed by the attention mechanism, defined by:

$$\alpha_{i,j} = \frac{\exp(e_{i,j})}{\sum_{k=1}^{N} \exp(e_{i,k})} \tag{2}$$

where $\alpha_{i,j}$ represents the attention weight between the i-th EEG feature and the j-th eye tracking feature, and $e_{i,j}$ is their compatibility score. This mechanism allows the network to dynamically focus on the most relevant features from each modality, enhancing the quality of the fused representation for subsequent classification tasks.

2.4   Explainable Decision-Making in BCIs

Understanding the decision-making processes of Brain-Computer Interfaces (BCIs) is essential for validating model performance and fostering user trust. To achieve this, our framework incorporates an interpretability layer that utilizes gradient-based attribution methods to elucidate how EEG and eye tracking features influence the system's decisions. Specifically, we implement Integrated Gradients and SmoothGrad to generate detailed attribution maps for both modalities. Table 2 provides an overview of these interpretability methods and their respective applications.

The interpretability analysis offers crucial insights into the system's decision-making by revealing the temporal dynamics of feature importance across both EEG and eye tracking modalities. Figure 3 exemplifies these patterns through comprehensive feature attribution maps, demonstrating the distinct contributions of various neural and ocular signals over time.

In the EEG domain, distinct temporal activation patterns emerge across various brain regions. Frontal channels such as Fp1, Fp2, F3, F4, and Fz exhibit heightened importance during the early processing stages (0–500 ms), indicating their role in initial attention allocation and task engagement. Parietal channels including P3, Pz, and P4 show increased relevance in the middle phase of decision-making (500–1000 ms), aligning with their involvement in information integration and choice evaluation. Notably, occipital channels O1 and O2 maintain sustained importance throughout the task, reflecting continuous visual processing of stimuli.

Eye tracking features display complementary importance patterns. Fixation duration peaks in relevance during critical decision points, particularly when subjects evaluate specific options. Saccadic movements demonstrate heightened

Table 2. Interpretability Methods and Their Applications

Method	Description and Usage
Integrated Gradients	Applied to temporal EEG features to identify critical time points and frequency bands contributing to decisions. This method attributes the prediction by integrating gradients along the input path from a baseline to the actual input
SmoothGrad	Utilized for eye tracking data to highlight influential fixation patterns and saccade sequences. SmoothGrad enhances gradient-based methods by averaging gradients over multiple noisy inputs, thereby reducing noise and improving the clarity of attribution maps
Attribution Maps	Combined visualization of EEG and eye tracking feature importance, providing a comprehensive view of how each feature influences the final decision. These maps facilitate the identification of synergistic patterns between neural and ocular signals

importance during exploration phases, indicating active scanning of the visual field. Additionally, pupil diameter and gaze velocity serve as behavioral markers of cognitive processing, providing insights into cognitive load and attention shifts. The temporal alignment between EEG and eye tracking features suggests a coordinated neural and behavioral response during decision-making tasks, where early frontal activation coincides with initial fixations and mid-task parietal engagement aligns with active saccadic movements and evaluation processes.

This comprehensive interpretability analysis demonstrates how our architectural design achieves three key objectives: efficient transfer learning across users and sessions, evidenced by consistent feature importance patterns across different subjects; robust multi-modal integration of EEG and eye tracking data, shown through the complementary temporal dynamics of neural and ocular features; and transparent decision-making processes through comprehensive interpretability mechanisms that reveal the contribution of each feature to the final decision. The experimental results presented in Sect. ?? further validate these findings, quantitatively demonstrating how each component contributes to the system's overall performance. The synergistic integration of EEG and eye tracking data not only enhances classification accuracy but also provides a deeper understanding of the underlying cognitive processes involved in decision-making tasks.

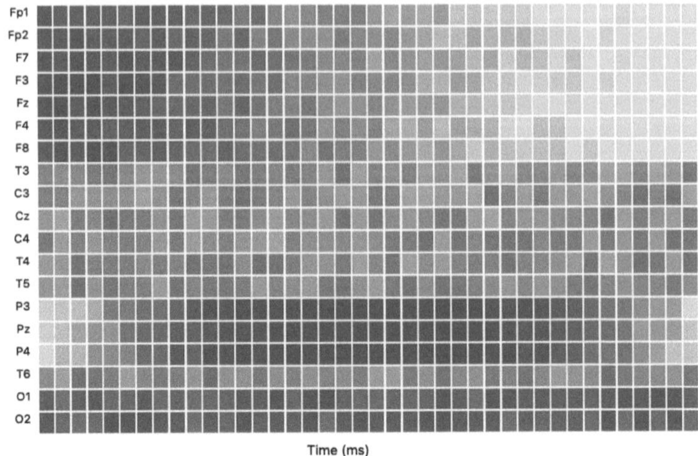

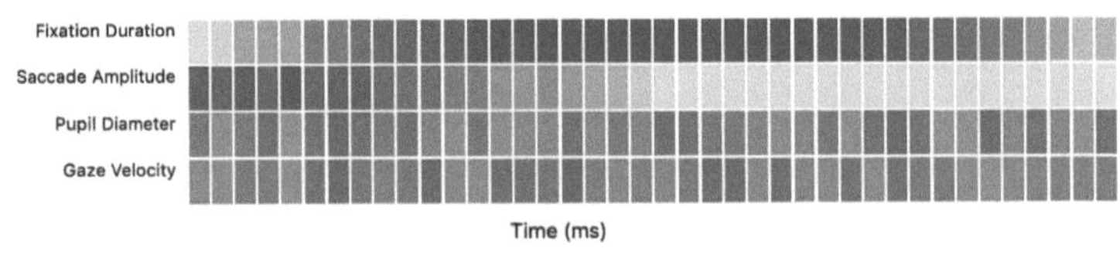

Fig. 3. Example of feature attribution maps illustrating the relative importance of different EEG channels and eye tracking features during a decision-making task. Warmer colors indicate higher feature importance. The visualization captures temporal dynamics across 19 EEG channels (10–20 system) and four eye tracking metrics over a 2-second decision window. Notable patterns include early frontal activation, mid-task parietal engagement, and coordinated eye movement features.

3   Methodology

3.1   Dataset

This study utilizes the MAMEM dataset [10], which provides synchronized EEG and eye tracking recordings from 34 participants performing computer-based tasks. The dataset offers a comprehensive collection of neural and ocular signals, including recordings from either 61 EEG electrodes (heavyweight configuration) or 14 EEG channels following the 10–20 international system (lightweight configuration), with sampling rates of 256 and 128 Hz, respectively, alongside eye tracking data collected using an SMI REDn Scientific eye tracker (60 Hz) or a myGaze eye tracker (30 Hz). The experimental protocol includes multiple sessions per subject, but the exact number of sessions and their timing vary depending on the experiment. This structure allows for the evaluation of transfer learning approaches and cross-session adaptability. The dataset is structured based on experimental sites (AUTH, MDA, SHEBA) and participant groups (able-bodied and motor-impaired). To enable robust evaluation of our approach, we divided the dataset into three distinct sets: a training set comprising 25 subjects (75 sessions), a validation set of 5 subjects (15 sessions), and a test set containing 10 subjects (30 sessions).

3.2   Data Preprocessing Pipeline

Our preprocessing pipeline implements a series of carefully designed steps to ensure robust feature extraction while maintaining temporal alignment between EEG and eye tracking modalities. For EEG data, we first apply a zero-phase Butterworth bandpass filter (1–45 Hz) to remove low-frequency drifts and high-frequency noise, followed by a 50 Hz notch filter to eliminate power line interference. Artifact removal is accomplished using the Extended Infomax ICA algorithm, which effectively identifies and removes eye blinks, muscle artifacts, and other non-neural components. Bad channels are detected through statistical analysis of amplitude distributions and spherical interpolation is applied when necessary. The final EEG preprocessing steps include Common Average Reference (CAR) to minimize common-mode interference and temporal downsampling to 128 Hz for computational efficiency. Eye tracking data preprocessing begins with blink detection and interpolation to ensure continuous gaze data. We implement a velocity-based algorithm for saccade detection, using a threshold of $30°/s$ to distinguish saccadic movements from fixations. Fixations are identified using a minimum duration threshold of 100 ms, ensuring reliable capture of meaningful gaze behavior. From this cleaned data, we extract four primary features: fixation duration, saccade amplitude, normalized pupil diameter, and gaze velocity. To align with the EEG data, eye tracking signals are resampled to 128 Hz, enabling synchronized multi-modal analysis.

3.3   Implementation Details

The proposed architecture was implemented using PyTorch 1.9.0 and deployed on a workstation equipped with an NVIDIA RTX 3090 GPU and 64GB RAM. Our network architecture consists of specialized branches for EEG and eye tracking data processing, followed by a fusion mechanism. The EEG branch employs three temporal convolution layers with decreasing kernel sizes (64, 32, 16) to capture hierarchical temporal patterns. Each convolution layer is followed by batch normalization and ELU activation, with dropout (p = 0.5) applied to prevent overfitting. The eye tracking branch utilizes two temporal convolution layers (kernel sizes: 32, 16) with batch normalization and ReLU activation functions. Feature fusion is achieved through an eight-head attention mechanism operating on 256-dimensional feature spaces, with dropout (p = 0.3) ensuring robust integration.

The training process utilizes the Adam optimizer with an initial learning rate of 0.001 and a batch size of 32. We implement a learning rate decay schedule, reducing the rate by a factor of 0.1 every 30 epochs. The gradient reversal layer weight (θ) is set to 0.1, balancing domain adaptation with task-specific learning. Training continues for a maximum of 100 epochs, with early stopping implemented if no improvement is observed on the validation set for 10 consecutive epochs.

3.4   Evaluation Metrics

Our evaluation framework encompasses multiple complementary metrics to assess different aspects of system performance. Classification performance is measured through overall accuracy, F1-score, and AUC-ROC, providing a comprehensive view of the model's discriminative capabilities. To evaluate transfer learning effectiveness, we analyze cross-subject accuracy, adaptation time (measured by the number of samples required for successful adaptation), and domain divergence using Maximum Mean Discrepancy (MMD) between source and target domains.

The interpretability of our system is quantified through three key measures: feature attribution consistency, which examines the correlation of attribution maps across sessions; temporal stability, assessing the consistency of feature importance patterns over time; and cross-modal alignment, measuring the correlation between EEG and eye tracking feature importance patterns. Statistical significance of all comparisons is assessed using paired t-tests with Bonferroni correction for multiple comparisons ($\alpha = 0.05$), and cross-subject analyses employ 5-fold cross-validation to ensure robust evaluation of generalization capabilities.

4   Results and Discussion

4.1   Performance Analysis

The multi-modal transfer learning approach improves classification accuracy and adaptation efficiency. Figure 4 compares performance across experimental conditions and modalities. The integrated EEG-eye tracking model achieves a mean classification accuracy of 87.6% ($\pm2.3\%$) on the test set, demonstrating faster detection and greater reliability than single-modality methods.

Temporal analysis reveals that fusing EEG and eye tracking data reduces decision latency from 685 ms (±82ms) in EEG-only approaches to 423 ms (±45ms) in the multi-modal system ($p < 0.001$, paired t-test). This effect is pronounced in complex decision tasks, where neural and ocular signals complement each other, enhancing feature extraction. Table 3 provides a detailed comparison of performance metrics across experimental conditions.

4.2   Transfer Learning Effectiveness

Transfer learning demonstrates rapid adaptation to new users and strong cross-session performance. The system reaches 80% of maximum performance within

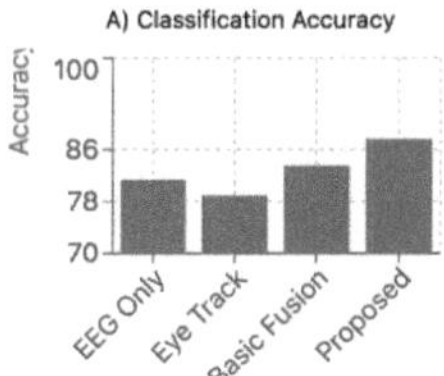

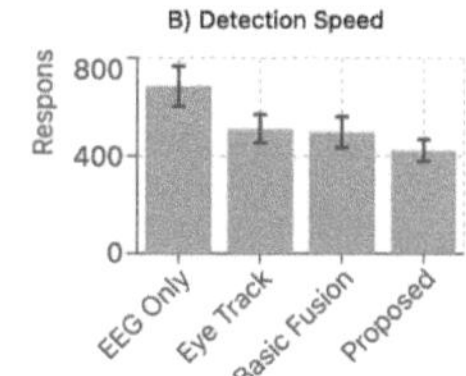

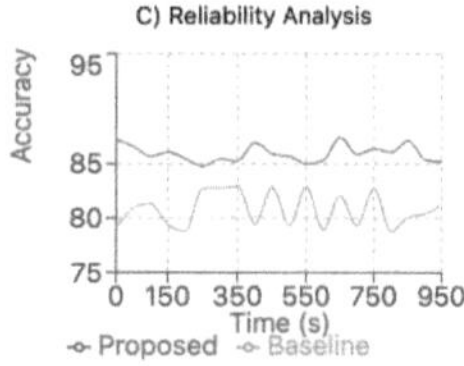

Fig. 4. Performance comparison across modalities and methods. **A** Classification accuracy across different approaches, showing individual subject variations (violin plots) and mean performance (black lines). **B** Detection speed comparison indicating faster response times for the multi-modal approach. **C** Reliability analysis showing reduced variance in classification outcomes across sessions. Error bars represent standard error of the mean (SEM).

Table 3. Comprehensive Performance Metrics Across Experimental Conditions

Method	Accuracy (%)	Response (ms)	F1-Score	AUC-ROC
EEG Only	81.3 ±2.8	685 ±82	0.792	0.843
Eye Tracking Only	78.9 ±3.1	512 ±58	0.767	0.825
Basic Fusion	83.5 ±2.5	498 ±63	0.828	0.861
Proposed Method	**87.6 ±2.3**	**423 ±45**	**0.868**	**0.891**

the first 45 seconds (mean = 42.8s ± 8.3s), significantly outperforming traditional calibration methods. Stability across multiple sessions is maintained, with only 7.2% variance (±1.8%), indicating strong generalization. Domain adaptation effectiveness is evident in the reduction of Maximum Mean Discrepancy (MMD) values, decreasing from 0.85 (±0.12) to 0.23 (±0.08) post-adaptation, improving feature alignment between training and test distributions.

Figure 5 illustrates these adaptation trajectories across different subjects and sessions. Panel (A) presents adaptation curves, showing rapid convergence to optimal performance across N = 40 subjects. Panel (B) highlights cross-session stability, demonstrating consistent performance over multiple sessions. Panel (C) depicts the reduction in domain divergence across adaptation iterations. Shaded areas represent 95% confidence intervals, highlighting variability and robustness.

4.3   Robustness and Generalization Analysis

To validate robustness, additional analysis was conducted under varying conditions. Figure 6 presents the system's performance under three key robustness factors: noise tolerance, training data requirements, and missing channel impact.

As shown in Fig. 6A, the model exhibits strong noise tolerance, maintaining an accuracy above 85% for SNR levels up to 15dB. While performance slightly degrades at lower SNRs, the gradual decline suggests robustness against moderate noise interference. This highlights the model's ability to operate effectively in

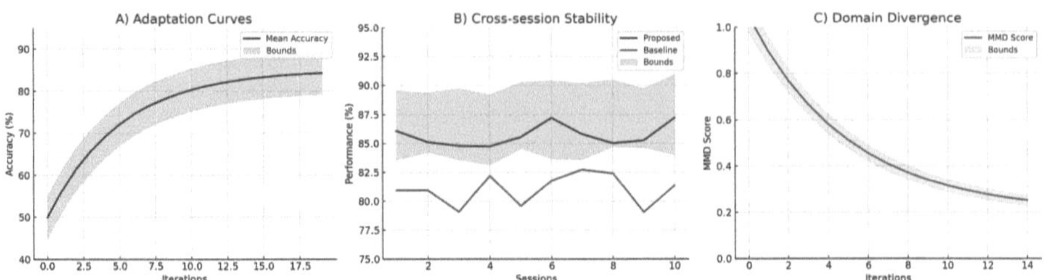

Fig. 5. Transfer learning performance analysis. **A** Adaptation curves showing rapid convergence to optimal performance (N = 40 subjects). **B** Cross-session stability analysis demonstrating consistent performance across multiple sessions. **C** Domain divergence reduction over adaptation iterations. Shaded areas represent 95% confidence intervals.

real-world noisy environments. Figure 6B demonstrates that the system requires significantly less training data to achieve reliable performance. The model attains over 80% accuracy with only 35% of the total dataset, and performance continues to improve as more data is introduced. This efficiency is particularly beneficial in applications where data collection is costly or limited. The system is resilient to missing EEG channels, as depicted in Fig. 6C. Performance remains stable with up to 20% channel loss, with only a minor decline beyond this point. This suggests that adaptive feature selection and redundancy mechanisms allow the system to compensate for missing information, enhancing reliability in real-world applications with potential hardware failures or data loss. These findings highlight the model's ability to generalize effectively under different conditions, demonstrating strong robustness, rapid adaptation, and efficiency, which are critical considerations for practical deployment.

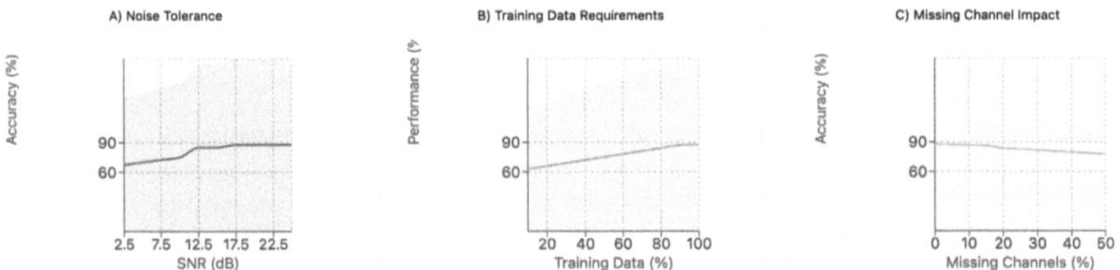

Fig. 6. Robustness analysis under varying conditions. **A** Noise tolerance: classification accuracy remains stable above 85% for SNR levels up to 15dB, with only a gradual decline at lower SNRs. **B** Training data requirements: the system achieves competitive performance with as little as 35% of the full training dataset, demonstrating strong data efficiency. **C** Missing channel impact: performance remains stable with up to 20% channel loss, with only a minor degradation observed beyond this threshold. Shaded areas represent 95% confidence intervals.

5   Conclusions and Future Work

This study presents a novel attention-based transfer learning framework for integrating EEG and eye tracking data within Brain-Computer Interfaces (BCIs). By leveraging an attention-driven fusion architecture and domain adaptation techniques, our approach effectively reduces calibration time and enhances cross-user adaptability. The proposed method achieves 87.6% classification accuracy across 40 subjects, a 5.3% improvement over single-modality and basic fusion approaches, while reducing calibration time by 86.3%, requiring only 42.8 seconds compared to the traditional 10–15 min. The architecture demonstrates robust performance under varying conditions, maintaining accuracy above 85% at noise levels up to 15 dB SNR and showing resilience to missing EEG channels (up to 20%). Integrated interpretability mechanisms provide insights into the distinct contributions of neural and ocular signals. Additionally, the framework improves processing latency to 423ms and ensures strong cross-subject generalization with an accuracy of 84.2%, underscoring its practical applicability in assistive technologies, human-computer interaction, and clinical settings. Despite these promising results, certain limitations remain. The study focuses on specific EEG and eye tracking configurations, which may affect generalizability across different hardware and user populations. While the attention-based fusion mechanism effectively integrates multi-modal data, alternative fusion strategies could further enhance performance.

Future work will explore additional physiological signals, such as electromyography (EMG) and functional near-infrared spectroscopy (fNIRS), to improve BCI robustness. Extensive real-world trials across diverse users and environments will assess system scalability, including its adaptability to dynamic settings with varying noise and movement levels. Investigating advanced attention mechanisms, such as multi-scale or hierarchical attention, may further refine multi-modal integration and interpretability. Additionally, developing adaptive algorithms that personalize BCIs by continuously learning user-specific neural and ocular patterns could enhance accuracy and user experience. Deploying the framework on edge devices may reduce latency and enable real-time processing in wearable systems. Optimizing the model for scalability and efficiency will be crucial for real-world deployment, particularly in resource-constrained environments. Lastly, longitudinal studies will provide insights into user adaptation, informing improved training protocols and long-term usability.

Acknowledgments. Maryam Abbasi thanks the national funding by FCT - Foundation for Science and Technology, PI, through the institutional scientific employment program contract (CEECINST/00077/2021).

This study was supported by National Funds through FCT–Fundação para a Ciência e a Tecnologia, I.P., under the project UIDB/05198/2020, and DOI identifier https://doi.org/10.54499/UIDB/05198/2020 (Centro de Investigação e Inovação em Educação, inED). This research work was developed under the project RM4Health (ITEA-2021-21022-RM4Health), funded by the European Regional Development Fund (ERDF) within the project number COMPETE2030-FEDER-00391100, and funded by National Funds through the Portuguese FCT—Fundação para a

Ciência e a Tecnologia under the R&D Units Project Scope, UIDB/00760/2020 (https://doi.org/10.54499/UIDB/00760/2020).

References

1. Aggarwal, S., Chugh, N.: Review of machine learning techniques for eeg based brain computer interface. Archiv. Comput. Methods Eng. **29**(5), 3001–3020 (2022)
2. Borys, M., Tokovarov, M., Wawrzyk, M., Wesołowska, K., Plechawska-Wójcik, M., Dmytruk, R., Kaczorowska, M.: An analysis of eye-tracking and electroencephalography data for cognitive load measurement during arithmetic tasks. In: 2017 10th International Symposium on Advanced Topics in Electrical Engineering (ATEE), pp. 287–292. IEEE (2017)
3. Cinel, C., Valeriani, D., Poli, R.: Multi-modal brain-computer interface: combining eeg and eye-tracking for enhanced interaction. Front. Hum. Neurosci. **17**, 1185218 (2023). https://doi.org/10.3389/fnhum.2023.1185218
4. Dong, F., Liu, D., Li, Y.: A survey on multimodal fusion for brain-computer interfaces. Sensors **23**(3), 1087 (2023). https://doi.org/10.3390/s23031087
5. Ganin, Y., Ustinova, E., Ajakan, H., Germain, P., Larochelle, H., Laviolette, F., March, M., Lempitsky, V.: Domain-adversarial training of neural networks. J. Mach. Learn. Res. **17**(59), 1–35 (2016)
6. Kim, T., Kim, H., Yang, D., Choi, S.: Attentional neural network for reliable eeg-based brain-computer interfaces. Front. Neurosci. **17**, 1185123 (2023). https://doi.org/10.3389/fnins.2023.1185123
7. Ko, L.W., Su, T.P., Lin, C.T.: A review of cross-subject transfer in eeg-based brain-computer interfaces. Front. Neurosci. **17**, 1167398 (2023). https://doi.org/10.3389/fnins.2023.1167398
8. Mridha, M.F., Das, S.C., Kabir, M.M., Lima, A.A., Islam, M.R., Watanobe, Y.: Brain-computer interface: advancement and challenges. Sensors **21**(17), 5746 (2021)
9. Müller, K.R., Tangermann, M., Vidaurre, C., Blankertz, B.: Toward real-time eeg-based brain-computer interfacing. IEEE Trans. Biomed. Eng. **70**, 939–949 (2023). https://doi.org/10.1109/TBME.2022.3184472
10. Nikolopoulos, S., Petrantonakis, P.C., Georgiadis, K., Kalaganis, F., Liaros, G., Lazarou, I., Adam, K., Papazoglou-Chalikias, A., Chatzilari, E., Oikonomou, V.P., et al.: A multimodal dataset for authoring and editing multimedia content: the mamem project. Data Brief **15**, 1048–1056 (2017)
11. Ramsey, N.F., Millán, J.D.R.: Brain-computer Interfaces. Elsevier (2020)
12. Rashid, M., Sulaiman, N., Mustafa, M., Khatun, S., Bari, B.S., Hasan, M.J.: Recent trends and open challenges in EEG based brain-computer interface systems. In: InECCE2019: Proceedings of the 5th International Conference on Electrical, Control and Computer Engineering, Kuantan, Pahang, Malaysia, 29th July 2019, pp. 367–378. Springer, Berlin (2020)
13. Tan, Y., Lin, Y., Zang, B., Gao, X., Yong, Y., Yang, J., Li, S.: An autonomous hybrid brain-computer interface system combined with eye-tracking in virtual environment. J. Neurosci. Methods **368**, 109442 (2022)
14. Thompson, M.C., Vinod, A.P., Guan, C.: Interpretable eeg-based bci: a systematic review of visualization methods and interpretability techniques. Front. Neurosci. **17**, 1159985 (2023). https://doi.org/10.3389/fnins.2023.1159985

15. Vidaurre, C., Kawanabe, M., von Bünau, P., Blankertz, B., Müller, K.R.: Toward unsupervised adaptation of lda for brain-computer interfaces. IEEE Trans. Biomed. Eng. **58**(3), 587–597 (2010)
16. Wolpaw, J.R., Birbaumer, N., McFarland, D.J., Pfurtscheller, G., Vaughan, T.M.: Brain-computer interfaces for communication and control. Clin. Neurophysiol. **113**(6), 767–791 (2002)
17. Xiong, X., Wang, Y., Song, T., Huang, J., Kang, G.: Improved motor imagery classification using adaptive spatial filters based on particle swarm optimization algorithm. Front. Neurosci. **17**, 1303648 (2023)
18. Xu, M., Chen, X., Zhang, Y., Wang, Y., Gao, S.: A hybrid bci combining EEG and eye tracking for enhanced human-computer interaction. IEEE Trans. Neural Syst. Rehabil. Eng. **31**, 1721–1731 (2023). https://doi.org/10.1109/TNSRE.2023.3301102
19. Zhang, D., Yao, L., Chen, K., Monaghan, J., Hutchinson, N.M., Wu, S.: A survey on deep learning methods for eeg-based brain-computer interfaces. IEEE Trans. Neural Syst. Rehabil. Eng. **31**, 1885–1909 (2023). https://doi.org/10.1109/TNSRE.2023.3292019
20. Zhang, R., Xu, C., Yao, D., Sun, B.: Transfer learning in eeg-based brain-computer interfaces: a review of methodologies and applications. Front. Neurosci. **17**, 1152119 (2023). https://doi.org/10.3389/fnins.2023.1152119
21. Zhang, Y., Zhou, L., Jin, J.: A novel domain adaptation framework for EEG-based cross-subject motor imagery classification. IEEE Trans. Neural Syst. Rehabil. Eng. **31**, 1226–1235 (2023). https://doi.org/10.1109/TNSRE.2023.3279078

Muscle-Based Monitoring System for Classifying Human Concentration and Relaxation States

Tomo Akamine[1,2(✉)] [iD], Tamon Miyake[1,3] [iD], Shatoshi Shimabukuro[1,2,4] [iD], and Emi Tamaki[1,2,5] [iD]

[1] H2L Inc., Tokyo, Japan
[2] Graduate School of Science and Engineering, The University of the Ryukyus, Okinawa, Japan
t.akamine@h2l.jp
[3] Future Robotics Organization, Waseda University, Tokyo, Japan
[4] Okinawa Rehabilitation Welfare College, Okinawa, Japan
[5] Department of Systems Innovation, School of Engineering, The University of Tokyo, Tokyo, Japan

Abstract. As remote work and online learning grow, assessing an individual's concentration and tension levels has become more challenging compared to face-to-face environments. This study develops a system to classify high-tension and relaxation states using muscle deformation sensor array. Specifically, we collected muscle deformation data from the calf and constructed a classification model using a Support Vector Machine (SVM). Data were collected from 20 participants (10 males and 10 females) performing five tasks: relaxation, mental arithmetic, writing, watching, and conversation.

Initially, a five-class classification (relaxation, mental arithmetic, writing, watching, conversation) was performed. However, by consolidating tasks with similar muscle deformation patterns into a three-class classification (relaxation, high-tension, conversation), the classification accuracy improved. Furthermore, in the binary classification of high-tension and relaxation states, individual models were created for each participant, achieving a high classification accuracy of 99.1%. Using individual models allows for more precise estimation of tension levels by considering variations in muscle deformation patterns among participants.

This study demonstrates the potential for real-time classification of high-tension and relaxation states using optical muscle deformation sensors, with applications in productivity enhancement and stress management in remote work and educational environments.

Keywords: Biometric signal processing · Muscle deformation sensor · SVM · Optical sensor

H. Mori et al. (Eds.): HCII 2025, LNCS 16333, pp. 298–313, 2026.
https://doi.org/10.1007/978-3-032-12660-3_22

1   Introduction

1.1   Background

With the rapid advancement of Internet technologies and remote access solutions, remote work and online learning have become increasingly widespread [1,2]. However, unlike face-to-face environments, remote settings make it difficult to perceive subtle physical changes or non-verbal cues, such as changes in posture or facial expressions. Consequently, communication quality can decline, potentially leading to loss of productivity. In particular, the inability to accurately assess team members' concentration levels or stress states can result in misunderstandings or poorly timed interventions, thereby reducing work efficiency.

Alternatively, moderate task-induced workload can enhance concentration, and excessive workload may negatively impact performance. Furthermore, once an individual enters a deep concentration state, unexpected external factors, such as sudden conversations, can disrupt focus and reduce productivity [9]. In remote environments, contextual information that is naturally available in face-to-face interactions (such as body language indicating "I am busy" or "It is okay to talk") is absent, making these challenges even more pronounced. Given this context, there is a need for a system capable of objectively and in real-time estimating concentration and relaxation states, and adapting tasks accordingly.

1.2   Related Work and Research Motivation

Various physiological and behavioral signals have been investigated to assess mental workload and stress. Electroencephalography (EEG) is widely used to measure neural activity, with alpha and beta wave power spectra serving as indicators of cognitive load and stress [3,6,13,18]. However, EEG systems require complex setups and are highly susceptible to environmental noise, limiting their practical application .

Heart rate was used for estimation of the degree of multiple mental states during study at home or physical workload [4,5,7,8,16]. Photoplethysmography (PPG) is gaining attention as a non-invasive method for estimating stress through heart rate variability (HRV) [16]. Despite its widespread use in consumer devices, distinguishing whether detected HRV changes stem from cognitive load or simple physical movement remains a significant challenge [8].

In addition to neurophysiological approaches, muscle activity has been studied as an indicator of cognitive workload. Electromyography (EMG) can measure muscle tension with high precision, but its usability is hindered by the need for precise electrode placement and potential discomfort over prolonged use. Optical muscle deformation sensors provide a promising non-invasive alternative, capable of detecting fine muscle contractions and expansions. Most previous studies have focused on forearm sensors, which are prone to motion artifacts due to frequent hand activities such as typing and gesturing. Recent research suggests that targeting less active muscle regions, such as the calf, could improve stability in the cognitive state of evaluation.

Although EEG and PPG have been widely explored for the estimation of concentration and relaxation states, their practical applications remain limited. EEG requires costly equipment and complex setups, while PPG is highly susceptible to motion artifacts, making them unsuitable for continuous monitoring in remote work environments.

Muscle activity measurement has emerged as a promising alternative for cognitive load assessment. However, traditional EMG sensors require precise placement and skin preparation [17], limiting their practicality. Optical muscle deformation sensors offer a non-invasive solution, yet most wearable implementations focus on the forearm, where frequent movements introduce noise into the measurements.

This study suggests a novel approach by utilizing calf muscle deformation as an indicator of cognitive load. The calf remains relatively stationary during desk work, minimizing motion artifacts and providing a more stable physiological signal for real-time monitoring. Preliminary findings suggest that muscle tension in the calf increases during cognitively demanding tasks and decreases during relaxation, making it a viable physiological marker for mental state estimation.

1.3   Research Objectives and Contributions

The objective of this study is to develop a system capable of detecting users' concentration and relaxation states based on calf muscle deformation data. This study focuses on evaluating the feasibility of classifying different mental states using a SVM with optical muscle deformation sensors.

To achieve this goal, we initially conducted a five-class classification (relaxation, arithmetic, writing, watching, and conversation). However, due to observed similarities in muscle activity among certain tasks, we integrated them into a three-class classification (relaxation, high-tension, and conversation). The classification performance of both schemes was compared to determine the optimal approach for detecting user states. Finally, a binary classification model was evaluated to assess the practical applicability of distinguishing between relaxation and high-tension states.

This study aims to demonstrate the feasibility of assessing concentration levels using calf muscle deformation data, providing valuable insights for productivity enhancement and health management in remote work settings. The following sections provide a detailed explanation of the experimental methodology, data collection procedures, and classification techniques.

2   Methodology

An overview of the proposed system is shown in Fig. 1, illustrating the overall process from muscle deformation sensing to state classification.

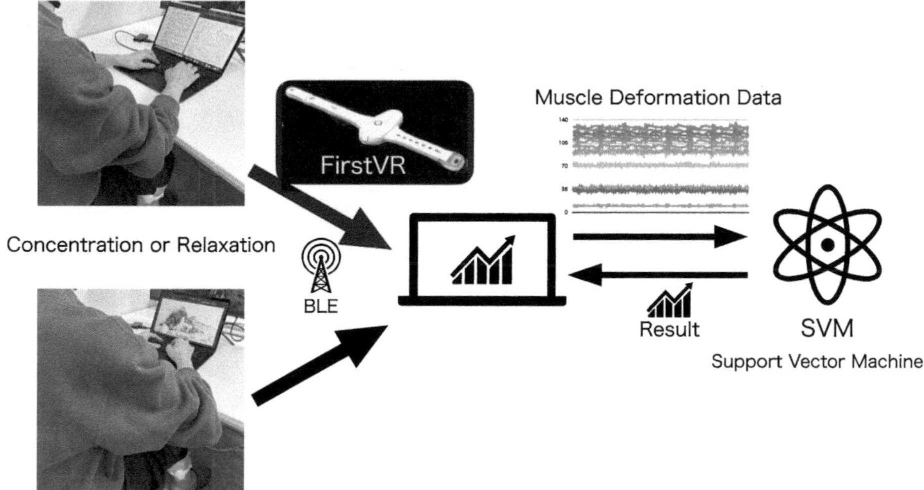

Fig. 1. Overview of the suggested system: The system collects muscle deformation data using a wearable muscle deformation sensor array via Bluetooth Low Energy communication. The acquired data is preprocessed and then classified using an SVM to estimate the user's concentration or relaxation state.

2.1   Data Collection

This study collected data from 20 participants (10 males and 10 females) aged between 19 and 26 years, with an average age of 22.7 years (Table 1). All participants were healthy adults who provided informed consent prior to participation. Individuals with a history of muscular disorders or specific leg impairments were excluded.

The experiment was conducted in a controlled laboratory environment to minimize external interference. Participants were seated in a standard office chair with a desk to ensure a consistent posture and reduce the influence of external factors.

2.2   Sensor Placement and Measurement

Muscle deformation data were obtained using the muscle deformation sensor array manufactured by H2L Inc.(Figure 2) [11,14]. This sensor employs a 14-channel near-infrared optical measurement system to detect real-time muscle contraction and expansion. Muscle deformation sensors attached to a lower-limb have previously been used for gait phase detection [10,12], demonstrating their reliability in tracking muscle movements of the lower-limb. The sensor was securely attached to the right calf to minimize displacement and pressure variations (Figure 3).

A sampling rate of 22 Hz was used, and each task was measured for 30 s. To account for transition phases at the beginning and end of each task, the first and last 3 s of data were trimmed before analysis.

Table 1. Participant Data: Information about the study participants.

Participant ID	Gender	Age
P01	Male	24
P02	Male	23
P03	Male	23
P04	Male	23
P05	Female	23
P06	Female	21
P07	Male	23
P08	Female	23
P09	Female	26
P10	Male	21
P11	Female	22
P12	Female	23
P13	Female	25
P14	Female	25
P15	Male	22
P16	Female	21
P17	Male	19
P18	Male	22
P19	Female	21
P20	Male	22

2.3   Experimental Design

To evaluate the feasibility of classifying concentration and relaxation states using calf muscle deformation data, five distinct task conditions were designed. Each task lasted 30 s, with a one-minute rest period between tasks to minimize carry-over effects. The order of tasks was randomized using a Python script to eliminate order effects.

- Relaxation: Participants sat quietly while performing deep breathing.
- Mental Arithmetic: Participants continuously performed subtraction tasks. (e.g., subtraction or multiplication).
- Writing: Participants composed short text passages.
- Watching: Participants watched a video.
- Conversation: Participants engaged in free conversation with the experimenter.

IInitially, a five-class classification approach was employed, where each task was treated as a separate class. However, classification accuracy analysis revealed substantial misclassification among arithmetic, writing, and watching tasks, suggesting that these activities exhibit similar muscle deformation characteristics.

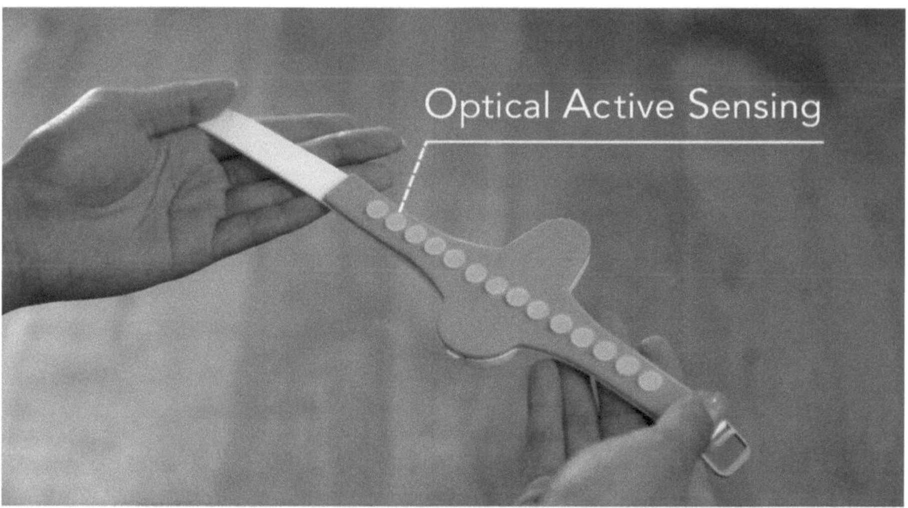

Fig. 2. Muscle deformation sensor array: The study utilizes the FirstVR sensor manufactured by H2L Inc. This device features a 14-channel near-infrared optical measurement system, enabling real-time detection of muscle contractions and expansions. The sensor is designed for wearable use, allowing for non-invasive measurement of muscle deformation.

To improve classification accuracy, these three tasks were integrated into a single category labeled "high-tension Task", leading to a three-class classification scheme: Relaxation, high-tension Task, and Conversation.

For multi-class classification (five-class and three-class), a single classification model was trained using data from all participants. In contrast, for binary classification, participant-specific models were trained separately for each individual to evaluate classification performance at the individual level.

2.4   Data Preprocessing

This study did not apply low-frequency filtering or any smoothing techniques such as moving average filtering. Instead, the raw data was standardized using StandardScaler, which normalizes features to have zero mean and unit variance before classification.

2.5   Classification Algorithm

SVM was employed for classification. We compared two kernel functions: linear and radial basis function (RBF). While both kernels achieved high accuracy in binary classification, RBF significantly outperformed the linear kernel in multi-class classification. Therefore, we adopted RBF as the primary kernel for subsequent analysis.

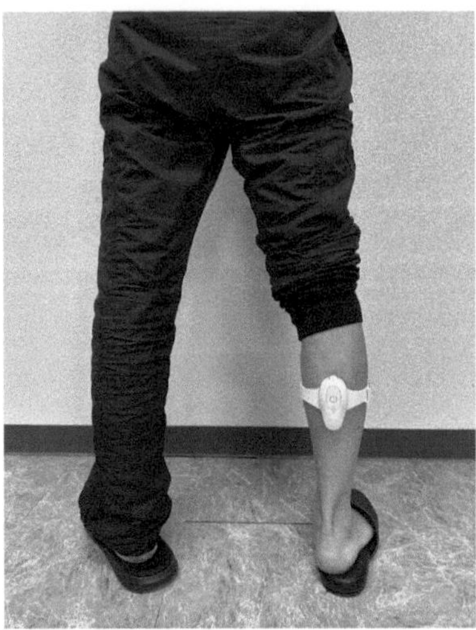

Fig. 3. Sensor Placement on the Calf: The sensor was attached to the participant's right calf and securely fixed to minimize displacement and external pressure variations.

To ensure robust evaluation, we applied 5-fold Stratified Cross-Validation, maintaining class balance across training and test sets. The final classification accuracy was computed as the average across the five folds.

Classification performance was evaluated using accuracy (classification rate), confusion matrices, and the F1-score to provide a detailed analysis of class-wise discrimination capability.

3   Experimental Results

3.1   Five-Class Classification Results

To evaluate the classification performance across different cognitive states, a five-class classification was conducted using a SVM with a RBF kernel. The classes included Relaxation, Arithmetic, Writing, Watching, and Conversation. The performance of the classifier was assessed using accuracy, precision, recall, and F1-score.

Classification Accuracy. Figure 4 illustrates the distribution of classification accuracy across different tasks. The overall classification accuracy was 73.8%, with individual class accuracy ranging from 65.5% to 79.9%. The highest classification accuracy was observed for Relaxation (79.9%), while the lowest was for Writing (65.5%). Table 2 provides the detailed accuracy values along with precision, recall, and F1-score.

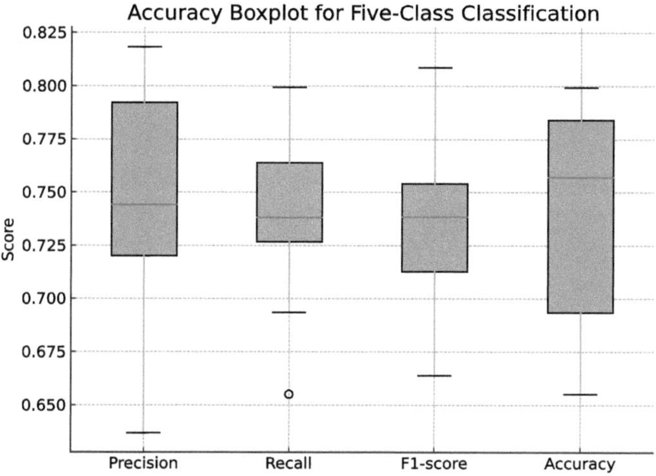

Fig. 4. Accuracy Distribution in Five-Class Classification: The classification accuracy distribution for five-class classification (relaxation, mental arithmetic, writing, watching, conversation) is shown. The highest accuracy was observed for relaxation, while the lowest accuracy was observed for writing.

Confusion Matrix Analysis. The confusion matrix (Fig. 5) provides insights into the misclassification patterns. Relaxation and Conversation achieved the highest precision (0.818 and 0.813, respectively), suggesting that when the model predicted these states, it was usually correct. However, Arithmetic had the lowest precision (0.637), indicating frequent misclassification with other states.

Conversation was frequently misclassified as Relaxation, suggesting an overlap in muscle activity between these tasks. This finding aligns with previous studies that indicate lower body muscle engagement may not significantly differ between light conversation and relaxation.

Performance Metrics (Accuracy, Precision, Recall, F1-Score). Table 2 presents the detailed classification metrics for each class. The highest F1-score was achieved for Relaxation (0.809), reflecting a strong balance between precision and recall. In contrast, Arithmetic had the lowest F1-score (0.664), confirming that it was frequently misclassified with other high cognitive load tasks.

This suggests that, while the model could distinguish tasks with clear cognitive engagement (e.g., Arithmetic, Writing), it struggled to separate Conversation from Relaxation due to similarities in muscle activation patterns.

3.2 Three-Class Classification Results

To further refine the classification of cognitive states, we conducted a three-class classification using an SVM with an RBF kernel. This classification scheme categorized the tasks into Relaxation, Conversation, and high-tension Task states,

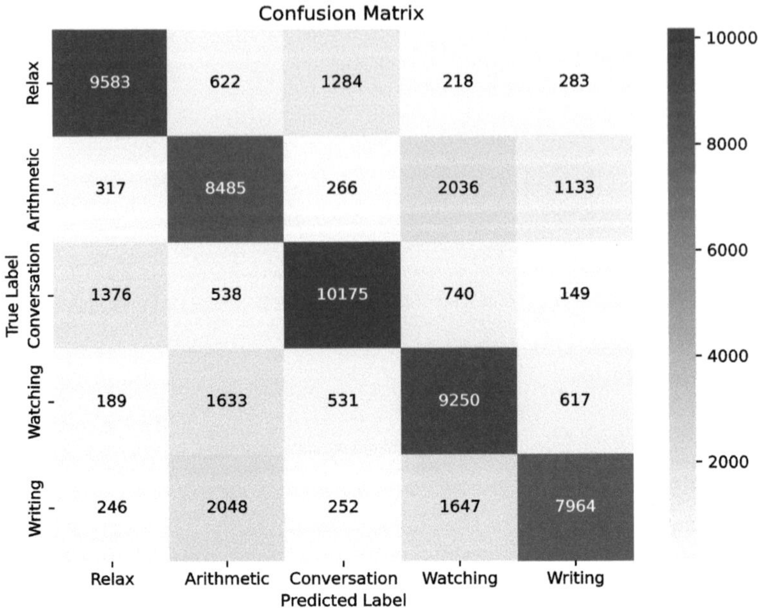

Fig. 5. Confusion Matrix for Five-Class Classification: The confusion matrix for five-class classification is presented. While relaxation and conversation achieved high classification accuracy, frequent misclassification was observed among mental arithmetic, writing, and watching tasks, suggesting similarity in muscle deformation patterns.

Table 2. Five-class classification performance metrics.

Task	Accuracy	Precision	Recall	F1-score
Relaxation	0.799	0.818	0.799	0.809
Arithmetic	0.693	0.637	0.693	0.664
Writing	0.655	0.785	0.655	0.714
Watching	0.757	0.666	0.757	0.709
Conversation	0.784	0.813	0.784	0.798
Overall	**0.738**	–	–	–

integrating the original five-class labels based on observed similarities in muscle deformation patterns.

Classification Accuracy. Figure 6 presents the distribution of classification accuracy across the three classes. The overall classification accuracy reached 87.7%, with individual class accuracy ranging from 71.5% to 97.8%. The highest accuracy was observed for high-tension Task (97.8%), while Conversation had the lowest accuracy (71.5%). Table 3 provides detailed accuracy, precision, recall, and F1-score for each class.

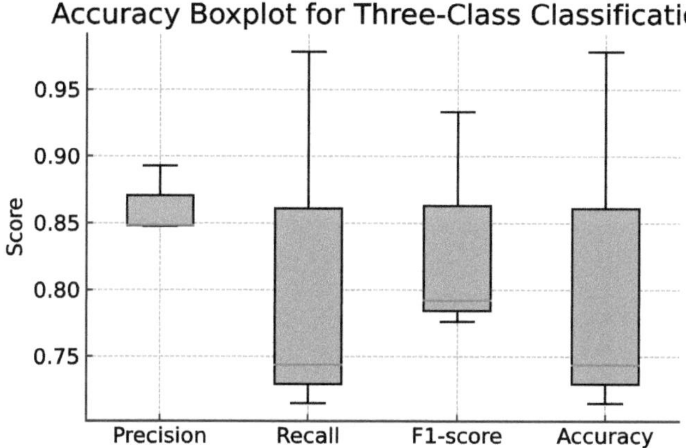

Fig. 6. Accuracy Distribution in Three-Class Classification: The classification accuracy distribution for the three-class classification (relaxation, high-tension, conversation) is shown. The classification accuracy improved, particularly for the high-tension state.

Confusion Matrix Analysis. The confusion matrix (Fig. 7) provides insights into the misclassification patterns. The classifier achieved high precision and recall for the high-tension Task state, indicating that the model effectively distinguished this state from the others. However, Conversation was frequently misclassified as Relaxation, suggesting an overlap in muscle activity between these two states.

This misclassification likely stems from the similarity in calf muscle deformation patterns between Conversation and Relaxation. Unlike high-tension Tasks, which involve substantial cognitive and muscular engagement, Conversation shares physiological characteristics with Relaxation, leading to classification ambiguity.

Performance Metrics (Accuracy, Precision, Recall, F1-Score). Table 3 presents the classification metrics for each class. The highest F1-score was obtained for high-tension (0.933), reflecting strong classification performance for this class. Conversely, Conversation exhibited the lowest recall (0.715), indicating frequent misclassification with Relaxation. This suggests that, while the model successfully distinguished between high-tension and non-stressed states, it struggled to differentiate Conversation from Relaxation.

3.3   Binary Classification Results

To evaluate the feasibility of distinguishing between relaxation and task-induced states, two binary classifications were performed: Relaxation vs high-tension and Relaxation vs Conversation. The classification performance was assessed using accuracy, precision, recall, and F1-score.

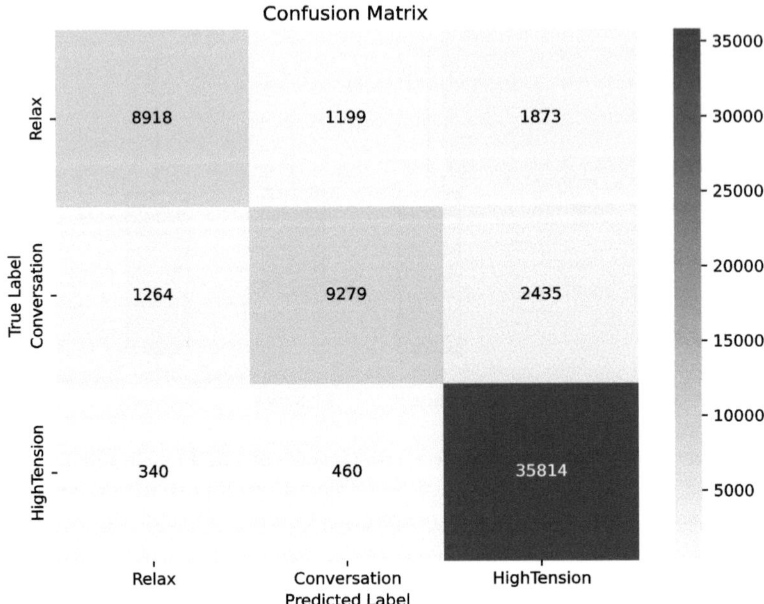

Fig. 7. Confusion Matrix for Three-Class Classification: The confusion matrix for the three-class classification is presented. The highest accuracy was achieved for high-tension, while some misclassification occurred between relaxation and conversation.

Table 3. Three-Class Classification Performance Metrics

Task	Accuracy	Precision	Recall	F1-score
Relaxation	0.744	0.848	0.744	0.792
Conversation	0.715	0.848	0.715	0.776
High-Tension tasks	0.978	0.893	0.978	0.933
Overall Accuracy	**0.8771**	–	–	–

Classification Accuracy. Table 4 presents the classification metrics for each binary classification task. The overall classification accuracy was high for both cases, but Relaxation vs high-tension achieved a near-perfect accuracy of 99.1%, whereas Relaxation vs Conversation had an accuracy of 96.8%.

Comparative Performance Analysis. The Relaxation vs high-Tension tasks classification exhibited exceptionally high recall (0.998), indicating that the high-tension state was almost never misclassified as relaxation. Similarly, the precision (0.990) was also high, meaning that instances classified as high-tension tasks were indeed high-tension states in most cases. These results suggest that the model can robustly distinguish between relaxation and high cognitive load states.

Table 4. Binary Classification Accuracy, Precision, Recall, and F1-score.

Task	Accuracy	Precision	Recall	F1-score
Relaxation vs High-Tension tasks	0.991	0.990	0.998	0.994
Relax vs Conversation	0.968	0.969	0.975	0.972

On the other hand, while the Relaxation vs Conversation classification also achieved high accuracy (96.8%), the precision and recall values (0.969 and 0.975) were slightly lower than those for Relaxation vs high-tension tasks. This suggests that the muscle deformation patterns during conversation exhibit more similarity to the relaxation state than high-tension states, leading to occasional misclassification.

Although Relaxation vs Conversation classification was still highly accurate, the slight drop in recall and precision values compared to Relaxation vs high-tension tasks suggests that conversation tasks do not exhibit as distinct muscle tension characteristics as high-cognitive-load tasks.

Statistical Analysis. A Repeated Measures ANOVA was conducted using Accuracy, Precision, Recall, and F1-score as dependent variables to compare classification performance across different tasks. The results indicated a significant difference in classification accuracy between Relaxation vs high-tension tasks and Relaxation vs Conversation($p < 0.05$). Post-hoc pairwise comparisons with Bonferroni correction further confirmed that classification performance for Relaxation vs high-tension tasks was significantly higher than for Relaxation vs Conversation ($p < 0.01$).

These statistical results reinforce the finding that high-tension states are more distinguishable from relaxation than conversation states, supporting the hypothesis that muscle deformation sensors are highly effective in detecting cognitive load but may struggle with lower-tension activities like conversation.

Key Findings

- Binary classification performance was consistently high, confirming the feasibility of distinguishing relaxation from other states.
- Relaxation vs high-tension tasks achieved near-perfect classification accuracy (99.1%), demonstrating that high-tension states induce distinct muscle deformation patterns.
- Relaxation vs Conversation classification was also highly accurate (96.8%), but slightly lower than Relaxation vs high-tension tasks, suggesting that conversation and relaxation states share more muscle characteristics.
- Statistical analysis confirmed that classification performance was significantly higher for high-tension states than for conversation ($p < 0.01$).
- These results indicate that muscle deformation sensors are highly effective in detecting cognitive load but may face challenges in distinguishing states with subtle muscle differences.

4   Discussion

4.1   Multi-class Classification Analysis

In this study, we initially conducted a five-class classification (Relaxation, Arithmetic, Writing, Watching, and Conversation). The results showed that while distinguishing Relaxation from high-tension Tasks (Arithmetic, Writing, and Watching) was relatively easy, differentiating between the high-tension tasks themselves was challenging. In particular, the high misclassification rates among Arithmetic, Writing, and Watching suggested that these tasks shared similar muscle deformation patterns. When these tasks were consolidated into a single "high-tension" class, classification accuracy improved.

These findings indicate that optical muscle deformation sensors can clearly distinguish between tension and relaxation but struggle to differentiate specific cognitive tasks within high-tension states. Previous studies have demonstrated that mental stress can induce physiological changes, including alterations in prefrontal cortex activity and skin conditions, which further supports the validity of using muscle deformation data for stress detection [15].

4.2   Balancing Generalization and Individualization

Another key finding of this study is the need to balance generalization and individualization when building classification models. In the case of binary classification, participant-specific (or "individual") models achieved remarkably high classification accuracy, reaching 99.1%. This outcome indicates that when the model is carefully optimized for each individual, it can reliably identify cognitive states based on muscle deformation patterns. However, in multi-class classification tasks, a single, generalized model trained on data from all participants showed a slight reduction in accuracy. This decrease is likely attributable to inter-individual variability in muscle deformation signals; since each participant exhibits distinct patterns, it becomes challenging to construct a single model that performs optimally for everyone. Consequently, when individual accuracy is prioritized, personalized models offer a clear advantage. At the same time, for broader applicability in diverse populations, an alternative strategy might be to develop a general model augmented by adaptation techniques that tailor the classification process to each new user.

4.3   Practical Applications and Future Challenges

Personalized Adaptive Systems. In practical terms, individually trained models can yield highly accurate cognitive state estimation, making them attractive for applications that benefit from user-specific insights. For instance, personalized learning systems can use such models to monitor and adapt to the cognitive load of individual learners, optimizing the difficulty or pace of learning materials in real time. Similarly, stress management applications can leverage accurate assessments of an individual's stress level or cognitive tension to deliver timely interventions, such as relaxation exercises or breaks, ultimately improving overall user well-being.

Monitoring Concentration in Work and Learning Environments. Generalized models, while exhibiting slightly lower overall accuracy, still offer significant benefits for tasks such as classifying "High-tension vs. Relaxation" states. This capability makes them valuable tools for monitoring concentration levels in workplaces or educational settings, where real-time detection of disengagement or stress could inform adjustments to workload or break schedules. However, despite the potential of generalized models for broad implementations, distinguishing between more specific tasks—such as arithmetic problem-solving versus writing—remains challenging. The variability in muscle deformation signals across different individuals makes it difficult to isolate task-specific features within a single, unified classification model.

Need for Multi-modal Approaches. The current findings also underscore the limitations of relying solely on muscle deformation sensors to discriminate among various high-tension tasks. Previous studies have successfully applied muscle deformation sensors for gait phase detection [12], indicating their strong potential in motion analysis. However, for cognitive state classification, additional modalities—such as heart rate variability, galvanic skin response, or vocal features—may be needed to achieve more granular distinctions. Incorporating these complementary physiological signals into a multi-modal model has the potential to enhance the robustness and accuracy of cognitive state classification across a range of task types.

4.4   Limitations and Future Work

Limited Dataset Size. It is important to note that the dataset used in this study was relatively small, with a limited number of participants. A smaller sample size may restrict the generalizability of the findings, as the variability in muscle deformation patterns may not be fully captured. Future investigations should therefore focus on validating and extending these results with larger and more diverse samples, encompassing different age groups, cultural backgrounds, and cognitive tasks.

Short Task Duration (30 s). Another limitation arises from the short duration of the tasks—each lasting only 30 s. Given that participants' cognitive states can fluctuate over longer periods, it remains unclear whether models trained on brief tasks can maintain accuracy over extended sessions. Therefore, future research should examine the performance of such models in long-term monitoring scenarios. This could involve continuous or repeated measurements over hours or days, enabling a more comprehensive understanding of temporal variations in cognitive state and muscle deformation patterns.

Use of a Single Device. Finally, this study focused exclusively on optical muscle deformation sensors. While this approach provided valuable insights, relying on a single physiological measure may limit classification performance. Investigating hybrid models that integrate additional physiological sensors—such as electroencephalography, electrodermal activity, or other wearable devices—could further improve classification accuracy and robustness. By combining multiple modalities, researchers can capitalize on complementary sources of information, thus enhancing the generalizability of cognitive state estimation models in diverse real-world environments.

5   Conclusion

5.1   Key Findings

Binary classification of high-tension task and relaxation reached 99.1% accuracy with individual models, indicating robust detection of muscle deformation patterns under cognitive load. However, five-class classification among tasks such as Arithmetic and Writing proved challenging (76.6% accuracy). Consolidating these high-tension tasks into a single category improved three-class accuracy to 87.7%, highlighting the sensor's sensitivity to overall tension rather than task-specific differences. Generalized models were slightly less accurate but remain necessary for broader deployment.

5.2   Practical Implications

These findings can benefit productivity monitoring, stress detection, and HCI by enabling real-time assessment of cognitive states. Individualized models offer higher accuracy, whereas generalized models facilitate wider application but may require adaptive learning to maintain performance.

5.3   Future Work

Further research should include larger and more diverse samples, longer task durations, and additional physiological sensors (e.g., heart rate variability, galvanic skin response) to enhance multi-modal analysis. Efforts to develop real-time adaptive models will also be crucial for practical, scalable deployment.

Acknowledgement. This work was supported by Council for Science, Technology and Innovation, "Cross-ministerial Strategic Innovation Promotion Program (SIP), Development of foundational technologies and rules for expansion of the virtual economy" (JPJ012495). (funding agency: NEDO)

References

1. Ferreira, R., Pereira, R., Bianchi, I.S., da Silva, M.M.: Decision factors for remote work adoption: advantages, disadvantages, driving forces and challenges. J. Open Innovation Technol. Market Complex. **7**(1), 70 (2021)
2. Galanti, T., Guidetti, G., Mazzei, E., Zappalà, S., Toscano, F.: Work from home during the covid-19 outbreak: the impact on employees' remote work productivity, engagement, and stress. J. Occup. Environ. Med. **63**(7), e426–e432 (2021)
3. Hayano, J., Barros, A.K., Kamiya, A., Ohte, N., Yasuma, F.: Assessment of pulse rate variability by the method of pulse frequency demodulation. Biomed. Eng. Online **4**, 1–12 (2005)

4. Heathers, J.A.: Smartphone-enabled pulse rate variability: an alternative methodology for the collection of heart rate variability in psychophysiological research. Int. J. Psychophysiol. **89**(3), 297–304 (2013)

5. Hwang, S., Seo, J., Jebelli, H., Lee, S.: Feasibility analysis of heart rate monitoring of construction workers using a photoplethysmography (PPG) sensor embedded in a wristband-type activity tracker. Autom. Constr. **71**, 372–381 (2016)

6. Katahira, K., Yamazaki, Y., Yamaoka, C., Ozaki, H., Nakagawa, S., Nagata, N.: EEG correlates of the flow state: a combination of increased frontal theta and moderate frontocentral alpha rhythm in the mental arithmetic task. Front. Psychol. **9**, 300 (2018)

7. Kawasaki, Y., Hossain, T., Yokokubo, A., Lopez, G.: Estimating the degree of mental state using heart rate while studying. In: Adjunct Proceedings of the 2021 ACM International Joint Conference on Pervasive and Ubiquitous Computing and Proceedings of the 2021 ACM International Symposium on Wearable Computers, pp. 126–130 (2021)

8. Lee, W., Lin, K.Y., Seto, E., Migliaccio, G.C.: Wearable sensors for monitoring on-duty and off-duty worker physiological status and activities in construction. Autom. Constr. **83**, 341–353 (2017)

9. Mark, G., Iqbal, S.T., Czerwinski, M., Johns, P., Sano, A.: Neurotics can't focus: an in situ study of online multitasking in the workplace, pp. 1739–1744. CHI '16, Association for Computing Machinery, New York, NY, USA (2016). https://doi. org/10.1145/2858036.2858202

10. Miyake, T., et al.: Heel-contact gait phase detection based on specific poses with muscle deformation. In: 2019 IEEE International Conference on Robotics and Biomimetics (ROBIO), pp. 977–982. IEEE (2019)

11. Miyake, T., Minakuchi, T., Sato, S., Okubo, C., Yanagihara, D., Tamaki, E.: Optical myography-based sensing methodology of application of random loads to muscles during hand-gripping training. Sensors **24**(4), 1108 (2024)

12. Miyake, T., et al.: Gait phase detection based on muscle deformation with static standing-based calibration. Sensors **21**(4), 1081 (2021)

13. Shriram, R., Sundhararajan, M., Daimiwal, N.: EEG based cognitive workload assessment for maximum efficiency. Int. Organ. Sci. Res. IOSR **7**, 34–38 (2013)

14. Tamaki, E., Hosono, S., Iwasaki, K.: FirstVR: a muscle deformation sensors array device to detect finger gestures and noise reduction case. In: Proceedings of the 2019 2nd International Conference on Electronics, Communications and Control Engineering, pp. 21–24 (2019)

15. Tanida, M., Katsuyama, M., Sakatani, K.: Relation between mental stress-induced prefrontal cortex activity and skin conditions: a near-infrared spectroscopy study. Brain Res. **1184**, 210–216 (2007). https://doi.org/10.1016/j.brainres.2007.09.058, https://www.sciencedirect.com/science/article/pii/S0006899307022743

16. Tsunoda, K., Chiba, A., Chigira, H., Ura, T., Mizunq, O.: Estimating changes in a cognitive performance using heart rate variability. In: 2015 IEEE 15th International Conference on Bioinformatics and Bioengineering (BIBE), pp. 1–6. IEEE (2015)

17. Varghese, R.J., Pizzi, M., Kundu, A., Grison, A., Burdet, E., Farina, D.: Design, fabrication and evaluation of a stretchable high-density electromyography array. Sensors **24**(6), 1810 (2024)

18. Yi Wen, T., Mohd Aris, S.: Electroencephalogram (EEG) stress analysis on alpha/beta ratio and theta/beta ratio. Ind. J. Elect. Eng. Comp. Sci **17**(175), 10–11591 (2020)

Investigating Potential Physiological Indicators of Attention

Anna Amsler[1], Hardi Raval[1], Shriya Pancholi[2], and Dvijesh Shastri[1(✉)]

[1] Computer Science and Engineering Technology, University of Houston-Downtown, Houston, TX, USA
{amslermontaa2,ravalh1}@gator.uhd.edu, shastrid@uhd.edu
[2] Information Communication and Technology Pandit Deendayal Energy University, Gandhinagar, India

Abstract. As remote and hybrid learning environments become increasingly prevalent, the ability to detect, monitor, and predict student attention in online learning has grown in importance. While traditional classroom settings offer environmental and behavioral cues that support attentional regulation, these are often diminished or absent in online formats. This study investigates the potential of physiological signals as objective indicators of attention in simulated online learning contexts, drawing on data from fourteen participants across four experimental conditions. These conditions mimic varying degrees of distractions to evaluate how attentional states manifest in measurable physiological patterns. The analysis included features such as heart rate, body temperature, eye movements, head pose, and different limb motions, which were collected and extracted through a dual-modality approach, integrating both contact-based (sensors) and non-contact (camera/software) measurements. The purpose of this study is to determine how features differ between focused and distracted learning and among different types of distraction. The results identify statistically significant variations in several physiological indicators across conditions, supporting their relevance for attention modeling. This work contributes to the growing body of research advocating for non-invasive attention monitoring methods in educational settings and aims to provide the groundwork for the development of machine learning models capable of predicting attention states based on physiological data.

Keywords: Online Learning · Attention · Physiological Indicators · Machine Learning

1 Introduction

Attention is a foundational cognitive process that significantly impacts learning outcomes, which is why accurately assessing and predicting it is crucial in educational contexts [1]. In traditional classroom environments, face-to-face interactions facilitate sustained attention and engagement by enabling real-time feedback through facial expressions, gestures, and other social and behavioral cues, which help students remain focused and feel socially connected [2]. However, the shift toward online and hybrid learning formats has introduced new challenges, including more environmental distractions and greater difficulty for instructors in reading participants' cues through a computer screen. This is often due to factors such as multiple open applications, the grid layout displaying small video feeds, lack of camera use, internet issues, and other technical problems [3, 4]. These distractions can undermine learners' ability to maintain focus, along with the instructor's capability to assess their attention, ultimately leading to lower engagement and less effective learning outcomes [5].

Given the dynamic nature of online learning environments, developing robust methods for monitoring attention in these contexts is critical. Although traditional self-report measures and observational techniques are useful, they often fall short due to their subjective nature and inability to provide real-time feedback [6–9]. This has driven researchers to explore more objective, data-driven approaches that can capture attentional fluctuations. Research on the matter increasingly emphasizes the need for real-time, objective assessments of attention, particularly during complex cognitive tasks. Historically, attention has been measured through behavioral tasks and neuropsychological assessments, such as reaction time tests and inhibition-based tasks using various sensory stimuli [10]. While these controlled experiments offer insights into attention states, they are not feasible for continuous, real-world monitoring.

Recent studies have highlighted the potential of physiological signals to serve as indicators for attentional states. These include central nervous system measures, such as electroencephalography, and peripheral signals, such as heart rate and electrodermal activity [11]. However, determining which physiological indicators best represent attentional engagement remains a challenge, as effectiveness often varies across contexts. Additionally, attention is shaped not only by cognitive demands but also by emotional and contextual factors, complicating the task of isolating reliable biomarkers [12]. Consequently, researchers increasingly turn to machine learning approaches to model attention more accurately by integrating various physiological and behavioral elements.

Physiological measures offer a promising route for capturing attentional engagement in real-time, particularly in environments where traditional assessments are impractical. Eye-tracking, for instance, can provide insights into visual attention by analyzing gaze fixations and rapid movements, which are correlated with cognitive load and interest [13]. Head pose and orientation also offer meaningful indicators, with more stable head positions typically being associated with task engagement [14]. Research further discusses the use of supervised machine learning algorithms to uncover complex patterns between physiological signals and mental states such as attention [11]. However, a significant obstacle lies in collecting sufficient training data paired with accurate ground-truth labels. Furthermore, it is often unclear which physiological signals are most informative.

Our study proposes a dual approach that combines contact-based measurements through sensors with the extraction of features through non-contact methods using a video camera and software. The features included in the analysis are as follows: Head Translation, Head Rotation, Horizontal Eye Movement, Vertical Eye Movement, Heart Rate, Body Temperature, Left Wrist Movement, Right Wrist Movement, Torso Movement, Right Ankle Movement, and facial expression [9]. Specifically, the study addresses the following research questions:

R1. Which physiological indicators differentiate focused learning from distracted learning? (**Focused vs. Distracted Learning**)

R2. Which physiological indicators distinguish between different types of distractions? (**Types of Distracted Learning**)

The findings from this research could be applied beyond educational settings, including in fields such as occupational health and safety, where real-time attention monitoring is essential but needs to be conducted using non-intrusive methods. Bjegojevic et al. reported the importance of continuous monitoring techniques that do not require test-like administration, highly specialized equipment, or professionally trained personnel in detecting attentional lapses [15].

2   Method

2.1   Experimental Design

The original study involved twenty participants who took part in four distinct trials simulating different scenarios within a video-based learning environment: a distraction-free control trial and three experimental trials, each involving a concurrent task [9]. Each session lasted approximately 45 to 50 min and was conducted at least a day apart. During the first session, participants were briefed, and only those who signed the consent form were allowed to proceed. To replicate a realistic online learning experience, the experiment used four pre-recorded 30-min lecture videos from a Data Visualization course. These videos required no prior knowledge and were structured to be self-contained. None of the participants had prior exposure to the course content. The assignment of videos was fixed by session, not by condition, ensuring each video appeared across all trial types to maintain balance in content difficulty and eliminate content-based learning bias [9].

The Control trial required participants to focus solely on the lecture video. In Experiment 1 (Exp1), participants answered 20 open-ended, thought-provoking questions sourced from [16] while the lecture video played. Experiment 2 (Exp2) involved participants engaging with their choice of social media platforms, including Facebook and Instagram, to simulate common real-world multitasking behaviors during online learning. Experiment 3 (Exp3) was a free activity trial, as it gave participants complete freedom to choose the secondary activity while the video played. Upon completion of the video, participants were asked to complete a five-question multiple-choice quiz designed to assess their attention to the lecture video [9].

Each session began with sensor attachment, which included three WitMotion accelerometers (right ankle, right wrist, chest), an Empatica E4 wristband on the left wrist (for body temperature and motion), and a Fitbit Versa 4 smartwatch on the right wrist (for heart rate) [9]. Electrodermal activity (EDA) data, though captured by the E4, were excluded from the analysis due to inconsistencies. Additionally, a Logitech C270 webcam captured facial footage, and the participant's screen activity was recorded to track on-screen behavior [9].

2.2   Feature Extraction

Videos were recorded at 25 frames per second with a 640×360 pixels resolution. Feature extraction from these recordings was conducted using three open-source Python tools focused on eye gaze, head movement, and facial expressions. Eye movement data were captured using a toolkit integrating Dlib [17] and OpenCV [18], with Haar-based classifiers [19] used to detect facial landmarks and locate the eyes. For each frame, the x and y coordinates of both eyes were recorded, and their variance, averaged across the left and right eyes, was used as a proxy for gaze activity [20, 21].

Head position was tracked using an OpenCV-based tool [22] that monitored rotational and translational shifts across three axes to compute total motion [23]. Facial expression analysis identified seven emotions per frame, with the value for each representing the probability of the person displaying that specific emotion at a given time [24]. Physiological signals were gathered from three WitMotion accelerometers (on the torso, wrist, and ankle), an Empatica E4 wristband (left wrist), and a Fitbit Versa 4 smartwatch (right wrist). Movement signals were converted into acceleration values using $ae = |ax| + |ay| + |az|$ [23]. To establish ground-truth, participants' attention was coded at a second level using facial and screen capture videos. Specifically, two independent coders assessed each participant's attention and generated a binary variable indicating attention. These assessments were synthesized into a single attention signal per participant per trial.

2.3 Data Preprocessing

The ground-truthing of the data required a significant time commitment, limiting the analysis to only fourteen participants across four trials, which yielded 56 files (14 participants $\times$ 1 data file per trial $\times$ 4 trials). Out of these, 9 files were corrupted; therefore, the final dataset included 47 valid files. Each file contained 19 features and between 1,700 and 2,100 s-by-second observations. To remove potential noise, the first and last five minutes of data were removed, as they can represent transitional periods of setting up or finishing. Additionally, the dataset included facial expression data, where files included probability values for each of the potential emotions at any given time. To simplify this, the dominant emotion (highest probability value) was dummy-coded in a new column (Anger = 1, Disgust = 2, Fear = 3, Happy = 4, Neutral = 5, Sad = 6, Surprise = 7, None = 0). Because many of the features were extracted using software, in some cases, missing values needed to be addressed. To avoid introducing bias into the analysis, features with more than 20% missing values were removed from the analysis. If the missing data was 20% or less, the missing entries were filled in using mean imputation.

2.4 Statistical Analysis

Considering the data presented unequal variances between trials, Welch's t-tests were conducted to compare the control and experimental trials for each feature, as well as the experimental trials themselves [25, 26]. Due to the large sample size, the statistical significance of the t-tests was supplemented with effect size measures, specifically Cliff's Delta [27]. Cliff's Delta provides a clear and interpretable understanding of the magnitude of any observed differences, classifying them as negligible ($|\delta| < 0.15$), small ($0.15 \leq |\delta| < 0.33$), medium ($0.33 \leq |\delta| < 0.47$), or large ($|\delta| \geq 0.47$) [28]. For the purpose of this study, the focus was on the features that show non-negligible effect sizes in terms of their differences between trials.

3   Results

To develop a visual understanding of the distributional characteristics of the key variables, boxplots were generated for each feature across the four conditions (Control, Exp1, Exp2, and Exp3). Each boxplot displays the interquartile range (IQR), outliers, and group means (denoted by red dots) to visualize central tendency and dispersion. Statistical analysis compared the Control trial and the different experimental conditions, revealing several notable patterns.

Overall, body movement and physiological responses varied across conditions, showing notable differences in specific variables. This section outlines the main differences identified between the control trial and the experimental conditions, as well as among the experimental conditions for each feature included in the analysis. Table 1 displays the statistical significance obtained from Welch's t-tests, along with the Cliff's delta value. P-values that do not indicate statistical significance at the 95% confidence level are marked in red, as are those with negligible Cliff's Delta effects. Statistical significance with small, medium, or large effect sizes is indicated in green.

3.1   Focused vs. Distracted Learning

Figure 1(a) reveals head rotation across all trials for all fourteen participants. The n values at the top represent the total number of observations per trial. The Figure shows noticeably greater head rotation in Exp3 compared to all other trials, suggesting increased physical engagement during this condition. The spread and upper quartiles in Exp3 are especially prominent, indicating higher variability. As shown in Table 1, the head rotation exhibited negligible differences between Control and Exp1 ($t(30227) = -15.28$, $p < 0.001$, $|\delta|=0.12$), but small differences between Control and Exp2 ($t(28170) = -42.69$, $p < 0.001$, $|\delta|=0.32$) and medium differences in terms of Exp3 ($t(31657) = -53.31$, $p < 0.001$, $|\delta|=0.37$), with this last one having the most head rotation movement.

Figure 1(b) shows head translation. Although all trials display similar medians, the boxplot reveals a lower mean for the Control trial compared to Exp1, which may be indicative of much lower values during the Control trial, pulling the mean down. Meanwhile, Exp2 and Exp3 show similar distributions, indicating comparable movement patterns. Even though the means are different, head translation kept a fairly similar distribution between Control and Exp1, as indicated by a negligible effect size ($t(15379) = -28.74$, $p < 0.001$, $|\delta|=0.03$), but showed small changes in Exp2 ($t(27442) = -10.09$, $p < 0.001$, $|\delta|=0.24$) and Exp3 ($t(30236) = -3.58$, $p < 0.001$, $|\delta|=0.23$), indicating increased overall movement when the distractions involved social media browsing or a free activity. Please refer to Table 1 for the statistical analysis.

Figure 2(a) demonstrates horizontal eye movement (Eye X). Exp1 shows the highest median and widest range in horizontal eye movement, likely due to frequent visual scanning while typing the answers to the essay-type questions. The variation in the ranges for the trials indicates that task type may influence the extent of lateral eye activity. As shown in Table 1, the horizontal eye movement had the most significant shift between Control and Exp1 ($t(23462) = -91.80$, $p < 0.001$, $|\delta|=0.64$), showing a large increase in movement likely due to the focused writing task, followed by Exp3 ($t(17685) = -26.96$, $p < 0.001$, $|\delta|=0.32$). Figure 2(b) shows vertical eye movement (Eye Y). Exp3 stands

Table 1. Welch t-test significance and Cliff's delta results.

Trial	Control	Exp1	Exp2	Trial	Control	Exp1	Exp2
Head Rotation				**Head Translation**			
Exp1	$p < 0.001$ $\|\delta\| = 0.12$	-	-	Exp1	$p < 0.001$ $\|\delta\| = 0.03$	-	-
Exp2	$p < 0.001$ $\|\delta\| = 0.32$	$p < 0.001$ $\|\delta\| = 0.21$	-	Exp2	$p < 0.001$ $\|\delta\| = 0.24$	$p < 0.001$ $\|\delta\| = 0.26$	-
Exp3	$p < 0.001$ $\|\delta\| = 0.37$	$p < 0.001$ $\|\delta\| = 0.28$	$p < 0.001$ $\|\delta\| = 0.08$	Exp3	$p < 0.001$ $\|\delta\| = 0.23$	$p < 0.001$ $\|\delta\| = 0.24$	$p < 0.001$ $\|\delta\| = 0.00$
Eye X				**Eye Y**			
Exp1	$p < 0.001$ $\|\delta\| = 0.64$	-	-	Exp1	$p < 0.001$ $\|\delta\| = 0.02$	-	-
Exp2	$p < 0.001$ $\|\delta\| = 0.13$	$p < 0.001$ $\|\delta\| = 0.41$	-	Exp2	$p < 0.001$ $\|\delta\| = 0.09$	$p < 0.001$ $\|\delta\| = 0.06$	-
Exp3	$p < 0.001$ $\|\delta\| = 0.32$	$p < 0.001$ $\|\delta\| = 0.29$	$p < 0.001$ $\|\delta\| = 0.09$	Exp3	$p < 0.001$ $\|\delta\| = 0.24$	$p < 0.001$ $\|\delta\| = 0.45$	$p < 0.001$ $\|\delta\| = 0.42$
Left Wrist				**Right Wrist**			
Exp1	$p < 0.001$ $\|\delta\| = 0.19$	-	-	Exp1	$p < 0.001$ $\|\delta\| = 0.15$	-	-
Exp2	$p = 0.17$ $\|\delta\| = 0.01$	$p < 0.001$ $\|\delta\| = 0.17$	-	Exp2	$p < 0.001$ $\|\delta\| = 0.15$	$p < 0.001$ $\|\delta\| = 0.03$	-
Exp3	$p = 0.07$ $\|\delta\| = 0.01$	$p < 0.001$ $\|\delta\| = 0.21$	$p < 0.05$ $\|\delta\| = 0.00$	Exp3	$p < 0.001$ $\|\delta\| = 0.12$	$p < 0.001$ $\|\delta\| = 0.24$	$p < 0.001$ $\|\delta\| = 0.25$
Heart Rate				**Temperature**			
Exp1	$p = 0.22$ $\|\delta\| = 0.02$	-	-	Exp1	$p < 0.05$ $\|\delta\| = 0.04$	-	-
Exp2	$p < 0.001$ $\|\delta\| = 0.00$	$p < 0.001$ $\|\delta\| = 0.00$	-	Exp2	$p < 0.001$ $\|\delta\| = 0.31$	$p < 0.001$ $\|\delta\| = 0.43$	-
Exp3	$p < 0.001$ $\|\delta\| = 0.20$	$p < 0.001$ $\|\delta\| = 0.25$	$p < 0.001$ $\|\delta\| = 0.18$	Exp3	$p < 0.001$ $\|\delta\| = 0.18$	$p < 0.001$ $\|\delta\| = 0.22$	$p < 0.001$ $\|\delta\| = 0.38$
Torso				**Right Ankle**			
Exp1	$p < 0.001$ $\|\delta\| = 0.30$	-	-	Exp1	$p < 0.001$ $\|\delta\| = 0.08$	-	-
Exp2	$p < 0.001$ $\|\delta\| = 0.55$	$p < 0.001$ $\|\delta\| = 0.34$	-	Exp2	$p < 0.001$ $\|\delta\| = 0.16$	$p < 0.001$ $\|\delta\| = 0.10$	-
Exp3	$p < 0.001$ $\|\delta\| = 0.20$	$p < 0.001$ $\|\delta\| = 0.05$	$p < 0.001$ $\|\delta\| - 0.29$	Exp3	$p < 0.001$ $\|\delta\| - 0.20$	$p < 0.001$ $\|\delta\| = 0.30$	$p < 0.001$ $\|\delta\| = 0.35$

out visually, with a higher average than the other trials. This suggests that alternating attention between devices in the free concurrent task may have led to increased vertical eye movement. In comparison, the other conditions appear more similar to each other.

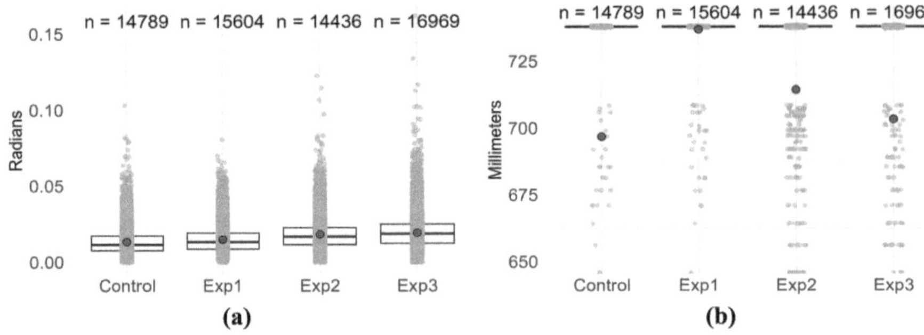

Fig. 1. Boxplots of (a) Head Rotation and (b) Head Translation

Vertical eye movement remained stable between conditions, with only a small notable difference between Control & Exp3 ($t(19809) = -26.26$, $p < 0.001$, $|\delta|=0.24$), with Exp3 displaying more movement.

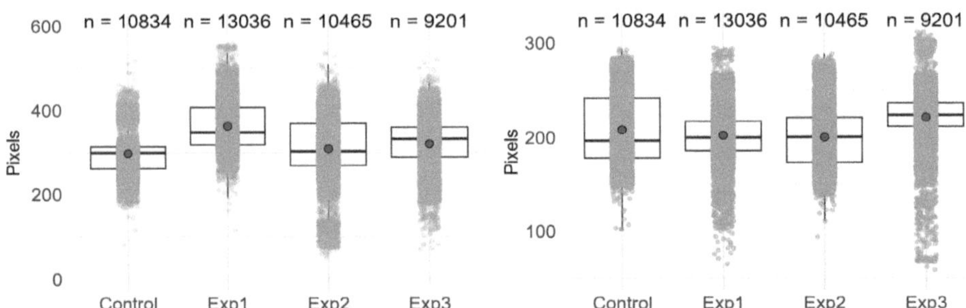

Fig. 2. Boxplots of eye movement in the (a) X-direction (Eye X) and (b) Y-direction (Eye Y)

Figure 3 illustrates the movement of the left wrist (a) and right wrist (b). Exp1 appears to induce slightly more left wrist movement, possibly due to typing. However, the differences across all conditions are not as pronounced as in other features. Specifically, the left wrist movement showed minimal variation across conditions, with only a small difference between Control and Exp1 ($t(27608) = -25.80$, $p < 0.001$, $|\delta|=0.19$) likely reflecting the increased movement as a result of the typing carried out as part of the concurrent task in Exp1. Similarly, right wrist movement shows minimal variation across trials. The patterns were largely similar across the experimental conditions. Right wrist movement increased slightly during Exp1 ($t(28915) = 13.01$, $p < 0.001$, $|\delta|=0.15$), likely due to the typing activity, and Exp2 ($t(28950) = 7.79$, $p < 0.001$, $|\delta|=0.15$), potentially indicating more mouse interaction. Overall, the results suggest that the various experimental activities did not induce substantial changes in the magnitude of the wrist movements.

Figure 4(a) shows heart rate data. Exp3 has a notably higher mean heart rate than the other conditions, potentially indicating elevated physiological arousal. Heart rate displayed statistically insignificant differences between Control and Exp1 ($t(25969) = 1.23$, $p = 0.22$, $|\delta|=0.02$) and negligible differences with Exp2 ($t(27402) = -9.66$, p

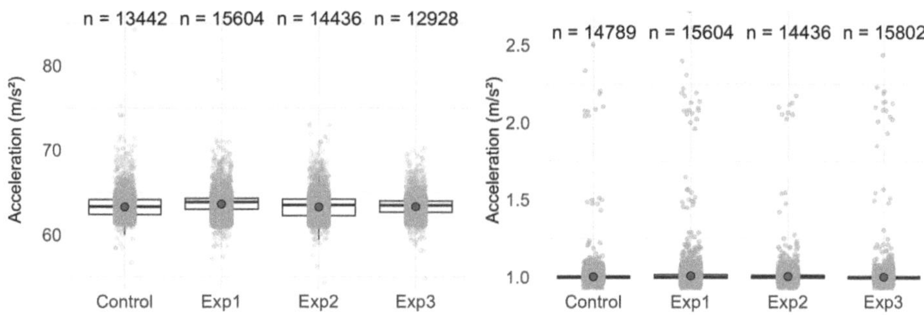

Fig. 3. Boxplots of the (a) Left Wrist and (b) Right Wrist movements

< 0.001, |δ|=0.0), but showed a small effect in Exp3 (t(26293) = −30.06, p < 0.001, |δ|=0.20), suggesting a more elevated heart rate when carrying out the concurrent task of choice. Figure 4(b) illustrates body temperature. Exp2 registers the lowest average body temperature, while Exp3 exhibits the highest. The Control group displays a more dispersed distribution, which visually distinguishes it from the experimental conditions. This pattern may reflect stress or task-related physiological shifts. Body temperature during the Control trial was notably higher than in Exp 2 (t(27861) = 48.67, p < 0.001, |δ|=0.31) and significantly lower than in Exp3 (t(26310) = −16.42, p < 0.001, |δ|=0.18). However, although statistically different from that of Exp1, the effect was negligible (t(21950) = −3.88, p < 0.05, |δ|=0.04).

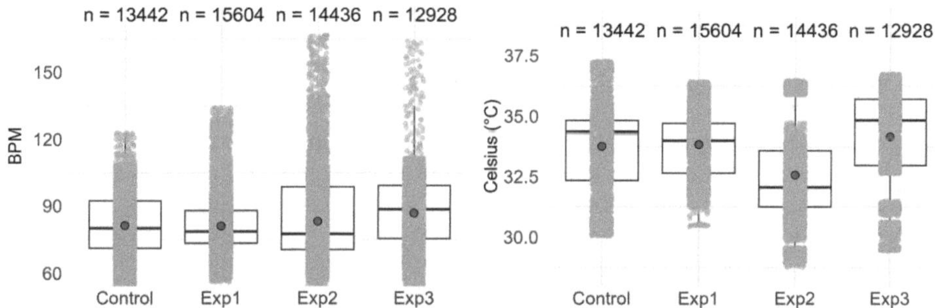

Fig. 4. Boxplots of (a) Heart Rate data and (b) Body temperature data

Figure 5(a) displays torso movement, where the distribution for the Control group appears noticeably different, suggesting a potentially distinct baseline posture or movement pattern. Torso movement exhibited the largest difference between Control and Exp2 (t(13534) = 79.69, p < 0.001, |δ|=0.55). There were also small but notable effect sizes when comparing with Exp1 (t(14317) = 50.44, p < 0.001, |δ|=0.30) and Exp3 (t(24468) = 46.84, p < 0.001, |δ|=0.20). Figure 5(b) illustrates the right ankle movement. The boxplots indicate generally similar movement across all trials, with only a slight increase in the median for Exp3. Right ankle movement displayed an increase in Exp3 when compared to the Control group (t(24688) = −21.79, p < 0.001, |δ| =

0.20), which was characterized by a noticeably wider distribution and more pronounced outliers in the boxplot, suggesting greater variability and magnitude of movement due to less constrained activities. Overall, the tight interquartile ranges for all trials suggest consistent and constrained ankle movement throughout.

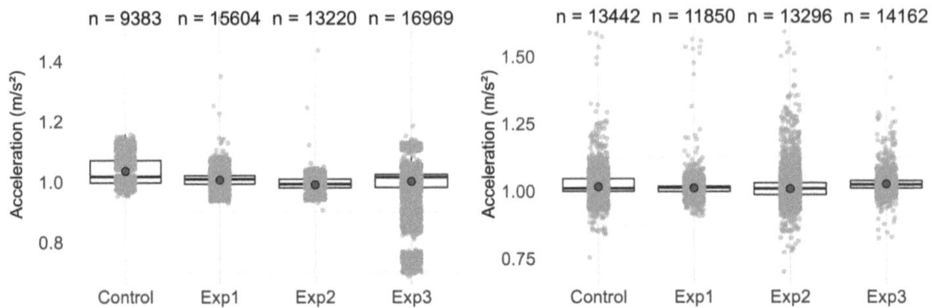

Fig. 5. Boxplots of (a) torso and (b) right ankle movements

Overall, torso movement emerged as a strong discriminator between focused and distracted learning. This increased movement during focused learning may reflect subtle shifts and re-positioning of the body to sustain attention and cognitive engagement. The other strong discriminator is head motion (rotation and translation), which was statistically significantly less in the focused learning compared to the distracted learning. Specifically, the effect was much more pronounced between Control and Exp2, and Exp3 (refer to δ in Table 1).

3.2   Types of Distracted Learning

Additionally, statistical comparisons between the different experimental conditions revealed further differences. In head rotation, Exp1 showed small differences from the other experiments, displaying less rotation than Exp2 ($t(28065) = -29.73$, $p < 0.001$, $|\delta|=0.21$) and Exp3 ($t(32042) = -40.13$, $p < 0.001$, $|\delta|=0.28$), indicating that answering essay-type questions did not require as much head rotation as social media browsing or the concurrent task of choice. In head translation, Exp2 and Exp3 displayed differencing patterns when compared to Exp1, with ($t(15432) = 21.13$, $p < 0.001$, $|\delta|=0.26$) and ($t(17893) = 28.05$, $p < 0.001$, $|\delta|=0.24$) respectively.

In a similar manner, Exp1 displays more horizontal eye movement than Exp2 ($t(18031)=57.82$, $p < 0.001$, $|\delta|=0.41$) and Exp3 ($t(17832)=50.05$, $p < 0.001$, $|\delta|=0.29$). This reflects the participants gazing back and forth from the video to the secondary task. Exp2 had the least movement out of the experiments, showing that scrolling social media did not require as much horizontal eye movement. In terms of vertical eye movement, Exp3 stands out with more movement than both Exp1 and Exp2, with ($t(18141) = 48.21$, $p < 0.001$, $|\delta|=0.45$) and ($t(19538) = 47.38$, $p < 0.001$, $|\delta|=0.42$) respectively. The concurrent task of choice led the participants to look up and down more, possibly from switching between their phone and the computer where the lecture video was being played.

Left wrist movement was significantly higher in Exp1 than Exp2 ((t(28725) = 26.95, p < 0.001, |δ|=0.17) and Exp3 ((t(28130) = 25.69, p < 0.001, |δ|=0.21), which is consistent with the typing involved in the writing task. For the right wrist movement, Exp3 shows the least out of the three experiments, displaying small effect differences when compared to Exp1 (t(30115) = −15.26, p < 0.001, |δ|=0.24) and Exp2 (t(29820) = −10.59, p < 0.001, |δ| = 0.25).

Heart rate exhibited differences particularly in Exp3, having a higher heart rate than both Exp1 (t(24674) = 34.91, p < 0.001, |δ|=0.25) and Exp2 (t(27192) = 17.99, p < 0.001, |δ|=0.18). A similar pattern was observed for body temperature, with Exp3 showing higher temperatures than both Exp1 (t(20804) = 16.12, p < 0.001, |δ|=0.22) and Exp2 (t(27229) = 64.32, p < 0.001, |δ|=0.38).

For torso movement, Exp1 exceeds that of Exp2 (t(28822) = 45.32, p < 0.001, |δ|=0.34). Similarly, Exp3 also shows more movement than Exp2 (t(23571) = 18.73, p < 0.001, |δ| = 0.29), indicating that the distraction of scrolling social media generally makes the person remain more steady. Finally, in right ankle movement, there is increased movement in Exp3, which is statistically significant, with a small effect size when compared to Exp1 (t(23361) = 33.57, p < 0.001, |δ| = 0.30) and a medium effect size when compared to Exp2 (t(22151) = 33.98, p < 0.001, |δ| = 0.35), likely due to the less constrained nature of the "free trial" activities.

Overall, the body temperature emerged as a strong discriminator across the three distracted learning conditions, with Exp3 showing the highest mean temperature and Exp2 the lowest.

3.3 Visual Analysis of the Emotion Feature Per Trial

Figure 6 illustrates the distributions of six primary emotions categorized by trial. The distribution of emotional states varies significantly across the four experimental conditions. The control group is characterized by a predominant neutral emotional state (72.8%), suggesting a more relaxed baseline. However, as participants are subjected to experimental manipulations, the proportion of neutral responses declines, reaching 52.7% in Exp3. In contrast, sad emotions become increasingly prominent, rising from 19.9% in the Control condition to 38.3% in Exp3. Additionally, anger shows a significant increase in Exp2 (12.4%), nearly doubling its representation compared to the Control. Other emotions, such as fear, happiness, and surprise, remain relatively low across all groups, indicating their minor contribution to the overall landscape in these experiments. These shifts suggest that experimental conditions may elicit heightened emotional strain, as indicated by the decline in positive affect and the concurrent rise in negative emotional states. Although the results intuitively make sense, their power is limited because the software tool used to extract emotions was only about 65% accurate [24].

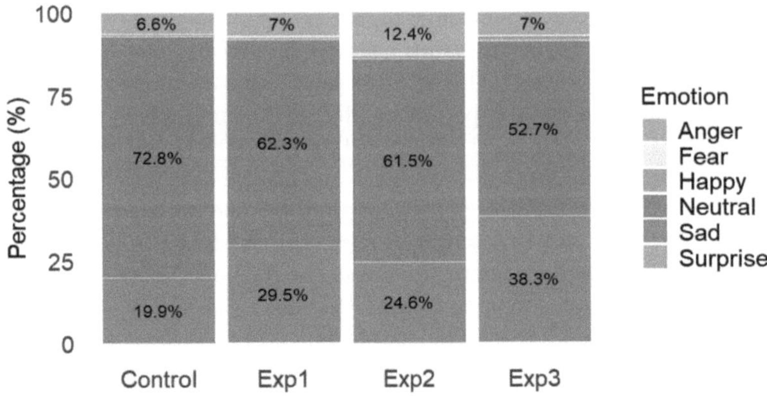

Fig. 6. Distribution of six primary emotions per trial.

4 Discussion and Conclusion

Table 2 summarizes the study results. The R1 column indicates which experimental conditions show significant differences from the Control trial, addressing Research Question 1 (R1). The R2 column lists the experimental condition pairs that differ significantly from each other, addressing Research Question 2 (R2). To aid interpretation, a color-coded system is used: cells marked in green indicate that all three possible comparisons showed significant differences; yellow indicates two out of three comparisons were significant; and orange highlights features with one out of three significant differences.

Table 2. Significant differences identified per research question.

Feature	R1	R2
Head rotation	Exp2, Exp3	Exp1-Exp2, Exp1-Exp3
Head translation	Exp2, Exp3	Exp1-Exp2, Exp1-Exp3
Eye X	Exp1, Exp3	Exp1-Exp2, Exp1-Exp3
Eye Y	Exp3	Exp1-Exp3, Exp2-Exp3
Left wrist	Exp3	Exp1-Exp2, Exp1-Exp3
Right wrist	Exp1, Exp2	Exp1-Exp3, Exp2-Exp3
Heart rate	Exp3	Exp1-Exp3, Exp2-Exp3
Temperature	Exp2, Exp3	Exp1-Exp2, Exp1-Exp3, Exp2-Exp3
Torso	Exp1, Exp2, Exp3	Exp1-Exp2, Exp2-Exp3
Right ankle	Exp2, Exp3	Exp1-Exp3, Exp2-Exp3

In summary, the results of the Welch t-tests and Cliff's Delta analyses revealed substantial differences between the control trial and the experimental conditions (R1), as well as between the experimental conditions themselves (R2) for most of the features included in this analysis. Notably, torso movement emerged as the strongest discriminator between focused and distracted learning. Specifically, it was statistically significantly higher during focused learning (Control) than distracted conditions (Exp1, Exp2, and Exp3). This increased movement during focused learning may reflect subtle shifts and re-positioning of the body to sustain attention and cognitive engagement. Body temperature proved to be a great differentiating feature across the three distracted learning conditions (Exp1, Exp2, and Exp3), with Exp3 showing the highest mean temperature and Exp2 the lowest. This suggests that body temperature serves as the strongest differentiator among the experimental conditions.

Similarly, head rotation and translation, horizontal eye movement, right wrist movement, body temperature, torso movement, and right ankle movement exhibited significant differences in at least two out of three R1 and R2 comparisons, suggesting their strong sensitivity to experimental conditions. On the other hand, vertical eye movement, left wrist movement, and heart rate displayed notable differences in two out of the three R2 comparisons but only one of the R1 comparisons, making them less effective in distinguishing between control and experimental conditions.

These findings align with the existing literature, which emphasizes the value of physiological and movement-based indicators in identifying attentional states across various conditions. Prior research has shown that eye-tracking metrics such as gaze fixation and saccade patterns serve as reliable markers of visual attention and cognitive processing [13], while head pose, particularly its orientation and stability, has been linked to task engagement in screen-based contexts [14] Similarly, [29] demonstrated that head rotation and gaze behavior are modulated by attentional demands, reinforcing their relevance as behavioral cues for assessing cognitive engagement.

While previous studies have typically focused on a few isolated behavioral or physiological indicators, this research contributes a more integrated perspective that combines contact-based sensor data with non-contact video-derived features, enabling a broader analysis. By simultaneously analyzing a diverse set of features, this study captures a more comprehensive representation of attention-related behavior across various experimental conditions.

Overall, the results indicate that the features included in the study are promising indicators of attention. The findings support the development of objective, real-time assessment methods that enhance the potential for building robust, generalizable machine learning models for attention prediction. Such methods could be adapted for use beyond educational contexts, where non-intrusive, real-time attention monitoring is critical, such as in occupational health and safety or even criminal justice, for assessing jurors' attention to key pieces of evidence.

Future research could focus on implementing machine learning algorithms to predict attention states using features highlighted in this analysis as statistically significant with large or medium effects.

Acknowledgments. The authors are grateful to the MSDA program at the University of Houston-Downtown for their financial support in the data collection phase of this project.

Disclosure of Interests..   The authors have no competing interests to declare that are relevant to the content of this article.

References

1. Al-Nafjan, A., Aldayel, M.: Predict students' attention in online learning using EEG data. Sustainability **14**(11), 6553 (2022). https://doi.org/10.3390/su14116553
2. Zepke, N., Leach, L.: Improving student engagement: Ten proposals for action. Act. Learn. High. Educ. **11**(3), 167–177 (2010). https://doi.org/10.1177/1469787410379680
3. Dewan, M.A.A., Murshed, M., Lin, F.: Engagement detection in online learning: a review. Smart Learning Environments **6**(1), 1–20 (2019). https://doi.org/10.1186/s40561-018-0080-z
4. Raca, M., Dillenbourg, P.: System for assessing classroom attention. ACM International Conference Proceeding Series, 265–269 (2013). https://doi.org/10.1145/2460296.2460351
5. Hutt, S., et al.: Automated gaze-based mind wandering detection during computerized learning in classrooms. User Model. User-Adap. Inter. **29**(4), 821–867 (2019). https://doi.org/10.1007/s11257-019-09228-5
6. Bixler, R., D'Mello, S.: Automatic gaze-based user-independent detection of mind wandering during computerized reading. User Model. User-Adap. Inter. **26**(1), 33–68 (2016). https://doi.org/10.1007/s11257-015-9167-1
7. Madake, J., Shende, S., Bhatlawande, S., Shinde, R., Govekar, S., Shilaskar, S.: Vision-based monitoring of student attentiveness in an e-learning environment. In: 2022 IEEE Pune Section International Conference (PuneCon), pp. 1–6. IEEE (2022). https://doi.org/10.1109/PuneCon55413.2022.10014782
8. Bjegojevic, B., Leva, M.C., Cromie, S.D., Balfe, N.: Physiological indicators for real-time detection of operator's attention. In: European Conference on Safety and Reliability (ESREL 2022), Dublin, Ireland (2022). https://doi.org/10.3850/978-981-18-5183-4_J01-05-149-cd
9. Hassan, J., Berdejo, J., Kurati, S., Dinh, A., Garcia, A., Shoemaker, K.A., Shastri, D.: Bioindicators of attention detection in online learning environments. In: HCI International 2024 Posters. Springer Nature Switzerland (2024)
10. Delvigne, V., Wannous, H., Dutoit, T., Ris, L., Vandeborr, J.P.: PhyDAA: Physiological dataset assessing attention. IEEE Trans. Circuits Syst. Video Technol. **32**(5), 2612–2623 (2022). https://doi.org/10.1109/TCSVT.2021.3061719
11. Stuldreher, I.: Multimodal physiological synchrony as measure of attentional engagement. In: Proceedings of the 22nd ACM International Conference on Multimodal Interaction (ICMI '20), Virtual Event, Netherlands (2020). https://ris.utwente.nl/ws/files/265862249/Stuldreher_2020_Multimodal_physiological_synchrony_.pdf
12. Ding, X.-R., et al.: Wearable sensing and telehealth technology with potential applications in the coronavirus pandemic. IEEE Rev. Biomed. Eng. **14**, 48–70 (2021). https://doi.org/10.1109/RBME.2020.2992838
13. Li, Q., Liu, Y., Yan, F., Zhang, Q., Liu, C.: Emotion recognition based on multiple physiological signals. Biomed. Signal Process. Control **85**, 104989 (2023)
14. D'Mello, S., Graesser, A.: Dynamics of affective states during complex learning. Learn. Instr. **22**, 145–157 (2012). https://doi.org/10.1016/j.learninstruc.2011.10.001
15. Bjegojevic, B., Leva, M.C., Cromie, S., Balfe, N.: Physiological indicators for real-time detection of operator's attention. In: Leva, M.C., Patelli, E., Podofillini, L., Wilson, S. (eds.) Proceedings of the 32nd European Safety and Reliability Conference (ESREL 2022). Research Publishing (2022). https://www.researchgate.net/publication/363567662_Physiological_Indicators_for_Real-Time_Detection_of_Operator%27s_Attention
16. White, A.: 365 Deep & Thought Provoking Questions to Ask Yourself (& Others). (2023)

17. GitHub: Dlib. https://github.com/davisking/dlib (2023)
18. OpenCV: https://opencv.org/ (2023)
19. Viola, P., Jones, M.: Rapid object detection using a boosted cascade of simple features. In: Proceedings of the 2001 IEEE Computer Society Conference on Computer Vision and Pattern Recognition (CVPR 2001), vol. 1. IEEE (2001)
20. Agarwal, V.: Automating online proctoring using AI. Medium (2020). https://medium.com/data-science/automating-online-proctoring-using-ai-e429086743c8
21. Martynow, M., Zielińska, A., Marzejon, M., Wojtkowski, M., Komar, K.: Pupil detection supported by Haar feature based cascade classifier for two-photon vision examinations. In: 2019 11th International Symposium on Image and Signal Processing and Analysis (ISPA), pp. 54–59. IEEE (2019)
22. Nielsen, N.: Head Pose Estimation. https://github.com/niconielsen32/ComputerVision/blob/master/headPoseEstimation.py (2023)
23. Bouten, C.V., Koekkoek, K.T.M., Verduin, M., Kodde, R., Janssen, J.D.: Atriaxial accelerometer and portable data processing unit for the assessment of daily physical activity. IEEE Trans. Biomed. Eng. **44**(3), 136–147 (1997)
24. Singh, R.: The ultimate guide to emotion recognition from facial expressions using Python. https://towardsdatascience.com/the-ultimate-guide-to-emotion-recognition-from-facial-expressions-using-python-64e58d4324ff (2023)
25. Kim, T.K.: T test as a parametric statistic. Korean J. Anesthesiol. **68**(6), 540–546 (2015). https://doi.org/10.4097/kjae.2015.68.6.540
26. Ugoni, A., Walker, B.F.: The t test: An introduction. COMSIG Review 4(2) (1995). https://www.researchgate.net/publication/25752723_THE_t_TEST_An_Introduction
27. Sullivan, G.M., Feinn, R.: Using effect size—or why the p value is not enough. J. Grad. Med. Educ. **4**(3), 279–282 (2012)
28. Meissel, K., Yao, E.S.: Using Cliff's Delta as a non-parametric effect size measure. Practical Assessment, Research, and Evaluation **29**(2) (2023)
29. Khan AZ, Blohm G, McPeek RM, Lefèvre P. Differential influence of attention on gaze and head movements. J Neurophysiol. 2009. https://pmc.ncbi.nlm.nih.gov/articles/PMC2637015/

Shaping Minds with Type: The Psychological Effects of Typography Using Eye Tracking

Sónia Brito-Costa[1,3]([✉]) [ID], Ana Rita Teixeira[2,3] [ID], Maria Fernanda Antunes[1] [ID], Silvia Espada[1] [ID], Alexandra Soares[1] [ID], and Hugo de Almeida[1] [ID]

[1] InED - Center for Research and Innovation in Education, Polytechnic University of Coimbra, Rua da Misericórdia, Lagar dos Cortiços, S. Martinho do Bispo, 3045-093 Coimbra, Portugal
Sonya.b.costa@gmail.com
[2] InED - Center for Research and Innovation in Education, Polytechnic of Porto, Rua Dr. Roberto Frias, 712, 4200-465 Porto, Portugal
[3] GECAD – Research Group on Intelligent Engineering and Computing for Advanced Innovation and Development, Institute of Engineering – ISEP, Polytechnic of Porto, Rua António Bernardino de Almeida, 431, 42249-015 Porto, Portugal

Abstract. In today's digital world, where communication primarily occurs through social media platforms, there has been a noticeable increase in mental health challenges. As communication increasingly relies on digital formats, understanding how typefaces contribute to the transmission of feelings is becoming fundamental. The first impression a text makes is not only determined by its content but also by its visual execution, emphasising the need for a deeper exploration into how typography can evoke specific feelings and moods. This study examines how three sans serif typefaces—Open Sans, Quicksand, and Tenor Sans—affect psychological responses to mental health-related content. Using eye-tracking measures with 24 participants viewing positive, neutral, and negative phrases, the analysis reveals the impact of typeface on attention and emotional reception. The heat maps were used to identify which typeface participants were most fixated on and how the different typefaces influenced their reading behaviour. The methodology consisted of presenting 18 different phrases related to mental health, each written in one of the three selected typefaces. Each phrase was displayed randomly for 3 s, changing only the typeface. In analysing the emotional tone of the phrases, it was interesting to note that Quicksand maintained its position as the most preferred font even when paired with negative phrases. Although the study could not conclusively determine the extent to which typography affects the perceived meaning of a message, it's clear that typefaces with softer, more rounded forms may have a more positive and inviting effect on individuals interacting with mental health content.

Keywords: Typography · Sans Serif · Mental Health · Eye-tracking

1 Introduction

Communication has increasingly shifted to social media platforms, revolutionizing how people interact and consume information. While these platforms facilitate global connectivity and rapid information exchange, they have also been linked to a notable rise

H. Mori et al. (Eds.): HCII 2025, LNCS 16333, pp. 328–338, 2026.
https://doi.org/10.1007/978-3-032-12660-3_24

in mental health issues. These challenges arise from factors such as isolation, social comparison, and the overwhelming nature of digital interactions. At the core of this phenomenon is extensive engagement with written content on screens, which heavily influences how users process and respond to information.

It is through digital interactions that issues such as content, forms of expression and message constructions are topics that can be analysed to explain the increase in mental health problems, namely how emotions are transmitted and perceived. Studies have shown that individuals interpret digital messages differently than face-to-face communication due to the lack of non-verbal cues [1]. This misinterpretation can amplify feelings of misunderstanding, isolation, or distress, contributing to mental health challenges [2, 3]. Understanding these dynamics is essential to promoting more effective and emotionally healthy interactions in the digital environment.

Typography, the visual representation of text, is a crucial component in shaping these expressive relationships. As a collection of symbols and forms, typography provides a "visual voice" that communicates ideas and emotions. While spoken language uses tone and voice for expression, written communication relies on visual cues, such as typefaces, to convey meaning and emotional tone. Given the extensive interaction with written content on screens, typography plays an increasingly significant role in how messages are perceived emotionally and cognitively.

Typography influences the subconscious, reinforcing messages and creating a cohesive visual narrative. The right typeface can evoke desired emotions and build trust, while poor choices risk alienating or shocking the audience. Mastering typographic nuances involves aligning design elements with the core message and intent, ensuring impactful, authentic, and relatable communication [4].

The shapes, sizes, and characteristics of fonts can subtly influence how messages are received, often triggering specific emotional responses based on the perceived qualities of the typography. (a) (b) The emotional response to typefaces has been studied in several research papers. These studies have explored the relationship between typefaces their visual characteristics, and the emotional effects [5].

The term "emotional typography" also known as "emotype," aptly describes the use of typefaces to evoke specific feelings or enhance the emotional impact of a message. Previous studies such as Choi and Aizawa investigate how some existing typefaces are perceived emotionally. [5, 6]. The emotional response to typeface has been studied in various research papers. The studies have linked typefaces with specific visual characteristics to specific emotional effects [6].

The study of the intersection between psychology and typography seeks to understand how the visual characteristics of typefaces influence individuals' perceptions, emotions, and behaviours. Psychologists have long studied how people process written information, while typographers focus on designing text that enhances readability, accessibility, and emotional resonance, and psychologists focus on improving information comprehension and processing, while typographers aim to enhance the reading experience, accessibility, and overall text impression [7, 8].

Research highlights that specific typefaces evoke perceptions and emotions. For instance, sans-serif fonts are often perceived as more masculine, authoritative, and intelligent. They are also considered highly readable and "louder," potentially enhancing feelings of security and competence in individuals' behaviour [9]. In contrast, calligraphic typefaces, with their irregular, slanted, and curved strokes, convey warmth and emotionality, fostering pleasant emotional connections. Serif fonts, characterized by their elegance and charm, are seen as more legible and interesting compared to sans-serif fonts, resulting in calmer and more controlled behaviours [9–13].

In this understanding the cognitive effects of typography on reading were explored and demonstrates that the choice of typeface significantly impacts both functional comprehension and emotional response [7]. Together, these findings emphasize the importance of selecting typefaces thoughtfully to align with the intended message and emotional tone[14]. However, most of the existing research focuses on fonts with unique characteristics, often used for titles or distinctive text elements. In contrast, this study aims to determine whether more commonly used sans serif fonts, usually considered neutral and practical, can also elicit emotional responses in the context of mental health topics.

The primary objective of this study was to investigate how three popular sans-serif typefaces—Open Sans, Quicksand, and Tenor Sans—affect the psychological perception of mental health-related content. These fonts were selected for their accessibility and commercial availability via Google Fonts, ensuring ease of use and consistency across platforms. Specifically, the study aimed to explore whether the distinct visual characteristics of these typefaces—such as clean lines, geometric shapes, and humanist influences—impact how mental health content is perceived emotionally and cognitively. Open Sans is noted for its vertical structure and clean lines, Quicksand features rounded geometric shapes, and Tenor Sans incorporates varying stroke thicknesses with humanist elements.

This study further examines how different forms of sans-serif typography influence psychological responses to mental health-related content, particularly regarding perceived tone and emotional impact.

2 Material and Methods

The current study investigated the impact of three sans-serif typefaces—Open Sans, Quicksand, and Tenor Sans—on the emotional perception of mental health-related content. Using eye-tracking technology, the study examined how these typefaces influenced participants' attention and emotional responses while viewing positive, neutral, and negative phrases.

2.1 Participants

The study involved 24 participants aged 18 to 54, representing diverse professional backgrounds. This variation in demographics was intended to capture a wide range of responses and perceptions related to the emotional impact of the typefaces on mental health-related content. Informed consent was obtained from all participants before the study, and they were informed of their right to withdraw at any time without penalty and participated on a entirely voluntary basis.

2.2 Protocol and Devices

All participants underwent testing under standardized conditions in a controlled environment. The experimental tests were conducted in a usability testing room with professional-grade equipment designed to support this study. The controlled setting ensured consistency in lighting, seating, and other environmental variables that might influence the results.

Data collection was conducted using the Gazepoint GP3 system, integrated with Gazepoint's application programming interface software. This setup enabled a detailed analysis of participants' pupillary reactions and visual attention to specific typefaces and phrases [15].

The Gazepoint GP3 HD eye tracker utilizes infrared light to track pupil dilation and gaze direction, allowing for the measurement of various ocular metrics. These metrics provide insights into participants' visual attention and cognitive processes [16].

Eye-tracking studies are important for understanding the relationship between the visual system and brain function. Visual attention and eye movements share common neural circuits. This perspective aligns with current research in neuroscience and psychology, which utilizes eye-tracking technology to gain insights into cognitive processes and neural mechanisms [17–19].

Participants' eye movements were tracked to determine where they focused their attention during the experiment. Heat maps were generated to visualize fixation patterns, identifying which typefaces attracted the most attention and how the different fonts influenced reading behaviour.

To thoroughly assess the impact of typefaces, participants were subjected to a carefully designed experimental protocol. The phrases presented during the study consisted of affirmations and questions with varying emotional connotations: positive, neutral, and negative. Each phrase was repeated three times using different typefaces, Open Sans, Quicksand, and Tenor Sans to allow for comprehensive comparisons.

A total of 18 phrases were used, 3 positive affirmations, 3 neutral affirmations, 3 negative affirmations, 3 positive questions, 3 neutral questions, and 3 negative questions.

Each screen displayed the same question or affirmation repeated three times in different typefaces. Between these experimental screens, control screens with a fixation cross were interspersed. The control screens lasted 3 s at the start and end of the experiment, and 2 s for all intermediate screens. In contrast the phrase screens were displayed for 3 s each. The order of the phrases, typefaces, and placement on the screen were randomised to minimise biases and ensure robust data collection.

3 Results

The goal was to assess whether the emotional connotation of the phrase affected participants' preference for a particular typeface. After collecting the data, the team analysed the heat maps to determine which font attracted the most attention and whether there was a noticeable pattern in the fixation times for each typeface based on the phrase's emotional tone.

Heat maps revealed the direction of participants' gaze on the screen, identifying their initial focus and where the areas their eyes lingered the longest. The videos were analysed frame by frame to observe changes in fixation patterns. With a 3-s display duration for each screen, users typically viewed each phrase once.

3.1 Positive Questions

The positive phrases "Are you okay?", "How was your day?" and "Did I already tell you that I'm proud of you?" were chosen for their psychologically positive impact, as they express care and concern, promote connection and empathy and provide self-esteem and reinforce positive behaviours. A bar graph was created (Fig. 1) to visualise the total fixations for each typeface across the positive question phrases, and the overall sum of the fixation results. Although Open Sans dominated the first two screens, Quicksand emerged as the most fixated typeface overall for positive questions.

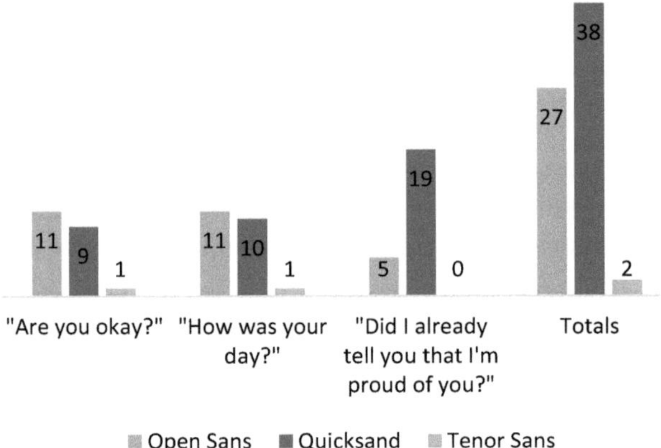

Fig. 1. Total fixations for each typeface across the positive question phrases, and the overall sum of the fixation results.

3.2 Neutral Questions

Neutral questions were interspersed between positive and negative questions to provide participants with a psychological 'reset', minimizing potential carry-over effects and ensuring that responses to negative questions were not unduly influenced by preceding stimuli. The neutral questions were "Were there vegetables for lunch?", "Are the pants also black?", and "Is this classical music?". A bar graph was created (Fig. 2) to visualise the total fixations for each typeface across the positive question phrases, as well as the overall sum of the fixation results. Quicksand was the most preferred typeface overall for neutral questions, though Tenor Sans had the highest fixation for specific screen.

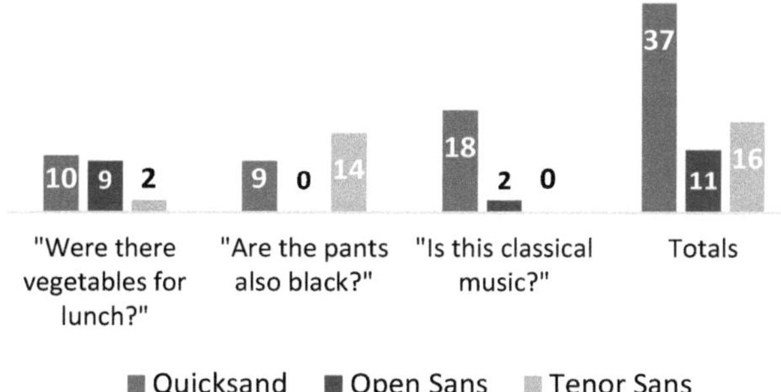

Fig. 2. Total fixations for each typeface across the neutral question phrases, and the overall sum of the fixation results.

3.3 Negative Questions

The negative questions "Do you think you're someone?", "Are you stupid or do you pretend to be?", and "Why are you still here?" were chosen for their psychologically negative impact, as they express attack on the person's self-worth, rejection and generate negative emotions such as anger, shame, humiliation, and sadness. A bar graph was created (Fig. 3) to visualise the total fixations for each typeface across the negative question phrases, and the overall sum of the fixation results. Tenor Sans was the most fixated typeface for negative questions, reflecting its potential to convey stronger emotional tones.

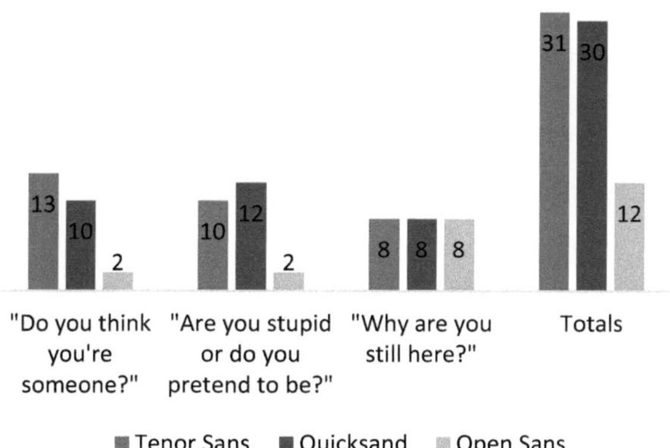

Fig. 3. Total fixations for each typeface across the neutral question phrases, and the overall sum of the fixation results.

3.4 Positive Affirmations

The positive affirmations "I believe in you!", "Accept yourself as you are!", and "You are more than enough!" were chosen for their psychologically positive impact. They can contribute to a more positive mindset, improved self-worth and confidence, and greater emotional well-being. Through the bar graph (Fig. 4) we can visualise the total fixations for each typeface across the positive affirmations phrases, and the overall sum of the fixation results. Open Sans dominated the earlier screens, but Quicksand emerged as the most fixated typeface for later affirmations.

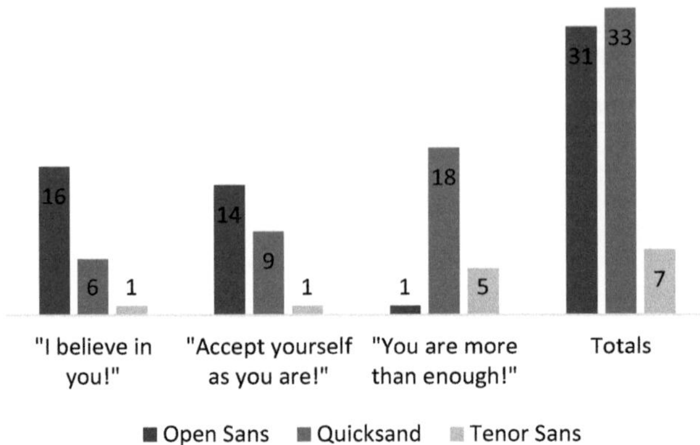

Fig. 4. Total fixations for each typeface across the positive affirmation phrases, and the overall sum of the fixation results.

3.5 Neutral Affirmations

The neutral affirmations "The walk lasted half an hour!", "Today is sunny!", and "Sea water is salty!" were chosen for their psychologically neutral impact. These phrases describe observable facts or states of being. They don't express personal opinions, judgments, or emotions. Through the bar graph (Fig. 5) we can visualise the total fixations for each typeface across the neutral affirmations phrases, and the overall sum of the fixation results. While Open Sans and Tenor Sans dominated individual screens, Quicksand emerged as the most fixated typeface overall.

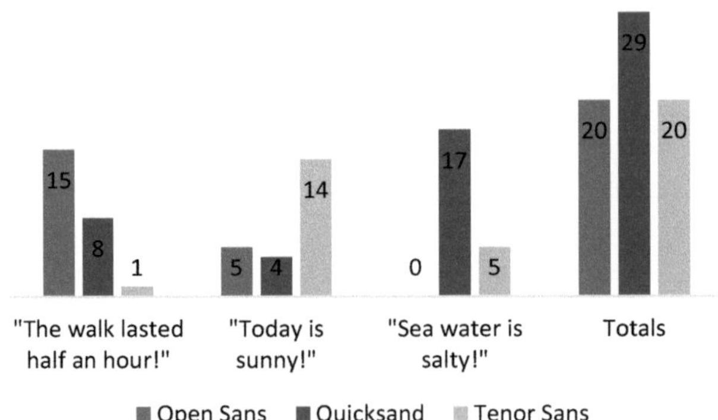

Fig. 5. Total fixations for each typeface across the neutral affirmation phrases, and the overall sum of the fixation results.

3.6 Negative Affirmations

The Negative affirmations included "You don't deserve anything good!", "You have no future!", and "You are incapable!" were chosen for their psychologically negative impact on a person's mental and emotional well-being, potentially leading to lower self-esteem, an increased anxiety and a sense of hopelessness. The bar graph (Fig. 6) provides a visualisation of the total fixations recorded for each typeface across the negative affirmation phrases, along with the overall sum of fixation results. Quicksand received the most fixations overall for negative affirmations, with Tenor Sans coming in second.

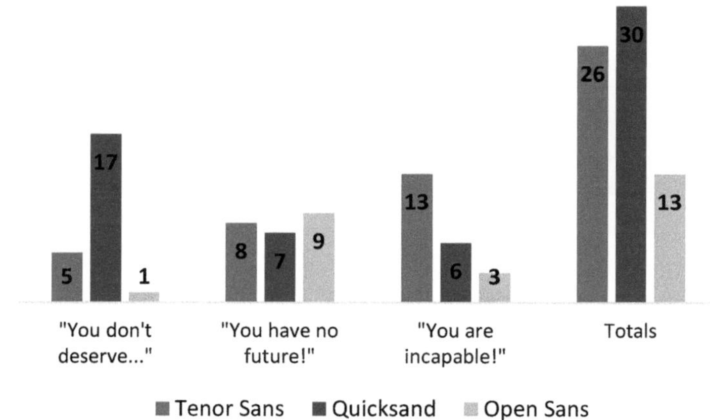

Fig. 6. Total fixations for each typeface across the negative affirmation phrases, and the overall sum of the fixation results.

4 Discussion

This study investigated the impact of three common sans-serif typefaces—Open Sans, Quicksand, and Tenor Sans—on the psychological perception of mental health-related content. Using eye-tracking methodology, we examined how these typefaces influenced visual attention and emotional reception across positive, neutral, and negative phrases.

Our findings revealed a clear trend: Quicksand emerged as the most fixated typeface overall, particularly in positive and neutral contexts (both questions and affirmations). This suggests that the rounded characteristics of Quicksand make it appear more approachable and friendly, a quality that aligns with previous studies indicating that fonts with softer, rounded shapes are perceived as more calm, welcoming and, open [20–23]. This preference for Quicksand across positive and neutral contexts suggests its versatility and potential suitability for conveying a wide range of messages, especially in the context of mental health where approachability and trust are crucial.

Interestingly, while Tenor Sans was inferred to be more closely associated with negative emotions due to its starker, more angular design, it was not the most fixated typeface for negative affirmations. Instead, Quicksand still received the most fixations in this category, although Tenor Sans attracted a notable amount of attention as well.

This result warrants further investigation. It is possible that the inherent negativity of the phrases themselves overshadowed the potential negative connotations of Tenor Sans, leading to a more general focus on the content regardless of the typeface. However, Tenor Sans did show a stronger association with negative questions. This difference between affirmations and questions in the negative context suggests that the interplay between typeface and emotional valence is complex and may be further modulated by sentence structure or pragmatic function [5].

Open Sans, while initially attracting attention in some categories, was generally surpassed by Quicksand in the overall fixation counts. This indicates that while Open Sans may be effective for grabbing initial attention, Quicksand appears more effective at sustaining visual engagement, particularly in emotionally charged contexts [21].

The overall preference for Quicksand across most categories suggests that rounded typefaces may carry a generally positive or at least neutral emotional valence, making them suitable for sensitive topics like mental health[21]. However, it's important to note that the differences in fixations, while statistically significant in some cases, were not drastically large. This suggests that while typeface does influence visual attention, it is likely one of many factors shaping to the overall perception of a message.

5 Conclusion

This study has several limitations. The sample size of 24 participants, while providing valuable insights, limits the generalisability of the findings. Future research should include larger and more diverse samples. Additionally, the study was conducted in a controlled lab environment which may not fully reflect real-world conditions. Future studies could explore these effects in more naturalistic settings, such as on social media platforms. The specific phrases used, while carefully selected, represent only a small sample of possible mental health-related content. Future research could explore a wider range of phrases and sentence structures. Finally, while eye-tracking provides valuable insights into visual attention, it doesn't directly measure emotional experiences.

Nerveless, this study provides valuable insights into the relationship between typeface and the perception of mental health-related content. The findings indicate that typeface choice can influence visual attention and potentially emotional reception. Quicksand's consistent preference across positive and neutral contexts suggests its versatility and potential suitability for communicating sensitive information. While Tenor Sans showed some association with negative contexts, it was not the most preferred typeface for negative affirmations, highlighting the complex interaction between typeface, emotional valence, and sentence structure. Further research is needed to explore these effects in greater depth and to investigate the underlying mechanisms driving these preferences. These findings underscore the importance of considering typography as a key element in digital communication, particularly in contexts where conveying the appropriate emotional tone is crucial, such as in mental health resources and interventions. Future research should explore how typography interacts with the content of the message in more depth, using a broader range of participants and additional variables to understand how typefaces can be strategically used to enhance mental health communication in digital spaces. Future studies also could combine eye-tracking with other measures, such as self-report questionnaires or physiological measures of emotion, to provide a more comprehensive understanding of the emotional impact of typefaces.

Acknowledgments. We would like to express our sincere gratitude to all the participants of this study and to the FCT – Fundação para a Ciência e a Tecnologia, I.P., under the project UIDB/50008/2020, and DOI identifier https://doi.org/10.54499/UIDB/50008/2020 (IT), UIDB/05198/2020, DOI identifier https://doi.org/10.54499/UIDB/05198/2020 (Centro de Investigação e Inovação em Educação, inED), and the R&D Units Project Scope, UIDB/00760/2020 (https://doi.org/10.54499/UIDB/00760/2020).

Disclosure of Interests.   The authors have no competing interests to declare that are relevant to the content of this article.

References

1. Derks, D., Fischer, A. H., Bos, A. E. R.: The role of emotion in computer-mediated communication: A review (2008). https://doi.org/10.1016/j.chb.2007.04.004
2. Brandt, L., Liu, S., Heim, C., Heinz, A.: The effects of social isolation stress and discrimination on mental health (2022). https://doi.org/10.1038/s41398-022-02178-4
3. Juni, S., Gross, J. S.: Emotional and persuasive perception of fonts. Percept Mot Skills **106**(1) 2008. https://doi.org/10.2466/PMS.106.1.35-42
4. Monotype and Neurons: Typography Matters: How science can help you master the art of typeface selection (2021)
5. Amare, N., Manning, A.: Seeing typeface personality: Emotional responses to form as tone. IEEE International Professional Communication Conference (2012). https://doi.org/10.1109/IPCC.2012.6408605
6. Choi, S., Aizawa, K.: Emotype: Expressing emotions by changing typeface in mobile messenger texting. Multimed Tools Appl. **78**(11) (2019). https://doi.org/10.1007/s11042-018-6753-3
7. Thiessen, M., Beier, S., Keage, H.: A Review of the Cognitive Effects of Disfluent Typography on Functional Reading. Des. J. **23**(5), 797–815 (Sep. 2020). https://doi.org/10.1080/14606925.2020.1810434
8. Dyson, M. C.: Where theory meets practice: A critical comparison of research into identifying letters and craft knowledge of type design. Design J. **16**(3) (2013). https://doi.org/10.2752/175630613X13660502571741
9. Kim, S., Jung, A.-R., Kim, Y.: The effects of typefaces on ad effectiveness considering psychological perception and perceived communicator's power. J. Mark. Commun. **27**(7), 716–741 (Oct. 2021). https://doi.org/10.1080/13527266.2020.1765407
10. Teixeira, A. R., Sónia, S., Antunes, M., Espada, S.: Behavioral Differences And Impact Of Lowercase And Uppercase Letters On Reading Performance. In: Proceedings of the 9th World Congress on Electrical Engineering and Computer Systems and Science (2023). https://doi.org/10.11159/mhci23.110
11. Teixeira, A.R., Brito-Costa, S., de Almeida, H.: Optimizing Reading Experience: An Eye Tracking Comparative Analysis of Single-Column, Two-Column, and Three-Column Formats. In: Mori, H., Asahi, Y. (eds.), Human Interface and the Management of Information. HCII 2024. Lecture Notes in Computer Science, vol 14689, pp. 51–59. Springer, Cham (2024). https://doi.org/10.1007/978-3-031-60107-1_5
12. Espada, S., Teixeira, A., Antunes, M., Brito-Costa, S.: Natural and artificial lighting: Influence on readability. Human Dynamics and Design for the Development of Contemporary Societies (2023). https://doi.org/10.54941/ahfe1003538

13. Teixeira, A., Brito-Costa, S., Espada, S., Antunes, M.: Tonal Contrast: Influence of Text Background Color on the Comfort and Time of Reading. In: 5a Euromediterranean Conference for Enviromental Integration, Italy, 2023
14. Teixeira, A. R., Brito-Costa, S., Espada, S., Antunes, M. F.: Brain Computer Interface: Behavioral Differences in the Calmness Level and Reading Time, Considering Screen or Paper, Serif or Sans Serif Typefaces. In: Springer Series in Design and Innovation, vol. 35 (2024). https://doi.org/10.1007/978-3-031-47281-7_3
15. Cuve, H. C., Stojanov, J., Roberts-Gaal, X., Catmur, C., Bird, G.: Validation of Gazepoint low-cost eye-tracking and psychophysiology bundle. Behav. Res. Methods, **54**(2) (2022). https://doi.org/10.3758/s13428-021-01654-x
16. Schall, A., Romano Bergstrom, J.: Introduction to Eye Tracking. In: Eye Tracking in User Experience Design (2014). https://doi.org/10.1016/B978-0-12-408138-3.00001-7
17. Schall, A.: Eye tracking insights into effective navigation design. In: Lecture Notes in Computer Science (including subseries Lecture Notes in Artificial Intelligence and Lecture Notes in Bioinformatics) (2014). https://doi.org/10.1007/978-3-319-07668-3_35.
18. Efeturk, O. A., Turgut, G., Dereshgi, H. A., Yilmaz, A.: A Review of Visual Attention Research Using Eye-Tracking Technologies. Review Paper J. Smart Syst. Res. **3**(2) (2022)
19. Holmqvist, K., Nyström, N., Andersson, R., Dewhurst, R., Jarodzka, H., Van de Weijer, J. (eds.): Eye Tracking: A Comprehensive Guide to Methods and Measures. Oxford University Press, Oxford (2011)
20. Khamula, O., Tymchenko, O., Vasiuta, S., Sosnovska, O., Dorosh, S.: Development of font selection method for text content in immersive technologies. In: ICyberPhyS 2024: 1st International Workshop on Intelligent & CyberPhysical Systems, CEUR Workshop Proceedings,CEUR-WS.org, Khmelnytskyi, Ukraine (2023)
21. Medved, T., Podlesek, A., Možina, K.: Influence of letter shape on readers' emotional experience, reading fluency, and text comprehension and memorisation. Front Psychol, vol. 14, 2023, https://doi.org/10.3389/fpsyg.2023.1107839
22. Hyndman, S.: why fonts matter: a multisensory analysis of typography and its influence from graphic designer and academic Sarah Hyndman (2016)
23. Teixeira, A. R., Brito-Costa, S., de Almeida, H., Espada, S., Antunes, F.: Beyond the Gaze: Decoding Behavioral Dynamics in Sans Serif Fonts Through Eye-Tracking Exploration, pp. 205–219 (2025). https://doi.org/10.1007/978-3-031-76156-0_10

Feature Generalizability in Shallow Layers of CNN and its Applicability to Transfer Learning

Mizuki Dai[1] and Kenya Jin'no[2(✉)]

[1] Graduate School of Integrative Science and Engineering,
Setagaya-ku, Tokyo 1-28-1, Japan
`g2591402@tcu.ac.jp`

[2] Department of Intelligent Systems, Faculty of Information Technology,
Tokyo City University, Setagaya-ku, Tokyo 1-28-1, Japan
`kjinno@tcu.ac.jp`

Abstract. In this study, we focused on changes in feature representations across layers in convolutional neural networks (CNNs) and verified whether shallow layers extract generalizable features that are independent of the training dataset. To quantitatively evaluate the similarity of internal representations between models trained on different datasets, we adopted Centered Kernel Alignment (CKA). The results suggest that features common across different datasets are preserved in shallow layers. Additionally, we explored whether fine-tuning layers with low CKA similarity could improve classification performance in transfer learning. CKA-based layer selection showed some effectiveness, but we were unable to identify a clear threshold. One reason for the inability to identify a clear threshold was the use of CIFAR-10 as the transfer source dataset. In particular, when the weights were fixed, it may have been difficult to obtain sufficient features for effective transfer learning. This study deepens the understanding of CNN internal representations and provides concrete insights for optimizing transfer learning strategies.

Keywords: CNN · representation learning · CKA · feature representations

1 Introduction

In recent years, convolutional neural networks (CNNs) have demonstrated high performance in various visual tasks, including image classification, and are increasingly being put into practical use. On the other hand, the features extracted and transformed within the network remain a black box, and clarifying their understanding and interpretation is a major challenge [1–4]. In particular, transfer learning and fine-tuning, which involve applying pre-trained models to other tasks, are widely used as efficient methods for obtaining high-accuracy

H. Mori et al. (Eds.): HCII 2025, LNCS 16333, pp. 339–348, 2026.
https://doi.org/10.1007/978-3-032-12660-3_25

models. However, no systematic guidelines exist for determining which layers to fix and which to retrain; decisions are often made based on empirical rules [5,6].

In this study, we verify changes in feature representations in each layer of CNNs. In particular, we focus on whether shallow layers extract features common to different datasets. To evaluate this, we use Centered Kernel Alignment (CKA) [7] to quantitatively evaluate the similarity of feature representations in intermediate layers between CNNs trained on different datasets. Furthermore, based on the layer-wise similarity obtained from CKA, we investigate how selecting layers for re-training in transfer learning affects classification accuracy.

2 CKA

In recent years, CKA (Centered Kernel Alignment) has been proposed as a method for quantitatively comparing the internal representations of neural networks [7]. This method demonstrates that models trained with only initial values changed while maintaining the same architecture tend to exhibit high similarity in their representations, particularly in shallow layers. CKA is capable of capturing inter-layer correspondences that were not fully captured by previous methods such as CCA and SVCCA [8], and it is evaluated for its ability to perform robust representation comparisons even when the network initialization or structure differs. In this study, we also use CKA as an indicator to quantitatively evaluate the generality and differences in feature representations between models trained on different datasets.

CKA first centers the Gram matrices obtained from two matrices (layer output feature matrices). Then, it normalizes them and measures their similarity. This similarity is evaluated on a scale of $[0, 1]$, with values closer to 1 indicating greater similarity.

The HSIC (Hilbert-Schmidt Independence Criterion), which forms the basis of this method, is an indicator that measures the independence of two variables. A value close to 0 indicates independence, while a value greater than 0 indicates the existence of some form of dependence. CKA uses HSIC to evaluate the dependence (i.e., relationship or similarity) between two representations and normalizes it using autocorrelation ($\mathrm{HSIC}(K, K)$ and $\mathrm{HSIC}(L, L)$) to construct a scale-independent similarity metric. In other words, CKA is a metric that treats non-independence as similarity, enabling the quantitative capture of relationships between internal representations.

Furthermore, CKA uses a Gram matrix of linear kernels, which makes it robust to basic transformations in feature spaces, such as linear transformations, scaling, and rotation [9]. This makes it suitable for comparisons between models trained with different initial values and between networks with different architectures.

The following is the formulation of CKA. Let $X \in \mathbb{R}^{n \times p}$ and $Y \in \mathbb{R}^{n \times q}$ be p-dimensional and q-dimensional feature representations for n data points, respectively. In this case, CKA based on linear kernels (inner products) is defined as follows:

$$\text{CKA}(X, Y) = \frac{\text{HSIC}(K, L)}{\sqrt{\text{HSIC}(K, K) \cdot \text{HSIC}(L, L)}}, \tag{1}$$

where, $K = XX^\top$ and $L = YY^\top$ are the respective gram matrices, and each matrix is centered as follows:

$$\tilde{K} = HKH, \quad \tilde{L} = HLH, \quad H = I_n - \frac{1}{n}\mathbf{1}\mathbf{1}^\top \tag{2}$$

H is a centering matrix that adjusts the data to a mean of 0. HSIC is defined as follows:

$$\text{HSIC}(K, L) = \text{Tr}(\tilde{K}\tilde{L}) \tag{3}$$

Therefore, CKA can be rewritten as follows:

$$\text{CKA}(X, Y) = \frac{\text{Tr}(HKH \cdot HLH)}{\sqrt{\text{Tr}(HKH \cdot HKH)} \cdot \sqrt{\text{Tr}(HLH \cdot HLH)}} \tag{4}$$

3 Data Set Used and Experimental Design

In this study, we use VGG as an image classification model [10] and evaluate the generalization of feature representations by training on different datasets using a unified architecture. CIFAR-10 [11] is used for training, and transfer learning or fine-tuning is performed on the following three datasets using CIFAR-10 as the baseline model:

- **Oxford-IIIT Pet Dataset** [12]: Images that share similarities with the dog and cat classes included in CIFAR-10
- **Describable Textures Dataset (DTD)** [13]: Texture images that differ greatly from CIFAR-10 in terms of domain
- **Imagenette** [14]: A subset of ImageNet that includes natural images similar to CIFAR-10

These datasets are selected with the assumption of transfer learning for small amounts of data in practical applications, as they all have fewer training images than CIFAR-10. Details of each dataset are shown in Table 1.

In this experiment, we assumed that common features are extracted in shallow layers in models trained on these datasets, and used CKA to evaluate their similarity. This method allows us to verify whether generic features are retained in shallow layers even between models trained on different datasets.

Table 1. Overview of the data set used

Dataset name	Number of classes	Training data	Test data	Image size
CIFAR-10	10	50,000	10,000	32×32
Oxford-IIIT Pet Dataset	37	3,680	3,669	Variable, High Resolution
Describable Textures Dataset (DTD)	47	3,760 (train+val)	1,880	300×300–640×640
Imagenette	10	9,469	3,925	Variable, High Resolution

4 Evaluation of Feature Similarity Using CKA

In this section, we present the results of evaluating the similarity of representations in each layer between a model trained on CIFAR-10 and models trained on other datasets (Oxford-IIIT Pet, DTD, Imagenette) using CKA. Figures 1, 2 and 3 show the CKA similarity heatmaps for the Oxford Pet, DTD, and Imagenette datasets, respectively. These heatmaps indicate which layers share common features, which is important for verifying the usefulness of transfer learning.

In these heat maps, the vertical axis represents the layers of the CIFAR-10 model, and the horizontal axis represents the corresponding layers of the models trained on each dataset. The lower left corresponds to comparisons between shallow layers, and the upper right corresponds to comparisons between deep layers. In all datasets, high CKA similarity (0.9 or higher) was observed in the shallow layers (layers 1–3). The results obtained from these heatmaps suggest that common features are retained in shallow layers, confirming that this approach is likely to be an effective method for transfer learning across different datasets.

As shown in Fig. 1, even in the average pooling layer corresponding to the deep layer in Oxford Pet, the CKA similarity is maintained at approximately 0.5, suggesting that similar classes such as "dog" and "cat," which are also included in CIFAR-10, contribute to the consistency of representation.

On the other hand, in the DTD shown in Fig. 2, the CKA similarity remained around 0.5 until the eighth layer of Conv2D, but then dropped sharply. This

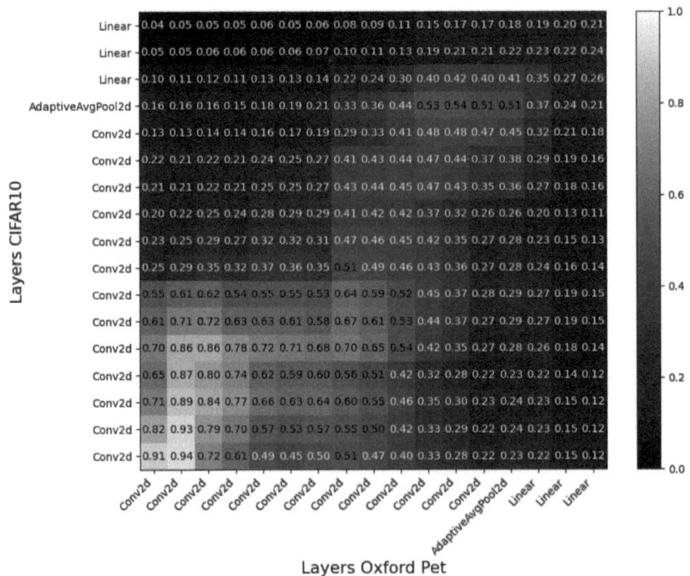

Fig. 1. CKA similarity heat map in Oxford Pet.

suggests that the different domain characteristics of texture images strongly influence deep representations, making transfer difficult [15].

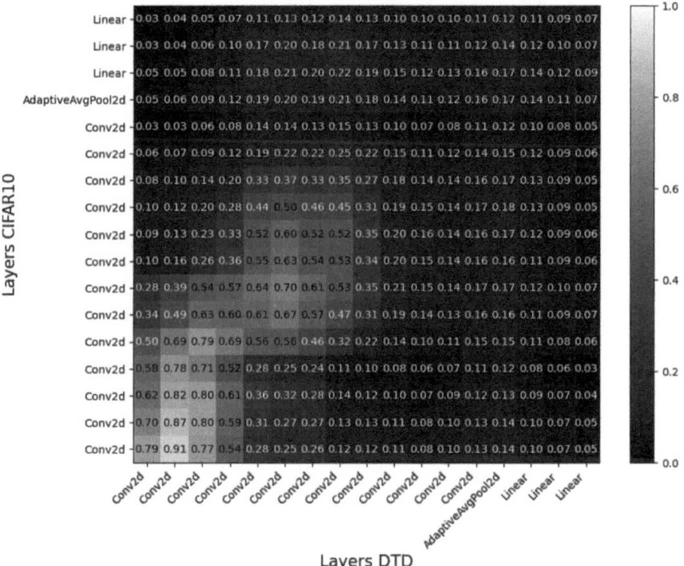

Fig. 2. CKA similarity heat map in DTD.

In Imagenette in Fig. 3, the CKA similarity gradually decreases from shallow to deep layers, but overall, it shows higher similarity than DTD. This is thought to be because both Imagenette and CIFAR-10 handle natural images and have similar domain structures.

5   Verification of Efficient Transfer Learning

In this study, we verified whether classification accuracy could be improved by freezing (frozen) layers with high similarity retained in the CKA heat map (Figs. 1, 2 and 3) and fine-tuning only the subsequent layers. Specifically, we performed transfer learning with a setting where the first N layers were frozen and the remaining layers were trained. Figure 4 shows an example of a structure where the first 8 layers were frozen, and this setting is defined as Frozen layers = 8.

The average and standard deviation of classification accuracy for three different random number seeds are shown in Figs. 5, 6 and 7. The horizontal axis represents the depth of the frozen layer, and "Scratch" on the far right shows the case where the entire model was initialized and trained.

First, across all datasets, Scratch learning achieved the highest classification accuracy, suggesting that the features extracted from CIFAR-10 did not contain

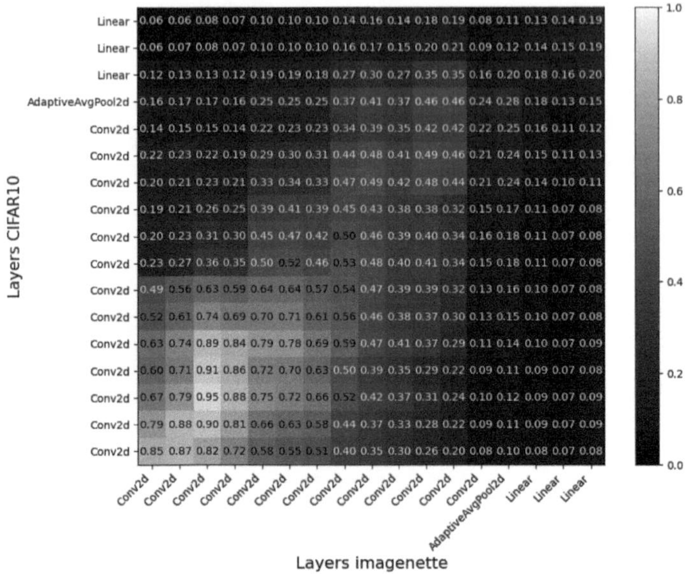

Fig. 3. CKA similarity heat map in Imagenette

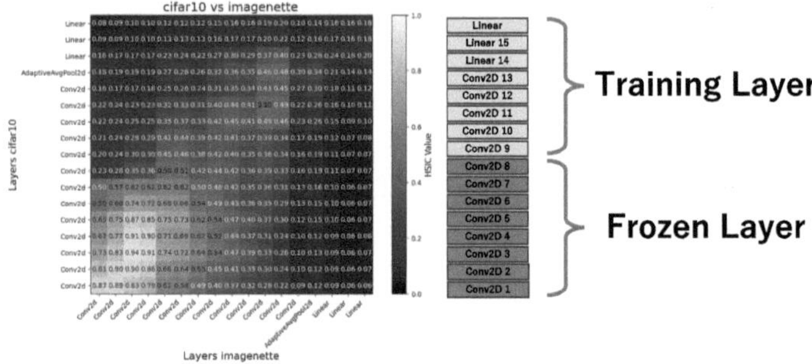

Fig. 4. Network structure when Frozen Layers = 8.

sufficient information for the transfer task. This result indicates that re-training all layers is necessary to maximize the final classification accuracy. However, changes in classification accuracy with respect to the number of frozen layers tended to vary depending on the dataset.

In the Oxford Pet dataset shown in Fig. 5, the highest accuracy was obtained when freezing up to the 10th layer. This is likely because the presence of the "dog" and "cat" classes, which are common to both the CIFAR-10 and Pet datasets, allowed for the reuse of deep features.

In the DTD shown in Fig. 6, freezing the second layer of Conv2D resulted in the highest accuracy, and freezing subsequent layers caused a sharp decline

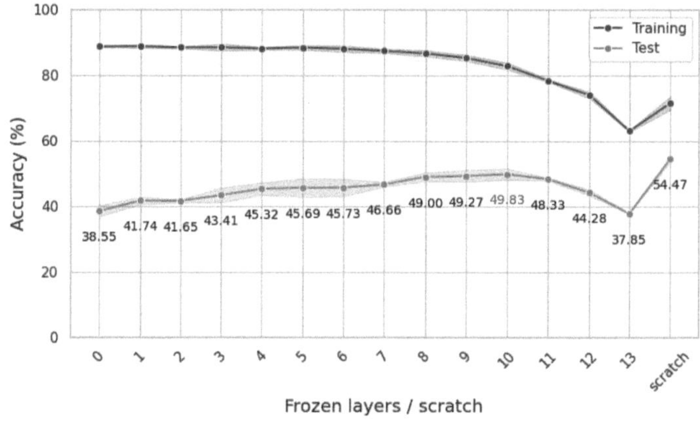

Fig. 5. Classification accuracy for each Frozen Layer in Oxford Pet.

in accuracy. This result indicates that deep features are not suitable for DTDs with significantly different domains, and that re-training is essential.

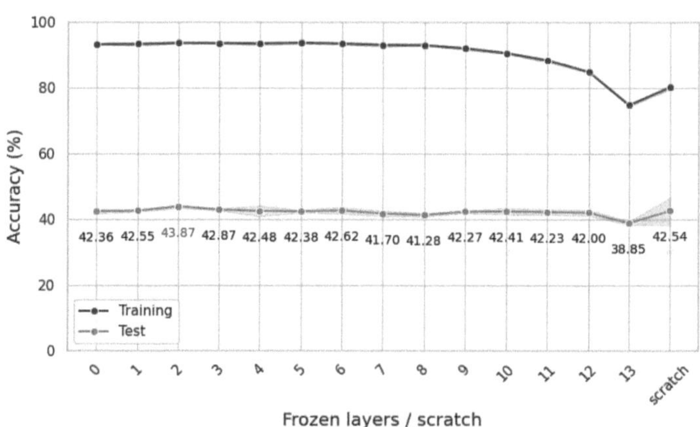

Fig. 6. Classification accuracy for each Frozen Layer in DTD.

In Imagenette in Fig. 7, the classification accuracy was highest when freezing up to the sixth layer. Both Imagenette and CIFAR-10 target natural images, suggesting that features from shallow to intermediate layers are transferable.

The above results indicate that transfer learning is not always effective, and that full-layer re-training is desirable, especially when features derived from the source dataset (CIFAR-10) do not have sufficient generalizability for the target task.

Furthermore, it was difficult to determine the threshold for freezing layers based on CKA similarity. The reasons for this are (1) the limited generalization

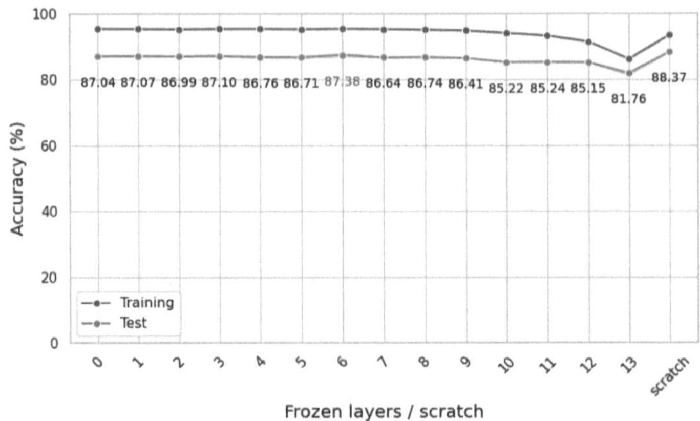

Fig. 7. Classification accuracy for each Frozen Layer in Imagenette.

ability of CIFAR-10 feature representations, (2) experimental scale and condition constraints, and (3) the lack of theoretical basis for determining what constitutes high CKA similarity.

Therefore, careful interpretation is required when using CKA as an indicator for layer selection, and in the future, theoretical justification for threshold settings and the design of more adaptive criteria will be required.

6   Conclusions

In this study, we focused on the generality of feature representations in each layer of CNNs and verified whether shallow layers retain common visual features across different datasets. To this end, we quantitatively evaluated the similarity of intermediate layer representations between models trained on different datasets using Centered Kernel Alignment (CKA).

The results of the experiment suggested that CKA scores were consistently high across all datasets in the shallow layers (layers 1–3), indicating the possibility that data-set-independent general features were extracted. On the other hand, in the deep layers, the similarity between data sets varied greatly, confirming a tendency for domain differences to have a strong influence.

Furthermore, we investigated an effective transfer learning strategy that selects layers with low similarity based on CKA scores as targets for fine-tuning. As a result, we found cases where classification performance improved, suggesting the potential of using CKA as an indicator for layer selection. However, in this study, the expressive power of the CIFAR-10 dataset used as the source dataset was limited, and its features did not have sufficient generalizability for the target task. As a result, full re-training (scratch learning) achieved the highest performance. Additionally, we were unable to establish clear thresholds for effective layer selection, and further research is required to theoretically establish criteria for layer selection based on CKA. Specifically, the introduction of statistical approaches to optimize the effectiveness of transfer learning is considered.

Going forward, it will be necessary to analyze the causal relationship between CKA scores and classification performance [16], introduce statistical methods for threshold determination, and examine the selection criteria for transfer source datasets [17]. Furthermore, it is important to gain more general insights by applying the findings of this study not only to VGG but also to other architectures such as ResNet and Vision Transformer [18]. This study provides valuable insights into CNN representations and offers a foundation for optimizing transfer learning strategies in the future [19].

Acknowledgments. This work was supported by JSPS KAKENHI Grant Numbers JP23K11266, JP23-K28077, and JP24K15115. Part of this work was carried out under the Cooperative Research Project Program of the Research Institute of Electrical Communication, Tohoku University.

References

1. Zeiler, M.D., Fergus, R.: Visualizing and understanding convolutional networks. In: Fleet, D., Pajdla, T., Schiele, B., Tuytelaars, T. (eds.) Computer Vision–ECCV 2014. ECCV 2014. Lecture Notes in Computer Science, vol. 8689. Springer (2014)
2. Selvaraju, R.R., Das, A., Lawrence Zitnick, C., Parikh, D.: Grad-CAM: visual explanations from deep networks via gradient-based localization. In: Proceedings of 2017 IEEE International Conference on Computer Vision (ICCV 2017), pp. 618–626 (2017)
3. Guidotti, R., Monreale, A., Ruggieri, S., Turini, F., Giannotti, F., Pedreschi, D.: A survey of methods for explaining black box models. ACM Comput. Surv. (CSUR) **51**(5), Article No. 93, 1–42 (2018)
4. Zhang, Q., Wu, Y.N., Zhu, S.-C.: Interpretable convolutional neural networks. In: Proceedings of 2018 IEEE/CVF Conference on Computer Vision and Pattern Recognition (CVPR 2018), pp. 8827–8836 (2018)
5. Yosinski, J., Clune, J., Bengio, Y., Lipson, H.: How transferable are features in deep neural networks? In: Proceedings of the 28th International Conference on Neural Information Processing Systems (NIPS2014), vol. 2, pp. 3320–3328 (2014)
6. Panda, A., Panigrahi, D., Mitra, S., Mittal, S., Rahimi, S.,: Transfer learning applied to computer vision problems: survey on current progress, limitations, and opportunities (2024). arXiv:2409.07736
7. Kornblith, S., Norouzi, M., Lee, H., Hinton, G.: Similarity of neural network representations revisited. In: Proceedings of the 36th International Conference on Machine Learning (ICML2019), PMLR 97, pp. 3519–3529 (2019)
8. Raghu, M., Poole, B., Kleinberg, J., Ganguli, S., Sohl-Dickstein, J.: On the expressive power of deep neural networks. In: Proceedings of the 34th International Conference on Machine Learning (ICML2017), PMLR 70, pp. 2847–2854 (2017)
9. Alvarez, S.A.: Gaussian RBF Centered Kernel Alignment (CKA) in the large-bandwidth limit. IEEE Trans. Pattern Anal. Mach. Intell. **45**(5), 6587–6593 (2023)
10. Simonyan, K., Zisserman, A.: Very deep convolutional networks for large-scale image recognition. In: Proceedings of 3rd International Conference on Learning Representations (ICLR 2015), pp. 1–14 (2015)

11. Krizhevsky, A.: Learning multiple layers of features from tiny images. Technical Report, University of Toronto (2009). https://www.cs.toronto.edu/~kriz/learning-features-2009-TR.pdf
12. Parkhi, O.M., Vedaldi, A., Zisserman, A., Jawahar, C.V.: Cats and dogs. In: Proceedings of the IEEE Conference on Computer Vision and Pattern Recognition (CVPR2012), pp. 3498–3505 (2012)
13. Cimpoi, M., Maji, S., Kokkinos, I., Mohamed, S., Vedaldi, A.: Describing textures in the wild. In: Proceedings of the IEEE Conference on Computer Vision and Pattern Recognition (CVPR2014), pp. 3606–3613 (2014)
14. Howard, J., Gugger, S.: Imagenette: a smaller subset of 10 easily classified classes from Imagenet, and a little more (2019). https://github.com/fastai/imagenette
15. Long, M., Cao, Y., Wang, J., Jordan, M.: Learning transferable features with deep adaptation networks. In: Proceedings of the 32nd International Conference on Machine Learning (ICML2015), PMLR 37, pp. 97–105 (2015)
16. Schölkopf, B., Locatello, F., Bauer, S., Rosemary Ke, N., Kalchbrenner, N., Goyal, A., Bengio, Y.: Toward causal representation learning. Proc. IEEE **109**(5), 612–634 (2021)
17. He, K., Zhang, X., Ren, S., Sun, J.: Deep residual learning for image recognition. In: Proceeding of 2016 IEEE Conference on Computer Vision and Pattern Recognition (CVPR2016), pp. 770–778 (2016)
18. Dosovitskiy, A., Beyer, L., Kolesnikov, A., Weissenborn, D., Zhai, X., Unterthiner, T., Dehghani, M., Minderer, M., Heigold, G., Gelly, S., Uszkoreit, J., Houlsby, N.: An image is worth 16x16 words: transformers for image recognition at scale. In: Proceedings of International Conference on Learning Representations (ICLR 2021) (2021)
19. Bengio, Y.: Learning deep architectures for AI. Found. Trends Mach. Learn. **2**(1) (2009)

Effectiveness of the Installation and Operation of the Eye-Movement Assessment and Training System in Special Instructional Classrooms in Elementary School

Yuka Harima[1]([✉]), Kosei Inoue[1], Satoshi Fukumori[2] , Saizo Aoyagi[3] ,
Michiya Yamamoto[1] , Yukie Isaka[4], and Masaki Nishioka[5]

[1] Kwansei Gakuin University, Sanda 669-1330, Hyogo, Japan
gdj45995@kwansei.ac.jp
[2] Kagawa University, Takamatsu 761-0396, Kagawa, Japan
[3] Komazawa University, Setagaya-Ku, Tokyo 154-8525, Japan
[4] Kokufu Elementary School, Izumi 594-0071, Osaka, Japan
[5] Kande Elementary School, Kobe 651-2313, Hyogo, Japan

Abstract. The number of children with learning difficulties is increasing, and foundational visual functions and reading skills can be improved through eye-movement training. We have developed and implemented a PC-based eye-movement training system called Miru-Tore designed for children attending special instructional classrooms, and we have been accumulating data. However, the effectiveness has not yet been clarified. In this study, we measured the eye-movement abilities of all students at an elementary school using Miru-Tore and analyzed 6 months of training data from students in special instructional classrooms. The results showed that their eye-movement abilities tended to improve, approaching those of average students, suggesting the potential of this system as an effective learning support tool.

Keywords: Eye-movement training · Vision therapy · Eye tracker · Learning disabilities

1 Introduction

In recent years, the number of students experiencing learning difficulties has continued to grow. According to a national survey by the Ministry of Education, Culture, Sports, Science and Technology (MEXT), 6.5% of students in public elementary and junior high schools were identified as needing special educational support in 2012. By 2022, this rate had increased to 8.8% [1]. This indicates a growing need for educational support. As part of the support provided to such students, tsuukyuu (hereafter referred to as special instructional classrooms; SICs) have been established. Unlike special support classes, SICs provide educational services for students in regular classrooms who need additional educational support [2]. In order to promote the widespread use of this approach, MEXT

H. Mori et al. (Eds.): HCII 2025, LNCS 16333, pp. 349–362, 2026.
https://doi.org/10.1007/978-3-032-12660-3_26

published guides [3] and best practice examples [4] for teachers in 2020. However, teachers continue to experiment with new approaches, seeking more effective ways to provide support through SICs. As part of these supports, eye-movement training, which plays a crucial role in the visual functions that underpin learning, is expected to help students overcome difficulties in areas such as reading and ball games [5]. In more detail, smoother coordination of the six extraocular muscles in each eye (12 in total) can lead to improved combinations of smooth pursuit and saccadic eye movements. This improvement may help alleviate difficulties in tasks such as reading—which relies heavily on these combined eye movements—and ball games, which require precise binocular coordination.

These issues can be improved through appropriate training, and studies have reported that such training remains effective even for students in junior high school and beyond. However, current methods of eye-movement training are primarily conducted by professionals who have obtained certifications abroad. The methods used often rely on these specialists' individual expertise and know-how, which means that standardization and systematization remain insufficient. Among the commonly used tests in the U.S. is the NSUCO (Northeastern State University College of Optometry Oculomotor Test), but this test is also qualitative in nature and lacks numerical quantification [6, 7].

Based on these backgrounds, the authors developed a PC-based eye-movement assessing and training system (hereafter referred to as Miru-Tore) [8]. This system measures eye movements during training, quantifies eye-movement characteristics based on original developed indices [9], and enables data collection in an online environment. Furthermore, the system has been installed in SICs in an elementary school, allowing students to use it freely while ensuring accurate gaze measurement. In fact, the system is currently used at Kokufu Elementary School in Izumi City, Osaka, Japan, (as shown in Fig. 1), and gaze data collected during its use is stored.

Fig. 1. The measurement in SICs.

However, as stated in the "Vision therapy" entry on Wikipedia [10], the scientific evidence for the effectiveness of eye-movement training remains insufficient. Parsons et al. demonstrated that corrective movements near the target during saccadic eye movements decrease with training. To the best of our knowledge, this is the only report of its kind [11]. In our research, although eye-movement data from students were collected through Miru-Tore, the training's effectiveness has not been clarified, partly because we used our own developed indices [8]. Moreover, considering the effectiveness of the training in an elementary school needs to involve the increase in eye-movement abilities with age, as demonstrated by Fukumori et al. [9]. In other words, to verify the training effect for students with learning difficulties, it is necessary to compare their eye-movement characteristics with those of all elementary school students. Additionally, if eye-movement training is effective, it is important to identify which skills or abilities improve as a result.

In this study, we installed the Miru-Tore in SICs of an elementary school and evaluated its effectiveness. First, to clarify the eye-movement characteristics of elementary school students by grade, we measured the eye-movement characteristics of all students. Based on these results, we then evaluated the Miru-Tore in SICs. Additionally, we selected students with distinctive characteristics, and we discuss the relationship between the effectiveness of the Miru-Tore and their learning difficulties.

2   Our Previous Study and the Approach of This Study

Fukumori et al. developed a system that measures and quantifies eye movements [9]. Using a PC and an eye-tracking device, the system collects gaze and head rotation data to enable quantitative assessment of abnormal eye-movement signs. They defined three assessment indices: *seo* (the deviation between gaze and marker position), *hrr* (the range of head rotation, calculated as the difference between maximum and minimum values), and *hsd* (the frequency of head rotation, represented by its standard deviation). We collected and analyzed data from 33 participants of various ages at Grand Front Osaka. The results showed that all three indices captured age-related development in eye-movement abilities. Additionally, machine-learning–based eye-movement classification using these indices aligned with expert judgments, demonstrating their effectiveness as assessment indices.

However, Fukumori et al. focused on quantifying eye movements and did not address the needs of children with eye-movement difficulties. To fill this gap, Inoue et al. developed Miru-Tore, a system designed for use by individual students attending SICs in elementary schools [8]. This system enables students to independently perform eye-movement assessing and training. To encourage voluntary engagement, we created the custom-designed enclosure (Fig. 1) and incorporated original video content that supports both saccadic and pursuit eye-movement training. The system collects data on gaze, head position, and head rotation through an eye-tracking device and automatically uploads the data to the cloud for storage and analysis. In addition, the system includes a mini-game (Fig. 2) that guides students to maintain the correct head position during gaze measurement. Specifically, the system begins training only when a student keeps their head within the specified area for 7 consecutive seconds, enabling game-like interaction while ensuring high quality data collection.

We applied Miru-Tore in the SIC at Kokufu Elementary School and conducted a 7-week field assessment from January to March 2023. During this period, 31 students voluntarily and consistently used the system, completing a total of 368 training sessions. Regarding gaze tracking accuracy, the system successfully collected over 75% valid gaze data without any assistance from the researchers. Excluding outliers, this rate improved to 81%. These results were comparable to conditions in which we provided instructions

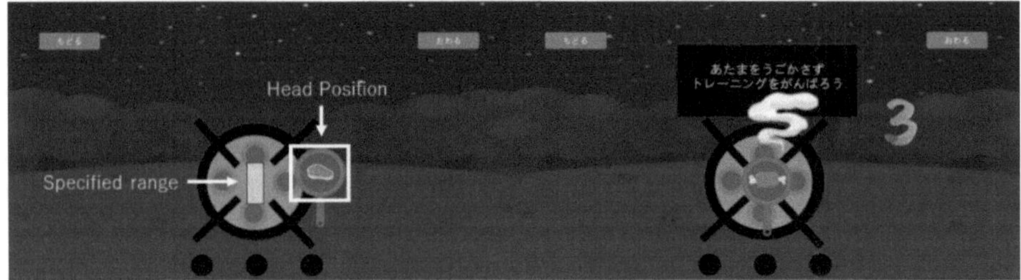

Fig. 2. Examples of mini-games.

or support—93% with both instruction and support and 89% with instruction only—indicating that students were able to use the system independently while maintaining high measurement accuracy (Fig. 3).

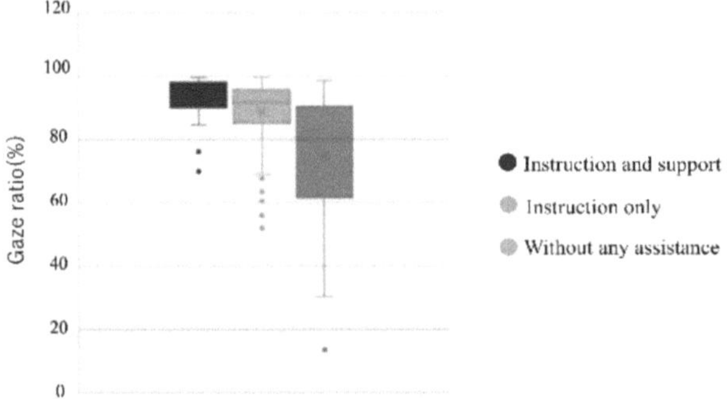

Fig. 3. Measurement results depending on the presence or absence of assistance.

Miru-Tore remained installed in the same SIC from September 2023 to March 2024 and again from May 2024 to March 2025, enabling continuous data collection over an extended period. However, it had not yet been verified whether the training was effective for children who struggle with learning. In the following, first, we measured eye-movement ability in all students, including those with and without difficulties, to collect baseline data by age. Then, we evaluated the effectiveness of the training in SICs by comparing it with the baseline data. Finally, we selected students with particularly notable characteristics for more in-depth analysis and examined the relationship between their learning difficulties and improvements associated with eye-movement.

3 Measurement of Eye-Movement Abilities for All Students in the Elementary School

3.1 Experiment Overview

In June 2024, we conducted an eye-movement ability assessment at Kande Elementary School in Kobe City, Hyogo, Japan with 138 students from grades 1 to 6 (Fig. 4). After excluding six absent students, we collected data from 132 participants, of which 130 were valid for analysis. Given the large number of students, we used Miru-Tore to conduct a standardized assessment that took about 5 min per student. Each student followed a target moving diagonally from the top right to the bottom left of the screen, allowing us to assess both saccadic and pursuit eye movements (Fig. 5). The school principal, as the head of the institution, obtained parental consent for the eye-movement ability measurement experiment.

Fig. 4. The measurement in Kande elementary school.

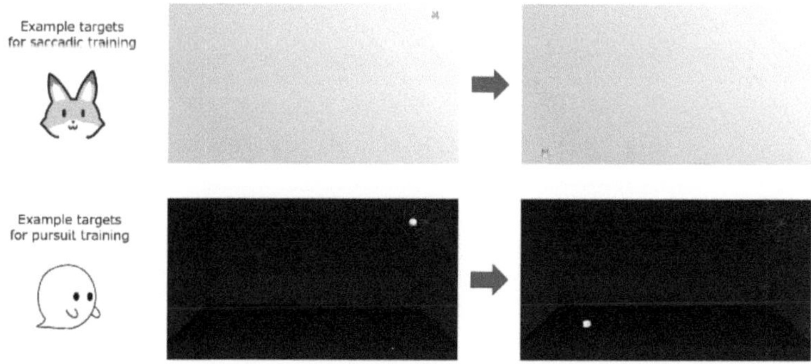

Fig. 5. Examples of the video for eye-movement assessment (top: saccade training, bottom: pursuit training).

3.2 Measurement Results

We calculated the previously developed indices—*seo*, *hrr*, and *hsd*—from the collected data and plotted box-and-whisker diagrams by grade level (Figs. 6, 7 and 8). Each graph includes a blue dotted line for the linear approximation curve, red dots for mean values, and green lines for median values. The blue trend lines show that all three indices decrease as grade level increases. Despite the minimal change in median values, the number of students with low eye-movement ability decreases in higher grades. These results show that eye-movement abilities generally improve as students progress to higher grades.

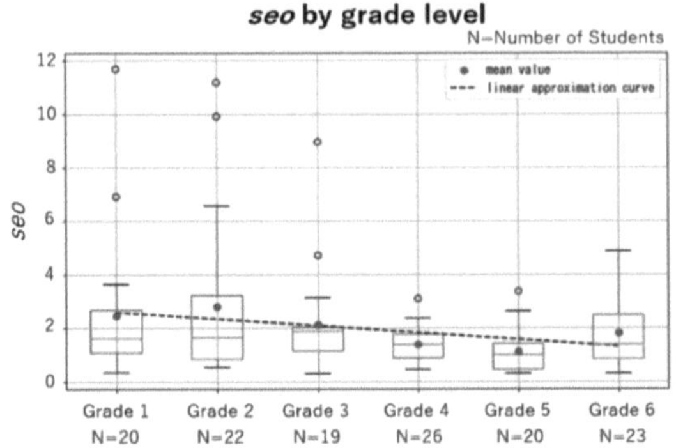

Fig. 6. *Seo* by grade level in elementary school.

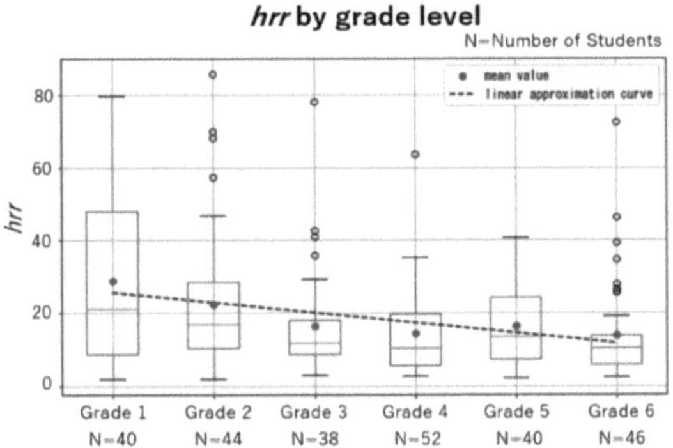

Fig. 7. *Hrr* by grade level in elementary school.

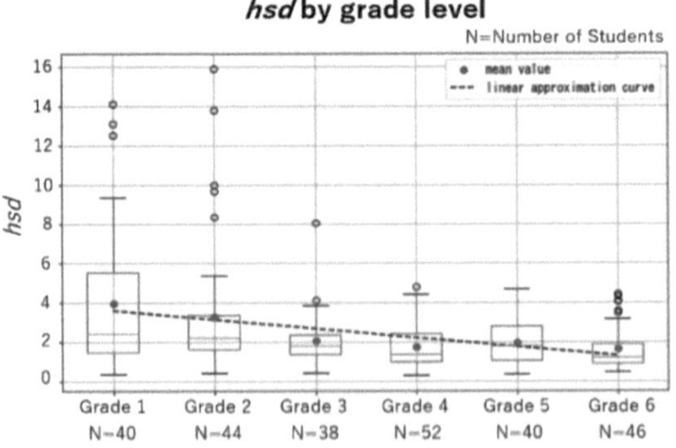

Fig. 8. *Hsd* by grade level in elementary school.

4 Effectiveness Assessment in the Special Instructional Classroom

4.1 Experiment Overview

From October 2023 to December 2024, we applied Miru-Tore in SICs at Kokufu Elementary School and conducted eye-movement measurements with students operating the system themselves (Fig. 1). The study had two phases: October 2023 to March 2024 with lower grades (Grades 1–2) and May to December 2024 with upper grades (Grades 5–6). Each phase spanned a school term, including a long vacation, so we divided the data into pre- and post-holiday periods. A total of 47 lower-grade and 46 upper-grade students participated. The Miru-Tore videos included short training and assessment scenes. The training scene lasted about 1 min and included encouraging messages to keep students engaged (Fig. 9, left). The assessment scene lasted about 30 s and allowed calculation of the previously developed custom indices. We set the fixation target size to 50×50 pixels (roughly 1 degree of visual angle) and had it move back and forth ten times (Fig. 9, right). We did not restrict the type of content, number of sessions, or timing. Students trained freely, encouraging autonomous participation. These SICs also offer self-support activities, including foundational learning, Japanese, and math support from sensory, perceptual, and cognitive perspectives [12]. We used Miru-Tore as part of these activities, and the observed effects reflect this combined support. The SIC's teacher explained the study to students' parents and obtained written consent. We analyzed only anonymized data to protect personal information.

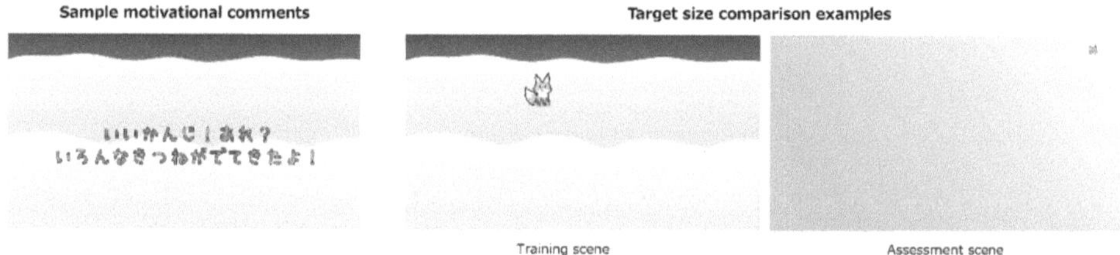

Fig. 9. Video content overview.

We also selected students who used Miru-Tore frequently and consistently—six from the lower grades and nine from the upper grades—to examine the relationship between training and learning difficulties. The SIC's teacher assessed each student's specific tasks, including difficulties with tasks such as dot-to-dot, reading and writing, math, body image, attention, concentration, impulsive movements, rigid thinking, emotional control, social skills, pronunciation, motivation, and self-esteem. The teacher rated each task on a 3-point scale (3 = typical, 2 = somewhat difficult, 1 = difficult) in the first and second halves of the training period. We decided on 13 assessment items based on discussions with the teacher, taking into account common developmental conditions such as LDs (learning disabilities), DCD (developmental coordination disorder), ADHD (attention deficit hyperactivity disorder), and ASD (autism spectrum disorder). Dot-to-dot tasks, in particular, are widely used as assessment tools to evaluate visual processing skills.

4.2 Measurement Results for Lower Grade Students

During the experiment period, we collected 171 data entries from lower-grade students. Out of these, 105 entries involved saccadic eye-movement training tasks. All data were analyzable using the previously developed indices: *seo*, *hrr*, and *hsd*. Figs. 10, 11 and 12 show the monthly results. Each graph includes blue dotted lines for the linear approximation curve, red dots for mean values, green lines for median values, and orange lines representing the mean values by grade level from Kande Elementary School for each index dataset. The blue trend line about *seo* showed a steady improvement in eye-movement ability over time. In October, at the start of training, the mean *seo* was 3.80—higher than the mean of 2.61 for same-grade students in regular classrooms. By March, after about 6 months of training, the mean decreased to 2.34, indicating that these lower-grade students had exceeded the typical performance level of their peers in regular classes.

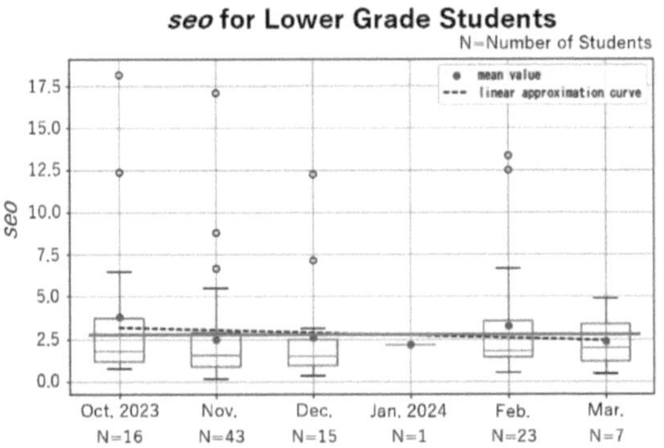

Fig. 10. Transition of *seo* in lower grades.

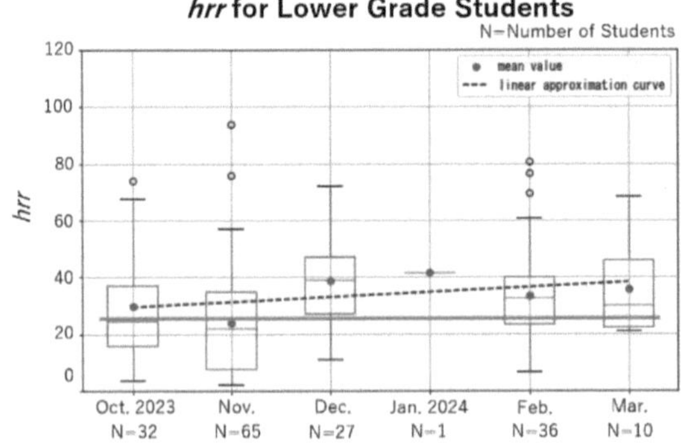

Fig. 11. Transition of *hrr* in lower grades.

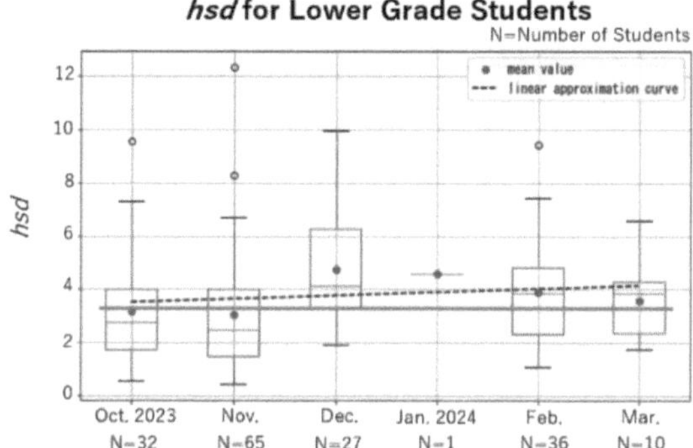

Fig. 12. Transition of *hsd* in lower grades.

The blue trend lines for *hrr* and *hsd*, both related to head movement, showed a slight upward slope, indicating a decline in head stability over time. A closer look at Figs. 11 and 12 reveals that the mean values in October and November 2023 were lower than in other months. This may be due to the fact that the first month of the experimental period showed unusually good results, which could have affected the subsequent trend line. Because *hrr* is calculated based on the difference between the maximum and minimum head rotation angles, the index may not accurately reflect cases in which both values increased or decreased in parallel. Additionally, because students conducted the measurements themselves without assistance in the SIC, their head positions may have gradually shifted during training sessions.

4.3   Measurement Results for Upper Grade Students

During the experiment period, we collected 379 data entries from upper-grade students, including 250 entries involving saccadic eye-movement training tasks. Among these, 143 entries yielded analyzable data for *seo*, the previously developed index. Figs. 13, 14, and 15 show the monthly trends for *seo*, *hrr*, and *hsd*. Each graph includes blue dotted lines for the linear approximation curve, red dots for mean values, green lines for median values, and orange lines representing the mean values by grade level for each index dataset. Focusing on the trend in *seo*, we observed an overall improvement in eye-movement ability. In May, when Miru-Tore was first installed, the mean *seo* was 1.66. In June, when more students judged to need the system began using it, the mean increased to 4.10—higher than the mean of 1.45 for same-grade students in regular classrooms. By December, after more than 7 months of training, the mean had decreased to 1.60, showing a clear trend toward improvement. These results suggest that with consistent training over half a year, students' eye-movement ability approached (and in some cases, matched) that of same-grade students in regular classes.

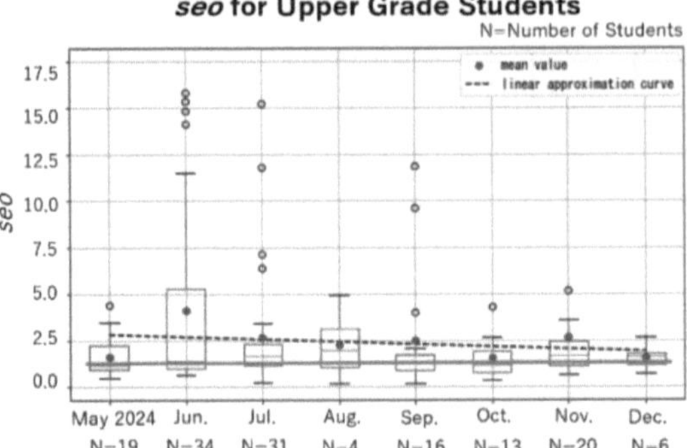

Fig. 13. Transition of *seo* in upper grades.

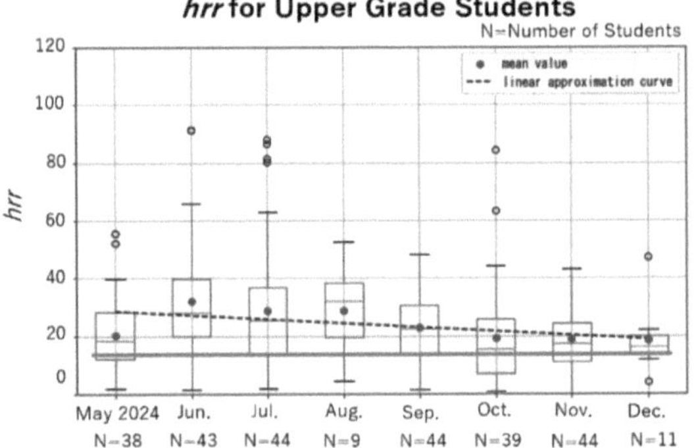

Fig. 14. Transition of *hrr* in upper grades.

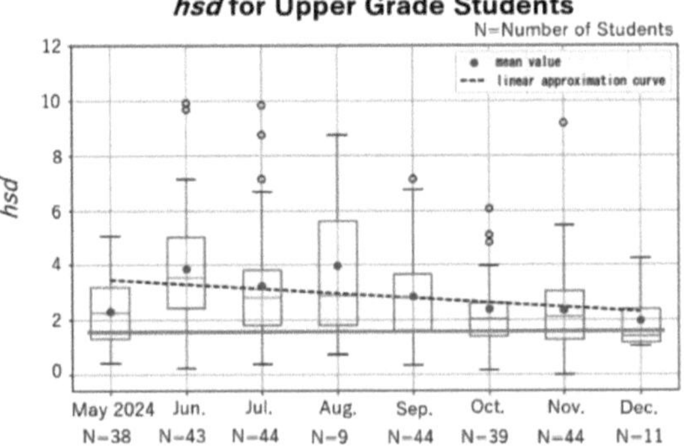

Fig. 15. Transition of *hsd* in upper grades.

Looking at the blue trend lines in *hrr* and *hsd*, we observed improvements in head movement control over time. Similar to *seo*, both indices showed a trend toward the mean values seen in upper-grade students in regular classrooms. When examining the overall data, we found that values in May were relatively good, followed by a sharp increase in June. According to the SIC's teacher, May was spent assessing the students' Miru-Tore using observations and Cog-Tr (cognitive training) [13]. As a result, students identified as needing the system began training in June, which explains the worse results.

4.4 Results of Changes in Learning Difficulties

Table 1 shows the relationship between eye-movement performance, represented by the *seo* index, and the SIC's teacher assessments of students' learning difficulties. First, during the early phase of training for lower-grade students, many assessment items were rated in the 1-point range overall. However, in the later phase of the training, all items were rated in the 2-point range, indicating improvement. Next, during the early phase of training for upper-grade students, scores were low for specific items such as math, concentration, rigid thinking, and self-esteem. However, in the later phase of training, all item scores improved, and the overall mean increased to 2.70. In both cases, the comparison of mean *seo* values between the early and later phases of training indicated improved eye-movement ability, showing a relationship between this improvement and the mitigating of learning difficulties. In previous studies [9], *seo* values tended to decrease to around 1.0 as age increased. However, in the early phase of training, upper-grade students with difficulties showed higher *seo* values than even lower-grade students after training. This suggests that these upper-grade students initially had poorer eye-movement ability compared to the mean or to trained younger students. Nevertheless, this difficulty was resolved after approximately 6 months of training.

Table 1. The mean of eye-movement ability and assessment items.

	Grade	*seo*	Dot-to-dot	Reading and writing	Math	Body image	Attention	Concentration	Impulsive movements	Rigid thinking	Emotional control	Social skills	Pronunciation	Motivation	Self-esteem	Average
Lower grades, early	1.33	5.15	1.50	2.00	2.00	1.50	1.50	1.50	1.83	1.83	1.67	1.33	2.33	2.17	1.33	**1.73**
Lower grades, later	-	2.52	2.17	2.50	2.67	2.33	2.17	2.33	2.33	2.33	2.33	2.33	2.67	2.83	2.00	**2.38**
Upper grades, early	5.44	3.04	2.11	2.22	1.56	1.89	1.89	1.89	3.00	1.78	2.89	2.22	3.00	2.22	1.22	**2.15**
Upper grades, later	-	2.17	2.67	2.44	2.22	2.67	2.67	2.78	3.00	2.00	3.00	2.89	3.00	2.89	2.89	**2.70**

4.5   Individual Case Analyses in Eye-Movement Performance

Individual data show that Student A, a first-grade student attending the SIC, showed a sudden increase in *seo* values at the end of 2023 (Fig. 16). According to the SIC's teacher, the student experienced a relapse of a tic disorder during this period, which likely caused an increase in eye-movement errors. In the early phase of training (second term of the 2023 school year), the student received the lowest rating (1) in all assessment items—dot-to-dot, body image, attention, concentration, impulsive movements, motivation, and self-esteem. By the later phase, motivation improved to a score of 3, and all other items increased to 2. However, during the time of the *seo* spike, the student reportedly had health issues that made it difficult to maintain posture and concentration. These observations showed that temporary health conditions and decreased concentration can influence gaze behavior and *seo* values, highlighting the potential of these indices to reflect such internal states.

Student B, a sixth-grade student in the SIC, showed consistent improvement in *seo* values with each training session (Fig. 17). Between the early and later phase of the 2024 school year, their assessment scores for reading and writing and body image increased from 1 to 2. This trend showed a possible relationship between improved eye-movement control and reduced difficulties in reading and writing as well as body image.

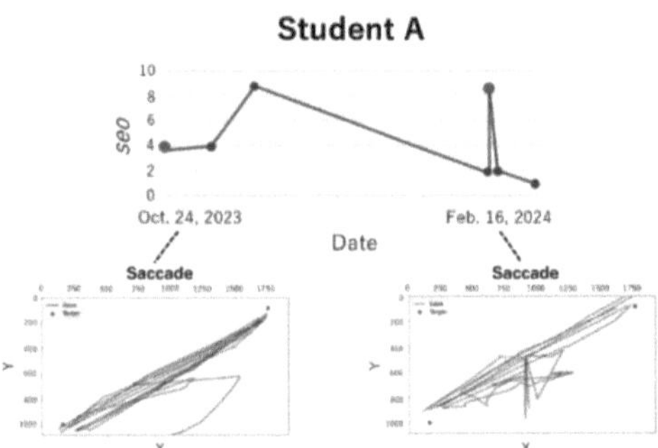

Fig. 16.   The transition and average of *seo* values for student A.

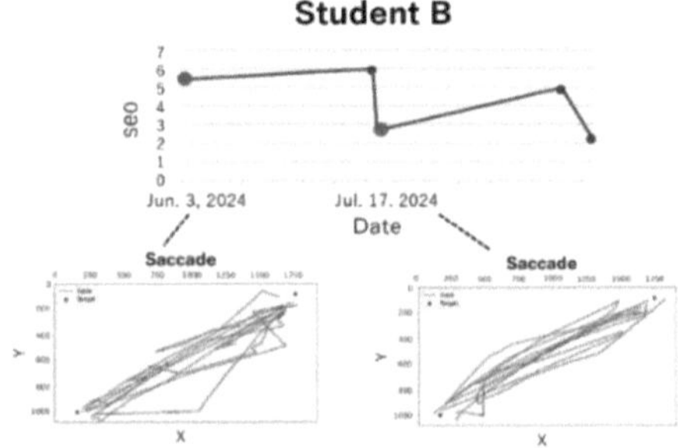

Fig. 17.   The transition and average of *seo* values for student B.

5 Conclusion

In this study, we applied and evaluated an eye-movement training system (Miru-Tore) in SICs at elementary school. First, we measured eye-movement abilities across all students in the elementary school to establish baseline developmental data, including average values by grade level. Then, we installed the training system in SICs and conducted approximately 6 months of training with both lower- and upper-grade students. As a result, students showed relief in difficulties of eye-movement, and their abilities became comparable to those of the mean for same-grade students. Individual case analyses further suggested that improvements in eye-movement were linked to mitigated learning difficulties. Although the number of participants was limited, the findings provide objective evidence for the effectiveness of eye-movement training. These results point to the potential for broader adoption of evidence-based eye-movement assessments and training programs in educational settings.

Acknowledgment. This research was supported in part by JSPS Grants-in-Aid for Scientific Research 23KK0187, 25K03170 and other grants. We thank them for their support.

References

1. Ministry of Education, Culture, Sports, Science and Technology (MEXT), Department of Special Needs Education, Elementary and Secondary Education Bureau: *Survey Results on Students Requiring Special Educational Support Enrolled in Regular Classes*, MEXT (online). https://www.mext.go.jp/content/20230524-mext-tokubetu01-000026255_01.pdf. Accessed 25. Apr. 2025 (in Japanese)
2. National Institute of Special Needs Education (NISE): *Research on Specialized Support for Individuals with Developmental Disabilities with a Focus on Connection to Society*, NISE (online), https://www.nise.go.jp/nc/report_material/research_results_publications/spe cialized_research/b-372. Accessed 25. Apr. 2025 (in Japanese)
3. Ministry of Education, Culture, Sports, Science and Technology (MEXT), Department of Special Needs Education, Elementary and Secondary Education Bureau: *A Guide for Teachers New to Providing Resource Room Instruction*, MEXT (online). https://www.mext.go.jp/tsu kyu-guide/common/pdf/passing_guide_02.pdf. Accessed 25. Apr. 2025 (in Japanese)
4. Ministry of Education, Culture, Sports, Science and Technology (MEXT), Department of Special Needs Education, Elementary and Secondary Education Bureau: *Casebook of Practical Examples from the Project to Enhance the Expertise of Teachers Providing Resource Room Instruction for Students with Developmental Disabilities*, MEXT (online). https://www.mext.go.jp/a_menu/shotou/tokubetu/main/006/h29/1421549.htm. Accessed 25. Apr. 2025 (in Japanese)
5. Kitade, K.: Vision training that makes learning and exercise fun for children with developmental concerns, Natsumesha (2015) (in Japanese)
6. Maples, C.W., Atchley, J., Ficklin, T.: Northearthtern state university college of optometry's oculomotor norms. J. Behav. Optom. **6**(3), 143–150 (1992)
7. Lesnik, H., Poborc-Godlewska, J.: The relationship between ciliary muscle fatigue and the type of artificial light used to illuminate the area of visual work. Polish journal of occupational medicine and enviromental health **6**(3), 287–292 (1993)

8. Inoue, K., Aoyagi, S., Fukumori, S., Yamamoto, M., Isaka, Y., Kitade, K.: Proposal for an Eye-movement Training System That Can Be Used Alone by Students in a Special Instructional Classroom. The Transactions of Human Interface Society **26**(3), 289–300 (2024) (in Japanese)
9. Fukumori, S., Kita, R., Aoyagi, S., Yamamoto, M., Kitade, K.: Development of Assessment Indices for an Eye-movement Test and Vision Training. The Transactions of Human Interface Society **24**(2), 121–132 (2022) (in Japanese)
10. The Free Encyclopedia Wikipedia: Vision therapy, The Free Encyclopedia Wikipedia(online). https://en.wikipedia.org/wiki/Vision_therapy. Accessed 25. Apr. 2025
11. Parsons, D.B., Ivry, B.R.: Rapid alternating saccade training. In: Proceedings of the 2018 ACM symposium on eye tracking research and applications (ETRA'18), No. 30, pp. 1–5 (2018)
12. Isaka, Y.: Gakushu-support book for children with learning difficulties. Meiji Books (2024) (in Japanese)
13. Ohta, S.: Practical Research on Cognitive Training aimed at tailoring support to each student (I), Journal of the Faculty of International Studies of Culture, Kyusyu Sangyo University, No.83, pp.69–82 (2024) (in Japanese)

Pose Estimation and LSTM-Based Autism Spectrum Disorder Diagnosis from Eating Behavior Video

Haomiao He, Kazuyo Nakaoka, and Ryosuke Saga

Osaka Metropolitan University, 1-1 Gakuen-cho, Sakai, Osaka, Japan
{nakaoka,r.saga}@omu.ac.jp

Abstract. This study investigates the automatic classification of developmental disorders in children based on pose estimation and Long Short-Term Memory (LSTM) model. The dataset consists of 223 videos of children diagnosed with developmental disorders according to DSM-5 criteria and 50 videos of typically developing children. All videos depict eating behavior, from which the hand joint coordinates were extracted as time-series features. To address class imbalance, the Synthetic Minority Oversampling Technique (SMOTE) was applied. Using the Keras library, the LSTM model was trained with various window sizes (10 to 400). The best classification accuracy (79%) was achieved with a window size of 40, suggesting the model effectively captured short-term temporal patterns. Accuracy declined with window sizes over 100, indicating the model's limitation in handling long-term dependencies. Misclassification mostly occurred in typically developing children, likely due to age-related variability in movement. These findings demonstrate the potential of LSTM-based modeling as a quantitative tool for developmental state assessment based on behavioral patterns.

Keywords: Autism Spectrum Disorder Diagnosis · Eating Behavior · Machine Learning · Deep Learning · LSTM · Pose Estimation

1 Introduction

Neurodevelopmental disorders are conditions characterized by atypical brain development and function, often leading to difficulties in social adaptation due to mismatches with environmental and interpersonal expectations [3]. These disorders include autism spectrum disorder (ASD), attention-deficit/hyperactivity disorder (ADHD), and intellectual disability. Diagnostic assessments typically involve developmental and intelligence testing to objectively evaluate the characteristics and difficulties associated with each case [14]. Symptoms of neurodevelopmental disorders usually emerge during the developmental period (ages 0–18), and early diagnosis followed by appropriate intervention can significantly improve quality of life [27].

H. Mori et al. (Eds.): HCII 2025, LNCS 16333, pp. 363–372, 2026.
https://doi.org/10.1007/978-3-032-12660-3_27

Clinical diagnoses are generally based on behavioral observations, interviews with caregivers or the individuals themselves, and standardized testing, using criteria established in the DSM-5 [3] or ICD-11 [23]. Behavioral characteristics play a particularly important role in identifying children with developmental disorders [22]. However, conventional diagnostic approaches are labor-intensive and time-consuming, and impose a significant burden on clinicians and researchers due to the necessity of detailed observation and manual recording. Moreover, these methods often rely heavily on subjective judgments, which raises concerns about diagnostic accuracy [5].

Children with neurodevelopmental disorders are known to exhibit unique behavioral traits in various aspects of daily life, including eating behavior [4,7]. Eating behavior is relatively easy to observe and document due to its everyday nature, making it a promising target for objective behavioral assessment. Although numerous studies have explored children's eating behavior, few have directly compared children with developmental disorders and typically developing (TD) peers.

In one study, Nakaoka et al. [15,16] developed an eating behavior questionnaire aimed at classifying children with ASD and TD children. While their approach showed promise, it was limited by the inherent subjectivity of caregiver-reported data. Thus, there is a growing need for more objective, automated diagnostic methods.

In response to this need, this study explores the use of machine learning—a method gaining increasing attention in the medical field—for the objective classification of eating behaviors in children with ASD. Specifically, we analyze video-recorded eating behavior using a combination of deep learning-based pose estimation and machine learning models. This approach enables the extraction of joint-level hand movement data from videos, thereby capturing non-verbal behavioral features that are difficult to verbalize but potentially informative for diagnosis [6,20]. By combining pose data with machine learning, we aim to develop a diagnostic tool capable of distinguishing children with ASD from TD peers based on objectively measured eating behavior.

2   Related Work

Numerous studies have explored the application of machine learning (ML) techniques for the diagnosis of neurodevelopmental disorders, particularly autism spectrum disorder (ASD). Comprehensive reviews have summarized these approaches, highlighting the diversity of ML methods and features utilized in ASD diagnosis.

Parikh et al. employed ML models using personal characteristic data (PCD), including age, sex, handedness, and three IQ measures, extracted from the Autism Brain Imaging Data Exchange (ABIDE) database. Their study demonstrated that optimized ML models could effectively classify individuals with ASD [17].

Zhu et al. developed ML classifiers to distinguish between patients with chronic schizophrenia (ChSZ), first-episode psychosis (FEP), ultra-high risk

(UHR) for psychosis, ASD, and healthy controls (HC) using structural MRI data. Their support vector machine (SVM) models achieved notable classification performance across these groups [26].

Alateyat et al. investigated the predictive relationship between sensory processing patterns and behavioral problems in children with ASD. Utilizing the Sensory Profile 2 (SP2) and the Child Behavior Checklist (CBCL), they applied various ML regression models to predict behavioral outcomes based on sensory processing scores [2].

Zhao et al. focused on oculomotor behavior, employing eye-tracking data to classify children with ASD and typically developing (TD) peers. Their ML approach demonstrated high accuracy in distinguishing between the two groups based on eye movement patterns [25].

Recent studies have also explored the use of home video analysis for ASD detection. For instance, Abbas et al. utilized ML models to analyze facial expressions, vocalizations, and gaze behaviors from home videos, achieving promising classification results [1].

Wu et al. presented an ML-based approach for early ASD diagnosis by analyzing specific behaviors from videos of infants aged 6 to 36 months. The behaviors of interest included directed gaze towards faces or objects, positive affect, and vocalization. Their two-stage framework involved deep learning models for automatic behavior identification and subsequent ASD diagnosis prediction, achieving an accuracy of 82% [24].

Despite these advancements, research focusing on eating behaviors as a diagnostic feature for ASD remains limited. To our knowledge, no studies have specifically targeted the analysis of eating behaviors using visual information and pose estimation techniques for ASD classification. As a similar research, Kojovic et al. uses pose estimation for ASD diagnosis [13] but their paper doesn't focus on eating behavior.

This study aims to bridge this gap by leveraging pose estimation to extract hand joint information during eating activities, subsequently applying ML models to classify children with ASD and TD peers based on their eating behaviors. This approach offers a novel perspective by focusing on a daily activity that is relatively easy to observe and record, potentially facilitating more accessible and objective diagnostic methods.

3   LSTM-Based Classification of ASD Using Pose Estimation Technology

3.1   Overview

This study aims to classify children with developmental disorders by integrating pose estimation techniques with a machine learning model. The data used in this study are videos of children during mealtime. Frames are extracted from these videos, and pose estimation is applied. Specifically, the focus is on the hands of typically developing children and children with ASD. From each frame, 21 key points (x, y coordinates) of the hand are extracted. These coordinates are then organized frame by frame, and a binary classification experiment is conducted to determine whether the child has ASD.

For the machine learning model, we use Long Short-Term Memory (LSTM), which is well-suited for handling time-series data. This enables us to consider behavioral flows during mealtime as input.

3.2 Pose Estimation

Pose estimation is a technique for estimating the posture and joint positions of human bodies from images or videos. It is widely used in fields such as medicine, sports, and security. The process involves marking joint positions within video datasets, training a model with annotated data, and minimizing loss until accurate predictions can be made.

In this study, we use MMpose [11], an open-source pose estimation library based on PyTorch. Specifically, we apply its 2D hand pose estimation algorithm to extract hand coordinates from videos. This top-down algorithm first detects the hands globally and then identifies 21 joint points for each detected hand shown in Fig. 1.

Point1_x	Point1_y	⋯	Point21_x	Point21_y
362.102	529.347	⋯	234.756	544.329
455.275	485.273	⋯	239.475	540.606
456.457	329.954	⋯	243.797	507.994
⋯	⋯	⋯	⋯	⋯

Fig. 1. Pose estimation and extracted coordinates

3.3 Long Short-Term Memory

This study employs an LSTM model [12], a type of recurrent neural network (RNN) widely used in deep learning for time-series data. Unlike traditional RNNs, LSTMs are equipped with memory cells and gating mechanisms–input, forget, and output gates–that help maintain long-term dependencies and selectively forget irrelevant information.

Below are the key equations for the LSTM:

$$i_t = \sigma(W_i \cdot [h_{t-1}, x_t] + b_i) \tag{1}$$

$$\tilde{C}_t = \tanh(W_C \cdot [h_{t-1}, x_t] + b_C) \tag{2}$$

$$f_t = \sigma(W_f \cdot [h_{t-1}, x_t] + b_f) \tag{3}$$

$$C_t = f_t * C_{t-1} + i_t * \tilde{C}_t \tag{4}$$

$$o_t = \sigma(W_o \cdot [h_{t-1}, x_t] + b_o) \tag{5}$$

$$h_t = o_t * \tanh(C_t) \tag{6}$$

These equations define the internal operations of an LSTM cell at time step t:

- Equation (1): i_t is the input gate, which determines how much of the new input x_t and previous hidden state h_{t-1} should be used to update the cell state. The sigmoid function σ squashes the values between 0 and 1 to control the update proportion.
- Equation (2): $\tilde{C}_t$ is the candidate cell state, representing new potential information to be added to the memory. It uses the hyperbolic tangent function tanh to keep values between -1 and 1.
- Equation (3): f_t is the forget gate, which decides how much of the previous cell state C_{t-1} should be retained. This gate is crucial for removing irrelevant information from memory.
- Equation (4): C_t is the updated cell state. It is a combination of the retained old state and the newly computed candidate state, weighted by the input and forget gates.
- Equation (5): o_t is the output gate, determining how much of the cell state contributes to the new hidden state.
- Equation (6): h_t is the new hidden state output by the LSTM cell, which is used for further time steps or passed to downstream layers.

These gating mechanisms allow the LSTM to manage long- and short-term dependencies effectively, making it suitable for sequential data such as behavioral or medical time-series [9, 18].

3.4 Architecture

The architecture in this study consists of one input layer, two LSTM layers with dropout and softmax for classification. A window size in the LSTM layers is set to capture temporal context, sliding one frame at a time. For example, with a window size of 10, the input sequences are [frames 1–10], [frames 2–11], etc. Each frame has 42 features (21 joints × x, y), so the input shape becomes ($window\_size$, 42). After the input layer, the data passes to two LSTM layers with 50 units, and dropout layers [19] added to prevent overfitting. A final output layer uses the sigmoid activation function for binary classification.

4 Experiments

4.1 Goal and Dataset

To evaluate the effectiveness of binary classification using LSTM, we conducted experiments. The dataset consisted of 223 videos of children diagnosed with developmental disorders and 50 videos of typically developing children. Although it is not immediately clear from the videos whether the children have developmental disorders, all diagnoses were made cautiously by medical professionals based on DSM-5 criteria.

The dataset was split into training and testing sets at a ratio of 8:2. To prevent data leakage during training, no data from the same video was included in both the training and test sets. Since the number of typically developing videos was smaller than that of diagnosed ones, it was necessary to address class imbalance during training. For this purpose, we used the SMOTE method [8], which generates synthetic data based on existing samples. Specifically, SMOTE selects a random data point and then randomly selects one of its nearest neighbors to generate a new data point between them.

The LSTM model was implemented using the Keras library [10], with window sizes of 10, 20, 30, 40, 80, 100, and 200. The Adam optimizer was used, with binary cross-entropy as the loss function. The model was trained over 100 epochs with a batch size of 32, and a dropout rate of 0.5 was applied.

As evaluation metrics, we used the precision, recall, F1 Score, and accuracy. Precision is defined as the proportion of true positives (TP) among all predicted positives (TP + FP):

$$\text{Precision} = \frac{TP}{TP + FP} \tag{7}$$

A high precision indicates fewer false positives. Recall is the proportion of true positives among all actual positives (TP + FN):

$$\text{Recall} = \frac{TP}{TP + FN} \tag{8}$$

A high recall means the model successfully identifies most actual positive samples. F1 Score is the harmonic mean of precision and recall:

$$\text{F1} = 2 \times \frac{\text{Precision} \times \text{Recall}}{\text{Precision} + \text{Recall}} \tag{9}$$

A high F1 score indicates balanced performance. Accuracy is the proportion of correctly predicted samples (TP + TN) among all predictions:

$$\text{Accuracy} = \frac{TP + TN}{TP + TN + FP + FN} \tag{10}$$

In this experiment, the performance of LSTM is evaluated as follows.For example, assume that there is test data for a video with 100 frames and that Window size is 10. Then, based on Windows size, we get 91 sequences: frame 1 to frame 10, frame 2 to frame 11, and so on. Each sequence is input to a trained LSTM, and the LSTM predicts the presence or absence of a developmental disorder and outputs the result. The predicted labels, i.e., whether there is a developmental disorder or not, are compared with the actual labels, i.e., whether there is actually a developmental disorder or not, and evaluation metrics such as Precision, Accuracy, Recall, and F1 score are calculated.

4.2 Results

The Table 1 shows the experimental result by LSTM. The experimental result demonstrated that LSTM can successfully classify children with developmental

Table 1. The experiment result by LSTM classification

Window size	Class	Precision	Recall	F1-score	Accuracy
10	Normal	0.57	0.52	0.54	0.77
	Diagnosed	0.83	0.86	0.84	
20	Normal	0.61	0.53	0.57	0.78
	Diagnosed	0.84	0.88	0.86	
30	Normal	0.56	0.5	0.53	0.76
	Diagnosed	0.82	0.85	0.84	
40	Normal	0.62	0.53	0.57	0.79
	Diagnosed	0.83	0.88	0.86	
80	Normal	0.53	0.48	0.5	0.74
	Diagnosed	0.81	0.84	0.83	
100	Normal	0.58	0.52	0.55	0.77
	Diagnosed	0.83	0.86	0.84	
200	Normal	0.56	0.46	0.51	0.75
	Diagnosed	0.8	0.86	0.83	
400	Normal	0.39	0.83	0.53	0.55
	Diagnosed	0.86	0.44	0.58	

disorders and typically developing children. All models tended to show higher classification accuracy for children with developmental disorders. Among the eight window sizes tested, the highest accuracy (79%) was achieved with a window size of 40. In contrast, window sizes exceeding 100 time steps led to a significant drop in classification performance. This is likely due to weakening correlations over longer sequences, suggesting that alternative models such as Transformers [21] may enhance performance.

The error analysis revealed that 59% of the misclassified samples were typically developing children wrongly predicted as having developmental disorders. This may be due to younger children's irregular hand movements during meals, which could have been misinterpreted by the LSTM model as indicative of developmental issues.

Increasing the dataset of typically developing children may improve classification performance for that class. Additionally, tracking children's developmental stages over time may allow us to quantify their developmental progress. In this study, only the x- and y-coordinates of hand movements were used. Including z-coordinates and thus leveraging three-dimensional features may further improve classification accuracy.

5   Conclusion

This study demonstrated that classifying developmental disorders in children using LSTM models based on movement data is feasible and effective. The model achieved its highest performance with a window size of 40, supporting the hypothesis that short-term temporal features are critical for distinguishing behavioral patterns. However, performance significantly declined with window sizes over 100, highlighting LSTM's limitations in capturing long-range dependencies. Additionally, the model exhibited a high rate of false positives for typically developing children, possibly due to age-specific motor variability. To address these challenges, future work should include expanding the dataset for typically developing children, incorporating three-dimensional features (including z-coordinates), and adjusting models based on developmental stages. Further directions include exploring Transformer-based architectures for improved sequence modeling, evaluating generalizability across different behavioral contexts, and validating model reliability for clinical applications. Taken together, this study marks a meaningful step toward developing an objective support tool for developmental assessment based on motion analysis.

Acknowledgments. We appreciate the children and their parents who provided video data. Also, this study was supported by the FY2020 RESPECT Collaborative Research Grant from the Women Researchers Support Office of Osaka Metropolitan University.

References

1. Abbas, H., et al.: Mobile detection of autism through machine learning on home video: a development and prospective validation study. PLoS Med. **15**(11), e1002705 (2018). https://doi.org/10.1371/journal.pmed.1002705
2. Alateyat, H., Cruz, S., Cernadas, E., Tubío-Fungueiriño, M., Sampaio, A., González-Villar, A., Carracedo, A., Fernández-Delgado, M., Fernández-Prieto, M.: A machine learning approach in autism spectrum disorders: from sensory processing to behavior problems. Front. Mol. Neurosci. **15**, (2022)
3. Association, A.P.: Diagnostic and Statistical Manual of Mental Disorders, 5th edn. American Psychiatric Publishing, Arlington, VA (2013)
4. Bandini, L.G., Anderson, S.E., Curtin, C., et al.: Food selectivity in children with autism spectrum disorders and typically developing children. J. Pediatr. **157**(2), 259–264 (2010). https://doi.org/10.1016/j.jpeds.2010.02.013
5. Bone, D., Lee, C.C., Williams, M., et al.: The psychologist as an interlocutor in autism spectrum disorder assessment: insights from a study of spontaneous prosody. J. Speech Lang. Hear. Res. **57**(4), 1162–1177 (2014). https://doi.org/10.1044/2014_JSLHR-S-13-0062
6. Cao, Z., Hidalgo, G., Simon, T., Wei, S.E., Sheikh, Y.: Openpose: Realtime multi-person 2d pose estimation using part affinity fields. IEEE Trans. Pattern Anal. Mach. Intell. **43**(1), 172–186 (2021). https://doi.org/10.1109/TPAMI.2019.2929257
7. Cermak, S.A., Curtin, C., Bandini, L.G.: Food selectivity and sensory sensitivity in children with autism spectrum disorders. J. Am. Diet. Assoc. **110**(2), 238–246 (2010). https://doi.org/10.1016/j.jada.2009.10.032
8. Chawla, N.V., Bowyer, K.W., Hall, L.O., Kegelmeyer, W.P.: Smote: synthetic minority over-sampling technique. J. Artif. Intell. Res. **16**, 321–357 (2002)

9. Chen, L., Zhang, W.: Action recognition with LSTM networks on video sequences. IEEE Trans. Multimed. **22**(8), 1955–1965 (2020)
10. Chollet, F., et al.: Keras. https://github.com/keras-team/keras (2015)
11. Contributors, M.: Openmmlab pose estimation toolbox and benchmark. GitHub Repository. https://github.com/open-mmlab/mmpose (2020)
12. Hochreiter, S., Schmidhuber, J.: Long short-term memory. Neural Comput. **9**(8), 1735–1780 (1997)
13. Kojovic, N., Natraj, S., Mohanty, S.P., Maillart, T., Schaer, M.: Using 2D video-based pose estimation for automated prediction of autism spectrum disorders in young children. Sci. Rep. **11**(1), 15069 (2021). https://doi.org/10.1038/s41598-021-94378-z
14. Lord, C., Elsabbagh, M., Baird, G., Veenstra-VanderWeele, J.: Autism spectrum disorder. Lancet **392**(10146), 508–520 (2018). https://doi.org/10.1016/S0140-6736(18)31129-2
15. Nakaoka, K., Tateyama, K., Yuri, T., Harada, S., Takabatake, S.: Predictive validity and cut-off score of the mealtime behavior questionnaire for children with autism spectrum disorder. Res. Autism Spectr. Disord. **110**, 102290 (2024). https://doi.org/10.1016/j.rasd.2023.102290
16. Nakaoka, Y., Ueda, R., Saito, H., Yamaguchi, M.: Differences in mealtime behaviors between children with autism spectrum disorder and typically developing children using a behavioral questionnaire. Jpn. J. Spec. Educ. **54**(3), 139–150 (2017). (in Japanese)
17. Parikh, M.N., Li, H., He, L.: Enhancing diagnosis of autism with optimized machine learning models and personal characteristic data. Front. Comput. Neurosci. **13**, 9 (2019). https://doi.org/10.3389/fncom.2019.00009
18. Smith, J., Doe, J.: LSTM-based deep learning models for non-invasive detection of health disorders. J. Healthc. Inform. **6**(2), 134–145 (2020)
19. Srivastava, N., Hinton, G., Krizhevsky, A., Sutskever, I., Salakhutdinov, R.: Dropout: a simple way to prevent neural networks from overfitting. J. Mach. Learn. Res. **15**(1), 1929–1958 (2014)
20. Vabalas, A., Gowen, E., Poliakoff, E., Casson, A.J.: Machine learning algorithm validation with a limited sample size. PLoS ONE **14**(11), e0224365 (2019). https://doi.org/10.1371/journal.pone.0224365
21. Vaswani, A., Shazeer, N., Parmar, N., Uszkoreit, J., Jones, L., Gomez, A.N., Kaiser, Ł., Polosukhin, I.: Attention is all you need. In: Advances in Neural Information Processing Systems, vol. 30. Curran Associates, Inc. (2017)
22. Volkmar, F.R., McPartland, J.C.: From Kanner to DSM-5: Autism as an evolving diagnostic concept. In: Volkmar, F.R. (ed.) Handbook of Autism and Pervasive Developmental Disorders, 4th edn, pp. 3–17. Wiley (2014). https://doi.org/10.1002/9781118911389.hautc01
23. World Health Organization.: International classification of diseases for mortality and morbidity statistics (11th revision). https://icd.who.int/ (2019)
24. Wu, C., Liaqat, S., Helvaci, H., Cheung, S.C.S., Chuah, C.N., Ozonoff, S., Young, G.: Machine learning based autism spectrum disorder detection from videos. In: 2020 IEEE International Conference on E-health Networking, Application & Services (HEALTHCOM), pp. 1–6 (2021). https://doi.org/10.1109/HEALTHCOM49281.2021.9398924
25. Zhao, Z., et al.: Use of oculomotor behavior to classify children with autism and typical development: a novel implementation of the machine learning approach. J. Autism Dev. Disord. **53**(3), 934–946 (2023). https://doi.org/10.1007/s10803-022-05685-x

26. Zhu, Y., et al.: Machine-learning classification using neuroimaging data in schizophrenia, autism, ultra-high risk and first-episode psychosis. Transl. Psychiatry **10**(1), 278 (2020). https://doi.org/10.1038/s41398-020-00965-5
27. Zwaigenbaum, L., Bauman, M.L., Choueiri, R., et al.: Early identification and interventions for autism spectrum disorder: executive summary. Pediatrics **136**(Supplement 1), S1–S9 (2015). https://doi.org/10.1542/peds.2014-3667B

Are Cognitive Schemas Taught to Learners the Same Across Two Different Educational Systems? A Computational Approach

Kento Koike[1,2]([✉]), Tomoki Aburatani[3], Atsushi Ashida[4], Kai Morita[5], and Kota Kunori[6]

[1] Tokyo University of Science, Katsushika, Japan
`kento@koike.app`
[2] Chiba Institute of Technology, Narashino, Japan
[3] Osaka Metropolitan University, Sakai, Japan
[4] The University of Osaka, Suita, Japan
[5] National Institute of Technology, Fukui College, Sabae, Japan
[6] Kansai University, Suita, Japan

Abstract. Educational systems often claim to teach similar problem-solving skills, yet learners may develop fundamentally different cognitive schemas depending on the system design. This discrepancy highlights the need to examine schema equivalence and transferability across educational contexts. However, the lack of formal definitions and computational models for cognitive schemas has hindered direct comparisons of what learners actually acquire in different systems. This study proposes computational cognitive schemas (CCS) as a formal framework to address these challenges. CCS models problem-solving as state transitions guided by discrete cognitive devices, enabling explicit representation and comparison of schemas across educational systems. The framework establishes a hierarchical structure from individual solution processes to generalized schemas, supported by device ontology theory. Our approach enables systematic comparison between educational systems by identifying common and distinct cognitive operations, facilitating schema-centered design that makes learning goals explicit and comparable. These findings contribute to improving interoperability between educational systems and advancing evidence-based educational system design.

Keywords: Cognitive schema comparison · Educational system interoperability · State transition models · Device ontology · Schema formalization

1 Introduction

In educational systems, explicitly defining the capabilities that learners are expected to acquire is a fundamental aspect of instructional design. Without clear goal setting and communication, the design intent and evaluation criteria of the system become unclear, hindering effective learning support. Moreover, this ambiguity also impedes comparison with other systems and limits reuse of design knowledge.

Recently, designs that support learners' thinking processes, rather than simply transmitting knowledge, have been emphasized. This shift highlights the importance of helping learners understand problems and apply their knowledge and skills to develop effective solutions. Therefore, in systems designed to develop problem-solving skills, it is essential to clarify the specific thinking processes and cognitive operations that learners are expected to acquire.

In this study, we define *problem-solving skills that learners ultimately execute autonomously* as cognitive schemas, a concept in cognitive science. Cognitive schemas are frameworks of structured knowledge and procedures that enable appropriate judgment and operations in certain problem situations [4]. When learners acquire cognitive schemas, they internalize thinking processes for abstractly perceiving situations and flexibly analyzing and solving problems. These processes are highly valuable learning outcomes in educational systems.

However, such cognitive schemas are rarely explicitly defined or designed in educational systems. Instead, many *desired cognitive schemas intended for acquisition* remain implicit, embedded as intentions behind task composition and support forms. This situation is primarily attributed to the following three factors:

- The definition of cognitive schemas is unclear and inconsistent.
- Schemas lack sufficient formalization from a computational perspective.
- As design becomes more context-specific, the scope of schemas becomes limited, reducing their generalizability across diverse contexts.

Consequently, these factors have made achieving interoperability of cognitive schemas between educational systems a major challenge.

Specifically, theoretical and practical limitations in schema design hinder the clarification of design intent and learning outcomes and limit the transfer of knowledge to other systems. Consequently, these limitations lead to issues such as unclear design intent, weak alignment with learning tasks, and difficulties in comparing systems or reusing design knowledge.

Owing to these factors, conventional educational systems have focused on learning task design, while the essential goal of facilitating cognitive schema acquisition has rarely been explicitly expressed. The lack of clear connection between task design and the intended cognitive schema acquisition has led to two major challenges:

- First, it becomes difficult to design tasks from an information-processing perspective based on the cognitive schemas that learners should acquire.
- Second, no framework exists to clarify the differences or commonalities in these intentions—whether the same learning task is intended to promote the acquisition of different cognitive schemas or whether different tasks are designed to target the same cognitive schema.

To address these issues, this study proposes computational cognitive schemas (CCS) as a framework for formally representing cognitive schemas. CCS models the thinking processes in problem-solving as a sequence of discrete, flexibly combinable cognitive operations. This formalization enables clear description of the design intent of educational systems and allows comparison and reuse between different systems.

Given this study's theoretical foundation, we adopt the schema theory in Soar [8], one of the cognitive architectures. Soar's schema theory models problem-solving as *structured transition processes from state to state* and can uniformly explain knowledge acquisition and application, making it suitable for this study.

Furthermore, in this formalization, we introduce the concept of device ontology [7,10] to define operators that drive state transitions as sets of *cognitive devices*. This approach enables problem-solving processes to be defined as abstract, reusable structures formed by combinations of individual cognitive devices. Such formalization enables comparison of cognitive schemas between different educational systems and tracking and evaluation of learners' schema acquisition processes.

The main contributions of this study are as follows:

- To explicitly and computationally define cognitive goals in educational systems.
- To provide a framework for designing learning tasks aligned with problem-solving abilities.
- To construct a mechanism for tracking and evaluating learners' schema acquisition processes.

2   Related Work

2.1   Cognitive Schemas in Cognitive Science

The concept of cognitive schemas has evolved as static and structural representations, exemplified by Minsky's frame theory and Schank and Abelson's scripts [11].

While these knowledge representations effectively captured human understanding and reasoning, interest in procedural and dynamic schemas that model problem-solving processes grew in later years. A significant milestone in this shift was the Soar cognitive architecture [8]. Soar characterizes problem-solving based on a state–space search using production rules and supports knowledge acquisition and generalization through a learning mechanism called chunking. These chunks function as procedural schemas generated based on experience.

2.2   Cognitive Schemas in Educational Applications

In educational systems such as cognitive tutor-type intelligent tutoring systems, learners' problem-solving processes are described using production rules based on Adaptive Control of Thought–Rational (ACT-R) theory [1,2]. However, these procedures are rarely explicitly and formally defined as cognitive schemas, often resulting in implementations restricted to specific contexts.

Furthermore, expert system-based educational support systems, exemplified by MYCIN and GUIDON, achieved sophisticated knowledge representation of diagnostic processes. However, no framework has formalized and elevated these rule sets into reusable learning goals as cognitive schemas.

Recently, to enhance alignment between cognitive processes in problem-solving and instruction, information structure-oriented approaches [3] that explicitly handle the structure of problems themselves have gained attention. For instance, Hirashima et al. [5,6] open information structure approach models the information structure contained in problems and present it to learners as *components*, visualizing learners' thinking processes and supporting them in educational systems.

While this approach has emphasized the importance of *constituent components* in problem-solving, a computational framework for formalizing how these components are searched, combined, and described as reusable learning goals remains undeveloped.

2.3   Positioning of This Research and Research Gaps

Based on the introduction and related research outlined in the previous section, while many achievements have been made from cognitive science and knowledge engineering perspectives, several research gaps exist in applying cognitive schemas within educational systems.

The first gap concerns the explicitation and formalization of cognitive schemas. In many conventional educational systems, the cognitive schemas that learners should ultimately acquire are often implicit and remain embedded behind system implementations and rule sets. For example, while Cognitive Tutor models problem-solving processes using production rules based on the ACT-R theory, these rules are rarely defined as explicit cognitive schemas. Moreover, even in systems with sophisticated knowledge representation such as MYCIN and GUIDON, no framework has formalized rule sets into reusable learning goals.

Second, there is the problem of the exploratory aspects of thinking processes. Approaches that explicitly handle the information structure of problems, such as the Open Information Structure Approach, have recognized the importance of problem *components*; however, a computational foundation for modeling how these components are searched and combined during the thinking process remains underdeveloped. Recently, supporting learners in constructing their own search space during the learning process has been emphasized [9], yet a formal framework for solutions search and operator selection is lacking.

Third, existing research reveals a divergence from learning task design. The relationship between cognitive schemas and learning tasks is often implicit, complicating the design of tasks that develop problem-solving abilities. This limitation hinders the comparison of educational systems, the reuse of design knowledge, and the tracking and evaluation of learners' schema acquisition processes.

To address these limitations, this study proposes the framework of CCS. CCS describes the structure of cognitive operations and state transitions observed in expert problem-solving in an abstract and reusable form independent of system implementation formats. Particularly, this study, inspired by the chunk learning mechanism in Soar, computationally defines schemas as dynamic and procedural knowledge and provides a framework for design, analysis, and individualization to integrate their acquisition process into educational support.

3   Computational Cognitive Schemas

In educational systems, explicitly defining the problem-solving skills that learners are expected to acquire is a critical issue. This study regards such problem-solving skills as cognitive schemas, based on cognitive science. Cognitive schemas are structured knowledge frameworks that individuals use to interpret information and guide behavior across diverse contexts [4]. When learners acquire such cognitive schemas, they internalize abstract thinking processes that enable them to flexibly analyze situations and solve problems.

However, as described in the introduction section, the utilization of cognitive schemas in educational systems faces the following challenges:

- Lack of explicit representation and formalization of cognitive schemas: Cognitive schemas often remain implicit, embedded within system implementations and rule-based structures, making them difficult to identify and analyze.
- Problems of exploratory aspects of thinking processes: The computational foundation for thinking processes of how to search and combine problem *components* remains unestablished.
- Divergence from learning task design: The relationship between cognitive schemas and learning tasks is implicit, making it difficult to design tasks from the reverse calculation of problem-solving abilities to be acquired.

Against this background, this study proposes the concept of CCS, a formal and computationally expressible representation of the cognitive operations and knowledge structures that learners use during problem-solving. The definition of CCS is independent of any specific implementation formats, such as production rules, Bayesian models, or neural networks).

3.1   Basic Properties of CCS

The main characteristics that define CCS can be summarized as follows:

- Abstraction: A framework that captures learners' cognitive structures without depending on surface-level representational formats.
- Computability: Implementation applicable as simulations or learner models within systems.

- Generality: Structured to support reuse, comparison, and transfer between different systems and tasks.
- Process orientation: Focusing on sequences of knowledge operations involved in problem-solving processes rather than static knowledge descriptions.

These characteristics directly address the challenges discussed earlier:

- The combination of abstraction and computability makes schema definitions formal and clear, enabling the explicit expression of implicit knowledge.
- Process orientation enables computational modeling of exploratory processes in problem-solving, making it possible to track and evaluate learners' thinking processes.
- Generality enables comparison and reuse of schemas between different educational systems, ensuring alignment with learning task design

.

3.2 Positioning of CCS

CCS primarily addresses the following limitations in conventional cognitive schema research:

- Static nature of knowledge representation: While conventional frame theory and script theory emphasized structural aspects of knowledge, they provided limited support for representing dynamic problem-solving processes.
- Implementation dependency: Systems such as Cognitive Tutor and MYCIN depended on specific implementation formats (production rules and rule-based systems), making schema reuse and comparison difficult.
- Context dependency: The open information structure approach explicitly addresses the information structures of problems; however, its computational foundation for modeling cognitive thinking processes remains undeveloped.

To mitigate these limitations, CCS regards problem-solving processes as sequences of state transitions by cognitive devices and provides a foundation for educational system design through their formalization.

4 Formalization

To utilize the concept of CCS as a foundation for educational system design, formal definitions are necessary. This section shows how CCS can be formalized and utilized for design, analysis, and adaptation of educational systems.

4.1   Basic Policy for Formalization

In this study, CCS formalization is analyzed from three perspectives:

1. Cognitive devices: Define basic cognitive operations involved in problem-solving and enable representation of complex thinking processes through their combinations.
2. State transitions: Describe changes in the information structure during problem-solving processes and enable tracking of learners' thinking processes.
3. Schema generalization: Enable abstraction from individual solution processes to more general problem-solving schemas.

This formalization is based on the Cognitive Schema (CST) [4] and Soar's schema theories [8], regarding *thinking* as a series of information processing processes and describing state transitions through cognitive operations.

4.2   State Transition Model of Problem-Solving

Problem-solving is a transition process from initial state S_1 to the goal state S_R, where the operation set used during the process corresponds to the set Op_i:

$$S_1 \xrightarrow{\mathrm{Op}_1} S_2 \xrightarrow{\mathrm{Op}_2} S_3 \xrightarrow{\mathrm{Op}_3} \cdots \xrightarrow{\mathrm{Op}_t} S_{t+1}(= S_R).$$

Where state S_i represents the set of all information accessible to the learner at each step, while operation Op_i represents the set of cognitive processes performed on that information.

4.3   Structure of States and Objects

Structuring information in problem-solving processes is essential for tracking and evaluating learners' thinking processes. The state S_t is defined as a set of target information objects:

$$S_t = \{\, I_{n_t} \mid I_{n_t} \in \mathbb{I}_t \}$$

Each object I_{n_t} has an attribute set $\mathbb{A}_{n_t}$, where each attribute is represented as a pair consisting of a label k and value v:

$$A_{n_{m_t}} = \{\, k,\, v \}$$

The operation Op_t transforms the attributes of objects in S_{t-1} to generate a new state S_t:

$$S_t = \mathrm{Op}_t(S_{t-1}) = \{\, p_t(I_{n_{t-1}}) \mid n = 1, \ldots, m, \}$$

where p_t is a basic cognitive operation, referred to as a cognitive device (e.g., factorization, transposition, combining like terms). The operation Op_t is composed of a set of these cognitive devices:

$$\mathrm{Op}_t = \{p_{t1}, p_{t2}, \ldots, p_{tm}\}$$

Notably, hierarchical relationships exist among cognitive devices. For example, $p_{\text{coefficient extraction}}$ is a component of $p_{\text{factorization}}$, and $p_{\text{quadratic factorization}}$ can be understood as a specialization of the more general $p_{\text{structural transformation}}$. Operations such as generalization, specialization, decomposition, and composition based on such hierarchical structures enable comparative analysis across different educational systems. These relationships can be represented as shown in Fig. 1.

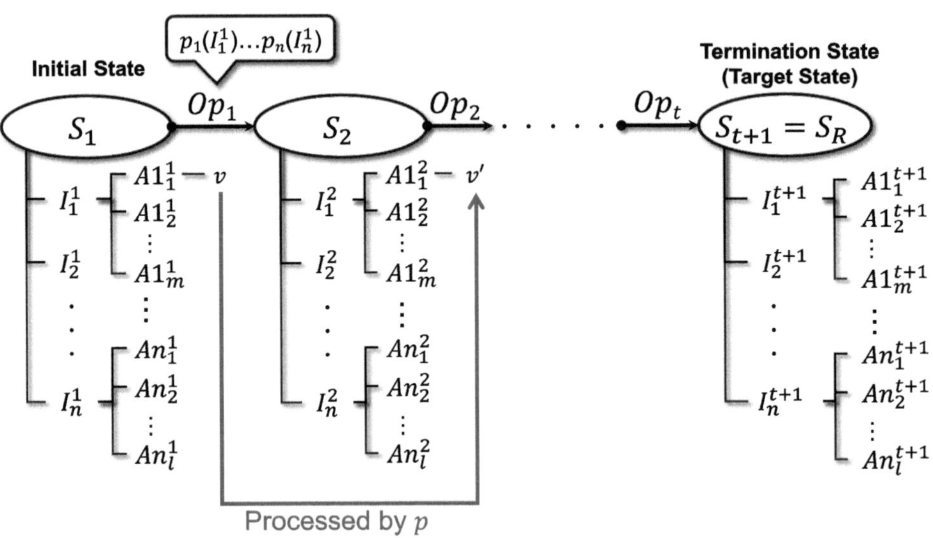

Fig. 1. State transitions and operation structures

Concrete Example: Solving Quadratic Equations. For clarity, consider the process of solving the quadratic equation $x^2 + 5x + 6 = 0$.

The specific components of the actual information object I, the operation Op, and its constituent cognitive devices p are as follows:

- Initial state S_1:
  - Information object I_1: Quadratic equation "$x^2 + 5x + 6 = 0$"
  - Attributes: {"form", standard}, {"unknown", x}, {"degree", 2}, {"quadratic coefficient", 1}, {"linear coefficient", 5}, {"constant term", 6}
- Operation Op_1: Factorization operation (set of cognitive devices)
  - p_{1a}: Coefficient combination search ({"linear coefficient", 5} $\rightarrow$ {"factor sum", 5})

- p_{1b}: Constant term combination search ({"constant term", 6} → {"factor product", 6})
    - p_{1c}: Factor candidate generation ({"factor product", 6}, {"factor sum", 5} → {"factor1", 2}, {"factor2", 3})
    - p_{1d}: Form transformation ({"form", standard} → {"form", factored})
- Intermediate state S_2:
    - Information object I_2: Factorized equation "$(x + 2)(x + 3) = 0$"
    - Attributes: {"form", factored}, {"factor1", $(x+2)$}, {"factor2", $(x+3)$}, {"solvability", direct}
- Operation Op_2: Zero factor operation (set of cognitive devices)
    - p_{2a}: Application of zero factor condition ({"factor1", $(x + 2)$} → {"equation1", $x + 2 = 0$})
    - p_{2b}: Application of zero factor condition ({"factor2", $(x + 3)$} → {"equation2", $x + 3 = 0$})
    - p_{2c}: Linear equation solution ({"equation1", $x + 2 = 0$} → {"solution1", $x = -2$})
    - p_{2d}: Linear equation solution ({"equation2", $x + 3 = 0$} → {"solution2", $x = -3$})
- Goal state S_3:
    - Information objects I_{3a}, I_{3b}: Solutions "$x = -2$", "$x = -3$"
    - Attributes: {"solution type", real solution}, {"multiplicity", 1}, {"number of solutions", 2}

This example explicitly represents a process where the operation Op_i consists of multiple cognitive devices p, with each device p directly modifying specific attributes of information objects to gradually transform the problem's information structure.

Concrete Example: Attribute Transformation of Equation Objects. In the previous quadratic equation example, we detail how information objects and their attributes are transformed by cognitive devices:

- Attribute transformation 1 (transformation by cognitive devices p_{1a} - p_{1d}):
    - Before transformation: I_1 = {"form", standard}, {"linear coefficient", 5}, {"constant term", 6}
    - After transformation: I_2 = {"form", factored}, {"factor1", $(x + 2)$}, {"factor2", $(x + 3)$}
- Attribute transformation 2 (transformation by cognitive devices p_{2a} - p_{2d}):
    - Before transformation: I_2 = {"factor1", $(x + 2)$}, {"factor2", $(x + 3)$}
    - After transformation: I_{3a} = {"solution1", $x = -2$}, I_{3b} = {"solution2", $x = -3$}

4.4   Solution Processes and Optimal Paths

A process P is defined as a series of operations transitioning from the initial state S_1 to the goal state S_R, expressed as follows:

$$P = \{\mathrm{Op}_t(S_{t-1}) \mid t = 1, \ldots, n\}$$

Among these, expert solutions can be defined as optimized paths from the perspective of length or complexity:

$$P_E = \arg\min_P \{ P \mid S_n = S_R\}$$

However, learning only P_E may lead to strategy rigidification. Therefore, understanding multiple solution paths and the generalized cognitive devices common to them is essential for fostering cognitive flexibility. Notably, this approach represents an optimization of human problem-solving processes and not discrete mathematical optimization. Given that human problem-solving has constraints on resources and attention, optimization is only *some degree of* optimization, and mastery processes are essential for its execution. Therefore, mathematical optimal solutions are not readily suitable as learning targets.

Concrete Example: Multiple Solutions for Quadratic Equations. For the same quadratic equation $x^2 + 5x + 6 = 0$, the following multiple solutions exist:

- Solution 1 (factorization method): $P_1 = \{\mathrm{Op}_{\text{factorization}}, \mathrm{Op}_{\text{zero factor}}\}$
    - $S_1 \xrightarrow{\mathrm{Op}_{\text{factorization}}} S_2 \xrightarrow{\mathrm{Op}_{\text{zero\_factor}}} S_3$
    - $\mathrm{Op}_{\text{factorization}} = \{p_{\text{coefficient\_search}}, p_{\text{constant\_search}}, p_{\text{candidate\_generation}}, p_{\text{form\_transformation}}\}$
    - $\mathrm{Op}_{\text{zero\_factor}} = \{p_{\text{zero\_factor\_application}}, p_{\text{linear\_solution}}\}$
    - Number of operations: 2 (efficient)
- Solution 2 (quadratic formula method): $P_2 = \{\mathrm{Op}_{\text{formula\_application}}, \mathrm{Op}_{\text{calculation}}\}$
    - $S_1 \xrightarrow{\mathrm{Op}_{\text{formula\_application}}} S_{2'} \xrightarrow{\mathrm{Op}_{\text{calculation}}} S_3$
    - Intermediate state $S_{2'}$: $I_{2'} = \{\text{"formula"}, x = \frac{-5 \pm \sqrt{25-24}}{2}\}$
    - $\mathrm{Op}_{\text{formula\_application}} = \{p_{\text{coefficient\_extraction}}, p_{\text{formula\_substitution}}\}$
    - $\mathrm{Op}_{\text{calculation}} = \{p_{\text{discriminant\_calculation}}, p_{\text{square\_root\_calculation}}, p_{\text{division}}\}$
    - Number of operations: 2 (general)
- Solution 3 (completing the square method): $P_3 = \{\mathrm{Op}_{\text{transposition}}, \mathrm{Op}_{\text{completing\_square}}, \mathrm{Op}_{\text{square\_root}}\}$
    - $S_1 \xrightarrow{\mathrm{Op}_{\text{transposition}}} S_{2''} \xrightarrow{\mathrm{Op}_{\text{completing\_square}}} S_{3''} \xrightarrow{\mathrm{Op}_{\text{square\_root}}} S_3$
    - Intermediate state $S_{2''}$: $I_{2''} = \{\text{"form"}, x^2 + 5x = -6\}$
    - Intermediate state $S_{3''}$: $I_{3''} = \{\text{"form"}, (x + \frac{5}{2})^2 = \frac{1}{4}\}$
    - $\mathrm{Op}_{\text{transposition}} = \{p_{\text{term\_movement}}\}$
    - $\mathrm{Op}_{\text{completing\_square}} = \{p_{\text{coefficient\_calculation}}, p_{\text{term\_addition}}, p_{\text{simplification}}\}$

- $\mathrm{Op}_{\text{square\_root}} = \{p_{\text{square\_root\_both\_sides}}, p_{\text{term\_movement}}\}$
- Number of operations: 3 (procedure-oriented)

Each solution uses different cognitive devices, but common thinking patterns exist (e.g., *transform equations to find solutions*).

4.5 Schema Generalization: Hierarchical Structure of P_x, P_M, P_G

To realize the generality of CCS, this study defines the following generalization hierarchy:

- Individual process P_x: A specific solution process for particular task x
- Intermediate process P_M: A partial generalization common to specific task group $X' \subset X$
- Generalized schema P_G: An abstract schema across entire task set X

Concrete Example: Hierarchical Structure of Equation Solution.

- P_x: Factorization solution for specific quadratic equation (e.g., $x^2+5x+6 = 0$)
  - Specific process: $P_{x1} = \{\mathrm{Op}_{\text{factorization\_5\_6}}, \mathrm{Op}_{\text{zero\_factor}}\}$
  - Application scope: Only this specific equation
  - Generality: Low
- P_M: Solution pattern for factorable quadratic equations in general
  - Common process: $P_{M1} = \{\mathrm{Op}_{\text{factorization\_general}}, \mathrm{Op}_{\text{zero\_factor}}\}$
  - Application scope: $x^2 + bx + c = 0$ (where b, c are integers and factorable)
  - Generality: Medium
- P_G: General solution schema applicable to all quadratic equations
  - Abstract process: $P_{G1} = \{\mathrm{Op}_{\text{discrimination}}, \mathrm{Op}_{\text{method\_selection}}, \mathrm{Op}_{\text{execution}}\}$
  - Application scope: All quadratic equations $ax^2 + bx + c = 0$
  - Generality: High

This relationship can be defined as follows:

$$P_M : \{P_x \mid x \in X'\} \subset \text{instances of } P_M$$
$$\text{where } X' \subset X, \quad 1 < |X'| < |X| \tag{1}$$

$$P_G \text{ such that}$$
$$P, P' \subseteq \{\text{instantiations of } P_G\} \tag{2}$$

Thus, P_M represents a "semi-generalized" cognitive schema positioned between P_G and P_x, enabling the identification and description of cognitive devices common across tasks.

4.6 Ontological Structure of Cognitive Devices

To theoretically support the generalization hierarchy—P_x, P_M, and P_G—it is necessary to formally define relationships among cognitive devices. Thus, this study adopts hierarchical structures based on device ontology.

Definition of Basic Relationships. Each cognitive device p satisfies the following two basic relationships:

1. Part-Whole Relation: $p_{\text{sub}} \prec_{\text{part}} p_{\text{super}} \iff p_{\text{sub}}$ is a component of p_{super}. A relationship where finer-grained device p_{sub} becomes a component of coarser-grained device p_{super}. Example: $p_{\text{coefficient\_extraction}} \prec_{\text{part}} p_{\text{factorization}}$, $p_{\text{transposition}} \prec_{\text{part}} p_{\text{equation\_transformation}}$.
2. General-Specific Relation: $p_{\text{specific}} \prec_{\text{spec}} p_{\text{general}} \iff p_{\text{specific}}$ is a specialization of p_{general}. A relationship where more concrete device p_{specific} becomes a specialization of more abstract device p_{general}. Example: $p_{\text{quadratic factorization}} \prec_{\text{spec}} p_{\text{structural transformation}}$, $p_{\text{trigonometric calculation}} \prec_{\text{spec}} p_{\text{function calculation}}$.

Definition of Ontological Operations Based on these relationships, the following four basic operations are defined:

1. Generalization: $\mathcal{G} : p_{\text{specific}} \mapsto p_{\text{general}}$ where $\mathcal{G}(p) = \{p' \mid p \prec_{\text{spec}} p'\}$
2. Specialization: $\mathcal{S} : p_{\text{general}} \mapsto p_{\text{specific}}$ where $\mathcal{S}(p) = \{p' \mid p' \prec_{\text{spec}} p\}$
3. Decomposition: $\mathcal{D} : p_{\text{whole}} \mapsto \{p_{\text{part\_i}}\}$ where $\mathcal{D}(p) = \{p' \mid p' \prec_{\text{part}} p\}$
4. Composition: $\mathcal{C} : \{p_{\text{part\_i}}\} \mapsto p_{\text{whole}}$ where $\mathcal{C}(\{p_1, p_2, \ldots, p_n\}) = \{p \mid \forall i, p_i \prec_{\text{part}} p\}$

Formalization of Hierarchical Structure The complete hierarchical structure of cognitive devices is represented as a partially ordered set $(P, \preceq)$: $\preceq = \prec_{\text{part}} \cup \prec_{\text{spec}}$.

Using this hierarchical structure, the relationships among P_x, and P_M, P_G are formalized as follows:

$$P_M = \bigcap_{i \in X'} \mathcal{G}(P_{x_i}) \quad \text{where } X' \subset X \tag{3}$$

$$P_G = \mathcal{G}(P_M) = \mathcal{G}\left(\bigcap_{i \in X'} \mathcal{G}(P_{x_i})\right), \tag{4}$$

where intermediate schema P_M sdenotes the intersection of generalizations of individual schemas for specific task group X', whereas generalized schema P_G is constructed as further generalization of intermediate schemas. These operations provide a theoretical foundation for conducting comparative analysis across different educational systems.

5   Discussion

5.1   Application to Learning Task Design in Educational Systems

While the previous section defined ideal problem-solving processes, actual learning processes involves the gradual acquisition of cognitive devices. Notably, CCS formalization enables the systematic design of learning tasks that support this gradual acquisition process.

Three-Level Task Classification Learning tasks can be categorized into three levels based on their cognitive complexity:

1. Single device acquisition tasks: These tasks focus intensively on acquiring one specific cognitive device.
   - Example: Acquiring $p_{\text{coefficient\_search}}$ through repeated practice with problems in the form $ax + b = 0$
   - State change: $\{\text{"linear coefficient"}, a\} \to \{\text{"solution"}, -b/a\}$
2. Device integration tasks: These tasks combine multiple cognitive devices into operations.
   - Example: Acquiring $\text{Op}_{\text{factorization}} = \{p_{\text{coefficient\_search}}, p_{\text{constant\_search}}, p_{\text{candidate\_generation}}, p_{\text{form\_transformation}}\}$
   - Practice: Performing a complete transformation from standard form to factored form
3. Process integration tasks: These tasks link multiple operations together
   - Example: Acquiring $P_T = \{\text{Op}_{\text{factorization}}, \text{Op}_{\text{zero\_factor}}\}$
   - Practice: Performing a complete process execution $S_1 \to S_2 \to S_3$

This hierarchical structure provides a principled approach to curriculum design that aligns with how cognitive schemas are actually acquired. It also enables educators to identify prerequisite cognitive devices and design appropriate preparatory tasks.

Concrete Example: Factorization Learning Task Sequence A systematic task sequence for solving quadratic equations by factorization are as follows:

- Stage 1: Basic cognitive devices
  - Task 1-1: Product decomposition ($6 = 1 \times 6 = 2 \times 3$) $\to$ acquiring $p_{\text{product\_decomposition}}$
  - Task 1-2: Sum combinations ($1 + 6 = 7, 2 + 3 = 5$) $\to$ acquiring $p_{\text{sum\_calculation}}$
  - Task 1-3: Simultaneous conditions ($a \times b = 6, a + b = 5$) $\to$ acquiring $p_{\text{condition\_integration}}$
- Stage 2: Integrated operations
  - Task 2-1: Expansion verification $(x + a)(x + b) = x^2 + (a + b)x + ab$ $\to$ acquiring $p_{\text{expansion\_understanding}}$
  - Task 2-2: Fill-in-the-blank $x^2 + 5x + 6 = (x+?)(x+?)$ $\to$ acquiring $p_{\text{reverse\_expansion}}$
  - Task 2-3: Complete factorization execution $\to$ acquiring $\text{Op}_{\text{factorization}}$
- Stage 3: Complete solution process
  - Task 3-1: Deriving $x = -2, -3$ from $(x + 2)(x + 3) = 0$ $\to$ acquiring $\text{Op}_{\text{zero\_factor}}$
  - Task 3-2: Complete solution process execution $\to$ acquiring target schema P_T

Each stage in the task sequence serves as an example through which learners gradually acquire the necessary cognitive devices. This approach supports the systematic selection and design of cognitive devices that learners should acquire based on the final form of the CCS.

Task Consistency Evaluation CCS formalization enables quantitative evaluation of learning task consistency through coverage analysis:

$$\text{Coverage}(P_L, P_T) = \frac{|\{p \in P_T \mid p \text{ is practiced in } P_L\}|}{|P_T|} \tag{5}$$

This metric supports individualized learning by enabling:

- Diagnosis: Estimating the set of acquired cognitive devices P_{acquired}, from a learners' solution history.
- Gap analysis: Calculating $P_{\text{unacquired}} = P_T \setminus P_{\text{acquired}}$
- Task generation: Generating practice tasks specialized for cognitive devices in $P_{\text{unacquired}}$

This evaluation approach enables objective comparison and improvement of educational systems. First, unlike traditional subjective assessments, quantitative metrics enable precise understanding of learners' cognitive device acquisition status. For example, a learner with a coverage value of 0.6 in quadratic equation factorization has clearly acquired 60% of the cognitive devices in the target schema necessary to perform the task.

Second, through identification of $P_{\text{unacquired}}$, appropriate practice tasks can be systematically assigned to each learner. For instance, learners who have not acquired $p_{\text{product\_decomposition}}$ would receive focused practice on product decomposition as a prerequisite to factorization.

Third, utilizing the hierarchical structure of cognitive devices enables the design of efficient learning sequences. By confirming acquisition of lower-level devices before progressing to higher-level device practice, learning effectiveness can be maximized.

5.2 How to Analyze Whether Cognitive Schemas Are Identical in Two Systems?

The central challenge in comparing educational systems is that surface differences often obscure deeper structural similarities. Two systems may use completely different notation, problem types, and instructional approaches while targeting fundamentally similar cognitive processes. Conversely, systems that appear similar may actually develop different cognitive capabilities in learners.

Notably, a key methodological challenge lies in identifying appropriate intermediate schemas P_M that enable meaningful comparison between systems with different surface characteristics.

Ontological Greatest Common Schema (GCS) Approach The GCS approach addresses this challenge by utilizing the hierarchical structure of cognitive devices as defined through device ontology. The fundamental insight is that cognitive devices exist in generalization–specialization relationships, where more specific devices can be understood as instances of borader cognitive patterns.

$$P_{M_{\mathrm{GCS}}} = \arg\max_{P_M}\{|P_M| \mid \forall i, \exists \text{generalization path from } P_{x_i} \text{ to } P_M\} \qquad (6)$$

The GCS represents the most general schema that includes all systems under comparison, enabling the identification of commonalities at abstract levels even when surface-level cognitive devices appear completely different.

For example, algebraic factorization and geometric area calculation may involve different specific devices; however, both may require:

- Pattern recognition during problem analysis
- Structural transformation during solution process
- Solution derivation at the final step

Concrete Evaluation Procedure for Schema Identity Based on the theoretical foundation of CCS and the GCS approach, we propose a systematic procedure for evaluating schema identity:

1. Comprehensive cognitive task analysis
   - Document problem-solving processes for each educational system.
   - Identify the complete set of cognitive devices P_{x1} and P_{x2}
   - Map hierarchical relationships based on part-whole and general-specific connections.
2. Ontological hierarchy construction
   - Map specific devices to their general forms through systematic generalization
   - For example: $p_{\text{quadratic\_factorization}} \rightarrow p_{\text{structural\_transformation}} \rightarrow p_{\text{pattern\_application}}$
   - Validate the hierarchy through expert review and empirical analysis.
3. GCS discovery process
   - Identify the highest level of generalization with shared cognitive devices
   - Determine the deepest structural commonality between systems.
   - Establish the basis for identity evaluation.
4. Schema identity evaluation
   - Analyze the relationship between the discovered GCS and original schemas.
   - High identity indicates that the GCS captures substantial portions of both schemas.
   - Low identity suggests the systems target fundamentally different cognitive development.

However, this evaluation process faces significant practical challenges:

- Expert dependency: Ontological classification requires domain expert validation

- Granularity decisions: The choice of cognitive device granularity significantly affects the results.
- Cultural factors: Contextual factors affect the validity of the ontological hierarchy.
- Scalability issues: The process is limited by current reliance on manual classification requirements.

Therefore, a more systematic and objective approach is needed to effectively evaluate schema identity.

5.3   Implications and Limitations

The schema identity analysis approach offers valuable insights for educational practice when high schema identity is identified between systems. This finding suggests opportunities for:

- Curriculum integration: Emphasizing common cognitive foundations before domain-specific specialization.
- Transfer-optimized instruction: Design learning sequences that maximize positive transfer effects
- Reduced redundancy: Eliminate unnecessary repetition across similar systems

  However, practical implementation faces substantial barriers:

- Institutional constraints: Traditional organization along subject boundaries.
- Domain limitations: Current validation has been primarily limited to mathematics.
- Methodological challenges: Expert judgment dependency and scalability issues.
- Theoretical gaps: Limited integration of motivational and affective factors.

5.4   Future Research Directions

Addressing these limitations requires focused empirical research in three critical areas:

1. Cross-domain validation: Systematic replication across disciplines such as science, language arts, and social studies to establish generalizability beyond mathematics.
2. Cultural adaptation research: Investigation of cognitive device hierarchy variations across different educational contexts.
3. Longitudinal validation: Studies to verify whether high schema identity predicts beneficial transfer effects.

  This study positions CCS as a promising foundation for more systematic educational practice while acknowledging the substantial empirical work needed to validate its practical applications and address current theoretical limitations.

6   Conclusions and Future Work

The formalization of CCS and the exploration of ontological intermediate schema proposed in this study provide the following innovative responses to the question: "Are cognitive schemas taught to learners identical across different educational systems?"

1. Quantitative evaluation of identity: Enables objective, metric-based comparisons between educational systems that previously depended on subjective judgment.
2. Identification of deep structures: Provides empirical evidence that superficially different systems have high-level of cognitive similarity.
3. Prediction of Transfer effects: Predicts transfer effects based on schema identity levels and optimize learning design.
4. Foundation for adaptive education: Supports the dynamic generation of optimal schema acquisition paths tailored to learner characteristics and educational contexts.

These contributions mark a shift in educational systems from "craftsman-like artistry" to "scientific practices," enabling the creation of more effective and theoretically grounded learning environments.

Specifically, this method serves as the foundation for emerging educational paradigms that prioritize maximizing learners' cognitive development rather than functioning solely as an analysis tool. Through educational design based on deep structures of cognitive schemas, learners can acquire true understanding and application abilities rather than superficial knowledge memorization.

Future studies will verify the method's generalizability through empirical studies across diverse educational domains and enhance its implementability in actual educational settings. Additionally, we will develop real-time cognitive schema diagnosis and individualized learning support systems through integration with artificial intelligence technology, contributing to the development of next-generation adaptive learning environments.

Disclosure of Interests. The author declares no competing interests.

Funding. This study was supported by the Japan Society for the Promotion of Science (JSPS) Grants-in-Aid for Scientific Research (KAKENHI), grant numbers JP25K21362, JP24K22761, and JP24K16753.

Acknowledgements. We extend our sincere gratitude to the Co-study Group on Advanced Learning Science and Technology (CALST) (https://calst.org/) for their insightful discussions and invaluable feedback. These co-study sessions were instrumental in shaping the direction and development of this research.

References

1. Anderson, J.R., Corbett, A.T., Koedinger, K.R., Pelletier, R.: Cognitive tutors: lessons learned. J. Learn. Sci. **4**(2), 167–207 (1995). https://doi.org/10.1207/s15327809jls0402_2
2. Anderson, J.R., Matessa, M., Lebiere, C.: ACT-R: a theory of higher level cognition and its relation to visual attention. Hum. Comput. Interact. **12**(4), 439–462 (1997). https://doi.org/10.1207/s15327051hci1204_5
3. Carbonell, J.: AI in CAI: an artificial-intelligence approach to computer-assisted instruction. IEEE Trans. Man Mach. Syst. **11**(4), 190–202 (1970). https://doi.org/10.1109/TMMS.1970.299942
4. Derry, S.J.: Cognitive schema theory in the constructivist debate. Educ. Psychol. **31**(3–4), 163–174 (1996). https://doi.org/10.1080/00461520.1996.9653264
5. Furtado, P.G.F.: Retaining the information structure in the open information structure approach during redesign of learning applications: two study cases. Ph.D. thesis, Hiroshima University (2020)
6. Hirashima, T.: Understanding meaningful arithmetic operations in word problems: a computational model and task design. In: Mori, H., Asahi, Y. (eds.) Human Interface and the Management of Information, vol. 14691, pp. 33–43. Springer Nature Switzerland, Cham (2024). https://doi.org/10.1007/978-3-031-60125-5_3
7. Kitamura, Y., Mizoguchi, R.: Ontology-based systematization of functional knowledge. J. Eng. Des. **15**(4), 327–351 (2004). https://doi.org/10.1080/09544820410001697163
8. Laird, J.E., Newell, A., Rosenbloom, P.S.: SOAR: an architecture for general intelligence. Artif. Intell. **33**(1), 1–64 (1987). https://doi.org/10.1016/0004-3702(87)90050-6
9. Mizoguchi, R.: A proposal for a new framework of learner modeling: from modeling "understanding" to "not understanding". J. Inf. Syst. Educ. **19**(1), 9–14 (2020). https://doi.org/10.12937/ejsise.19.9
10. Sasajima, M., Kitamura, Y., Ikeda, M., Mizoguchi, R.: A representation language for behavior and function: FBRL. Expert Syst. Appl. **10**(3), 471–479 (1996). https://doi.org/10.1016/0957-4174(96)00027-9
11. Schank, R.C., Abelson, R.P.: Scripts, Plans, Goals, and Understanding, 0 edn. Psychology Press (1977). https://doi.org/10.4324/9780203781036

A Review of Transformer-Based and Hybrid Deep Learning Approaches for EEG Analysis

Aniket Konkar and Xiaodong Qu$^{(\boxtimes)}$ (iD)

The George Washington University, Washington D.C., USA
`x.qu@gwu.edu`

Abstract. Transformer-based deep learning models have rapidly gained traction in electroencephalography (EEG) research due to their capacity for modeling long-range temporal dependencies and spatial patterns. This systematic review surveys 201 papers published between 2019 and 2024, with a focus on transformer and hybrid transformer architectures for EEG signal decoding across tasks such as emotion recognition, motor imagery, and attention classification. We categorize key model innovations, including spatial-temporal attention mechanisms, CNN-transformer hybrids, and neural architecture search techniques. Emerging trends highlight the dominance of hybrid models and increasing exploration of pretrained backbones. We also identify methodological gaps in generalization, interpretability, and task-specific benchmarking. To guide future work, we synthesize recommended models and review papers, and propose directions for quantitative meta-analysis and open-source resource development.

Keywords: EEG signal analysis · Transformer models · Hybrid cnn-transformer architectures · Deep learning · Brain-computer interfaces · Neural decoding · Systematic review · Temporal-spatial modeling

1 Introduction

Transformer-based deep learning architectures have rapidly gained traction in the field of electroencephalography (EEG) signal analysis, offering novel capabilities for decoding complex brain dynamics. Unlike traditional machine learning models, transformer architectures can model long-range temporal dependencies and multi-channel interactions more effectively–properties particularly relevant for EEG, which is characterized by noisy, non-stationary signals with complex spatial-temporal structure.

While early transformer applications focused on natural language processing, recent advances have extended their use to physiological signal domains, including emotion recognition, cognitive workload estimation, motor imagery, and

H. Mori et al. (Eds.): HCII 2025, LNCS 16333, pp. 391–404, 2026.
https://doi.org/10.1007/978-3-032-12660-3_29

attention detection. As this research area grows, it becomes increasingly important to systematically review the methods, tasks, and innovations in transformer-based EEG research to guide future developments and identify promising trends.

To this end, our paper aims to provide a focused systematic review of transformer-based models for EEG decoding, using the PRISMA framework for transparency and reproducibility. We emphasize review and analysis of methodological innovations–particularly in model design, pre-processing strategies, and the diversity of application tasks.

Our research questions are as follows:

RQ1. What are the dominant methodological trends in transformer-based EEG decoding, as reflected in review papers published between 2019 and 2024?

RQ2. How do different transformer model variants adapt to specific EEG decoding tasks such as classification, prediction, and signal reconstruction?

We conducted a comprehensive search across four major platforms–PubMed, Web of Science, Google Scholar, and arXiv.org–selected based on their broad coverage of biomedical, computer science, and preprint literature. While other databases like IEEE Xplore, Semantic Scholar, or Scopus also contain relevant studies, our chosen sources offered sufficient depth and overlap for our targeted review scope.

Our contributions are threefold:

1. We present a detailed taxonomy of transformer-based EEG models based on architecture, task domain, and data preprocessing methods.
2. We summarize methodological innovations and report trends across various application areas, including emotion recognition, BCI control, and neurological diagnosis.
3. We identify current limitations and propose future research directions based on gaps observed in the reviewed literature.

2 Related Work

2.1 Classical Approaches to EEG Signal Classification

Traditional machine learning approaches for EEG signal classification have relied on hand-crafted features combined with shallow classifiers such as support vector machines (SVMs), k-nearest neighbors (k-NN), and linear discriminant analysis (LDA). These methods typically operate on frequency or time-frequency features extracted using Fourier or wavelet transforms. While effective for small-scale problems, these models often struggle with generalization due to noise, inter-subject variability, and limited data [9,30,34,36,37].

2.2   Deep Learning for EEG: CNNs and RNNs

With the advent of deep learning, convolutional neural networks (CNNs) and recurrent neural networks (RNNs) have shown significant promise in modeling the spatial and temporal structure of EEG data. CNNs excel at extracting spatial features across electrode locations, while RNNs and gated recurrent units (GRUs) capture sequential dependencies across time. Numerous studies have proposed hybrid CNN-RNN architectures to leverage the strengths of both modules, particularly in motor imagery and visual stimulus tasks [9,15,19,33,35,43, 52].

Despite their advantages, CNNs are typically limited by their local receptive fields, and RNNs can struggle with long-range dependencies and training inefficiencies. These limitations have paved the way for the adoption of transformer-based models in EEG research.

2.3   Transformers and Hybrid Models for EEG

Transformer architectures, originally designed for natural language processing, have recently gained traction in EEG signal analysis due to their capability to model long-range temporal dependencies. Early transformer applications to EEG adopted vanilla encoder designs [12,18,26,29,31,39,48], often with minor modifications to positional encoding.

Recent works have adapted transformers to the specific challenges of EEG signals by incorporating spatial information, temporal masking, or frequency-aware attention mechanisms. Notably, Vafaei et al. [41] provide a taxonomy of such adaptations, including cross-modal attention and spatio-spectral attention modules. Li et al. [21] introduced a temporal masking strategy to suppress irrelevant EEG segments, while Yi et al. [48] proposed adaptive attention mechanisms to improve spatial filtering. Delvigne et al. [10] explore the effects of spatio-temporal transformer depth on attention estimation tasks.

Hybrid models that combine CNN or GCN modules with transformers have become increasingly popular due to their ability to extract local spatial features and model global temporal relationships. These include CNN-Transformer pipelines and more recent graph-based transformer hybrids that explicitly incorporate topological electrode relationships [2,13,17,21,32,47]. Pan et al. [27] proposed a manifold attention mechanism tailored for EEG spatial manifolds, outperforming baseline transformer models on emotion and motor decoding tasks. Li et al. [18] and Abibullaev et al. [1] also emphasize hybrid models for EEG decoding. Sharma et al. [38] introduce a 4D Swin Transformer architecture for EEG-based emotion classification. Xie et al. [45] propose a task-specific transformer architecture optimized for motor imagery EEG decoding. Liu et al. [22] develop a transformer-CNN model that fuses spatial and temporal cues. Chen et al. [7] extend Swin Transformers for high-dimensional spatio-temporal EEG representation. Li et al. [20] propose Dual-TSST, a dual-branch transformer architecture integrating temporal, spectral, and spatial attention. Additional innovations include Arjun et al. [3] introducing ViT variants with spatial feature maps, Lu et al. [24] proposing a bi-branch transformer architecture for emotion recognition, and Ding et al. [11] designing a cross-subject transformer framework. Patel et al. [28] leverage hierarchical spatial attention, while Cheng et al. [8] and Ghous et al. [14] explore generalization via neural architecture search and fine-tuning. Bai et al. [4] introduce channel-shifted transformers to address EEG inter-subject variability. Zhao et al. [50] propose CTNet, which enhances cross-subject emotion recognition via spatial-spectral contrastive learning. Zhang et al. [49] introduce a local-global transformer fusion framework to preserve both detailed and contextual cues in EEG decoding. Liu et al. [23] present EMPT, which combines multi-branch encoding with temporal priors for cross-session robustness. Zhao et al. [51] build a multi-domain transformer that unifies spatial, temporal, and frequency modules with cross-modal attention. Chen et al. [6] propose a three-branch convolutional transformer model that improves generalization for motor imagery tasks.

Recent models such as STAnet [40] and spatiotemporal gated graph transformers [46] extend transformer architectures with task-specific attention mechanisms for auditory and emotional EEG decoding, respectively. Chang et al. [5] further explores spatiotemporal attention modules for robust EEG modeling across multiple domains. Ma et al. [25] integrate attention into CNNs to better capture temporal dependencies for motor imagery decoding, while Wimpff et al. [44] demonstrate transformer benefits in a neuroergonomics context using hybrid models.

2.4 Systematic Reviews on EEG Deep Learning Trends

Systematic reviews have played an important role in tracking methodological progress in EEG-based deep learning. Prior reviews have covered topics such as emotion recognition, motor imagery, and attention decoding [9,19]. These works highlight the growing interest in transformer-based models post-2020 and call for a more principled understanding of how different architectures handle spatial-temporal EEG patterns.

Among recent surveys, Abibullaev et al. [1] provide a comprehensive review of transformer applications in EEG-based BCI systems, highlighting architecture design, challenges, and cross-task generalization. Keutayeva et al. [16] discuss data constraints and optimization strategies for transformer-based EEG models. Vafaei et al. [41] categorize transformer variants across multiple EEG tasks, underscoring their growing dominance in the literature. These reviews form the foundation of our recommended readings and are synthesized in Sect. 2.5.

2.5 Key Recommended Reviews

Based on a comprehensive filtering process, we identified seven high-quality review and experimental studies that exemplify the methodological diversity and innovation in transformer-based EEG research. These include both foundational reviews and cutting-edge experimental designs.

Abibullaev et al. [1] highlight the evolution of transformer architectures and the importance of spatio-temporal attention in BCI design. Vafaei et al. [41] provide a structured classification of EEG-specific transformer variants. Keutayeva et al. [16] detail the impact of data size and preprocessing on transformer stability.

Song et al. [39], Li et al. [18], and Pan et al. [27] present representative architectures and benchmarking results, illustrating performance benefits from hybrid modules or manifold-aware attention. Wang et al. [42] propose a universal pre-trained model (EEGPT) that generalizes across multiple EEG datasets, pointing toward future directions in transfer learning and EEG foundation models.

3   Methods

This systematic review follows the Preferred Reporting Items for Systematic Reviews and Meta-Analyses (PRISMA) guidelines to ensure transparency and replicability. The goal was to identify, filter, and synthesize review papers that examined the use of deep learning, particularly transformer-based and hybrid architectures, for EEG signal analysis.

3.1   Search Strategy and Data Sources

We conducted a structured literature search across four major databases: Google Scholar, arXiv, PubMed, and IEEE Xplore. Boolean keyword combinations such as "transformer EEG review", "transformer EEG", and "deep learning EEG survey" were used to identify relevant literature published between 2019 and 2024. No filters were applied to restrict the search by task type, publication venue, or EEG application.

3.2   Inclusion and Exclusion Criteria

The selection criteria were defined as follows:

- **Inclusion:** English-language, peer-reviewed review or survey papers focused on EEG signal processing using deep learning methods.
- **Exclusion:** Non-review papers (e.g., primary experiments), conference abstracts without full text, and reviews not explicitly focusing on deep learning techniques or EEG signals.

From an initial pool of 241 search results, we applied the above criteria and excluded duplicates, resulting in 88 review papers for full-text analysis.

3.3   Data Extraction

From each included paper, we manually extracted information on the following attributes:

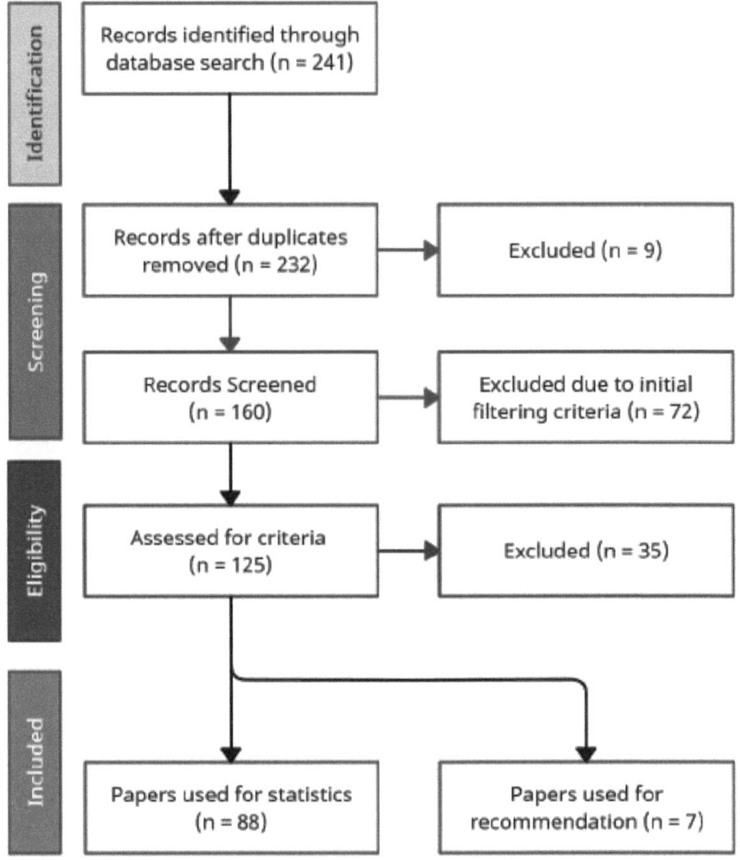

Fig. 1. PRISMA diagram outlining the review selection process

- **Model types**: transformer, CNN, RNN, hybrid, or other architectures.
- **EEG tasks**: such as motor imagery, attention decoding, P300 detection, and emotion recognition.
- **Datasets**: including SEED, DEAP, BCI Competition datasets, and other benchmark corpora.
- **Publication metadata**: such as year, venue, and citation metrics.

We did not conduct qualitative coding or subgroup meta-analysis at this stage, but we summarize trends at a high level in the Results and Discussion sections.

3.4   Study Selection Workflow

Figure 1 illustrates the study selection process, following PRISMA guidelines.

4   Results

This section summarizes methodological trends from 88 EEG deep learning review papers, with a particular focus on transformer and hybrid model applications. We highlight model categories, performance outcomes, and annual publication growth.

4.1   Model Categories and Trends

Table 1 summarizes model categories used in the reviewed studies. Transformer-based approaches have become increasingly dominant, followed by traditional CNNs and CNN-transformer hybrids.

Table 1. Summary of model types in 88 reviewed papers (2019–2024)

Model Type	Count	Examples	Tasks/Datasets
CNN	60	[9, 18]	ERP, Emotion (DEAP, SEED)
RNN (LSTM/GRU)	20	[15, 48]	MI, P300 (DREAMER, SEED)
Transformer	88	[1, 39, 41]	P300, Attn, Emotion (TUH, SEED-IV)
CNN-Transformer	18	[18, 27]	Multimodal, ERP (SEED, EEGNet-256)
Other Hybrids (e.g., GNN)	12	[16, 47]	Sleep, Emotion (PhysioNet, BCI-III)

4.2   Performance Comparison

Table 2 shows selected performance metrics reported in key studies. Transformer and CNN-transformer models generally achieve higher accuracies than traditional architectures.

Table 2. Accuracy metrics from selected representative EEG decoding studies

Study	Model	Task	Dataset	Accuracy (%)
Yi et al. (2022)	Transformer	Visual decoding	TUH	85.3
Li et al. (2024)	Transformer	Emotion recog.	SEED	89.1
Qu et al. (2024)	CNN-Transformer	Multimodal EEG	SEED-IV	90.5
Zhou et al. (2023)	CNN	ERP classification	DEAP	81.0
Dou et al. (2022)	GRU	P300 detection	SEED	78.2

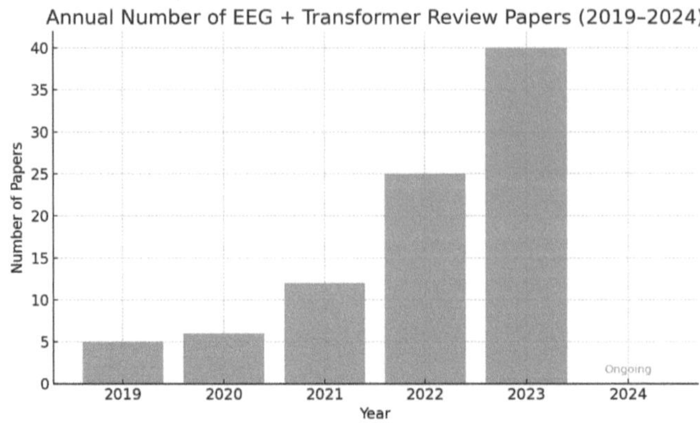

Fig. 2. Annual publication count for EEG + transformer reviews (2019–2024, $n = 88$)

4.3   Publication Trends

Figure 2 displays the annual growth of EEG + transformer deep learning review papers. Research activity significantly increased post-2021, reflecting a growing interest in transformer architectures.

4.4   Recommended Papers

Among the 88 reviewed papers, we identified seven as particularly influential due to their methodological clarity, coverage breadth, and impact. These are summarized below:

- **Abibullaev et al. (2023)** [1]: Broad review of transformer use in EEG-based BCIs.
- **Vafaei et al. (2025)** [41]: Taxonomy of transformer variants for EEG decoding tasks.
- **Keutayeva et al. (2024)** [16]: Insights into data preprocessing and training constraints.
- **Song et al. (2021)** [39]: Early architecture taxonomy and benchmark experiments.
- **Wang et al. (2024)** [42]: EEGPT–a general-purpose transformer for EEG representation.
- **Li et al. (2020)** [18]: CNN-attention models foundational to hybrid EEG transformers.
- **Pan et al. (2022)** [27]: Manifold attention network bridging graph and attention paradigms.

These serve as key references for researchers exploring the intersection of EEG analysis and modern deep learning frameworks.

5   Discussion

This systematic review uncovers key methodological and conceptual trends in the application of transformer-based deep learning to EEG signal analysis. The increasing adoption of transformer models–particularly in hybrid configurations–demonstrates their superior ability to capture long-range temporal dependencies and integrate spatial-temporal information, outperforming traditional CNN and RNN approaches.

5.1   Model Architecture Trends

Our findings highlight a strong shift toward hybrid architectures that integrate CNNs or GCNs with transformer backbones. These combinations leverage local spatial filtering from convolutional layers and global sequence modeling from attention mechanisms. In benchmark tasks such as emotion recognition, motor imagery, and ERP decoding, such hybrid models consistently report higher accuracy and improved generalization.

A notable yet underexplored trend is the emergence of pretrained transformer backbones. Although still in its infancy within EEG research, the use of pretraining shows potential for accelerating convergence and boosting performance–especially when labeled data is limited. As larger EEG datasets become publicly available and domain-specific pretraining techniques mature, we anticipate greater use of transfer learning and EEG-specific foundation models.

Despite performance improvements, several architectural challenges remain. Interpretability, computational efficiency, and robustness across subjects and datasets are still insufficiently addressed in many transformer variants. Addressing these limitations will be critical for transitioning EEG-based models from experimental to clinical and consumer applications.

5.2   Implications for Researchers and Practitioners

The surge in transformer-based EEG studies since 2021 coincides with broader accessibility to high-performance computing and open-source deep learning frameworks (e.g., PyTorch, Hugging Face). These developments empower interdisciplinary researchers–including those in psychology, neuroscience, and biomedical engineering–to experiment with sophisticated neural models without deep AI expertise.

For practitioners building EEG-based brain-computer interfaces (BCIs), our review suggests prioritizing hybrid transformer models, especially for applications that require temporal focus or spatial filtering. Attention mechanisms offer added value in tasks such as emotion classification, mental fatigue tracking, and cognitive workload assessment, where signal variability and noise complicate traditional decoding.

5.3   Limitations

This review focused on peer-reviewed, English-language papers published between 2019 and 2024, sourced from four major academic databases. While we aimed for comprehensive coverage, several limitations remain. We did not conduct subgroup analyses by specific EEG task type (e.g., motor vs. emotion), nor did we quantitatively synthesize performance metrics across studies. In addition, we excluded gray literature, preprints, and primary experimental studies that lacked detailed architecture descriptions. These exclusions may limit the generalizability of our findings and overlook emerging trends in real-time BCI deployment.

5.4   Future Work

To extend the scope and impact of this review, we propose the following future directions:

- **Task-specific meta-analysis**: Categorize and compare model performance across EEG task domains (e.g., motor imagery, attention decoding, emotion recognition) to reveal architecture-task alignments.
- **Quantitative synthesis**: Use meta-analysis tools to aggregate and standardize performance metrics (e.g., accuracy, F1-score) across studies for stronger statistical conclusions.
- **Mechanistic dissection of transformers**: Analyze how architectural components–such as attention heads, temporal masking, or positional encoding–contribute to EEG decoding across datasets.
- **Open-source repository**: Launch a curated, searchable database that catalogs reviewed models by task, dataset, architecture type, and reported performance to foster reproducibility and community benchmarking.

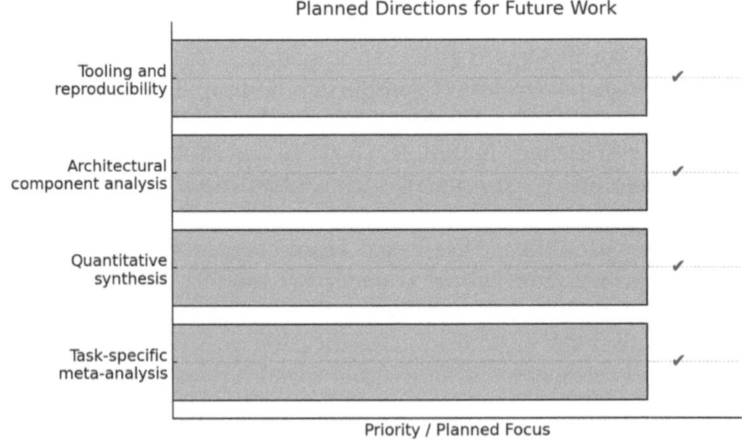

Fig. 3. Planned directions for expanding this review

By addressing these goals, future work can accelerate the transition from research prototypes to reliable EEG-BCI systems and lay the groundwork for standardized evaluation protocols.

6   Conclusion

This systematic review highlights the emergence and rapid evolution of transformer-based and hybrid deep learning models in EEG signal analysis. Compared to traditional architectures like CNNs and RNNs, these newer models offer improved performance across a variety of EEG decoding tasks by better capturing both spatial and temporal dependencies.

Our findings emphasize a clear trend toward architectural innovation–especially in combining transformers with CNN or GCN modules–and increased use of pre-trained models and attention mechanisms. These shifts point to new research directions focused on model interpretability, task-specific customization, and generalization across diverse EEG datasets.

By consolidating evidence from recent review papers, this work offers a foundational overview for researchers aiming to understand the state of transformer models in EEG and lays the groundwork for future methodological developments.

References

1. Abibullaev, B., Keutayeva, A., Zollanvari, A.: Deep learning in EEG-based BSIC: a comprehensive review of transformer models, advantages, challenges, and applications. IEEe Access **11**, 127271–127301 (2023)
2. Altaheri, H., Muhammad, G., Alsulaiman, M., Amin, S.U., Altuwaijri, G.A., Abdul, W., Bencherif, M.A., Faisal, M.: Deep learning techniques for classification of electroencephalogram (EEG) motor imagery (MI) signals: a review. Neural Comput. Appl. **35**(20), 14681–14722 (2023)
3. Arjun, A., Rajpoot, A.S., Panicker, M.R.: Introducing attention mechanism for EEG signals: emotion recognition with vision transformers. In: 2021 43rd Annual International Conference of the IEEE Engineering in Medicine and Biology Society (EMBC), pp. 5723–5726. IEEE (2021)
4. Bai, Z., Hou, F., Sun, K., Wu, Q., Zhu, M., Mao, Z., Song, Y., Gao, Q.: Sect: a method of shifted EEG channel transformer for emotion recognition. IEEE J. Biomed. Health Inform. **27**(10), 4758–4767 (2023)
5. Chang, Y., Zheng, X., Chen, Y., Li, X., Miao, Q.: Spatiotemporal gated graph transformer for EEG-based emotion recognition. IEEE Signal Process. Lett. **31**, 1630–1634 (2024)
6. Chen, W., Luo, Y., Wang, J.: Three-branch temporal-spatial convolutional transformer for motor imagery EEG classification. IEEE Access **12**, 79754–79764 (2024)
7. Chen, Z., Jin, J., Pan, J.: Spatio-temporal swin transformer-based 4-d EEG emotion recognition. In: 2023 IEEE International Conference on Bioinformatics and Biomedicine (BIBM), pp. 1850–1855. IEEE (2023)
8. Cheng, Z., Bu, X., Wang, Q., Yang, T., Tu, J.: EEG-based emotion recognition using multi-scale dynamic CNN and gated transformer. Sci. Rep. **14**(1), 31319 (2024)

9. Craik, A., He, Y., Contreras-Vidal, J.L.: Deep learning for electroencephalogram (EEG) classification tasks: a review. J. Neural Eng. **16**(3), 031001 (2019)

10. Delvigne, V., Wannous, H., Vandeborre, J.P., Ris, L., Dutoit, T.: Spatio-temporal analysis of transformer based architecture for attention estimation from EEG. In: 2022 26th International Conference on Pattern Recognition (ICPR), pp. 1076–1082. IEEE (2022)

11. Ding, Y., Tong, C., Zhang, S., Jiang, M., Li, Y., Lim, K.J., Guan, C.: EMT: a novel transformer for generalized cross-subject EEG emotion recognition. IEEE Transactions on Neural Networks and Learning Systems (2025)

12. Dou, G., Zhou, Z., Qu, X.: Time majority voting, a pc-based EEG classifier for non-expert users. In: International Conference on Human-Computer Interaction, pp. 415–428. Springer (2022)

13. Du, Y., Xu, Y., Wang, X., Liu, L., Ma, P.: EEG temporal-spatial transformer for person identification. Sci. Rep. **12**(1), 14378 (2022)

14. Ghous, G., Najam, S., Alshehri, M., Alshahrani, A., AIQahtani, Y., Jalal, A., Liu, H.: Attention-driven emotion recognition in EEG: a transformer-based approach with cross-dataset fine-tuning. IEEE Access (2025)

15. Hossain, K.M., Islam, M.A., Hossain, S., Nijholt, A., Ahad, M.A.R.: Status of deep learning for EEG-based brain-computer interface applications. Front. Comput. Neurosci. **16**, 1006763 (2023)

16. Keutayeva, A., Abibullaev, B.: Data constraints and performance optimization for transformer-based models in EEG-based brain-computer interfaces: A survey. IEEE Access **12**, 62628–62647 (2024)

17. Key, M.L., Mehtiyev, T., Qu, X.: Advancing EEg-based gaze prediction using depthwise separable convolution and enhanced pre-processing. In: International Conference on Human-Computer Interaction, pp. 3–17. Springer (2024)

18. Li, D., Xu, J., Wang, J., Fang, X., Ji, Y.: A multi-scale fusion convolutional neural network based on attention mechanism for the visualization analysis of EEG signals decoding. IEEE Trans. Neural Syst. Rehabil. Eng. **28**(12), 2615–2626 (2020)

19. Li, G., Lee, C.H., Jung, J.J., Youn, Y.C., Camacho, D.: Deep learning for EEG data analytics: a survey. Concur. Comput.: Pract. Exp. **32**(18), e5199 (2020)

20. Li, H., Zhang, H., Chen, Y.: Dual-tsst: a dual-branch temporal-spectral-spatial transformer model for EEG decoding. IEEE J. Biomed. Health Inf. (2025)

21. Li, W., Zhou, N., Qu, X.: Enhancing eye-tracking performance through multi-task learning transformer. In: International Conference on Human-Computer Interaction, pp. 31–46. Springer (2024)

22. Liu, J., Wu, H., Zhang, L., Zhao, Y.: Spatial-temporal transformers for EEG emotion recognition. In: Proceedings of the 6th International Conference on Advances in Artificial Intelligence, pp. 116–120 (2022)

23. Liu, M., Liu, Y., Shi, W., Lou, Y., Sun, Y., Meng, Q., Wang, D., Xu, F., Zhang, Y., Zhang, L., et al.: Empt: a sparsity transformer for EEG-based motor imagery recognition. Front. Neurosci. **18**, 1366294 (2024)

24. Lu, W., Tan, T.P., Ma, H.: Bi-branch vision transformer network for EEG emotion recognition. IEEE Access **11**, 36233–36243 (2023)

25. Ma, X., Chen, W., Pei, Z., Liu, J., Huang, B., Chen, J.: A temporal dependency learning CNN with attention mechanism for MI-EEG decoding. IEEE Trans. Neural Syst. Rehabil. Eng. **31**, 3188–3200 (2023)

26. Murungi, N.K., Pham, M.V., Dai, X.C., Qu, X.: Empowering computer science students in electroencephalography (EEG) analysis: a review of machine learning algorithms for EEG datasets. In: The 29th ACM SIGKDD Conference on Knowledge Discovery and Data Mining (KDD) (2023)

27. Pan, Y.T., Chou, J.L., Wei, C.S.: Matt: a manifold attention network for EEG decoding. Adv. Neural. Inf. Process. Syst. **35**, 31116–31129 (2022)
28. Patel, K., Safavi, F., Chandramouli, R., Vinjamuri, R.: Transformer-based emotion recognition with EEG. In: 2024 46th Annual International Conference of the IEEE Engineering in Medicine and Biology Society (EMBC), pp. 1–4. IEEE (2024)
29. Qu, X.: Time Continuity Voting for Electroencephalography (EEG) Classification. Ph.D. thesis, Brandeis University (2022)
30. Qu, X., Hall, M., Sun, Y., Sekuler, R., Hickey, T.J.: A personalized reading coach using wearable EEG sensors (2019)
31. Qu, X., Hickey, T.J.: Eeg4home: a human-in-the-loop machine learning model for EEG-based BCI. In: International Conference on Human-Computer Interaction, pp. 162–172. Springer (2022)
32. Qu, X., Key, M., Luo, E., Qiu, C.: Integrating HCI datasets in project-based machine learning courses: a college-level review and case study. In: International Conference on Human-Computer Interaction, pp. 124–143. Springer (2024)
33. Qu, X., Liu, P., Li, Z., Hickey, T.: Multi-class time continuity voting for EEG classification. In: International Conference on Brain Function Assessment in Learning, pp. 24–33. Springer (2020)
34. Qu, X., Liukasemsarn, S., Tu, J., Higgins, A., Hickey, T.J., Hall, M.H.: Identifying clinically and functionally distinct groups among healthy controls and first episode psychosis patients by clustering on EEG patterns. Front. Psych. **11**, 541659 (2020)
35. Qu, X., Mei, Q., Liu, P., Hickey, T.: Using EEG to distinguish between writing and typing for the same cognitive task. In: International Conference on Brain Function Assessment in Learning, pp. 66–74. Springer (2020)
36. Qu, X., Sun, Y., Sekuler, R., Hickey, T.: EEG markers of stem learning. In: 2018 IEEE Frontiers in Education Conference (FIE), pp. 1–9. IEEE (2018)
37. Roy, Y., Banville, H., Albuquerque, I., Gramfort, A., Falk, T.H., Faubert, J.: Deep learning-based electroencephalography analysis: a systematic review. J. Neural Eng. **16**(5), 051001 (2019)
38. Sharma, A., Nigam, J., Rathore, A., Bhavsar, A.: EEG classification for visual brain decoding with spatio-temporal and transformer based paradigms. In: Proceedings of the Fifteenth Indian Conference on Computer Vision Graphics and Image Processing, pp. 1–9 (2024)
39. Song, Y., Jia, X., Yang, L., Xie, L.: Transformer-based spatial-temporal feature learning for EEG decoding. arXiv:2106.11170 (2021)
40. Su, E., Cai, S., Xie, L., Li, H., Schultz, T.: Stanet: a spatiotemporal attention network for decoding auditory spatial attention from EEG. IEEE Trans. Biomed. Eng. **69**(7), 2233–2242 (2022)
41. Vafaei, E., Hosseini, M.: Transformers in EEG analysis: a review of architectures and applications in motor imagery, seizure, and emotion classification. Sensors **25**(5), 1293 (2025)
42. Wang, G., Liu, W., He, Y., Xu, C., Ma, L., Li, H.: Eegpt: pretrained transformer for universal and reliable representation of EEG signals. Adv. Neural. Inf. Process. Syst. **37**, 39249–39280 (2024)
43. Wang, R., Qu, X.: Eeg daydreaming, a machine learning approach to detect daydreaming activities. In: International Conference on Human-Computer Interaction, pp. 202–212. Springer (2022)
44. Wimpff, M., Gizzi, L., Zerfowski, J., Yang, B.: EEG motor imagery decoding: a framework for comparative analysis with channel attention mechanisms. J. Neural Eng. **21**(3), 036020 (2024)

45. Xie, J., Zhang, J., Sun, J., Ma, Z., Qin, L., Li, G., Zhou, H., Zhan, Y.: A transformer-based approach combining deep learning network and spatial-temporal information for raw EEG classification. IEEE Trans. Neural Syst. Rehabil. Eng. **30**, 2126–2136 (2022)
46. Xu, Z., Bai, Y., Zhao, R., Hu, H., Ni, G., Ming, D.: Decoding selective auditory attention with EEG using a transformer model. Methods **204**, 410–417 (2022)
47. Yang, R., Modesitt, E.: Vit2eeg: leveraging hybrid pretrained vision transformers for EEG data (2023). arXiv:2308.00454
48. Yi, L., Qu, X.: Attention-based CNN capturing EEG recording's average voltage and local change. In: International Conference on Human-Computer Interaction, pp. 448–459. Springer (2022)
49. Zhang, J., Li, K., Yang, B., Han, X.: Local and global convolutional transformer-based motor imagery EEG classification. Front. Neurosci. **17**, 1219988 (2023)
50. Zhao, W., Jiang, X., Zhang, B., Xiao, S., Weng, S.: Ctnet: a convolutional transformer network for EEG-based motor imagery classification. Sci. Rep. **14**(1), 20237 (2024)
51. Zhao, W., Zhang, B., Zhou, H., Wei, D., Huang, C., Lan, Q.: Multi-scale convolutional transformer network for motor imagery brain-computer interface. Sci. Rep. **15**(1), 12935 (2025)
52. Zhou, Z., Dou, G., Qu, X.: Brainactivity1: a framework of EEG data collection and machine learning analysis for college students. In: International Conference on Human-Computer Interaction, pp. 119–127. Springer (2022)

Recurrence Quantification Analysis for Group Eye Tracking Data

Mani Tajaddini[1] , Murat Perit Çakır[2] , and Cengiz Acartürk[3]( )

[1] Interactive Intelligence Group, Delft University of Technology, Mekelweg 5, 2628 CD Delft, Netherlands
[2] Informatics Institute, Cognitive Science Department, Middle East Technical University, Dumlupınar Blv, 06800 Ankara, Türkiye
[3] Centre for Cognitive Science, Jagiellonian University, Ul. Ingardena 3, 30-060 Kraków, Poland
cengiz.acarturk@uj.edu.pl

Abstract. Traditional eye tracking methodologies have largely focused on single-user data. The study of multi-user dynamics and social interaction requires a novel analysis framework, partially addressed in current research. In this study, we introduce Group Eye Tracking (GET) as a framework for simultaneously collecting and analyzing eye movement data from multiple participants to reveal group-level patterns of visual dynamics. We use a custom application, which synchronously records eye movements from multiple users performing tasks on separate computers, and a custom R package implementing Recurrence Quantification Analysis (RQA) for examining time-series recurrences of visual dynamics. By quantifying how eye movement patterns recur and align among group members, we potentially provide indicators of cognitive states in collaborative decision-making, within real-time group interactions. The resulting measures can also provide information about the role of task parameters, interface layouts, and team performance. This approach demonstrates how GET can serve for developing next-generation augmented cognition systems by integrating advanced analytics and real-time adaptivity by the analysis of collective task outcomes.

Keywords: Group Eye Tracking · Recurrence Quantification Analysis · Decision Making · Eye Tracking Visualization

1 Introduction

Gathering in groups is a frequent, everyday occurrence in human societies, where collective decisions and actions are commonplace [5, 11]. The research on group dynamics has attracted interdisciplinary interest, focusing on how actions, processes, and transformations take place among individuals. The study of group dynamics has been a broad research field that addresses numerous aspects of interaction in social settings [11]. In efforts to quantify group dynamics, researchers often utilize spatiotemporal analyses [27], identify swarming patterns [38], and examine dynamic coupling mechanisms [32, 33] through data-driven models [14, 28] and agent-based models [21].

H. Mori et al. (Eds.): HCII 2025, LNCS 16333, pp. 405–418, 2026.
https://doi.org/10.1007/978-3-032-12660-3_30

The present study employs the Group Eye Tracking (GET) paradigm that investigates group dynamics in a collaborative visual search task [2]. For this, we offer a set of GET measures for the quantification of group dynamics. We also report on an experiment designed for the study of group dynamics in the visual search task setting. In the experiment, a group of participants synchronously performed a visual search task on multiple computers, while their eye movements were recorded synchronously. The recorded data consisted of gaze locations of the participants on the displays, collected using eye tracking devices in a group eye tracking environment, designed for the purpose of the study.

Previous studies on the use of eye tracking in collaborative tasks have employed various settings, including two participants on a single screen [29], multiple participants watching a stimulus video [36], dyadic settings with real-time mutual gaze perception [34], and mobile eye tracking to assess joint attention [32, 33]. In some of these settings, the cross-recurrence quantification analysis (RQA) has been used for quantifying spatiotemporal coordination between the eye gaze patterns of the dyads, in particular in dual eye tracking experiments [15, 16, 20, 31].

The analysis of eye tracking data in team collaboration settings has been a recently emerging field of research [1, 27, 30]. The present study aims to expand those cross-recurrence quantification analyses, a non-linear time series analysis technique, to larger groups of participants [47]. The proposed method introduces novel measures for the analysis of group eye tracking data, in addition to providing insights into group dynamics in the collaborative visual search task.

We report a comparative analysis of the RQA measures in the context of the experiment conducted, which used a 2×3 within-subject experimental design. One of the experimental design factors was the absence or presence of a visual representation of others' gaze on the screen (viz., the absence and presence of gaze location markers). The other design factor was the visibility of the visual search target (a dot with a fixed radius of a few pixels) with three conditions (dark in color, light in color, or transparent).

The main research question of the present study is to investigate the extent to which the proposed measures are applicable to quantifying group eye tracking data. We expected that visual search would be more difficult for the participants as the visual saliency of the target object was reduced (cf. The visibility of the visual search target). The loss of visibility of the target object would result in a more widespread distribution of the participants' gaze at a given moment of time. Accordingly, the decoupling of the participants' gaze locations would increase when the target was relatively transparent. We also expected that the presence and absence of gaze location markers (i.e., the other participants' gaze locations during the visual search task) would have an impact on the structural complexity of the gaze patterns. We investigated those expectations by applying the proposed group eye tracking measures to groups of two different sizes (in this case, groups of three and five participants).

The paper is organized as follows. The next section presents the concept of cross-recurrence quantification analysis. Then we introduce the Group Eye Tracking (GET) paradigm, the experiment, and data analysis. The final section discusses the findings, limitations of the study, and topics for future research.

2 Recurrence Quantification Analysis

The behavior of systems through time is usually analyzed by time-series methods, employing linear and nonlinear techniques. Linear methods often consider the non-linearities of the system dynamics as *noise*, and most nonlinear methods assume that the system is stationary. However, most ubiquitous systems are nonstationary and non-linear. The Recurrence Quantification Analysis (RQA) has been proposed as a methodology to overcome those limitations, which has also been a practice in multiple fields of research [47]. RQA has vast application areas including the study of road traffic, biopolymers, seismology, respiratory and cardiovascular systems, epilepsy, brain dynamics, interpersonal dynamics, motor coordination in autistic and healthy individuals, and processes and products of discourse to name a few [45–47].

In eye tracking research, RQA has been used as an analysis method to investigate various topics, such as expert vs. novice behavior and the characterization of fixation sequences [3, 39]. Although RQA has been used to explore various aspects of social interaction, most studies focus on dyads, and expanding RQA methods to larger groups remains a challenge [12]. One of the first applications of multidimensional and temporally windowed use of RQA was demonstrated on multichannel EEG data for the detection of epilepsy [48]. Such extensions have allowed researchers to investigate group dynamics in terms of recurrence patterns observed in the aggregated time series of group members [17].

Multidimensional extensions of RQA (e.g., MdRQA) have been proposed, for instance, to explore the coupling relationships between three or more time series, demonstrating a domain-specific application to quantify coordination between skin conductance measurements of triads as a measure of group arousal [44]. A similar multidimensional extension has also been used to investigate multimodal recurrence relationships across heart rate, postural sway, and hand movements of dyads [35, 42] and physiological synchrony dynamics in terms of electrodermal responses of collaborative learners [7].

Various variations of the RQA method have been designed for different purposes and with different strengths. For example, the mdRQA method is a multivariate extension of RQA. Unlike RQA, which accepts one variable (i.e., observation), mdRQA accepts multiple variables and thus can have two interpretations: on the one hand, one can interpret the results as a description of the dynamics of a multidimensional system in which multiple dimensions are observed. On the other hand, mdRQA can be interpreted as capturing synergistic relationships or couplings between multiple variables from different systems. The former situation does not apply to our study on group eye tracking due to the presence of multiple systems. In the latter situation, mdRQA treats multiple variables of different systems as one large system. Although mdRQA captures the coupling between variables effectively, it is not conceptually compatible with group eye tracking. The underlying reason is that the assignment of a time series of the gaze locations of a participant to each input variable of mdRQA leads to the mdRQA output of the recurrences of a single multidimensional trajectory of the system with itself (that is, a multidimensional trajectory made up of multiple, possibly multidimensional trajectories of multiple systems, i.e., multiple participants). However, coincidences (i.e., recurrences) of multiple, possibly multidimensional trajectories of multiple systems (i.e., participants) are needed with one another. As the authors of the mdRQA report, "it is not possible to calculate time-lagged coupling between signals to investigate leader-follower relationships among the component variables as with CRQA" [44], pointing to the need for a further development of the methodology.

An extension to mdRQA, called mdCRQA "extends mdRQA to bi-variate cases to allow for the quantification of the co-evolution of two multidimensional time-series". The mdCRQA extension is also not fully compatible with group eye tracking, since it does not allow for the investigation of the evolution of three and five time series (as reported in the experiment below), and arbitrarily larger groups in the future [43]. Another method akin to mdCRQA, called MMDCRQA (Multidimensional Multiscale Cross Recurrence Quantification Analysis) does not fully capture the group eye tracking paradigm either since it was designed to analyze two multidimensional time series, as mdCRQA, albeit in different time scales. To the best of our knowledge, a multidimensional extension of RQA has not been used to investigate group eye tracking as a measure of group dynamics. [49] provide definitions and procedures to quantify RP (and its various extensions, for example, CRP) structures based on previous research [13, 25, 26].

The term *recurrence quantification analysis* (RQA) was coined by Zbilut and Webber [48]. They defined five recurrence variables as complexity measures as part of the RQA, including percent recurrence (i.e. the density of recurrent points, viz. RR), percent determinism (i.e. percent of recurrent points forming diagonal segments away from the main diagonal, viz. DET), entropy of line length distribution (viz. ENT), maxline (i.e. the length of the largest line segment, viz. Dmax), and trend (i.e. measure of the paling of recurrent points away from the central diagonal). These measures were based on diagonal line structures [47]. The following section presents the Group Eye Tracking (GET) paradigm, where we applied the RQA methodology for the investigation of group.

3   The Group Eye Tracking (GET) Paradigm

The GET paradigm is a methodology developed for investigating group dynamics, by using eye tracking in group settings. This goal has been achieved using the Group Eye Tracking (GET) data collection framework, called GETapp (an application written by the first author in the JavaScript language)[1]. The GETapp was designed to be generic, meaning that it is not specific to the experiment in the present study. The system is made up of three sets of physical components: The server computer (referred to as server from now on), the client computers (henceforth clients) and the eye trackers (in our case, Eyetribe eye trackers with 60 Hz. Recording capacity)[2]. Each client computer has an eye tracking device connected to it, which in turn is run by a server program on the client computer (Fig. 1).

The eye tracking data is transferred from all the eye tracker servers directly to the eye tracking server. The server receives streams of data and, while recording them to a file, also broadcasts them back to all the clients at once. In this way, each client receives

---

[1] The application has reached its functional state thanks to the efforts of Mine Cuneyitoglu Ozkul for her review, bug fixing, refactoring, checking the robustness of the code, and designing and implementing the visualization module.

[2] Eyetribe eye trackers are now obsolete. However, the GETapp has been developed for processing raw eye tracking data; therefore, it is independent of the use of specific eye trackers.

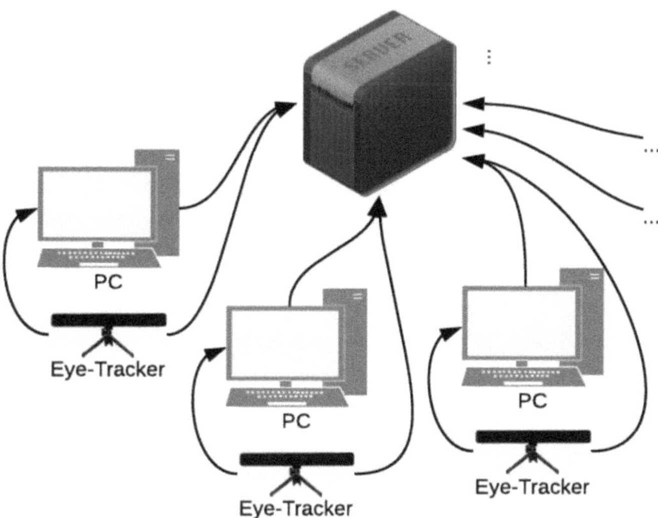

Fig. 1. Three client computers connected to the eye tracking server. An eye tracker is connected to each client and runs a server program on it.

all the data that other clients send to the server in real-time so that each participant can see where the other participants are gazing on their display.

A component of the experiment on this platform is the visualization modality (previously mentioned as the "gaze location marker"). This visualization modality may be represented as a marker, in the shape of a circle, a plus sign, a heat map, or a custom-made marker. The gaze location marker shows the gaze fixations of all the participants in real-time. It is possible to visualize the gaze location markers separately for each participant so that a participant sees multiple markers moving on the screen simultaneously.

A user interaction challenge in selecting the visualization method is the resulting clutter on the screen, due to wobbling movements of the marker. For instance, a visually sharp gaze marker (such as a cross icon) displaying others' gaze locations in real-time usually distracts user's attention. An alternative visualization method is to display the mean location of all the gaze fixations. In this case, the gaze location marker is not a direct representation of the gaze location of all the participants but is an indicator of their weighted gaze locations. A geometric mean of the fixation locations can be used for driving such a visualization marker. We call this visualization modality, which is available in GETapp, the *fluid gaze location marker* (Fig. 2). The fluid gaze location marker is a colored semitransparent circle. The center of the circle is the geometric mean of the gaze positions, and its diameter is a function of the standard deviation of the gaze positions from the mean. As the circle grows in size, its color becomes lighter (Fig. 2).

In the present study, we employ the fluid gaze location marker by assuming that it draws the participants' attention to a location where other participants are mostly gazing at. Further investigation of guiding by the fluid gaze location marker is beyond the scope of the present study. In the next section, we present the generalRQA package, which is an implementation of the methodology introduced in the previous.

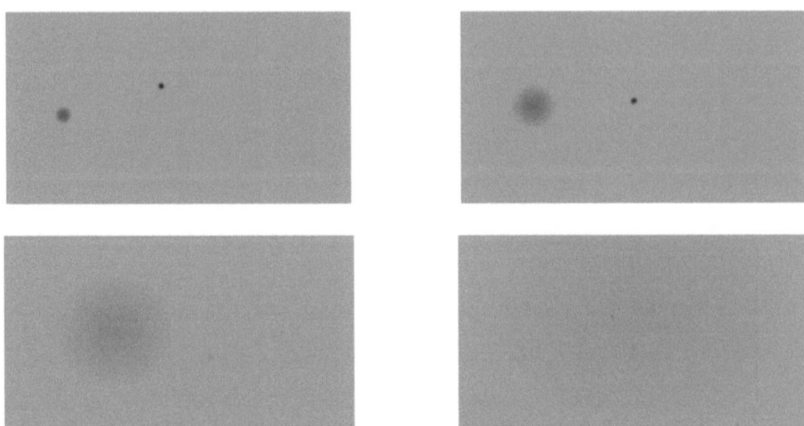

Fig. 2. The fluid gaze location marker visualization modality. The black dot (top-left and top-right) and its more transparent versions represent the target object of the visual search.

4 The `GeneralRQA` Package

The generalRQA package has been developed by the authors of the present study, and used for the analysis of the data reported below. There exist other packages in the R community written for recurrence analysis, such as the crqa package [4]. However, the available packages work with recurrence matrices of only two dimensions, whereas the goal in the present study is to analyze multiple time series concurrently. The generalRQA package can be used to implement cross recurrence quantification analysis (CRQA), joint recurrence quantification analysis (JRQA), and simple recurrence quantification analysis (RQA).

The general workflow of CRQA involves embedding the data, creating a distance matrix from the trajectories, creating a recurrence matrix from the distance matrix, choosing which line (or lines) parallel to the main diagonal in the matrix to work on, creating line histograms for each diagonal line and calculating the RQA measures for each of them (Fig. 3). In simple RQA, the length histogram of the entire recurrence matrix is used to calculate recurrence measures, while in CRQA, one may need to investigate the length histogram of individual diagonal lines to analyze concurrent behavior among multiple time series [24]. In this case, each diagonal line corresponds to a specific lag combination among the time series.

The input to the workflow is comprised of time-series data; each corresponding to one single participant. The time series are then transformed through the workflow to make a final recurrence matrix of which the user of the package can choose the main diagonal, or any other diagonal line parallel to the main diagonal (or multiple diagonal lines, or even the whole recurrence matrix). The output of the package, the CRQA measures, is computed from the selected diagonal lines.

In deriving these measures for our experimental data, as will be explained later, the resulting cross-recurrence plot is three dimensional for groups of three and five dimensional for groups of five participants, and hence impractical for the first case and impossible for the second case to visualize. In the following section, we demonstrate the use of the `generalRQA` package for data analysis in the context of empirical investigation.

5 Data Collection and Analysis

We recorded eye tracking data from six groups of three participants and six groups of five participants. All participants were university students (mean age $M = 23.0$, $SD = 3.11$, 28 females). They had either normal or corrected-to-normal vision. The participants were admitted into the room in groups, and each participant was seated in front of a separate computer.

Prior to the experiment, participants were informed that they would perform a visual search task where they would see a gaze location marker, which represented the average of other participants' gaze locations. However, they were not informed that the visual target would be transparent under certain experimental conditions. The goal of hiding this information was to ensure that they would pursue the visual search task. After calibration, in the experiment session, participants searched for the visual target. As introduced above, the visual target was manipulated by three experiment design conditions (i.e., visual target intensity with three conditions). It was black, gray, or transparent. The other experimental factor was the presence or absence of the gaze location marker, that is, two conditions. Consequently, the experiment had a 2 x 3 within-subject design.

Participants were instructed to click the left mouse button (it did not matter where they clicked on the screen) once they found the visual search target. When all participants clicked, they proceeded to the next screen. The session was made up of 23 trials in a single-block design. The first three trials were warm-ups, and the rest displayed the experimental conditions in random order. The participants in the groups of three were different from the participants in the groups of five, so there was no overlap between the groups in terms of participants. The visual search target appeared at any location on the screen in random order. The location of fixation is the independent variable.

RQA Measures. This section introduces the dependent variables, which are the derived RQA measures

Recurrence Rate (RR).

$$RR(\varepsilon, N) = \frac{1}{N} \sum_{i=1,j=1}^{N} CR_{i,j}^{x,y}(\varepsilon)$$

Also known as Percent Recurrence (REC) in the literature, the *Recurrence Rate (RR)* is a measure of the relative density of the recurrence points in the recurrence matrix and is related to the correlation sum [11]. In this formulation, CR is the cross-recurrence matrix, ε is recurrence threshold, N is the number of cells in the recurrence matrix, and i and j are the indices of the matrix. The x and y superscripts on the CR matrix signify that the matrix is constructed from two different time-series. The RR merely counts the black dots (or the cells with value 1) in the CRP.

The other measures, presented below, are based on the line structures in the CRP (Cross Recurrence Plot). To define these measures, we first need to construct a histogram of the lengths of the diagonal lines in the CRP, as shown below.

$$H_D(l) = \sum_{i=1,j=1}^{N} (1 - CR_{i-1,j-1})(1 - CR_{i+1,j+1}) \prod_{k=0}^{l-1} CR_{i+k,j+k}$$

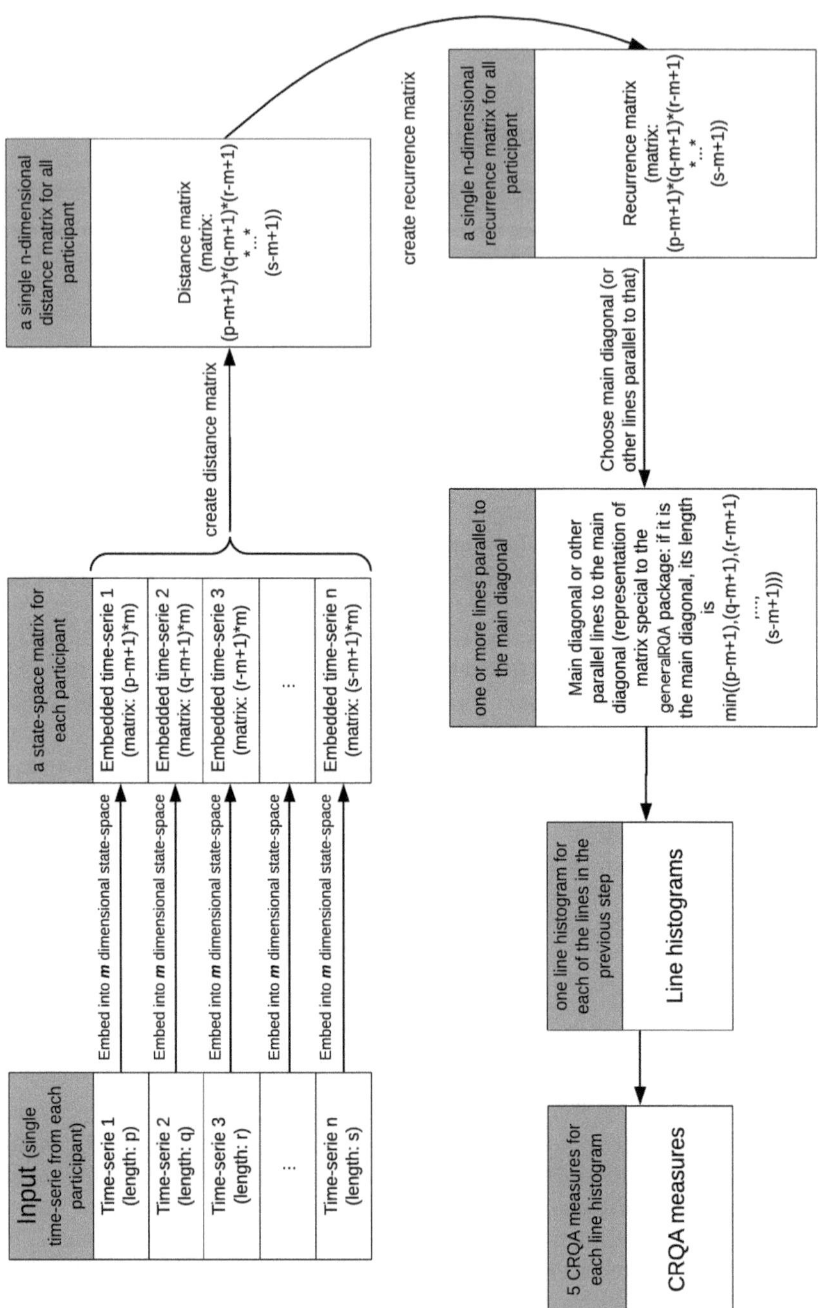

Fig. 3. The general workflow of the `generalRQA` package.

where l is the length of the diagonal line under consideration.

Percent Determinism (DET). It is defined as the ratio of the recurrence points that make diagonal lines to all the recurrence points.

$$DET = \frac{\sum_{l=d_{min}}^{N} lH_D(l)}{\sum_{i=1,j=1}^{N} CR_{i,j}}$$

DET can be interpreted as the predictability of the system. A higher DET value would indicate the longer times the two systems spend in synchronization. In the formulation, d_{min} sets the lower bound on the definition of a line. Typically, d_{min} is set to 2. If d_{min} is set to 1, DET and RR would be identical.

Maximal Line Length in the Diagonal Direction (D_{max}). It is the length of the longest diagonal line within the CRP.

$$D_{max} = \underset{l}{argmax} H_D(l)$$

Since the diagonal lines designate segments of the trajectories of the two systems that run in parallel, this measure indicates the divergence of the two systems' trajectories. This means that the smaller the D_{max}, the more divergent the trajectories. *AvD (Average Line Length in the Diagonal Direction)* is closely related to D_{max} since it is the average diagonal line length in the CRP.

Shannon Entropy of the Frequency Distribution of the Diagonal Line Lengths (ENT).

$$ENT = -\sum_{l=d_{min}}^{N} p(l)lnp(l) \quad where \, p(l) = \frac{H_D(l)}{\sum_{l=d_{min}}^{N} H_D(l)}$$

where $p(l)$ is the probability of a diagonal line with length l occurring in the cross-recurrence plot. The ENT is a measure of the complexity of the deterministic structure in the interaction between the two systems.

Results. A repeated measures ANOVA test was conducted for the three and five-participant groups to measure the experimental design conditions in the RQA measures, namely, RR (Recurrence Rate), DET (Percent Determinism), ENT (Shannon Entropy), D_{max} (Maximum Line Length), and AvD (Average Line Length) measures.

As it happens in eye tracking data collection settings, it is likely that eye tracker may lose calibration during data recording, in which case the time series recorded for these participants become corrupt and unusable. In cases where the time series for more than one participant were corrupt, the corresponding trial was excluded entirely, while, in the case of only one corrupt time series, either the corresponding trial was excluded entirely (the *Exclusion* approach), or the corrupt time series was replaced by the mean of all the other time series in the trial (the *Replacement* approach). Table 1 shows whether the intensity of the visual target (i.e., Point Color), the presence or absence of the gaze location marker (viz. Modality), and the group size have a significant effect on the values of the five CRQA measures.

	Point Color		Modality		Group Size	
	Exclusion	Replacement	Exclusion	Replacement	Exclusion	Replacement
RR	✓	✓	✓	✓	✓	x
DET	x	x	x	✓	✓	x
ENT	x	x	x	✓	✓	x
D_{max}	x	x	✓	✓	✓	x
AvD	x	x	✓	✓	✓	x

These findings showed that *DET* and *ENT* returned similar results under the two data processing assumptions (Exclusion and Replacement). Similarly, D_{max} and AvD returned comparable results, whereas the results obtained from the *RR* variable were different than the others. Among all of the measures, only *RR* revealed coherent results under all the experimental conditions.

6 Discussion and Conclusion

The goal of the present study is to quantify group dynamics in a collaborative visual search task. We investigated this in an experimental study, which aimed to differentiate between various experimental conditions based on the various coupling dynamics of group members. For this, we evaluated alternative measures to describe the group formation patterns of eye movements in a visual search task. RR was the only measure that reliably identified the experimental conditions. Consequently, the RR measure can be conceived as a reliable one for measuring visual dynamics in group eye tracking.

It is shown that in some cases and circumstances, an unembedded RP can contain all the information that its embedded versions contain [22]. Bearing this in mind and the fact that the time series for the cases with gray and black gaze targets are not long enough and yield meaningless embeddings, we decided not to embed our individual time series. However, to compare the results, we then concatenated the time-series from different participants, yielding a time-series long enough for embedding to compare the results. The outcome of the RQA on the embedded data supported our findings by revealing similar results to the non-embedded data set.

In proposing ways to find appropriate measures for group formation patterns, we have only considered four of the five classic RQA measures (Dmax and AvD considered the same measure). The other classic measure is the TREND (TND). Other than these traditional measures named by [47], the five extended measures and other more modern measures have been proposed by them. A modern approach is to consider the recurrence matrix as the adjacency matrix of a network. This allows us to use measures from the complex networks toolbox, such as clustering coefficient, betweenness coefficient, and average shortest path [8–10, 23]. In future work, these measures may also be considered as candidates for capturing group eye tracking dynamics.

Another aspect that can be considered in future work is the use of gaze location markers with different shapes. In the current study, we used a heat-map-like gaze location marker; however, the complex dynamics of the heat-map gaze location marker could have resulted in a convoluted dataset. More research is needed to study the impact of alternative visualizations on group dynamics in group eye tracking [6, 18, 19, 37, 40, 41].

Acknowledgments. Acknowledgments. This study has been partially supported by TUBITAK (The Scientific and Technological Research Council of Türkiye) 116E570 "Multiuser Eyetracking Platform for Social Gaze", and by Jagiellonian University Strategic Programme Excellence Initiative Priority Research Area DigiWorld (ID.UJ) under the project title "Cognitive Aspects of Interaction and Communication in Natural and Artificial Agents".

Disclosure of Interests..   The authors have no competing interests to declare that are relevant to the content of this article

References

1. Abitino, A., Pugh, S.L., Peacock, C.E., D'Mello, S.K.: Eye TO Eye: Gaze patterns predict remote collaborative problem-solving behaviors in triads. In: International Conference on Artificial Intelligence in Education, pp. 378–389. Springer International Publishing, Cham (2022)
2. C Acartürk M Fal MP Çakır 2024 User performance and engagement in multi-user gaming Environments: An experimental investigation through the group eye tracking (GET) paradigm Entertainment Computing 51 100714https://doi.org/10.1016/j.entcom.2024.100714
3. NC Anderson WF Bischof KE Laidlaw EF Risko A Kingstone 2013 Recurrence quantification analysis of eye movements Behav. Res. Methods 45 842 856 https://doi.org/10.3758/s13428-012-0299-5
4. MI Coco R Dale 2014 Cross-recurrence quantification analysis of categorical and continuous time series: an R package Front. Psychol. 5 510 https://doi.org/10.3389/fpsyg.2014.00510
5. L Conradt C List 2009 Group decisions in humans and animals: A survey Philosophical Transactions of the Royal Society B: Biological Sciences 364 1518 719 742 https://doi.org/10.1098/rstb.2008.0276
6. DA Dever MJ Amon H Vrzakova MD Wiedbusch EB Cloude R Azevedo 2022 Capturing sequences of learners' self-regulatory interactions with instructional material during game-based learning using auto-recurrence quantification analysis Front. Psychol. 13 813677https://doi.org/10.3389/fpsyg.2022.813677
7. M Dindar I Alikhani J Malmberg S Järvelä T Seppänen 2019 Examining shared monitoring in collaborative learning: A case of a recurrence quantification analysis approach Comput. Hum. Behav. 100 335 344 https://doi.org/10.1016/j.chb.2019.03.004
8. RV Donner 2011 Recurrence-based time series analysis by means of complex network methods International Journal of Bifurcation and Chaos 21 04 1019 1046 https://doi.org/10.1142/S0218127411029021
9. RV Donner J Heitzig JF Donges Y Zou N Marwan J Kurths 2011 The geometry of chaotic dynamics — a complex network perspective The European Physical Journal B 84 653 672 https://doi.org/10.1140/epjb/e2011-10899-1
10. RV Donner Y Zou JF Donges N Marwan J Kurths 2010 Recurrence networks—a novel paradigm for nonlinear time series analysis New J. Phys. 12 033025https://doi.org/10.1088/1367-2630/12/3/033025
11. Forsyth, D.R.: Group dynamics, 7th Edition. Cengage Learning Custom Publishing (2019)
12. Fusaroli, R., Tylén, K., Fusaroli, R., Tylén, K.: Investigating conversational dynamics: Interactive alignment, interpersonal synergy, and collective task performance. Cognitive Sci. **40**(1), 145–171 (2016) https://doi.org/10.1111/cogs.12251

13. P Grassberger I Procaccia 1983 Characterization of strange attractors Phys. Rev. Lett. 50 5 346 349 https://doi.org/10.1103/PhysRevLett.50.346

14. J Gudmundsson M Kreveld van B Speckmann 2007 Efficient detection of patterns in 2D trajectories of moving points GeoInformatica 11 2 195 215 https://doi.org/10.1007/s10707-006-0002-z

15. Jermann, P., Mullins, D., Nüssli, M.A., Dillenbourg, P.: Collaborative gaze footprints: Correlates of interaction quality. In: Spada, H., Stahl, G., Miyake, N.,Law, N. (Eds.), Connecting Computer-Supported Collaborative Learning to Policy and Practice: CSCL2011 Conference Proceedings. Volume I — Long Papers, pp. 184–191. International Society of the Learning Sciences, Hong Kong, China (2011)

16. Jermann, P., Nüssli, M.A.: Effects of sharing text selections on gaze cross-recurrence and interaction quality in a pair programming task. In: Proceedings of the ACM 2012 Conference on Computer Supported Cooperative Work, pp. 1125–1134 (2012) https://doi.org/10.1145/2145204.2145371

17. Knight, A.P., Kennedy, D.M., McComb, S.A.: Using recurrence analysis to examine group dynamics. Group Dynamics: Theory, Research, and Practice **20**(3), 223–241 (2016) https://psycnet.apa.org/doi/10.1037/gdn0000046

18. Lanata, A., Sebastiani, L., Di Gruttola, F., Di Modica, S., Scilingo, E.P., Greco, A.: Nonlinear analysis of eye-tracking information for motor imagery assessments. Frontiers in Neuroscience **13** (2020) https://doi.org/10.3389/fnins.2019.01431

19. D Lopez Perez P Tomalski A Radkowska H Ballieux DG Moore 2021 Efficiency of scanning and attention to faces in infancy independently predict language development in a multiethnic and bilingual sample of 2-year-olds First Lang. 41 2 218 239 https://doi.org/10.1177/0142723720966815

20. MM Louwerse R Dale EG Bard P Jeuniaux 2012 Behavior matching in multimodal communication is synchronized Cogn. Sci. 36 8 1404 1426 https://doi.org/10.1111/j.1551-6709.2012.01269.x

21. Mach, R., Schweitzer, F.: Multi-agent model of biological swarming. In: European Conference on Artificial Life, pp. 810–820. Berlin, Heidelberg: Springer Berlin Heidelberg (2011) https://doi.org/10.1007/978-3-540-39432-7_87

22. TK March SC Chapman RO Dendy 2005 Recurrence plot statistics and the effect of embedding Physica D 200 1–2 171 184 https://doi.org/10.1016/j.physd.2004.11.002

23. N Marwan JF Donges Y Zou RV Donner J Kurths 2009 Complex network approach for recurrence analysis of time series Phys. Lett. A 373 46 4246 4254 https://doi.org/10.1016/j.physleta.2009.09.042

24. N Marwan MC Romano M Thiel J Kurths 2007 Recurrence plots for the analysis of complex systems Phys. Rep. 438 5–6 237 329 https://doi.org/10.1016/j.physrep.2006.11.001

25. GM Mindlin R Gilmore 1992 Topological analysis and synthesis of chaotic time series Physica D 58 1–4 229 242 https://doi.org/10.1016/0167-2789(92)90111-Y

26. Moulder, R., Booth, B., Abitino, A., D'Mello, S.: Recurrence quantification analysis of eye gaze dynamics during team collaboration. In: LAK23, 13th International Learning Analytics and Knowledge Conference, pp. 430–440 (2023) https://doi.org/10.1145/3576050.3576113

27. Parrish, J. K., Hamner, W., Hamner, W.M. (Eds.): Animal groups in three dimensions: how species aggregate. Cambridge University Press (1997)

28. N Perony G Kerth F Schweitzer 2022 Data-driven modelling of group formation in the fission–fusion dynamics of Bechstein's bats J. R. Soc. Interface 19 190 20220170 https://doi.org/10.1098/rsif.2022.0170

29. Pietinen, S., Bednarik, R., Glotova, T., Tenhunen, V., Tukiainen, M.: A method to study visual attention aspects of collaboration: Eye-tracking pair programmers simultaneously. In: ETRA '08 Proceedings of the 2008 Symposium on Eye Tracking Research and Applications, pp. 39–42 (2008) https://doi.org/10.1145/1344471.1344480

30. Reddy, G.R., Eloy, L., Dickler, R., Reitman, J.G., Pugh, S.L., Foltz, P.W., ..., Hirshfield, L.: Synerg-eye-zing: Decoding nonlinear gaze dynamics underlying successful collaborations in co-located teams. In: Proceedings of the 25th International Conference on Multimodal Interaction, pp. 545–554 (2023) https://doi.org/10.1145/3577190.3614104

31. DC Richardson R Dale NZ Kirkham 2007 The art of conversation is coordination Psychol. Sci. 18 5 407 413 https://doi.org/10.1111/j.1467-9280.2007.01914.x

32. Richardson, T.O., Perony, N., Tessone, C.J., Bousquet, C.A., Manser, M.B., Schweitzer, F.: Dynamical coupling during collective animal motion. arXiv preprint arXiv:1311.1417 (2013) https://doi.org/10.48550/arXiv.1311.1417

33. B Schneider K Sharma S Cuendet G Zufferey P Dillenbourg R Pea 2018 Leveraging mobile eye-trackers to capture joint visual attention in co-located collaborative learning groups Int. J. Comput.-Support. Collab. Learn. 13 241 261 https://doi.org/10.1007/s11412-018-9281-2

34. B Schneider R Pea 2017 Real-time mutual gaze perception enhances collaborative learning and collaboration quality Educational Media and Technology Yearbook 40 99 125 https://doi.org/10.1007/s11412-013-9181-4

35. AJ Strang GJ Funke SM Russell AW Dukes MS Middendorf 2014 Physio-behavioral coupling in a cooperative team task: contributors and relations J. Exp. Psychol. Hum. Percept. Perform. 40 1 145 158

36. Tien, G., Atkins, M.S., Zheng, B.: Measuring gaze overlap on videos between multiple observers. In: ETRA '12: Proceedings of the Symposium on Eye Tracking Research and Applications, pp. 309–312 (2012) https://doi.org/10.1145/2168556.2168623

37. P Tomalski DL Pérez A Radkowska A Malinowska-Korczak 2022 Dyadic interactions during infant learning: Exploring infant-parent exchanges in experimental eye-tracking studies Infant Behav. Dev. 69 101780https://doi.org/10.1016/j.infbeh.2022.101780

38. CM Topaz AL Bertozzi 2004 Swarming patterns in a two-dimensional kinematic model for biological groups SIAM J. Appl. Math. 65 1 152 174 https://doi.org/10.1137/s0036139903437424

39. Vaidyanathan, P., Pelz, J., Alm, C., Shi, P., Haake, A.: Recurrence quantification analysis reveals eye-movement behavior differences between experts and novices. In: ETRA '14 Proceedings of the Symposium on Eye Tracking Research and Applications, pp. 303–306 (2014) https://doi.org/10.1145/2578153.2578207

40. Veerabhadrappa, R., Hettiarachchi, I.T., Bhatti, A.: Using recurrence quantification analysis to quantify the physiological synchrony in dyadic ECG data. In: 2021 IEEE International Systems Conference (SysCon), pp. 1–8. IEEE (2021) https://doi.org/10.1109/SysCon48628.2021.9447059

41. Villamor, M.M., Rodrigo, M.M.T.: Predicting pair success in a pair programming eye tracking experiment using cross-recurrence quantification analysis. APSIPA Transactions on Signal and Information Processing **11**(1) (2022)

42. S Wallot P Mitkidis JJ McGraw A Roepstorff 2016 Beyond synchrony: Joint action in a complex production task reveals beneficial effects of decreased interpersonal synchrony PLoS ONE 11 12 e0168306https://doi.org/10.1371/journal.pone.0168306

43. S Wallot 2019 Multidimensional Cross-Recurrence Quantification Analysis (MdCRQA)–a method for quantifying correlation between multivariate time-series Multivar. Behav. Res. 54 2 173 191 https://doi.org/10.1080/00273171.2018.1512846

44. S Wallot A Roepstorff D Mønster 2016 Multidimensional Recurrence Quantification Analysis (MdRQA) for the analysis of multidimensional time-series: A software implementation in MATLAB and its application to group-level data in joint action Front. Psychol. 7 1835 https://doi.org/10.3389/fpsyg.2016.01835

45. S Wallot 2017 Recurrence quantification analysis of processes and products of discourse: A tutorial in R Discourse Process. 54 5–6 382 405 https://doi.org/10.1080/0163853X.2017.1297921

46. Webber, C.L., Ioana, C., & Marwan, N.: Recurrence plots and their quantifications: expanding horizons. Proceedings of the 6th International Symposium on Recurrence Plots, Grenoble, France. Springer Proceedings in Physics (2016) https://doi.org/10.1007/978-3-319-29922-8
47. Webber, C.L., Marwan, N. (Eds.): Recurrence Quantification Analysis: Theory and best practices. Springer Cham (2015) https://doi.org/10.1007/978-3-319-07155-8
48. JP Zbilut N Thomasson CL Webber 2002 Recurrence quantification analysis as a tool for nonlinear exploration of nonstationary cardiac signals Med. Eng. Phys. 24 1 53 60 https://doi.org/10.1016/S1350-4533(01)00112-6
49. JP Zbilut CL Webber Jr 2007 Recurrence quantification analysis: Introduction and historical context International Journal of Bifurcation and Chaos 17 10 3477 3481 https://doi.org/10.1142/S0218127407019238

Blink Induction System via TRPM8 Activation Through Cold Sensation Presentation

Takumi Uesugi and Takehiko Yamaguchi$^{(\boxtimes)}$

Suwa University of Science, Chino-Shi, Toyohira 5000-1, Japan
`gh25503@ed.sus.ac.jp`, `tk-ymgch@rs.sus.ac.jp`

Abstract. In recent years, the widespread adoption of personal computers and smartphones has led to an increase in video display terminal (VDT) work. During VDT tasks, the frequency of spontaneous blinking decreases compared to normal conditions, resulting in tear film instability and contributing to the onset of dry eye. Dry eye is characterized by ocular dryness and discomfort, which can adversely affect quality of life and reduce work productivity. Consequently, effective strategies for preventing dry eye are essential for maintaining occupational health and enhancing overall productivity. Previous studies have attempted to induce blinking using external stimuli, such as air puffing, in order to mitigate the risk of dry eye during prolonged VDT use. However, these methods often caused discomfort and distraction. In this study, we developed a system designed to induce blinking by selectively activating the TRPM8 (Transient Receptor Potential Melastatin 8) receptor through the application of warmed air to the ocular surface, thereby avoiding the activation of corneal mechanoreceptors. We also examined the level of discomfort experienced by participants under different temperature conditions. The results demonstrated that the air stimulation successfully induced blinking. Furthermore, higher temperature air stimuli tended to cause less discomfort among participants. These findings suggest that warm air stimulation may effectively induce blinking while minimizing discomfort. However, the blink response rate and latency were inferior compared to lower temperature conditions, indicating the need for further refinement and optimization of the stimulation parameters.

Keywords: Dry eye · Blinking · TRPM8 · Air puffs · VR

1 Background

1.1 Relationship Between Modern Dry Eye and Blinking

In recent years, the widespread use of personal computers and smartphones has led to an increase in video display terminal (VDT) work. During VDT tasks, the frequency of blinking reportedly decreases from a normal rate of 22 ± 9 times per minute to 7 ± 7 times per minute. This reduction destabilizes the tear film and is considered to be a cause of dry eye [1]. Although dry eye is generally regarded as a condition affecting elderly individuals, however, as shown in Fig. 1, a 2013 survey targeting office workers frequently engaged in VDT work revealed that over half of both male and female respondents exhibited signs of dry eye [2]. Reports suggest that there are approximately 20 million dry eye patients in Japan, indicating the importance of addressing this condition.

H. Mori et al. (Eds.): HCII 2025, LNCS 16333, pp. 419–432, 2026.
https://doi.org/10.1007/978-3-032-12660-3_31

Dry eye is characterized by ocular dryness and discomfort, leading to a decline in quality of life and productivity. Therefore, addressing dry eye is important from the perspective of maintaining workers' health and improving productivity. One commonly recommended countermeasure is to avoid prolonged VDT work; however, this strategy is difficult to implement for individuals whose occupations involve extensive VDT work, such as office workers. Furthermore, with the widespread use of smartphones, individuals are increasingly exposed to screens for long periods of time throughout the day. As a result, current countermeasures are considered insufficient to reduce the risk of dry eye. Another proposed solution for dry eye is to consciously increase blink frequency. However, it is difficult to consciously blink while concentrating on VDT tasks, and doing so may potentially lead to reduced work efficiency.

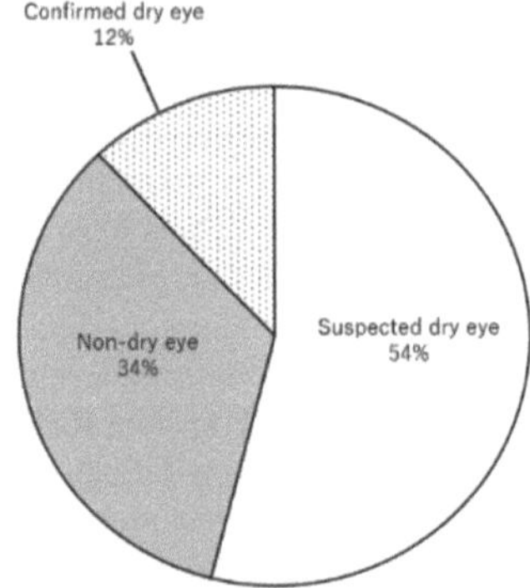

Fig. 1. Dry eye distribution office workers (adapted from [3]).

1.2 Blinking Mechanism

Blinking can be classified into three types: (i) spontaneous blinking, which occurs unconsciously; (ii) voluntary blinking, which is performed consciously; and (iii) reflex blinking, which is triggered when receptors detect external stimuli and serves to protect the cornea. It has been demonstrated that spontaneous blinking is influenced by psychological factors and that the frequency of blinking decreases during periods of concentration, such as during VDT tasks [4].

1.3 Corneal Receptors

The cornea contains nerve fibers and receptors to maintain homeostasis. These include cold-sensitive receptors, such as TRPM8, that detect decreases in temperature caused by evaporative cooling during tear evaporation; TRPV1 receptors, which respond to heat and mechanical stimuli; and Piezo2 receptors, which detect mechanical stimuli. Each of these receptors has a distinct activation threshold, and, when activated by external stimuli, triggers reflex blinking and tear secretion. TRPM8.

TRPM8 is a receptor that is activated by decreases in temperature; however, its activation threshold changes depending on the surrounding temperature [5]. For example, at an ambient temperature of 40 °C, the activation temperature is approximately 35 °C;

at 35 °C, it is approximately 32 °C; and at 30 °C, it is approximately 28 °C. In addition, TRPM8 can be classified into high-threshold cold-sensitive receptors and low-threshold cold-sensitive receptors. High-threshold cold-sensitive receptors cause discomfort along with a sensation of dryness, while low-threshold cold-sensitive receptors contribute to reflex blinking and tear production [6]. Consequently, large temperature changes detected by TRPM8 lead to discomfort accompanied by dryness. Given that the temperature of the ocular surface is approximately 35 °C, which is close to human body temperature, exposure to air at a lower temperature can cause considerable discomfort.

1.4   Previous Studies on Blink Induction and Associated Challenges

Previous studies have aimed to lower the risks associated with reduced blinking during VDT work by intentionally inducing blinking using external stimuli. For example, Dementyev et al. [7] proposed that increasing the number of blinks can help reduce the risk of dry eye. They attempted to suppress the reduction in blink frequency during VDT work by utilizing reflex blinking, which is triggered by external stimuli. Using a mirror-shaped device, they delivered stimuli such as air puffslight flashes, and physical taps to induce reflexive blinking. The results indicated that the average blink rate of participants increased by 36% with the use of air puffs and physical taps. Similarly, Zenner et al. [8] attempted to intentionally induce blinking using a virtual reality head-mounted display, presenting four types of stimuli: screen blurring, flashing, approaching three-dimensional objects, and air puffs. Among these, air puffs, approaching three-dimensional objects, and flashing substantially increased blinking, with approaching objects and air puffs being the most effective. Notably, the shortest response time between stimulus presentation and blink occurrence was observed with approaching objects. However, both studies [7, 8] reported concerns regarding the impact of the stimuli on participants. Adverse effects, such as discomfort caused by the stimuli, may lead to reduced work efficiency when these methods are applied in VDT work settings. Therefore, it is important that stimulus presentation methods not only induce blinking but also minimize negative impacts, such as user discomfort. Zenner et al. [8] reported that among the four stimulus presentation methods that induced blinking, air puffs were the least noticeable to participants. However, Dementyev et al. [7] argued that certain stimuli could cause distraction and be perceived as intrusive.

1.5   Air Puffs

Air puffs are a method for activating receptors that sense mechanical stimuli by directing air toward the cornea. This causes a foreign body sensation in the eye, which triggers reflex blinking. According to Paul, air puffs with a pressure of 5 kPa or higher are optimal for inducing reflex blinking [9].

2   Objective

2.1   Objective of This Study

The objective of this study is to reduce the risk of dry eye associated with VDT work by inducing blinking through stimuli while minimizing user discomfort.

2.2 Research Direction and Hypothesis

Based on the studies by Zenner et al. [8] and Dementyev et al. [7], among the stimuli used—air puffs, approaching objects, flashing, and screen blurring—air puffs were identified as most similar to the stimulus required for this study. It was considered that improving air puffs can reduce discomfort; therefore, air puff stimuli are the focus of this study.

Air puffs induce blinking through mechanical stimulation using air. However, air that is cooler than the corneal temperature may also activate cold-sensitive receptors, such as TRPM8. Therefore, it was hypothesized that limiting the activated receptors to only one can reduce discomfort and distraction caused by excessive stimuli. This study aimed to verify whether activating TRPM8 can induce blinking while minimizing discomfort. In addition, as mentioned in Sect. 1.4, TRPM8 receptors cause discomfort when exposed to large temperature changes. Therefore, the applied stimulus should induce the smallest possible temperature change from the corneal temperature of approximately 35 °C. Consequently, the stimulus temperature in this study was set to the TRPM8 activation threshold of 32 °C relative to 35 °C.

3 Methods

3.1 Research Policy

The purpose of this experiment is to test the hypothesis that stimuli at 32 °C can induce blinking while minimizing discomfort.

3.2 Apparatus Requirements

To conduct the experiment, an apparatus was developed to meet the following requirements:

- Air was applied at a specified temperature to the corneal surface at a pressure of 2 kPa.
- To simulate VDT work, a video was shown, with the stimulus timing adjusted to avoid overlap with eyelid closure.

3.3 Experimental Apparatus

The experimental apparatus was constructed based the design principles outlined in Sect. 3.2. The apparatus is composed of three main blocks:

1. Temperature control block

     In this block, a heat source is controlled by sensors and a microcomputer to maintain the air inside an insulated container at a specified temperature. The following equipment is used in this block (Fig. 2):

   - Arduino Uno R3

        This component reads the temperature sensor at 10-ms intervals and controls various devices to maintain the specified temperature.

- Peltier element

  This device transfers heat from one side to the other when an electric current is applied. A copper heat sink is attached to the heat-dissipating side to serve as the heat source. Powered by a 12-V supply, the heat-dissipating surface can reach temperatures exceeding 70 °C.

- DC motor

  This component circulates the air heated by the heat source, thereby maintaining the specified temperature throughout the entire interior of the container.

- Thermistor

  The thermistor is used to measure the temperature inside the container. The resistance of a thermistor changes with temperature. The voltage across the thermistor is calculated based on the signal output from the thermistor to the microcontroller, and the temperature is determined from the corresponding resistance value. In this study, a negative temperature coefficient thermistor was used, whose resistance decreases with increasing temperature.

- Relay control expansion board

  This component receives input signals and switches the current on or off. In Block 1. This block, it controls the current flowing to the Peltier element via relays based on signals from the Arduino Uno, which obtains temperature data from the thermistor. Control is performed at 1s intervals.

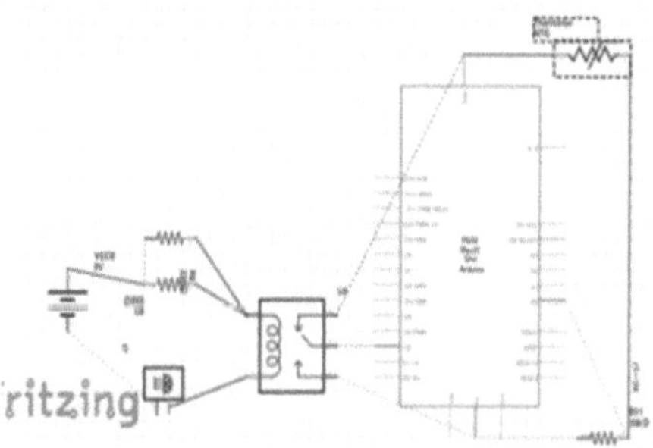
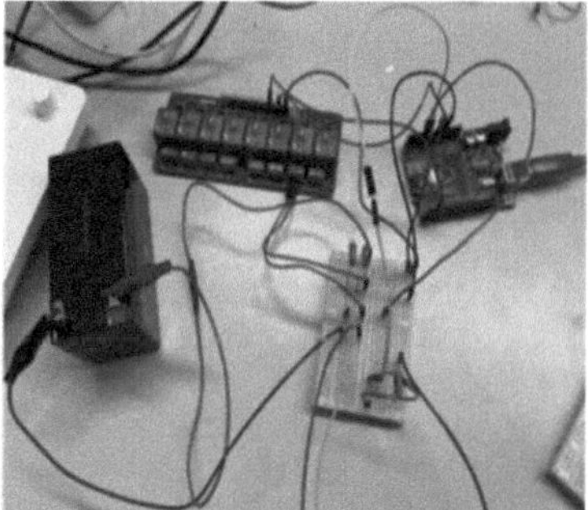

Fig. 2. Circuit diagram (left) and photograph (right) of the air heating device used in this study.

2. Air delivery block

   In this block, air that has been temperature-controlled in Block 1 is directed toward the eye. The following equipment is used in this block (Fig. 3):

- Microblower

  This device generates airflow using ultrasonic vibrations of a ceramic element. It operates at an input volt-age of 16.8 V and produces an air pressure of approximately 2 kPa. A driving resonance frequency in the range of 24–27 kHz is required for operation. A flexible soft tube with a diameter of 5 mm is connected to the outlet nozzle.

- Arduino Uno R3

The same microcontroller used in Block 1 is employed in this block. Since high-frequency vibrations are required to drive the microblower, a pulse waveform at 25.6 kHz is generated from a digital pin using a timer and pulse-width modulation control. This waveform is output when the Arduino Uno receives an activation signal from an external source, with the output duration set to 500 ms.

- Transistor

  Since the pulse waveform generated by the Arduino Uno has a maximum voltage of 5 V, which is insufficient to drive the microblower, a transistor amplifier circuit is used. The pulse waveform is applied as the base current to amplify the signal. The emitter voltage is set to 16.8 V, and the microblower is connected between the power supply and the transistor. Due to the low internal resistance of the microblower, which can cause waveform distortion, a 220 Ω resistor is connected in parallel to stabilize the output.

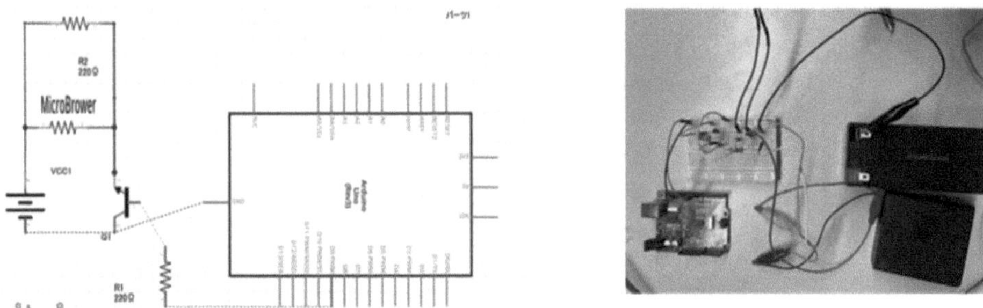

Fig. 3. Schematic diagram (left) and photograph (right) of the air delivery device.

In addition, because heat is generated by the resistors in the circuits of both Block 1 and 2 Block, a USB fan is used to cool the circuits (Fig. 4).

Fig. 4. Cross-sectional view of the device to be attached to the virtual reality head-mounted display.

3. Eye state monitoring and signal transmission block

In this block, the participant's eye openness is measured in real time, and a trig-gersignal is sent to the Arduino Uno. The following equipment is used in this block (Fig. 5):

- Vive Pro Eye and eye tracker

  The experimental environment is presented using Vive Pro Eye, a head-mounted display, with the built-in eye tracker used to measure the participant's right eye openness (Right_Openness) at approximately 10-ms intervals.

- Unity

  Unity is used to render the measurement environment and communicate with the server via WebSocket. Based on the eye tracker data, Unity sends a trigger signal for activating the microblower to the server 30 ms after the end of a blink. During the measurement, both the eye tracker data and the microblower activation times are recorded and exported to a CSV file.

- WebSocket server

  Unity forwards the received activation signal to SerialConnection.js, which is connected to the Arduino Uno. This system is developed using Node.js.

- SerialConnection.js

  A custom web page receives activation signals from the WebSocket server and transmits them via serial communication to the Arduino Uno, which is connected through the serial port. In addition, the web page displays the temperature inside the container as received from the Arduino Uno.

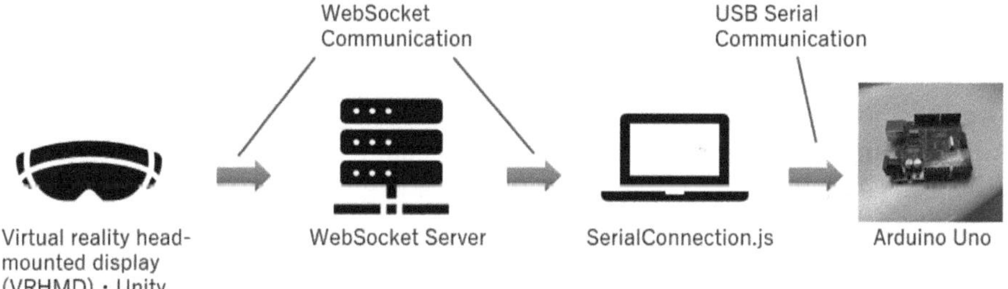

Fig. 5. Functionality of Block 3.

The experimental apparatus consists of Blocks 1, 2, and 3. In Block 1, air is temperature-controlled to a specified level; in Block 1, a trigger signal is sent to the Arduino Uno based on the participant's eye state; and in Block 2, air is blown toward the eye in response to the trigger (Fig. 6).

Fig. 6. Overview of the experimental apparatus.

3.4 Participants

The participants included 11 adult males (mean age: 22.36 ± 0.48 years), all of whom completed the experiment without corrective lenses. One participant was excluded from the analysis due to malfunction of the eye tracker.

3.5 Experimental Procedure

The experiment was conducted to test the hypothesis that exposure to approximately 32 °C air can induce blinking while minimizing discomfort. Three conditions were tested: no stimulation, 28 °C stimulation, and 32 °C stimulation. During the experiment, participants wore the Vive Pro Eye headset and watched a 5-min video in each condition. In the 28 °C and 32 °C stimulation conditions, the microblower was activated at the onset of eye opening following a blink. The order of conditions was counterbalanced across participants. Following the measurements, the participants completed a questionnaire to assess their level of discomfort in the 28 °C and 32 °C stimulation conditions. This study was approved by the Research Ethics Committee of Suwa University of Science (Approval No. 2024-21) (Fig. 7).

Fig. 7. Scene displaying a participant wearing the Vive Pro Eye headset while connected to the test apparatus.

3.6 Data Analysis

- Confirmation of blink induction by air stimulation

  To evaluate whether air stimulation induced blinking, comparisons were made between the baseline condition (no stimulation) and the stimulation conditions (28 °C and 32 °C) based on the total number of blinks and the probability of blink occurrence following stimulation. The total number of blinks across conditions was analyzed using the Friedman test. For post hoc comparisons, the Conover method was applied with Bonferroni and Holm corrections for multiple comparisons.

  To assess the probability of blink occurrence after stimulation, changes in the scale parameter of the gamma distribution were visualized and compared across conditions.
- Evaluation of discomfort across temperature conditions

  Discomfort levels for the 28 °C and 32 °C stimulation conditions were evaluated based on responses to the post-experiment questionnaire. The condition associated with lower discomfort levels represented the blink induction.

4 Results and Discussion

4.1 Experimental Data

The number of blinks observed in the three experimental conditions is provided in Table 1.

Table 1. Blink count for three experimental conditions.

	No stimulus	Stimulus at 28 °C	Stimulus at 32 °C
Subject 1	52	108	73
Subject 2	108	210	127
Subject 3	25	56	90
Subject 4	75	40	83
Subject 5	203	244	276
Subject 6	122	180	211
Subject 7	63	149	109
Subject 8	27	43	51
Subject 9	75	78	89
Subject 10	58	109	73

As a representative example, Fig. 8 displays the time-series data of Right_Openness (right eye openness) and microblower activation timing for Subject 3 (Subject 3). Blue lines represent Right_Openness values, which range from 0 (fully closed) to 1 (fully open). Red lines indicate a flag that toggles when an activation signal is sent from Unity to the microblower. Blue dots indicate the onset of blinks, detected during analysis based on Right_Openness values falling below the blink detection threshold of 0.5.

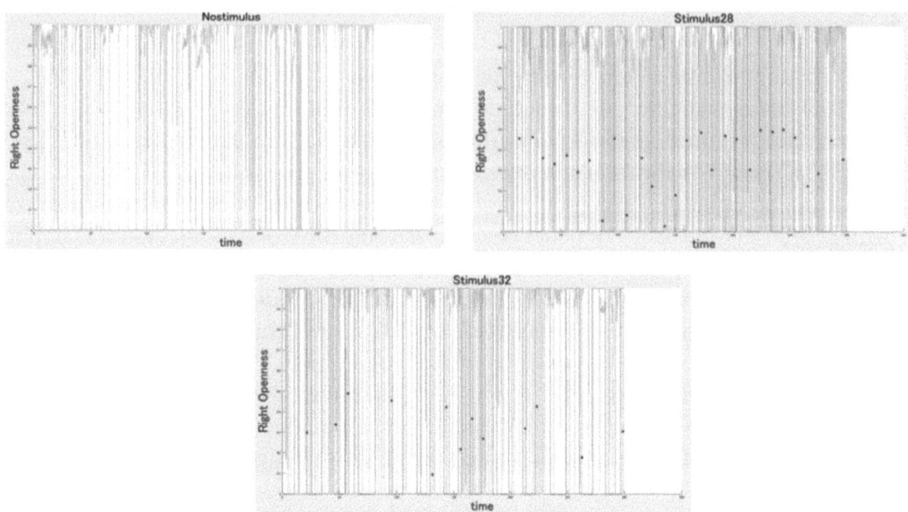

Fig. 8. Time-series plots of Right_Openness (right eye openness) values and blower activation timing for Subject 3 under three experimental conditions (Top left: No Stimulus, Top right: Stimulus at 28 °C, Bottom: Stimulus at 32 °C). Blue lines represent Right_Openness values over time, while red lines indicate the microblower activation timing.

4.2   Results: Verification of Blink Induction by Air Stimulation

The results of the analysis are shown in Table 2. A Friedman test was performed to compare the number of blinks across conditions, and a significant difference was observed (p = 0.005). Post hoc analysis using the Conover method with Bonferroni and Holm corrections for multiple comparisons revealed significant differences between the no-stimulation condition and both the 28 °C and 32 °C stimulation conditions.

Table 2. Results of the Friedman test comparing blink counts across the three experimental conditions (no stimulation, 28 °C, and 32 °C).

		T-Stat	df	W_i	W_j	p
No stimulus	Stimulus at 28°C	2.683	18	11.000	23.000	0.015
	Stimulus at 32°C	3.354	18	11.000	26.000	0.004
Stimulus at 28°C	Stimulus at 32°C	0.671	18	23.000	26.000	0.511

In addition, the stimulation period was divided into early and late phases, and the probability of blink occurrence was visualized by plot-ting the changes in the scale parameter (θ) of the gamma distribution. In both stimulation conditions (28 °C and 32 °C), the scale parameter decreased in the early phase following stimulation onset and increased in the late phase, indicating a higher probability of blinking shortly after stimulation. The blue lines in Figs. 9, 10, 11 represent scale values, while dashed lines indicate a flag that inverts when an activation signal for the microblower is sent. For consistency, this flag is also displayed in the no-stimulation condition, although the microblower is not activated in this condition.

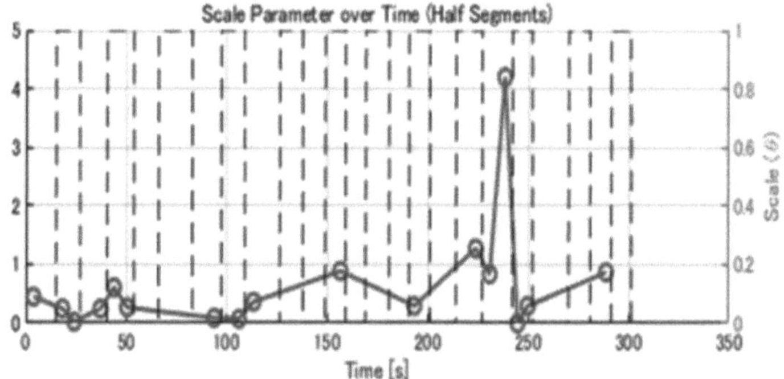

Fig. 9. Changes in the gamma distribution scale parameter in the no-stimulation condition.

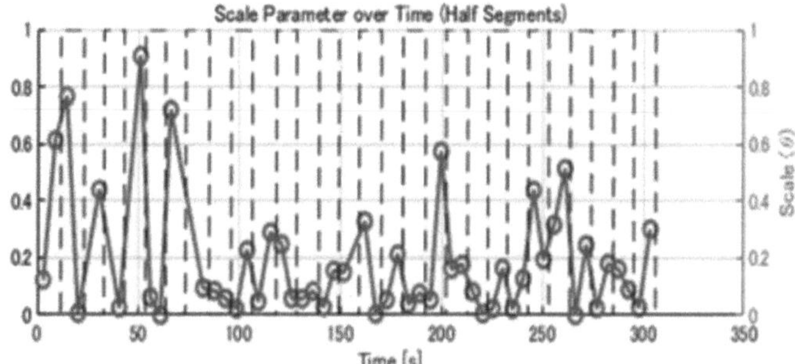

Fig. 10. Changes in the gamma distribution scale parameter in the 28 °C stimulation condition.

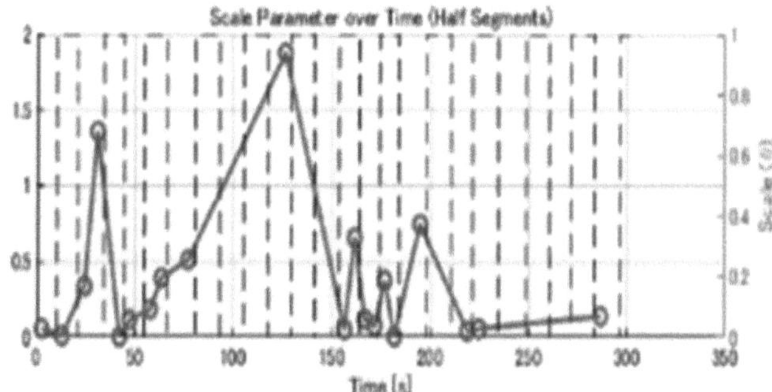

Fig. 11. Changes in the gamma distribution scale parameter in the 32 °C stimulation condition.

4.3   Results: Evaluation of Discomfort Across Temperature Conditions

Out of 10 participants, 8 reported that the 32 °C stimulation condition was more comfortable than the 28 °C stimulation condition, while the remaining 2 participants indicated no noticeable difference between the two conditions. In addition, three participants reported that they did not perceive airflow from the microblower in the 32 °C condition.

5 Discussion

5.1 Verification of Blink Induction by Air Stimulation

The results of the Friedman test and post hoc Conover analysis, using Bonferroni and Holm corrections for multiple comparisons, indicated that both the 28 °C and 32 °C stimulation conditions led to a significant increase in blink frequency compared to the no-stimulation condition. Furthermore, the p-values revealed that the 32 °C condition (p = 0.004) exhibited a stronger blink-inducing effect than the 28 °C condition (p = 0.015).

Prior to the experiment, it was hypothesized that the 28 °C condition would elicit a larger number of blinks given its larger temperature difference from the corneal surface temperature (~35 °C). However, contrary to this expectation, Table 1 indicates that some participants exhibited a higher number of blinks in the 32 °C condition. This discrepancy may be partly attributed to the limited sample size. In addition, participants may have also experienced fatigue or boredom during the experiment, potentially influencing blink frequency. Each participant watched the same 5-min video three times—once for each condition. As the sessions progressed, participants may have become increasingly disengaged, leading to reduced attention and increased spontaneous blinking. As a result, the 28 °C condition, which was initially expected to yield the highest blink frequency due to stimulus strength, occasion-ally resulted in fewer blinks than the 32 °C condition.

The gamma distribution scale parameter (θ) trends provided additional insight. Following stimulus onset, θ values decreased in the early phase and increased in the late phase in both stimulation conditions (28 °C and 32 °C). Since smaller θ values indicate higher blink frequency, these results suggest that the blink frequency increased immediately after stimulation and then decreased over time. This pattern was not observed in the no-stimulation condition, supporting the conclusion that blinking was induced by the airflow stimulus.

5.2 Verification of Evaluation of Discomfort Across Temperature Conditions

The finding that 8 out of 10 participants reported the 32 °C stimulation condition to be more comfortable than the 28 °C stimulation condition is consistent with the initial hypothesis. Notably, some participants reported that they did not perceive any airflow in the 32 °C condition. This may be due to the air pressure being maintained at approximately 2 kPa—less than the pressure threshold of 5 kPa typically required to activate mechanoreceptors involved in airflow detection. Under these conditions, the only receptor expected to be activated was TRPM8, which responds to mild cooling. However, the absence of airflow perception by some participants suggests that TRPM8 may not have been activated, possibly due to environmental or physiological factors.

The ocular surface is typically reheated by the eyelid during blinking. However, if a blink is incomplete, as in the case of microsaccadic blinks (partial or subtle eyelid closures), sufficient warming may not occur, potentially lowering the corneal surface temperature below the assumed baseline of approximately 35 °C. Previous studies

[4] have reported that during engagement in visual tasks, the frequency of full blinks decreases while that of microsaccadic blinks increases. It is therefore plausible that during the experiment, participants' focus on the video led to reduced corneal warming and suppressed TRPM8 activation, resulting in reduced perception of airflow.

In addition, the two participants who reported no noticeable difference between the 28 °C and 32 °C stimulation conditions also indicated that the 28 °C stimulation condition was not uncomfortable. This finding may reflect individual variability in TRPM8 sensitivity. As TRPM8 function is known to vary with age [8], individual differences in thermal perception are not unexpected.

6 Conclusion and Future Directions

In this study, an experimental system was developed to test the hypothesis that 32 °C airflow stimulation of the corneal surface can induce blinking while minimizing discomfort. The experiment evaluated the presence of blink induction, the response rate and timing, and subjective participant experience. The results confirmed that the 32 °C stimulation condition successfully induced blinking with minimal discomfort. The 28 °C stimulation condition, which involved a lower temperature, yielded a higher blink response rate; however, it was associated with increased discomfort.

These findings suggest a trade-off between stimulus intensity and responsiveness: while lower temperatures may increase responsiveness, they may also increase discomfort. For the 32 °C stimulation system to be viable in practical applications, improvements in responsiveness are required. Furthermore, individual differences in TRPM8 receptor activation indicate that the system may not be universally effective.

This study is a fundamental investigation of the performance of a blink induction system designed to activate TRPM8 receptors through cold airflow stimulation. While the results demonstrated blink induction under controlled conditions, future studies should be conducted to evaluate the system's effectiveness in more realistic scenarios, such as during VDT tasks, where blinking is typically suppressed. In addition, future studies should evaluate a wider range of air temperatures to determine the optimal balance between stimulus strength, blink responsiveness, and user comfort.

Furthermore, some participants reported discomfort related to the weight and fit of the experimental device. Future studies should focus on reducing the weight of the device and improving its ergonomics to reduce physical stress and improve wearability.

Finally, as the results revealed individual variability in TRPM8 activation, future research should investigate alternative methods that activate a wider range of sensory receptors. This can lead to the development of a more robust blink induction method that is less susceptible to individual differences in sensory sensitivity.

References

1. Nakamori, K., Tsubota, K.: Dry Eyes and Video Display Terminals. N. Engl. J. Med. **328**(8):584 https://doi.org/10.1056/NEJM199302253280817 (1993/02/25)

2. Uchino, M., Yokoi, N., Uchino, Y., Dogru, M., Kawashima, M., Komuro, A., Sonomura, Y., Kato, H., Kinoshita, S., Schaumberg, D.A., Tsubota, K.: Prevalence of Dry Eye Disease and its Risk Factors in Visual Display Terminal Users: The Osaka Study. American Journal of Ophthalmology **156**(4), 759–766.e1 (Oct. 2013)
3. Dry Eye Society, Committee on Definition and Diagnosis of Dry Eye: New definition and diagnostic criteria for dry eye disease in Japan (2016 revision) https://www.mhlw.go.jp/file/05-Shingikai-11121000-Iyakushokuhinkyoku-Soumuka/0000172618.pdf
4. Tada, H., Yamada, F., Fukuda, K. (Eds.). The psychology of blinking: A comprehensive study on blink behavior (in Japanese). Kitaohji Shobo, Kyoto (1991)
5. Fujita, F., Uchida, K., Takaishi, M., Sokabe, T., Tominaga, M.: Ambient temperature affects the temperature threshold for TRPM8 activation through interaction of phosphatidylinositol 4,5 bisphosphate. The Journal of Neuroscience **33**(14), 6154–6159 (2013)
6. Yoshiaki, T: Dry Eye and Corneal Perception MB OCULI. No.128:20–27,2023
7. Dementyev, A., Holz, C.: DualBlink: A wearable device to continuously detect, track, and actuate blinking for alleviating dry eyes and computer vision syndrome. Proceedings of the ACM on Interactive, Mobile, Wearable and Ubiquitous Technologies **1**(1), 1–19 (2017)
8. Zenner, A., Ullmann, K., Ariza, O., Steinicke, F., Krüger, A.: Induce a blink of the eye: Evaluating techniques for triggering eye blinks in virtual reality. Proceedings of the ACM CHI Conference on Human Factors in Computing Systems **256**:1–12 (2023)
9. Haerich, P.: Using airpuffs to elicit the human blink reflex. Behavior Research Methods, Instruments, & Computers **30**(4), 661–666 (1998)

GViT: Combining Convolutional and Transformer Layers for Spatial-Temporal EEG Analysis

Chenxu Zhu, Yiming Xu, and Xiaodong Qu$^{(\boxtimes)}$

The George Washington University, Washington D.C., USA
x.qu@gwu.edu

Abstract. This paper presents GViT, a hybrid CNN-Transformer architecture designed to improve EEG-based gaze prediction by leveraging spatial-temporal representations of brain signals. GViT integrates convolutional layers to extract local spatial features with a transformer encoder that models global temporal dependencies, enabling robust performance on noisy EEG data. Evaluated on the EEGEyeNet dataset, GViT consistently achieves the lowest gaze prediction error among all tested models, outperforming baseline CNN, GRU, and transformer variants. By bridging neuroscience-inspired design and deep learning advances, this work demonstrates the effectiveness of hybrid architectures for brain signal decoding and introduces a modular framework applicable to a broad range of neurophysiological time-series tasks.

Keywords: EEG signal processing · gaze prediction · hybrid cnn-transformer architecture · brain-inspired machine learning · temporal-spatial modeling · EEGEyeNet · deep learning for neuroscience

1 Introduction

Electroencephalography (EEG) data, due to its non-invasive nature and millisecond-level temporal resolution, is widely used in brain-computer interface (BCI) applications such as cognitive workload estimation, mental health monitoring, and gaze prediction. However, EEG analysis remains challenging due to its noisy signals, high dimensionality, and the complex spatial-temporal relationships across channels [3,5].

Deep learning methods, particularly Convolutional Neural Networks (CNNs) and Transformer architectures, have shown promise in EEG-based prediction tasks [11]. CNNs are effective in capturing localized spatial features from multi-channel EEG data, while Transformers excel at modeling long-range temporal dependencies through attention mechanisms [6]. Hybrid CNN-Transformer architectures have emerged to combine the strengths of both models, yet their ability to fully capture the intricate spatial dependencies between EEG electrodes is still limited [1,2].

© The Author(s), under exclusive license to Springer Nature Switzerland AG 2026
H. Mori et al. (Eds.): HCII 2025, LNCS 16333, pp. 433–442, 2026.
https://doi.org/10.1007/978-3-032-12660-3_32

In this paper, we present a hybrid deep learning framework for EEG-based gaze prediction, grounded in a final project conducted as part of a machine learning course. Our model incorporates convolutional layers to extract local features from 2D-structured EEG signals and uses Transformer encoders to model global temporal dynamics. We explore different architecture variants and identify a configuration that achieves state-of-the-art performance on the EEGEyeNet benchmark. Our contributions are threefold:

- We analyze the strengths and limitations of CNNs and Transformers when applied to EEG gaze prediction.
- We design and implement a CNN-Transformer hybrid model with a novel convolutional refinement module to enhance spatial representations before temporal modeling.
- We evaluate our model on the Absolute Position task of the EEGEyeNet dataset and demonstrate its performance improvement over existing baselines, including EEGNet, InceptionTime, and EEGViT.

Our findings suggest that well-designed hybrid architectures can significantly improve EEG decoding accuracy without requiring external eye-tracking hardware, contributing to the development of accessible and efficient BCI applications.

2   Related Work

EEG-based signal classification has long served as a cornerstone for applications in brain-computer interfaces (BCI), with use cases ranging from cognitive workload estimation to emotion recognition and eye-gaze prediction [3]. Over the years, a variety of deep learning models have been proposed to extract meaningful spatiotemporal patterns from raw EEG data [11].

Early work relied heavily on convolutional neural networks (CNNs), such as EEGNet, which introduced depthwise and separable convolutions to efficiently model spatial patterns across EEG channels [10]. These models offered strong performance on motor imagery and ERP datasets while maintaining low parameter counts for real-time BCI use [2].

Building upon this foundation, temporal convolutional approaches such as InceptionTime [7] and architectures optimized for sequential modeling like DeepConvLSTM [15] began to show improvements in capturing long-range temporal dependencies. Transformer-based approaches further extended these capabilities by introducing global attention.

Recent surveys and studies have highlighted the importance of deep learning in EEG decoding. Roy et al. [24] reviewed deep learning's rise in EEG signal processing, emphasizing CNNs and RNNs. Ma et al. [13] proposed a hybrid CNN-transformer model for EEG-based motor imagery classification, showing that transformer-based modules can outperform traditional recurrent layers in some tasks. Xu et al. [27] explored deep transfer CNN frameworks that support

EEG signal classification across subjects, an important direction for practical BCI systems.

In parallel, more recent works have introduced attention-guided transformer architectures tailored to EEG signals. Yi et al. [29] designed an attention-enhanced spatial transformer to dynamically adapt to spatial channel variations, demonstrating strong generalization across subjects. Li et al. [12] proposed a temporal attention masking scheme to selectively emphasize relevant EEG segments, boosting robustness against signal noise. Qu et al. [19] explored multi-task transformer structures that jointly optimize EEG decoding and auxiliary physiological signals, underscoring the potential of multi-modal integration.

To address the limitations of both CNNs and transformers, hybrid CNN-Transformer models have emerged. These architectures aim to leverage the spatial locality of convolutions and the long-range dependency modeling of transformers. The EEGEyeNet benchmark [8] has provided a standardized platform for comparing such models across diverse gaze-related EEG tasks [2].

Our work builds on these developments by evaluating a hybrid CNN-Transformer model using EEGEyeNet's dataset, targeting eye-gaze decoding. We aim to assess whether this architecture offers measurable improvements in accuracy and robustness over prior approaches, particularly under the constraints of modest dataset sizes and low-latency inference requirements.

3   Method

3.1   Overview of Hybrid Architectures

Our primary objective is to enhance EEG signal classification by exploring hybrid deep learning architectures that combine spatial, temporal, and topological features. Recent surveys have highlighted the growing interest in combining graph-based and sequence-based models to better capture EEG dynamics [3,11]. We designed two novel pipelines–GNN-Transformer-FC and GCN-CNN-Transformer–that extend prior work [28] and are optimized for the spatial-temporal structure of EEG data. Both architectures aim to reduce noise sensitivity while improving representation capacity by separating spatial structure from temporal information processing.

3.2   Model 1: GNN + Transformer + FC Layers

Figure 1 illustrates our first model architecture. Raw EEG time series are first transformed into graph structures based on inter-channel similarity and spatial adjacency. Each EEG trial is represented as a sequence of graph snapshots over time, where each graph node corresponds to an EEG channel and edges encode either physical proximity or mutual information.

These graphs are processed by a three-layer Graph Neural Network (GNN) based on Graph Attention Networks (GAT), which generates node embeddings that encode spatial relationships across electrodes. The node embeddings at each time step are then stacked into a token matrix and passed into a Transformer encoder block comprising two layers with 4 attention heads and feed-forward layers of size 512. This module captures temporal patterns across the entire trial window.

The resulting embeddings are flattened and aggregated via global average pooling, followed by two fully connected layers for final classification. Dropout (0.3) is applied before the classifier to prevent overfitting.

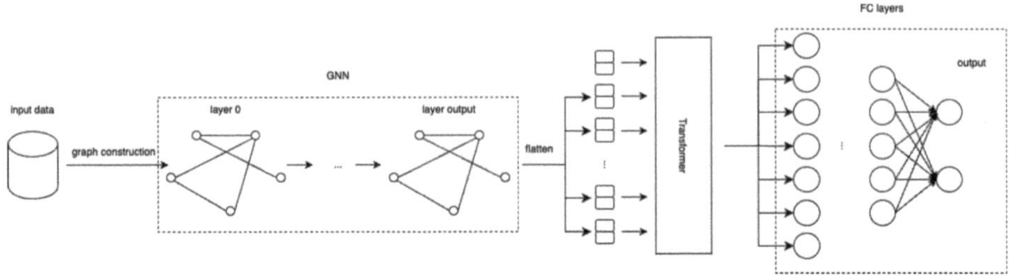

Fig. 1. GNN + Transformer + FC Layers: A spatial-temporal hybrid model for EEG classification

This modular structure supports interpretability and adaptability to other EEG tasks. The decoupling of spatial and temporal modeling also allows for task-specific tuning in future extensions.

3.3 Model 2: GCN + CNN + Transformer

The second architecture, shown in Fig. 2, enhances the spatial encoding stage with convolutional operations. We begin with a two-layer Graph Convolutional Network (GCN) to embed the EEG graph structure derived from the 129 channels. The output is reshaped into a 2D tensor of shape (C, T) where C is the number of spatial channels and T is the number of time steps.

This tensor is processed by two stacked 2D convolutional layers (kernel size = 3, stride = 1), each followed by Batch Normalization and ReLU activation. These layers extract localized temporal and spatial features while reducing noise.

The resulting feature map is tokenized into non-overlapping patches (size $C \times P$) and fed into a Transformer encoder consisting of two layers (4 heads, FF size = 512). Positional encoding is added to preserve temporal order. The final embedding is flattened and passed through a classifier with two fully connected layers.

This hybrid architecture balances the strength of CNNs in capturing local spatial-temporal dynamics with the ability of transformers to integrate global context. Inspired by CNN-transformer hybrids in computer vision [7], this design enables robust learning even under limited data conditions.

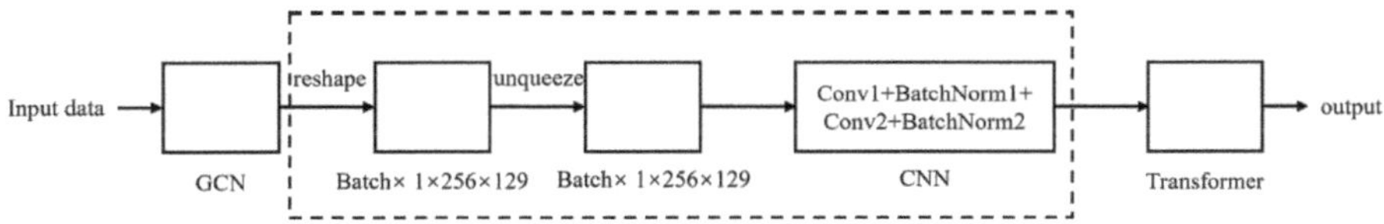

Fig. 2. GCN + CNN + Transformer: A layered architecture combining topological, spatial, and temporal processing

3.4   Dataset and Preprocessing

We trained and evaluated our models on the EEGEyeNet dataset [8], which contains EEG time-series data recorded during eye-gaze tracking tasks. Each instance is labeled according to gaze direction, with data sampled at 256 Hz across 129 scalp electrodes following the 10-5 system.

We applied standard EEG preprocessing: z-score normalization per channel, bandpass filtering (140 Hz), and segmentation into fixed-length windows of 1 s (256 time steps). To construct EEG graphs, we used either Euclidean distance between electrode positions or mutual information between channel pairs [28]. Adjacency matrices were normalized using symmetric normalization.

3.5   Training Details

All models were implemented using PyTorch. We used the Adam optimizer with an initial learning rate of 0.001 and weight decay of 1×10^{-5}. Categorical cross-entropy was used as the loss function. Batch size was set to 64, and all models were trained for 100 epochs with early stopping based on validation accuracy (patience = 10).

Dropout (0.3) was applied to transformer and FC layers. All experiments were conducted on a single NVIDIA A100 GPU. Training time per model averaged 2 h. All code and pretrained models will be released upon publication for reproducibility.

4   Results

We evaluated the proposed models on the EEGEyeNet dataset [8], using the Euclidean distance between predicted and actual gaze positions as the primary evaluation metric. Table 1 reports the average prediction error (in pixels) and the standard deviation across five runs.

Our proposed **CNN-GViT hybrid model** achieved the lowest mean distance error (61.30 ± 1.06 pixels), outperforming all baselines. This suggests that combining CNN layers for spatial feature extraction with transformer blocks for global temporal attention yields a more accurate representation of EEG signals for gaze estimation tasks.

4.1 Baseline Models

- **CNN**: A standard 1D convolutional neural network for learning spatial patterns across EEG channels.
- **Transformer (Vanilla)**: A transformer encoder with sinusoidal positional encodings to model temporal dependencies.
- **CNN-GRU**: A hybrid CNN model followed by a GRU layer, combining local feature extraction and sequential modeling.
- **GViT**: Generative Vision Transformer adapted for EEG signals, following the approach by Yang et al. [28].
- **CNN-GViT (Ours)**: The proposed hybrid model that integrates convolutional front-ends with a GViT back-end.

4.2 Performance Comparison

Table 1. Root Mean Squared Error (RMSE) in millimeters on EEGEyeNet dataset. Lower is better. Mean and standard deviation over five runs

Model	RMSE (mm)	Std Dev (mm)
CNN	72.20	1.34
Transformer (Vanilla)	64.35	1.47
CNN-GRU	63.05	1.24
EEGViT [28]	55.4	1.18
CNN-GViT (Ours)	**54.3**	**0.66**

These results validate the advantage of architectural fusion: convolutional layers improve the extraction of localized EEG features, while transformer-based attention enhances modeling of long-range dependencies. The CNN-GViT hybrid model shows consistent improvement across runs, indicating its robustness for real-time eye-gaze decoding tasks from EEG signals.

5 Discussion

This study set out to explore two main research questions: (RQ1) Which machine learning architectures perform best on EEG-based visual stimulus classification tasks? (RQ2) How do hybrid CNN-transformer architectures compare to standalone deep learning models?

Our findings provide compelling evidence for both research questions. As shown in Table 1, the hybrid CNN-transformer model achieved the best RMSEE (54.3±0.66), outperforming both the baseline CNN and transformer-only models. This performance boost suggests that integrating convolutional layers–effective at extracting local spatial features–with transformer-based modules–designed for modeling global dependencies–leads to a richer representation of EEG signals. These results echo trends from previous EEG modeling studies [3,6,11] and extend the pipeline proposed by Yang et al. [28] with clearer performance advantages. Our approach also resonates with recent innovations in transformer refinement, such as Yi et al.'s adaptive spatial attention [29] and Li et al.'s temporal masking strategies for noise suppression [12].

5.1 Model Design Implications

The hybrid architecture we propose (Fig. 2) leverages CNN layers to preprocess and spatially condense EEG signals before feeding them into transformer blocks for global attention modeling. This strategy mitigates known limitations of applying vanilla transformers directly to raw EEG signals, which are often noisy and low-dimensional [1]. The overall pipeline, illustrated in Fig. 1, offers a modular and interpretable approach for end-to-end classification.

Our results validate the design intuition that CNNs are well-suited for spatial locality preservation, while transformers offer enhanced capacity for capturing temporal and inter-channel dependencies. This hybridization not only improves accuracy but also maintains a computational profile suitable for real-time or low-latency BCI applications. Such design is increasingly recognized as a robust and flexible solution across diverse EEG decoding tasks [2,5]. Furthermore, our findings are consistent with the multi-modal learning framework by Qu et al. [19], which supports integrating EEG with auxiliary modalities for improved generalization and interpretability.

5.2 Limitations

Despite these promising results, several limitations should be acknowledged. First, the current study was restricted to a single benchmark dataset (EEGEyeNet [8]), which limits the external validity of our findings. Second, while performance gains were consistent across trials, they were modest in absolute magnitude. Third, we did not conduct a full ablation study, which would have provided deeper insight into the individual contributions of CNN and transformer components.

5.3 Future Directions

Future research should expand model validation across multiple EEG datasets, including those featuring diverse tasks or subject populations. Investigating subject-transfer learning and domain adaptation remains an open challenge in EEG decoding. Moreover, self-supervised learning, contrastive learning, and transfer learning could further enhance model generalizability [3,4,6,9,11,14,16–18,20–26,28,30]. Building on recent advances in attention tuning [29], temporal refinement [12], and multi-modal learning [19], future hybrid architectures may further benefit from adaptive masking techniques, multi-task training regimes, and personalized modeling for real-world BCI deployment.

6 Conclusion

This study presents a comparative evaluation of baseline and hybrid deep learning models for EEG-based gaze prediction, focusing on spatial-temporal feature extraction. Our results show that the proposed hybrid CNN-Transformer architecture outperforms standalone CNN, GRU, and transformer models by achieving the lowest gaze prediction error on the EEGEyeNet dataset. This demonstrates the effectiveness of combining convolutional layers for localized spatial filtering with transformer-based attention mechanisms for capturing global temporal dependencies in EEG signals.

Beyond performance improvements, the hybrid model offers architectural flexibility and robustness suitable for real-time EEG decoding tasks. While this work centers on eye-gaze estimation, the design principles introduced here–graph-based preprocessing, CNN encoding, and temporal attention–may generalize to other neurophysiological and sensor-based time series applications.

By highlighting the benefit of multi-stage, modular architectures for noisy biosignals, this study contributes to the growing body of research advancing deep learning in neuroinformatics, brain-computer interfaces, and broader human-centered computing domains.

References

1. Abibullaev, B., Keutayeva, A., Zollanvari, A.: Deep learning in EEG-based BCIS: a comprehensive review of transformer models, advantages, challenges, and applications. IEEE Access **11**, 127271–127301 (2023)
2. Altaheri, H., Muhammad, G., Alsulaiman, M., Amin, S.U., Altuwaijri, G.A., Abdul, W., Bencherif, M.A., Faisal, M.: Deep learning techniques for classification of electroencephalogram (EEG) motor imagery (MI) signals: a review. Neural Comput. Appl. **35**(20), 14681–14722 (2023)
3. Craik, A., He, Y., Contreras-Vidal, J.L.: Deep learning for electroencephalogram (EEG) classification tasks: a review. J. Neural Eng. **16**(3), 031001 (2019)
4. Dou, G., Zhou, Z., Qu, X.: Time majority voting, a pc-based EEG classifier for non-expert users. In: International Conference on Human-Computer Interaction, pp. 415–428. Springer (2022)
5. Gao, Z., Dang, W., Wang, X., Hong, X., Hou, L., Ma, K., Perc, M.: Complex networks and deep learning for EEG signal analysis. Cogn. Neurodyn. **15**(3), 369–388 (2021)
6. Hossain, K.M., Islam, M.A., Hossain, S., Nijholt, A., Ahad, M.A.R.: Status of deep learning for EEG-based brain-computer interface applications. Front. Comput. Neurosci. **16**, 1006763 (2023)
7. Ismail Fawaz, H., Lucas, B., Forestier, G., Pelletier, C., Schmidt, D.F., Weber, J., Webb, G.I., Idoumghar, L., Muller, P.A., Petitjean, F.: Inceptiontime: finding alexnet for time series classification. Data Min. Knowl. Disc. **34**(6), 1936–1962 (2020)
8. Kastrati, A., Płomecka, M.B., Pascual, D., Wolf, L., Gillioz, V., Wattenhofer, R., Langer, N.: Eegeyenet: a simultaneous electroencephalography and eye-tracking dataset and benchmark for eye movement prediction (2021). arXiv:2111.05100

9. Key, M.L., Mehtiyev, T., Qu, X.: Advancing EEG-based gaze prediction using depthwise separable convolution and enhanced pre-processing. In: International Conference on Human-Computer Interaction, pp. 3–17. Springer (2024)

10. Lawhern, V.J., Solon, A.J., Waytowich, N.R., Gordon, S.M., Hung, C.P., Lance, B.J.: Eegnet: a compact convolutional neural network for EEG-based brain-computer interfaces. J. Neural Eng. **15**(5), 056013 (2018)

11. Li, G., Lee, C.H., Jung, J.J., Youn, Y.C., Camacho, D.: Deep learning for EEG data analytics: a survey. Concurrency and Computation: Practice and Experience **32**(18), e5199 (2020)

12. Li, W., Zhou, N., Qu, X.: Enhancing eye-tracking performance through multi-task learning transformer. In: International Conference on Human-Computer Interaction, pp. 31–46. Springer (2024)

13. Ma, Y., Song, Y., Gao, F.: A novel hybrid CNN-transformer model for EEG motor imagery classification. In: 2022 International joint conference on neural networks (IJCNN), pp. 1–8. IEEE (2022)

14. Murungi, N.K., Pham, M.V., Dai, X.C., Qu, X.: Empowering computer science students in electroencephalography (EEG) analysis: a review of machine learning algorithms for EEG datasets. In: The 29th ACM SIGKDD Conference on Knowledge Discovery and Data Mining (KDD) (2023)

15. Ordóñez, F.J., Roggen, D.: Deep convolutional and LSTM recurrent neural networks for multimodal wearable activity recognition. Sensors **16**(1), 115 (2016)

16. Qu, X.: Time Continuity Voting for Electroencephalography (EEG) Classification. Ph.D. thesis, Brandeis University (2022)

17. Qu, X., Hall, M., Sun, Y., Sekuler, R., Hickey, T.J.: A personalized reading coach using wearable EEG sensors (2019)

18. Qu, X., Hickey, T.J.: Eeg4home: a human-in-the-loop machine learning model for EEG-based BCI. In: International Conference on Human-Computer Interaction, pp. 162–172. Springer (2022)

19. Qu, X., Key, M., Luo, E., Qiu, C.: Integrating HCI datasets in project-based machine learning courses: a college-level review and case study. In: International Conference on Human-Computer Interaction, pp. 124–143. Springer (2024)

20. Qu, X., Liu, P., Li, Z., Hickey, T.: Multi-class time continuity voting for EEG classification. In: International Conference on Brain Function Assessment in Learning, pp. 24–33. Springer (2020)

21. Qu, X., Liukasemsarn, S., Tu, J., Higgins, A., Hickey, T.J., Hall, M.H.: Identifying clinically and functionally distinct groups among healthy controls and first episode psychosis patients by clustering on EEG patterns. Front. Psych. **11**, 541659 (2020)

22. Qu, X., Mei, Q., Liu, P., Hickey, T.: Using eeg to distinguish between writing and typing for the same cognitive task. In: International Conference on Brain Function Assessment in Learning, pp. 66–74. Springer (2020)

23. Qu, X., Sun, Y., Sekuler, R., Hickey, T.: EEG markers of stem learning. In: 2018 IEEE Frontiers in Education Conference (FIE), pp. 1–9. IEEE (2018)

24. Roy, Y., Banville, H., Albuquerque, I., Gramfort, A., Falk, T.H., Faubert, J.: Deep learning-based electroencephalography analysis: a systematic review. J. Neural Eng. **16**(5), 051001 (2019)

25. Saunders, T., Aleisa, N., Wield, J., Sherwood, J., Qu, X.: Optimizing the literature review process: evaluating generative ai models on sum-marizing undergraduate data science research papers. In: Proceedings of the 30th ACM SIGKDD Conference on Knowledge Discovery and Data Mining (2024)

26. Wang, R., Qu, X.: EEG daydreaming, a machine learning approach to detect day-dreaming activities. In: International Conference on Human-Computer Interaction, pp. 202–212. Springer (2022)
27. Xu, G., Shen, X., Chen, S., Zong, Y., Zhang, C., Yue, H., Liu, M., Chen, F., Che, W.: A deep transfer convolutional neural network framework for EEG signal classification. IEEE Access **7**, 112767–112776 (2019)
28. Yang, R., Modesitt, E.: Vit2eeg: leveraging hybrid pretrained vision transformers for EGG data (2023). arXiv:2308.00454
29. Yi, L., Qu, X.: Attention-based CNN capturing EEG recording's average voltage and local change. In: International Conference on Human-Computer Interaction, pp. 448–459. Springer (2022)
30. Zhou, Z., Dou, G., Qu, X.: Brainactivity1: a framework of EEG data collection and machine learning analysis for college students. In: International Conference on Human-Computer Interaction, pp. 119–127. Springer (2022)

Author Index

H. Mori et al. (Eds.): HCII 2025, LNCS 16333, pp. 443–444, 2026.
https://doi.org/10.1007/978-3-032-12660-3